conceptual art

**conceptual art:** a critical anthology

edited by alexander alberro and blake stimson

the MIT press · cambridge, massachusetts · london, england

This book was set in Adobe Garamond and Trade Gothic by Graphic Composition, Inc. and was printed and bound in the United States of America.

Library of Congress Cataloging-in-Publication Data

Conceptual art : a critical anthology / edited by Alexander Alberro and Blake Stimson.
     p.  cm.
  Includes bibliographical references and index.
  ISBN 0-262-01173-5 (hc : alk. paper)
  1. Conceptual art.   I. Alberro, Alexander.   II. Stimson, Blake.
N6494.C63C597   1999
  700—dc21                                             98-52388
                                                            CIP

# contents

# illustrations

# preface

Compared to other neo-avant-garde movements that emerged during the 1960s, conceptual art is conspicuous by virtue of the lack of serious discussion by art historians and critics over the last two decades. This gap in the reception is particularly ironic given the tremendous influence conceptual art has had on subsequent artistic developments, on the critical discussion surrounding the concept of postmodernism, and on the recognition and use, more generally, of various forms of theory by artists, curators, critics, and historians.

There are signs that this deficiency is being remedied, however, with the recent publication of the writings of a growing number of conceptual artists and the staging of large exhibitions surveying conceptualism at major museums. The MIT Press has played a crucial role in supporting this renewed interest, so we were delighted when it agreed to publish this collection. Our hope is that it will make a valuable contribution to this resurgence, serving teachers and students of the period as well as artists, historians, and critics.

Included in our selection are some of the best-known texts of conceptual art, a number of lesser-known, previously unpublished or untranslated materials, as well as articles and interviews produced specifically for this volume. Each of these, in its own way, provides considerable insight into the period.

The volume is organized chronologically from 1966 to 1977. The final two sections present memoirs by artists involved in the initial historical moment and a selection of the most important critical and scholarly histories of conceptual art written to date. The images we have chosen to include are not meant to function as illustrations but as separate, stand-alone documents augmenting the written material.

We are grateful to the authors and publishers of the texts and illustrations for granting us permission to reproduce their material. For clerical and editorial support, we are indebted to Diana Dopson and Lora Rempel. For translation assistance, we thank Nora M. Alter, Trilce Navarrete, and Maya Rabasa. For photographic expertise, we are grateful to Anne Naldrett. For recommendations of specific texts and the overall scope of the project, we are obliged to Benjamin H. D. Buchloh, Hal Foster, Charles Harrison, Lucy R. Lippard, Juan Maidagan, Mari Carmen Ramírez, Martha Rosler, and Dolores Zinny. Finally, we would like to thank Roger Conover at the MIT Press, whose consistent patience and guidance throughout every step of this project made the realization of this volume possible.

# reconsidering conceptual art, 1966–1977
## alexander alberro

From its inception, and continuing to this very day, conceptual art has been entangled in controversy by those who stake claims to its foundational moment.[1] This phenomenon is highly paradoxical given that, as with avant-garde practice in general, the emergence of conceptual art was the result of complicated processes of selection, fusion, and rejection of antecedent forms and strategies.[2] Claims for the clarity and purity of the foundational lineage of conceptual art, therefore, should be considered with skepticism, since they are so limited, confusing, and often explicitly constructed in order to promote a particular, partial legacy. Of course, this is not uncommon in the history of modern art, but it is remarkably blatant at the moment of conceptual art.

Let me begin by delineating various art-historical genealogies that led to the increasing conceptualization of artistic practices in the 1960s. In particular, four trajectories can be singled out as strong precursors of conceptual art. The first includes the self-reflexivity of modernist painting and sculpture that systematically problematizes and dismantles the integral elements of the traditional structure of the artwork. One of the recurring characteristics in much art that is referred to as conceptual is the consideration of every one of the constituting elements of the artwork as equal components. In the process, the valuation of technical manual skill is largely (if not entirely) abandoned, as well as the notion of an original, cohesive work. In turn, serial and highly schematic structures emerge, placing the inherently hierarchical concept of quality under duress. The second trajectory, what can be termed "reductivism," will push the conventional objectness of the artwork toward the threshold of a complete dematerialization. Increasingly, in works following this strand, the visual elements of an artwork are challenged, the prominence of text expands, and the degree to which viewing is dependent upon the integration of contingent and contextual elements becomes a focal point. The negation of aesthetic content marks a third genealogy of conceptualism. This is an antecedent that can ultimately be traced back to the work of Marcel Duchamp and which, by way of a series of mediations throughout the twentieth century, places art at the threshold of information. The fourth trajectory that leads to conceptual art is one that problematizes placement. Here, the subject of the work becomes both a reflection on the conventions that will frame it or situate it, and a self-questioning of how it will be communicated or displayed. Among the results of this lineage will be the melding of the work with the surrounding architectural environment, and its integration within the context of publicity (including newspapers, magazines, books, even advertisement billboards). In its broadest possible definition, then, the conceptual in art means an expanded critique of the cohesiveness and materiality of the art object, a growing wariness toward definitions of artistic practice as purely visual, a fusion of the work with its site and context of display, and an increased emphasis on the possibilities of publicness and distribution.[3]

Given the complexity of genealogical strands and avant-garde strategies that combined to comprise what came to be referred to as conceptual art, it is not surprising that conceptualism during the mid to late 1960s was a contested field of multiple and opposing practices, rather than a single, unified artistic discourse and theory. Be that as it may, there are several aesthetic theories or models of conceptual art that can be discerned to have a certain preeminence or predominance as shaping or influencing forces. One of the most significant of these is represented by the work of Joseph Kosuth, Christine Kozlov, and the Art & Language group. Kosuth describes the distinguishing characteristics of this aesthetic theory that I will refer to as "linguistic conceptualism" in his three-part essay "Art After Philosophy" (1969), where he advances an exposition of conceptualism undergirded by the tenets of logical positivism, in particular A. J. Ayer's *Language, Truth and Logic* (1936).[4] According to Kosuth's thesis, questioning the nature of art should be the main concern of artists. Remaining within traditional categories of painting and sculpture, however, obstructs such inquiry since these artistic categories are conventional and their legitimacy is taken for granted. Thus these categories should be disavowed, regarded as anachronistic, useless, even detrimental, to artists.

This main line of argument leads Kosuth to reconsider the history of modern art as it is conventionally narrated, and to dismiss the relevance of artists such as Edouard Manet, Paul Cézanne, and the cubists, whose work as art he deems valid only on morphological grounds, that is, only insofar as they remained tied to the medium of painting. Instead Kosuth champions an alternate canon of art—one that is characterized by the subversion of the old classifications—represented by his understanding of the legacy of Marcel Duchamp. "The 'value' of particular artists after Duchamp," he writes, can be weighed according to how much they rejected "the handed-down 'language' of traditional art" and thereby freed from morphological constrictions inquiry into the meaning of art.[5] Given this formulation, in which a work's importance is exclusively located in its meaning, the problem of referentiality arises. Presumably, prioritizing the conceptual content of art, its intelligibility, requires an account that is more than self-reflexive.

It is in this connection that Kosuth introduces Ayer's evaluation of Immanuel Kant's distinction between analytic and synthetic propositions. Following Ayer, Kosuth argues that forms of art that depend for their validity on being verified by the world and "the 'infinite space' of the human condition" are synthetic propositions while "forms of art most clearly finally referable only to art" are analytic propositions.[6] Then, making the unlikely pairing of analytic proposition and meaning on the one hand, and synthetic proposition and language on the other, Kosuth brackets off and expels any questions of a referential dimension from his theoretical model, concluding that "art's only claim is for art. Art is the definition of art."[7]

This last point bears elaborating, and perhaps can best be understood by comparing Kosuth's claims about his own work with the theoretical underpinnings of the work of his closest associates in the early 1970s, Terry Atkinson, Michael Baldwin, and the Art & Language group. The main corpus of the latter in the late 1960s consists of numerous texts presented in an art context as analytic arguments about the nature of art objects and assertions about art. As early as 1967, these artists articulated a position that parallels the claims Kosuth was to make in the next couple of years, for example their shared repudiation of art legitimated on the basis of morphology, and their avowal of what Atkinson referred to as a "declarative methodology" whereby artworks are deemed to achieve their status as such by the nominal, metalinguistic act of asserting their "art-context." But while Kosuth's investigations, as I noted earlier, interrogate the nature of art, Art & Language's work focuses on an analysis of "the linguistic usage of both plastic art itself and its support languages, namely word-language."[8]

If Kosuth's point of departure is his rejection of formalist art legitimated only by its morphological similarity to previous art, Art & Language's point of departure is the rejection of the simple materiality of minimal art. For, as Baldwin noted in an early expository article on his and Atkinson's "Air-Conditioning Show," even the site-specific work of minimalism depends on the visual dimension for cognition.[9] Indeed, Baldwin's comments in this article summon a range of issues that concerned the Art & Language group in the following years. First, there is the issue of reductivism. Baldwin traces the development of reductivism that characterizes avant-garde practice in New York in the preceding years—from self-sufficient objects placed within a gallery, to site-specific artworks visible in the gallery space, to the invisible site-specific artwork—and places the notion of an "Air-Conditioning Show" firmly within that trajectory. At the same time, the idea proposed by Baldwin of an invisible art shifts the cognitive emphasis of the artwork from material vehicle to conceptual content in a way that parallels Kosuth's arguments for the deemphasis of language in favor of meaning. And finally, there is the issue of language. For if the material employed in the "Air-Conditioning Show" discussed by Baldwin is perceptually invisible, it is so only if one expects art to be solely a matter of "'looking at' objects" rather than "'reading from' objects," as Atkinson phrased it.[10] But if one accepts written language—"i.e., paper with ink lines upon it"—to be physically and visually perusable, then not only do works such as the "Air-Conditioning Show" become visible, but nothing prevents the idea of art from broadening to include critical or theoretical speculations on art as an art material as well.[11] And of course once art language is considered "inside the framework of 'conceptual art,'" the distinction between work and text becomes blurred, leading to questions about the status of artworks such as the following, posed by Atkinson in the first issue of *Art-Language: The Journal of Conceptual Art:* "Can this editorial," asks Atkinson rhetorically, "in itself an attempt to evince some outlines as to what 'conceptual art' is, come up for the count as a work of conceptual art?"[12]

Similar to Atkinson's and Baldwin's, Kosuth's starting point, as I suggested earlier, is also in the declarative act of deeming art objects, or in Kosuth's terms "art-propositions," meaningful as such. But that nominal act reaches its threshold much earlier in Kosuth's art practice than it does in Atkinson's and Baldwin's. Whereas the latter are concerned primarily with the function of the metalanguage in which the physical art objects reside, Kosuth's exclusive concern is with the nature of the thing declared an art object. To put this another way, unlike Atkinson and Baldwin's inquiry into the relationship between the specific artwork and the more general art discourse ("the language-use of the art society," as Atkinson once pithily put it), Kosuth's project is concerned with the relation of the definition of art to art, which he locates exclusively in the completeness of the artist's idea of art.[13]

Although the model of conceptualism articulated and given form by Kosuth and the Art & Language group quickly became, and has remained, the dominant one, the conceptualist work of Mel Bochner, Hanne Darboven, Sol LeWitt, Lee Lozano, Brian O'Doherty, and others in the mid to late 1960s deals with different—even opposed—sets of interests than those of linguistic conceptualism. LeWitt, for example, argued that the elimination of the perceptual object in favor of an emphasis on the conceptual process was a way of dismantling myths of integrated subjectivity. In what stands as the first manifesto of conceptual art, "Paragraphs on Conceptual Art" of 1967, LeWitt sets up a binary between expressionist art which requires rational decisions to be made throughout the process of an artwork's execution, and conceptual art in which all decisions about execution are made in advance. By extension, LeWitt differentiates between perceptual art that depends on visual forms and conceptual art that is "made to engage the mind of the viewer rather than his eye." LeWitt's account of conceptual art, then, proposes that the concept determines what the artwork will look like. The idea, he writes, becomes "a machine that makes the art," a logical operation that "eliminates the arbitrary, capricious, and the subjective as much as possible."[14] But, unlike Kosuth's aesthetic theory, which posits that the idea itself can be considered the art, for LeWitt the process of conception stands in a complementary relation to the process of realization, mutually supplying each other's lack, and thus of equal importance.

Basically, I interpret LeWitt's aesthetic theory as opposed to Kosuth's. Whereas the latter's is characterized by a rational mode of artistic production that affirms the centered and authorial artist—the decisionmaker from beginning to end—LeWitt's theory proposes a mode of production that is opposed to rationalism; the work is produced following a logical sequence that does not require intuition, creativity, or rational thought. Thus the work reads without the testimony of the privileged artist; this process of production is fundamentally, in a word, irrational.[15] Furthermore, consistent with his rational standpoint, Kosuth's aesthetic theory clearly restricts viewing experience to two possibilities: the viewer either comprehends the idea, or does not. As he states polemically in a 1969 interview, "The public's not interested in art anyway. . . . No more interested in art than they are with physics."[16] In contrast, LeWitt's model of conceptualism posits an unlimited public. The content of artworks produced following this model is more than the private history of the artist and allows a multiplicity of readings. In this respect, whereas Kosuth formulates an aesthetic theory based upon the epitome of positivist thinking—the tautological model—LeWitt's aesthetic theory references positivism only to break out of it by introducing the subjective dimension of the beholder. "Once out of his hand," LeWitt writes, "the artist has no control over the way a viewer will perceive the work. Different people will understand the same thing in a different way."[17]

It is in this context that the early work of artists such as Bas Jan Ader, Adrian Piper, Christopher D'Arcangelo, Vito Acconci, and others who steered conceptual art toward an increasing emphasis on the body ought chiefly to be seen. Acconci's *Following Piece* of 1969, for instance, provides a concrete example of a type of work that integrates the decentering of the artist into its formal and constitutive elements while incorporating the artist's body into the work. *Following Piece* is essentially a chronological list that meticulously describes the public activities of an anonymous urban dweller on a particular day during the month of October 1969. Each day in this month, Acconci would follow a randomly chosen person in the streets of New York City as long as he could, until the person followed entered a private place. Thus by their very nature variants of *Following Piece* differ in length. Some last for only two or three minutes—that is until the person followed enters their home and closes the door, or enters their car and speeds off; others last seven or eight hours, continuing as the person goes to various public places such as a restaurant, movie, or store.

In addition, by rejecting all manual intrusion on the part of the artist, relying instead on an a priori scheme that generates itself once the person to be followed is (randomly) selected, Acconci's *Following Piece* also effects the total depersonalization of the work. It is mechanical and irrational: it does not require the artist to make choices. The artist is carried along through the streets of the city by the activities of another (anonymous) person; decisions of time and space are out of his hands, as it were, and he virtually disappears behind the system's self-generation. Once produced, variants of *Following Piece* could then be reactivated or performed by the artist or any other interested party at will. The work is thus reduced to a purely descriptive analysis of an episode, and all composition, narrative, and interiority is negated. In what is now the inverse of a work that functions as "a working out, a thinking out, of all the implications of all aspects of the concept 'art,'" as Kosuth puts it, the process of decentering is absolute in *Following Piece*—there is no connection back to the artist through the work. Rather it is the contingent experience of the person reactivating the work that becomes the focus, while the physical space of the city becomes the ground of the work.

xxii

If, however, we turn to the late 1960s work of Lawrence Weiner and Douglas Huebler, another model of conceptual art can be discerned—one that integrates the decentering of the artist into its formal and constitutive elements in an attempt to democratize the production and reception of art. Weiner's art practice of this period is characterized by a radical dislocation of the notion of the sign. Rather than functioning as a general sign, presenting the physical art object and the conceptual information that supplements and closes the art object, Weiner most often presents the information of the work only in the form of a statement. These statements define linguistically the material structure of the work, presenting in the past participle facts about its materials and processes of production. A case in point is "One Hole in the Ground Approximately 1′ × 1′ × 1′. One Gallon Water Based White Paint Poured into this Hole." The use of the past participle is in itself significant insofar as it simultaneously allows for the conclusiveness of the description as well as the prospect of a future realization. Importantly, Weiner does not write, for example, "dig a hole in the ground, and take a gallon of water-based white paint and pour it into this hole," but chooses the past tense exclusively because, as he put it, "To use the imperative would be for me fascistic. . . . The tone of command is the tone of tyranny."[18] But one of the remarkable features of Weiner's art is that it is equally valid whether communicated verbally or materially documented.[19] In this sense, the hole into which a gallon of water-based white paint was poured is not a discrete work but one link in a chain of signifiers that summon and refer to one another—a metonymic chain that includes the oral communication, the published statement, the process of carrying out the declaration, the residue of this act, the photographic documentation, and so on. In short, the work could take innumerable physical forms.[20]

Even more problematic, perhaps, is Weiner's assertion that the work does not have to take form. For at this time Weiner also formulated the by now infamous "declaration of intent" that has been the criteria for the execution of his work since late 1968:

*1. The artist may construct the piece*
*2. The piece may be fabricated*
*3. The piece need not be built*
*Each being equal and consistent with the intent of the artist, the decision as to condition rests with the receiver upon the occasion of receivership.*[21]

In light of the interpretation of Weiner's art that has so far emerged, several aspects of this proclamation seem particularly significant. For one thing, it posits either the artist or somebody else fabricating or describing the piece as equal conditions for the production of his work, thereby abolishing the traditional notion of artist-centered production.[22] For another, the proclamation indicates that the artwork requires that one try to diminish the distance between beholding and producing, joining the beholder and the work in a single signifying practice. Further, Weiner's instructions are for any interested body, collector or otherwise, and hence destabilize the myth of authority and authorship. The work thus represents a method of art production, distribution, and consumption with a degree of egalitarianism that is virtually unprecedented in the history of twentieth-century art.[23]

The inversion of traditional practices of fabricating, exhibiting, and distributing works of art put into operation by Weiner's theoretical model of conceptualism places his work outside the parameters of LeWitt's aesthetic theory of conceptual art. For although LeWitt eliminated rational decisionmaking from the manufacture stage of the work, thereby separating execution from artistic value, he maintained that the work should still take on a physical form. Weiner's work of the late 1960s, I am suggesting, is set apart from LeWitt's because the participatory model is pushed to its logical conclusion. Now one of the explicit conditions of the work is that it need not be built, and the decision of whether to actually give the piece physical form is left completely up to the viewer, or in the terminology of Weiner at the time, the "receiver."[24] The activation of the receiver is the direct result of the eclipse of the authorial figure of the artist.[25]

But I want to go further and propose that when exhibited, the self-reflexivity of Weiner's work touches on the work's value as economic exchange. Indeed, a typical characteristic of Weiner's exhibited works in the late 1960s was the accompanying acknowledgment of the collector who owned the piece. Those works yet unsold were cited as in a "private collection," and one in every ten or so was referenced as in "public freehold." Insofar as in its production the work is deprivileged in every respect, the ever-present proprietary supplement renders the logic of the exchange in the market a subject of contemplation.[26] From here it's only a step to suggest that whereas the aesthetic use value of one of Weiner's works is democratized, the operation of the work emphasizes the exclusivity of a certain experience—the experience of ownership. And it requires only a slightly greater step to conclude that it's essentially a mechanism of economic exchange that allows a gesture to circulate as an artwork in the culture.

What makes Weiner's work of the late 1960s so suggestive is the introduction it provides for an analysis of an even more radical alternative to what later came to be the dominant theoretical model of conceptualism. In contrast to the other strands of conceptualism I have thus far examined, this one did not stop its interrogation of the underlying essence of an artwork at linguistic or economic conditions. Rather, artists such as Daniel Buren, Marcel Broodthaers, Hans Haacke, and various collective groups formed in the early 1970s around *The Fox,* or the activist Artists Meeting for Cultural Change in New York, deemed the ideological conditions of the institution of art to be fundamental to the validation of artworks. This development was part of a larger shift from the primacy of works that critiqued the idea of autonomous art and authoritative artists toward works that addressed the invisible institutional mechanisms that structure and define art in advanced capitalist society—more accurately, from work that decentered the artist to work that commented on the decentered artist.[27] From this point of view, artistic production is considered to be overdetermined by the underlying system of rules of the institution of art. The individuality and creativity of artists capable of producing and exhibiting works, indeed everything that had been attributed to artistic subjectivity, now came to be considered residual, alienated phenomena.

Haacke's model of conceptualism developed over the course of the 1960s.[28] As the decade unfolded, however, the emphasis in his work shifted from natural and biological systems to social systems. Part and parcel of this shift was the diminished role of the artist, culminating in works that virtually produce themselves such as *MoMA-Poll* (1970) and *Gallery-Visitor's Profile* (1969–73), which employ systemic methods for gathering data on social phenomena. In addition to the reduced role of the artist as producer, these works also problematize the networks of relationships through which power is exercised in the art world and expose the social, economic, and political bases of that power.

In this connection it is revealing to look briefly at one of Haacke's earliest conceptualist works, the *Gallery-Visitor's Profile.* Haacke's schema reflects upon the characteristics of the people who attend the site where the artwork is exhibited. *Gallery-Visitor's Profile* employs an empiricist method of accumulating information to compose a statistical breakdown of the gallery-goer: according to age, gender, religious belief, ethnicity, class, occupation, and so on. The result is a work that explicitly recognizes that the work of art's status as such arises not from characteristics of its own inner logic, nor from the nominal act of the autonomous agent in absolute control of his creative impulses, but, in the first place, from the "relative ideological frame" of the privileged social group that constitutes the art audience and administers the discourse of art in our society, and second, from the gallery-museum power nexus that bestows value upon a work of art. With *Gallery-Visitor's Profile,* then, we are a long way from ideas of the work of art as an analytic proposition. In fact, Haacke's work is closer to what Kosuth had categorized as a "synthetic" proposition. For rather than posing the artwork and art world as an isolated circuit, these works clearly transcend their context and intersect with the ideological values of the culture at large.

In a similar way, Daniel Buren's late 1960s work integrates the framing conventions not only of the art object but also of the art world in general into its formal and thematic content. At the same time, Buren's work unsettles myths of integrated subjectivity and the authorial role of the artist, thereby echoing the work of his U.S. counterparts such as LeWitt and Weiner. But whereas the latter maintained their investigations on the abstract level, Buren turned instead to submitting the constant of his stripe motif to an ever-changing variety of contexts. In the resulting dialectical relation between the aesthetic sign and its environment, not only the artistic traditions that artists are located in, the "inter-text" as it were, but also the effect the institutional container of art—that is, the museum, gallery, or other display mechanism—has upon the designation and design of artworks themselves is problematized, and subverted from within.[29]

In his writings of the late 1960s, Buren argues that the interior space of the artwork, its "content," has been decimated by institutional mechanisms that regulate the exhibition and distribution of artworks in our society. Under these catastrophic conditions, Buren claims, art comes to buttress the existing order of things by offering proof that fine art is thriving and well.[30] Furthermore, any form art takes, however unconventional, is acceptable because the institutional network or structure of art has so thoroughly taken hold of the development of culture that even the most avant-garde gestures are immediately appropriated.[31] Buren's response to these conditions is to deemphasize the importance of the art object per se, focusing instead on the means by which the art system affirms the art object as significant, or meaningful, avant-garde art.

Thus, Buren rejects the idea that the art object could have an inherent subject—a denial not unlike that proposed by the work of Kosuth or LeWitt. But the institution-critical dimension of the latter quickly reaches its limit, I would argue, insofar as the notion that the artwork could have a concrete relation to the problematic of display is excluded from both the operation of this work and the supplementary texts the artists produce to explain it. In contrast, the very inadequacy of the striped canvases (or posters) Buren exhibits as art index his interventions in the media in the form of writings, which, as I just noted, expound a theoretical position that critically analyzes, and prompts reflection on, the containment of art by institutional techniques and means.

But perhaps the most extreme alternatives to models of analytic conceptualism in the late 1960s and early 1970s are those that developed in the deteriorating political and economic climate of a number of Latin American countries including Argentina, Brazil, Uruguay, and Chile. We get an early glimpse of the development of conceptual art in Latin America in the manifesto "A Media Art," written in 1966 by Eduardo Costa, Raúl Escari, and Roberto Jacoby. Recognizing the power of the media in constructing artistic events, these artists propose to "de-realize" objects by presenting accounts to newspapers and magazines of artistic exhibitions and events that did not in fact take place. Underpinned by an understanding of the profound impact of the media in late twentieth-century society, the stated aim of the authors of the "Media Art" manifesto is to "unchain" (*desencadenar*) information communicated through the media, and produce work that is nothing but the act of that unchaining. Such a *détournement* of the media, to employ the terminology of another group of radical theorists of the era, the European situationists, was conceived as capable of empowering the spectator to construct the substance of the nonexistent work, based on the information received and depending on the particular way that information signifies for him or her.[32] Here, then, in a completely different geographical context, we have the unfolding of a media art that at once parallels artistic practices developing in North America that come to be defined as nascent conceptual art, such as Dan Graham's "works for magazine pages" that take place entirely within the structure of communication—the magazine system—and post-conceptual practices that emerge in the 1970s that problematize that most hallowed principle of art: originality.[33]

But in Argentina the abstracted appropriation and manipulation of readymade media forms and structures did not last long, as the increasingly repressive social and political reality of the late 1960s made such passive engagements with the prevailing system seem woefully inadequate and led to more politically aggressive art interventions. Indeed, the swift shift in focus from a conceptualism that questions the ideological conditions of bourgeois art to an art that questions all the institutions that represent bourgeois culture, evident in the context of Latin American conceptual art, is perhaps best exemplified by the "Tucumán Burns" manifesto. Collectively written and first published as a mimeograph by the Argentinean General Confederation of Labor in 1968, the manifesto postulates that the first step to a truly "revolutionary art" is the "awareness of the actual reality of the artist as an individual inside the political and social context that surrounds him." This would lead artists with truly avant-garde and thus revolutionary aims to destroy bourgeois forms of art that "reinforce the institution of individual property and the personal pleasure of the unique art object" by constructing artistic objects capable of producing modifications in society as efficaciously as political acts.[34]

What is particularly relevant in this context of an articulation of moves toward conceptual art is that, like other conceptual art models that dissolve the work of art into a tool of communication, integrating the work within the context of publicity, the writers of "Tucumán Burns" also call for a relation between the work of art and the mass media. According to the manifesto, revolutionary art consists of the creation of "informational circuits" of particular realities (such as the appalling conditions of the working population of Tucumán) capable of de-mythifying the dominant (i.e., bourgeois) mass-media image of those realities. The assault on the media image advocated by this group of artists, however, is characterized by an awareness not only of the power of the media, but also of its "susceptibility to being charged with different kinds of content."[35] These are characteristics that, as we shall shortly see, will come to define 1970s practices of conceptualism, or post-conceptualism, in a variety of contexts.

A similar interest in the discursive potential of systems of distribution pervades Brazilian strands of conceptual art in the 1960s. One of these is articulated in the manifesto "General Scheme of the New Objectivity," printed in the catalogue accompanying the 1967 exhibition "Brazilian New Objectivity" in Rio de Janeiro. Written by Hélio Oiticica, the manifesto charts out the principal characteristics of the new art, which include "the participation of the spectator (bodily, tactile, visual, semantic, etc.)," "an engagement and a position on political, social and ethical problems," a "tendency towards collective propositions," and "a revival of, and new formulations in, the concept of anti-art."[36] The impact that the standpoints advanced in this manifesto were to have on a generation of artists in Brazil and elsewhere on the continent cannot be underestimated, all the more because of the extremely volatile and dangerous circumstances surrounding artistic production under military dictatorship. One of the artists upon whom Oiticica's manifesto, combined with the heightened level of artistic repression, had an obvious and profound impact was Cildo Meireles, whose work of the late 1960s and early 1970s fuses conceptual art with political activism. A case in point is Meireles's series of *Inserções em circuitos ideológicos* (Insertions into ideological circuits). Arising out of what Meireles retrospectively described as the need "to create a system for the circulation and exchange of information that did not depend on any kind of centralized control," the *Inserções* series transmitted information through a variety of alternative "circuits."[37] For instance, *Insertion—Coca-Cola* (1970) consisted of printing messages and critical opinions about Brazilian politics and the politics of imperialism onto the sides of empty Coca-Cola bottles in vitreous white ink to match the bottles' logo, and then reintroducing the bottles into circulation. The texts were virtually invisible when the bottles were empty, but as they were filled in the factory, the information became legible. In this manner, these works inverted the idea of the readymade that had characterized pop and, in its own way, minimal art. Instead of inserting the commodity object into the space of the gallery, the work returned the Coca-Cola bottles to their original system of circulation—albeit in a radically altered form. As such, the work not only attempts an ambitiously egalitarian form of distribution, but also critiques the imperialism of advanced capitalism that Coca-Cola represented.[38]

Several artistic practices emerge in the 1970s that at once follow logically from and challenge many of the claims of conceptual art. In particular, I want to single out three post-conceptual models of the 1970s and '80s that, though significantly different from each other, share the conceptualist belief that all art is dependent upon institutional practices, forms of distribution, and a structure that is preestablished by discursive and institutional conventions. The first is exemplified by the work of artists such as Mike Bidlo, John Knight, Louise Lawler, Sherrie Levine, Allan McCollum, and Richard Prince. What is most striking about these works, I want to suggest, is their exploration of structure, as well as their critique of authenticity and originality. In the conceptualist tradition of the effacement of authorial presence, Bidlo's and Levine's works, for instance, absolutely fuse with objects made by artists working in completely different historical contexts, and overtly undermine the credibility of artistic agency in the contemporary art world. Similarly, the focus on preexisting institutional and discursive formations— whether that of the museum or gallery (e.g., Lawler, McCollum), art history (e.g., Levine, Bidlo), or advertising (e.g., Knight, Prince)—singled out as the sites where their own cultural production will be determined, controlled, placed, and eventually threatened, characterizes the work of other artists that adopt this artistic model. What all these works share is that they again reposition the role of the artist, and problematize notions of uniqueness and originality.

The second model, comprised of the work of Victor Burgin, Jenny Holzer, Mary Kelly, and Barbara Kruger, among others, evolves in the same artistic context, and engages critically with similar issues. What is addressed now more programatically and forcefully than in the work of the artists discussed above, however, is the construction of the subject through various overdetermining forms. Particular focus is placed on the complex link between text and image, and between language and subjectivity. And this points to one of the distinct differences between this model of post-conceptual art and the linguistic conceptualism of the late 1960s. The latter, with its emphasis on a purely formal language, as much as on the belief that linguistically stated analytic propositions are capable of displacing traditional models of visuality, is clearly based on a modernist model of language, one that correlates historically with the legacies of reductivism and self-reflexivity. By contrast, artists such as Burgin, Holzer, Kelly, and Kruger theorize language beyond the purely analytic and formal, situating it within a synthetic, discursive practice determined by a system of control and domination.[39] From this perspective, language is perceived as in and of itself the very medium by which ideological subjectivity is always already constructed. In other words, in direct response to the formal neutrality of conceptual art of the late 1960s, the post-conceptual work of artists such as Burgin, Holzer, Kelly, and Kruger in the 1970s argues that language is inextricably bound to ideology.[40] Which is in turn a point of view that the latter share with the first group of post-conceptual artists discussed above—namely, that all art is dependent upon preestablished discursive structures and institutional conventions.[41]

And it was precisely in those terms that the works of these artists were criticized by producers of a third and in many ways antithetical model of mid-1970s post-conceptualist artistic practice.[42] In particular, what artists such as Fred Lonidier, Martha Rosler, Allan Sekula, and Phil Steinmetz consider problematic in the work produced by the first model, and, though to a lesser extent, by that of Burgin, Holzer, Kelly, and Kruger, is precisely that in their collapse of individual subjectivity and overdetermined patterns of behavior, they deny authorial intervention and political agency. Echoing the artistic practices of Latin American conceptualists of the 1960s, as well as that of many of the artists involved with *The Fox* and the activist Artists Meeting for Cultural Change in New York in the 1970s, the implication of the work of Lonidier, Rosler, Sekula, and Steinmetz is that self-determination and communication, even in advanced forms of capitalist control, is still a historical option and artistic possibility.

This opposition to the pessimism that characterizes the approach of artists of the first two models of post-conceptualist artistic practice is perhaps most clearly discerned in works such as Rosler's photo-text, *The Bowery in Two Inadequate Descriptive Systems* of 1974. A sequence of twenty-four panels, and subsequently produced and distributed as a book, the work consists of a juxtaposition of texts and close-focus black-and-white photographs. In the first three panels, texts are juxtaposed with blanks; the rest alternate image and text constellations, sometimes positioning the image on the right, sometimes on the left. The photographic side of the panels features frontal views of storefronts and walls in the Bowery, evoking a large archive of representations of this district of Manhattan. Words and phrases that contain familiar idioms used to describe alcoholics, inebriation, and alcoholism in detail and in general are accumulated on the textual side of the panels. Thus both the linguistic and the visual provide detailed information without ultimately explaining their subject. In turn, assumptions about the neutrality of visual representation (and more specifically photographic imagery) and language are questioned and problematized. Neither of these "descriptive systems," Rosler's work implies, is adequate for a rendering or presentation of the complexities of the subject in question. Instead of describing the Bowery, Rosler's project stakes it out as a territory for an exploration of two ubiquitous forms of representation and their inherent limitations.

In this sense, *The Bowery in Two Inadequate Descriptive Systems* parallels the work of other post-conceptual artists. But rather than stopping at an analysis of the system of representation itself, such works have a clear political subtext.[43] For if the post-conceptual models of artistic practice that I outlined earlier question and deny the possibility of rational communication within the contemporary public sphere, the work of Lonidier, Rosler, Sekula, and Steinmetz is characterized by an attempt to elicit dialogue, as much as political change, via redemption of critical, reflexive, activist modes of thought that combine theory with practice.[44] And it is precisely that ambition to communicate, to politically intervene within existing institutions of the democratic public sphere, that makes the work of these artists so different from that of their post-conceptualist peers.

The moment of conceptual art was relatively short-lived, barely spanning a full decade. And yet its legacy is wide-ranging, covering a vast terrain in terms of its effect on traditional modes and categories of artistic production, exhibition, and distribution. Indeed, one could argue that the influence of conceptualism can be found in almost all ambitious contemporary art practices—from the most obvious direct lineage of "neo-conceptualism" to the more obscure links of contemporary video, performance, and public art. As an international movement that transcended national borders voicing common concerns about the role of the artist, the artwork, the public, and the institutions involved, the questions and problematics posed by conceptual art continue to be as important today as when they were initially raised in the 1960s and 1970s.

**NOTES**

1. See, for instance, Joseph Kosuth's assertions in "Art After Philosophy, Part II" (1969), reprinted in part III of this volume, and the debate that followed: Michel Claura, "Conceptual Misconceptions," *Studio International,* 179:918 (January 1970), pp. 5–6; Dore Ashton, "Kosuth: The Facts," *Studio International,* 179:919 (February 1970), p. 44; Joseph Kosuth, "Kosuth Replies to Claura," *Studio International,* 179:919 (February 1970), p. 44; Joseph Kosuth, "An Answer to Criticisms," *Studio International,* 179:923 (June 1970), p. 245; Barbara Reise, "Joseph Kosuth," *Studio International,* 180:925 (September 1970), p. 71.

See also the debate following the initial publication of Benjamin H. D. Buchloh, "Conceptual Art 1962–1969: From the Aesthetic of Administration to the Critique of Institutions," in Claude Gintz, *L'art conceptuel: Une perspective,* ex. cat. (Paris: Musée d'Art Moderne de la Ville de Paris, 1989), pp. 25–54, compiled in *October,* no. 57 (Summer 1991), pp. 152–161, and the collection of documents pertaining to "the present Art & Language history war," as Terry

Atkinson refers to it, compiled in Dave Rushton, *Don Quixote's Art & Television* (Edinburgh: Institute of Local Television, 1998), esp. pp. 33–41, and Terry Atkinson's "Introduction" to Rushton's volume, pp. xi–xiv.

2. The key essays in this context are reproduced in "Critical Histories of Conceptual Art," part VIII of this anthology, to which this essay is indebted.

3. To a considerable extent, these general definitions of conceptual art informed the most important book on the movement to date. Written by the art critic with the greatest amount of influence and insight in the tumultuous art world of the late 1960s, Lucy Lippard, *Six Years: The Dematerialization of the Art Object, 1966–72* (1973) suggests that the notion that the work of art by necessity employs a certain type of materiality, visuality, and aesthetic quality is far from assured. On the contrary, in tracking various artistic developments of the preceding half-decade, she discovers that such categories and assumptions can in fact be questioned, challenged, and in some cases altogether dismantled. Several texts by Lippard are republished in this anthology, including excerpts from "The Dematerialization of Art" (1967–68), co-written with John Chandler (in part II), and the "Postface" to *Six Years* (in part V).

4. The thesis that Kosuth develops has at its core a pursuit parallel to that of the logical positivists. Whereas the primary concern of the latter is in the search for the "meaning of our meaning systems," Kosuth presents his work as in search of the "art of our art systems" (which is what Kosuth means when he says that "art is the definition of art"). See Joseph Kosuth, "Art After Philosophy: Part 1" (1969), reprinted in part III of this volume.

5. Ibid.

6. Ibid. Citing Ayer, Kosuth writes: "A proposition is analytic when its validity depends solely on the definitions of the symbols it contains, and synthetic when its validity is determined by the facts of experience."

7. Ibid. A single long quotation conveys the gist of his argument: "The validity of artistic propositions is not dependent on any empirical, much less any aesthetic, presupposition about the nature of things. For the artist, as an analyst, is not directly concerned with the physical properties of things. He is concerned with the way (1) in which art is capable of conceptual growth and (2) how his propositions are capable logically of following that growth. In other words, the propositions of art are not factual, but linguistic in character—that is, they do not describe the behavior of physical, or even mental objects; they express definitions of art, or the formal consequences of definitions of art."

8. Art & Language, "Introduction," *Art-Language: The Journal of Conceptual Art* (1969), reprinted in part III of this volume. I take this introduction, written primarily by Terry Atkinson, to represent the standpoint of the early Art & Language. Needless to say, it is a point of view that,

like all of those presented from the 1960s in this essay, will evolve considerably over the next decades. On the early history of Art & Language, see Charles Harrison and Fred Orton, *A Provisional History of Art & Language* (Paris: Editions E. Fabre, 1982).

9. Michael Baldwin, "Remarks On Air-Conditioning" (1967), reprinted in part I of this volume. Baldwin writes: "It has been customary to regard 'exhibitions' as those situations where various objects are in discrete occupation of a room, site, etc.: perceptions appear, to peruse. In the case of so-called 'environmental' exhibitions, it is easily shown that aspects of the discrete arrangement remain. Instead of inflected, dominating surfaces, etc., there are inflected, dominating sites. . . . It is absurd to suggest that spatial considerations are all bound to the relations of things at a certain level above that of a minimum visibility."

10. Terry Atkinson in a polemical letter to Lucy R. Lippard and John Chandler following the publication of their article "The Dematerialization of Art" (1967–68), excerpts of which are reprinted in part II of this volume. Atkinson's letter, dated 23 March 1968, is also republished in this anthology.

11. Art & Language, "Introduction."

12. Ibid.

13. As Kosuth stated in a 1970 radio interview with Jeanne Siegel: "I call it art and it came out of art. I have had a traditional, even classical, art education." See "Joseph Kosuth: Art as Idea as Idea," in Jeanne Siegel, *Artwords: Discourse on the 60s and 70s* (New York: Da Capo, 1985), p. 228.

14. Sol LeWitt, "Paragraphs on Conceptual Art" (1967), reprinted in part I of this volume.

15. Patsy Norvell, interview with Sol LeWitt, 10 April 1969, unpublished (in Patsy Norvell archives, New York: "LeWitt: This kind of art that I'm doing, I don't think of it as being rational at all. I think of it as being irrational. Formalist art, where the artist decides and makes decisions all the way down the line, that's a rationalistic kind of way of thinking about art. I don't think mine is at all. . . . What I'm doing is much more complex. It's much more irrational." My account of the difference between rational and logical operations in LeWitt's artistic practice is informed by Rosalind Krauss, "The Mind/Body Problem: Robert Morris in Series," in *Robert Morris: The Mind/Body Problem,* ex. cat. (New York: Solomon R. Guggenheim Museum, 1994), p. 11.

16. Norvell, interview with Joseph Kosuth.

17. LeWitt, "Paragraphs on Conceptual Art."

18. John Anthony Thwaites, "Lawrence Weiner: An Interview and an Interpretation," *Art and Artists,* 7:5 (August 1972), p. 23.

19. "I don't care aesthetically which of the three conditions the work exists in," Weiner stressed in an early interview. "It would be a fascist gesture on my part if I were to say you can accept

the things only on a verbal information level, which would be type on the page, or you can accept them only on an oral information level. It doesn't matter if it's physically conveyed or whether it's conveyed verbally or orally." See Willoughby Sharp, "Lawrence Weiner at Amsterdam," *Avalanche,* 4 (Spring 1972), p. 66.

20. As Weiner once remarked about his work, "There's no way to build a piece incorrectly." Ibid. p. 69.

21. This statement of intent was first published in the catalogue for the exhibition "January 5–31, 1969" (New York: Seth Siegelaub, 1969), n.p.

22. "Anyone who imposes a unique condition for receivership, for interpretation, for seeing a work, is placing art within a context that is almost 19th century. There is the specific, unique, emotional object produced by a prophet, produced by the only person who can make this. It becomes Expressionist to say: 'I am the only one who can make this work, there's not other viable means of doing it.' I find Expressionism related to aesthetic fascism. And being basically a Marxist, I find any kind of Expressionism fascist, and repugnant. It becomes a moral issue as well as an aesthetic one." Sharp, "Lawrence Weiner at Amsterdam," p. 70.

23. Weiner repeatedly emphasized this characteristic of his work in the late 1960s. For example, in an unpublished interview with Patsy Norvell (3 June 1969, in Patsy Norvell archives, New York), he states: "I want the art to be accessible. . . . The price becomes almost unimportant because all the art's given away when you think about it. I go through a lot of trouble to get things published all the time. So the pieces are published, the information is public, anybody that really is excited can make a reproduction. So, in fact, the art is all freehold."

24. Weiner describes some of the motivations for the dismantling of agency and subjectivity in his work in the late 1960s in the following way: "I refuse to make any definite [decision about] . . . the presentation, because then it would become an art decision. But if I accept all of the variables of presentation, then it's not an art decision because it has nothing to do with the art. The art is as validly communicated orally, verbally, or physically. It's all the same. So I can't make a decision one way or the other without lending weight to it. It also takes the expressionism out of the work for me, . . . whereby my emotional state would be interfering with the art, and leaves it in the hands of whoever is receiving it, the interested party. And they can do with it as they choose." Norvell, interview with Lawrence Weiner, unpublished.

25. Only a couple of years earlier than Weiner, Roland Barthes theorized (and called for) this transition from author to reader in "The Death of the Author," trans. Richard Howard, *Aspen 5+6,* ed. Brian O'Doherty (Fall/Winter 1967), n.p.: "The birth of the reader must be ransomed by the death of the Author."

26. In a 1969 interview with Ursula Meyer, Weiner described the program of production and distribution of his work: "People . . . can take [my work] wherever they go and can rebuild it if they choose. If they keep it in their heads, that's fine too. They don't have to buy it to have it— they can have it just by knowing it. Anyone making a reproduction of my art is making art just as valid as art as if I had made it." Ursula Meyer, "Lawrence Weiner, October 12, 1969," in *Conceptual Art* (New York: Dutton, 1972), p. 217.

27. See Benjamin H. D. Buchloh, "Conceptual Art 1962–1969: From the Aesthetic of Adminis-tration to the Critique of Institutions" (1989), an extract of which is reprinted in part VIII of this volume.

28. Throughout most of the 1960s, Haacke produced an art that explored natural systems. The systems were of physical phenomena such as wind, water, and air, as well as biological events. It should be stressed, however, that in all of these works with extant systems, the artist's role only consists of selecting the system to be demonstrated and organizing a convenient method of exhibiting it. Which is to say that a similar decentering of the artist to what we saw earlier in LeWitt's work takes place in these works by Haacke. This feature of Haacke's work was noted as early as 1966 by Mel Bochner who, in a review of Haacke's show at Harold Wise Gallery in New York, observed: "Duplicating nature in her operations . . . is what Haacke sets out to do. But at the same time he attempts to conceal the hand and personality of the maker." See Mel Bochner, "In the Galleries: Hans Haacke, Gerald Oster," *Arts Magazine,* 40:5 (March 1966), p. 58.

29. I borrow the term "inter-text" from Roland Barthes's "The Wisdom of Art" (1979): "The inter-text . . . is that circulation of anterior (or contemporary) texts in the artist's head (or hand)." *The Responsibility of Forms,* trans. Richard Howard (Berkeley: University of California Press, 1991), p. 190.

30. "The work of art . . . in seemingly by-passing all difficulties, attains full freedom, thus in fact nourishing the prevailing ideology. It functions as a security valve for the system, an image of freedom in the midst of general alienation and finally as a bourgeois concept supposedly be-yond all criticism, natural, above and beyond all ideology." Daniel Buren, "Critical Limits" (1970), in Buren, *Five Texts,* trans. Laurent Sauerwein (New York: John Weber Gallery, 1973), p. 45.

31. "The Museum/Gallery, for lack of being taken into consideration, is the framework, the habit, . . . the inescapable "support" on which art history is 'painted.' . . . The museum is thus an excellent weapon in the hands of the bourgeoisie because its role, at first sight, is not tyrannical. It is indeterminate and self-evident. It preserves. Also, access to privilege of the Museum/Gallery is often submission to vigilance over what the system considers dangerous. One sees clearly here the political interest which there is for established order to privilege that which it fears might

escape it. The museum can assess in its own time what is presented, including that which has no a priori value (of an aesthetic-saleable kind), and will succeed all the more easily as everyone lends himself to this process, and no one notices this phenomenon or else considers it as inevitable and self-evident." Ibid., p. 39.

32. See Eduardo Costa, Raúl Escari, Roberto Jacoby, "A Media Art (Manifesto)" (1966), included in part I of this volume.

33. For Dan Graham's employment of media systems for the production, exhibition, and distribution of his art in the 1960s, see his "My Works for Magazine Pages: 'A History of Conceptual Art'" (1985), reprinted in part VII of this volume. See also Benjamin H. D. Buchloh, "Moments of History in the Work of Dan Graham" (1977), in part VI of this volume.

34. See María Teresa Gramuglio and Nicolás Rosa, "Tucumán Burns" (1968), included in part II of this volume. In Tucumán, a province in northwestern Argentina, the harsh plan of economic rationalization introduced by the military government of Juan Carlos Ongania in 1966 closed the majority of its sugar refineries. As these were the province's principal source of income, with their demise the area was soon abandoned, leaving it poverty-stricken and without a labor force to protest conditions. The government in turn, with the cooperation of the press, promoted its "Operativo Tucumán" in an attempt to conceal the conditions of extreme poverty rampant in the province. A massive publicity campaign was launched that announced a largely mythical industrialization project based on creating new capital industries throughout Tucumán that would soon lead to prosperity. Thus the pressing reality of the social conditions in Tucumán was downplayed and deferred.

In response to this phenomenon, a group of artists from Rosario, Sante Fe, and Buenos Aires formed the Group of Avant-Garde Artists (Grupo de Artistas de Vanguardia) and affiliated themselves with the Argentinean General Confederation of Labor (Confederación General del Trabajo, or CGT). This culminated in the 1968 action entitled "Tucumán Burns" (*Tucumán Arde*) that sought to subvert the mythical nature of official media information with counterinformation in order to expose the catastrophic situation in the province. Not only the present situation but, more significantly, the factors that led up to this situation were publicized. Following an intense period of research systematically undertaken by the Group, posters and fliers of Tucumán were distributed through Rosario and Sante Fe. Soon, though, the Group decided to mount the work in the form of large multimedia exhibitions within main union halls of the CGT in Rosario and Buenos Aires.

The exhibitions featured all-over interior environments made up of posters, placards, photomurals, newspaper montages, and an array of statistical graphs indicating rates of infant mortality, tuberculosis, illiteracy, and the like, in the region of Tucumán. Juxtaposed to this information was the full range of government-sponsored misinformation. The huge discrepancy between official and actual information was theorized by the group as having the potential not only to educate but to heighten the political consciousness of the spectators. But even with the direct engagement of the exhibitions' visitors, the high level of media attention the shows would attract was posited by the Group as an important vehicle for the dissemination of information. The movement from handbills to exhibition displays to media stratagems underscored the growing savviness of these artists to the increased role of media in production, transmission, and, ultimately, control of information about art and politics alike.

35. Ibid.

36. Hélio Oiticica, "General Scheme of the New Objectivity" (1967), republished in part I of this volume.

37. See Cildo Meireles, "Statements" (1981), reprinted in part VII of this volume.

38. See Cildo Meireles, "Insertions in Ideological Circuits" (1970), reprinted in part IV of this volume. Also see Mari Carmen Ramírez, "Blueprint Circuits: Conceptual Art and Politics in Latin America" (1993), in part VIII of this volume.

In Brazil, the military coup that toppled the constitutional regime in 1964 was followed by a resurgence of dictatorship in 1968. The latter, in tandem with Brazilian censors, immediately imposed a dramatic crackdown on the arts. Seen from this perspective, the radically transformed bottles that comprise the *Insertion—Coca-Cola* project function to communicate a revolutionary, anti-imperialist message to a potentially enormous public at a time when the dictatorial regime was vigilantly monitoring all the conventional channels of communication.

39. As Mary Kelly puts it in the interview with Terry Smith, first published in part VII of this anthology, "When I started work on *Post-Partum Document* in 1973 I was curious about the parallels with Art & Language work in England. They were very influential, as was the work of Kosuth in New York. I did want to shift the emphasis from the notion of the analytical proposition to a more synthetic process."

40. Clearly these are works that criticize both the analytic model of linguistic conceptualism in which language displaces the visual, and the more synthetic models of conceptualism of the 1960s and early 1970s where the displacement of the visual by language is coupled with the opening up of the work to allow the spectator/reader to become an active performer.

41. As was noted at the time by contemporary critics, many of these developments can be attributed to the influence of French structural and poststructural philosophy and theory. See, for example, Douglas Crimp, "Pictures" (1977–79), in *October,* no. 8 (Spring 1979), pp. 75–88, Craig Owens, "The Discourse of Others: Feminists and Postmodernism" (1983), in *Beyond Rec-*

*ognition: Representation, Power, Culture* (Berkeley: University of California Press, 1992), pp. 166–190, and Abigail Solomon-Godeau, "Living with Contradictions: Critical Practices in the Age of Supply-Side Aesthetics" (1987), in *Photography at the Dock: Essays on Photographic History, Institutions, and Practices* (Minneapolis: University of Minnesota Press, 1991), pp. 124–148.

42. See in particular Martha Rosler, "Notes on Quotes" (1981–82), *Wedge,* no. 2 (Fall 1982), pp. 68–73, and Allan Sekula, "Dismantling Modernism, Reinventing Documentary (Notes on the Politics of Representation)" (1976–78), in Sekula, *Photography Against the Grain: Essays and Photoworks 1973–1983* (Halifax: The Press of Nova Scotia College of Art and Design, 1984), pp. 53–75.

43. As Sekula notes in "Dismantling Modernism," *The Bowery in Two Inadequate Descriptive Systems* distinctly registers an intersection of class and language. "The pool of language that Rosler has tapped," Sekula writes, "is largely the socio-linguistic property of the working class and poor. This language attempts to handle an irreconcilable tension between bliss and self-destruction in a society of closed options" (p. 62).

44. Particularly crucial for this generation of artists are intersubjective theories of communicative action, such as those advanced by Jürgen Habermas, and the Birmingham school's pursuit of spaces where alternative political discourse and action can occur. Communication and progressive social change, Habermas maintains in "An Alternative Way out of the Philosophy of the Subject: Communication versus Subject-Centered Reason," in *The Philosophical Discourse of Modernity,* trans. Fredrick G. Lawrence (Cambridge, Mass.: MIT Press, 1987), esp. pp. 321–326, can be achieved if one is willing to engage in rational discourse on topics of controversy, to attempt to understand the issues and arguments, to yield to the force of the better argument, and to accept a rational consensus. And it is precisely this pursuit of communication and social change that characterizes the work of Lonidier, Rosler, Sekula, and Steinmetz.

# the promise of conceptual art

## blake stimson

It's like everything that happened in 1968, at Columbia and Paris and all other symbolic places is finally being understood, and it all REALLY meant something and it really will result in something because it already has in this show.

—Gregory Battcock reviewing the work of Robert Barry, Douglas Huebler, Joseph Kosuth, and Lawrence Weiner in Seth Siegelaub's exhibition "January 5–31, 1969," 1969

Looking back in 1975 on the art movement he helped found, Joseph Kosuth offered the following summary explanation of conceptual art's accomplishment: "It is impossible to understand" what conceptualism achieved, he announced to readers of the journal *The Fox*, "without understanding the sixties, and appreciat[ing] CA for what it was: the art of the Vietnam war era."[1] As historical observers we have to agree with Kosuth's claimed link between conceptual art and the new social movements of the same moment. Conceptual artists of all varieties shared with others of their generation an unequaled sense of opportunity and obligation to question the authority of the institutions that superintended their social roles, and the ambition to develop alternative means of negotiating their interests within the larger social order. Just as the Black Panthers felt the need and the capacity to challenge the racism of the police and, thereby, of society as a whole, by posing as a substitute armed force, just as antiwar activists were able to question the legitimacy of the war and circumvent the draft by various means, just as hippies dropped out of the existing civil society and instituted various countercultural mores, and just as women's liberation and gay power advocates called into question the institution of the patriarchal family and its extension in the larger social order and developed alternative structures of support and agency, so conceptualism challenged the authority of the institutional apparatus framing its place in society and sought out other means for art to function in the world.

For this reason, conceptual art occupies a position of unique importance in recent art history—it stands as an exemplary test case, a rare opportunity to evaluate the state of the relations between modernist aesthetics and an emergent leftist political culture. Like the artistic developments allied with the political events of 1789, 1848, and 1917 (the canonical works of David, Courbet, or Tatlin, for example)—conceptual art provides occasion to evaluate the social and political ambitions and effects of an art movement whose aesthetic radicalism and critical intent have allowed it to claim the mantle of 1968. For our purpose of attempting to gain historical understanding, that claim continues to be of central importance. This is equally true for readers inclined to evaluate conceptual art's success or failure by the modernist criterion of avant-gardism as it is for those predisposed to judge it by its contribution to a larger rupture in that tradition. For better or worse, conceptual art and its reception in a host of neo-conceptualisms carry on what one critic has disparaged as "the discourse of the last partisans of the avante-garde."[2]

Regardless of varying critical perspectives now, however, conceptual art did earn its claim on history in several consequential respects. Like many of the other revolts of the late 1960s that rejected existing authorities and realized new means of self-governance from that rejection, conceptualism successfully renegotiated its place in the social order, gaining new authority for art and artists in the process and, at least momentarily, redefining the social function of art. As Ian Burn noted in retrospect, it is "hard to imagine conceptual art" as

*the product of a moment other than the late sixties. While anti-authoritarian social movements throughout that decade demonstrated their power by occupation of the streets, buildings and universities, artists of the (late) avant-garde asserted their power by creating art which aggressively occupied the spaces of institutions, intervened in the marketplace and contested the intellectual spaces of art.*[3]

For a critical moment these ambitions were realized, and in several parts of the world simultaneously. The early organizer and promoter of conceptual art in New York, Seth Siegelaub, and the artists that worked with him, for example, successfully developed innovative distribution systems that restructured the relations among artists, their audiences, and the various intermediaries. Collective statements and working relationships were developed by the English group Art & Language, the Canadian group General Idea, and French conceptualist Daniel Buren and his early associates (Olivier Mosset, Michel Parmentier, and Niele Toroni) that modified existing expectations about artistic creativity and production. The form of most conceptual art was capable of being distributed much more broadly and efficiently and therefore, in theory, more democratically (one particularly popular idea of the period, for example, was that an entire exhibition could be carried around in a manila folder). And the new emphasis on transmission of ideas rather than objects helped to shift focus from the works' formal properties and their place in a history of style to the more immediate contextual frame where such conventions were legitimated and consumed.[4]

This last accomplishment was realized first in its most radical form in November 1968 when a group of artists in Rosario, Argentina, many of whom had been working through aesthetic issues raised by New York–based happenings, pop art, and minimalism, dropped the dada influence shared by these movements from the early 1960s and switched en masse to an agit-prop aesthetic. This new position, "born from an awareness of the actual reality of the artist as an individual inside the political and social context that surrounds him," was reminiscent of many of the historical avant-garde movements of the 1920s and 30s.[5] The "context" they were addressing was the impact of government planning on sugar industry laborers in the remote province of Tucumán. Their activism on behalf of working-class, non-art interests also anticipated a turn many of the New York–based conceptualists would make in the mid-1970s and one made by the conceptualism-derived "synthetic" practices of artists such as Hans Haacke, Mary Kelly, Martha Rosler, Fred Lonidier, and Allan Sekula in the early 1970s.[6]

Just as there are a variety of ways to explain the emergence of the larger New Left political culture of the 1960s, so there are many ways to account for the particular radicalism of conceptual art. The sense of security and willingness to take risks that come from a robust economy might be considered, for example, or the high level of education achieved by many of the artists that emerged in the 1960s, or the heightened critical acumen gained from the recently revitalized tradition of the artist-critic, or the renewed influence of dada and constructivism afforded by several important and timely books and exhibitions.[7] One crucial factor, however, was conceptualism's clear picture of the established interests it was fighting and defining itself against. That picture was described well by Kosuth in retrospect:

*In the late sixties and early seventies in New York there was somewhat of a 'junta' atmosphere in the art world. The Greenberg gang was attempting with great success to initiate an Official History gestalt, and there wasn't much generosity toward us 'novelty' artists that didn't happen to fit into the prescribed historical continuum.*[8]

Kosuth was not alone in targeting Greenberg and particularly his heir Michael Fried: such was the burden or complex of an entire generation.[9]

Conceptualism's promise is best understood in relation to this particular Oedipal struggle. Kosuth's 1970 statement, "Conceptual art annexes the function of the critic . . . ; [it] makes the middle-man unnecessary,"[10] is the best-known and most concise expression of the ambition, but the emphasis on artists realizing their autonomy by taking over the role of the critic had already been introduced as a reason-for-being of conceptualism by Sol LeWitt in the opening sentences of his 1967 manifesto for the movement, "Paragraphs on Conceptual Art." "I will refer to the kind of art in which I am involved as conceptual art," he wrote, responding to a sympathetic editor who shared his opposition to "the notion that the artist is a kind of ape that has to be explained by the civilized critic." There is "a secret language that art critics use when communicating with each other through the medium of art magazines," LeWitt insisted, "but I have not discovered any [artist] who admits to doing this kind of thing" or to making work that fits the critics' categories. The "idea itself" ("as much a work of art as any finished product") not only "eliminates the arbitrary, the capricious, and the subjective," it also presents the work of art in already-interpreted form, obviating the need for a professional interpreter or critic.[11]

More than any other of conceptualism's distinctive qualities, thus, it was its *intellectualism* that made it radical and empowered its momentary takeover of the institutions of art. The burden of the endless philosophizing about the meaning of art, the burden of the shift from object-based aestheticism to a language- and theory-based anti-aestheticism, the burden of the rejection of the street coding of happenings, the commercial coding of pop, and the industrial coding of minimalism in favor of academic philosophical, literary, and scientific associations, was to aggressively usurp the authority to interpret and evaluate art assumed to be the privileged domain of scholarly critics and historians. Such was the liberation on offer from conceptualism; such was the insurrection it promised a generation of artists and that allowed it the claim, as Gregory Battcock gushed, that "everything that happened in 1968, at Columbia and Paris and all other symbolic places . . . REALLY meant something and . . . really will result in something," because its significance had already been realized in conceptual art.[12]

As appealing as this picture of liberation is, however, and as consistent as it is with precedents established within the modernist tradition, that claim has never rested easy. Emerging quite early on, often from within conceptualism itself, a discourse of "failure" developed alongside claims for the radical character of its criticality. This position differed from the considerable critical response that dismissed the project wholesale, often accusing it—as pop and minimalism had been before it—of banalizing art.[13] Those who spoke of conceptualism's "failure" chose their term of opprobrium specifically for its suggestion of the promise and seriousness of purpose they held out as the movement's mandate.[14]

At issue on both sides of the question of failure was the most politicized among the various ambitions driving conceptual art: the critique and transformation of the existing institutions of art.[15] Museums, galleries, and auction houses, the patrons and audiences they served, the artists and intellectuals who worked for them, and the aesthetic criteria that governed and legitimated their social function and status, all served, from this critical perspective, as art world outposts of the larger "establishment" called into question by the greater New Left political culture of the 1960s. It is here that conceptual art showed its ambition to be consistent with the avant-garde tradition: at its most focused its aim was not simply to shock the bourgeoisie but to recast its art institutions in more democratic form. The burden for conceptualism, the test of its own critical legitimation, thus, was the extent to which it succeeded in challenging and transforming the functioning of that apparatus. It has been on just such grounds that conceptualism's most sympathetic and perceptive critics have evaluated its contribution and raised the specter of "failure."

An early and important critical reevaluation of conceptualism came from one of its initial, most enthusiastic, and most influential champions, Lucy Lippard. After helping to give definition and seriousness to the movement in 1968 by invoking the promise of renaissance—"The studio is again becoming a study" is how she and John Chandler characterized the state of artistic development in their inaugural review, "The Dematerialization of Art"—she concluded her 1973 anthology of excerpts from conceptual art's still-warm history, *Six Years,* with grave doubts about the ultimate benefit of such a development. For "the most part," she reflected in retrospect, "the artists have been confined to art quarters, usually by choice." Artists were now engaged with issues and problems that extended beyond their own immediate technical domain, but a "ghetto mentality" persisted in a "narrow and incestuous art world," and artists had little choice but to maintain their "resentful reliance on a very small group of dealers, curators, critics, editors and collectors who are all too frequently and often unknowingly bound by invisible apron strings to the 'real world's' power structure." The move from studio to study and from the language of painterly and sculptural form to various philosophical, scientific, and other academic lexicons, Lippard now felt, had not given artists any more of a foothold in the world around them than they had had before. Indeed, it was "unlikely," she lamented, "that conceptual art will be any better equipped to affect the world any different than, or even as much as, its less ephemeral counterparts."[16]

Similarly, Seth Siegelaub, the organizer-entrepreneur who was, perhaps, the single most influential figure associated with the movement,[17] argued a related point at the end of a 1973 discussion about "the success of conceptual art" with Michel Claura: "the economic pattern associated with conceptual art is remarkably similar to that of other artistic movements: to purchase a unique work cheap and resell it at a high price." His remarks also betrayed more resentment than Lippard and a greater sense of having been let down by the movement:

*Conceptual art, more than all previous types of art, questions the fundamental nature of art. Unhappily, the question is strictly limited to the exclusive domain of fine art. There is still potential of it enabling an examination of all that surrounds art, but in reality, conceptual artists are dedicated only to exploring avant-garde aesthetic problems.*[18]

Around the same time that Lippard and Siegelaub were working through their doubts, part-time conceptualist Robert Smithson developed a similar but more extreme critique suggesting that conceptual art not only was unable to achieve its aims but also was unknowingly reaffirming the political and economic interests of the very institutions it was posturing against. The central premise of conceptualism, he argued in 1972, was not art for art's sake but even worse: "production for production's sake." Where art for art's sake had still relied on a notion of "quality" (albeit a very mystified and abstract one) to justify itself in social terms, production for production's sake could dispense with the interests of the audience altogether and justify itself simply on the basis of its own activity: it assumed that conceptualizing was valuable on its own, was "productive," without any consideration for whether or not the particular concepts produced served specific social needs or functions. The conceptual artist presents him or herself "like a B. F. Skinner rat doing his 'tough' little tricks."[19] As in the lab rat's compliance with the dictates of the scientist, Smithson argued, conceptual art served the business needs of galleries and collectors in the wake of the 1960s boom in the art market: "Because galleries and museums have been victims of 'cut-backs,'" he wrote, "they need a cheaper product—objects are thus reduced to 'ideas,' and as a result we get 'Conceptual Art.' Compared to isolated objects, isolated ideas in the metaphysical context of a gallery offer . . . an aesthetic bargain."[20]

The various ways in which conceptualism distanced itself from the material quality and commodity status of art—its rejection of art's conventional object status, for example, and its attempt to eliminate or appropriate many of the institutions of art, such as the critic and the gallery—were, he thought, based on naive assumptions about the potential for avant-garde autonomy. It's "silly," he said in a different context in 1972, "for artists to try to overcome that, because they will just be absorbed . . . , they'll just be integrated into the whole thing, so there's no viable alternative. . . . Their purity is the opiate, the reward they get . . . religion functioned in that way too."[21] Or again in 1973 he said: "I think it is time we realized that there is no point in trying to transcend those realms. Industry, commercialism, and the bourgeoisie are very much with us. . . . this whole notion of trying to form a cult that tries to transcend all this strikes me as a kind of religion in drag."[22]

By 1975 uncertainty about conceptualism's accomplishments and the critique of its claim to autonomy had become a focal point and inspiration for a group of first- and second-generation conceptual artists based in New York when they joined together under the name of the English conceptual art group Art & Language and began publishing *The Fox.* Advertising their first issue in 1975, the *Fox* group promised to investigate "the failure of Conceptual Art," asking "What good is a critique of institutions?" (taking the most politicized tendency within conceptual art as their object of critique), and "Does this art now stand for the total ossification of any conditions of a feasible non-bureaucratic ideology?"[23] This sense of crisis was inflected with an even greater self-critical tone by *Fox* affiliate and first-generation conceptual artist Ian Burn in a much-discussed *Artforum* essay that began with the following framing statement: "WHILE WE'VE BEEN ADMIRING OUR NAVELS / WE HAVE BEEN CAPITALIZED AND MARKETED / BUT THROUGH REALIZING OUR SOCIALIZATION / MIGHT WE BE ABLE TO TRANSFORM OUR REALITY?"[24] By the second issue of *The Fox,* the editorial orientation had shifted its emphasis away from self-doubt and toward a call for proactive social intervention and pointed critique of artistic "indolence."

*If you are concerned with trying to reclaim art as an instrument of social and cultural transformation, in exposing the domination of the culture/administrative apparatus as well as art which indolently reflects that apparatus, you are urged to participate in this journal. Its editorial thrust is ideological: it aims at a contribution to the wider movement of social criticism/ transformation.*[25]

By the third and final issue of *The Fox* in 1976, the new consensus—that art should be explicitly political and attempt to contribute to "the wider movement of social criticism/

transformation"—had been undermined by personal and ideological conflicts within the group. The disagreements between a newly strident faction of mostly second-generation conceptualists and several old-guard factions of mostly first-generation figures would lead to the breakup of what had become a quite large alliance.[26]

The undoing of *The Fox* marked the end of an initial period of loose consensus about what art should be or do (or at least about what it should *not* be and do) in the name of conceptualism. Many of those involved abandoned anti-aestheticism as their primary emphasis at this point and sought out new directions. Some simply dropped out of the art world altogether, while others carried on with their careers by reorienting their work around the emerging critical rubric of postmodernism.[27] Several of those who became politicized in the mid-1970s removed themselves as far as possible from art world institutions while still attempting to function as artists and actively sought out new forms of patronage, primarily from labor unions.[28] Finally, those who chose to carry on the Art & Language name found new purpose and a new aesthetic direction in ridiculing the workerism they witnessed in their former affiliates.[29]

This turning point in the history of conceptual art in the mid-1970s may also be understood to reflect more general changes in artists' social ambition from the critique of its own institutions to a critique of larger social processes on behalf of specific, non-artist constituencies. The rise of feminist art and the Chicano mural movement, the organization of the many activist groups such as PAD/D and Group Material, the myriad new, politically oriented art journals such as *Left Curve* (1974), *Praxis* (1975), *October* (1976), *Red Herring* (1977), *Heresies* (1977), *Block* (1979), and *Wedge* (1982), the reworking of reportage aesthetics by Haacke, Kelly, Sekula, and others, the opening up of dada found-object aesthetics into critical appropriation in the work of artists such as Cindy Sherman, Sherrie Levine, Richard Prince, Barbara Kruger, and Jenny Holzer, all contributed to a sense that art had expanded its ambition beyond the critique of institutionalized aestheticism that had dominated most of conceptualism in the late 1960s.

In its historic moment, however, the moment in which it emerged as the new hegemonic vanguard in the capital of the international art market, in 1968, 1969, and 1970 as the new left political culture was exploding onto streets and campuses, conceptual art had not, in the main, adapted itself to the new political-cultural climate. "The split between art and real problems emerged in the sixties in an essentially apolitical and asocial art," Ian Burn and Karl Beveridge argued in 1975.[30] "Given the estrangement of the avant-garde from real politics," Burn noted later, conceptual art "was very much an 'in-house' revolt—doing what you could with what you had to work with."[31] Ultimately, most conceptual art confined itself to the laboratory of the art world at a time when such professional specialization had little valence or currency. By and large, it did not use the social unrest of the period—as artists had in 1789, 1848, and 1917—to reach out to new audiences and to establish new avenues of patronage.

Retrospective laments focusing on this question of artist-audience relations have come from many quarters. I have already cited several who abandoned conceptualism for other, more politicized practices (Lippard, Siegelaub, and Burn, for example). Those who continued to work under the name Art & Language (and thereby carry on the legacy of conceptualism closest to its original form) have also raised similar concerns in their retrospective accounts. "Realistically," Charles Harrison has written, for example, Art & Language "could identify *no* actual alternative public which was not composed of the participants in its own projects and deliberations."[32] In a recent, collectively attributed lecture, the group addressed the issue of audience as follows: "A combination of ludicrous (perhaps) theoretical adventurism plus a suspicious malingering (perhaps) around the boundaries of philosophy, sociology, mathematical logic, aesthetics and art criticism amounted to, though did not set out as, a suppressive revolt against the spectator."[33] Michael Baldwin raised a similar concern by focusing on the self-instituting or bureaucratic function of conceptualism's colonization of its own critical reception: "what we were creating was an iconography of *administration.* The artist turned businessman and worse is one of the legacies of conceptual art. Refuse as we might."[34] Finally, Mel Ramsden was even more baleful: conceptual art, he wrote in 1975, "was basically limited to insular-tautological spectacle. It wasn't *enough;* it was a diversification, not a contradiction . . . our mode of operation is 'professionalized,' specialized, autonomous, and essentially quaintly harmless (but essential) to the mode of operation of the market-structures. . . . The situation becomes, to me, even more vain as we ourselves finally become our own entrepreneurs-pundits, the middle-life of the market our sole reality."[35]

The modernist art movements of the late 1960s—conceptual art in particular—were different in tone and ambition from earlier artistic movements associated with emergent leftist political cultures. As the discourse developed from happenings and pop to minimalism to conceptualism, it came to have less and less of the bravado, less of the emotional force and scale, less of the claim to historical agency that had once characterized David's memorial to Marat as the martyred saint of the revolution, for example, or Courbet's projection of the citizens of Ornans into the elevated realm of history painting, or Tatlin's proposed monument to the Third International as historical transformation institutionalized. As both Jeff Wall and Benjamin Buchloh point out, conceptual art had little of the social utopianism that drove the historical avant-gardes of the 1910s, 1920s, and 1930s outside of their regular circles, leading them to define their roles as designers and propagandists for the emergent leftist political cultures of their time.[36] "The audience of conceptual art is composed primarily of artists," Kosuth wrote, staking out his turf and ambition in the wake of 1968; "an audience separate from the participants doesn't exist."[37]

This would change and even start off on very different footing in, for example, the work of Hans Haacke in New York and the "Tucumán Burns" group in Argentina. But on the whole, in the work of those artists around the world who had come of age with the neo-avant-garde movements of the early 1960s and were attempting to move beyond them with a more radical refusal of the aestheticism of the previous generation, a kind of professional entrenchment ensued that gave conceptual art a distant and, at moments, disdainful tone. By "turning their backs on the political culture of the time,"[38] as Charles Harrison has written, the conceptualists were able to do little more than pose as melancholy reflections of the loss of utopian ideals historically associated with avant-garde ambition at precisely the same moment that the riotous utopianism of the New Left political culture—and with it, at least potentially, a new audience and new social function for art and its institutions—was opening up alongside it.

The question such comparisons raise, of course, is *why?* Why was there such a gap in tone and ambition between the modernist art and the new social movements of the late 1960s? Why did artists not come to serve the new political culture directly as their modernist forebears had in the past? The answer is by no means clear, but it is well worth considering in relation to the materials collected in this volume. At stake in such considerations, after all, are issues fundamental to the conceptualist project in all its variants: What is the place or function of art in society? What is its relationship to its supporting institutions? Who is its audience? What is it that makes art's contribution to society in its present historical circumstances distinctive and valuable? A central ambition for this collection is that it might aid in rethinking these core artistic issues through the prism of 1968 as an epochal historical *and* art-historical moment. In the end such a project is of equal value to the "last partisans of the avant-garde" as it is to the partisans of its demise. Conceptualism's promise, after all, has always turned on its claim to have emerged as the art of a time in which such concerns with institutions and audiences were unusually pressing and exceptionally available to reevaluation. Whether its legacy as the art of 1968 will be to pass its inherited ideal forward through neo-conceptualism and on to a future moment when avant-gardism might once again be viable, or whether it will mark a point in the history of modernism when that ideal passed into irrelevance, remains an open question.

## NOTES

1. Joseph Kosuth, "1975," reprinted in part VI of this volume.

2. Thierry de Duve, *Kant After Duchamp* (Cambridge: MIT Press, 1996), p. 455.

3. Ian Burn, "Abstracts of Perception," *Flash Art* (November/December 1988), p. 109.

4. See the discussion of the "success of conceptual art" between Seth Siegelaub and Michel Claura in their 1973 essay "Conceptual Art," included in part V of this volume.

5. See the manifesto by María Teresa Gramuglio and Nicolás Rosa on behalf of the Rosario group, "Tucumán Burns," and my interview with Luis Camnitzer, "'Dada—Situationism/Tupamaros—Conceptualism,'" included in parts II and VII of this volume.

6. See Terry Smith's discussion of synthetic vs. analytic practices in Mary Kelly and Terry Smith, "A Conversation about Conceptual Art, Subjectivity and *The Post-Partum Document*," included in part VII of this volume.

7. These are the most common explanations given by art historians. Among others, see Thomas Crow's account: "By the mid 1960s, certainly, a stark choice existed between the demands of 'the Movement' and the demands of a career in art, however radically conceived." Thomas Crow, *The Rise of the Sixties: American and European Art in the Era of Dissent* (New York: Abrams, 1996), p. 180.

8. Kosuth, "1975."

9. The best-known of such responses to Fried—"the orthodox modernist, the keeper of the gospel of Clement Greenberg, . . . the Marxist saint"—is Robert Smithson's letter to the editor of *Artforum* (October 1967) in response to Fried's "Art and Objecthood" (*Artforum,* June 1967). Smithson's letter is reprinted in Jack Flam, ed., *Robert Smithson: The Collected Writings* (Berkeley: University of California Press, 1996), pp. 66–67. See also the many disparaging comments by those associated with Art & Language, including their comparison of Greenberg and Lenin in a 1971 interview with Catherine Millet translated in this volume.

10. Joseph Kosuth, "Introductory Note to *Art-Language* by the American Editor," *Art Language,* 1:2 (February 1970), reprinted in *Art After Philosophy and After: Collected Writings, 1966–1990* (Cambridge: MIT Press, 1993), p. 39, emphasis added.

11. Sol LeWitt, "Paragraphs on Conceptual Art," reprinted in part I of this volume. This was a point Barbara Rose also raised prior to Kosuth's manifesto: "By making immaterial, ephemeral or extra-objective work, the artist eliminates intrinsic quality. This challenges not only the market mechanism, but also the authority of the critic by rendering superfluous or irrelevant his role of connoisseur of value or gourmet of quality." Barbara Rose, "The Politics of Art Part III," *Artforum* (May 1969), p. 46.

12. Gregory Battcock, "Painting Is Obsolete," reprinted in part III of this volume.

13. See, for example, Dore Ashton, "New York Commentary," *Studio International* (March 1969); Hilton Kramer, "Art: Xeroxophilia Rages out of Control," *New York Times* (11 April 1970); Robert Hughes, "The Decline and Fall of the Avant-Garde," *Time* (18 December 1972); Tom Wolfe, *The Painted Word* (New York: Farrar, Straus and Giroux, 1975).

14. Lumping sympathetic and antagonistic critics together is one of the limitations of Gabriele Guercio's review of conceptualism's critical reception, "Formed in Résistance: Barry, Huebler, Kosuth and Weiner vs. the American Press," in Claude Gintz, *L'art conceptuel: Une perspective,* ex. cat. (Paris: Musée d'Art Moderne de la Ville de Paris, 1989), pp. 74–81). Another limitation is the way in which he, apparently naively, plays into the charge of simple self-indulgence levied by critics like Kramer and Hughes when he defines conceptual art as a would-be artist's rights movement whose main accomplishment was to "defend the right to self-reflexivity and the freedom to define art" for oneself.

15. For very different analyses of competing critical and aesthetic tendencies within American and European conceptualism as a whole, see Joseph Kosuth's distinction between "SCA" (stylistic conceptual art) and "TCA" (theoretical conceptual art) in "1975," and Benjamin H. D. Buchloh's distinction between the "aesthetic of administration" and the "critique of institutions" in "Conceptual Art 1962–1969: From the Aesthetic of Administration to the Critique of Institutions," reprinted in part VIII of this volume. For more recent and comprehensive critical accounts of the various tendencies that made up conceptual art, see Alexander Alberro, "Deprivileging Art: Seth Siegelaub and the Politics of Conceptual Art," Ph.D. diss. (Northwestern University, Evanston, III., 1996), and his introduction to this volume. All of these accounts base their analyses in New York. For alternative accounts that delineate various conceptualist approaches within a perspective that includes work produced in Argentina and Brazil, see Mari Carmen Ramírez, "Blueprint Circuits: Conceptual Art and Politics in Latin America," reprinted in part VIII of this volume, and my interview with Luis Camnitzer, published in part VII of this volume.

16. Lucy Lippard, "Postface," reprinted in part V of this volume.

17. For an extensive study of Siegelaub's accomplishments, see Alberro, "Deprivileging Art."

18. Seth Siegelaub in Siegelaub and Michel Claura, "L'art conceptual" (1973), my translation, published in part V of this volume.

19. Quoted by Hughes, "The Decline and Fall of the Avant-Garde."

20. Robert Smithson, "Production for Production's Sake," reprinted in part V of this volume.

21. Robert Smithson interviewed by Bruce Kurtz in 1972, first published in *The Fox,* no. 2 (1975) and reprinted in Smithson, *Collected Writings,* pp. 264–265.

22. Smithson in an interview with Moira Roth, "Robert Smithson on Duchamp," published in *Artforum* (October 1973) and reprinted in Smithson, *Collected Writings,* p. 312. Smithson developed his own aesthetic position against both conceptualism's naive separatism and the culture of political protest developed by, particularly, the antiwar and environmental movements. For example, when asked to speak as a representative artist among *Vogue*'s January 1970 "Best Bets for the 70s," he chose to characterize what was needed for "the monuments of the future" as follows: "Art exists in thousands of dollars," he said, "but to give art real importance and timelessness artists have to begin to think in terms of millions." To that end he began soliciting funding for his earthworks from mining companies in early 1970s, offering to transform their mining pits into art. "His desire," according to his widow Nancy Holt, was "to have art be a necessary part of society" ("Biographical Note," in Smithson, *Collected Writings,* p. xxviii.) Of course, it was a very particular part of society that he chose to ally himself with. For more on the development of Smithson's aesthetic position in the early 1970s, see my "Sinking into the 'Slough of Decayed Language': Robert Smithson and the Impact of Conceptualism on the Social Function of Art," unpublished, and "An Art and Its Public/A Public and Its Art: Robert Smithson vs. the Environmentalists," *Collapse,* 2 (1997).

23. Indeed, it was precisely this claim of failure that would prompt Kosuth to raise his "reservations" about the claim, at least insofar as it pertained to his work, and defend conceptualism as the art of the Vietnam War era in the second issue of *The Fox.*

24. Ian Burn, "The Art Market: Affluence and Degradation," reprinted in part VI of this volume.

25. The poster advertising the first issue of *The Fox* promised investigations of "Art and power," "Art and economics," "The bankruptcy of art education," "the cultural responsibilities of art in the postmodern period," and the "failure of conceptual art," among other themes. See the advertisement in *Artforum* (April 1975), p. 87. The editorial is in *The Fox,* no. 2 (1975), inside front cover.

26. For retrospective accounts of this moment see Charles Harrison and Fred Orton, *A Provisional History of Art & Language* (Paris: E. Fabre, 1982), Terry Smith interviewed by Jelana Stojanovic, "Conceptual Art: Then and Since," *Agenda: Contemporary Art,* 26–27 (November/December 1992–January/February 1993), supplement, pp. 19–34, and Michael Corris, "Inside a New York Art Gang: Selected Documents of Art & Language, New York," reprinted in part VII of this volume.

27. See, for example, Joseph Kosuth, "Necrophilia Mon Amour," *Artforum* (May 1982), pp. 58–63.

28. For one account of this development by one of its leading figures, see Ian Burn, "Artists

in the Labour Movement," *Dialogue: Writings in Art History* (Sydney: Allen & Unwin, 1991), pp. 140–151.

29. This critique would be expressed in its most schematic form by mixing references to American postwar, anticommunist aestheticism with socialist realist iconography in a series of portraits of Lenin painted in Pollock-style drips and drabs. (See, for example, *Portrait of V. I. Lenin in July 1917 Disguised by a Wig and Working Man's Clothes in the Style of Jackson Pollock II,* 1980.)

30. Karl Beveridge and Ian Burn, "Donald Judd," *The Fox,* no. 2 (1975), p. 129.

31. Burn, "Abstracts of Perception," p. 109.

32. Charles Harrison, "Art Object and Artwork," in Gintz, *L'art conceptuel,* p. 63. Harrison has also said, "The work was not done to enfranchise a new public. On the other hand, I suspect that it would not have been done at all if it had not at some level been responsive to the insights of an actual constituency—a constituency unrepresented in the dominant culture but necessary to the maintenance of that culture's vitality. In its English form at least, Conceptual Art was a *class* activity, intended to destroy the already-aestheticized objects of thought, on the grounds that the linguistic rituals of their appreciation served mindlessly to consolidate social power." "The Legacy of Conceptual Art," in *Place, Position, Presentation, Public,* ed. Ine Gevers (Maastricht: Jan Van Eyck Akademie; Amsterdam: De Balie, 1993), pp. 42–59. Or, in a related manner: "All art idealizes a public in some form. It would be true to say that the public envisaged for or presupposed by the Conceptual Art of Art & Language was one which only a social transformation could conceivably bring to the foreground of culture (though this is not to deny that public a continuing and significant presence both in imagination and in the actual margins of social life). To that extent the movement recapitulated the critical utopianism of those earlier phases of Modernism which had been marginalized in orthodox art history and art criticism by the cultural protocols of the Cold War." "Conceptual Art and the Suppression of the Beholder," in *Essays on Art & Language* (Oxford: Blackwell, 1991), p. 61.

33. "Remembering Conceptual Art," delivered by Art & Language to the conference "Who's Afraid of Conceptual Art" (19 March 1995, Institute of Contemporary Arts, London), pp. 9–10.

34. *Flash Art* (November–December 1988), p. 106.

35. Mel Ramsden, "On Practice," *The Fox,* no. 1 (1975), p. 83.

36. It was "precisely the utopianism of earlier avant-garde movements," Buchloh argues, "that was manifestly absent from Conceptual Art throughout its history" (Buchloh, "Conceptual Art 1962–1969"). Similarly, Jeff Wall has made a related general argument: "The social indifference of [Conceptual Art] is a reflex of the trauma of the collapse, circa 1939, of the ideal of an

integrated modernist art which could speak critically about the world." The "missing term," he writes, was "the absent revolutionary teleology." Wall, "Kammerspiel," reprinted in part VIII of this volume.

37. Kosuth, "Introductory Note to *Art-Language* by the American Editor," p. 39. This sense of a self-sustaining art subculture was reasserted in 1990 during a panel discussion when an audience member commented that "one of the dominant features of conceptual art was that the public felt more cut off from art than it had before" and Lawrence Weiner interrupted another panelist to respond "*We* are the public." Judith Mastai, ed., "Evening Forum: Terry Atkinson, Jeff Wall, Ian Wallace, Lawrence Weiner, moderated by Willard Holmes" (Vancouver: Vancouver Art Gallery, 1990), p. 10.

38. Harrison, "Art Object and Artwork," p. 61.

eduardo costa, raúl escari, roberto jacoby, christine kozlov, hélio oiticica, sol lewitt, sigmund bode, mel bochner, daniel buren, olivier mosset, michel parmentier, niele toroni, michel claura, michael baldwin, adrian piper

**1966–1967**

# a media art (manifesto)

## eduardo costa, raúl escari, roberto jacoby

In a mass society, the public is not in direct contact with cultural activities but is informed of them through the media. For example, the mass audience does not see an exhibition; it doesn't experience a happening or a soccer match first hand but, instead, sees its projection in the news. Real artistic production stops having importance with its diffusion since it can only reach a diminished public. "To distribute two thousand copies in a big modern city is like shooting a bullet into the air and waiting for the pigeons to fall," said Nam June Paik. Ultimately, information consumers are not interested in whether or not an exhibition occurs; it is only the image the media constructs of the artistic event that matters.

Contemporary art (principally Pop Art) sometimes makes use of mass media elements and techniques, divorcing them from their natural context (in, for example, the work of Lichtenstein or in D'Arcangelo's road series). Unlike Pop Art, we aim to make works of art utilizing the qualities fundamental to this medium. In this way, we undertake to give to the press the written and photographic report of a happening that has not occurred. This false report would include the names of the participants, an indication of the time and location in which it took place and a description of the spectacle that is supposed to have happened, with pictures taken of the supposed participants in other circumstances. In this way of transmitting the information, in this way of "realizing" the nonexistent event, in the differences that would arise from the separate versions that each transmission would make from the same event, the sense of the art work would appear. The work would begin to exist in the same moment that the consciousness of the spectator constitutes it as having been accomplished.

Therefore there is a triple creation:

— *the formation of the false report*
— *the transmission of the report through the existing channels of information*[1]
— *the reception by the spectator who constructs—based on the information received and depending on the manner that information signifies for him—the substance of a nonexistent reality which he would imagine as truthful.*

This way we take on the ultimate characteristic of the media: the de-realization of objects. In this way the moment of transmission of the work of art is more privileged than its production. The creation consists of liberating its production from its transmission.

Currently, the work of art is a combination of results from a process that starts with the realization of a work (traditional) and continues until such work is converted into material transmitted by the media. Now we propose a work of art in which the moment of production disappears. In this way it will be made clear that works of art are, in reality, pretexts to start up the apparatus of the media.

From the spectator's point of view it is possible, for this kind of work of art, to have two readings: on one side, the reading of the spectator who trusts the media and believes in what he sees; on the other side, the reading of the informed spectator who is conscious of the nonexistence of the art work that is being transmitted.

In this way the possibility of a new genre is open: the art of the media where "what is said" is not fundamentally important but instead thematizes the media as media.

This report addresses not only the second type of reader but also "notifies" some other readers and thereby also performs the first part of the work that we described.

**NOTES**
1. The message would vary, depending on the material characteristics of the transmitting channel. "The medium is the message" (McLuhan).

4    This text was written in Buenos Aires in July 1966, and published in Oscar Masotta, ed., *Happenings* (Buenos Aires: Jorge Alvarez, 1967), pp. 119–122. Translated by Trilce Navarrete, this is its first publication in English. The editors are grateful to Mari Carmen Ramírez for pointing out the importance of this text to Latin American conceptualism.

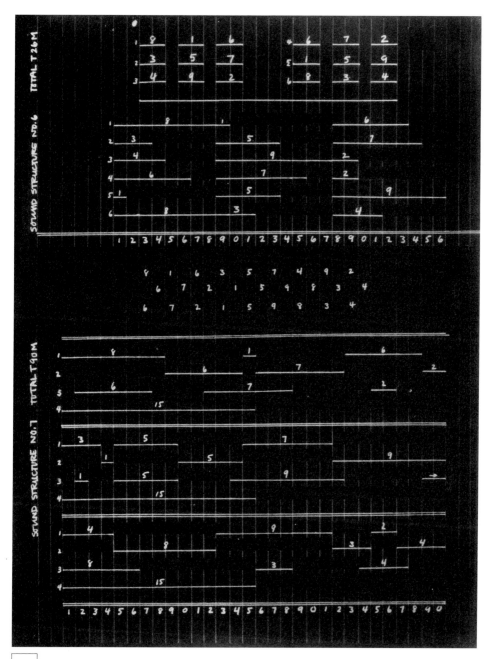

Christine Kozlov, *Sound Structure*, 1965–66.

# compositions for audio structures

## christine kozlov

The numbers on the left indicate the different sounds. The horizontals corresponding to each number indicate both placement (in relation to the other sounds) and duration in counts of sound (the numbers on top of the horizontals). In structure number 1, for instance, number 1's first duration is 12 counts of sound, stopping for 1 count, continuing for 11, stopping for 2, continuing for 10, and so on.

The sounds sounding together are realized by reading downward until the sound-indicating numbers repeat; so that again in structure number 1, the first 6 counts of sound, sound 1, 3 and 5 (the constant) are sounding; at the end of count 6 sound 4 enters lasting for 12½ counts, or until the middle of sound 1 and 3's second duration; after sound 1 and 3's first stop and until sound 1 and 3 start again sound 2 is sounding.

The structures are concerned with symmetry, asymmetry, progression, or with their own intrinsic logic.

The structure's development in sound would incorporate either constant sounds, or sounds with equal beat durations or both.

This text appeared in the catalogue for the exhibition "Nonanthropomorphic Art by Four Young Artists," held at the Lannis Gallery in New York City in February and March 1967. Unpaginated.

# position and program
## hélio oiticica

Anti-art, in which the artist understands his/her position not any longer as a creator for contemplation, but as an instigator of creation—"creation" as such: this process completes itself through the dynamic participation of the "spectator," now considered as "participator." Anti-art answers the collective need for creative activity which is latent and can be activated in a certain way by the artist. The metaphysical, intellectualist and aestheticist positions thus become invalidated—there is no proposal to "elevate the spectator to a level of creation," to a "meta-reality," or to impose upon him an "idea" or "aesthetic model" corresponding to those art concepts, but to give him a simple opportunity to participate, so that he "finds" there something he may want to realize. What the artist proposes is, thus, a "creative realization," a realization exempt from moral, intellectual or aesthetic premises—anti-art is exempt from these—it is a simple position of man within himself and in his vital creative possibilities. "Not to find" is an equally important participation, since it defines the freedom of "choosing" of anyone to whom participation is proposed. The artist's work, in whatever fixed aspects it may have, only takes meaning and completes itself through the attitude of each participator—it is he who attributes the corresponding signifiers to it: something is anticipated by the artist, but the attributed signifiers are unanticipated possibilities, generated by the work—and this includes non-participation among its innumerable possibilities. The issue of knowing whether art is "this" or "that," or whether it ceases to be, is not raised: there is no definition of what art is. (. . .)

. . . There is such a freedom of means that the very act of not creating already counts as a creative manifestation. An ethical necessity of another kind comes into being here, which I would also include in the environmental, since its means are realized through the word, written or spoken, and in a more complex way through discourse: This is the social manifestation, incorporating an ethical (as well as political) position which comes together as manifestations of individual behavior. I should make it a bit clearer, first of all, that such a position can only be a totally anarchic position, such is the degree of liberty implicit in it. It is against everything that is oppressive, socially and individually—all the fixed and decadent forms of government, or reigning social structures. The "socio-environmental" position is the starting point for all social and political changes, or the fermenting of them at least—it is incompatible with any law which is not determined by a defined interior need, laws being constantly remade—it is the retaking of confidence by the individual in his or her intuitions and most precious aspirations.

Politically, this position is that of all of the genuine lefts of this world—not of course the oppressive lefts (of which Stalinism is an example). It could not possibly be otherwise. For me, the most complete expression of this entire concept of "environmentation" was the formulation of what I called *Parangolé*. This is much more than a term which defines a series of typical works: the capes, banners and tent. *Parangolé* is the definitive formulation of what environmental anti-art is, precisely because, in these works, I was given the opportunity, the idea, of fusing together color, structures, poetic sense, dance, words, photography—it was the definitive pact with what I define as totality-work, if one may speak of pacts in this regard. I will therefore from now on call *Parangolé* all the definitive principles formulated here, including that of the nonformulation of concepts, which is the most important. I do not want or intend to create, as it were, a "new anti-art aesthetic," since this would already be an outdated and conformist position. *Parangolé* is anti-art par excellence; and I intend to extend the practice of *appropriation* to things of the world which I come across in the streets, vacant lots, fields, the ambient world, things which would not be transportable, but which I would invite the public to participate in. This would be a fatal blow to the concept of the museum, art gallery, etc., and to the very concept of "exhibition." Either we change it, or we remain as we are. Museum is the world: daily experience. (. . .)

This text is dated July 1966. It was first published in the catalogue for the exhibition "Aspiro ao Grande Labirinto" (Rio de Janeiro, 1986), and republished in Guy Brett et al., *Hélio Oiticica* (Rotterdam: Witte de With; Minneapolis: Walker Art Center, 1992), pp. 100–105, from where the present extracts are taken.

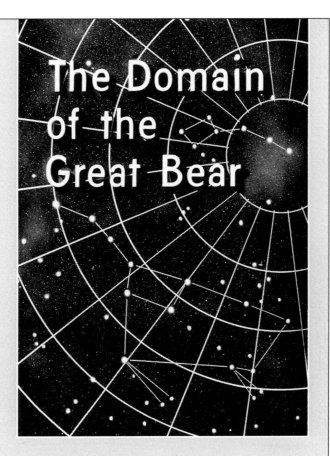

# The Domain of the Great Bear

### By Mel Bochner & Robert Smithson

FOR SOME, INFINITY IS THE PLANETARIUM, A FROZEN WHIRLPOOL AT THE END OF THE WORLD, A VAST STRUCTURE OF CONCENTRIC CIRCLES, ROUND WHOSE BORDERS ONE MAY FIND AN INTERMINABLE COLLECTION OF IDEAS AS OBJECTS, A REPOSITORY OF MODEL UNIVERSES. HERE ALSO IS THE DOMAIN OF THE GREAT BEAR.

Mel Bochner and Robert Smithson, *The Domain of the Great Bear,* 1966. First page of an article published in *Art Voices,* no. 5 (Fall 1966).

# paragraphs on conceptual art
## sol lewitt

The editor has written me that he is in favor of avoiding "the notion that the artist is a kind of ape that has to be explained by the civilized critic." This should be good news to both artists and apes. With this assurance I hope to justify his confidence. To continue a baseball metaphor (one artist wanted to hit the ball out of the park, another to stay loose at the plate and hit the ball where it was pitched), I am grateful for the opportunity to strike out for myself.

I will refer to the kind of art in which I am involved as conceptual art. In conceptual art the idea of concept is the most important aspect of the work.[1] When an artist uses a conceptual form of art, it means that all of the planning and decisions are made beforehand and the execution is a perfunctory affair. The idea becomes a machine that makes the art. This kind of art is not theoretical or illustrative of theories; it is intuitive, it is involved with all types of mental processes and it is purposeless. It is usually free from the dependence on the skill of the artist as a craftsman. It is the objective of the artist who is concerned with conceptual art to make his work mentally interesting to the spectator, and therefore usually he would want it to become emotionally dry. There is no reason to suppose, however, that the conceptual artist is out to bore the viewer. It is only the expectation of an emotional kick, to which one conditioned to expressionist art is accustomed, that would deter the viewer from perceiving this art.

Conceptual art is not necessarily logical. The logic of a piece or series of pieces is a device that is used at times only to be ruined. Logic may be used to camouflage the real intent of the artist, to lull the viewer into the belief that he understands the work, or to infer a paradoxical situation (such as logic vs. illogic).[2] The ideas need not be complex. Most ideas that are successful are ludicrously simple. Successful ideas generally have the appearance of simplicity because they seem inevitable. In terms of idea the artist is free to even surprise himself. Ideas are discovered by intuition.

What the work of art looks like isn't too important. It has to look like something if it has physical form. No matter what form it may finally have it must begin with an idea. It is the process of conception and realization with which the artist is concerned. Once given physical reality by the artist the work is open to the perception of all, including the artist. (I use the word "perception" to mean the apprehension of the sense data, the objective understanding of the idea and simultaneously a subjective interpretation of both.) The work of art can only be perceived after it is completed.

Art that is meant for the sensation of the eye primarily would be called perceptual rather than conceptual. This would include most optical, kinetic, light and color art.

Since the functions of conception and perception are contradictory (one pre-, the other post-fact) the artist would mitigate his idea by applying subjective judgement to it. If the artist wishes to explore his idea thoroughly, then arbitrary or chance decisions would be kept to a minimum, while caprice, taste and other whimsies would be eliminated from the making of the art. The work does not necessarily have to be rejected if it does not look well. Sometimes what is initially thought to be awkward will eventually be visually pleasing.

To work with a plan that is pre-set is one way of avoiding subjectivity. It also obviates the necessity of designing each work in turn. The plan would design the work. Some plans would require millions of variations, and some a limited number, but both are finite. Other plans imply infinity. In each case, however, the artist would select the basic form and rules that would govern the solution of the problem. After that the fewer decisions made in the course of completing the work, the better. This eliminates the arbitrary, the capricious, and the subjective as much as possible. That is the reason for using this method.

When an artist uses a multiple modular method he usually chooses a simple and readily available form. The form itself is of very limited importance; it becomes the grammar for the total work. In fact it is best that the basic unit be deliberately uninteresting so that it may more easily become an intrinsic part of the entire work. Using complex basic forms only disrupts the unity of the whole. Using a simple form repeatedly narrows the field of the work and concentrates the intensity to the arrangement of the form. This arrangement becomes the end while the form becomes the means.

Conceptual art doesn't really have much to do with mathematics, philosophy or any other mental discipline. The mathematics used by most artists is simple arithmetic or simple number systems. The philosophy of the work is implicit in the work and is not an illustration of any system of philosophy.

It doesn't really matter if the viewer understands the concepts of the artist by seeing the art. Once out of his hand the artist has no control over the way a viewer will perceive the work. Different people will understand the same thing in a different way.

Recently there has been much written about minimal art, but I have not discovered anyone who admits to doing this kind of thing. There are other art forms around called primary structures, reductive, rejective, cool, and mini-art. No artist I know will own up to any of these either. Therefore I conclude that it is part of a secret language that art critics use when communicating with each other through the medium of art magazines. Mini-art is best because it reminds one of the mini-skirts and long-legged girls. It must refer to very small works of art. This is a very good idea. Perhaps "mini-art" shows could be sent around the country in matchboxes. Or maybe the mini-artist is a very small person, say under five feet tall. If so, much good work will be found in the primary schools (primary school primary structures).

If the artist carries through his idea and makes it into visible form, then all the steps in the process are of importance. The idea itself, even if not made visual, is as much a work of art as any finished product. All intervening steps—scribbles, sketches, drawings, failed work, models, studies, thought, conversations—are of interest. Those that show the thought process of the artist are sometimes more interesting than the final product.

Determining what size a piece should be is difficult. If an idea requires three dimensions then it would seem any size would do. The question would be what size is best. If the thing were made gigantic then the size alone would be impressive and the idea may be lost entirely. Again, if it is too small, it may become inconsequential. The height of the viewer may have some bearing on the work and also the size of the space into which it will be placed. The artist may wish to place objects higher than the eye level of the viewer, or lower. I think the piece must be large enough to give the viewer whatever information he needs to understand the work and placed in such a way that will facilitate this understanding. (Unless the idea is of impediment and requires difficulty of vision or access.)

Space can be thought of as the cubic area occupied by a three-dimensional volume. Any volume would occupy space. It is air and cannot be seen. It is the interval between things that can be measured. The intervals and measurements can be important to a work of art. If certain distances are important they will be made obvious in the piece. If space is relatively unimportant it can be regularized and made equal (things placed equal distances apart), to mitigate any interest in interval. Regular space might also become a metric time element, a kind of regular beat or pulse. When the interval is kept regular whatever is irregular gains more importance.

Architecture and three-dimensional art are of completely opposite natures. The former is concerned with making an area with a specific function. Architecture, whether it is a work of art or not, must be utilitarian or else fail completely. Art is not utilitarian. When three-dimensional art starts to take on some of the characteristics of architecture such as forming utilitarian areas it weakens its function as art. When the viewer is dwarfed by the large size of a piece this domination emphasizes the physical and emotive power of the form at the expense of losing the idea of the piece.

New materials are one of the great afflictions of contemporary art. Some artists confuse new materials with new ideas. There is nothing worse than seeing art that wallows in gaudy baubles. By and large most artists who are attracted to these materials are the ones that lack the stringency of mind that would enable them to use the materials well. It takes a good artist to use new materials and make them into a work of art. The danger is, I think, in making the physicality of the material so important that it becomes the idea of the work (another kind of expressionism).

Three-dimensional art of any kind is a physical fact. This physicality is its most obvious and expressive content. Conceptual art is made to engage the mind of the viewer rather than his eye or emotions. The physicality of a three-dimensional object then becomes a contradiction to its non-emotive intent. Color, surface, texture, and shape only emphasize the physical aspects of the work. Anything that calls attention to and interests the viewer in this physicality is a deterrent to our understanding of the idea and is used as an expressive device. The conceptual artist would want to ameliorate this emphasis on materiality as much as possible or to use it in a paradoxical way. (To convert it into an idea.) This kind of art, then, should be stated with the most economy of means. Any idea that is better stated in two dimensions should not be in three dimensions. Ideas may also be stated with numbers, photographs, or words or any way the artist chooses, the form being unimportant.

These paragraphs are not intended as categorical imperatives but the ideas stated are as close as possible to my thinking at this time.[3] These ideas are the result of my work as an artist and are subject to change as my experience changes. I have tried to state them with as much clarity as possible. If the statements I made are unclear it may mean the thinking is unclear.

Even while writing these ideas there seemed to be obvious inconsistencies (which I have tried to correct, but others will probably slip by). I do not advocate a conceptual form of art for all artists. I have found that it has worked well for me while other ways have not. It is one way of making art; other ways suit other artists. Nor do I think all conceptual art merits the viewer's attention. Conceptual art is only good when the idea is good.

**NOTES**

1. In other forms of art the concept may be changed in the process of execution.

2. Some ideas are logical in conception and illogical perceptually.

3. I dislike the term "work of art" because I am not in favor of work and the term sounds pretentious. But I don't know what other term to use.

This text first appeared in *Artforum,* 5:10 (Summer 1967), pp. 79–84.

# excerpt from *placement as language* (1928)
## sigmund bode

It should be possible to construe a situation in which persons, things, abstractions, become simply nouns and are thus potentially objectified. As "objects" they may be heaped or dumped in any way (a definition of life?). Or they may perhaps be conjugated in such a way that their *positions* imply "verbs" in the spaces (silences) between them.

This invisible grammar can be read within and between categories. As a function of placement, it can be permitted to imply different systems, i. e., languages. Some of these languages we have not yet deciphered, i. e., invented. To identify such a grammar, to read such a language constitutes a test for the reader. . . .

This linguistics of interval and position is usually closed off by themes and titles, complex nouns that immobilize a system in a particular attitude. In this sense, explanations are modes of concealing what is accessible by removing concepts to the area of other concepts (initiating that process which eventually leads to "meaning" in the least fortunate academic sense). . . .

Placement as a grammatical concept can be extended to any abstraction . . . to a degree we may speak of meaning as a system of permutations, as a mathematics of placement. . . . It is, of course, also possible to consider how placement is concealed, how the objectified unit (a person, a concept, a period) can conceivably occur without dimensions, in no place and in no time, and thus approach the condition of art.

This text serves as the introduction to *Aspen,* 5–6 (Fall-Winter 1967), guest edited by Brian O'Doherty (a.k.a. Sigmund Bode). Unpaginated.

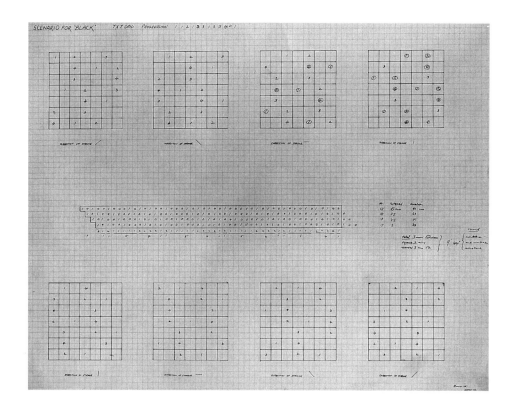

3

Brian O'Doherty, *Scenario for Black*, 1967.

# the serial attitude
## mel bochner

**What order-type is universally present wherever there is any order in the world? The answer is, serial order. What is a series? Any row, array, rank, order of precedence, numerical or quantitative set of values, any straight line, any geometrical figure employing straight lines, and yes, all space and all time.**

—Josiah Royce, *Principles of Logic*

Serial order is a method, not a style. The results of this method are surprising and diverse. Edward Muybridge's photographs, Thomas Eakins' perspective studies, Jasper Johns' numerals, Alfred Jensen's polyptychs, Larry Poons' circles, dots and ellipsoids, Donald Judd's painted wall pieces, Sol LeWitt's orthogonal multi-part floor structures all are works employing serial logics. This is not a stylistic phenomenon. Variousness of the above kind is sufficient grounds for suggesting that rather than a style we are dealing with an attitude. The serial attitude is a concern with how order of a specific type is manifest.

Many artists work "in series." That is, they make different versions of a basic theme; Morandi's bottles or de Kooning's women, for example. This falls outside the area of concern here. Three basic operating assumptions separate serially ordered works from multiple variants:

*1 — The derivation of the terms or interior divisions of the work is by means of a numerical or otherwise systematically predetermined process (permutation, progression, rotation, reversal).*

*2 — The order takes precedence over the execution.*

*3 — The completed work is fundamentally parsimonious and systematically self-exhausting.*

Serial ideas have occurred in numerous places and in various forms. Muybridge's photographs are an instance of the serialization of time through the systematic subtraction of duration from event. Muybridge simultaneously photographed the same activity from 180°, 90°, and 45° and printed the three sets of photographs parallel horizontally. By setting up alternative reading logics within a visually discontinuous sequence he completely fragmented perception into what Stockhausen called, in another context, a "directionless time-field."

Robert Rauschenberg's *Seven White Panels* and Ellsworth Kelly's orthogonal eight-foot-square *Sixty-Four* are anomalous works of the early 1950s. Both paintings fall within a generalized concept of arrays, which is serial, although their concerns were primarily modular. Modular works are based on the repetition of a standard unit. The unit, which may be anything (Andre's bricks, Morris's truncated volumes, Warhol's soup cans) does not alter its basic form, although it may appear to vary by the way in which units are adjoined. While the addition of identical units may modify simple gestalt viewing, this is a relatively uncomplex order form. Modularity has a history in the "cultural methods of forming" and architectural practice. Frank Stella has often worked within a modular set, although in his concentric square paintings he appears to have serialized color arrangement with the addition of random blank spaces. Some of the early black paintings, like *Die Fahne Hoch,* employed rotational procedures in the organization of quadrants.

Logics which precede the work may be absurdly simple and available. In Jasper Johns' number and alphabet paintings the prime set is either the letters A-Z or the numbers 0–9. Johns chose to utilize convention. The convention happened to be serial. Without deviating from the accustomed order of precedence he painted all the numbers or letters, in turn, beginning again at the end of each sequence until all the available spaces on the canvas were filled. The procedure was self-exhausting and solipsistic. Other works of Johns are noteworthy in this context, especially his *Three Flags,* which is based on size diminution and, of course, the map paintings. His drawings in which all the integers 0–9 are superimposed are examples of a straightforward use of simultaneity.

An earlier example of simultaneity appears in Marcel Duchamp's *Nude Descending a Staircase.* Using the technique of superimposition and transparency he divided the assigned canvas into a succession of time intervals. Due to the slight variation in density it is impossible to visualize specific changes as such. Alternations are leveled to a single information which subverts experiential time. Duchamp has said the idea was suggested to him by the experiments of Dr. Etienne Jules Marey (1830–1904). Marey, a French physiologist, began with ideas derived from the work of Muybridge, but made a number of significant conceptual and mechanical changes. He invented an ingenious optical device based on principles of revolution similar to Gatling's machine gun. This device enabled him to photograph multiple points of view on one plate. In 1890 he invented his "chronophotograph," which was capable of recording, in succession, 120 separate photos per second. He attempted to visualize the passage of time by placing a clock within camera range, obtaining by this method a remarkable "dissociation of time and image."

Types of order are forms of thoughts. They can be studied apart from whatever physical form they may assume. Before observing some further usages of seriality in the visual arts, it will be helpful to survey several other areas where parallel ideas and approaches also exist. In doing this I wish to imply neither metaphor nor analogy.

**My desire was for a *conscious control* over the new means and forms that arise in every artist's mind.**

—Arnold Schoenberg

Music has been consistently engaged with serial ideas. Although the term "serial music" is relatively contemporary, it could be easily applied to Bach or even Beethoven. In a serial or Dodecaphonic (twelve tone) composition, the order of the notes throughout the piece is a consequence of an initially chosen and ordered set (the semitonal scale arranged in a definite linear order). Note distribution is then arrived at by permuting this prime set. Any series of notes (or numbers) can be subjected to permutation as follows: 2 numbers have only 2 permutations (1, 2; 2, 1); 3 numbers have 6 (1, 2, 3; 1, 3, 2; 2, 1, 3; 2, 3, 1; 3, 1, 2; 3, 2, 1); 4 numbers have 24; . . . 12 numbers have 479,001,600. Other similarly produced numerical sequences and a group of pre-established procedures give the exact place in time for each sound, the coincidence of sounds, their duration, timbre and pitch.

The American serial composer Milton Babbit's *Three Compositions for Piano* can be used as a simplified example of this method (see George Perle's *Serial Composition and Atonality* for a more detailed analysis). The prime set is represented by these integers: P = 5, 1, 2, 4. By subtracting each number in turn from a constant of such value that the resulting series introduces no numbers not already given, an inversion results (in this case the constant is 6): I = 1, 5, 4, 2. A rotational procedure applied to P and I yields the third and fourth set forms: Rp = 2, 4, 5, 1; Ri = 4, 2, 1, 5.

**Mathematics—or more correctly arithmetic—is used as a compositional device, resulting in the most literal sort of "programme music," but one whose course is determined by a numerical rather than a narrative or descriptive "Programme."**
—Milton Babbit

The composer is freed from individual note-to-note decisions which are self-generating within the system he devises. The music thus attains a high degree of conceptual coherence, even if it sometimes sounds "aimless and fragmentary."

**The adaptation of the serial concept of composition by incorporating the more general notion of permutation into structural organization—a permutation the limits of which are rigorously defined in terms of the restrictions placed on its self-determination constitutes a logical and fully justified development, since both morphology and rhetoric are governed by one and the same principle.**
—Pierre Boulez

**The form itself is of very limited importance, it becomes the grammar for the total work.**
—Sol LeWitt

**Language can be approached in either of two ways, as a set of culturally transmitted behavior patterns shared by a group or as a system conforming to the rules which constitute its grammar.**
—Joseph Greenberg, *Essays in Linguistics*

In linguistic analysis, language is often considered as a system of elements without assigned meanings ("uninterpreted systems"). Such systems are completely permutational, having grammatical but not semantic rules. Since there can be no system without rules of arrangement, this amounts to the handling of language as a set of probabilities. Many interesting observations have been made about uninterpreted systems which are directly applicable to the investigation of any array of elements obeying fixed rules of combination. Studies of isomorphic (correspondence) relationships are especially interesting.

Practically all systems can be rendered isomorphic with a system containing only one serial relation. For instance, elements can be reordered into a single line, i. e., single serial relation by arranging them according to their coordinates. In the following two-dimensional array, the coordinates of C are (1, 3), of T (3, 2):

$$R \quad P \quad D$$
$$L \quad B \quad T$$
$$C \quad U \quad O$$

Isomorphs could be written as: R, L, C, P, B, U, D, T, O or R, P, D, L, B, T, C, U, O. An example of this in language is the ordering in time of speech to correspond to the ordering of direction in writing. All the forms of cryptography from crossword puzzles to highly sophisticated codes depend on systematic relationships of this kind.

**The limits of my language are the limits of my world.**
—Ludwig Wittgenstein

(. . .)

**The structure of an artificial optic array may, but need not, specify a source. A wholly invented structure need not specify anything. This would be a case of structure as such. It contains information, but not information *about,* and it affords perception but not perception of.**
—James J. Gibson, *The Senses Considered as Perceptual Systems*

Perspective, almost universally dismissed as a concern in recent art, is a fascinating example of the application of prefabricated systems. In the work of artists like Ucello, Dürer, Piero, Saendredam, Eakins (especially their drawings), it can be seen to exist entirely as methodology. It demonstrates not how things appear but rather the workings of its own strict postulates. As it is, these postulates are serial.

Perspective has had an oddly circular history. Girard Desargues (1593–1662) based his non-Euclidean geometry on an intuition derived directly from perspective. Instead of beginning with the unverifiable Euclidean axiom that parallel lines never meet, he accepted instead the visual evidence that they do meet at the point where they intersect on the horizon line (the "vanishing point" or "infinity" of perspective). Out of his investigations of "visual" (as opposed to "tactile") geometry came the field of projective geometry. Projective geometry investigates such problems as the means of projecting figures from the surface of three-dimensional objects to two-dimensional planes. It has led to the solution of some of the problems in mapmaking. Maps are highly abstract systems, but since distortion of some sort must occur in the transformation from three to two dimensions, maps are never completely accurate. To compensate for distortion, various systems have been devised. On a topographical map, for example, the lines indicating levels (contour lines) run through points which represent physical points on the surface mapped so that an isomorphic relation can be established. Parallels of latitude, isobars, isothermal lines and other grid coordinate denotations, all serialized, are further cases of the application of external structure systems to order the unordered.

Another serial aspect of mapmaking is a hypothesis in topology about color. It states that with only four colors all the countries on any map can be differentiated without any color having to appear adjacent to itself. (One wonders what the results might look like if all the paintings in the history of art were repainted to conform to the conditions of this hypothesis.) (. . .)

This text was published in *Artforum,* 6:4 (December 1967), pp. 28–33.

# statement

## daniel buren, olivier mosset, michel parmentier, niele toroni

Art is the illusion of disorientation, the illusion of liberty, the illusion of presence, the illusion of the sacred, the illusion of Nature. . . . Not the painting of Buren, Mosset, Parmentier or Toroni. . . . Art is a distraction, art is false. Painting begins with Buren, Mosset, Parmentier, Toroni.

This text appeared in the form of a three-minute audio tape loop synchronized to a series of slides (of flowers, a striptease, a bullfight, views of St. Tropez, and more) projected onto paintings by the four artists at the Paris Biennale in October 1967. The present translation is taken from Lucy R. Lippard, *Six Years: The Dematerialization of the Art Object from 1966 to 1972* (New York: Praeger, 1973), p. 30.

# buren, mosset, toroni or anybody
michel claura

In order to discuss a forgery, one must refer to an original. In the case of Buren, Mosset, Toroni, where is the original work? . . . Who is to say whether from the beginning they have not been doing each other's canvases? And if we compare all the canvases with vertical bands, all those with a central circle, all those with the regular imprints, who can distinguish between Buren, or Mosset, or Toroni as the author? For there is an *absolute* identity among all the canvases of each "type," whoever happened to be the author of any one of them. . . . "Real" or "False" are notions that cannot be adapted to the painting of Buren, Mosset, Toroni. . . . For the first time, with Buren, Mosset, Toroni, painting *is*. The experiment proposed to us carries a supplementary proof. One could search endlessly for a work which would lend itself to this demonstration. Why bother. Art exists as it is and it would be useless to establish a comparison between art and the painting of Buren, Mosset, Toroni.

This text appeared in the form of a brochure distributed independently by the artists in the Fall of 1967, and at an exhibition by Buren and Toroni in Lugano in December 1967. The present translation is taken from the Lucy R. Lippard papers, Archives of American Art, uncataloged recent acquisition.

The content of this painting is invisible; the character and dimension of the content are to be kept permanently secret, known only to the artist.

Mel Ramsden, *Secret Painting*, 1967–68.

# remarks on air-conditioning: an extravaganza of blandness
## michael baldwin

It has been customary to regard "exhibitions" as those situations where various objects are in discrete occupation of a room or site, etc.: perceptors appear, to peruse. In the case of so-called "environmental" exhibitions, it is easily shown that aspects of the discrete arrangement remain. Instead of inflected, dominating surfaces, etc., there are inflected dominating sites, etc. Objections to this view which call up questions of degree (in respect of fineness of supported detail) are irrelevant here since they are integral to the discrete situation, only serving to distinguish one mode from another there.

It is absurd to suggest that spatial considerations are at all bound to the relations of things at a certain level above that of a minimum visibility.

Our proposals so far concern an interior situation: to declare open a volume of (free) air would be to acquire administrative problems which inform a further decomplexity. (A distinction, as appropriate to these proposals, between, say, designator and designandum is beyond the scope of this writing ) Administrative problems are anyway only partially distinguished in a formal sense from others concerning requirements of specificity, etc. Inside, dimensional aspects remain physically explicit; "air-conditioning" itself acquires a contextual decorum.

It is traditional to expect so–called ordinary things to be identifiable: there is nothing in the instrumental situation which demands identifiability. It may be true that the situation will remain only partially interpreted along many axes: there is a lack of a system of rules like those of correspondence.

A "complete" interpretation in terms of operations with sensitive instruments, etc., would amount to showing a veneer over the extended possibilities which the work supports. It is easy to define what is meant by saying that a magnitude which is only "computable" with the help of, say, instruments and one which one can take a ruler to are nonetheless values of the same physical magnitude. It means that the visible or stated relations of the functor to other physical functors are the same. Obviously, anyway, one is still with experience.

Ornamental detail in the rooms may be objected to on the grounds that it offers a "strong" experiential competitiveness which would never be supported by the air medium (the competition would never be met). Here, the all-black, all-gray, all-white, etc., environmental situations inform ornamental values. Extremes of air temperature (either very hot or very cold) are cut out for several reasons: one is that to allow the air to become self– importantly hot or cold indicates an insistence upon just one of its properties; another, which is secondary here, is that extremes of high or low temperature make us dwell on tactile experience. Any sound coming from the equipment is not ornamental so long as it is consistent with the functioning of that equipment. Terry Atkinson has written: "Sounds from outside should be eliminated, although sounds from outside kept at a very low level might well be consistent with the super-usual quality."

The demand made of the equipment would be that it keep the temperature constant: this is another reason for going inside. Prescriptions which go much further in specifying the dress of the room are mostly useless; it has to be looked at *mutatis mutandis.*

Terms like "neutral" are irrelevant in this context except perhaps with one application— a "social" one. There the term might indicate an absence of the feeling that what was occurring was technologically miraculous (such feelings are engendered by air-conditioning in, say, London, whereas people are used to it in New York).

Rubrics like "Non Exhibition," etc., are not inaccurate, they are just nonsensical. Obviously, there are cases where, for instance, sense is not exhibited, but the usage of the term itself is not similar to the present one.

It can't be said that we are relying on old-fashioned logical postulates (The Bellman's map in *The Hunting of The Snark*),[1] or that the experiences offered are in any sense cut down, rather they rely less on the vagaries of a detailed situation.

**NOTES**

1. "Other maps are such shapes, with their islands and capes!

   But we've got our brave captain to thank."

   (So the crew would protest) "that he's bought us the best—

   A perfect and absolute blank!"


This text was first published in *Arts Magazine,* 42:2 (November 1967), pp. 22–23.

# a defense of the "conceptual" process in art
adrian piper

I am very much aware of the thorniness (at this late date!) of using words like "detached" or "objective" in relation to an artist's work or attitude about his work. I've often attempted to plow through people's protests about the vulgarity of an artist's non-involvement in his work supposedly implied in the use of such terms. However, that is not at all what those words mean to me; on the contrary—I think that a greater total involvement in one's work is possible when one attempts to be objective than when one does not. I have found that the limitations imposed by decisions based on my personal "tastes" are absolutely stifling. Choices made through the criteria of subjective likes and dislikes are to me nothing more than a kind of therapeutic ego-titillation that only inhibit further the possibility of sharing an artistic vision (as if it weren't difficult enough a thing to do as it is).

Besides, I really believe that truly good art is always made of broader stuff than the personality of the artist. Think of all the hangups Cézanne had that he managed to transcend in his work! I don't mean to imply that great artists of the past necessarily knew and consciously strove for this kind of objectivity—I don't presume to know whether they did or not—but I think that the mere fact of their work's ability to affect us on any level is an indication that they attained and shared this breadth of vision. The new terminology—"cool," "rational," "reductive" art—simply corroborates my opinion that the necessity for this transcendence of subjectivity has been recognized, and that attempts are being made to facilitate the process.

To me, people who complain about the "anti-humanism" of conceptual art are missing the point. Any kind of objectivity—whether it is in the formulation of a concretized system, a rational decision-making method, conceptual clarity—can serve only to facilitate the final emergence, in as pure a form as possible, of the artistic idea, which is almost always basically intuitive in nature. It is only when one subordinates the original intuition to the subjective distillations and limitations of one's own personality that one need be finally confronted with a kind of mirror image of one's egoistical conflicts as an end product.

I think that the best thing an artist can do for his creative development is allow his intuitions as full an actualization as possible—unhampered by ultimately unavoidable limitations of personality and material. (. . .) I have found that the best way for me to deal with my own subjective limitations is in the process of conceptual formulation. (. . .)

Only the intuitive is truly unlimited. I see all art as basically an intuitive process, regardless of how obliquely it has been dealt with in the past. Within this context, I think "conceptual art" is the most adequate way of liberating the creative process so that the artist may approach and realize his work—or himself—on the purest possible level.

This text is dated 1967. It was first published in Adrian Piper, *Out of Order, Out of Sight. Volume II: Selected Writings in Art Criticism 1967–1992* (Cambridge: MIT Press, 1996), pp. 3–4.

Hans Haacke, *Live Airborne System,* 1965–68. Photograph of seagulls attracted by bread thrown out on the ocean at Coney Island, 30 November 1968.

# general scheme of the new objectivity
## hélio oiticica

A typical state of current Brazilian avant-garde art could be formulated as "New Objectivity." Its principal characteristics are: 1) general constructive will; 2) a move towards the object, as easel painting is negated and superceded; 3) the participation of the spectator (bodily, tactile, visual, semantic, etc.); 4) an engagement and a position on political, social and ethical problems; 5) a tendency towards collective propositions and consequently the abolition, in the art of today, of "isms," so characteristic of the first half of the century (a tendency which can be encompassed by Mário Pedrosa's concept of "Post-Modern Art"); 6) a revival of, and new formulations in, the concept of anti-art.

"New Objectivity" therefore, as a typical state of current Brazilian art, likewise distinguishes itself on the international plane from the two main currents of today: Pop and Op, and also from those connected to them: Nouveau Réalisme and Primary Structures (Hard Edge).

"New Objectivity" being a state, and not a dogmatic, aestheticist movement (as Cubism was, for instance, or any of the other "isms" constituted as a "unity of thought," but unified nevertheless by a general verification of these multiple tendencies grouped into general tendencies). One may find, if one wishes, a simile in Dada, keeping in mind the distances and differences. (...)

The problem of spectator participation is more complex, since this participation, which from the beginning was opposed to pure transcendental contemplation, manifests itself in many ways. There are, however, two well-defined modes of participation: one is that which involves "manipulation" or "sensorial-corporal participation"; the other, that which involves a "semantic" participation. These two modes of participation seek, as it were, a fundamental, total, significant, nonfractioned participation, involving the two processes; that is, they are not reducible to the purely mechanical participation, but concentrate on new meanings, differing from pure transcendental contemplation. From the "playful" propositions to those of the "act," from the "pure word" semantic propositions to those of the "word in the object," in "narrative" works and works of political or social protest, what is being sought is an objective mode of participation. This would be the internal search, inside the object, desired by the proposition of active spectator participation in the process: the individual to whom the work is addressed is invited to complete the meanings proposed by it—it is thus an open work. (. . .) It is useless to outline here a history of the phases and appearances of spectator participation, but it can be found in all the new manifestations of our avant-garde, from the individual works to the collective (e.g. "happenings"). Experiences of both an individualized and a collective nature tend towards increasingly more open propositions in the sense of this participation, including those which tend to give the individual the opportunity to "create" his work. Likewise, the preoccupation with serial production of works (which would be the playful sense elevated to the highest degree) is an important take-off point for this problem.

There is currently in Brazil the need to take positions in regard to political, social, and ethical problems, a need which increases daily and requires urgent formulation, since it is the crucial issue in the creative field: the so-called plastic arts, literature, etc. (. . .)

There are two ways to propose a collective art: the first would be to throw individual productions into contact with the public in the streets (naturally, productions created for this, not conventional productions adapted); the other is to propose creative activities to this public, in the actual creation of the work. In Brazil, the tendency towards a collective art is what really concerns our avant-garde artists. (. . .)

. . . In Brazil, the roles take on the following pattern: how to, in an underdeveloped country, explain and justify the appearance of an avant-garde, not as a symptom of alienation, but as a decisive factor in its collective progress? How to situate the artist's activity there? The problem could be tackled by another question: who does the artist make his work for? It can be seen, thus, that this artist feels a greater need, not only simply to "create," but to "communicate" something which for him is fundamental, but this communication would have to be large-scale, not for an elite reduced to "experts," but even "against" this elite, with the proposition of unfinished, "open" works. This is the fundamental key to the new concept of anti-art: not only to hammer away at the art of the past, or against the old concepts (as before, still an attitude based upon transcendentalism), but to create new experimental conditions where the artist takes on the role of "proposer," or "entrepreneur," or even "educator." The old problem of "making a new art," or of knocking down cultures, is no longer formulated in this way— the correct formulation would be to ask: what propositions, promotions and measures must one draw upon to create a wide-ranging condition of popular participation in these new open propositions, in the creative sphere to which these artists elected themselves. Upon this depends their very survival, and that of the people in this sense. (. . .)

. . . In conclusion, I want to evoke a sentence which, I believe, could very well represent the spirit of "New Objectivity," a fundamental sentence which, in a way, represents a synthesis of all these points and the current situation (condition) of the Brazilian avant-garde; it could serve as a motto, the rallying cry of "New Objectivity"—here it is: OF ADVERSITY WE LIVE!

This text first appeared in the catalogue for the exhibition "Nova Objetividade Brasileira" (Rio de Janeiro: Museu de Arte Moderna, 1967), and was republished in Guy Brett et al., *Hélio Oiticica* (Rotterdam: Witte de With: Minneapolis: Walker Art Center, 1992), pp. 110–120, from where the present extracts are taken.

lucy r. lippard, john chandler, terry atkinson, yvonne rainer, hanne darboven, georges boudaille, maría teresa gramuglio, nicolás rosa

**II** 1968

# the dematerialization of art
## lucy r. lippard and john chandler

During the 1960's, the anti-intellectual, emotional/intuitive processes of art-making character-istic of the last two decades have begun to give way to an ultra-conceptual art that emphasizes the thinking process almost exclusively. As more and more work is designed in the studio but executed elsewhere by professional craftsmen, as the object becomes merely the end product, a number of artists are losing interest in the physical evolution of the work of art. The studio is again becoming a study. Such a trend appears to be provoking a profound dematerialization of art, especially of art as object, and if it continues to prevail, it may result in the object's becoming wholly obsolete. (. . .)

A highly conceptual art, like an extremely rejective art or an apparently random art, upsets detractors because there is "not enough to look at," or rather not enough of what they are accustomed to looking *for*. Monotonal or extremely simple-looking painting and totally "dumb" objects exist in time as well as in space because of two aspects of the viewing experi-ence. First, they demand more participation by the viewer, despite their apparent hostility (which is not hostility so much as aloofness and self-containment). More time must be spent in experience of a detail-less work, for the viewer is used to focusing on details and absorbing an impression of the piece with the help of these details. Secondly, the time spent looking at an "empty" work, or one with a minimum of action, seems infinitely longer than action-and-detail-filled time. This time element is, of course, psychological, but it allows the artist an alternative to or extension of the serial method. Painter-sculptor Michael Snow's film *Wavelength,* for instance, is tortuously extended within its 45–minute span. By the time the camera, zeroing in very slowly from the back of a large loft, reaches a series of windows and finally a photograph of water surface, or waves, between two of them, and by the time that photograph gradually fills the screen, the viewer is aware of an almost unbearable anticipation that seems the result of an equally unbearable length of time stretched out at a less than normal rate of looking; the intensity is reinforced by the sound, which during most of the film is monotonal, moving up in pitch and up in volume until at the end it is a shrill hum, both exciting and painful.

Joseph Schillinger, a minor American Cubist who wrote, over a twenty-five year period, an often extraordinary book called *The Mathematical Basis of the Arts,* divided the historical evolution of art into five "zones," which replace each other with increasing acceleration: 1. pre-aesthetic, a biological stage of mimicry; 2. traditional-aesthetic, a magic, ritual-religious art; 3. emotional-aesthetic, artistic expressions of emotions, self-expression, art for art's sake; 4. rational-aesthetic, characterized by empiricism, experimental art, novel art; 5. scientific, post-aesthetic, which will make possible the manufacture, distribution and consumption of a perfect art product and will be characterized by a fusion of the art forms and materials, and, finally, a "disintegration of art," the "abstraction and liberation of the idea."[1]

Given this framework, we could now be in a transitional period between the last two phases, though one can hardly conceive of them as literally the last phases the visual arts will go through. After the intuitive process of recreating aesthetic realities through man's own body, the process of reproduction or imitation, mathematical logic enters into art. (The Bauhaus dictum "Less is More" was anticipated by William of Occam when he wrote: "What can be explained by fewer principles is explained needlessly by more"; Nominalism and Minimalism have more in common than alliteration.) From then on, man became increasingly conscious of the course of his evolution, beginning to create directly from principles without the intercession of reproductive reality. This clearly corresponds to the Greenbergian interpretation of Modernism (a word used long before Greenberg, though his disciples insist on attributing it to him). The final "post-aesthetic" phase supersedes this self-conscious, self-critical art that answers other art according to a determinist schedule. Involved with opening up rather than narrowing down, the newer work offers a curious kind of Utopianism which should not be confused with Nihilism except in that, like all Utopias, it indirectly advocates a *tabula rasa;* like most Utopias, it has no concrete expression.

Dematerialized art is post-aesthetic only in its increasingly non-visual emphases. The aesthetic of principle is still an aesthetic, as implied by frequent statements by mathematicians and scientists about the *beauty* of an equation, formula or solution: "Why should an aesthetic criterion be so successful so often? Is it just that it satisfies physicists? I think there is only one answer—nature is inherently beautiful" (physicist Murray Gell-Mann); "In this case, there was a moment when I knew how nature worked. It had elegance and beauty. The goddam thing was gleaming" (Nobel prizewinner Richard Feynman).[2] The more one reads these statements, the more apparent it becomes that the scientist's attempt to discover, perhaps even to impose order and structure on the universe, rests on assumptions that are essentially aesthetic. Order itself, and its implied simplicity and unity, are aesthetic criteria.

The disintegration Schillinger predicted is obviously implicit in the break-up since 1958 or so of traditional media, and in the introduction of electronics, light, sound, and, more important, performance attitudes into painting and sculpture—the so far unrealized intermedia revolution whose prophet is John Cage. It is also implied by the current international obsession with entropy. According to Wylie Sypher, for example: "The future is that in which time becomes effective, and the mark of time is the increasing disorder toward which our system tends. . . . During the course of time, entropy increases. Time can be measured by the loss of structure in our system, its tendency to sink back into that original chaos from which it may have emerged. . . . One meaning of time is a drift toward inertia."[3]

Today many artists are interested in an order that incorporates implications of disorder and chance, in a negation of actively ordering parts in favor of the presentation of a whole.[4] Earlier in the 20th century the announcement of an element of indeterminacy and relativity in the scientific system was a factor in the rise of an irrational abstraction. Plato's anti-art statements, his opposition to imitative and representational art, and his contempt for the products of artists, whom he considered insane, are too familiar to review here, but they are interesting to note again in view of the current trend back to "normalcy," as evidenced by the provocative opening show of the East Village cooperative Lannis Museum of Normal Art, where several of the works discussed here were seen. Actually, the "museum" would be better called the Museum of Adnormal Art, since it pays unobtrusive homage to the late Ad Reinhardt and to his insistence that only "art-as-art" is normal for art. (The painter-director, Joseph Kosuth, admits his pedantic tendency, also relatable to Reinhardt's dogmas, in the pun on normal schools.) However, "no idea" was one of Reinhardt's Rules and his ideal did not include the ultra-conceptual. When works of art, like words, are signs that convey ideas, they are not things in themselves but symbols or representatives of things. Such a work is a medium rather than an end in itself or "art-as-art." The medium need not be the message, and some ultra-conceptual art seems to declare that the conventional art media are no longer adequate as media to be messages in themselves. (. . .)

Idea art has been seen as art about criticism rather than art-as-art or even art about art. On the contrary, the dematerialization of the object might eventually lead to the disintegration of criticism as it is known today. The pedantic or didactic or dogmatic basis insisted on by many of these artists is incorporated in the art. It bypasses criticism as such. Judgment of ideas is less interesting than following the ideas through. In the process, one might discover that something is either a good idea, that is, fertile and open enough to suggest infinite possibilities, or a mediocre idea, that is, exhaustible, or a bad idea, that is, already exhausted or with so little substance that it can be taken no further. (The same can be applied to style in the formal sense, and style except as an individual trademark tends to disappear in the path of novelty.) If the object becomes obsolete, objective distance becomes obsolete. Sometime in the near future it may be necessary for the writer to be an artist as well as for the artist to be a writer. There will still be scholars and historians of art, but the contemporary critic may have to choose between a creative originality and explanatory historicism.

Ultra-conceptual art will be thought of by some as "formalist" because of the spareness and austerity it shares with the best of painting and sculpture at the moment. Actually, it is as anti-formal as the most amorphous or journalistic expressionism. It represents a suspension of realism, even formal realism, color realism, and all the other "new realisms." However, the idea that art can be experienced in order to extract an idea or underlying intellectual scheme as well as to perceive its formal essence *continues from* the opposing formalist premise that painting and sculpture should be looked at as objects *per se* rather than as references to other images and representation. As visual art, a highly conceptual work still stands or falls by what it looks like, but the primary, rejective trends in their emphasis on singleness and autonomy have limited the amount of information given, and therefore the amount of formal analysis possible. They have set critic and viewer thinking about what they see rather than simply weighing the formal or emotive impact. Intellectual and aesthetic pleasure can merge in this experience when the work is both visually strong and theoretically complex.

Some thirty years ago, Ortega wrote about the "new art": "The task it sets itself is enormous; it wants to create from nought. Later, I expect, it will be content with less and achieve more."[5] Fully aware of the difficulty of the new art, he would probably not have been surprised to find that a generation or more later the artist has achieved more with less, has continued to make something of "nought" fifty years after Malevich's *White on White* seemed to have defined nought for once and for all. We still do not know how much less "nothing" can be. Has an ultimate zero point been arrived at with black paintings, white paintings, light beams, transparent film, silent concerts, invisible sculpture, or any of the other projects mentioned above? It hardly seems likely.

**NOTES**

1. Joseph Schillinger, *The Mathematical Basis of the Arts* (New York: Philosophical Library, 1948), p. 17.

2. Quoted in Lee Edson, "Two Men in Search of the Quark," *New York Times Magazine* (8 October 1967).

3. Wylie Sypher, *Loss of Self in Modern Literature and Art* (New York: Vintage, 1962), pp. 73–74. The word has also been applied to differing areas of recent art by Robert Smithson and Piero Gilardi; it appears as the title of short stories as well, for instance, by Thomas Pynchon.

4. In the New York art world, the idea seems to have originated with Don Judd.

5. José Ortega y Gasset, *The Dehumanization of Art* (New York: Doubleday Anchor, 1956), p. 50.

This essay was written in late 1967 and first published in *Art International,* 12:2 (February 1968), pp. 31–36.

# concerning the article "the dematerialization of art"

terry atkinson

(. . .)

I have some inquiries I wish to advance relating to the usage of the word "dematerialization" with precise regard as to its correctness in describing and relating the process of disestablishing a precept which had been assumed to be a necessary condition of the visual art menage (i.e. that there be a "looking at" object). There seems to be in your article a strongly emphasized paleontological framework of reference according to the data you offer from Schillinger's evolutionary categorical chronology of art-making procedures, hence I deduce that you are using "dematerialization" to describe a process which has connections with processes which have been slowly forming its own structure. Nevertheless, after careful consideration, I can only perceive that your usage of "dematerialization" is a metaphorical one (I know that I am pointing out what is probably the most obvious of facts); there is not, I realize, anything of necessity wrong with metaphorical usage. But I think in the case of the process I understand your article to be concerned with, such a usage has a number of shortcomings in as far as the process of dematerialization is not in any strict sense the process (I emphasize as I understand it) you are describing. (. . .)

...The Oxford English Dictionary defines "dematerialization" as "to deprive of material qualities." It would seem appropriate here to define matter as follows: a specialized form of energy which has the attributes of mass and extension in time, and with which we become acquainted through our bodily senses. It is more than plain then that when a material entity becomes dematerialized it does not simply become non-visible (as opposed to invisible), it becomes an entity which cannot be perceived by any of our senses. As far as material qualities go it is simply a non-entity. Thus it seems to me that if you are talking about art-objects dematerializing,[1] then you would be obliged to talk about objects of which there was now no material trace; if, on the other hand, you are talking or implying, by virtue of the metaphorical license, that some artists today are using immaterial entities to demonstrate ideas, then you would be talking of ideas that had never had any material concretization. It certainly does not follow that because an object is invisible, or is less visible[2] than it was, or is less visible than another object,[3] that any process of dematerialization has taken place. If I might be permitted to make more specific reference to your article I would like to continue in the postliminary manner.

All the examples of art-works (ideas) you refer to in your article are, with few exceptions, art-objects. They may not be an art-object as we know it in its traditional matter-state, but they are nevertheless matter in one of its forms, either solid-state, gas-state, liquid-state. And it is on this question of matter-state[4] that my caution with regard to the metaphorical usage of dematerialization is centered upon. (. . .) I consider your article to be an important document in pointing out some recently developed directions of artistic sensibility (and which appears to be carrying the extensions of art more and more into areas regarded previously as not the business of the artist). But I think that any elucidation, extrapolation, explication, formulation, etc. of such a development will itself have to develop and use a far more stringent terminology and dialectic than that traditionally used to describe the acts and resultant objects of an embroilment in what are called artmaking procedures; procedures which, after all, have a blatant and rabid poetic and romantic basis. (It may be more than a possibility that a lot of what is considered to be great art criticism may yet turn out to be great art fiction.)[5]

I wish at this point to reiterate briefly some of the aspects of your article which have interested me and which I have touched upon in the foregoing. Matter is a specialized form of energy, radiant energy is the only form in which energy can exist in the absence of matter. Thus when dematerialization takes place it means, in terms of physical phenomena, the conversion (I use this word guardedly) of a state of matter into that of radiant energy; this follows as energy can never be created or destroyed. But further, if one were to speak of an art-form that used radiant energy, then one would be committed to the contradiction of speaking of a formless form, and one can imagine the verbal acrobatics that might take place when the romantic metaphor was put to work on questions concerning formless-forms (non-material) and material forms. The philosophy of what is called aesthetics relying finally, as it does, on what it has called the content of the art work is at the most only fitted with the philosophical tools to deal with problems of an art that absolutely counts upon the production of matter-state entities. The shortcomings of such philosophical tools are plain enough to see inside this limit of material objects. Once this limit is broken these shortcomings hardly seem worth considering, as the sophistry of the whole framework is dismissed as being not applicable to an art procedure that records its information in words, and the consequent material qualities of the entity produced (i.e. typewritten sheet, etc.) do not necessarily have anything to do with the idea. That is, the idea is "read about" rather than "looked at." That some art should be directly material and that other art should produce a material entity only as a necessary by-product of the need to record the idea is not at all to say that the latter is connected by any process of dematerialization to the former.

Here in England, I have been and still am a participant in what could loosely be called a think-tank[6] (at the risk of being accused of using metaphorical technological jargon reminiscent of McLuhan) which had been working with "objectless" quiddities (I use this phrase for the patent want of a better one) developed inside what I can, at the moment, only call a framework of mention.[7] Such a framework uses only theoretical entities and as such does not come up for the count as either material or immaterial art. The ideas are recorded in typewritten word form as the nature of the ideas can only be satisfactorily developed in such a form (or in audio form on magnetic tape). One reads the written information just as one reads any written information. (. . .)

. . . At the moment I can only refer to the technique that Michael Baldwin and myself have used in attempting to formulate the theoretical entities constructed in the "Air-Conditioning Show," the "Air Show" and the "Time Show" as a technique where the content is separated off from the notion of making an art-object. Maybe something like a technique of content-isolation (I am wary of such a description; but I must admit, at the cost of being a little anecdotal, that the term appeals to me by virtue of the fact that Clement Greenberg has pontificated to the effect that it is no use talking about the content of an art-work, which if I guess correctly means he can't talk about these particular works at all.) It is, to put it more approximately than precisely, the artist working with what, in the visual art-context, is traditionally recognized as the medium of the art-critic and art-historian. Perhaps I can explicate the methodology of such a technique a little more. If it is pointed out in the theoretical frameworks (used by Michael Baldwin and myself) that the situations are no more than synallagmatically related to the internal introduction (i.e. inside the framework of what I call mention) of new descriptive terms, etc. which provide a consistent and appropriate noneliminative context for nomological implication (i.e. if there are any rules governing such a framework they are, in consequence of the nature of the structure of the framework, open-ended and thus difficult to identify as rules), then questions about objects made will, obviously, be seen to entail answers, the natures of which will in the end only be cognizable with objects produced as a by-product of the need to record the content of the idea, hence to consider the objects produced within the framework (i.e. typewritten sheets) as "looking-at" objects rather than "reading-about" objects is to look for 1st-order-visual information where there is no intention to produce such information.[8]

In view of the immediately preceding paragraph I wish to develop a few ideas and thoughts with regard to another interesting postulation you have made in the "Dematerialization" article. I quote, "that dematerialized art is post-aesthetic only in its increasing non-visual emphases. . . ." Nobody concerned with problems (pertaining to your article) that I know of here in England is likely to want to make a major issue of argument over whether or not "the aesthetic of principle is still an aesthetic";[9] however, I have a few reflective notes which may be of some small relevance here. Equations, formulae, theoretical entities, etc. are normally recorded in written-sign-word form and obviously any aesthetic criteria applied to them are usually related to how effectively the written format expresses the information relevant to the state, situation, etc. it is seeking to describe/explain. If I may be allowed to pursue an analogy here, consider the following. A man has in his possession a map which he knows contains the information instructing him how to get from A to B, but because he has not had an adequate course in map-reading he cannot read the map. If he then says the map has great beauty, then he cannot be judging this map to have beauty according to the information presented by the map as a map, but is talking of the map in some other way. Now when a scientist talks of the beauty of an equation, his beauty is judged according to the nature of his course in equation-reading[10] which provides him with the basis for making judgements concerning how good an equation is. If he is simply looking at the object "equation" rather than reading-looking at the object "equation" then his judgement of the beauty of the equation is according some other kind of beauty to it. If, for instance, the scientist is reading-looking at the equation, then if he is reading it wrongly then he is not applying criteria according to another kind of beauty;

rather, questions of true or false come in here. Judgements pertaining to another kind of beauty bring in questions relating to relevant or irrelevant before questions of truth or falsehood are examined. I quote further from your article ". . . The more one reads these statements, the more apparent it becomes that the scientist's attempt to discover, perhaps even to impose order and structure on the universe, rests on assumptions that are essentially aesthetic. Order itself, and its implied simplicity and unity, are essentially aesthetic criteria." Now the search for a completely coherent theory of anti-matter (i.e. quark theory) is a fascinating one, and I certainly would not dispute Richard Feynman's claim that he has experienced revelata and therefore is aware of certain things or phenomena that most of us are not. But, and I think it is a considerable but, statements such as "nature is inherently beautiful" (Gell-Mann), and "It had elegance and beauty. The goddamn thing was gleaming," whilst maybe showing evidence of the two physicists' "aesthetic" sophistication do not in themselves have anything to do with the effectiveness of an equation, formula, theory, etc.

The principles of aesthetics are an accepted area of philosophical investigation,[11] but the aesthetic of principle is quite another. I wonder if there is (to use a metaphor) a danger of putting the cart before the horse. Obviously, I am open to any discussion you wish to raise. By using a phrase such as "the aesthetic of principle"[12] do you somehow intend to imply the principle of the aesthetic of beauty? Are you hinting at some kind of meta-aesthetic? It seems that here we are not only up against the difficulty of constructing a framework allowing a general definition of goodness and its consequent directive to examine the varieties of goodness,[13] but also, here, you seem to be implying that our seeking after a thorough analysis of our compulsion to seek after what we think is goodness is not the sole area that comes under the heading of aesthetics, but that aesthetics is extended to the construction of the aesthetic of principle theory (a kind of theory of principles?) in addition to its more conventional applications. Such a notion implies that the framework that is set up to examine what the nature of aesthetics is has the nature (framework) of what it is trying to examine as the foundations of its own framework. There is, obviously, something not quite right here. A principle is defined, in one sense at least, as a theoretical basis. An aesthetic of theoretical basis? Imagine books written entitled, *The Aesthetic of the Principles of Literary Criticism* or *The Aesthetics of the Principles of Thermodynamics*. What is often judged as good about a principle is that it is the foundation of a certain theory(ies) or construct. Would then two books, to be purely speculative, trace the origins of, say, the principles of literary criticism and those of thermodynamics to the same principle of principles? I am open to your suggestions on such a point, but I think that such a usage of aesthetic as the aesthetic of principle calls for a stringent examination of whether there is any valid hierarchy in the concepts of principle, aesthetics and criteria. I will be in New York over Easter. I would welcome an exchange of views with you.

Yours in good faith. Terry Atkinson

P.S. Although neither David Bainbridge, Michael Baldwin nor Harold Hurrell have seen this letter, I sign with some considerable confidence for them.

**NOTES**

1. Dematerialization especially relates to the form of radiant energy as this is the only form in which energy can exist in the absence of matter. Such a factor is discussed in a little more detail later in this paper.

2. When I use the term "less visible" I admit to a somewhat everyday usage of the description of the quality of being visible. There are more fundamental questions implied here than I have gone into. For example, when we say a car is less visible in a fog than it is on a clear day, it does not mean that we see any the worse on a foggy day (i.e. our seeing mechanism is not functioning any the worse). On a foggy day we see the unclear image of the car just as clearly as we see the distinct image of the car on a clear day.

3. (Relating to note 2.) That is we see that the object that is less visible is as clearly less visible as the object that is more visible is as clearly more visible.

4. There is a modest theory-object pertaining to the use of a solid-state to liquid-state to gas-state conversion process which I sketched together in May, 1967. I may yet publish it along with the other small theories, theory-objects I worked upon between February and May of 1967. I would not include in this category the "Air-conditioning Show" that I worked upon with Michael Baldwin during this period nor many of the still not formulated ideas I worked upon (and still am working upon) with both David Bainbridge and Michael Baldwin, as I think these ideas are of a much more comprehensive nature.

5. Archaeologists of the future will no doubt not find such criticism any the less interesting if it should turn out to belong to the category of the novelette.

6. I am using the term "think-tank" here to refer to the loose confederation that has existed between Harold Hurrell, David Bainbridge, Michael Baldwin and myself. On the "Air-conditioning Show," "Air Show" and "Time Show" and also on "Frameworks" Michael Baldwin

and myself worked particularly closely together, and the present project concerning the hardware MI in the main engineered by David Bainbridge has entailed much explication and theorizing by all four of us.

7. The concept of "framework of mention" was as far as I know first used by Michael Baldwin in the context of the "Air Show" that he and myself worked upon during September and October 1967. Since we have formulated some considerable explication and extrapolation of the device in "Frameworks."

8. Consequently there is a section in "Frameworks" in 2nd order visual-information form explaining that in the "Air-conditioning," "Air" and "Time" shows there is no intention to present 1st order visual information forms.

9. It should be noted here that I am assuming when you use "the aesthetic of principle" you are stating an aesthetic that is judged by you to be post-visual-aesthetic. The question of the aesthetic of principle is dealt with in a little more detail later in the paper.

10. Perhaps it is as well here to confirm that I am aware that to interpret art-objects (1st order visual information) it is obviously a considerable help to have had an adequate course in art-object reading, thus it should be clear that I am not maintaining, when I call art-objects 1st order visual information, that I am maintaining that a comprehensive reading of an art-object can be done naively, but rather one is reading about the object one is looking at through this act of "looking at." Whereas if, say, one is reading-looking at the letter R, usually one is not examining the form of the R (except that it be recognizable as R) but rather seeing how it fits in aggregate with other letters to form, for example, the word red.

11. E. g. *Principia Ethica*. G. E. Moore. (etc. etc. etc.)

12. Refer note 9.

13. Georg Henrik von Wright, *The Varieties of Goodness* (London: Routledge and Kegan Paul, 1963).

This letter-essay was written in response to Lippard and Chandler's "The Dematerialization of Art," and dated 23 March 1968. A shortened version was published in Lippard's *Six Years* (1973), pp. 43–44. The entire text, excerpts of which we reproduce here, is in Lucy R. Lippard papers, Archives of American Art, uncataloged recent acquisition.

ASH, W. *Marxism and Moral Concepts.* New York: Monthly Review Press, 1964. xvii, 204 pp. $3.50—Although Ash (an American living in England) does put the Marxist position in language familiar to the English reader, both Marxism and moral concepts are not treated in depth. Marxism (which according to Ash asks to be judged on results in socialist countries) is primarily a theory which holds values are based in a direct way on economic relations. Recent advances in Marx scholarship or discussions with the Marxist movement are ignored as the attack is focused on the capitalist order. — K. A. M.

BAHM, A. J. *The World's Living Religions: A Searching Comparison of the Faiths of East and West.* New York: Dell Publishing Co., 1964. 384 pp. Paper, $.75—After an introduction about the nature of religion and primitive religion, the author discusses the Indian religions: Hinduism, Jainism, Buddhism, and Vedantism and Yoga. How Vedantism and Yoga could be considered as a religion different from Hinduism is not clear. In the second part the author studies the religions of China and Japan. Taoism, Confucianism, Buddhism, and Shintoism are represented. As the representative religions of Western civilization he has chosen Judaism, Christianity, Islam, and Humanism. The norm the author has adopted to distinguish between the Eastern and Western religions is questionable. The concluding chapter discusses syncretic tendencies and the pursuit of comparative studies that might eventually help to form a World Religion. — J. K.

Art & Language (Michael Baldwin), *Abstract Art No. 2,* 1968.

# statement
## yvonne rainer

The choices in my work are predicated on my own peculiar resources—obsessions of imagination, you might say—and also on an ongoing argument with, love of, and contempt for dancing. If my rage at the impoverishment of ideas, narcissism, and disguised sexual exhibitionism of most dancing can be considered puritan moralizing, it is also true that I love the body—its actual weight, mass, and unenhanced physicality. It is my overall concern to reveal people as they are engaged in various kinds of activities—alone, with each other, with objects—and to weigh the quality of the human body toward that of objects and away from the super-stylization of the dancer. Interaction and cooperation on the one hand; substantiality and inertia on the other. Movement invention, i. e. "dancing" in a strict sense, is but one of the several factors in the work. (. . .)

The condition of making my stuff lies in the continuation of my interest and energy. Just as ideological issues have no bearing on the nature of the work, neither does the tenor of current political and social conditions have any bearing on its execution. The world disintegrates around me. My connection to the world-in-crisis remains tenuous and remote. I can foresee a time when this remoteness must necessarily end, though I cannot foresee exactly when or how the relationship will change, or what circumstances will incite me to a different kind of action. Perhaps nothing short of universal female military conscription will affect my function (the ipso facto physical fitness of dancers will make them the first victims); or a call for a world-wide cessation of individual functions, to include the termination of genocide. This statement is not an apology. It is a reflection of a state of mind that reacts with horror and disbelief upon seeing a Vietnamese shot dead on TV—not at the sight of death, however, but at the fact that the TV can be shut off afterwards as after a bad Western. My body remains the enduring reality.

Written in March, 1968, this text was distributed in the program accompanying Rainer's "The Mind Is a Muscle." According to Rainer, "it is not necessary to read this prior to observation" of the performance. The text was subsequently published in Yvonne Rainer, *Yvonne Rainer: Work 1961–73* (Halifax: The Press of Nova Scotia College of Art and Design, 1974), p. 71.

# statement to lucy lippard
## hanne darboven

I build something up by disturbing something (destruction—structure—construction).

A system became necessary; how else could I see more concentratedly, find some interest, continue at all? Contemplation had to be interrupted by action as a means of accepting anything among everything. No acceptance at all = chaos. In my work I try to move, to expand and contract as far as possible between more or less known and unknown limits. I couldn't talk about any limits, I know generally, I just can say I feel at times closer while doing a series or afterwards. But whether coming closer once or not, it is still one experience. Whether positive or negative, I know it then. Everything is in so far in a proof, for the negative that a positive exists, and vice versa.

A circle as a symbol of infinity, everything; what is beginning, where? What is end, where?

I couldn't recreate my so-called system; it depends on things done previously. The materials consist of paper and pencil with which I draw my conceptions, write words and numbers, which are the simplest means for putting down my ideas; for ideas do not depend on materials. The nature of ideas is immateriality.

Things have plenty of variations and varieties, so they can be changed. At this moment I know about what I have done, what I am doing; I shall see what will happen next.

This statement, sent by Darboven to Lippard in 1968, is previously unpublished. It is presently in Lucy R. Lippard papers, Archives of American Art, uncataloged recent acquisition.

EVERYTHING IS PURGED FROM THIS PAINTING
BUT ART, NO IDEAS HAVE ENTERED THIS WORK.

7

# interview with daniel buren: art is no longer justifiable or setting the record straight
## georges boudaille

(. . .)

Georges Boudaille: Before any discussion, we should agree on the meaning of certain terms. First, what is art?

Daniel Buren: I agree with Rosenberg's text that says anything is art as soon as it is put in a museum. And that is why artists are such appalling things, since they are responsible for this state of affairs in art. Duchamp realized that there was something false in art, but his limitation was that, rather than demystifying, he amplified it. By taking a manufactured object and placing it out of context, he quite simply symbolized art. His actions tended to "represent" and not "present" the object. Duchamp, like all artists, could not "present" anything at all without "re-presenting" it. And if he symbolized art in this way, it was because as soon as he exhibited a bottle rack, a shovel, or a urinal, he was really stating that anything was art as soon as you pointed at it. By extension, and this is very important, that means that *a cow in a field becomes art in a painting, a tree by Courbet becomes art, and a woman by Rubens becomes art;* now this cow, this tree, and this woman exist in another way. Duchamp dismantled this process supposedly to take away its sanctity, but he went about it in such a way that by being against art, he was in art. Let's clarify an important point right away: Duchamp is not anti-art. He belongs to art. The art of extolling the consumer society. Reassuring art. Putting a shovel in a gallery or museum signified "this shovel has become art." And it actually was. The action itself is art, because the artist projects himself in choosing the shovel, and especially in *placing it out of context*. It is art in the sense that the imprint of a hand in a cave is art, the *Mona Lisa* is art, a happening is art, etc. It is a problem that touches on the ethics and function of the artist: he assumes the right to have this supra-human calling that allows him to say to others, "everything that I touch with my hand is transformed into art." The artist imposes his anguish, his vision of the world, and himself on others. *The artist emasculates the observer.* Maybe he thinks that the latter deserves no better . . . The artist assumes the right to show you what you can see for yourself, what you could obviously see much more clearly without his intervention. *I contest this right.*

G. B.: So you are questioning the misuse of power by those whom we call artists and the respect that society gives them, even when society contests it. What is interesting, and what I would like you to explain more precisely, is your notion of art. Today we take an old yoke, stand it up, and it seems just as beautiful as an African sculpture.

D. B.: You say "today." I say that artists have always proceeded in this manner. What's more, you say . . . "just as beautiful" . . . which implies a notion that may be the one most commonly associated with the idea of art, namely beauty. Artists have shown us beauty in all its aspects, including its most ugly ones. Beauty equals ugliness equals art, and it's no longer my problem. Furthermore, it's high time we left yokes where they belong!

G. B.: To continue, I would like you to contrast two different points of view. On the one hand, an object is taken and transformed by being put in another context and sometimes by being placed in another position. Conversely, the view of the new realists is to return the object to its original function. You must not put nails on an iron as Man Ray did—Arman's iron only has value as an iron and should not be surrounded by pretension.

D. B.: First of all, as I indicated a few moments ago, it is known that an object taken out of context, whether or not it is altered, no longer has the same meaning, and right away it is automatically surrounded by pretension. However, when there is not one but a dozen irons together, the problem changes. There is organization of these irons in a space as there is organization with Mondrian's lines and Piero della Francesca's characters. In short, there is art. There is always the same cry of the artist who says, "Look! Everything around you that I have transformed is remarkable." There is always the same need: "Look, you have the good fortune to have artists in your society to show you their subway, their one-way streets, their cultural revolution, their high-rises, their sex, their Coca-Cola, and their problems. Accept theirs as your own, accept your artists."

(. . .)

In spite of their good intentions, artists cannot change society's structures because they accept them from the start. The deception consists of making others accept them through the artifice of art.

*All illusion must be eliminated*

G. B.: Getting back to you, when you take a canvas window shade, does this window shade exist for itself, do you want to attract our attention to the beauty of the window shade?

D. B.: No, I make you see the stripes. I don't think that a striped canvas is of any particular interest. You can call it a canvas window shade, that doesn't bother me. On the contrary, I prefer, if I have the choice, that you say canvas window shade rather than Buren. When it's called a "Buren," this instantly reveals an artistic pretension. Moreover, the work that I do on the canvas is not primarily to change the canvas; I cover the two bands on the edges with paint. If everything is covered, the medium is hidden and transformed, and thus an illusion is created. All of the particulars must be legible. The observer cannot even imagine the medium, he sees it, and there is no mystery.

G. B.: But does putting something on it manifest a human intervention, therefore going against your idea?

D. B.: Of course it is human, but this wouldn't change the problem if a machine were doing it. In this sense, what is to be seen is *something done* and not *something done by someone*. One way of showing this position was to initially present this painting and another showing paint brush imprints in a quincunx arrangement done by Buren and Toroni, then by extension done and signed by anyone at all. This wasn't to demonstrate that anyone at all could do it, this is *obvious* and *of no interest*. Anyone can do an accumulation, a target, or a dripping. It was above all to try to make clearer the fact that it is not the least bit important that this painting was done by someone named Buren, Toroni, or Boudaille. As far as we're concerned, saying that it's a Toroni is archaic and false. Saying that it's a Matisse is proper because Matisse has projection and a vision of the world. Illusion must be eliminated whatever it may be, as well as aestheticism, sensitivity, and individual expression, which of course doesn't mean that work must be done in groups, but that the piece becomes the *reality, raw thought,* and consequently *anonymous.* I insist that expression be eliminated. As long as people express themselves for others by means of the plastic arts, they will be unable to get out of the realm of illusion, because the work created will always be an "expressive" screen upon which any object projected will appear in the form of its own illusion. Those who see salvation in manufactured objects or technologically and scientifically inspired works have absolutely not resolved the problem. The artist expresses himself and "loads" the manufactured object by shifting it away from its function. It may happen that the object is factory-made solely because the artist ordered it, in other words the object will have an "artistic" function from the moment it is made. Needless to say in his order the artist will not have failed to express himself. And even if, "resolutely objective," he gives the company complete freedom to create the object, then it is an anonymous worker that he allows to express himself. The artist, through the artifice of this fraud, will claim that he did not express himself!

The only solution resides in the creation—if the word can still be used—of a thing totally disconnected with the person working on it, in which this person has not had any input whatsoever, the thing thus *expressing itself for nothing.* The *artistic communication is cut:* it no longer exists. The object presented no longer has any aesthetic, moral, marketable, or consumable function. It is solely and undisputedly there for nothing. The observer finds that he is *alone with himself and confronted with himself* in front of an *anonymous* thing that gives him no solution. Art is no longer there. It's about *something else.*

G. B.: So your position would aim at a desacralization of art?

D. B.: Yes, obviously, and of the artist as well. My position is the logical conclusion of theoretical reflection based on art history and its apparent contradictions. It is interesting to realize that art has never been a problem of content, but one of form. This may explain the anarchic side of its evolution, one form shoving another aside. Chance, inspiration, and the right moment must be forsaken for a theory, and art is not capable of this.

## SYSTEMATIC REPETITION

G. B.: But . . . judging by what you have shown at the Musée des Arts Décoratifs at the Biennale exhibition, then on Rue Montfaucon, under the pretext of forcing us to reflect, you lock yourself into a pattern and you eliminate all possibility of development. I know that there is no progress in art . . . but . . .

D. B.: I have actually been doing the same thing for two years now. There must be about 170 identical paintings. As soon as the visible shape is neutral, it is no longer *evolutive,* meaning that a neutral shape can be followed by another identical or different neutral shape. If these two shapes are truly neutral, one cannot be better than the other, they cannot be perfected. If they become so, it is because they are not neutral. From this time on, one notices a certain repetition. It is not *a priori, it is necessary.* The most important point is really the awareness that the *concept of progress,* of perfectibility, has been eliminated. Repetition also removes the object's quality of being a unique work that, whatever it may be, can be retrieved one day by art because of its uniqueness. The first stage is to systematically repeat one single thing, the most simplistic way of not "evolving." Clearly it is not a case of copying oneself, of repeating the same thing *a priori* for ten months, ten years, or thirty years, this being at the very most an accumulation through time taking us back to a familiar concept in art. Systematic repetition put forth as *a priori* is unjustified and is of no interest in the sense that it is only an action, a gamble on the future. If this action were interesting, it would allow any type of illustration. What difference would there be then between an individual indefinitely repeating the painting of a small rabbit on a canvas and one who would repeat *a priori* his own notion of the neutral shape? There would be no difference at all. In both cases a fantasy would be projected, a personal view would take precedence over what is shown. However, it is understood that the thing to be viewed must *signify itself without the help of the creator,* regardless of the relevance or the beauty of this individual's personal view. This attitude immediately leads back to a hieratic art. Repetition is worthwhile only if it does not take on meaning in itself, so that it in turn doesn't become mythical. The second stage, and the most important, is to question the repetitive concept in its primary stage in order to have it pass from the mythical to the *historical.*

G. B.: What meaning then do you attach to the word repetition?

D. B.: Repetition should essentially be understood as meaning: *Non Perfectible.* An evolution, neither progressive nor perfectible, can be envisaged by passing from one neutral shape to another equally neutral. For example, there is no qualitative difference whatsoever between a black circle in the middle of a white square, flat brush imprints in a quincunx arrangement on white plastic, or a striped painting with borders covered with paint, and this is why Mosset, Toroni and I did not hesitate, each one doing these three different designs, to *depersonalize* what were from the outset, although neutral, our own personal designs. There is no evolution at all from one design to another: there is repetition since, for the observer, the thing has not changed: but *there is no longer a personal claim* to this thing because it is *anyone's,* really and truly impersonal. This is the only way that repetition does not become the expression of one specific person who, endlessly repeating even a neutral thing, will necessarily make it valid because it is repeated and therefore filled with intention. At the same time it loses its quality of being a common object and will become Mr. So-and-so's neutral painting. The fact of repeating must entail a total depersonalization of the thing displayed, and not become a ritual that would only have the function of re-sacralizing art. What counts is the object displayed, whether it is two- or three-dimensional, of fabric or plastic, wood or iron, cut out or pasted, electric or not, kinetic or motionless. From the moment it is neutral, anonymous, and refers to nothing but itself, an object has value for and through itself, whether it is 1.034 or 1.

G. B.: At this stage, art would become truly democratic since the layman and the specialist would be equal in front of the work. Do you want to force the spectator to see only what is visible, and not what the visible may suggest?

D. B.: I don't want to force the spectator to do anything. I present a thing that distracts in no way from this thing: *this thing is this thing.* You look at it, examine it, the expression "you contemplate it" can no longer be used. What I attempt to do is to question the content of the painting rather than its form, the latter being the artist's problem.

Questioning art risks *ineffectiveness.* The shape that will appear suggesting nothing apart from itself will lose effectiveness, a vital element of art, in order to become *neutral,* and therefore conventional, if it is compared to the artistic form which itself must be original. Neutrality and effectiveness are incompatible.

G. B.: Is abstract art not an art, precisely, in which what is to be seen is only what is on the canvas?

D. B.: No. It is not by taking away figurative images that all images are removed. There is no abstract or concrete art. Whether art is figurative, abstract, objective, kinetic, or in any kind of "ism," all artists have the same purpose: to exercise the will to express, to communicate. There are screens, windows, dreams, entertainment and spectacle. There is especially *contempt of others.*

G. B.: Your position interests me because it seems to be motivated by currently existing art forms. I would like us to go over them and you to tell me what you think of them.

## ART TODAY IS STAGNATING

D. B.: I am no longer directly concerned about art in general and contemporary art in particular. Art interests me, namely its history and developments, just as tribal customs interest ethnologists. It seems to me the only way to envisage the possibility of *a theory.* Art history is a succession of experiments in form that are sometimes justifiable by their structures and their era.

In the same way, human sacrifice was justifiable for the Aztecs. Much more than being pushed by the desire to change art structures, I notice that these structures have changed. Art can no longer be accepted. *Art is no longer justifiable.* In this sense, art today is very instructive, since every day it confirms my point of view, whether it is noticed in New York, Milan, London, Tokyo, Paris . . . The formal evolution that can be followed from Cézanne to cubism, Mondrian, Pollock, and Newman no longer even exists. There is stagnation. The lessons of the past are rehashed for us with new materials.

I believe that any material can be used. For example, we can use ready-made paint—it would be stupid to want to make our own! But using the latest technical discovery for its novelty seems foolish. We can speak of "con art." In this sense, artists of all eras have never proceeded otherwise, but today the illusion has been stripped bare. On the other hand, if this state of affairs exists, it is not because artists today are less clever than their predecessors. Perhaps they simply lack lucidity, they are unaware. As for some, and not the lesser artists, they find that illusionism still works rather well, therefore they have no reason to deprive themselves of it. I believe that it is not a question of a shortage of ideas as some would have us believe, but of an inherent process in art. Modern art has the great advantage of making evident why *art of all times has been futile.* The most intuitive among today's artists, sensing their uselessness and not accepting it, resort to methods of diversion, either by adding heterogeneous elements— noises, television, smell—to art which is already hybrid by nature or by realizing, in spite of all their contortions, the ineffectiveness (historically understood) of their works compared to Matisse or Pollock, by turning to expressions that they believe are new, because they discover them, namely cinema, choreography, light, movement . . . They de-bone art and, unwittingly or not, make it evident that art is an "emollient," a hoax, and unacceptable.

Thanks to Rembrandt, Picasso, Schoeffer, Ucello, Chapelain-Midy, Stella, Rubens, Churchill, Gilardi, Johns, Monet, Pollock, Jacquet, Schneider, Judd, etc., for showing us everything that we must no longer do and furthermore what should never have been done. I don't doubt for a second that Giotto today would have used electricity or electro-magnets. It is not because they are being used that anything is being questioned. There is nothing revolutionary about their use, and it must not distract art critics or scare them away, whether they are "for-and-blind" and speak of inherent artistic revolution, or "against-and-blind" and speak anti-art, of betrayal. Open your eyes. *It is only art.* And full-fledged art, just as Cézanne or Mondrian are full-fledged artists.

G. B.: It is true that the artist, regardless of the style he chooses to work in, always suggests a dimension beyond, and he obliges the spectator to adopt his thought patterns. He leads, channels the spectator's thoughts down the route that he wishes.

D. B.: I call that the "reactionary" role of the artist. When you believe in art, certain things are seen in relation to it—if not, they don't exist, which seems absurd to me. Art is, as they say, a truth that, by symbolization, development and organization, shows that the exterior world exists and is beautiful, and wouldn't be so if art were not. This is actually what art is and what we must revolt against. Thinking and saying that "there was no London fog before Turner" is very pretty and poetic, but it is *outrageous.* It's an attack on the mind of the individual. It forces him to have the same dream as you. After seeing Cézanne, that is how I became one of these mental prisoners who believed they saw Sainte-Victoire Mountain as he represented it. *I believed "in" art.* When I lost the faith, I noticed that the mountain had disappeared. At last I saw Sainte-Victoire Mountain.

*Art distorts things.* It doesn't make you aware of things.

## CREATING SOMETHING "NEUTRAL"

G. B.: Do you regret man's impossibility of conceiving and creating something that was not given to him from the exterior world?

D. B.: I don't regret anything. I ascertain that art is false.

G. B.: Are you a prisoner of the fact that a thing is always taken in context, in relation to something else?

D. B.: In relation to art. If you must insist on comparing, let's say that artists display their responses, formal responses to their anguish, to their problems, in relation to the world, and to their life calling. What *we* present in relation to these responses is a *question.* But if you look objectively at my painting, without comparing, you will see that there is neither response nor question, but a raw, neutral fact, as it is.

G. B.: Some endeavor to supply a response. But you wish to ask questions?

D. B.: Yes, if you like.

G. B.: Can you tell me how you see the future, your future? I imagine that you don't sell many of your paintings . . . the striped ones, etc., while your past works have won you some success and even prizes. You are condemning yourself to not sell, and so starve, or do something else. Well?

D. B.: It's true that I don't sell anything, but I didn't sell anything in the past either when I had "some success" as you put it. It's a habit, even if I am aware that it's a very bad one! Furthermore, selling or not selling doesn't change the problem at all. Things are there, they exist and I have no illusions. Even if what I show can be sold, our society is strong enough to swallow the worst garbage without flinching. As for the future, you'd have to ask a clairvoyant! I am not a prophet, critic, or philosopher. I will continue as long as I can. Right now, there is only what is shown, nothing more, nothing less, something that has meaning in itself. Whatever idea we may have about this thing, *it is an essential reality,* even if it is ephemeral. I maintain that our paintings, as such, are the only ones that can be displayed without being *an insult to the potential observer.*

It's something not good or bad, right or wrong, question or answer, all or nothing, for or against, art or anti-art. It's something neutral that exists once seen, something irreducible. The supposed observer is finally free, lucid, and mature. He can choose.

I must insist that, besides this oft-repeated "thing" displayed, there is the way it is presented. I'll call this the packaging. This goes from the place where paintings are presented, to the show that reprimands the public, and even the interview that we are now having. The packaging is an important point, since its aim is to clarify things, to set the record straight. But obviously it must not be confused with what is displayed. There is the painting, and there is the packaging: I claim the latter because it is consistent with the former. Consequently, the packaging is acceptable because the painting is justifiable. Besides this, and as a point of comparison, I will say that art is only packaging. . . .

This interview was first published as "Entretien avec Daniel Buren: L'art n'est plus justifiable ou les points sur les 'i'," in *Les Lettres Francaises* (Paris, 13 March 1968), pp. 28–29. Translated by Alex Alberro, this is its first publication in English.

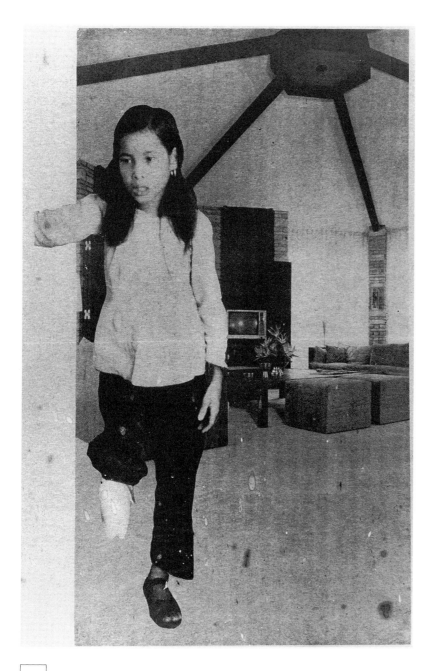

Martha Rosler, *Bringing the War Home,* 1968.

# tucumán burns

## maría teresa gramuglio and nicolás rosa

Beginning in 1968, a series of aesthetic works started to be produced in the Argentinean art world which broke with the avant-gardist pretense of the artists associated with the Di Tella Institute. Until then, this institution had adjudicated responsibility for legislating and proposing new models of engagement, not only for the artists linked to it, but for all new artistic affairs that arose in the country.

These works ruptured the celebrated and precious aesthetic atmosphere of the false avant-garde events produced in the official cultural institutions and began to suggest the emergence of a new attitude that would lead to the deployment of artistic phenomena as positive and real actions intended to initiate a modification of the environment in which they were generated.

This attitude pointed towards the development of implicit political content in all works of art, and to propose them as actively and violently charged so that the work of the artist would be incorporated into reality with a truly avant-garde and, thus, revolutionary intention. Aesthetic works that denounced the cruelty of the Vietnam War or the radical falsity of American policies would speak directly to the necessity of creating not only a relation between the work of art and the mass media, but an artistic object capable, on its own, to produce modifications as effective as a political act.

The recognition of this new conception drove a group of artists to postulate aesthetic creation as a *collective and violent* act destroying the bourgeois myth of the new forms of art. To be violent in this manner is to possess and destroy the old forms of art that reinforce the institution of individual property and the personal pleasure of the unique art object. Violence is now a creative act with new content: it destroys the system of the official culture, opposing it with a subversive culture that integrates the process of transformation, creating a truly revolutionary art.

Revolutionary art is born from an awareness of the actual reality of the artist as an individual inside the political and social context that surrounds him.

Revolutionary art proposes the aesthetic work as a hub that integrates and unifies all the elements that conform to human reality: economic, social, and political. It is an integration of the contributions of the different disciplines eliminating the separation between artists, intellectuals and technicians in a unitary action of all of them directed to modify the totality of the social structure—that is to say, it is a *total art*.

Revolutionary art activates reality through a process of collecting the elements that compose it, through a extraordinary ideological conception based on the principles of materialist reason.

Revolutionary art, in this way, presents itself as a partial form of reality that integrates itself into total reality, destroying the idealistic separation between the work and the world, as it maintains a truthful transformation of the social structures—that is to say, it is a *transformative art*.

Revolutionary art is the manifestation of those political contents that fight to destroy the obsolete artistic and aesthetic philosophy of bourgeois society, integrating into the revolutionary forces that fight the forms of economic dependency and class oppression—it is, therefore, a *social art*.

The work that is realized by this group of avant-garde artists is the continuation of a series of acts of aggression aimed at institutions that represent bourgeois culture, for example the nonparticipation and boycott of the Braque Prize, instituted by the Cultural Service of the French Embassy, which culminated with the detention of several artists that settled their rejection violently.

The collective work that realizes and supports itself in the actual Argentinean situation was radicalized in one of its poorest provinces, Tucumán, subjugated by a long tradition of underdevelopment and economic oppression. The Argentinean government, determined to carry out a disastrous colonizing policy, had proceeded to close the majority of Tucumán's sugar refineries, a vital resource in the province's economy, spreading hunger, unemployment and all their social consequences. A "Tucumán Operation," developed by government economists, is intended to obscure this attack on the working class with a sham economic development plan based on the creation of new and hypothetical industries financed by North American capital. The truth hidden behind this operation is the following: it attempts to destroy a real and explosive union extending across northwestern Argentina, breaking up worker groups by balkanizing them through small acts of industrial exploitation and obliging workers to relocate to other regions to look for temporary work that is poorly paid and without stability. One of the consequences that arise from this fact is the dissolution of the worker's nuclear family, left to improvisation and luck to survive. The economic politics the government has followed in the province of Tucumán has the character of a pilot program which it is using to evaluate the level of resistance of the worker population, that will, subsequently, result in the neutralization of union opposition, and which could be transported to other provinces that represent similar social and economic characteristics.

This "Tucumán Operation" is reinforced by a "silencing operation" organized by government institutions in order to confuse and stifle the serious Tucumán situation to which the "free press" has been subject to for reasons of common class interests.

In light of this situation, and assuming the responsibility of artists compromised by a social reality that includes them, avant-garde artists have responded to this "silencing operation" with the production of the work "TUCUMAN ARDE".

The work consists of the creation of an *informational circuit* to demonstrate the distortion that the activities in Tucumán suffer from a mass media that holds official power along with the bourgeois class. The media is a powerful interceding element, susceptible to being charged with different kinds of content; the positive influence that the media produces in society depends on the realism and truthfulness of its content. The information about the facts produced in Tucumán given by the government and the official media tend to silence the serious social problem unleashed by the closing of the sugar refineries, and give a false image of economic recuperation in the province which the real facts refute in a shocking manner. To gather these facts and make evident the false contradiction of the government and its supporting class, a group of avant-garde artists traveled to Tucumán, along with technicians and specialists, and proceeded to verify the social reality in the province. The artists' program reached a high point with a press conference, where their repudiation of the actions by the official authorities and the complicity of the media that collaborated in maintaining a shameful and degrading state for the working population of Tucumán was made public in a violent manner.

The artists worked in collaboration with student and worker groups with that collaboration being integrated into the artistic process.

The artists traveled to Tucumán with extensive documentation of the economic and social problems of the province and a detailed knowledge of all the information that the media had produced regarding the problems. This last body of information had previously been submitted to critical analysis in order to evaluate its degree of distortion. In a second instance, the information gathered by the artists and technicians was developed for the exhibit that is presented at the workers' union hall. And finally, the information that the media has produced about the artists' activities in Tucumán is to be incorporated into the informational circuit of the first phase.

The second part of the work is the presentation of all the information gathered about the situation and about the performance of the artists in Tucumán, part of which would be disseminated in union halls and in student and cultural centers in the same audiovisual form as the show at the General Confederation of Labor of the Argentineans in the city of Rosario, and subsequently in Buenos Aires.

The informational circuit, whose basic intention is to promote a de-alienation of the mass-media image of the Tucumán reality, would reach a high point in the third and last phase of generating publicity in a formal publication where all the processes of conception and realization of the work would be described as well as all the documentation produced, along with a final evaluation.

The position adopted by the avant-garde artists demands that their work not be incorporated into the official institutions of bourgeois culture, and establishes the necessity of having them transferred to other contexts. This exhibition is happening, then, at the General Confederation of Labor of the Argentineans because it is the institution that functions as the nucleus of the vanguard class in a fight whose ultimate objectives are shared by the authors of this work. (. . .)

This text was published as a mimeo by the General Confederation of Labor of the Argentineans in Rosario, Argentina, in 1968. Translated by Trilce Navarrete, this is its first appearance in English.

michel claura, gregory battcock, dan graham, editors of art-language, sol lewitt, ian burn, lee lozano, mierle laderman ukeles, john murphy, piero gilardi, jean clay, rolf wedewer, daniel buren, joseph kosuth, lucy r. lippard

**III 1969**

# paris commentary
## michel claura

There are, I feel, a few basic ideas to be considered before discussing the work of Buren and his friends. First of all, these ideas are the outcome of an objective look at art from its beginnings. Each work of art is the fruition of its creator's sensitivity and is directed at the sensitivity of the beholder.

The forms taken by an artist's sensitivity, and indeed by its opposite, can be manifold, but it determines his choice of subject—flowers, a woman, war, his environment, movement, the contrast or harmony of colors, the contrast or harmony of form—and whatever his subject the artist's aim is to translate his personal feelings into a work of art. Artistic creation thus boils down to the exploitation of his personal problems, either by translating his problems into universal terms or sinking his own inhibitions in his work. "Everybody, hence me," or "me, hence everybody." *To express himself the artist must both receive and transmit.*

If art is both an illusion in itself and the illusion of communication, what does it mean to the public? A doubtless unconscious complicity is established between artist and spectator. The artist offers an illusion which the public accepts. In so doing, the public, consciously or otherwise, in fact rejects reality. Which reduces art to the level of entertainment.

During the time that a spectator takes to look at, or even to think of, a work of art, he is no longer quite alone, alone with himself, alone in a hostile environment. Thus the complicity between the artist and his public reaches a state of blindness—the one blinding and the other allowing himself to be blinded.

It is, however, possible to find another criterion—which alone explains the fact that there is a history of art. The artist is constantly striving for greater perfection of expression. His aim is to progress, to reduce the distance between the significant and the expressed and to give greater universality to his own problems. Problems are not hard to acquire. They have not noticeably changed since man first made hand imprints on cave walls. The only development, the only progress that has been made, is exclusively in the means of expression. Thus, when all is said and done, our advance has been of a technical nature only. So far as art is concerned, the change has been in form without affecting the fundamentals. It is a purely technical development. *The history of art is the history of the technique of art.* Illusion's great attraction remains undiminished because techniques have continuously developed. Thus the outcome of the creative act can only be illusion, in that an artist's job is to select from his environment or from within himself an object, a light, a form, a movement, and to remove them from their context in order to transform them into a work of art. The illusion lies in the fact that a work of art is a space in which material or spiritual odds and ends taken out of context are deposited and which, we are persuaded, form an entity. This problem of illusion in art is the problem of communication. As art has always been a pseudo-realistic or symbolic representation of non-communicable feelings, what else could it be but the illusion of communication?

Communication takes place at the level of the artist's own proclaimed beliefs, and to see something more than this in a work of art is to bring one's own sensitivity into play. But by clinging to an illusion, this very sensitivity will be lost in the gulf which separates the significant from the expressed, intent from deed. The beholder will have had no more than the illusion of communication.

This cursory but fundamental analysis of art is possible today because art is more in evidence than ever. It is an obvious illusion, an illusion of communication, an aesthetic hedge against inflation, a technical entertainment: today art is more self-conscious than ever. Seen in this context, the attitudes of Buren and his friends are perhaps more comprehensible. On the one hand they present an objective analysis of art and on the other new concepts which, to my mind, are connected with art only insofar as they fundamentally question the whole role of art.

For more than a year Buren and three friends put on a series of demonstrations. On January 3, 1967, at the "Salon de la Jeune Peinture" at the Paris Museum of Modern Art, the four of them painted in public from eleven in the morning until eight in the evening to show how simple their techniques are. They also distributed a leaflet which said:

*Because painting is a game,*

*Because painting is the application (consciously or otherwise) of the rules of composition,*

*Because painting is the freezing of movement,*

*Because painting is the representation (or interpretation or appropriation or disputation or presentation) of objects,*

*Because painting is a springboard for the imagination,*

*Because painting is spiritual illustration,*

*Because painting is justification,*

*Because painting serves an end,*

*Because to paint is to give aesthetic value to flowers, women, eroticism, the daily environment, art, dadaism, psychoanalysis and the war in Vietnam,*

We are not painters.

Throughout the day a tape-recording in French, English and Spanish repeated "Buren, Mosset, Parmentier and Toroni advise you to use your intelligence." That evening they withdrew their canvases from the "Salon" saying they opposed Paris salons as the "heritage of nineteenth-century salons" and "galleries which abet public laziness (each gallery being a place of pilgrimage for a public intent on self-consolation)."

On June 2, 1967, at 9 p.m. in the auditorium of the Musée des Arts Décoratifs (entrance 5 Fr.), four canvases by Buren, Mosset, Parmentier and Toroni were displayed on a platform before 150 spectators. Nothing happened. The public waited a quarter of an hour, half an hour, an hour; still nothing happened. At a quarter past ten a leaflet was distributed which read:

*Obviously you have come here to look at canvases by Buren, Mosset, Parmentier and Toroni. What you must look at is:*

*a canvas 2.50 m × 2.50 m divided into twenty-nine equal vertical red and white stripes of which the two outer stripes are white (Buren);*

*a black circle (interior radius 4.5 cm, exterior radius 7.8 cm), centered on a white canvas 2.50 m × 2.50 m (Mosset);*

*alternate gray and white horizontal stripes each 38 cm apart on a canvas 2.50 m × 2.50 m (Parmentier);*

*eighty-five regular blue imprints of a flat brush each 30 cm apart on a white surface 2.50 m × 2.50 m (Toroni).*

In October 1967 at the Fifth Paris Biennale, the four paintings were again displayed but this time photographs were projected onto them to the accompaniment of a recorded text:

| Photographs | Text |
|---|---|
| Views of St. Tropez | Art is the illusion of being somewhere else. It is not a painting by Buren (spotlight projected onto his canvas), by Mosset (idem), by Parmentier (idem), by Toroni (idem). Art is the illusion of freedom. It is not etc. |
| Little Red Riding Hood | Art is the illusion of dreaming. It is not etc. |
| Shots of a bullfight | Art is the illusion of sacredness. It is not etc. |
| Shots of the Versailles fountains | Art is the illusion of the marvelous. It is not etc. |
| Striptease | Art is the illusion of escape. It is not etc. |
| Flowers | Art is the illusion of nature. It is not etc. |
| No projection | Art is entertainment, art is false. Painting begins with Buren, Mosset, Parmentier and Toroni. |

After a three-minute interval, the whole thing began again, and continued throughout the exhibition.

In December 1967, three of them—Buren, Mosset and Toroni—put on a new exhibition at the former "J" Gallery in Paris. I should add here that these three had been painting the same three pictures for more than a year. In order to stress the "autonomy" of their canvases, each artist painted and presented both his picture and those of the other two. They stated:

*The logic of our activities up to the present leads us today to say that to call a Buren a Buren, a Mosset a Mosset or a Toroni a Toroni is nothing but an abuse of language.*
*Buren presents a Buren, a Mosset and a Toroni. But all three canvases were painted by Buren.*
*Mosset presents a Mosset, a Buren and a Toroni. But all three canvases were painted by Mosset.*
*Toroni presents a Toroni, a Buren and a Mosset. But all three canvases were painted by Toroni.*
*This demonstration adds nothing to the paintings by Buren, Mosset and Toroni. It is an exhibition of three Burens, three Mossets and three Toronis.*

Also in December 1967, Buren and Toroni held a joint exhibition at the Flaviana Gallery in Lugano. They carried their logic a stage further and entitled the show "Buren or Toroni or

Any One Else." "Anyone else" was invited to paint either of the pictures usually done by Buren or Toroni and to sign it with his own name, appropriating the picture simply by painting it. There is nothing to distinguish any of the canvases, no matter who painted them. *In this demonstration the two artists are stating as clearly as possible that the thing they are painting IS.* It is therefore of little significance whether it was painted by one of themselves by someone else or by a machine. In two successive interviews which appeared in *La Galerie des Arts* (February 1968) and *Les Lettres Françaises* (March 13, 1968) Buren once again stated his case. Clearly it is no longer an artist talking, but a theoretician. Theory and art are incompatible.

The actual canvases shown by Buren, Toroni and Mosset are completely lacking in sensitivity. Humor, discomfort, anxiety, joy, calm, serenity—every human feeling is absent. This first point alone challenges our basic concept of art. To reject sensitivity means abandoning personal problems. And abandoning what I have called "personal problems" results in a picture which is no longer a transformation—by the artist—of reality into illusion.

Perhaps these attempts should be placed on a linguistic level, the search for a language which would, for the first time, specifically belong to the plastic arts. There is no longer a question of a work of art being limited to a given space, for example, where everything or nothing can be put, but of a work conceived in itself without ever taking anything whatever (being, object, idea) out of context. The result is a thing to be looked at for its own sake. It no longer represents, expresses, etc. It is no longer an illusion.

These canvases introduce a new concept of art which means that the relations between the work and the public will be changed. The problem of communication—even of non-communication—will no longer exist. There is no didactic intent. The spectator sees a work in itself, nothing else, nothing more. Buren, Mosset, Parmentier and Toroni will not be there to entertain you because the entertainment aspect of art is the transformation of what is all too true into illusion. Or, put another way, illusion is eliminated because no outside elements are introduced.

What happens to technique in their painting? It can no longer be the means by which an object is transformed into the representation of an object, into the illusion of an object, because there is no longer an object to recreate. In fact their technique is extremely simple, and if the work remains a composition (in that everything is "composed") it has nonetheless taken on a completely new meaning. The technique is *within* the work but no longer *is* the work.

To go back once again to the Buren-Toroni exhibition at Lugano, which was, I think, the most important they have ever presented, their canvases are "autonomous." Hence they were able to ask literally anyone to produce them and claim them as their own. They had in fact eliminated the artist's "expression," since whoever produces one of these is not expressing himself. If there were any self-expression, the work could only be imitated, but if in addition to Buren and Toroni, absolutely anyone can produce the "*same*" canvas, this means that the painter never expresses himself on any level, whether his name is Buren, Toroni or Any One Else. If the canvas is always identical, it is because it *is, immutably.* The artist is insignificant. Thus the system of references which constitutes the language of art is no longer acceptable.

This contention supports—and is supported by—the fact that the very concept of art is fundamentally questioned and in the course of being replaced by a new proposition. Because, let us not forget, these pictures existed before we came to talk about them. Logically (according to their own lights), they have painted innumerable copies of one canvas for nearly two years. Logically, because if they limited themselves to a single copy each this would have to be considered as a unique work, as *the* masterpiece, a concept they have also rejected. We do not have to consider their future. We can limit ourselves to what they show us, to their canvases. Their existence-in-themselves could be related to formalist mathematics.

We are no longer in the domain of art. But we are faced with a questioning of the whole basis of art.

Since this article was written, Buren in particular has been able to demonstrate at what point his action was coherent. He continues to prove that it is possible to elaborate a practical theory in art, on condition that one ceases to be just an artist or, in other words, that one has a *total* and specific vision of the innumerable problems posed by the work and its communication. Using the same material, Buren has, since March 1968, produced the same stripes printed on paper. In April he pasted pieces of paper on advertisement hoardings in Paris, showing nothing but the stripes themselves. At "Prospect '68'" in Dusseldorf he pasted similar pieces of paper on a surface 26 by 32 ft. (September 1968). In October, in an article in *Galerie des Arts,* Buren, discussing specific and marginal problems of art teaching, described the mechanics of creation as a social act. In the same month he had an exhibition at the Galerie Apollinaire in Milan, and used the gallery as a kind of background support rather than as an exhibition space.

This text first appeared in *Studio International,* 177:907 (January 1969), pp. 47–49.

# painting is obsolete

## gregory battcock

An exhibition that is entitled "0 OBJECTS, 0 PAINTERS, 0 SCULPTURES . . ." has been organized by Seth Siegelaub, a pleasant sort of sexy chap, and can be seen at 44 East 52nd St. until January 31, 1969. Anyone who doesn't go needs his head examined because this is perhaps the first exhibit this season that really goes someplace and offers something a little bit new and something that really matters. It's like everything that happened in 1968, at Columbia and Paris and all other symbolic places is finally being understood, and it all REALLY meant something and it really will result in something because it already has in this show. Finally in art, the revolution that one sometimes briefly understands at perhaps the Fillmore, or late at night on WBAI, or in weird, unexpected glimpses at surprising places around town, or watching a Warhol movie or in unplanned encounters with sex or metaphysics or acid or grass or just nice people—it's here, in art. A beautiful exhibit that makes so much sense right now, and that is so clear and frank and simple and has such a nice smile—is offered by four artists and finally there is an exhibit that doesn't have any junk in it, doesn't have anything at all really. If that doesn't fuck up all those nice comfortable minds that like art to have big dollar signs, and armed guards, and ticket takers and don't (or do) touch, and that most annoying of all demands some modern art tries to make, *experience.* Why do we have to experience anything. I don't like playing with buttons and little balls, and opening little doors, and patting slimy surfaces or listening to gurgling or popping sounds when I'm around art. I can do all that, even better, with real things and if art is anything remotely like imitation of reality then I don't like it since I don't like imitations.

The stuff in this show leaves you alone, more or less, and it only grabs your mind, which is fine, and when you leave you really feel like you've been through something and you have a lot of ideas, which you can think about or throw out and it doesn't matter which you decide to do, despite my aged philosophy professor at NYU who says that, in this day and age, drugs have resulted in the modern condition of "intellectual perversion" because people are all hung up on experience itself, and after all experience itself is no good if it doesn't lead to positive learning. Which only shows that someone should turn the old goat on but nobody will because it's hard to turn somebody on if they live in a closet, which he does even though they call it University Village and he drags himself to Europe every summer and has tenure. Nothing is going to change really in the American University until they get rid of everybody who is on tenure. Just the fact that a college teacher would WANT to have tenure is enough reason to fire him or at least disqualify him from teaching. Only the prof who doesn't care about his job or the false "security" it affords is in a position to recognize the real things that are happening, but that most people cannot, must not, see.

It would be nice to compare Godard's *A Movie Like Any Other* with this new exhibition I'm writing about because there must be some pretty interesting reasons for a comparison but the editor of this rag keeps telling me not to write about movies, for some reason, so back to art, which is O. K. when it's this type of art. The works in the show are ideas that are not intended to be any more than ideas. As such they are pretty much invisible, which itself is a good idea. We've suspected, for some time now, that art perhaps can be invisible and now it is. Therefore there's nothing to steal, nothing to damage, no images to remember later, and we don't have to worry about slides and lighting. If 69 contributes to the history of art invisibility, art history students from now on will remember us fondly.

Another thing about this show is that perhaps it isn't art and maybe it's art criticism, which would be something I've suspected all along, that the painter and sculptor have been moving further and further away from art and in the end perhaps all that would remain is art criticism. (. . .) What a show like this does is, in one stroke not only demolish the Museum of Modern Art (the Whitney demolished itself last week) but all those painting courses they are still cranking out in the "art" schools, which were doomed a decade ago but nobody noticed, oh well it's too bad, after spending all that money on paints and everything. (. . .)

This review was published in *New York Free Press,* 23 January 1969, p. 7.

Luis Camnitzer, *Dictionary*, 1969.

# art workers' coalition open hearing presentation
## dan graham

The subject is the artist, the object is to make art *free*.

The art world stinks; it is made of people who collectively dig the shit; now seems to be the time to get the collective shit out of the system.

Where does the cycle begin? Let's begin with the individual painter or sculptor ensconced "high" in his loft world, making his pile of shit (perhaps he is really shitting, in his mind's eye, on the world) having ingested art information and raw material from the shared world, pissing his time away, the labor of his love perhaps to be redeemed, to be *realized* at some other time.

The stuff is transformed when it is transposed into imposed "higher" values. First, a gallery, then, perhaps a museum, and further extended by translation into the data of art information when reproduced in an art magazine; at which point the artist, seeing the transposition, is pissed off. As time is transposed, money is transposed into private worth for the artist and a "high" *quality* for the collector and art critic in this business society. The art world is a collection of people who dig the dirt, or pay the artist to dig it for him, to get a "piece" of the action—the games people play—for personal fun and profit ("a profitable experience").

Everybody has their private part (parts) to contribute—for the media it's just another slice of life/entertainment.

It's time it seems to leave all this shit behind; the art world is poisoned; get out to the country or take a radical stance. (According to the dictionary, "root," the root of radical and the root of root are the same—does dirt or evil really have roots?)

*Should art be a lever against the Establishment? Make art dangerous?* but art is only one item among the dangerous commodities being circulated in this society and, unattractive as it may be, one of the less lethal. *Withhold?*—a closed system dies of suffocation.

The writer in the past has been presented with an analogous problem. All magazines in order to survive are forced to present a well-known point of view to identify readers with advertisements just as in the past the structure of the book as object functioned to re-press the author's private, interior perspective or vision of life to the private reader who has bought the unique illusion as he reads through the narrative—linear, progressive, continuous from beginning to vanishing end point—his perspective is supposed to be altered by a novel insight into the world; he is changed; in Marx, Zola and Brecht's time he was hopefully motivated to change affect into effecting changes back in the *outside* world. Magazines—art magazines—continued this fiction of assuming private points-of-view whose sum they must assume to be the collective view of its readership and advertisers. They depend exclusively for their economic existence on selling ads to galleries for the most part. For what it's worth to the readers who will buy it, the critic who must sell it, quality in art is all that counts (time is money which counts/man is the measure of all things). For the writer, and recently, some so-called conceptual artists, there is a simple solution: buy the ads himself—the cycle thus feeds back on itself; invest in oneself—it's a free society.

Actually, it's not the artists, the galleries, the collectors, the critics or the art magazines who support the structure at all—but the United States government—you and me—geared to corporate needs—which through the tax structure make it profitable to run a non-profitable art "business" to buy and donate "works" to museums (in the process serving the soul purpose of feeding artists and Madison Avenue types in the overall process of making a lot of money for yourself), etc., etc.

The conceptual artist conceives of a pure art without material base, conceived simply by giving birth to new ideas—an art that would ideally mean and not be of baseball or Monopoly in the den, a game without ball, bat, gravity, dice or money. But it's free and like sex, with a minimum of two people (subject/object; inside/outside; yin/yang; receiver/sender; people who take pictures of each other just to prove that they really existed) anyone can play, making their rules as they go along.

The artist labored under the myth of trying to define himself (and his time) in terms of his work—his unique contribution—his *raison d'etre;* rather than be defined by society in their image.

But art is an inevitable part of the larger order of society, its language and world shared and interdependent with the language, "vision" and stuff of its specific Time, Life, place and function.

All human brains perceive and think partially in symbols which have a relationship to external signs available to all which reduce to various interrelated language systems which relate to the larger social order at a given moment.

What does the artist have in common with his friends, his public, his society? Information about himself, themselves and all ourselves—which is not reduced to ideas or material, but shares in both categories as it has a past, present and future time/space. It is neither subjective or objective "truth;" it simply is—it is both a residue "object" and neutral "ethereal" media transcribed—transcribed upon/translation—translating the content of single and collective man's internal and external position, work, ideas, activities.

The artist is not a machine; the artist shares in mankind's various media of expression having no better "secrets" or necessarily seeing more inside or outside of things than any other person; often he is more calculating; he wants things to be as interesting as possible; to give and have return pleasure; to contribute to the life-enhancing social covenant. Perhaps young artists, with their new naivete have replaced the old naivete of their fathers.

My opinion (more later): we must go back to the old notion of socially "good works" as against the private, aesthetic notion of "good work"—i.e.: art to go public.

These comments were first presented at the Art Workers' Coalition "Open Hearing" on 10 April 1969. They were subsequently published in Art Workers' Coalition, *An Open Hearing on the Subject: What Should Be the Program of the Art Workers Regarding Museum Reform and to Establish the Program of an Open Art Workers' Coalition* (New York: Art Workers' Coalition, 1969), n.p.

10

## DETUMESCENCE

I had in mind a page, describing in clinical language the typical emotional and physiological aspects of post-climax in the sexual experience of the human male. It was noted that no description exists anywhere in the literature, as it is "anti-romantic." It may be culturally suppressed — a structural "hole" in the psycho-sexual-social conditioning of behavior. I wanted the "piece" to be, simply, this psycho-sexual-social "hole" — truncated on the page alone as printed matter. To create it, I advertised in several places. In late 1966 I advertised for a qualified medical writer in the "National Tatler" (a sex tabuloid). In early 1969 "The New York Review of Sex" gave me an ad. As both of these ads were somewhat edited, I bought an ad in "SCREW" in mid-1969. I HAVE RECEIVED NO RESPONSES.

Dan Graham, *Detumescence,* 1969.

# introduction
## editors of *art-language*

This editorial is not intended to serve as a thorough compendium of the activity within the field of conceptual art; if it was, it would possess lamentable shortcomings. Neither does it presume to represent conceptual artists in the U.S.A., nor many of those in Britain. There are three contributions from American artists in this issue; it is hoped that contributions from American artists will be maintained and increased and it is also an aim of this magazine to furnish a comprehensive report of conceptual art in the U.S.A. in one of the future issues this year. The essay below is specifically directed toward indicating the development of a number of artists in Britain who have worked in this field for the past two years. The formation of this magazine is part of that development and the work discussed in this essay is the work of the founders of this magazine. The essay will point out some differences, in an indirect way, between American and British conceptual art, but it should not be seen to indicate a clear and definite boundary between them; there are British artists working in this field who show more affinity with American conceptual art than with what is, here, called British conceptual art. The editor-founders of this magazine have, for example, maintained close contact over the past year and a half with Sol LeWitt and Dan Graham. Their position is not at all seen by them to be one of isolation.

Suppose the following hypothesis is advanced: that this editorial, in itself an attempt to evince some outlines as to what "conceptual art" is, is held out as a "conceptual art" work. At first glance this seems to be a parallel case to many past situations within the determined limits of visual art, for example the first Cubist painting might be said to have attempted to evince some outlines as to what visual art is, whilst, obviously, being held out as a work of visual art. But the difference here is one of what shall be called "the form of the work." Initially what conceptual art seems to be doing is questioning the condition that seems to rigidly govern the form of visual art—that visual art remains visual.

During the past two years, a number of artists have developed projects and theses, the earliest of which were initially housed pretty solidly within the established constructs of visual art. Many of these projects etc. have evolved in such a manner that their relationship to visual art conventions has become increasingly tenuous. The later projects particularly are represented through objects, the visual form of which is governed by the form of the conventional signs of written language (in this case English). The content of the artist's idea is expressed through the semantic qualities of the written language. As such, many people would judge that this tendency is better described by the category-name "art theory" or "art criticism;" there can be little doubt that works of "conceptual art" can be seen to include both the periphery of art criticism and of art theory, and this tendency may well be amplified. With regard to this particular point, criteria bearing upon the chronology of art theory may have to be more severely and stringently accounted for, particularly in terms of evolutionary analogies. For example, the question is not simply: "Are works of art theory part of the kit of the conceptual artist, and as such can such a work, when advanced by a conceptual artist, come up for the count as a work of conceptual art?" But also: "Are past works of art theory now to be counted as works of conceptual art?" What has to be considered here is the intention of the conceptual artist. It is very doubtful whether an art theoretician could have advanced one of his works as a work of "conceptual art" (say) in 1964, as the first rudiments of at least an embryonic awareness of the notion of "conceptual art" were not evident until 1966. The intention of the "conceptual artist" has been separated off from that of the art theoretician because of their previously different relationships and standpoint toward art, that is, the nature of their involvement in it.

If the question is formed the other way round, that is, not as "Does art theory come up for the count as a possible sector of 'conceptual art?'" but as, "Does 'conceptual art' come up for the count as a possible sector of art theory?" then a rather vaguely defined category is being advanced as a possible member of a more established one. Perhaps some qualification can be made for such an assertion. The development of some work by certain artists both in Britain and the U.S.A. does not, if their intentions are to be taken into account, simply mean a matter of a transfer of function from that of artist to that of art theoretician, it has necessarily involved the intention of the artist to count various theoretical constructs as art works. This had contingently meant either (1) If they are to be "left alone" as separate, then re-defining carefully the definitions of both art and art theory, in order to assign more clearly what kind of entity belongs to which category. If this is taken up it usually means that the definition of art is expanded, and art theoreticians then discuss the consequences and possibilities of the new definitions, the traditional format of the art theoretician discussing what the artist has implied, entailed etc., by his "creative act." Or (2) To allow the peripheral area between the two categories some latitude of interpretation and consequently account the category "art theory" a category which the category "art" might expand to include. The category "maker of visual art" has been traditionally regarded as solely the domain of the visual-art object producer (i.e. the visual-art artist). There has been a hierarchy of languages headed by the "direct read-out from the object" language which has served as the creative core, and then various support languages acting as explicative and elucidatory tools to the central creative core. The initial language has been what is called "visual," the support languages have taken on what shall be called here "conventional written sign" language-form. What is surprising is that although the central core has been seen to be an ever-evolving language, no account up to the present seems to have taken up the possibility of this central core evolving to include and assimilate one or other or all of the support languages. It is through the nature of the evolution of the works of "conceptual art" that the implicated artists have been obliged to take account of this possibility. Hence these artists do not see the appropriateness of the label "art theoretician" necessarily eliminating the appropriateness of the label "artist." Inside the framework of "conceptual art" the making of art and the making of a certain kind of art theory are often the same procedure.

With a context such as this the initial question can be posed with a view to a more specific inquiry. The question: "Can this editorial, in itself an attempt to evince some outlines as to what 'conceptual art' is, come up for the count as a work of conceptual art?" Firstly, the established notions of what the presentation of art and the procedures of art-making entail have to be surveyed. The question "Can this editorial come up for the count as a work of art within a developed framework of the visual art convention?" can only be answered providing some thorough account is given of what is meant by "developed" here. At the present we do not, as a norm, expect to find works of visual art in magazines, we expect critical, historical, etc. comment upon them, photographic reproductions etc. The structures of the identity of art-objects have consecutively been placed under stress by each new movement in art, and the succession of new movements has become more rapid this century. In view of these phenomena perhaps the above question can be altered to: "Can this editorial come up for the count as a member of the extended class 'visual art work?'" Here "extended" replaces "developed" and can, perhaps, be made to point out the problem as follows:

Suppose an artist exhibits an essay in an art exhibition (like a print might be exhibited). The pages are simply laid out flat in reading order behind glass within a frame. The spectator is intended to read the essay "straight," like a notice might be read, but because the essay is mounted in an art ambience it is implied that the object (paper with print upon it) carries conventional visual art content. The spectator being puzzled at not really being able to grasp any direct visual art read-out meaning starts to read it (as a notice might be read). It goes as follows:

"On why this is an essay"

The appearance of this essay is unimportant in any strong sense of visual-art appearance criteria. The prime requirement in regard to this essay's appearance is that it is reasonably legible. Any decisions apart from this have been taken with a view to what it should not look like as a point of emphasis over what it should look like. These secondary decisions are aimed at eliminating as many appearance similarities to established art-objects as possible.

Thus if the essay is to be evaluated in terms of the content expressed in the writing (*which it is*), then in an obvious established sense many people would say that if it has a connection with art at all, that it fits better into the category "art criticism" or "art theory." Such a statement at least admits the observation that when an artist uses "(a piece of) writing" in this context then he is not using such an object in the way that art audiences are accustomed to it being used. But further it admits of a rather more bigoted view, that is this essay belongs more to art criticism or art theory because it is formed of writing and in this sense it looks more like art criticism or art theory than it looks like art; that is, that this object (a piece of writing) does not have sufficient appearance criteria to be identified as a member of the class "art object"— it does not look like art. This observation has a strong assumption behind it that the making of a traditional art object (i.e. one to be judged within the visual evaluative framework) is a necessary condition for the making of art. Suppose there are some areas (say) pertaining to art at present which are of such a nature that they need not, maybe cannot, any longer meet the requirements which have previously been required as a necessary mode of an object coming up for the count as a member of the class "art work." This necessary mode is formulated as follows, (say) the recognition of art in the object is through some aspect(s) of the visual qualities of the object as they are directly perceived.

The question of "recognition" is a crucial one here. There has been a constantly developing series of methods throughout the evolution of the art whereby the artist has attempted to construct various devices to ensure that his intention to count the object as an art object is recognized. This has not always been "given" within the object itself. The more recently established ones have not necessarily, and justifiably so, meant the obsolescence of the older methods. (. . .)

. . . Once having established writing as a method of specifying points in an inquiry of this kind, there seems no reason to assume that inquiries pertaining to the art area should necessarily have to use theoretical objects simply because art in the past has required the presence of a concrete object before art can be thought of as "taking place"; having gained the use of such a wide-ranging instrument as "straight" writing, then objects, concrete and theoretical, are only two types of entity which can count; a whole range of other types of entities become candidates for art usage. Some of the British artists involved in this area have constructed a number of hypotheses using entities which might be regarded as alien to art. Most of these inquiries do not exhibit the framework of the established art-to-object relationship and (if you like) they are not categorically asserted as members of the class "art object," nor for that matter is there a categorical assertion that they are art ("work"); but such a lack of absolute assertion does not prohibit them from being tentatively asserted as having some important interpellations for the art area.

This concept of presenting an essay in an art gallery, the essay being concerned with itself in relation to it being in an art gallery, helps fix its meaning. When it is used as it is in this editorial, then the art gallery component has to be specified. The art gallery component in the first essay is a concrete entity, the art gallery component in the second case (here) is a theoretical component, the concrete component is the words "in an art gallery." (. . .)

The British "conceptual artists" are still attempting to go into this notion of the meta-stratas of art-language. Duchamp wrote early in the century that he "wanted to put painting back into the service of the mind." There are two things to be especially taken into account here, "painting" and "the mind." Leaving aside here ontological questions concerning "the mind," what the British artists have, rightly or wrongly, analyzed out and constructed might be summarized in words something like: "There is no question of putting painting, sculpture, *et al.,* back in the service of the mind (because as painting and sculpture it has only served the mind within the limits of the language of painting and sculpture and the mind cannot do anything about the limits of painting and sculpture after a certain physical point, simply because those are the limits of painting and sculpture). Painting and sculpture have physical limits and the limit of what can be said in them is finally decided by precisely those physical limits." Painting and sculpture, *et al.,* have never been out of the service of the mind, but they can only serve the mind to the limits of what they are. The British conceptual artists found at a certain point that the nature of their involvements exceeded the language limits of the concrete object; soon after they found the same thing with regard to theoretical objects, and both put precise limits on what kind of concepts can be used. There has never been any question of these latter projects coming for the count as members of the class "painting" or the class "sculpture," or the class "art object" which envelops the classes "painting" and "sculpture." There is some question of these latter projects coming up for the count as members of the class "art work." A little has to be said of Duchamp's work here for other reasons besides those already stated. It has been maintained by some commentators upon early American and British conceptual work that Duchamp's influence is all-pervasive and his aesthetics are totally absorbed and accepted by the younger generation of artist today. If this is meant to mean that Duchamp is treated uncritically as a kind of "gospel" then it is certain that at least the British group will disagree with this assessment. (. . .)

Something might now be said noting the relationship of the psychology of perception with regard to "conceptual art." It is today widely agreed that the psychology of perception is of some importance in the study of visual art. The practice of this study by art theoreticians, for example Ehrenzweig, Arnheim, etc., has at least clarified some questions within the context of visual "visual art" which have enabled the conceptual artists today these (such and such) projects have not such and such characteristics, in this way they have influenced what the formulative hypotheses of some of conceptual art are not about. Such concepts as whether art consecrates our ordinary modes of seeing and whether or not we are able, in the presence of art, to suspend our ordinary habits of seeing are strongly linked with inquiries into Gestalt hypotheses and other theories of perception; the limits of visual art are often underlined in inquiries into how we see. The British group have noted particularly and with deep interest the various Gestalt hypotheses that Robert Morris (for example) had developed in the notes on his sculpture-objects. These notes seem to have been developed as a support and an elucidation for Morris' sculpture. The type of analysis that the British group have spent some considerable time upon is that concerning the linguistic usage of both plastic art itself and of its support languages. These theses have tended to use the language form of the support languages, namely work-language, and not for any arbitrary reason, but for the reason that this form seems to offer the most penetrating and flexible tool with regard to some prime problems in art today. Merleau-Ponty is one of the more recent contributors to a long line of philosophers who have in various ways stressed the role of visual art as a corrective to the abstractness and generality of conceptual thought—but what is visual art correcting conceptual thought out of—into? In the final analysis such corrective tendencies may simply turn out to be no more than a "what we have we hold" conservatism without any acknowledgement as to how art can develop. Richard Wollheim has written, ". . . but it is quite another matter, and one I suggest, beyond the bounds of sense, even to entertain the idea that a form of art could maintain itself outside a society of language-users." I would suggest it is not beyond the bounds of sense to maintain that an art form can evolve by taking as a point of initial inquiry the language-use of the art society.

This text served as the introduction to the first volume of *Art-Language: The Journal of Conceptual Art,* 1:1 (May 1969), pp. 1–10.

# sentences on conceptual art
## sol lewitt

1 — *Conceptual Artists are mystics rather than rationalists. They leap to conclusions that logic cannot reach.*

2 — *Rational judgements repeat rational judgements.*

3 — *Illogical judgements lead to new experience.*

4 — *Formal Art is essentially rational.*

5 — *Irrational thoughts should be followed absolutely and logically.*

6 — *If the artist changes his mind midway through the execution of the piece he compromises the result and repeats past results.*

7 — *The artist's will is secondary to the process he initiates from idea to completion. His willfulness may only be ego.*

8 — *When words such as painting and sculpture are used, they connote a whole tradition and imply a consequent acceptance of this tradition, thus placing limitations on the artist who would be reluctant to make art that goes beyond the limitations.*

9 — *The concept and idea are different. The former implies a general direction while the latter is the components. Ideas implement the concept.*

10 — *Ideas alone can be works of art; they are in a chain of development that may eventually find some form. All ideas need not be made physical.*

11 — *Ideas do not necessarily proceed in logical order. They may set one off in unexpected directions but an idea must necessarily be completed in the mind before the next one is formed.*

12 — *For each work of art that becomes physical there are many variations that do not.*

13 — *A work of art may be understood as a conductor from the artist's mind to the viewers. But it may never reach the viewer, or it may never leave the artist's mind.*

14 — *The words of one artist to another may induce an ideas chain, if they share the same concept.*

15 — *Since no form is intrinsically superior to another, the artist may use any form, from an expression of words (written or spoken), to physical reality, equally.*

16 — *If words are used, and they proceed from ideas about art, then they are art and not literature; numbers are not mathematics.*

17 — *All ideas are art if they are concerned with art and fall within the conventions of art.*

18 — *One usually understands the art of the past by applying the conventions of the present thus misunderstanding the art of the past.*

19 — *The conventions of art are altered by works of art.*

20 — *Successful art changes our understanding of the conventions by altering our perceptions.*

21 — *Perception of ideas leads to new ideas.*

22 — *The artist cannot imagine his art, and cannot perceive it until it is complete.*

23 — *One artist may mis-perceive (understand it differently than the artist) a work of art but still be set off in his own chain of thought by that misconstrual.*

24 — *Perception is subjective.*

25 — *The artist may not necessarily understand his own art. His perception is neither better nor worse than that of others.*

26 — *An artist may perceive the art of others better than his own.*

27 — *The concept of a work of art may involve the matter of the piece or the process in which it is made.*

28 — *Once the idea of the piece is established in the artist's mind and the final form is decided, the process is carried out blindly. There are many side effects that the artist cannot imagine. These may be used as ideas for new works.*

29 — *The process is mechanical and should not be tampered with. It should run its course.*

30 — *There are many elements involved in a work of art. The most important are the most obvious.*

31 — *If an artist uses the same form in a group of works, and changes the material, one would assume the artist's concept involved the material.*

*32 — Banal ideas cannot be rescued by beautiful execution.*

*33 — It is difficult to bungle a good idea.*

*34 — When an artist learns his craft too well he makes slick art.*

*35 — These sentences comment on art, but are not art.*

This text first appeared in *0–9*, no. 5 (January 1969), pp. 3–5.

THE GARB AGE COLLECTION---Green Plastic Dispoables

Have people collect all the plastic garbage bags
in an area and pile them all together in a giant
pile.Perhaps in a busy area on Yonge st.

Photos of garbage bags mounted on board and shown
in a strip...like a street.Make some blow ups of
a couple of the photos.Make actual recostructions
of some of the sites shown in the photos and place
bags in them.Make enlarged scale drawings of some
of the photos and ...blue or black printed.Tinted
blow ups.Many different shot of same bags. Maps??

General Idea, *The Garb Age Collection*, 1969.

# dialogue
## ian burn

*1 — Artists are exploring language to create access to ways of seeing.*

*2 — Perception is no longer a direct and unified act; through language it has become fragmented and dispersed.*

*3 — Language has become an integral part and tool of activity.*

*1 — Language and the product are separate and independent.*

*2 — Language influences and alters the perceiving and recognizing of material and products.*

*3 — Language reduces the role of perception and brings into use new material, areas for ideas and processes beyond previous perceiving.*

*1 — Language has more relevance in terms of idea.*

*2 — The product ceases to have a focal center: perceiving becomes scanning rather than focusing, taking in a field of no particular emphasis rather than directing interest.*

*3 — The viewing is an experience outside of the idea and its structure, visual interest has become arbitrary.*

*1 — Language suggests, through the idea and viewer, a kind of dialogue or "conversation."*

*2 — This creates an actual area of the work.*

*3 — Participating in a dialogue gives the viewer a new significance; rather than listening, he becomes involved in reproducing and inventing part of that dialogue.*

This text appeared in the untitled mimeograph periodical *Art Press*, published in New York in July 1969 by The Society for Theoretical Art & Analysis of which Burn was a founding member.

# dialogue piece
## lee lozano

(Started April 21, 69) OR VERBALL. CALL (OR WRITE/SPEAK TO) PEOPLE FOR THE SPECIFIC PUR-
POSE OF INVITING THEM TO YR LOFT FOR A DIALOGUE. IN PROCESS FOR THE REST OF "LIFE".
(printed in the notebook's margin) NOTE: DEFINITION OF "DIALOGUE" REMAINS OPEN. VERBALL
GIVES SOME INDICATION.

| | |
|---|---|
| *April 21, 69—* | *Call Moose (Robt Morris). Leave name & number with his answering service.* |
| *May 11, 69—* | *Call Walter DeMaria. Leave name only with A.S.* |
| *May 13, 69—* | *Call Walter DeMaria. Leave name & number with A.S.* |
| *May 14, 69—* | *Call Jap, (Jasper Johns) at Castelli Gallery. Leave name & no. with David White who promises to get message to Jap although Jap is "very busy & in & out of town this week".* |
| *May 14, 69—* | *Call Poonsie (Larry Poons). He answers phone, we make a date for May 21 (Wed), 4 P.M.* |

NOTE: START WRITE UP OF PIECE WHEN YOU HAVE MADE THE FIRST "CONTACT". SO FAR THE PEOPLE CALLED ARE THOSE WITH WHOM A DIALOGUE HAS ALREADY BEEN STARTED IN THE "PAST", A DIALOGUE WHICH MIGHT BE INTERESTING TO PURSUE.

May 16, 69—        *Moose ret'ns call. We make a date for May 17 (Sat), 5 P.M.*

May 17, 69—        *Moose visits, then we go to his crib, turn on and have a great dialogue, that is, a long intense talk without too much tension during which we exchange many ideas.*

NOTE: THE PURPOSE OF THIS PIECE IS TO HAVE A DIALOGUE WITH AS MANY PEOPLE AS POSSIBLE, NOT TO MAKE A PIECE. ANY PERSONAL INFORMATION EXCHANGED DURING DIALOGUE WILL BE PROTECTED BY MY CONFIDENCE. IF ANYONE WISHES IDEAS TO BE PASSED ON I SHALL COMPLY. As much as poss.

May 18—        *Call John Giomo, leave name & no. w/ A. S.*

"        *Call Claus Oldenburg. Speak to Patty who will pass message on to Claus when he gets back to N. Y. In 2 wks.*

"        *Call Yvonne Rainer. We make date for Sun, May 25.*

"        *Call my mother, who is ill. She is having first drug experience & I invite her to have dialogue by long-dist. phone.*

"        *Attend opening of Lucy's show at Paula Coopees. Speak to at least 13 people whom I'll call for a dialogue.*

May 19, 69—        *John Giorno ret'ns call, will call Wed or Thur.*

"        *Call Heizer to acknowledge rec't of repros, Invite him for dialogue, he'll call soon and bring more prints to show me.*

"        *Call Ian Wilson, leave name/no. w/ his wife?*

" 20, 69        *David Lee calls from downstairs waking me up & we have a beautiful two hour dialogue (before I even have a chance to take a shit).*

"        *Ian Wilson returns call. After a very unpleasant conversation he refuses to visit. I suggest taking a walk, he refuses and can't wait to get off phone. The conversation yielded an enormous amount of information in spite of his being adamant about not believing in "passing information", and some of his questions forced me to think more about what I am doing. He put his ideas into art mag jargon: "Are you setting up an environment?" He said something about the first "conversation" we had (abt a yr ago, at Longview, thru Lucy's suggesting that he talk to me), that it made him vomit, or something we talked about concerning art mags which I don't recall. I must now decide what to "do". Note: Mention inviting an animal to I. W. during this call.*

May 21—    *No word from Poonsie. Call him at 6:16 P.M. He said (a bit fakely) "Oh this is Wednesday isn't it", that he was "inta sumpthin", could I call next Tues, I said I'd be glad to call next week, and he called me "Dear".*

May 22—    *John Torreanot calls, I invite him over & we have a dialogue on grass he brought. At end he stays too long but then I am so tired, I would not have been "up" to anything today. It was a good dialogue, very "dense", I clarified some important ideas.*

DECIDE TO INVITE A CAT & A BABY FOR A DIALOGUE EACH. (May 22, 69)

May 23—    *Call Larry Weiner (as I promised at Cooper opening). Make date for visit Mon, May 26, 4 P.M.*

May 24—    *Kaltenbach comes at last for our first "official" dialogue. We trade a lot of our art ideas & discuss doing a piece together when he returns from Cal. (He leaves on June 3 for teaching job).*

May 24, 69    *When I call Claire Copley to apologize for abrupt departure last night from LaMonte's I invite her & we make date for Wed, May 28, after 7 P.M.*

" 25    *Call Yvonne around 2 P.M., no answer. Again later (to be correct) at 6:15. No answer.*

" 25    *Call David Diau, he'll call very soon for a visit.*

" 25    *Call Alan Saret, he will come tonight at 9.00. Later. It was very sluggish dialogue but I learn more than can be expressed verbally from Alan (a lot abt his no-scene), and about this time & place in history. Also realize I have no floor-pad for stoned guests stretching.*

" 28    *Larry Weiner & I have a "fast-paced" dialogue. He seems to behave as though to let the other person talk is to let the other person win. The*

|  |  |
|---|---|
|  | *"element" missing from this dialogue which happened to be present in all the previous dialogues was love.* |
| *" 28* | *Claire Copley mostly talks during dialogue, is interested in learning, she said.* |
| *" 30* | *Dan Graham & I have important dialogue in that definite changes were immediately effected because of it.* |
| *June 2, 60* | *Call Poons, leave name & no. w/ A.S.* |
| *"* | *Call Brice, make date for June 3 (Tue), 8:30. Will Brice Marden bring his old lady I wonder?* |
| *" 3* | *No Brice doesn't come with Helen & we discuss "the Revolution", Brice talking almost entirely abt shitty business practices in the art world, & shitty treatment of artists by each other.* |
| *" 4* | *Larry Stafford who is in bldg to visit Ray Sieminowski knocks on my door & we have spontaneous dialogue, much abt gallery & dealer pitfalls.* |
| *" 5&6* | *Alan Saret returns both these nights & we continue dialogue. More later re this.* |
| *" 6* | *Vogels visit, we have long "dialogue".* |
| *" 7* | *Serra comes over a little high on beer & no food. Just into a dialogue with him (we've been smoking Saret's hash) when he gets an attack (too stoned), falls off chair to floor with a crash, has "convulsions" & passes out. Later he feels sick, lies down on bed until Saret comes over.* |
| *" 9* | *Call more people for dialogue. From now on I won't enter these calls in* Piece *but only dialogues per se, & calls when they are relevant.* |
| *" 10* | *Meet with Dick Anderson. We walk to 8th st. bkstores & return to his loft for rest of "dialogue". He talks continuously.* |
| *June 16, 69* | *Gary Bower comes for dialogue at 3:00 P.M. & leaves at 9:00 P.M. It was engaging almost the whole time.* |
| *" 17* | *Gary Stevens talks abt his job at mental hosp. & other interesting subjects but I sense something (resistance, tension)? which keeps him at a distance. Perhaps he was just uncomfortable?* |
| *" 18* | *Send following postcard to Walter De Maria: "The reason I called you twice to which you have not been gracious enough to reply was to invite* |

|  |  |
|---|---|
|  | *you for a dialogue. Love, Lozano". (Walter replies by letter before he leaves town for summer. July.)* |
| " 23 | *Felix Roth comes for a "dialogue", laying on me all the problems of the middle class including operations.* |
| " 24 | *Jake (neighbor, 2 loft bldgs east of mine) unexpectedly drops in thru fire escape door which I open in hot weather. We have dialogue including stock market info & drug info.* |
| " 30 | *I receive a visit from Romy McDonald & her friend Margo who were given my name in England by Tim Head. Pass info.* |
| July 9, 69 | *Jason Crum comes & is interesting but we do not have dialogue.* |
| " 9 | *Arthur Berman comes & is not very interesting but we do not have dialogue. (see July 17).* |
| " 10 | *Kass Zapkus & I have terrific dialogue, much abt art workers coalition, but then our dialogues have always been good & are mellow by now.* |
| " 11 | *Start dialogue with Hugo the Cat, who will live here for a while while his owners (neighbors Bill & Charlotte Sayler) are out of town. He mauls my arm as a start but the dialogue progresses slightly to a good fighting dialogue. One wkend is all I can take with Hugo.* |
| " 15 | *Bob Hout comes. We have rather stiff formal exchange. I try an abrupt move to wake him up.* |
| " 16 | *Bob (Smitty) Smithson arrives early. It is a matter of discomfort I think. But I got a lot of info out. (He wants my info.)* |
| " 17 | *Arthur Berman brings Doc Hughes. Doc does his rapp & then goes to sleep. Have better talk with Arthur.* |
| " 24 | *Receive a visit from Phyllis Rosen & Portia Harcus, who have galleries in Boston. We talk a lot & I learn a lot, it was a good dialogue (trialogue). Abt 3 hrs, maybe more.* |
| " 25 | *Weston Naef has his own info but also allows himself to be drenched by my info. 4 hrs.* |
| " 28 | *Marcia Tucker stays 3 hrs, asks good questions, intense if somewhat gossipish dialogue, but she enjoys the play. Dialogue meaning.* |
| Aug 1, 69 | *Mike Shore & I were falling asleep from boredom with "conversation" so I suggested we go out & we ran around doing errands & stopping in stores, especially the bicycle store in E. Village.* |

| | |
|---|---|
| Aug 8, 69 | Kent Cunow. Told a great "How I got my 1. Y. rating" story. |
| Aug 19, 69 | Jim Harithas is as modern & interesting as ever—we have very good dialogue. Info from the world of museums, trustees & "political heavies". |
| Aug 28, 69 | Larry Stafford ret'ns. |
| Sept 2— | David Lee ret'ns. Contrast with his visit May 20, 69. |
| Sept 10— | Jerry Kastner comes back to pick up dope. This visit was slightly better than last time he came to see me. |
| Sept 10— | Ted Castle. For some reason, I no longer get turned on by his ideas, but he wasn't relaxed. |
| Sept 11— | David Levin, faggot, ex-Andover, stays 6 hrs, honest talk. |
| Sept 19— | Jillen Lowe comes to see wk (she's a double Leo). |
| Sept 20— | Ted Castle ret'ns once more for a brief visit. |
| Sept 21— | James Lee Bryars stretches out on bad for entire dialogue enjoying window view, bourbon, grass, etc. |
| Sept 22— | Jillen Lowe ret'ns bringing Baron & Baroness John & Helen Von Echt (both rich, young, beautiful & a lot of fun). For a change a pleasurable exchange with collectors. |
| Sept 29— | Jillen Lowe brings Jeff Paley. This was more of a trilogue. Jeff Paley was more interest (ed) than (ing). |
| Oct 1— | Clement Meadmore brings the Englishwoman Jennifer A. Towndrow for a brief, packed dialogue betw. them & my work. She's with Studio Vista publ., London. |
| Oct 1— | Keith Sonnier & I on some previous visits he made here had more fun talking than we did today, but it was okay. |
| Oct 8— | Billy Bryant Copley & I has as good a dialogue today as any previously & we didn't even turn on till the end. |
| Oct 12— | Miles Forst hasn't been here for a long time but unfortunately I was too tired to be enthusiastic. |
| Oct 14— | Gregorie Muller & Whee Kim come unannounced (from Paris) given my name by Bellamy. Dan Graham happened to be here & he & I both dumped our own info in them. Gregorie says I am the only artist enthusiastic abt N.Y.C. |
| Oct 16— | Max Hutchinson from Australia invites me to join gallery he's opening |

| | |
|---|---|
| | *here but I tell him at present I don't want to join any gallery. Dialogue mostly about galleries. Jolly Max.* |
| *Oct 16—* | *Miles Forst & I have a much better talk, a lot about teaching.* |
| *Oct 22—* | *Have we of the best dialogues I've had in a long time: Murray Hochman.* |
| *Oct 27, 69* | *Mac Dody (from Whitney Mus.) doesn't get turned on by abstract painting but sure digs my comix. That's all right. Belts two bourbons for his trip to the suburbs.* |
| *Nov 1, 69* | *Larry Stafford ret'ns & we are both more relaxed & have more fun.* |
| *Nov 7, 69—* | *Rolfe Ricke brings friend Hans, from Germany.* |
| *Nov 8—* | *Amanda (Mackie?) from Wheaton College visits as a result of the colloquium there on Nov 6. She is bright & sophisticated, pretty, family lives in N.Y.C. (16th & Ave A?). We have very good talk especially towards end. She has her own grass & we get smashed on it. Her (male) family picks her up (her mother calls when she is here).* |
| *Nov 10—* | *Alan Bayman (Baiman?) who was sent by Jillen Lowe is very draggy, from Brooklyn (but not Jewish, but I never know who is & who isn't).* |
| *Nov 11—* | *Connie Bower visits to pick drawings for "Art Resources Center of the Whitney Museum of American Art" (Nov 22–Dec 6, 185 Cherry St. near Manhattan Bridge & South St).* |
| *Nov 11—* | *Brief dialogue with Jerry "Walker" to whom I give some acid (instead of ass. As Kaltenbach said). Pick up from St. Adrian's.* |
| *Nov 16—* | *Kass-Kes Zapkus brings over Mr & Mrs Frankel. The Frankels, from Chicago, to turn them on. They got high just fine, offer me <u>money</u> which I refuse telling them I'm insulted that they offered, & we part sugarly.* |
| *Nov 17—* | *Cindy Nemser. Aries. I like Aries women, they're not sentimental. The big Brooklyn rebellion.* |
| *Nov 18—* | *Larry Frifeld (sp?) drops in, <u>good talk.</u>* |
| *Nov 19—* | *George ("Dick") Bellamy comes again, slightly less hard work than last time he was here, enigma at end (both very high), inscrutable as sometimes before.* |
| *Nov 20, 69—* | *Finally a group dialogue. Gary Bower brings kids from <u>Arts Resources Center of Whitney Mus</u>, for a terrific experience for me. About 18 kids. Talk mostly to a boy\* who's going back to his farm in Mich., said he's the* |

*only one who's not staying in N.Y.C. of his group. Said mine of all their symposiums so far was most "disorderly", the least "strict". *Bill Goers.*

Nov 28, 69— *Dr & Mrs Milton Brutton from Philadelphia. Dr Brutten, a child psychologist, wanted to talk about art & I wanted to talk abt psychology, which seems like the conditions favorable to a good dialogue.*

Dec 4, 69— *Fred Gutzeit & I have instant good Scorpio communication.*

Dec 5, 69— *Agnes Denes tells me abt Dialectic Triangulation, her do-it-yrself philosophy.*

Dec 5, 69— *Eric, a student, comes by with Kaltenbach & the dialogue is mostly non-verbal.*

Dec 8, 69— *Ed Shostak, an old friend, gives a very generous & high-info dialogue which I enjoyed.*

Dec 12, 69— *Gary Bower ret'ns for a 7-hr dialogue this time. I thank him for letting me get out so many ideas.*

Dec 13, 69— *Lefty (Sebastian) Adler & I were just getting into a dialogue when Bob Stanley who brought him drags him away.*

Dec 18, 69— *Dine at Ed & Cindy Feldman's where the most exquisite dialogue takes place.*

This text was begun by Lozano in April 1969. It has never before been published in its entirety.

("QUOTE"): SOUND OF "DAISY" FADING IN BACKGROUND FOLLOWED BY SOUND OF
"ALSO SPRACH ZARATHUSTRA"(R.STRAUSS) FOLLOWED BY SOUND OF
"THE BLUE DANUBE" (J. STRAUSS) — SOUNDTRACK, 2001 (S. KUBRICK)

## GENERAL STRIKE PIECE (STARTED FEB. 8, '69)*

GRADUALLY BUT DETERMINEDLY AVOID BEING PRESENT
AT OFFICIAL OR PUBLIC "UPTOWN" FUNCTIONS OR
GATHERINGS† RELATED TO THE "ART WORLD" IN ORDER
TO PURSUE INVESTIGATION OF TOTAL PERSONAL &
PUBLIC REVOLUTION.° EXHIBIT IN PUBLIC ONLY PIECES
WHICH FURTHER SHARING OF IDEAS & INFORMATION
RELATED TO TOTAL PERSONAL & PUBLIC REVOLUTION.⁴

IN PROCESS AT LEAST THROUGH SUMMER, '69.

* WITHDRAWAL FROM 3-MAN SHOW COMPILED BY RICHARD BELLAMY,
GOLDOWSKY GALLERY, 1078 MADISON AVE.
† DATE OF LAST VISIT TO UPTOWN GALLERIES FOR PERUSAL OF ART — FEB. 13 OR 14, 69
  "   "   "   "   "   A MUSEUM — MARCH 24, 69
  "   "   "   "   " UPTOWN GALLERY OPENING — MARCH 15, 69
  "   "   "   "   " A BAR — APRIL 5, 69
  "   "   " ATTENDANCE AT A CONCERT — APRIL 18, 69
  "   "   "   "   "   " FILM SHOWING — APRIL 4, 69
  "   "   "   "   " AN "EVENT" — APRIL 18, 69
  "   "   "   "   " A BIG PARTY — MARCH 15, 69
° TERMS OF TOTAL PERSONAL & PUBLIC REVOLUTION SET FORTH IN BRIEF
STATEMENT READ AT OPEN PUBLIC HEARING, ART WORKERS COALITION,
SCHOOL OF VISUAL ARTS, APRIL 10, 69. FURTHER PARTICIPATION IN
ART WORKERS COALITION OR ANY OTHER GROUP DECLINED AS PART OF
GENERAL STRIKE PIECE. THIS INCLUDES ARTISTS AGAINST THE EXPRESSWAY
GROUP & OTHERS.
⁴ FIRST PIECE EXHIBITED AT ART/PEACE EVENT, N.Y. SHAKESPEARE FESTIVAL,
PUBLIC THEATER, MARCH 5, 69. GRASS PIECE & NO-GRASS PIECE EXHIBITED IN
NUMBER 7 SHOW COMPILED BY LUCY LIPPARD, PAULA COOPER, MAY 18, 69.
INVESTMENT PIECE & CASH PIECE EXHIBITED IN LANGUAGE III SHOW, DWAN GALLERY,
MAY 24, 69.

LEE LOZANO, JUNE 12, 69.

Lee Lozano, *General Strike Piece*, 1969.

# "maintenance art manifesto: proposal for an exhibition, 'CARE'"
## mierle laderman ukeles

## I. IDEAS

A.   The Death Instinct and the Life Instinct:

The Death Instinct: separation; individuality; Avant-Garde par excellence; to follow one's own path to death—do your own thing; dynamic change.

The Life Instinct: unification; the eternal return; the perpetuation and MAINTENANCE of the species; survival systems and operations; equilibrium.

B.   Two basic systems: Development and Maintenance. The sourball of every revolution: after the revolution, who's going to pick up the garbage on Monday morning?

Development: pure individual creation; the new; change; progress; advance; excitement; flight or fleeing.

Maintenance: keep the dust off the pure individual creation; preserve the new; sustain the change; protect progress; defend and prolong the advance; renew the excitement; repeat the flight:: show your work—show it again keep the contemporaryartmuseum groovy keep the home fires burning

Development systems are partial feedback systems with major room for change.
Maintenance systems are direct feedback systems with little room for alteration.

C.    Maintenance is a drag; it takes all the fucking time (lit.)
The mind boggles and chafes at the boredom. The culture confers lousy status on maintenance jobs minimum wages, housewives = no pay.

*clean your desk, wash the dishes, clean the floor, wash your clothes, wash your toes, changes the baby's diaper, finish the report, correct the typos, mend the fence, keep the customer happy, throw out the stinking garbage, watch out don't put things in your nose, what shall I wear, I have no sox, pay your bills, don't litter, save string, wash your hair, change the sheets, go to the store, I'm out of perfume, say it again—'he doesn't understand,' seal it again—it leaks, go to work, this art is dusty, clear the table, call him again, flush the toilet, stay young.*

D.    Art:
Everything I say is Art is Art. Everything I do is Art is Art. "We have no Art, we try to do everything well." (Balinese saying).

Avant-garde art, which claims utter development, is infected by strains of maintenance ideas, maintenance activities, and maintenance materials.
Conceptual & Process art, especially, claim pure development and change, yet employ almost purely maintenance processes.

E.    The exhibition of Maintenance Art, 'CARE,' would zero in on pure maintenance, exhibit it as contemporary art, and yield, by utter opposition, clarity of issues.

## II.  THE MAINTENANCE ART EXHIBITION: *"CARE"*

Three parts: Personal, General, and Earth Maintenance.

A.  <u>Part One: Personal</u>

I am an artist. I am a woman. I am a wife. I am a mother. (Random order).

I do a hell of a lot of washing, cleaning, cooking. renewing, supporting, preserving, etc. Also, (up to now separately) I "do" Art.

Now, I will simply do these maintenance everyday things, and flush them up to consciousness, exhibit them, as Art. I will live in the museum as I customarily do at home with my husband and my baby, for the duration of the exhibition (Right? or if you don't want me around at night I would come in every day), and do all these things as public Art activities: I will sweep and wax the floors, dust everything, wash the walls (i.e. "floor paintings, dust works, soapsculpture, wall–paintings"), cook, invite people, to eat, make agglomerations and dispositions of all functional refuse.

The exhibition area might look "empty" of art, but it will be maintained in full public view.

MY WORKING WILL BE THE WORK.

B.  <u>Part Two: General</u>

Everyone does a hell of a lot of noodling maintenance work. The general part of the exhibition would consist of interviews of two kinds.

*1. — Previous individual interviews, typed and exhibited.*

> *Interviewees come from, say, 50 different classes and kinds of occupations that run a gamut from maintenance "man," maid, sanitation "man," mail "man," union "man," construction worker, librarian, grocerystore "man," nurse, doctor, teacher, museum director, baseball player, sales "man," child, criminal, bank president, mayor, moviestar, artist, etc., about:*

*—what you think maintenance is; —how you feel about spending whatever parts of your life you spend on maintenance activities; —what is the relationship between maintenance and freedom; —what is the relationship between maintenance and life's dreams.*

*2. — Interview Room—for spectators at the Exhibition:*

*A room of desks and chairs where professional (7) interviewers will interview the spectators at the exhibition along same questions as typed interviews. The responses should be personal.*

*These interviews are taped and replayed throughout the exhibition area.*

C.   Part Three: Earth Maintenance

Everyday, containers of the following kinds of refuse will be delivered to the Museum:

— *the contents of one sanitation truck;*
— *a container of polluted air;*
— *a container of polluted Hudson River;*
— *a container of ravaged land.*

Once at the exhibition, each container will be serviced:

*purified, de–polluted, rehabilitated, recycled, and conserved*
*by various technical (and/or pseudo–technical) procedures either by myself or scientists.*
*These servicing procedures are repeated throughout the duration of the exhibition.*

This text was written in 1969, and functioned as a manifesto for Ukeles's work. It is here published in its entirety.

# patron's statement for "when attitudes become form"

## john murphy

The works assembled for this exhibit have been grouped by many observers of the art scene under the heading "new art." We at Philip Morris feel it is appropriate that we participate in bringing these works to the attention of the public, for there is a key element in this "new art" which has its counterpart in the business world. That element is innovation—without which it would be impossible for progress to be made in any segment of society.

Just as the artist endeavors to improve his interpretation and conceptions through innovation, the commercial entity strives to improve its end product or service through experimentation with new methods and materials. Our constant search for a new and better way in which to perform and produce is akin to the questionings of the artists whose works are represented here.

For a number of years, we have been involved in sponsorship of the arts in its many diverse forms—through purchase of works, commissioning of young artists, presentation of major exhibits, and so forth.

These activities are not adjuncts to our commercial function, but rather an integral part. As businessmen in tune with our times, we at Philip Morris are committed to support the experimental. We hope that those who attend this exhibit will be as stimulated while viewing it as we have been during its preparation.

This text first appeared as a preface by the sponsor, Phillip Morris Europe, of the international exhibition "When Attitudes Become Form: Works, Concepts, Processes, Situations," first staged at the Bern Kunsthalle (22 March–27 April 1969), and then in a slightly revised form at the Institute of Contemporary Arts in London (28 September–27 October 1969).

# politics and the avant-garde
## piero gilardi

At the beginning of the 60's, pop and nouveaux realists looked at "mass-media" as a clarifying force in human relationships; intuition of the objectivity of the relationship induced by the technological system seemed to open up new avenues of freedom for the individual; the myth of a classless society, encouraged by the planning of consumption, lifted the artist out of the anguish of an ideological debate embroiled in abstractions and frustrations without end.

The explosion of Pop Art with its "naive" vigor gave new-Dada language a fresh and vital taste; Nouveau Realisme, more timid and intellectually inclined, was interpreted by Restany as the artistic beginning of a new technological humanism.

Neofigurazione, New Expressionism and Nouveausurrealisme used the iconography of the mass-media with the old aim of social criticism, an inheritance of abstract art.

It was the moment of a renewed cultural faith in technology. The instruments wielded by technology had lost all sense of magic and empiricism, and had become part of the social picture; neocapitalism was waxing stronger and "information" was passing from the infrastructure to the structure of society.

Artists, together with a fair sprinkling of intellectuals, were convinced that the technological society, with its own new internal logic, would solve the general problem of association; programming and planning were creating a platform for human relationships that was both unified and objective. The dazzling nature of this psychological discovery was such that the problems presented by technological progress and by its inherent social contradictions were overlooked. From the first moment of this discovery, artists such as Lichtenstein, Warhol, Wesselmann, Hamilton, Christo and Raysse penetrated ever more deeply into the linguistic mechanism employed by the media of commerce; the initial approach of the new-Dada group was abandoned in favor of structural and ideological adherence to the consumer society.

This work was continued by Oldenburg, Dine, Rosenquist, Pistoletto, Fahlstrom and Arman in terms that were either more analytical or more romantic but were in any case detached from the intrinsic logic of the media themselves.

The kinetic artists developed a view of technological society based on an ideology that was both static and preconstituted; the political conscience that they proclaimed was inefficient and, for them, artistic discovery resolved itself into an attempt to import a degree of humanistic rationalization into the alienating factors presented by the new dimension.

The Pop dimension has spread from 1965 onwards; its content has been reduced to essentials; the reductive experience of Primary Structures and Minimal Art has been born.

The ideology of the consumer and of the information society remains; artists, however, having pursued their analysis of its iconography to the limit, now concentrate their attention on its entropic structure.

The language formally employed undergoes a startling change, though its meaning remains within the ambit of the technological dimension; we pass from the "fullness" of the repeated image, presented by Warhol, to the "emptiness" of Morris' geometrical bodies; from space to time by way of "obsolescence"; yet, this is a bodily void whose "material" is supplied by technology; it is represented in the dramatized language of Morris, Judd, Flavin, Andre and Grosvenor or in the calculated speech of Sol LeWitt, Smithson and Snelson; in the case of Europe, we may mention the names of King, Tucker and Heerich.

McLuhan's analysis of contemporary media has given support to the intuitions of these artists. (. . .)

The Press has seen the Chinese cultural revolution as a move aimed at mobilizing the young to strengthen the personal power of Mao. Yet some of the more profound features of this event must be seen against the background of the newer and more radical problem of existence faced by the entire technological society; permanent political mobilization itself has brought into being a climate of extroversion and extraordinarily perceptive fluidity among the youth of China.

The most serious error committed by Western observers has been that of assigning too much importance to symbolic and ritual factors. In schools, factories and hospitals, work is suspended for the choral recitation of Mao's verses with complete disregard for the pressing needs of the moment or for the demands imposed by technological rhythms; only if we succeed in looking beyond the symbolic content of this action shall we get a clear idea of its function as a "horizontal" emotive relationship and as a psychic decontamination from structural and technological work. In the technocratic or capitalist system, decontamination of this type enters into the program in the guise of the entertainment industry with its release and escapist fare. One of Mao's sayings is: "Wouldst thou know the apple? Eat it"; the content of his verses is cathartic in the sense that the simple, but nevertheless conscious gesture of eating the apple brings the individual into touch with reality on the plane of time: the external stimulus and the inner sensation are seen as the same, with no intrusion from the abstract relativism of the mind. This attitude is as far from Zen as it is from Western empiricism, but stands close to the perceptive dimension of the artistic and political avant-gardes that lie outside the system.

Many persons, "progressive" and at the same time ambiguous, spoke of the May barricades in Paris as a great Happening; their interpretation of the facts sought, by way of a distorting rationalization, to carry over to the language of the theater an event born of the creative forces of life: life, indeed, was involved, political life in its most all-embracing and real form; the element of creativity was to be found in the emotional relationship uniting those who took part and in the individual simultaneity of thought and action. During May, the Latin Quarter, as well as other parts of Paris, was flooded with mural graffiti and manifestoes; the latter were extremely terse and violent and extended the range of the face-to-face communication being made during the action in the streets. They were generally published, at the rate of about 10 per night, by the Atelier Populaire des Beaux Arts.

European students have also developed political discussion in the market-place in another fashion; in the squares of Paris, groups of 10–12 would trace a circle on the ground and begin a discussion called "The truth game": after an hour or so, they would move away leaving the square full of people engaged in animated discussion; in Italy, students have chosen the big stores as places in which to "interrogate" each other in public, or to act sketches dealing with recent events, such as the procession of the previous day or their companions in prison.

In New York, some Greenwich Village groups have established communication in the streets by means of "shock tactics." At Central Station, a group of marine commandos carried out a quick and highly realistic "shooting" of a Vietnamese girl; one of these groups, closer to the language of the visual avant-garde, uses the *Village Voice* for publicizing its environments; a famous example is the house in the downtown Puerto Rican section which was taken over as a living museum, with each stick of filthy furniture idiotically labeled "art object," "serial work," etc.; political message and the demystification of art were united via an intense unity of awareness typical of the moral climate of New York.

Although not politically aligned, the underground cinema is a phenomenon that must be linked to the cultural revolution; the New American Cinema, in particular, arose with premises that stamped it as an "off" phenomenon far superior in range to any other phenomenon of the same type; recently, due to that attitude of creative naiveté common to a good part of the American visual avant-garde, its impulses have become clothed in moralism and the phenomenon itself has been institutionalized. In his European lectures, Mekas said that the New American Cinema was like one of nature's creative forces. Today the vital ferments of the underground cinema are the "newsreel" films prepared by two identically-named cooperatives in New York and San Francisco; their documentary set-up is forming a new creative unit between art and politics.

In the widest sense, the cultural revolution has little to do with culture, though some of its phases are an experiment in the creative dimension that the avant-garde artists have also reached by way of individual maturation.

No ideology filters through the relationships between the new political avant-gardes and reality; the "strategy" and "tactics" of practical action remain; in the same way, "poetry" has fallen from grace in the case of the artistic avant-garde, behavior and communication remain; the symbols of the cultural revolution have no greater importance than the "signs" of the artistic avant-garde.

The strategy and the tactics involved in the relationship between artists and reality can be traced out via their own words, especially in the case of those uttered over the last couple of years; Pistoletto has written: "After every action, I step to one side and proceed in a direction different from that formulated by my subject, since I refuse to accept it as an answer"; Artschwager, referring to one of his environments composed of small black signs scattered all around and extending outside the bounds of the gallery itself, declared ". . . the space that they [the signals] take in transcends its own physical limits and stretches out into mental and total space"; Walter de Maria has said: "Something always enters in a streak of non-purity. It's that point, where warm meets cold, action meets inaction, that's what interests me."

Emilio Prini states: "creative action must join hands with reality in every one of its aspects—climate, the people and things that stand around it"; Ger van Elk, speaking of the "verbal action" prepared by Dibbets for German TV, said ". . . there will not be any communication between Dibbets and the public since the latter will be but an instrument in an act of mental and total creativity"; William Wiley says: "When I get up each day, I reinvent my life minute by minute"; speaking of the question "To find the time or let it find me?," Steve Kaltembach wrote: "It is possible to manipulate an object so as to achieve an alteration in the perception of the object or the environment; an object may also be manipulated to bring about an alteration in perception itself"; finally, we may quote a reasoned statement made by Boezem: ". . . the whole scene is open and there is an evolution by individuals who find that they are 'stuff' outside the cadre of art-history. And just that is the 'news' in it—the engagement with total reality."

In the case of the art-trade establishment in New York and, at second remove, the whole of western avant-garde market, the driving force is no longer financial gain but the acquisition of cultural power as an end in itself; the gallery owners of the avant-garde are interested in controlling the informative structure of an artistic movement or of a group of artists; the making of a profit is a matter of secondary consideration.

It is well known that the majority of the avant-garde galleries in the States run at a loss. Their financing, via the assistance of a notorious clause in the tax legislation, offers one of the many safety-valves for exuberant capital spending; at the same time, the avant-garde is held on a leash, channeled into political neutrality and, in a word, absorbed into the ideology of the "system."

The work of museums of modern art is equally tied to social structures, but is clearly less sensitive to the strains of the struggle for cultural power and free from commercial interests; in the U.S., museums, like galleries, are closely bound up with the private economy; the galleries look upon museums interested in avant-garde art as an instrument for enhancing the prestige of their own artists.

The most functional contribution being made by the museums of the United States and northern Europe is that of impartial analysis of single sectors or situations of avant-garde research; exhibitions with a historical or comprehensive panorama are always heavy; today, one-man shows stand for cultural mystification that is a contradiction of the new environmental content offered by the avant-garde.

The crisis facing the large official exhibitions came to a head in 1963 with the storm that raged round the Venice Biennale; a timid protest also disturbed the opening of the Kassel Documenta 4 exhibition, a grandiose affair laid on with the aid of public funds, but lacking an objectivity.

Exhibitions inspired with the breath of novelty have been organized by the Albright Knox Foundation, Buffalo, by the Pasadena Museum and the Berne Kunsthalle; but artists have found their most effective freedom of action in mixed-art festivals, in action meetings and one-day group shows; in Italy, the most successful exhibition has been that of the "Poor Actions" festival at Amalfi.

Less intensive, but free and uninterrupted work on the artistic community level has been carried on by the Art Departments of American universities and in some European schools of art.

In concluding a lecture in a school of figurative art, Herbert Marcuse said: ". . . in that case, art with all its affirmative force would form part of the liberating power of the negative and would serve to set free the unconscious and the conscious, both of them mutilated, that lend strength to repressive institutions. I believe that modern art is discharging this duty with greater awareness and method than before. The rest is not within the purlieu of the artist. Implementation and the real change that would set free both men and things are left for the field of political action; the artist does not take part therein as such. Today, however, this external activity is, perhaps, closely linked with the position held by art and perhaps with the achievement of the ends of art itself." Marcuse has here laid his finger on something that is both different and positive in the new position adopted by art; his is not a full understanding, however, since he is still impeded by "vertical" logic; the cathartic function and the world of the negative are real but nevertheless obvious features of the present avant-garde; the connection between art and politics is not to be thought of as an infrastructure but as falling on a horizontal plane in the form of mental and emotional "closeness"; art, in its linguistic and structural aspects, is already finished—absorbed into the entropy of the system.

The only reason why free artists still express themselves through the medium of signs is that their consciousness has not yet brought forth a globality that is "functional" by nature; avant-garde artists at one with the establishment take on more and more the appearance of isolated, mechanical extensions of the body of the system; for the rest, entire experience is already a mental reality, "functional" experience is not: psychoanalytical and sociological obstacles continue to call for resort on the part of the individual artist to the "defense" offered by signs; the condition of entire being, as opposed to the unidimensionality of the system, has only been spasmodically experimented.

Between today and the achievement of the "global continuum" of art-life lies a series of "economic" actions that must be undertaken: participation in the revolutionary praxis, demystification of the cultural dialogue, and "epidermic contact" between artists all over the world.

This text appeared in the catalogue for the exhibition "Op Losse Schroeven: situaties en cryptostructuren," staged at the Stedelijk Museum, Amsterdam, 15 March–27 April 1969. Unpaginated.

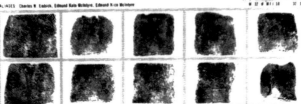

Duration Piece #15
Global

Beginning on January 1, 1970 a reward of $1,100.00 will be paid to the person who
provides the information resulting in the arrest and conviction of Edmund Kite McIntyre
wanted by the Federal Bureau of Investigation for Bank Robbery (Title 18 U.S. Code
Sections 2113a and 2113d) On February 1, 1970 $100.00 will be reduced from that first
offer making it $1,000.00. it will be reduced another $100.00 on the first day of each
subsequent month until there will exist no reward at all on January 1, 1971
I (Douglas Huebler) guarantee (by my signature below) the full payment of the reward
offered above. In the event that this piece has been purchased from me at any time
between September 1969 and January 1971 the then owner will have assumed
responsibility for payment of such a reward
(The price for this piece is $1,000.00 from that sum I will reimburse its owner any amount
that he pays as a reward in completing the destiny of its design.)

This statement and the "Wanted" publication (FBI No. 342.327) will constitute the finished
form of this piece on January 1, 1971 unless Mr. McIntyre is apprehended and convicted in
which case copies of all attendant documents concerning his conviction will join
altogether to form the piece

September 1969

Douglas Huebler, *Duration Piece #15, Global*, 1969.

# art tamed and wild
## jean clay

May 1968 was a decisive traumatic experience for the Parisian art world. Now that everything is "back to normal," some artists, heads bowed, have returned to the gallery fold; others have sought fresh areas of expression. All, however, have been forced to choose between a "cultural" conception of the artist as a professional engaged upon pure investigation, and a conception of the artist as a person actuated by a critical approach to the static nature of the social conditions in which he lives. In May 1968, students and para-artistic groups, by contributing their political initiative, proved that they can introduce an imaginative note into the often calcified methods used by trade unions and political parties in their campaigns. A case in point was the activity of the literature faculty at Nanterre where the influence of the Situationist group was considerable. As long ago as August 1964 Debord and his friends wrote in the review, *L'internationale situationniste,*

*A large part of Situationist criticism of the consumer society consists in showing how far contemporary artists, in abandoning the extraordinary wealth (not always utilized, it is true) of the period 1910–25 have, for the most part, condemned themselves to producing art as one might produce any other commodity. Since then, artistic movements have been nothing more than the imaginary fallout of an explosion that never happened, but which threatened—and threatens—*

*the whole structure of our society. The result of such an abandonment and its contradictory impli-cations (the emptiness and the desire to return to the initial eruption) makes the* Internationale situationniste *the only movement capable of identifying with the needs of the true artist by inte-grating the survival of art with the art of living. In other words, we are artists only insofar as we are no longer artists; we live* art.

This attitude to "cultural" art is provoked by a consideration of some of the major twentieth-century art movements, all of which placed great emphasis on pure investigation on a collective basis, and all of which were eventually brought back to the well-marked terrain of culture for culture's sake where the artist could, at his leisure, *play* at freedom instead of *living* it. Italian Futurism, Russian Cubo-futurism, Dadaism and even the Bauhaus started off with broader ambitions than a mere limited aesthetic objective. All were keen to argue about and dynamize the real world around them. Yet all were brought back, little by little, to established, commer-cialized, tamed art or—in the case of the Russians—were suppressed. The recent experience of the Visual Arts Research Group (GRAV) in Paris confirms this. Despite its socially active program calling for the "return to the people of their feeling of power over the real world" and their utilization to this end of such collective demonstrations as rooms of games, mazes, days in the streets and so on, the six GRAV artists gradually found themselves back within the gallery system. The latter had put on sale the purely functional articles invented by the GRAV artists solely to stress the passivity of contemporary man. As a result the group lost all signifi-cance and disintegrated some months ago.

From all this it has slowly become clear that the galleries, notably in Paris where they are particularly ossified, are playing an increasingly harmful and reactionary role vis-à-vis the development of modern art, especially where this development shows signs of expanding be-yond its cultural confines. The gallery system gives rise to "pure" inoffensive artists. As Edoardo Sanguinetti wrote: "In bourgeois society, the intellectual is the one who is paid and encouraged by kicks on the backside to picture or describe the role of a free man."

Or the galleries may, in the post-war tradition, simply deny the existence of new move-ments and sell post-tachist, neodada, post-surrealist and post–Paris-school pictures. Such gal-leries are becoming increasingly like antique shops. Or, more cleverly, they may set out to deprive the most advanced creations of their meaning. Certain handicraft galleries, for ex-ample, are going over to selling gadgets via limited multiples, an intermediary stage on the path to "democratic" distribution through the modern furniture chain-stores and the super-markets. The work of the artist is vetted; his output is reduced to articles of a "reasonable" size which will fit easily into a conventional domestic collection.

In a period of gigantic ephemeral works, auto-destructive works, oeuvres-concepts and uncontrollable expansions—all attempts to escape from the cultural ghetto—the luxury trade in multiples has the primary effect of thrusting the artist constantly back into his past. He is plunged back into what was a necessary but passing phase during which, often due to lack of means, he tried out his ideas on small-scale pieces. Hence the proliferation of Mannerist multiples, those recapitulatory variations on old and already assimilated themes which have therefore become "exploitable." While multiples may have a use in ensuring the artist's daily bread, they are obviously no way to new developments.

What we are at present witnessing is the metamorphosis of "handicraft" galleries into neo-capitalist enterprises requiring considerable investment, and thus frequently assistance from banks. Through take-overs and mergers their activities extend to cover both sides of the Atlantic. Dealers grow less and less like Père Vollard and more and more like international businessmen who, with the aid of publicity in specialist reviews, play upon the mimetic reflexes of cultural institutions and private collectors to "send into orbit" a product symbolizing daring, culture, a modern outlook. . . . The idea is implanted that X or Y is quite indispensable to any modern collection; in the present state of the world market with its increasingly standardized tastes this is tantamount to several thousand orders. When saturation point for one product is reached, another is launched.

It happens that the logic of this art commerce is that galleries, diverted from their original aims, create visual incidents and large-scale demonstrations openly designed to attract publicity. A massive show concentrates attention on a product which elsewhere is sold in driblets. The last Documenta Trade Fair in Kassel showed how the method works. On their ground-floor stands, American dealers displayed outsize works which could be acquired in the basement in miniature versions, as lithographs, sketches, micro-sculptures, etc.

More serious, as Piero Gilardi has explained in *Robho* (No. 5), are the aims of "cultural" enterprises to emasculate the revolutionary potential of the avant-garde.

*The ambition of certain American galleries is not to make money out of art but to establish a* position of power *within the art world. This ambition is increasingly shared by fund trustees and collectors. The establishment as a whole exercises very solid social control over the avant-garde in the West. At the cost of a slight deficit to the galleries (which can in any case be offset against taxes), its destructive potential is suitably canalized. Control is exercised by capitalist art-lovers, through the financial and social backing of artists and through the manipulation of information on the arts.*

*The nonrevolutionary artist is expected to work solely to be hung in the "appropriate" gallery for his works. The gallery takes over full responsibility, including cultural responsibility, for introducing the artist to the changing world of artistic fashions. Of course, certain unstated "conditions" apply to the would-be entrant into the social integration mechanism of avant-garde art. The most important of these is that his artistic expression be* in a phase of initial purity and neutrality *similar to the laboratory research stage of the scientist's work.*

*Should the artist's mode of expression already imply real intervention in social life or direct political action, then there is no chance of integration. His conscience will break upon the ideology of the system.*

Gilardi's analysis is borne out remarkably by an exhibition of funk art in Berne financed by the Philip Morris Company on the theme "When attitudes become form." As Mr. Murphy, president of the European section of Philip Morris, stated in his introduction to the catalogue: "Just as the artist endeavors to improve his interpretation and conceptions through innovation, the commercial entity strives to improve its end product or service, through experimentation with new methods and materials. Our constant search for a new and better way in which to perform and produce is akin to the questionings of the artists whose works are presented here. . . . As businessmen in tune with our times, we at Philip Morris are committed to support the experimental."

Art courtesy of Philip Morris or art in the service of Philip Morris, one can agree with Gilardi, could do no harm to anyone. (. . .)

It is certainly no answer to transfer gallery conditions to the streets. If, in the course of an open-air vernissage—like Fromanger's in Paris at the Place d'Alésia last October—the artist shows his latest creations to the press and to art-lovers, he is not in fact escaping the confines of a conventional gallery exhibition. Only the walls are missing; there an object is closed in upon itself; the experience is without possibility of real development and lacks any participation on the part of the public. Nothing new has happened. Segregation has been maintained. THE DYNAMICS OF THE ARTISTIC PROCESS ARE STILL DIVORCED FROM THE DYNAMICS OF THE SOCIAL PROCESS.

To compensate for this, in the numerous cases where artistic enterprise is condemned for practical or repressive reasons to separation in a cultural ghetto, it can still from within its confines make systematic attempts to distribute its products in the outside world by means of loudspeakers, *objets perdus,* leaflets, balloons and so on. The expansion of a free concept is the consequence of a program of action.

There has been a noticeable *increase in public action* in the most advanced works—an action which in fact amounts to participation in the evolutionary process. It more and more takes charge, changing its transient or long-term significance. This is another factor which forces the creative proposition beyond cultural boundaries; it engenders *irreversible processes* in which the artist is no longer master of his work.

Public participation involves the desacralization and the desegregation of the work of art (at the same time it debunks the idea of the artist as a semi-sacred personality). In the hands of the public, the contention gains a didactic value. It teaches freedom of action. All life's phenomena can be transformed: why not those governing social conditions? We can change those too.

These influences serve not to eliminate the activity of the artist (as those may desire for whom "art is dead") but to inject modern creative activity, by an increasingly rapid chain-reaction, right into the heart of the social process.

"Culture for culture's sake," like the "ideology of leisure" (after work) aims at hermetically partitioning the intellectual sphere from the social. What the ruling class wants is an inoffensive artist, brushes in hand, shut away in his golden cage. Picturesque poverty is an acceptable alternative. Let him paint and draw—it will at least make for one protester less. Shut the "creator" up behind bars of words. In his pretty isolation, he will favor the designs of the official ideology. Troublemakers can be eliminated by bribery or suppression. See that no disturbance troubles the somnolent mastication of uni-dimensional man, both producer and consumer of blinkers, the intoxicated slave of the so-called abundant society. Repression of the bizarre protagonists of "wild art" will increasingly go hand in hand with social repression.

To summarize the hypothesis: IN SUPPORTING THE SYSTEMATIC AND UNLIMITED EXPANSION AND PROLIFERATION OF WORKS OF ART ALONG WITH OPEN PARTICIPATION, ARTISTS WILL FIND THEMSELVES IN DUE COURSE OFF THE BEATEN CULTURAL TRACKS, OUTSIDE THE SEGREGATED CIRCUITS DESIGNED TO CONFINE THEM. Within the logic of its current development out of the "art object," THE AESTHETIC PROCESS FLOWS EVER STRAIGHTER TO THE HEART OF SOCIAL REALITY, LIKE A RIVER TO THE SEA, CREATING AN INDEFINITE, INTERMEDIARY ZONE WHERE INHERITED CATEGORIES NO LONGER APPLY. And this not by betraying the language of art—as happened with Socialist Realism and Narrative painting, both of which used iconographic methods borrowed from the past—but by keeping straight along the main lines of artistic evolution. As the object is freed of its pedestal, so culture is freed of its confines. To go . . . ?

This text appeared in *Studio International*, 177:912 (June 1969), pp. 261–265.

# introduction to *konzeption/conception*
## rolf wedewer

Conceptual art is not only a name for one of the youngest and probably one of the most radical movements in art, but, in addition, this term also draws attention to a general change in art as well as to a change in its conceptualization. Its designation marks an opening of new perspectives which may lead to a form of art which cannot be judged and understood on the basis of its concrete and manifest creations, but—similar to other communication media—based on its procedural potentials. In other words, the changes that can be vaguely perceived through the name not only concern forms and topics of art, but are of structural, that is fundamental, nature.

It all started with the so-called Earth- or Land-art, with Earth-sculptures that were created in the form of long trenches or walls built in an open terrain. Since they cannot be moved, they were substituted very early by planning designs—descriptions or sketches—that replaced the actual work of art by its sketch. Out of this emerged Conceptual art that, for the first time, represents an art that only consists of planning sketches whose execution and transformation into the final work of art is considered of secondary importance and, therefore, can be dismissed. Moreover, the sketches and designs of Conceptual art no longer refer to concrete objects waiting to be turned into an art object—as was the case with Land art—their references are instead unspecified events or processes.

Following Georg Jappe's formula, one could say that Conceptual art substitutes the object-like ("verdinglichte") final work by a creative process. This implies, to be sure, a recourse to subjectivity, a rediscovery of an individualistic gesture without fixed meaning. However, to see in this only a new version of the subjective structures of Art Informel means to ignore the completely different structural perspective through which the subjective gesture can obtain a universal, that is, procedural, meaning.

Since the sketch replaces the final work of art, art does without its traditional finalized form and, therefore, assigns a new role not only to the artist, but also to the viewer. The artist gives only a hint, an indication or general direction, and the viewer is no longer reduced to merely perceiving the finalized work and to interpreting what he sees. He is exposed to the necessity and, at the same time, the possibility, to reflect upon the indications the sketch provides him with following his own ideas and associations. In the case of Conceptual art the creative process does not end with a final product, but stays within the field of open forms, representing an ongoing process.

Independent of the individual idea in a concrete conceptual design and notwithstanding the fact that one may judge a concrete conceptual design as meaningful or nonsensical, one thing is sure: a new procedure becomes visible within this form of art that has the potential for entirely new artistic developments, even if they will lead to different artistic practices than the ones represented in present Conceptual art. In this understanding, present Conceptual art is neither perceived as the paradigmatic contemporary art form nor is it promoted to represent any transcendent meanings or aspirations; however, by understanding Conceptual art as a new artistic procedure, its significance lies in being something like a theoretical art.

This text served as the introduction for the catalogue to the exhibition "Konzeption/Conception," organized by Rolf Wedewer and Konrad Fischer and staged at the Städtischen Museum in Leverkusen, October-November 1969. Translated by Nora M. Alter, this is its first publication in English.

# beware
## daniel buren

This text was written for the exhibition "Conception" at Leverkusen (subsequently reprinted by A 379089 of Antwerp), before I had seen the works which were "exhibited" there. My skepticism in certain respects proved justified. Given that this text is neither a profession of faith nor a bible nor a model for others, but merely a reflection upon work in progress, I have wished, for this new context, to change certain words, delete or restate certain phrases or to go more thoroughly into certain particular points with respect to the original text. Alterations or additions to the original are set in italics and placed in square brackets.

## I. WARNING

A concept may be understood as being "the general mental and abstract representation of an object" (see *Le Petit Robert Dictionary;* "an abstract general notion of conception"—*Dictionary of the English Language*). Although this word is a matter for philosophical discussion, its meaning is still restricted; concept has never meant "horse." Now, considering the success which this word has obtained in art circles, considering what is and what will be grouped under this word, it seems necessary to begin by saying here what is meant by "concept" in para-artistic language.

We can distinguish [*four*] different meanings that we shall find in the various "conceptual" demonstrations, from which we shall proceed to draw [*four*] considerations which will serve as a warning.

(1.) *Concept/Project:* Certain works which until now were considered only as rough outlines or drawings for works to be executed on another scale, will henceforth be raised to the rank of "concepts." That which was only a means becomes an end through the miraculous use of one word. There is absolutely no question of just any sort of concept, but quite simply of an object which cannot be made life-size through lack of technical or financial means.

(2.) *Concept/Mannerism:* Under the pretext of "context" the anecdotal is going to flourish again and with it, academic art. It will no longer of course be a question of representing to the nearest one the number of gilt buttons on a soldier's tunic, nor of picturing the rustling of the undergrowth, but of discoursing upon the number of feet in a kilometer, upon Mr. X's vacation of Popocatépetl, or the temperature read at such and such a place. The "realistic" painters, whether it be Bouguereau, painters of socialist realism, or Pop artists, have hardly acted otherwise under the pretext of striving after reality. [*In order, no doubt, to get closer to "reality," the "conceptual" artist becomes gardener, scientist, sociologist, philosopher, storyteller, chemist, sportsman.*] It is a way—still another—for the artist to display his talents as conjurer. In a way, the vague concept of the word "concept" itself implies a return to Romanticism.

[*(2a.) Concept/Verbiage: To lend support to their pseudo-cultural references and to their bluffing games, with a complacent display of questionable scholarship, certain artists attempt to explain to us what a conceptual art would be, could be, or should be—thus making a conceptual work. There is no lack of vulgarity in pretension. We are witnessing the transformation of a pictorial illusion into a verbal illusion. In place of unpretentious inquiry we are subjected to a hodgepodge of explanations and justifications which serve as obfuscation in the attempt to convince us of the existence of a thought. For these, conceptual art has become "verbiage art." They are no longer living in the twentieth century, but wish to revive the eighteenth.*]

(3.) *Concept/Idea/Art:* Lastly, more than one person will be tempted to take any sort of an "idea," to make art of it and to call it "concept." It is this procedure which seems to us to be the most dangerous, because it is more difficult to dislodge, because it is very attractive, because it raises a problem which really does exist: how to dispose of the object? We will attempt, as we proceed, to clarify this notion of object. Let us merely observe henceforth that it seems to us that to exhibit (*exposer*[1]) or set forth a concept is, at the very least, a fundamental misconception right from the start and one which can, if one doesn't take care, involve us in a succession of false arguments. To exhibit a "concept," or to use the word concept to signify art, comes to the same thing as putting the concept itself on a level with the object. This would be to suggest that we must think in terms of a "concept-object"—which would be an aberration.[2]

This warning appears necessary to us because if it can be admitted that [*these interpretations are not relevant for all representatives of this tendency*] we can affirm that at least nine-tenths of the works gathered together for [*the exhibition at Leverkusen*] (or its counterparts) [*relied on one of the four points*] raised above or even, for some people, [*partook subtly of all four at once*]. They rely on the traditional and "evergreen" in art or, if you like, rely on idealism or utopianism, the original defects which art has not yet succeeded in eradicating.[3] We know from experience that at the time of a manifestation of this kind, people are only too quick to impose the image of the majority upon any work shown. In this particular case, this image will be approximately as described above, i.e. that of the new avant-garde which has become "conceptual." This is nothing more than to identify, in a more or less new form, the *prevailing ideology.* Therefore, *although concerned with confronting problems,* let us henceforth suspend judgement of the way in which they are approached or solved in the majority of cases. Moreover our present task is not to solve any enigmas, but rather to try to understand/to recognize the problems which arise. It is much more a question of a method of work than the proposal of a new intellectual gadget.

Vertically striped sheets of paper, the bands of which are 8.7 cms. wide, alternate white and colored, are stuck over internal and external surfaces: walls, fences, display windows, etc.; and/or cloth/canvas support, vertical stripes, white and colored bands each 8.7 cms., the two ends covered with dull white paint.

I record that this is my work for the last four years without any evolution or way out. This is the past: it does not imply either that it will be the same for another ten or fifteen years or that it will change tomorrow.

The perspective we are beginning to have, thanks to these past four years, allows a few considerations on the direct and indirect implications for the very conception of art. This apparent break (no research, nor any formal evolution for four years) offers a platform that we shall situate at zero level, when the observations both internal (conceptual transformation as regards the action/praxis of a similar form) and external (work/production presented by others) are numerous and rendered all the easier as they are not invested in the various surrounding movements, but are rather derived from their absence.

Every act is political and, whether one is conscious of it or not, the presentation of one's work is no exception. Any production, any work of art is social, has a political significance. We are obliged to pass over the sociological aspect of the proposition before us due to lack of space and considerations of priority among the questions to be analyzed.

The points to be examined are described below and each will require examination separately and more thoroughly later. [*This is still valid nowadays.*]

(a) *The Object, the Real, Illusion:* Any art tends to decipher the world, to visualize an emotion, nature, the subconscious, etc. . . . Can we pose a question rather than replying always in terms of hallucinations? This question would be: can one create something which is real, non-illusionistic and therefore not an art object? One might reply—and this is a real temptation for an artist—in a direct and basic fashion to this question and fall instantly into one of the traps mentioned [*in the first section*]; i.e. believe the problem *solved,* because it was *raised,* and [*for example*] present no object but a concept. This is responding too directly to need, it is mistaking a desire for reality, it is making like an artist. In fact, instead of questioning or acquainting oneself with the problem raised, one provides a solution, and what a solution! One avoids the issue and passes on to something else. Thus does art progress from form to form, from problems raised to problems solved, accruing successive layers of concealment. To do away with the object as an illusion—the real problem—through its replacement by a "concept" [*or an idea*]—utopian or ideal(istic) or imaginary solution—is to believe in a moon made of green cheese, to achieve one of those conjuring tricks so beloved of twentieth-century art. Moreover it can be affirmed, with reasonable confidence, that as soon as a concept is announced, and especially when it is "exhibited as art," under the desire to do away with the object, *one merely replaces it* in fact. The exhibited "concept" becomes *ideal-object,* which brings us once again to art as it is, i.e. the illusion of something and not the thing itself. In the same way that writing is less and less a matter of verbal transcription, painting should no longer be the vague vision/illusion, even mental, of a phenomenon (nature, subconsciousness, geometry . . .) but VISUALITY *of the painting itself.* In this way we arrive at a notion which is thus allied more to a method and not to any particular inspiration; a method which requires—in order to make a direct attack on the problems of the object properly so-called—that painting itself should create a mode, a specific system, which would no longer direct attention, but which is "produced to be looked at."

(b) *The Form:* As to the internal structure of the proposition, the contradictions are removed from it; no "tragedy" occurs on the reading surface, no horizontal line, for example, chances to cut through a vertical line. Only the imaginary horizontal line of delimitation of the work at the top and at the bottom "exists," but in the same way that it "exists" only by mental reconstruction, it is mentally demolished simultaneously, as it is evident that the external size is arbitrary (a point which we shall explain later on).

The succession of vertical bands is also arranged methodically, always the same [*x,y,x,y,x, y,x,y,x,y,x, etc.* . . .], thus creating no composition on the inside of the surface or area to be looked at, or, if you like, a minimum or zero or neutral composition. These notions are understood in relation to art in general and not through internal considerations. This neutral painting is not however freed from obligations; quite on the contrary, thanks to its neutrality or absence of style, it is extremely rich in information about itself (its exact position as regards other work) and especially information about other work; thanks to the lack or absence of any formal problem its potency is all expended upon the realms of thought. One may also say that this painting no longer has any plastic character, but that it is *indicative* or *critical;* among other things, indicative/critical of its own process. This zero/neutral degree of form is "binding" in the sense that the total absence of conflict eliminates all concealment (all mythification or secrecy) and consequently brings silence. One should not take neutral painting for uncommitted painting.

Lastly, this formal neutrality would not be formal at all if the internal structure of which we have just spoken (vertical white and colored bands) was linked to the external form (size of the surface presented to view). The internal structure being immutable, if the exterior form were equally so, one would soon arrive at the creation of a quasi–religious archetype which, instead of being neutral, would become burdened with a whole weight of meanings, one of which—and not the least—would be as the idealized image of neutrality. On the other hand, the continual variation of the external form implies that it has no influence on the internal structure, which remains the same in every case. The internal structure remains uncomposed and without conflict. If, however, the external form or shape did not vary, a conflict would immediately be established between the combination or fixed relationship of the band–widths, their spacing (internal structure) and the general size of the work. This type of relationship would be inconsistent with an ambition to avoid the creation of an illusion. We would be presented with a problem all too clearly defined—here that of neutrality to zero degree—and no longer with the thing itself posing a question, in its own terms.

Finally, we believe confidently in the validity of a work or framework questioning its own existence, presented to the eye. The framework which we have just analyzed clinically has in fact no importance whatsoever in terms of form or shape; it is at zero level, a minimum but *essential* level. We shall see later how we shall work to cancel out the form itself as far as possible. In other words, it is time to assert *that formal problems have ceased to interest us.* This assertion is the logical consequence of actual work produced over four years where the formal problem was forced out and disqualified as a pole of interest.

Art is the form which it takes. The form must unceasingly renew itself to ensure the development of what we call new art. A change of form has so often led us to speak of a new art that one might think that inner meaning and form were/are linked together in the mind of the majority—artists and critics. Now, if we start from the assumption that new, i.e. "other," art is in fact never more than the same thing in a new guise, the heart of the problem is exposed. To abandon the search for a new form at any price means trying to abandon the history of art as we know it: it means passing from the *Mythical* to the *Historical,* from the *Illusion* to the *Real.*

(c) *Color:* In the same way that the work which we propose could not possibly be the image of some thing (except itself, of course), and for the reasons defined above could not possibly have a finalized external form, there cannot be one single and definitive color. The color, if it was fixed, would mythify the proposition and would become the zero degree of color X, just as there is navy blue, emerald green or canary yellow.

One color and one color only, repeated indefinitely or at least a great number of times, would then take on multiple and incongruous meanings.[4] All the colors are therefore used simultaneously, without any order of preference, but systematically.

That said, we note that if the problem of form (as pole of interest) is dissolved by itself, the problem of color considered as subordinate or as self–generating at the outset of the work and by the way it is used, is seen to be of great importance. The problem is to divest it of all emotional or anecdotal import.

We shall not further develop this question here, since it has only recently become of moment and we lack the required elements and perspective for a serious analysis. At all events, we record its existence and its undeniable interest. We can merely say that every time the proposition is put to the eye, only one color (repeated on one band out of two, the other being white) is visible and that it is without relation to the internal structure or the external form which supports it and that, consequently, it is established *a priori* that: white=red=black=blue=yellow=green=violet, etc.

(d) *Repetition:* The consistency—i.e. the exposure to view in different places and at different times, as well as the personal work, for four years—obliges us to recognize manifest visual repetition at first glance. We say at "first glance," as we have already learned from sections (a) and (b) that there are divergencies between one work and another; however, the essential, that is to say the internal structure, remains immutable. One may therefore, with certain reservations, speak of repetition. This repetition provokes two apparently contradictory considerations: on the one hand, the reality of a certain form (described above), and on the other hand, its *canceling–out* by successive and identical confrontations which themselves negate any originality which might be found in this form, despite the systematization of the work. We know that a single and unique "picture" as described above, although neutral, would be charged by its very uniqueness with a symbolic force which would destroy its vocation of neutrality. Likewise by repeating an identical form, or identical color, we would fall into the pitfalls mentioned in sections (b) and (c). Moreover we would be burdened with every unwanted religious tension if we undertook to idealize such a proposition or allowed the work to take on the anecdotal interest of a test of strength in response to a stupid bet.

There remains only one possibility; the repetition of this neutral form, with the divergencies we have already mentioned. This repetition, thus conceived, has the effect of reducing to a minimum the potency, however slight, of the proposed form such as it is, of revealing that the external form (shifting) has no effect on the internal structure (alternate repetition of the bands) and of highlighting the problem raised by the color in itself. This repetition also reveals in point of fact that visually there is *no formal evolution*—even though there is a change—and that, in the same way that no "tragedy" or composition or tension is to be seen in the clearly defined scope of the work exposed to view (or presented to the eye), no tragedy nor tension is perceptible in relation to the creation itself. The tensions abolished in the very surface of the "picture" have also been abolished—up to now—in the time–category of this production. *The repetition is the ineluctable means of legibility of the proposition itself.*

This is why, if certain isolated artistic forms have raised the problem of neutrality, they have never been pursued in depth to the full extent of their proper meaning. By remaining "unique" they have lost the neutrality we believe we can discern in them. (Among others, we are thinking of certain canvases by Cezanne, Mondrian, Pollock, Newman, Stella.)

Repetition also teaches us that there is no perfectibility. A work is at zero level or it is not at zero level. To approximate means nothing. In these terms, the few canvases of the artists mentioned can be considered only as empirical approaches to the problem. Because of their empiricism they have been unable to divert the course of the "history" of art, but have rather strengthened the idealistic nature of art history as a whole.

(e) *Differences:* With reference to the preceding section, we may consider that repetition would be the right way (or one of the right ways) to put forward our work in the internal logic of its own endeavor. Repetition, apart from what its use revealed to us, should, in fact, be envisaged as a Method and not as an end—a Method which definitively rejects, as we have seen, any repetition of the mechanical type, i.e. the geometric repetition (superimposable in every way, including color) of a like thing (color + form/shape). To repeat in this sense would be to prove that a single example already has an energy which denies all neutrality, and that repetition could change nothing.

One rabbit repeated 10,000 times would give no notion whatever of neutrality or zero degree, but eventually the identical image, 10,000 times, of the same rabbit. The repetition which concerns us is therefore fundamentally the presentation of the same thing, but under an objectively *different* aspect. To sum up, manifestly it appears to us of no interest always to show precisely the same thing and from that to deduce that there is repetition. The repetition which interests us is that of a method and not a mannerism (or trick): it is a repetition with differences. One could even say that it is these differences which make the repetition and that it is not a question of doing the same in order to say that it is identical to the previous—which is a tautology (redundancy)—but rather a *repetition of differences with a view to a same (thing).*

*[This repetition is an attempt to cover, little by little, all the avenues of inquiry. One might equally say that the work is an attempt to close off in order the better to disclose.*

*(e2) Canceling–out: We would like to return to the idea of canceling-out, briefly touched upon in sections (b) and (d).*

*The systematic repetition, which allows the differences to become visible each time, is used as a method and not considered as an end, in conscience of the danger that, in art, a form/thing—since there is a form/thing—can become, even if it is physically, aesthetically, objectively insignificant, an object of reference and of value. Furthermore, we can affirm that objects apparently insignificant and reduced are more greatly endangered than others of more elaborate appearance, and this is a result of (or thanks to) the fact that the object/idea/concept of the artist is only considered from a single viewpoint (a real or ideal viewpoint, cf. section (g) and with a view to their consummation in the artistic milieu.*

*A repetition which is ever divergent and non– mechanical, used as a method, allows a systematic closing– off and, in the same moment that things are closed off (lest we should omit anything from our attempts at inquiry), they are canceled out. Canceled out through lack of importance. One cannot rest content once and for all with a form which is insignificant and impersonal in itself—we have just exposed the danger of it. We know from experience, that is to say theoretically, that the system of art can extrapolate by licensing every kind of impersonal aspect to assume the role of model. Now, we can have no model, rest assured, unless it is a model of the model itself. Knowing what is ventured by the impersonal object, we must submit it—our method—to the test of repetition. This repetition should lead to its disappearance/obliteration. Disappearance in terms of significant form as much as insignificant form.*

*The possibility of the disappearance of form as a pole of interest—disappearance of the object as an image of something—is "visible" in the single work, but should also be visible through the total work, that is to say in our practice according to and in every situation.*

*What is being attempted, as we already understand, is the elimination of the imprint of form, together with the disappearance of form (of all form). This involves the disappearance of "signature," of style, of recollection/derivation. A unique work (in the original sense), by virtue of its character, will be conserved. The imprint exists in a way which is evident/insistent at the moment when it is, like form itself, a response to a problem or the demonstration of a subject or the representation of an attitude. If, however, the "print" of the imprint presents itself as a possible means of canceling-out and not as something privileged/conserved—in fact, if the imprint, rather than being the glorious or triumphant demonstration of authorship, appears as a means of questioning its own disappearance/ insignificance—one might then speak of canceling–out indeed; or, if you like, destruction of the imprint, as a sign of any value, through differentiated repetition of itself rendering void each time anew, or each time a little more, the value which it might previously have maintained. There must be no let–up in the process of canceling–out, in order to "blow" the form/thing, its idea, its value and its significance to the limits of possibility.*

*We can say (cf. section (f)) that the author/creator (we prefer the idea of "person responsible" or "producer") can "efface himself" behind the work which he makes (or which makes him), but that this would be no more than a good intention, consequent upon the work itself (and hence a minor consideration) unless one takes into consideration the endless canceling–out of the form itself, the ceaseless posing of the question of its presence; and thence that of its disappearance. This going and coming, once again non– mechanical, never bears upon the succeeding stage in the process. Everyday phenomena alone remain perceptible, never the extraordinary.]*

*[(e3) Vulgarization: The canceling–out, through successive repetitions in different locations of a proposition, of an identity which is constant by virtue of its difference in relation to a sameness, hints at that which is generally considered typical of a minor or bad art, that is to say vulgarization considered here as a method. It is a question of drawing out from its respectable shelter of originality or rarity a work which, in essence, aims at neither respect nor honors. The canceling–out or the disappearance of form through repetition gives rise to the appearance, at the same moment, of pro- fuseness and ephemerality. The rarefaction of a thing produced augments its value (saleable, visual, palpable . . .). We consider that the "vulgarization" of the work which concerns us is a matter of necessity, due to the fact that this work is made manifest only that it shall have being, and disappears in its own multiple being.*

*In art, Banality soon becomes Extraordinary. The instances are numerous. We consider that at this time the essential risk that must be taken—a stage in our proposition—is the vulgarization of the work itself, in order to tire out every eye that stakes all on the satisfaction of a retinal (aesthetic) shock, however slight. The visibility of this form must not attract the gaze. Once the dwindling form/ imprint/gesture have been rendered impotent/invisible, the proposition has/will have some chance to become dazzling. The repetition of a neutral from, such as we are attempting to grasp and to put into practice, does not lay emphasis upon the work, but rather tends to efface it. We should stress that the effacement involved is of interest to us insofar as it makes manifest, once again, the disappearance of form (in painting) as a pole of attraction of interest, that is to say makes manifest our questioning of the concept of the painting in particular and the concept of art in general.*

*This questioning is absolutely alien to the habits of responding, implies thousands of fresh responses, and implies therefore the end of formalism, the end of the mania for responding (art).*

*Vulgarization through repetition is already calling in question the further banality of art.]*

(f) *Anonymity:* From the [seven] preceding sections there emerges a relationship which itself leads to certain considerations; this is the relationship which may exist between the "creator" and the proposition we are attempting to define. First fact to be established: *he is no longer the owner of his work.* Furthermore, it is not *his* work, but *a* work. The neutrality of the purpose—"painting as the subject of painting"—and the absence from it of considerations of style, forces us to acknowledge a certain anonymity. This is obviously not anonymity in the person who proposes this work, which once again would be to solve a problem by presenting it in a false light—why should we be concerned to know the name of the painter of the Avignon Pieta—*but of the anonymity of the work itself as presented.* This work being considered as common property, there can be no question of claiming the authorship thereof, possessively, in the sense that there are authentic paintings of Courbet and valueless forgeries. As we have remarked, the projection of the individual is nil; we cannot see how he could claim his work as *belonging* to him. In the same way we suggest that the same proposition made by X or Y would be identical to that made by the author of this text. If you like, the study of past work forces us to admit that there is no longer, as regards the form defined above—when it is presented—any truth or falsity in terms of conventional meaning, which can be applied to both these terms relating to a work of art.[5] [*The making of the work has no more than a relative interest, and in consequence he who makes the work has no more than a relative, quasi-anecdotal interest and cannot at any time make use of it to glorify "his" product.*] It may also be said that the work of which we speak, because neutral/anonymous, is indeed the work of someone, but that this someone has no importance whatsoever [*since he never reveals himself*], or, if you like, the importance he may have is totally archaic. Whether he signs "his" work or not, it nevertheless remains anonymous.

(g) *The Viewpoint—The Location:* Lastly, one of the external consequences of our proposition is the problem raised by the location where the work is shown. In fact the work, as it is seen to be without composition and as it presents no accident to divert the eye, becomes itself the accident in relation to the place where it is presented. The incident of any form considered *as such,* and the judgement against such forms on the facts established in the preceding paragraphs, leads us to question the finite space in which this form is seen. It is established that the proposition, in whatever location it be presented, does not "disturb" that location. The place in question appears as it is. It is seen in its actuality. This is partly due to the fact that the proposition is not distracting. Furthermore, being only its own subject-matter, its own location is the proposition itself. Which makes it possible to say, paradoxically: the proposition in question "has no real location."[6]

In a certain sense, one of the characteristics of the proposition is to reveal the "container" in which it is sheltered. One also realizes that the influence of the location upon the significance of the work is as slight as that of the work upon the location.

This consideration, in course of work, has led us to present the proposition in a number of very varied places. If it is possible to imagine a constant relationship between the container (location) and the contents (the total proposition), this relationship is always annulled or reinvoked by the next presentation. This relationship then leads to two inextricably linked although apparently contradictory problems:

(i) revelation of the location itself as a new space to be deciphered;

(ii) the questioning of the proposition itself, insofar as its repetition (see sections (d) and (e)) in different "contexts," visible from different viewpoints, leads us back to the central issue: What is exposed to view? What is the nature of it? The multifariousness of the locations where the proposition is visible permits us to assert the unassailable persistence which it displays in the very moment when its non-style appearance merges it with its support.

It is important to demonstrate that while remaining in a very well defined cultural field—as if one could do otherwise—it is possible to go outside the cultural location in the primary sense (gallery, museum, catalogue . . .) without the proposition, considered as such, immediately giving way.[7] This strengthens our conviction that the work proposed, insofar as it raises the question of viewpoint, is posing what is in effect a new question, since it has been commonly assumed that the answer follows as a matter of course.

We cannot get bogged down here in the implications of this idea: we will merely observe for the record that all the works which claim to do away with the object (conceptual or otherwise) are essentially dependent *upon the single viewpoint* from which they are "visible," *a priori* considered (or even not considered at all) as ineluctable. A considerable number of works of art (the most exclusively idealist, e.g. ready-mades of all kinds) "exist" only because the location in which they are seen is taken for granted as a matter of course.

In this way, the location assumes considerable importance by its fixity and its inevitability; becomes the "frame" (*and the security that pre-supposes*) at the very moment when they would have us believe that what takes place inside shatters all the existing frames (manacles) in the attaining of pure "freedom." A clear eye will recognize what is meant by freedom in art, but an eye which is a little less educated will see better what it is all about when it has adopted the following idea: that the location (outside or inside) where a work is seen is its frame (its *boundary*).

## II. PREAMBLE

One might ask why so many precautions must be taken instead of merely putting one's work out in the normal fashion, leaving comment to the "critics" and other professional gossip-columnists. The answer is very simple: complete rupture with art—such as it is envisaged, such as it is known, such as it is practiced—has become the only possible means of proceeding along the path of no return upon which thought must embark; and this requires a few explanations. This rupture requires as a first priority the revision of the History of Art as we know it or, if you like, its radical dissolution. Then if one rediscovers any *durable and indispensable criteria* they must be used not as a release from the need to imitate or to sublimate, but as a [*reality*] which should be restated. A [*reality*] in fact which, although already "discovered," would have to be challenged, therefore to be created. For it may be suggested that, at the present time, [*all the realities*] which it has been possible to point out to us or which have been recognized, are not *known*. To recognize the existence of a problem certainly does not mean the same as to know it. Indeed, if some problems have been solved empirically (or by rule-of-thumb), we cannot then say that we know them, as the very empiricism which presides over this kind of discovery obscures the solution in a maze of carefully maintained enigmas.

But art works and the practice of art have served throughout, in a parallel direction, to signal the existence of certain problems. This recognition of their existence can be called practice. The exact knowledge of these problems will be called theory (not to be confused with all the aesthetic "theories" which have been bequeathed to us by the history of art). It is this *knowledge* or *theory* which is now indispensable for a perspective upon the rupture—a rupture which can then pass into the realm of fact. *The mere recognition* of the existence of pertinent problems *will not suffice for us*. It may be affirmed that all art up to the present day has been created on the one hand only *empirically* and on the other out of idealistic thinking. If it is possible to think again or to think and create theoretically/scientifically, the *rupture* will be achieved and thus the word art will have lost the meanings—numerous and divergent—which at present encumber it. We can say, on the basis of the foregoing, that the rupture, if any, can be (can only be) epistemological. This rupture is/will be the resulting logic of a theoretical work at the moment when the history of art (which is still to be made) and its application are/will be envisaged theoretically: theory and theory alone, as we well know, can make possible a revolutionary practice. Furthermore, not only is/will theory be indissociable from its own practice, but again it may/will be able to give rise to other original kinds of practice.

Finally, as far as we are concerned, *it must be clearly understood that when theory is considered as producer/creator, the only theory or theoretic practice is the result presented/the painting* or, according to Althusser's definition: "Theory: a specific form of practice."

We are aware that this exposition of facts may be somewhat didactic; nevertheless we consider it indispensable to proceed in this way at this time.

July/August 1969 and January 1970

## NOTES

1. Whether there is a material object or not, as soon as a thing, an idea or a "concept" is re-removed from its context, it is indeed a question of its exposition, in the traditional sense of this term.

2. This approach is not only aberrant (nonsense) but typically regressive, considering that the very concepts of art, of works of art . . . are in the course of being dissolved.

3. To deny this would be to call in question all the notions sustaining the word art.

4. We may here mention the false problem raised/solved by the monochrome: ". . . The monochrome canvas as subject-picture refers back—and refers back in the end only to that metaphysical background against which are outlined the figures of the type of painting called realist, which is really only illusionist." Marcelin Pleynet in *Les Lettres Françaises* no. 1177.

5. See "Buren or Toroni or no matter who," demonstration, Lugano, December 1967.

6. See Michel Claura in *Les Lettres Françaises* No. 1277.

7. As an example and by comparison, what has become of Duchamp's urinal since it was returned to the public lavatories?

The first version of this text, "Mise en garde," first appeared in catalogue for the exhibition "Konzeption/Conception, staged at the Städtischen Museum in Leverkusen, October-November 1969. This version, completed in January 1970, was entitled "Mise en garde #3" and first published in *VH101,* no. 1 (Spring 1970), pp. 97–103. The present translation, by Charles Harrison and Peter Townsend, first appeared in *Studio International,* 179:920 (March 1970), pp. 100–104.

White and blue vertical stripes were visible at:

20.9.69     Kunsthalle, Düsseldorf

30.9.69     Konrad Fischer's, 12 Neubrück Street, Düsseldorf

30.9.69     4 Ratinger Street (outside), Düsseldorf

2.10.69     3 Rhein Street, Gästehaus Nina, room no. 5, Düsseldorf

3.10.69     3 pieces, parking lot, Düsseldorf (photo)

5.10.69     Dr. Hock's, 53 Kleidbruch Street, Krefeld

6.10.69     2 pieces, 35 Stern Street, Düsseldorf

6.10.69     advertising pillar, Rochus Street, Düsseldorf

7.10.69     on 2 advertising pillars, Prinz-Georg Street, Düsseldorf

Daniel Buren, *Recapitulation,* 1969.

# art after philosophy

joseph kosuth

## PART I

The fact that it has recently become fashionable for physicists themselves to be sympathetic towards religion . . . marks the physicists' own lack of confidence in the validity of their hypotheses, which is a reaction on their part from the anti-religious dogmatism of nineteenth-century scientists, and a natural outcome of the crisis through which physics has just passed.

— A. J. Ayer

. . . Once one has understood the *Tractatus* there will be no temptation to concern oneself any more with philosophy, which is neither empirical like science nor tautological like mathematics; one will, like Wittgenstein in 1918, abandon philosophy, which, as traditionally understood, is rooted in confusion.

— J. O. Urmson

Traditional philosophy, almost by definition, has concerned itself with the *unsaid*. The nearly exclusive focus on the *said* by twentieth-century analytical linguistic philosophers is the shared contention that the *unsaid* is *unsaid* because it is *unsayable*. Hegelian philosophy made sense in the nineteenth century and must have been soothing to a century that was barely getting over Hume, the Enlightenment, and Kant.[1] Hegel's philosophy was also capable of giving cover for a defense of religious beliefs, supplying an alternative to Newtonian mechanics, and fitting in with the growth of history as a discipline, as well as accepting Darwinian biology.[2] He appeared to give an acceptable resolution to the conflict between theology and science, as well.

The result of Hegel's influence has been that a great majority of contemporary philosophers are really little more than *historians* of philosophy, Librarians of the Truth, so to speak. One begins to get the impression that there "is nothing more to be said." And certainly if one realizes the implications of Wittgenstein's thinking, and the thinking influenced by him and after him, "Continental" philosophy need not seriously be considered here.[3]

Is there a reason for the "unreality" of philosophy in our time? Perhaps this can be answered by looking into the difference between our time and the centuries preceding us. In the past, man's conclusions about the world were based on the information he had about it—if not specifically like the Empiricists, then generally like the Rationalists. Often, the closeness between science and philosophy was so great that scientists and philosophers were one and the same person. In fact, from the time of Thales, Epicurus, Heraclitus, and Aristotle to Descartes and Leibniz, "the great names in philosophy were often great names in science as well."[4]

That the world as perceived by twentieth-century science is vastly more different than the one of its preceding century, need not be proved here. Is it possible, then, that in effect man has learned so much, as his "intelligence" is such, that he cannot *believe* the reasoning of traditional philosophy? That perhaps he knows too much about the world to make those kinds of conclusions? As Sir James Jeans has stated:

*. . . When philosophy has availed itself of the results of science, it has not been by borrowing the abstract mathematical description of the pattern of events, but by borrowing the then current pictorial description of this pattern; thus it has not appropriated certain knowledge but conjectures. These conjectures were often good enough for the man-sized world, but not, as we now know, for those ultimate processes of nature which control the happenings of the man-sized world, and bring us nearest to the true nature of reality.*[5]

He continues:

*One consequence of this is that the standard philosophical discussions of many problems, such as those of causality and freewill or of materialism or mentalism, are based on an interpretation of the pattern of events which is no longer tenable. The scientific basis of these older discussions has been washed away, and with their disappearance have gone all the arguments.*[6]

The twentieth century brought in a time which could be called "the end of philosophy and the beginning of art." I do not mean this, of course, strictly speaking, but rather as the "tendency" of the situation. Certainly linguistic philosophy can be considered the heir to empiricism, but it's a philosophy in one gear.[7] And there is certainly an "art condition" to art preceding Duchamp, but its other functions or reasons-to-be are so pronounced that its ability to function clearly as art limits its art condition so drastically that it's only minimally art.[8] In no mechanistic sense is there a connection between philosophy's "ending" and art's "beginning," but I don't find this occurrence entirely coincidental. Though the same reasons may be responsible for both occurrences, the connection is made by me. I bring this all up to analyze art's function and subsequently its viability. And I do so to enable others to understand the reasoning of my art and, by extension, other artists', as well as to provide a clearer understanding of the term "Conceptual art."[9]

## The Function of Art

**The main qualifications to the lesser position of painting is that advances in art are certainly not always formal ones.**
 —Donald Judd (1963)

**Half or more of the best new work in the last few years has been neither painting nor sculpture.**
 —Donald Judd (1965)

**Everything sculpture has, my work doesn't.**
 —Donald Judd (1967)

**The idea becomes a machine that makes the art.**
 —Sol LeWitt (1967)

The one thing to say about art is that it is one thing. Art is art-as-art and everything else is everything else. Art as art is nothing but art. Art is not what is not art.
> —Ad Reinhardt (1963)

The meaning is the use.
> —Wittgenstein

A more functional approach to the study of concepts has tended to replace the method of introspection. Instead of attempting to grasp or describe concepts bare, so to speak, the psychologist investigates the way in which they function as ingredients in beliefs and in judgements.
> —Irving M. Copi

Meaning is always a presupposition of function.
> —T. Segerstedt

. . . the subject-matter of conceptual investigations is the meaning of certain words and expressions—and not the things and states of affairs themselves about which we talk, when using those words and expressions.
> —G. H. Von Wright

Thinking is radically metaphoric. Linkage by analogy is its constituent law or principle, its causal nexus, since meaning only arises through the causal contexts by which a sign stands for (takes the place of) an instance of a sort. To think of anything is to take it as of a sort (as a such and such) and that "as" brings in (openly or in disguise) the analogy, the parallel, the metaphoric grapple or ground or grasp or draw by which alone the mind takes hold. It takes no hold if there is nothing for it to haul from, for its thinking is the haul, the attraction of likes.
> —I. A. Richards

In this section I will discuss the separation between aesthetics and art; consider briefly Formalist art (because it is a leading proponent of the idea of aesthetics as art), and assert that art is analogous to an analytic proposition, and that it is art's existence as a tautology which enables art to remain "aloof" from philosophical presumptions.

It is necessary to separate aesthetics from art because aesthetics deals with opinions on perception of the world in general. In the past one of the two prongs of art's function was its value as decoration. So any branch of philosophy which dealt with "beauty" and thus, taste, was inevitably duty-bound to discuss art as well. Out of this "habit" grew the notion that there was a conceptual connection between art and aesthetics, which is not true. This idea never drastically conflicted with artistic considerations before recent times, not only because the morphological characteristics of art perpetuated the continuity of this error, but also because the apparent other "functions" of art (depiction of religious themes, portraiture of aristocrats, detailing of architecture, etc.) used art to cover up art.

When objects are presented within the context of art (and until recently objects always have been used) they are as eligible for aesthetic consideration as are any objects in the world, and an aesthetic consideration of an object existing in the realm of art means that the object's existence or functioning in an art context is irrelevant to the aesthetic judgement.

The relation of aesthetics to art is not unlike that of aesthetics to architecture, in that architecture has a very specific *function* and how "good" its design is is *primarily* related to how well it performs its function. Thus, judgements on what it looks like correspond to taste, and we can see that throughout history different examples of architecture are praised at different times depending on the aesthetics of particular epochs. Aesthetic thinking has even gone so far as to make examples of architecture not related to "art" at all, works of art in themselves (e.g. the pyramids of Egypt).

Aesthetic considerations are indeed *always* extraneous to an object's function or "reason to be." Unless of course, the object's "reason to be" is strictly aesthetic. An example of a purely aesthetic object is a decorative object, for decoration's primary function is "to add something to so as to make more attractive; adorn; ornament,"[10] and this relates directly to taste. And this leads us directly to "Formalist" art and criticism.[11] Formalist art (painting and sculpture) is the vanguard of decoration, and, strictly speaking, one could reasonably assert that its art condition is so minimal that for all functional purposes it is not art at all, but pure exercises in aesthetics. Above all things Clement Greenberg is the critic of taste. Behind every one of his decisions there is an aesthetic judgement, with those judgements reflecting his taste. And what does his taste reflect? The period he grew up in as a critic, the period "real" for him: the fifties.[12] Given his theories (if they have any logic to them at all) how else can one account for his disinterest in Frank Stella, Ad Reinhardt, and others applicable to his historical scheme? Is it because he is ". . . basically unsympathetic on personally experiential grounds"?[13] Or, in other words, their work doesn't suit his taste?

But in the philosophic *tabula rasa* of art, "if someone calls it art," as Don Judd has said, "it's art." Given this, formalist painting and sculpture activity can be granted an "art condition," but only by virtue of its presentation in terms of its art idea (e.g. a rectangularly-shaped canvas stretched over wooden supports and stained with such and such colors, using such and such forms, giving such and such a visual experience, etc.). Looking at contemporary art in this light, one realizes the minimal creative effort taken on the part of formalist artists specifically, and all painters and sculptors (working as such today) generally.

This brings us to the realization that formalist art and criticism accept as a definition of art one which exists solely on morphological grounds. While a vast quantity of similarly looking objects or images (or visually related objects or images) may seem to be related (or connected) because of a similarity of visual/experiential "readings," one cannot claim from this an artistic or conceptual relationship.

It is obvious then that formalist criticism's reliance on morphology leads necessarily with a bias toward the morphology of traditional art. And in this sense such criticism is not related to a "scientific method" or any sort of empiricism (as Michael Fried, with his detailed descriptions of paintings and other "scholarly" paraphernalia would want us to believe). Formalist criticism is no more than an analysis of the physical attributes of particular objects which happen to exist in a morphological context. But this doesn't add any knowledge (or facts) to our understanding of the nature or function of art. Nor does it comment on whether or not the objects analyzed are even works of art, since formalist critics always bypass the conceptual element in works of art. Exactly why they don't comment on the conceptual element in works of art is precisely because formalist art becomes art only by virtue of its resemblance to earlier works of art. It's a mindless art. Or, as Lucy Lippard so succinctly described Jules Olitski's paintings: "they're visual *Muzak*."[14]

Formalist critics and artists alike do not question the nature of art, but as I have said elsewhere: "Being an artist now means to question the nature of art. If one is questioning the nature of painting, one cannot be questioning the nature of art. If an artist accepts painting (or sculpture) he is accepting the tradition that goes with it. That's because the word art is general and the word painting is specific. Painting is a *kind* of art. If you make paintings you are already accepting (not questioning) the nature of art. One is then accepting the nature of art to be the European tradition of a painting-sculpture dichotomy."[15]

The strongest objection one can raise against a morphological justification for traditional art is that morphological notions of art embody an implied *a priori* concept of art's possibilities. But such an *a priori* concept of the nature of art (as separate from analytically framed art propositions or "work" which I will discuss later) makes it, indeed, *a priori:* impossible to question the nature of art. And this questioning of the nature of art is a very important concept in understanding the function of art.

The function of art, as a question, was first raised by Marcel Duchamp. In fact it is Marcel Duchamp whom we can credit with giving art its own identity. (One can certainly see a tendency toward this self-identification of art beginning with Manet and Cézanne through to Cubism,[16] but their works are timid and ambiguous by comparison with Duchamp's.) "Modern" art and the work before seemed connected by virtue of their morphology. Another way of putting it would be that art's "language" remained the same, but it was saying new things. The event that made conceivable the realization that it was possible to "speak another language" and still make sense in art was Marcel Duchamp's first unassisted readymade. With the unassisted readymade, art changed its focus from the form of the language to what was being said. Which means that it changed the nature of art from a question of morphology to a question of function. This change—one from "appearance" to "conception"—was the beginning of "modern" art and the beginning of "conceptual" art. All art (after Duchamp) is conceptual (in nature) because art only exists conceptually.

The "value" of particular artists after Duchamp can be weighed according to how much they questioned the nature of art; which is another way of saying "what they *added* to the conception of art" or what wasn't there before they started. Artists question the nature of art by presenting new propositions as to art's nature. And to do this one cannot concern oneself with the handed-down "language" of traditional art, since this activity is based on the assumption that there is only one way of framing art propositions. But the very stuff of art is indeed greatly related to "creating" new propositions.

The case is often made—particularly in reference to Duchamp—that objects of art (such as the readymades, of course, but all art is implied in this) are judged as *objets d'art* in later years and the artists' *intentions* become irrelevant. Such an argument is the case of a pre-conceived notion of art ordering together not necessarily related facts. The point is this: aesthetics, as we have pointed out, are conceptually irrelevant to art. Thus, any physical thing can become *objet d'art,* that is to say, can be considered tasteful, aesthetically pleasing, etc. But this has no bearing on the object's application to an art context; that is, its *functioning* in an art context. (E.g. if a collector takes a painting, attaches legs, and uses it as a dining-table it's an act unrelated to art or the artist because, as art, that wasn't the artist's *intention.*)

And what holds true for Duchamp's work applies as well to most of the art after him. In other words, the value of Cubism is its idea in the realm of art, not the physical or visual qualities seen in a specific painting, or the particularization of certain colors or shapes. For these colors and shapes are the art's "language," not its meaning conceptually as art. To look upon a Cubist "masterwork" *now* as art is nonsensical, conceptually speaking, as far as art is concerned. (That visual information which was unique in Cubism's language has now been generally absorbed and has a lot to do with the way in which one deals with painting "linguistically." [E.g. what a Cubist painting meant experimentally and conceptually to, say, Gertrude Stein, is beyond our speculation because the same painting then "meant" something different than it does now.]) The "value" now of an original Cubist painting is not unlike, in most respects, an original manuscript by Lord Byron, or *The Spirit of St. Louis* as it is seen in the Smithsonian Institution. (Indeed, museums fill the very same function as the Smithsonian Institution—why else would the *Jeu de Paume* wing of the Louvre exhibit Cézanne's and Van Gogh's palettes as proudly as they do their paintings?) Actual works of art are little more than historical curiosities. As far as *art* is concerned Van Gogh's paintings aren't worth any more than his palette is. They are both "collector's items."[17]

Art "lives" through influencing other art, not by existing as the physical residue of an artist's ideas. The reason why different artists from the past are "brought alive" again is because some aspect of their work becomes "usable" by living artists. That there is no "truth" as to what art is seems quite unrealized.

What is the function of art, or the nature of art? If we continue our analogy of the forms art takes as being art's *language* one can realize then that a work of art is a kind of *proposition* presented within the context of art as a comment on art. We can then go further and analyze the types of "propositions."

A. J. Ayer's evaluation of Kant's distinction between analytic and synthetic is useful to us here: "A proposition is analytic when its validity depends solely on the definitions of the symbols it contains, and synthetic when its validity is determined by the facts of experience."[18] The analogy I will attempt to make is one between the art condition and the condition of the analytic proposition. In that they don't appear to be believable as anything else, nor about anything (other than art), the forms of art most clearly finally referable only to art have been forms closest to analytical propositions.

Works of art are analytic propositions. That is, if viewed within their context—as art—they provide no information what-so-ever about any matter of fact. A work of art is a tautology in that it is a presentation of the artist's intention, that is, he is saying that a particular work of art is art, which means, is a *definition* of art. Thus, that it is art is true *a priori* (which is what Judd means when he states that "if someone calls it art, it's art").

Indeed, it is nearly impossible to discuss art in general terms without talking in tautologies—for to attempt to "grasp" art by any other "handle" is to merely focus on another aspect or quality of the proposition which is usually irrelevant to the art work's "art condition." One begins to realize that art's "art condition" is a conceptual state. That the language forms which the artist frames his propositions in are often "private" codes or languages is an inevitable outcome of art's freedom from morphological constrictions; and it follows from this that one has to be familiar with contemporary art to appreciate it and understand it. Likewise one understands why the "man on the street" is intolerant to artistic art and always demands art in a traditional "language." (And one understands why formalist art "sells like hot cakes.") Only in painting and sculpture did the artists all speak the same language. What is called "Novelty Art" by the formalists is often the attempt to find new languages, although a new language doesn't necessarily mean the framing of new propositions: e.g. most kinetic and electronic art.

Another way of stating in relation to art what Ayer asserted about the analytic method in the context of language would be the following: The validity of artistic propositions is not dependent on any empirical, much less any aesthetic, presupposition about the nature of things. For the artist, as an analyst, is not directly concerned with the physical properties of things. He is concerned only with the way (1) in which art is capable of conceptual growth and (2) how his propositions are capable of logically following that growth.[19] In other words, the propositions of art are not factual, but linguistic in *character*—that is, they do not describe the behavior of physical, or even mental objects; they express definitions of art, or the formal consequences of definitions of art. Accordingly, we can say that art operates on a logic. For we shall see that the characteristic mark of a purely logical inquiry is that it is concerned with the formal consequences of our definitions (of art) and not with questions of empirical fact.[20]

To repeat, what art has in common with logic and mathematics is that it is a tautology; i.e., the "art idea" (or "work") and art are the same and can be appreciated as art without going outside the context of art for verification.

On the other hand, let us consider why art cannot be (or has difficulty when it attempts to be) a synthetic proposition. Or, that is to say, when the truth or falsity of its assertion is verifiable on empirical grounds. Ayer states:

> . . . *The criterion by which we determine the validity of an* a priori *or analytical proposition is not sufficient to determine the validity of an empirical or synthetic proposition. For it is characteristic of empirical propositions that their validity is not purely formal. To say that a geometrical proposition, or a system of geometrical propositions, is false, is to say that it is self-contradictory.*

*But an empirical proposition, or a system of empirical propositions, may be free from contradiction, and still be false. It is said to be false, not because it is formally defective, but because it fails to satisfy some material criterion.*[21]

The unreality of "realistic" art is due to its framing as an art proposition in synthetic terms: one is always tempted to "verify" the proposition empirically. Realism's synthetic state does not bring one to a circular swing back into a dialogue with the larger framework of questions about the nature of *art* (as does the work of Malevich, Mondrian, Pollock, Reinhardt, early Rauschenberg, Johns, Lichtenstein, Warhol, Andre, Judd, Flavin, LeWitt, Morris, and others), but rather, one is flung out of art's "orbit" into the "infinite space" of the human condition.

Pure Expressionism, continuing with Ayer's terms, could be considered as such: "A sentence which consisted of demonstrative symbols would not express a genuine proposition. It would be a mere ejaculation, in no way characterizing that to which it was supposed to refer." Expressionist works are usually such "ejaculations" presented in the morphological language of traditional art. If Pollock is important it is because he painted on loose canvas horizontally to the floor. What *isn't* important is that he later put those drippings over stretchers and hung them parallel to the wall. (In other words, what is important in art is what one *brings* to it, not one's adoption of what was previously existing.) What is even less important to art is Pollock's notions of "self-expression" because those *kinds* of subjective meanings are useless to anyone other than those involved with him personally. And their "specific" quality puts them outside of art's context.

"I do not make art," Richard Serra says, "I am engaged in an activity; if someone wants to call it art, that's his business, but it's not up to me to decide that. That's all figured out later." Serra, then, is very much aware of the implications of his work. If Serra is indeed just "figuring out what lead does" (gravitationally, molecularly, etc.) why should *anyone* think of it as art? If he doesn't take the responsibility of it being art, who can, or should? His work certainly appears to be empirically verifiable: lead can do and be used for many physical activities. In itself this does anything but lead us into a dialogue about the nature of art. In a sense then he is a primitive. He has no idea about art. How is it then that we know about "his activity"? Because he has told us it is art by his actions *after* "his activity" has taken place. That is, by the fact he is with several galleries, puts the physical residue of his activity in museums (and sells them to art collectors—but as we have pointed out, collectors are irrelevant to the "condition of art" of a work). That he denies his work is art but plays the artist is more than just a paradox. Serra secretly feels that "arthood" is arrived at empirically. Thus, as Ayer has stated: "There are no absolutely certain empirical propositions. It is only tautologies that are certain. Empirical questions are one and all hypotheses, which may be confirmed or discredited in actual sense-experience. And the propositions in which we record the observations that verify these hypotheses are themselves hypotheses which are subject to the test of further sense-experience. Thus there is no final proposition."[22]

What one finds all throughout the writings of Ad Reinhardt is this very similar thesis of "art-as-art," and that "art is always dead, and a 'living' art is a deception."[23] Reinhardt had a very clear idea about the nature of art, and his importance is far from being recognized.

Forms of art that can be considered synthetic propositions are verifiable by the world, that is to say, to understand these propositions one must leave the tautological-like framework of art and consider "outside" information. But to consider it as art it is necessary to ignore this same outside information, because outside information (experiential qualities, to note) has its own intrinsic worth. And to comprehend this worth one does not need a state of "art condition."

From this it is easy to realize that art's viability is not connected to the presentation of visual (or other) kinds of experience. That this may have been one of art's extraneous functions in the preceding centuries is not unlikely. After all, man in even the nineteenth century lived in a fairly standardized visual environment. That is, it was ordinarily predictable as to what he would be coming into contact with day after day. His visual environment in the part of the world in which he lived was fairly consistent. In our time we have an experientially drastically richer environment. One can fly all over the earth in a matter of hours and days, not months. We have the cinema, and color television, as well as the man-made spectacle of the lights of Las Vegas or the skyscrapers of New York City. The whole world is there to be seen, and the whole world can watch man walk on the moon from their living rooms. Certainly art or objects of painting and sculpture cannot be expected to compete experientially with this?

The notion of "use" is relevant to art and its "language." Recently the box or cube form has been used a great deal within the context of art. (Take for instance its use by Judd, Morris, LeWitt, Bladen, Smith, Bell, and McCracken—not to mention the quantity of boxes and cubes that came after.) The difference between all the various uses of the box or cube form is directly related to the differences in the intentions of the artists. Further, as is particularly seen in Judd's work, the use of the box or cube form illustrates very well our earlier claim that an object is only art when placed in the context of art.

A few examples will point this out. One could say that if one of Judd's box forms was seen filled with debris, seen placed in an industrial setting, or even merely seen sitting on a street corner, it would not be identified with art. It follows then that understanding and consideration of it as an art work is necessary *a priori* to viewing it in order to "see" it as a work of art. Advance information about the concept of art and about an artist's concepts is necessary to the appreciation and understanding of contemporary art. Any and all of the physical attributes (qualities) of contemporary works if considered separately and/or specifically are irrelevant to the art concept. The art concept (as Judd said, though he didn't mean it this way) must be considered in its whole. To consider a concept's parts is invariably to consider aspects that are irrelevant to its art condition—or like reading *parts* of a definition.

It comes as no surprise that the art with the least fixed morphology is the example from which we decipher the nature of the general term "art." For where there is a context existing separately of its morphology and consisting of its function one is more likely to find results less conforming and predictable. It is in modern art's possession of a "language" with the shortest history that the plausibility of the abandonment of that "language" becomes most possible. It is understandable then that the art that came out of Western painting and sculpture is the most energetic, questioning (of its nature), and the least assuming of all the general "art" concerns. In the final analysis, however, all of the arts have but (in Wittgenstein's terms) a "family" resemblance.

Yet the various qualities relatable to an "art condition" possessed by poetry, the novel, the cinema, the theatre, and various forms of music, etc., is that aspect of them most reliable to the function of art as asserted here.

Is not the decline of poetry relatable to the implied metaphysics from poetry's use of "common" language as an art language?[24] In New York the last decadent stages of poetry can be seen in the move by "Concrete" poets recently toward the use of actual objects and theatre.[25] Can it be that they feel the unreality of their art form?

**We see now that the axioms of a geometry are simply definitions, and that the theorems of a geometry are simply the logical consequences of these definitions. A geometry is not in itself about physical space; in itself it cannot be said to be "about" anything. But we can use a geometry to reason about physical space. That is to say, once we have given the axioms a physical interpretation, we can proceed to apply the theorems to the objects which satisfy the axioms. Whether a geometry can be applied to the actual physical world or not, is an empirical question which falls outside the scope of geometry itself. There is no sense, therefore, in asking which of the various geometries known to us are false and which are true. Insofar as they are all free from contradiction, they are all true. The proposition which states that a certain application of a geometry is possible**

is not itself a proposition of that geometry. All that the geometry itself tells us is that if anything can be brought under the definitions, it will also satisfy the theorems. It is therefore a purely logical system, and its propositions are purely analytic propositions.

—A. J. Ayer[26]

Here then I propose rests the viability of art. In an age when traditional philosophy is unreal because of its assumptions, art's ability to exist will depend not only on its *not* performing a service—as entertainment, visual (or other) experience, or decoration—which is something easily replaced by kitsch culture and technology, but rather, it will remain viable by *not* assuming a philosophical stance; for in art's unique character is the capacity to remain aloof from philosophical judgements. It is in this context that art shares similarities with logic, mathematics and, as well, science. But whereas the other endeavors are useful, art is not. Art indeed exists for its own sake.

In this period of man, after philosophy and religion, art may possibly be one endeavor that fulfills what another age might have called "man's spiritual needs." Or, another way of putting it might be that art deals analogously with the state of things "beyond physics" where philosophy had to make assertions. And art's strength is that even the preceding sentence is an assertion, and cannot be verified by art. Art's only claim is for art. Art is the definition of art.

## PART II
"Conceptual Art" and Recent Art

The disinterest in painting and sculpture is a disinterest in doing it again, not in it as it is being done by those who developed the last advanced versions. New work always involves objections to the old. They are part of it. If the earlier work is first rate it is complete.

—Donald Judd (1965)

Abstract art or nonpictorial art is as old as this century, and though more specialized than previous art, is clearer and more complete, and like all modern thought and knowledge, more demanding in its grasp of relations.

—Ad Reinhardt (1948)

In France there is an old saying, "stupid like a painter." The painter was considered stupid, but the poet and writer very intelligent. I wanted to be intelligent. I had to have the idea of inventing. It is nothing to do what your father did. It is nothing to be another Cézanne. In my visual period there is a little of that stupidity of the painter. All my work in the period before the Nude was visual painting. Then I came to the idea. I thought the ideatic formulation a way to get away from influences.

—Marcel Duchamp

For each work of art that becomes physical there are many variations that do not.

—Sol LeWitt

The main virtue of geometric shapes is that they aren't organic, as all art otherwise is. A form that's neither geometric or organic would be a great discovery.

—Donald Judd (1967)

The one thing to say about art is its breathlessness, lifelessness, deathlessness, contentlessness, formlessness, spacelessness, and timelessness. This is always the end of art.

—Ad Reinhardt (1962)

Note: The discussion in the previous part does more than merely "justify" the recent art called "conceptual." It points out, I feel, some of the confused thinking which has gone on in regards to past—but particularly—present activity in art. This article is not intended to give evidence of a "movement." But as an early advocate (through works of art and conversation) of a particular kind of art best described as "conceptual" I have become increasingly concerned by the nearly arbitrary application of this term to an assortment of art interests—many of which I would never want to be connected with, and logically shouldn't be.

The "purest" definition of conceptual art would be that it is inquiry into the foundations of the concept "art," as it has come to mean. Like most terms with fairly specific meanings generally applied, "conceptual art" is often considered as a *tendency*. In one sense it is a tendency of course because the "definition" of "Conceptual Art" is very close to the meanings of art itself.

But the reasoning behind the notion of such a tendency, I am afraid, is still connected to the fallacy of morphological characteristics as a connective between what are really disparate activities. In this case it is an attempt to detect stylehood. In assuming a primary cause-effect relationship to "final outcomes," such criticism bypasses a particular artist's intents (concepts) to deal exclusively with his "final outcome." Indeed most criticism has dealt with only one very superficial aspect of this "final outcome," and that is the apparent "immateriality" or "anti-object" similarity amongst most "conceptual" works of art. But this can only be important if one assumes that objects are necessary to art—or to phrase it better, that they have a definitive relation to art. And in this case such criticism would be focusing on a negative aspect of the art.

If one has followed my thinking (in part one) one can understand my assertion that objects are conceptually irrelevant to the condition of art. This is not to say that a particular "art investigation" may or may not employ objects, material substances, etc. within the confines of its investigation. Certainly the investigations carried out by Bainbridge and Hurrell are excellent examples of such a use.[27] Although I have proposed that all art is finally conceptual, some recent work is clearly conceptual in intent whereas other examples of recent art are only related to conceptual art in a superficial manner. And although this work is in most cases an advance over Formalist or "Anti-Formalist" (Morris, Serra, Sonnier, Hesse, and others) tendencies, it should not be considered "Conceptual Art" in the *purer* sense of the term.

Three artists often associated with me (through Seth Siegelaub's projects)—Douglas Huebler, Robert Barry, and Lawrence Weiner—are not concerned with, I do not think, "Conceptual Art" as it was previously stated. Douglas Huebler, who was in the "Primary Structures" show at the Jewish Museum (New York), uses a non-morphologically art-like form of presentation (photographs, maps, mailings) to answer iconic, structural sculpture issues directly related to his formica sculpture (which he was making as late as 1968). This is pointed out by the artist in the opening sentence of the catalogue of his "one-man show" (which was organized by Seth Siegelaub and existed only as a catalogue of documentation): "The existence of each sculpture is documented by its documentation." It is not my intention to point out a *negative* aspect of the work, but only to show that Huebler—who is in his mid-forties and much older than most of the artists discussed here—has not as much in common with the aims in the *purer* versions of "Conceptual Art" as it would superficially seem.

The other men—Robert Barry and Lawrence Weiner—have watched their work take on a "Conceptual Art" association almost by accident. Barry, whose painting was seen in the "Systemic Painting" show at the Guggenheim Museum, has in common with Weiner the fact that the "path" to conceptual art came via decisions related to choices of art materials and processes. Barry's post-Newman/Reinhardt paintings "reduced" (in physical material, not "meaning") along a path from two-inch square paintings, to single lines of wire between architectural points, to radio-wave beams, to inert gases, and finally to "brain energy." His work then seems to exist conceptually only because the material is invisible. But his art does have a physical state, which is different than work which only exists conceptually.

Lawrence Weiner, who gave up painting in the spring of 1968, changed his notion of "place" (in an Andrean sense) from the context of the canvas (which could only be specific) to a context which was "general," yet all the while continuing his concern with specific materials and processes. It became obvious to him that if one is not concerned with "appearance" (which he wasn't, and in this regard he preceded most of the "Anti-Form" artists) there was not only no need for the fabrication (such as in his studio) of his work, but—more important—such fabrication would again invariably give his work's "place" a specific context. Thus, by the summer of 1968, he decided to have his work exist only as a proposal in his notebook—that is, until a "reason" (museum, gallery, or collector) or as he called them, a "receiver" necessitated his work to be made. It was in the late fall of that same year that Weiner went one step further in deciding that it didn't matter whether it was made or not. In that sense his private notebooks became public.[28]

*Purely* conceptual art is first seen concurrently in the work of Terry Atkinson and Michael Baldwin in Coventry, England; and with my own work done in New York City, all generally around 1966.[29] On Kawara, a Japanese artist who has been continuously travelling around the world since 1959, has been doing a highly conceptualized kind of art since 1964.

On Kawara, who began with paintings lettered with one simple word, went to "questions" and "codes," and paintings such as the listing of a spot on the Sahara Desert in terms of its longitude and latitude, is most well known for his "date" paintings. The "date" paintings consist of the lettering (in paint on canvas) of that day's date on which the painting is executed. If a painting is not "finished" on the day that it is started (that is, by 12:00 midnight) it is destroyed. Although he still does the date paintings (he spent last year travelling to every country in South America) he has begun doing other projects as well in the past couple of years. These include a *One-hundred year calendar,* a daily listing of everyone he meets each day (*I met*) which is kept in notebooks, as is *I went* which is a calendar of maps of the cities he is in with the marked streets where he traveled. He also mails daily postcards giving the time he woke up that morning. On Kawara's reasons for his art are extremely private, and he has consciously stayed away from any publicity or public art-world exposure. His continued use of "painting" as a medium is, I think, a pun on the morphological characteristics of traditional art, rather than an interest in painting "proper."

Terry Atkinson and Michael Baldwin's work, presented as a collaboration, began in 1966 consisting of projects such as: a rectangle with linear depictions of the states of Kentucky and Iowa, titled *Map to not include: Canada, James Bay, Ontario, Quebec, St. Lawrence River, New Brunswick* . . . and so on; conceptual drawings based on various serial and conceptual schemes;

a map of a 36–square-mile area of the Pacific Ocean, west of Oahu, scale 3 inches to the mile (an empty square). Works from 1967 were the "Air- Conditioning Show" and the "Air Show." The "Air Show" as described by Terry Atkinson was, "A series of assertions concerning a theoretical usage of a column of air comprising a base of one square mile and of unspecified distance in the vertical dimension."[30]

No particular square mile of the earth's surface was specified. The concept did not entail any such particular location. Also such works as *Frameworks, Hot-cold,* and *22 sentences: the French army* are examples of their more recent collaborations.[31] Atkinson and Baldwin in the past year have formed, along with David Bainbridge and Harold Hurrell, the Art & Language Press. From this press is published *Art-Language,* (a journal of conceptual art),[32] as well as other publications related to this inquiry.

Christine Kozlov has been working along conceptual lines as well since late 1966. Some of her work has consisted of a "conceptual" film, using clear Leder tape; *Compositions for audio structures*—a coding system for sound; a stack of several hundred blank sheets of paper—one for each day on which a concept is rejected; *Figurative work,* which is a listing of everything she ate for a period of six months; and a study of crime as an art activity.

The Canadian Iain Baxter has been doing a "conceptual" sort of work since late 1967. As have the Americans James Byars and Frederic Barthelme; and the French and German artists Bernar Venet and Hanne Darboven. And certainly the books of Edward Ruscha since around that time are relevant too. As are *some* of Bruce Nauman's, Barry Flanagan's, Bruce McLean's, and Richard Long's works. Steven Kaltenbach *Time capsules* from 1968, and much of his work since is relatable. And Ian Wilson's post-Kaprow *Conversations* are conceptually presented.

The German artist Franz E. Walther in his work since 1965 has treated objects in a much different way than they are usually treated in an art context.

Within the past year other artists, though some only related peripherally, have begun a more "conceptual" form of work. Mel Bochner gave up work heavily influenced by "Minimal" art and began such work. And certainly some of the work by Jan Dibbets, Eric Orr, Allen Ruppersberg, and Dennis Oppenheim could be considered within a conceptual framework. Donald Burgy's work in the past year as well uses a conceptual format. One can also see a development in a *purer* form of "conceptual" art in the recent beginnings of work by younger artists such as Saul Ostrow, Adrian Piper, and Perpetua Butler. Interesting work in this "purer" sense is being done, as well, by a group consisting of an Australian and two Englishmen (all living in New York): Ian Burn, Mel Ramsden, and Roger Cutforth. (Although the amusing pop paintings of John Baldessari allude to this sort of work by being "conceptual" cartoons of actual conceptual art, they are not really relevant to this discussion.)

Terry Atkinson has suggested, and I agree with him, that Sol LeWitt is notably responsible for creating an environment which made our art acceptable, if not conceivable. (I would hastily add to that, however, that I was certainly much more influenced by Ad Reinhardt, Duchamp via Johns and Morris, and by Donald Judd than I ever was specifically by LeWitt.) Perhaps added to conceptual art's history would be certainly early works by Robert Morris, particularly the *Card File* (1962). Much of Rauschenberg's early work such as his *Portrait of Iris Clert* and his *Erased De Kooning Drawing* are some important examples of a conceptual kind of art. And the Europeans Klein and Manzoni fit into this history somewhere, too. And in Jasper Johns' work—such as his *Target* and *Flag* paintings and his ale cans—one has a particularly good example of art existing as an analytical proposition. Johns and Reinhardt are probably the last two painters that were legitimate *artists* as well.[33] Robert Smithson, *had* he recognized his articles in magazines as being his work (as he could have, and should have) and his "work" serving as illustrations for them, his influence would be more relevant.[34]

Andre, Flavin, and Judd have exerted tremendous influence on recent art, though probably more as examples of high standards and clear thinking than in any specific way. Pollock and Judd are, I feel, the beginning and end of American dominance in art; partly due to the ability of many of the younger artists in Europe to "purge" themselves of their traditions, but most likely due to the fact that nationalism is as out of place in art as it is in any other field. Seth Siegelaub, a former art dealer who now functions as a curator-at-large and was the first exhibition organizer to "specialize" in this area of recent art, has had many group exhibitions that existed no *place* (other than in the catalogue). As Siegelaub has stated: "I am very interested in conveying the idea that the artist can live where he wants to—not necessarily in New York or London or Paris as he has had to in the past—but *anywhere* and still make important art."

## NOTES

1. Morton White, *The Age of Analysis* (New York: Mentor Books, 1955), p. 14.

2. Ibid., p. 15.

3. I mean by this Existentialism and Phenomenology. Even Merleau-Ponty, with his middle-of-the-road position between Empiricism and Rationalism, cannot express his philosophy without the use of words (thus using concepts); and following this, how can one discuss experience without sharp distinctions between ourselves and the world?

4. Sir James Jeans, *Physics and Philosophy* (New York: Macmillan, 1946), p. 17.

5. Ibid., p. 190.

6. Ibid., p. 190.

7. The task such philosophy has taken upon itself is the only "function" it could perform without making philosophic assertions.

8. This is dealt with in the following section.

9. I would like to make it clear, however, that I intend to speak for no one else. I arrived at these conclusions alone, and indeed, it is from this thinking that my art since 1966 (if not before) evolved. Only recently did I realize after meeting Terry Atkinson that he and Michael Baldwin share similar, though certainly not identical, opinions to mine.

10. *Webster's New World Dictionary of the American Language* (1962), s. v. "decoration."

11. The conceptual level of the work of Kenneth Noland, Jules Olitski, Morris Louis, Ron Davis, Anthony Caro, John Hoyland, Dan Christensen, et al. is so dismally low, that any that is there is supplied by the critics promoting it. This is seen later.

12. Michael Fried's reasons for using Greenberg's rationale reflect his background (and most of the other formalist critics) as a "scholar," but more of it is due to his desire, I suspect, to bring his scholarly studies into the modern world. One can easily sympathize with his desire to connect, say, Tiepolo with Jules Olitski. One should never forget, however, that an historian loves history more than anything, even art.

13. Lucy Lippard uses this quotation in *Ad Reinhardt: Paintings* [exhibition catalogue] (New York: Jewish Museum, 1966), p. 28.

14. Lucy Lippard again, in "Constellation by Harsh Daylight: The Whitney Annual" [review], *Hudson Review* 21, no. 1 (Spring 1968), p. 180.

15. Arthur R. Rose, "Four Interviews," *Arts Magazine* 43, no. 4 (February 1969), p. 23.

16. As Terry Atkinson pointed out in his introduction to *Art-Language* 1 no. 1, the Cubists never questioned *if* art had morphological characteristics, but *which* ones in *painting* were acceptable.

17. When someone "buys" a Flavin he isn't buying a light show, for if he was he could just go to a hardware store and get the goods for considerably less. He isn't "buying" anything. He is subsidizing Flavin's activity as an artist.

18. A. J. Ayer, *Language, Truth, and Logic* (New York: Dover, 1946), p. 78.

19. Ibid., p. 57.

20. Ibid., p. 57.

21. Ibid., p. 90.

22. Ibid., p. 94.

23. *Ad Reinhardt: Paintings,* p. 12.

24. It is poetry's use of common language to attempt to *say the unsayable* which is problematic, not any inherent problem in the use of language within the context of art.

25. Ironically, many of them call themselves "Conceptual Poets." Much of this work is very similar to Walter de Maria's work and this is not coincidental; de Maria's work functions as a kind of "object" poetry, and his intentions are very poetic: he really wants his work to change men's lives.

26. Ayer, p. 82.

27. *Art-Language* 1, no. 1.

28. I did not (and still do not) understand this last decision. Since I first met Weiner, he defended his position (quite alien to mine) of being a "Materialist." I always found this last direction (e.g. *Statements*) sensical in *my* terms, but I never understood how it was in his.

29. I began dating my work with the *Art as Idea as Idea* series.

30. Atkinson, pp. 5–6.

31  All obtainable from Art & Language Press, 84 Jubilee Crescent, Coventry, England.

32. (Of which the author is the American editor.)

33. And Stella, too, of course. But Stella's work, which was greatly weakened by being painting, was made obsolete very quickly by Judd and others.

34. Smithson of course did spearhead the Earthwork activity—but his only disciple, Michael Heizer, is a "one idea" artist who hasn't contributed much. If you have thirty men digging holes and nothing develops out of that idea you haven't got much, have you? A very large ditch, maybe.

This text was first published in three parts in *Studio International,* 178:915–917 (October, November, December 1969), pp. 134–137, 160–161, 212–213. Included here are the first two of the three parts.

# introduction to *557,087*
## lucy r. lippard

**Benevolent societies seem persistently engaged in bringing things together that are apart, and taking things apart that are together, thus fostering the perceptual mobility of art which is destructive of genuine concentration.**

—Edgar Wind

Art has never succeeded in changing or integrating with society. Recently artists (Cage, Kaprow, Rauschenberg, Oldenburg, Rainer) have moved to encompass the world (or be encompassed by it) on a more fundamental level. Experience and awareness are, after all, shared by everyone. Art intended as pure experience doesn't exist until someone experiences it, defying ownership, reproduction, sameness. Intangible art could break down the artificial imposition of "culture" and provide a broader audience for a tangible, object art. When automation frees millions of hours for leisure, art should gain rather than diminish in importance, for while art is not just play, it is the counterpoint to work. The time may come when art is everyone's daily occupation, though there is no reason to think this activity will be called art.

\* \* \*

The experiences and motivations of a visual artist still differ from those of a poet, though as the media continue to mesh and the performing arts provide an increasingly relevant bridge between concrete art and concrete poetry, transitional figures continue to emerge (see the work of poets Acconci, Graham, and Perreault or artists Nauman, Wilson, and Barthelme in this exhibition).

At the moment the performance media offer extensions rather than alternatives to visual artists, since they are generally interested in the sensation of a kind of stopped or scrambled, unlinear time, not open to the performing arts, which exist in real time. Some of this comes in from literature like that of the very visually oriented Robbe-Grillet, but music and dance have also moved increasingly nearer to the plastic arts in their fascination with silence and near stasis, or very slow, extended and repetitive movement. Visual art retains no "purity of medium," but an autonomy of viewpoint remains, and is best translated into film.

\*  \*  \*

**Capitalist progress . . . not only reduces the environment of freedom, the "open space" of the human existence, but also the "longing," the need for such an environment.**
—Herbert Marcuse

**The engaged position is to run along the earth. . . . My ideal piece of sculpture is a road.**
—Carl Andre

The major sculptural innovation of the 60's is the horizontal viewpoint opened to a traditionally vertical art form, a fact that finally distinguishes sculpture from most architecture and, except for the linear, perspective depth implied, from painting. Vertical alignment is anthropomorphic, immediate, but static; the horizontal incorporates time distance, and is experienced and measured, kinesthetically. This is a logical result of the jet age. Floor sculpture is seen from an aerial viewpoint. Man sees everything differently once he has flown.

\*  \*  \*

Why did the chicken cross the road? To get to the other side.

**The course of development: Sculpture as form, Sculpture as structure, Sculpture as place.**
—Carl Andre

Sense of place varies: Baxter claims ready-made natural or artificial places. Andre's places are localized by his "found" or indigent materials and by his use of sculptural energy. *Lever* (1966) ran through a doorway; the line of hay bales at Windham (1968) began in the woods and moved into an open field. Smithson localizes place, though in a manner that incorporates (shrinks) long distance between site and nonsite, landscape and its test–tube counterpart (rock samples). Huebler's place is generalized when he imposes a geometrical or serial plan on large areas, times, distances, demanding no physical proof of their characteristics, but marking duration or extension by document. Richard Long's ten–mile walking tour sculpture (1967) was both local and general; despite the distance, a very regional sense was retained by the choice of area in which to walk.

\*   \*   \*

**Start a rumor.**
  —Steve Kaltenbach

**Live in your head.**
  —Keith Sonnier

**Art is only memory anyway.**
  —Michael Heizer

Ian Wilson, whose medium is "oral communication," preserves his apparently ephemeral art by "making it mnemonic . . . transcending particular times and particular places." How many people have seen Angkor Wat or the Isenheim Altarpiece more than once? Temporary art exists for less time but is no less accessible by photographic record. A "memorable art" is accessible to anyone who wants it enough to store it away. When computers provide artificial memories, our "private collections" will be unlimited, and the mind will be freer to pursue its own expanding awareness.

Idea or conceptual art, like that of Darboven, Atkinson, Baldwin, Borofsky, Kawara or Kosuth, and physically extant but imperceptible art like Barry's, share basic conditions with all previous art. What is radically new is its context, the exhibition and dissemination possibilities (c.f. Seth Siegelaub's March and Summer shows, 1969, which took place all over the world—simultaneously or however the artists chose to govern their time).

\*   \*   \*

Photography is a product of the non–relational aesthetic that pervades the 60's, and its ramifications for all the arts are innumerable. Still photography is notoriously unselective; though it can be made to falsify or over–dramatize its subject, once a viewpoint is chosen extraneous detail cannot be omitted, nor reality re– arranged. It can bring art to the level of everything else (Ruscha's books) or ricochet off reality (Baxter) or prove that the work of art exists specifically (Ruppersberg, Morris) or generally (Smithson, Huebler). Bruce Nauman extracts the punning potential of photography, as he dealt with puns in his seminal piled, random rubber sculpture (he, Hesse and Viner were the first abstract artists to work significantly with soft materials), then in his elaborately titled "representational" pieces, in photographs ("flour arrangement") and now in holograms. His films and tapes play deadpan act on timely fiction (fact taken on faith): "The True Artist Helps the World by Revealing Mystic Truths." "Do you believe that?" "I don't know. I think we should leave that open."

* * *

**Chance brings us closer to Nature in her manner of operation.**
     —John Cage

The more technologically sophisticated we become, the more we are able to plug into extant natural systems. Ecology, the relationship between an organism and its environment, interests some artists as a framework for control and change, others as a means of exploring the ratio of order and lack of order in nature. Haacke's "Live Airborne Systems" (1968) documents the movements of gulls taking bread from the sea. He has also worked with frost, condensation, evaporation, snow, mist, grass, representing the laboratory aspect of the more physically assertive earth sculpture. Hesse, Serra and Saret, in varying degrees of dematerialization, explore the effects of natural forces and controlled randomness on materials, while Ruscha's inclusiveness ("All the Buildings on the Sunset Strip") applies a similar idea to the artificial environment; Artschwager's "bips" and Buren's posters accent urban ecology.

* * *

**A word is worth 1,000th of a picture.**
     —Iain Baxter

The visual artist uses words to convey information about sensorial or potentially perceptible phenomena; his current preoccupation with linguistics, semantics, and social structures as exposed by anthropology is not surprising. The fact that it is indeed structural patterns that are the basis of these fields brings them into visual range.

**People deny that words have anything to do with pictures. I don't accept that. They do. Art is a source of information . . . the work concerns itself with things whose interrelationship is beyond perceptual experience. Because the work is beyond perceptual experience, awareness of the work depends on a system of documentation . . . photographs, maps, drawings and descriptive language.**

—Douglas Huebler

**All art originates in the human mind, in our reaction to the world rather than in the visible world in itself.**

—Ernst Gombrich

\*   \*   \*

If the insistent physical presence of the primary structures is a time–stopping device that resists the modern world's flux by creating new, frontal, static monuments to the present, most of the work here deals with energy, animation, non–sequential and relatively irrational lines of time and material. It can, however, be speculatively concrete, even when it is invisible. Despite deceptively scientific or pragmatic presentations, the artists generally accept and are involved with the unknown on a different level than scientists. Artists do not analyze circumstances with progress in mind so much as expose them, making themselves and their audience aware of things previously disregarded, information already in the environment which can be harnessed into aesthetic experience. And what can't be?

**The structures within which man functions should not be fortresses which exclude the external world, but interacting systems through which his life is made possible. Living and working space will then become organizational entities that will change as humans and the natural environment evolve.**

—The Pulsa Group

\*   \*   \*

The conviction that geometry is the most neutral vehicle for either physical or conceptual art ideas has been more directly transferred from minimal art into the new forms than is immediately obvious. Morris' felt is cut in rectangular sections before it assumes its own shapes; Smithson, Huebler, Baxter, Arnatt, Louw and others impose geometric overlays on space. If Morris is trying to expose the fallibility of order by refusing "to continue aestheticizing form by dealing with it as a prescribed end," a "systems aesthetic" continues the traditional artistic task of discovering underlying order in the world. Though the order found is far from traditionally constructed: "The special function of modern didactic art has been to show that art does not reside in material entities, but in relations between people and between people and the components of their environments" (Jack Burnham). Thus social comment (Oppenheim's extermination piece, Baldessari's ghetto boundaries) is possible, as well as a "regional art" made by foreigners through remote control (Ferrer's memorial to a Seattle engineer; McLean's Lake Washington piece).

*    *    *

**The most important question is Why? all the answers belong to What? and every real interest pertains to How?**
—Frederick Castle

When the artist determines the materials and allows the materials to determine the final shape or shape possibilities, he is dealing with a set of factors producing difficulties new to contemporary art. The Surrealists, and Pollock, had in mind an often unarticulated image context within a broad Freudian or Jungian framework, even when this content was not immediately recognizable.

The new "materialist," experience–oriented art has a recognizable content only in that it summons up a how–to–do– it picture of its execution in the viewer's mind. The lead was spattered against the wall with such and such a gesture; the rubber was poured and allowed to run off the edge of the mold this way; the sand was dumped that way and has spread according to succeeding events in its space. Ryman, the only painter involved, states unequivocally by his negation of the object quality of painting, that the path of what brush in what paint to produce what kind of surface is what matters.

*    *    *

Deliberately low-keyed art often resembles ruins, like neolithic rather than classical monuments, amalgams of past and future, remains of something "more," vestiges of some unknown venture. The ghost of content continues to hover over the most obdurately abstract art. The more open, or ambiguous, the experience offered, the more the viewer is forced to depend upon his own perceptions.

**I cannot experience your experience. You cannot experience my experience. We are both invisible men. All men are invisible to one another. Experience is man's invisibility to**

man. . . . Since your and their experience is invisible to me as mine is to you and them, I seek to make evident to the others, through their experience of my behavior, what I infer of your experience, through my experience of your behavior.

This is the crux of social phenomenology.

—R. D. Laing

\* \* \*

Pop Art questioned the subject matter and materials of art. Earthworks, outdoor projects, documentary and some "antiform" sculpture question the experience of art; they suggest that like the tree falling in the forest, art can be anything perceived as art by anyone at that time. An artist can make his own or his environment's presence felt by dropping a point, a line, an accent, a word into the world, embracing all or parts of any area or period at any place or time. Concurrently, the area's or period's importance can be neutralized until the art becomes more abstract than ever, even when it is virtually inseparable from life. The implication is that what we now consider art will eventually be unrecognizable. On the other hand, the boundaries of seeing, like the perceptible aspects of nature or outer space, seem to extend as infinitely as man's experience and experiments can take them.

Art teaches people how to see.

—Ad Reinhardt

\* \* \*

Freedom is a negative, it's freedom *from* something.

—Ad Reinhardt

The world is full of objects, more or less interesting, I do not wish to add any more. I prefer, simply, to state the existence of things in terms of time and/or place.

—Douglas Huebler

Andre's use of his materials as "the cut in space" has been extended by Weiner's "removals" and Heizer's "negative objects" (trenches, holes). Freeing the world from an inundation of "precious objects" is only a by– product, but it has also freed younger artists from restrictions imposed by traditional definitions of the plastic arts. Kosuth, who began with Reinhardtian negative photostats of these definitions, wants "to remove the experience from the work of art. . . . Non-artists often insist on something along with the art because they are not excited by the idea of art. They need that physical excitation along with the art to keep them interested.

But the artist has that same obsessed interest in art that the physicist has in physics and the philosopher in philosophy."

(. . .)

This text served as the introduction to the catalogue for the exhibition "557,087," organized by Lucy R. Lippard and staged at the Seattle Art Museum (5 September–5 October 1969). Lippard's introduction consists of twenty 4" × 6" index cards in random order; the catalogue as a whole consists of ninety-five text cards. The show and exhibition catalogue were subsequently retitled "955,000," when they traveled to the Vancouver Art Gallery (13 January–8 February 1970).

ian burn, mel bochner, charles harrison, seth siegelaub, athena tacha spear, kynaston mcshine, jack burnham, harold rosenberg, luis camnitzer, cildo meireles

**IV** 1970

# conceptual art as art

## ian burn

This article is an attempt to outline some general features of that which, during the past two or three years, has come to be known as Conceptual Art. It is the nature of this art that it replaces the customary visual object constructs with arguments about art, and this article will follow that pattern. Consequently, it is difficult to prepare a framework for an article in a country where the "advanced" in art is presented through the aesthetics of Modernist (or Formalist) painting and sculpture. Through the proliferation of such conceptually timid art (and I shall substantiate this later) one must conclude that, within the art-society, there is little acknowledgement that the "language" of painting and sculpture (i.e. aesthetics-as-art) has, during the past few years, been seriously questioned within the major (i.e. the conceptually germane) art of our time. I shall therefore begin with some background remarks concerning some recent art activities.

Contrary to what the professional art magazines convey, aesthetics is an issue only in Formalist art in which a direct function of the work is to be aesthetic. During the past decade, since the advent of the art of Judd, Morris, Flavin, LeWitt, Andre etc.,[1] the morphologically bounded "language" of painting etc. has ceased to be able to provide a basis for the introduction of a *conceptually new* art. As Donald Judd stated in 1963, "painting has to be as powerful as any kind of art; it can't claim a special identity, an existence for its own sake as a medium. If it does it will end up like lithography and etching." In other words, for painting to be "real," its problems must be problems of art. But neither painting nor sculpture is synonymous with art, though they may be *used* as art. To confuse the appearance of painting with art is to mistake the identity of a class of things with art itself (which of course has no appearance). Accepting such a basis for one's art entails advocating an *a priori* concept of what art can be and how it should appear.

The critical role sustaining the function of Formalist art depends on the Formalist presenting the "experience" and the critics presenting the "ideas." Such artists appear to have abandoned responsibility for their ideas in order to allow the critic to analyze (or interpret) the experience provided by the art. In addition, a whole hierarchy of roles is being maintained through this attitude; for example, galleries, museum officials, critics etc., who do not want art to change its traditional identity, depend for their vocation on the institutionalization of experience-as-art, aesthetics-as-art, and even investments-as-art. As such, art functions through polite and cultured "experiences" and this function is governed by an *a priori* concept of what art should be. It is precisely such a regulated function that Conceptual Art's "strict and radical extreme" seeks to usurp.

During the twentieth century, all innovations in art have been conceptual; to mistake as such the changing of say hard-edge to soft-edge is to have a peculiarly telescoped view of one's "language" and to confuse art's function with a kind of rearrangement of furniture. Since Cubism and Malevich's *Black Square,* through Reinhardt's Invisible Paintings, there has been an obsessive desire to abstract; that is, artists have wanted to remove their art from "the green world of flesh and bones" and purge it of anything that was recognizable (be it flying angels or abstract imagery). Anything in art that was not strictly art was progressively eliminated. Conceptual Art can be seen within this tradition; not only does it remove morphological significance as art, but it isolates "the art" from the form of presentation altogether.

The influence of Minimalism[2] on the thinking of certain of the Conceptual artists has been to bring about an awareness that the art-object is not self-supporting. One of Andre's Floors is art in the Dwan Gallery, but not necessarily if placed on a sidewalk; i.e. this object, lacking an identifiable morphology, now depends upon its context to be *seen* as art.[3] One such context is the "linguistic support" that the art-society provides for its art-works; and through such supports we identify an art-work as an art-work. In other words, "what is singled out depends entirely upon *how* one does one's singling out." Conceptual Art shifts the focus from what is said through the language to an investigation of the language itself;[4] it expands the art ideas beyond the limits of visual-object-making and in doing so repudiates all formal aesthetic considerations.

To put forward a generalized argument then, one could say that, following Minimalism, the artist's choice was either to "conceptualize" and discard the whole object framework or to "retinalize" and "return to Abstract Expressionism" etc. (the latter direction is well behaved and within the traditional visual status of art, hence it is well supported critically; in fact, such art-confectionery has reached pollution-level in New York where it is extravagantly promoted by the new galleries, the Whitney Annual et al.).

Today, many of the traditional functions of art, such as to provide cultural entertainment and decoration, have been supplanted by the modern world. If this world can provide us with aesthetic spectacles like the Empire State Building and TV relays from Mars, then is there any need for an art form restricted to similar macroscopic maneuvers? Once art is abstracted from its form of presentation and becomes strictly the artist's idea of art, it can, like science and philosophy, become serious and completely concerned with its own problems.

Once one understands that art is not *in* objects but in the completeness of the artist's *concept* of art, then the other functions can be eradicated and art can become more wholly art. (. . .)

## NOTES

1. This selection has been based on what has been conceptually relevant during the past few years. The "famous" Formalist artists (Noland, Stella, Olitski, Caro, etc.) have contributed little, in fact no *conceptually new* Formalist painting has emerged during the past decade, probably since Stella's paintings of 1959.

2. Minimal art has gathered little critical response and this is probably why it seems not to have been understood in Australia. Minimal artists are concerned enough with the conceptual content of their art to write about it themselves; they do not need critics to write it for them.

3. Greenberg's oft quoted dictum that "art is strictly a matter of experience" is the antipathy of Conceptual Art and apparently an attempt to see art-objects as empirical entities, outside of the artist's cognitive domain and in the domain (one assumes) of good food, mountains and thunderstorms!

4. The use of words is in itself of no importance. What is important is the art information carried by the words. The presentation of art writing "as art" does not mean that the form of the words is aesthetically significant.

This text was published in *Art and Australia*, 8:2 (September 1970), pp. 167–170.

# excerpts from speculation (1967–1970)
## mel bochner

For a variety of reasons I do not like the term "conceptual art." Connotations of an easy dichotomy with perception are obvious and inappropriate. The unfortunate implication is of a somewhat magical/mystical leap from one mode of existence to another. The problem is the confusion of idealism and intention. By creating an original fiction, "conceptualism" posits its special non-empirical existence as a positive (transcendent) value. But no amount of qualification (or documentation) can change the situation. Outside the spoken word, no thought can exist without a sustaining support.

*A fundamental assumption in much recent past art was that things have stable properties, i.e. boundaries. This seemingly simple premise became the basis for a spiraling series of conclusions. Boundaries, however, are only the fabrication of our desire to detect them . . . a tradeoff between seeing something and wanting to enclose it. For example, what we attribute to objects as "constancy of size," during their progressive diminution when we walk away from them, is not a set of snapshot images gradually blending together. Concentration produces the illusion of consistency. Sight itself is pre-logical and without constants (out-of-focus). The problem is that surrendering the stability of objects immediately subverts any control we think we have over situations. Consider the possibility that the need to identify with objects is probably the outgrowth of the need to assign our feelings to the things that prompt them.*

The "history of art" and the "history of painting and sculpture" are not the same, but merely coincident at some points.

*Immediate experience will not cohere as an independent domain. Memories tend to be remains, not of past sensations, but past verbalizations. The discussion of much recent art has attempted the substitution of stimulus information for sensation (exterior vs. interiorization). This has not resolved discreteness with continuity. Perception of an object is generally pre-conceived as taking place within a point by point time. This disconnected time, a lingering bias of tense in language, restricts our experiencing the conjunction between object and observation. When this conjunction is acknowledged, "things" become indistinguishable from events. Carried to its conclusion, physicality, or what separates the material from the non-material (the object from our observation), is merely a contextual detail.*

*A structure that concerns the non-object-oriented artist is the language which he uses to formulate his thoughts. There is nothing inherently anti-visual about this pursuit. Works of art are not illustrations of ideas.*

If, as it has been said, time presupposes a view of time, perception also includes its presuppositions. Perception is geared to cancel out whatever is stray or unaccountable. "Background" is characterized negatively as the unclear, indistinct, and nonarticulated. But background is neither the margin nor fringe of the implicit. It is only through the function of its "opening out" that we are presented with a passage to the density of things. The realm of ideas is the operative link preceding any of the forms of objectness: it is an expanse of directions, not dimensions; of settings, not points; of regions, not planes; of routes, not distances. Beneath materiality are not merely facts but a radiation spreading out beyond dimensionality, involvement, and signification.

*What if we were to only think about the place from which works of art enter our consciousness? Five possibilities come to mind:*

*1 — that which we look up at*
*2 — that which we look down upon*
*3 — that which we see straight on*
*4 — that which we are surrounded by*
*5 — that which is not seen by looking*

*(One dividend of such an approach could be the erasure from our minds of all vestiges of the listless "object quality" of paintings, or the leaden "specific materials" of sculpture.) We could then simply concentrate on where we are looking. Consideration of "where" implies more than an ontology of position. It suggests that differentiations by style need not be made and then transformed into values. All art exists as it exists within its own described set of conditions. The only aesthetic question is recognition . . . re-cognition . . . thinking it again.*

A desire to eliminate "furniture" from art is not nihilistic. What does initially appear "sterile" is an attitude that establishes nothing, produces little, and by its very nature cancels out results. Also there is the gratuitousness of being unwilling to transform the world or accumulate in it . . .

*At the risk of appearing self-contradictory, I do not believe art is understood through intellectual operations, but rather that we intercept the outline of a certain manner of treating (being in) the world.*

Thinking via the constant intervention of procedures, one over another, filters out the arbitrariness of conventional thought patterns. Any sort of in-formation or re-formation can be diverted by externally maintained constants. The fascination with seriality and modular form (which continues, disguised, in the work of many artists) made it possible, at one point, to clarify and distinguish the processes involved in the realization of the work of art. Ordered proceduralism often led to an inversely proportional visual complexity. Suppression of internal relational concerns opened the way for the involvement with ideas beyond the concentricity of objects. It became apparent that the entire foundation of art experienced from a "point-of-view" was irrelevant to art of attenuated size or total surround, i.e., works without experienced centers. A case in point is the work made in and for a single place. Wall-works, for example, simply bypass double supports. Marks on the wall, here forward and in view, there only peripherally visible, held where they are by the wall's mass . . . spread *along* the surface. They cannot be "held," only seen. As such they are neither copy nor paradigm. Art of this nature is not secondly present. Its uniqueness (single-placedness) is its co-existent unity with its own appearance.

*Formalist art is predicated on a congruency between form and content. Any artist who considers this dichotomy either irreconcilable (or desirable) is no longer interested in formal relationships. For this artist the activity of making is not equivalent to the informing of content (a more appropriate word would be "intent"). Certain intents are capable of various equally viable realizations.*

Imagination is a word that has been generally banned from the vocabulary of recent art. Associations with any notion of special power reserved for artists or of a "poetical world" of half dreams seem particularly unattractive. There is, however, within the unspecified usage of the word a function which infuses the process of making and seeing art. The root word "image" need not be used only to mean representation (in the sense of one thing referring to something other than itself). To re-present can be defined as the shift in referential frames of the viewer from the space of events to the space of statements or vice versa. Imagining (as opposed to imaging) is not a pictorial pre-occupation. Imagination is a projection, the exteriorizing of ideas about the nature of things seen. It re-produces that which is initially without product. A good deal of what we are "seeing" we are, in this sense, actually imagining. There is an overlap in the mind of these two dissimilar activities. We cannot see what we cannot imagine.

*One does not frequently think with his eyes closed, although what one is thinking at any moment need not be directly concerned with what one is looking at. A non-visual thought (one without back-ground) seems highly unlikely.*

Ultimately, description as a critical method fails. Pretending to a non-subjective rendering of the object, it cuts off the peripheral pressures of experience. When visual data is accepted as the only basis of apprehension, there is no possibility for an account of intentions. At the same time, descriptive self-enclosure does not create itself as its own sole recipient.

*Would anything change if sensible things were conceived of as "across" space, rather than "in" space? First, objects would cease to be the locus of sight. Then, no longer centers in themselves, they would demand to be perceived as the organization by everything around them. What might result from this conjecture is a sense of trajectory rather than of identity. That which common sense has always presented as a unity (objects) become only the negatives in a field of determinants. Opaque, yet fragmented, what is seen is only what stops my view beyond . . . it is in front of me but without being in depth. Profiled in this way, matter surrenders its obstinate chunkiness to reveal only a position in a cross section of orientations and levels, these levels merge on but one plane into dimensional sense data. And even on this plane, thought can efface them.*

Aprocedural work of art is initiated without a set product in mind. In a piece of this kind the interest is only in knowing that the procedures, step by step, have been carefully and thoroughly carried through. The specific nature of any result is contingent on the time and place of implementation, and is interesting as such. It is the "proceeding" that establishes it.

*On approaching the threshold of non-enduring art, we can easily postulate an art of micro-seconds . . . but rarely see it. Why does art have to be any more distinct than peripheral vision? I do not mean this in the sense of "now-you-see-it-now-you-don't." I am imagining an art which by taking up all the expected requirements of our basic modes of perception would, in so doing, render itself invisible.*

In the context of visual art what could the term "de-materialization" mean? I find that it contains an essential contradiction which renders it useless as an idea. The inherent weakness is revealed when the derivation of the term is examined. Tracing the origin of the idea leads one back to the basic confusion in the notion of "abstraction." All "abstract art" is premised on the belief in a first-level reality composed of constituent and separate qualities. In order to arrive at a truer "reality," the abstract artist must take apart this composite structure. The act of disjointure was to result in an intensification of the abstracted quality (color, shape, texture, etc.). This then became the material for further manipulation. The entire substructure of this concept is flawed. It simply is not possible to break things down into classifiable components, at least not without destroying the essential unity that is their existence. The blue of my typewriter is inseparable from its smooth surface. The blue-smooth surface was not created by combining a blue with a "smooth." Abstraction is an analytical method and not a reversible equation. One further step along this same line of reasoning yields "de-materialization." If all qualities are taken away, you have de(no)-materialization (components). But given the evidence that abstraction itself is without credible grounds, can one derive from it a second level . . . a completely non-ontological art? My disagreement with de-materialization goes beyond a squabble with terms. There is no art which does not bear some burden of physicality. To deny it is to descend to irony. Words set up circumstances for understanding, and this particular one only perpetuates old confusions. It is misleading to the intentions of artists finding different ways for art to come into being . . . and both how and how long it stays there.

This text was published in *Artforum,* 8:9 (May 1970), pp. 70–73.

Progress Report: daily record of performance time:
First month (February 1970):

| Date | Duration |
|---|---|
| Feb. 1 | 3 min. 20 sec. |
| 2 | 3 min. 40 sec. |
| 3 | 3 min. 8 sec. |
| 4 | 3 min. 12 sec. |
| 5 | 3 min. 20 sec. |
| 6 | 3 min. 16 sec. |
| 7 | 6 min. 36 sec. |
| 8 | 8 min. 0 sec. |
| 9 | 8 min. 48 sec. |
| 10 | 3 min. 52 sec. |
| 11 | 9 min. 8 sec. |
| 12 | 9 min. 0 sec. |
| 13 | 10 min. 12 sec. |
| 14 | 10 min. 44 sec. |
| 15 | 11 min. 12 sec. |
| 16 | 11 min. 40 sec. |
| 17 | 13 min. 20 sec. |
| 18 | 13 min. 48 sec. |
| 19 | 14 min. 40 sec. |
| 20 | 14 min. 52 sec. |
| 21 | 15 min. 40 sec. |
| 22 | 17 min. 24 sec. |
| 23 | 18 min. 8 sec. |
| 24 | 19 min. 12 sec. |
| 25 | 20 min. 36 sec. |
| 26 | 21 min. 16 sec. |
| 27 | 21 min. 48 sec. |
| 28 | 23 min. 0 sec. |

An 18-inch stool is set up in my apartment and used as a step.

Each morning, during the designated months, I step up and down the stool at the rate of 30 steps per minute. Each day, I step up and down until I can't go on and I am forced to stop.

Improvement, and the ability to sustain improvement, is put to the test: after the first month's activity, there's a one-month layoff, then a three-month layoff.

(Announcements are sent out inviting the public to come see the activity in my apartment any day during the designated months. At the end of each month's activity, a progress report is sent out to the public.)

Vito Acconci, *Step Piece (Steps: Stepping-Off Place),* Apartment 6B, 102 Christopher Street, New York City, 1970. Activity/Performance, 4 months (February, April, July, November); varying times each day.

# on exhibitions and the world at large

## charles harrison and seth siegelaub

(. . .)

Charles Harrison: Do you think exhibitions affect looking at art?

Seth Siegelaub: They can. But usually pejoratively. In a large sense, everything is situation. In an exhibition situation the context—other artists, specific works—begins to imply, from without, certain things about any art work. The less standard the exhibition situation becomes, the more difficult to "see" the individual work of art. So that an exhibition with six works of one artist and one of another begins to bring to bear on the art pre-exhibition values that prejudice the "seeing" process. All choices in the predetermination of the exhibition hinder the viewing of the intrinsic value of each work of art. Themes, judgmental criticism, preferences for individual artists expressed by differences in the number of works, all prejudge art.

C. H.: Can exhibitions ever serve the intentions of the artist, and if so, how?

S. S.: When artists show together their art shares a common space and time. This situation makes differences more obvious—if only by proximity. If all the conditions for making art were standard for all artists—same materials, size, color, etc.—there would still be great artists and lesser artists. The question of context has always been important. The nature of the exhibition situation begins to assume a "neutral" condition as one standardizes the elements in the environment in which art is "seen." I think exhibitions can function to clarify or focus in on certain dominant interests of an artist. As we know now, things that look alike are not necessarily alike. Certain exhibitions present differences better than others. Most exhibitions stress similarities, at the expense of the individual works.

C. H.: If the responsibility of the organizer is to standardize, what sort of choices can he take upon himself?

S. S.: The choice of specific artists and of the environment in which their work is to be placed.

C. H.: What conditions these decisions?

S. S.: The personal sensibility of the organizer, obviously. We're all critics, the most important criticism being "yes" or "no." After that his decisions should be in the realm of the practical and logistical, not the aesthetic. The organizer should have as little responsibility as possible for the specific art.

C. H.: Have the conditions for exhibitions changed as art has changed, and if so, how?

S. S.: Until 1967, the problems of exhibition of art were quite clear, because at that time the "art" of art and the "presentation" of art were coincident. When a painting was hung, all the necessary intrinsic art information was there. But gradually there developed an "art" which didn't need to be hung. An art wherein the problem of presentation paralleled one of the problems previously involved in the making and exhibition of a painting: i.e. *to make someone else aware that an artist had done anything at all.* Because the work was not visual in nature, it did not require the traditional means of exhibition, but a means that would present the intrinsic ideas of the art.

For many years it has been well known that more people are aware of an artist's work through (1) the printed media or (2) conversation than by direct confrontation with the art itself. For painting and sculpture, where: the visual presence—color, scale, size, location—is important to the work, the photograph or verbalization of that work is a bastardization of the art. But when art concerns itself with things not germane to physical presence its intrinsic (communicative) value is not altered by its presentation in printed media. The use of catalogues and books to communicate (and disseminate) art is the most neutral means to present the new art. The catalogue can now act as primary information for the exhibition, as opposed to secondary information *about* art in magazines, catalogues, etc., and in some cases the "exhibition" can be the "catalogue." I might add that presentation—"how you are made aware of the art"—

is common property, the same way that paint colors or bronze are common property to all painters or sculptors. Whether the artist chooses to present the work as a book or magazine or through an interview or with sticker labels or on billboards, it is not to be mistaken for the "art" ("subject matter"?).

C. H.: The organizer's response to an art "idea" is still primary. Where no other information is available, the man who takes responsibility for making someone else aware that an artist has done something can still make his own response absolutely intrusive; a kind of filter between the work and everyone else.

S. S.: It's a question of where an artist will give up his choice. This is a vitally important difference between the new work and what has preceded it. Whereas painters have generally never specified how much light their paintings should be seen by, what size wall they should be hung on—they have left it up to you *implicitly*—this new body of work *explicitly* denies any responsibility for presentation. All you need to see a painting is light. This new work doesn't even concern itself with that. The question of what environment you see the work in has nothing to do with what has been done. If it is made clear that the presentation of the work is not to be confused with the work itself, then there can be no misreadings of it. If an audience is made aware of an artist's work and he knows that *how* he is made aware is not within the artist's control or concern, then its specific presentation can be taken for granted.

C. H.: How do you make it clear?

S. S.: The standardizing of the exhibition situation begins to make the specific intentions of the artists clearer.

C. H.: Do you feel that this new work cannot, by its very nature, be misused as earlier work has often been in mixed exhibitions?

S. S.: No. By selection you could choose ideas between artists that parallel each other, just as you could pick up fifty stripe paintings and make them look more alike than they really are. You could load any exhibition situation in the same way. Orienting a show is not any more or less possible than it was when painting was painting and sculpture was sculpture. You can still make anything look like what you want it to. Figures don't lie; accountants do.

C. H.: So how has your function as an exhibition organizer been different from anyone else's?

S. S.: By keeping the exhibition situation as uniform as possible for each and all of the artists in the exhibition and not relying on outside verbal information like catalogue introductions, thematic titles, etc., I've tried to avoid prejudicing the viewing situation.

C. H.: This holds good as long as no one can begin to identify a "house style" in what you do.

S. S.: True. Failure is imminent. Unfortunately over a period of twenty exhibitions one begins to *become* the theme and the cement; which begins to be as offensive as prefaces, thematic titles etc.

C. H.: Do you think then that every exhibition organizer has only a limited time before his activity becomes harmful to the artist?

S. S.: Only if he's successful. Yes. Because his opinions begin to become more important than what his opinions are about.

C. H.: Important for whom?

S. S.: For the people who are aware of the exhibitions he is doing.

C. H.: Do you think the development of this situation can affect the artists?

S. S.: It can only be detrimental to the artists for the same reasons.

C. H.: Do you think this now means that it is dangerous for artists to be associated with you?

S. S.: I don't know. Certainly right now it is. I may be a total bind. I don't really know. There are certain artists who interest me right now who would conceivably be the focus for some interests of mine. I feel my dilemma now is to be able to deal with art generally but not get involved specifically with specific artists. Everyone's pushing artists; which is OK, but I want to move away from that.

C. H.: Is there anything to move into?

S. S.: I don't know. I'm still interested in distributing art and art information. I personally value my network of booksellers and my mailing list throughout the world as a very important aspect of what I do. I am concerned with getting art out into the world and plan to continue publishing in multilingual editions to further this end. This is a very important communications consideration. American museums, with typical chauvinism, never publish in more than one language—just English.

C. H.: This implies that despite being a New Yorker, you are interested in decentralization.

S. S.: I think that New York is beginning to break down as a center. Not that there will be another city to replace it, but rather that where any artist is will be the center. International activity. It is more important to send artists to exhibitions than to send art. Art centers arise because artists go there. They go there because of (1) geographic and climatic factors (2) access to other artists (3) access to information and power channels and (4) money. These factors are now becoming balanced throughout the world. To be part of this changing situation interests me very much.

C. H.: Do you think the new art has forced a new relationship between artists and those involved in art in a secondary capacity—dealers, critics, exhibition organizers, etc.?

S. S.: Yes, very definitely. I doubt whether artists have ever been so articulate about what they're doing as they are right now.[1]

C. H.: So what's the nature of the new relationship?

S. S.: There are really two types of people: artists and everyone else.

C. H.: Artists have art and everyone else has relative amounts of power to manipulate or promote art. So where's the relationship and what's new about it?

S. S.: The need for an intermediary begins to become lessened. The new work is more accessible as art to the community: it needs fewer interpretive explanations.

C. H.: Do you think art ever needed interpretive explanations?

S. S.: I don't know anything about history, but the art we're talking about seems to be much more self-explanatory than any other. It just goes from mind to mind as directly as possible. The need for a community of critics to explain it seems obviously superfluous right now.

C. H.: Is this perhaps because they have fewer specifics to deal with?

S. S.: Yes. I think a basic underlying tendency in all art today is the ability of the artist to set general limits and not care about being specific. The tendency in practically all art today is towards generality about how things look rather than what specific things look like.

C. H.: How can this be made explicit in exhibitions?

S. S.: By organizing exhibitions in which the general conditions are proposed to the artists and the decisions about specifics are left entirely to them. Artists are the best judges of their own work. The general feeling one got from Harald Szeemann's show "When Attitudes become Form"[2]—the nonchalance of it—did much to enhance the viewing situation for individual works.

C. H.: Maybe the most important thing a critic or organizer or whatever can do is to draw attention to what is art by isolating what is not and acting to devalue it.[3]

**NOTES**

1. "What I say is part of the art work. I don't look to critics to say things about my work. I tell them what it's about."—Douglas Huebler

2. "When Attitudes Become Form" was first shown at the Kunsthalle, Berne, in March/April 1969, and has also been seen in Krefeld and at the ICA in London (August/September 1969).
3. "I want to remove the experience from the work of art."—Joseph Kosuth

This interview was first published in *Studio International,* 178:917 (December 1969), pp. 202–203.

# notes towards art work

## charles harrison

Art now has no object in view.

Some withdrawals are more operative than most engagements.

**Is it that the only useful thing a sculptor can do, being a three-dimensional thinker and therefore one hopes a responsible thinker, is to assert himself twice as hard in a negative way?**

    —Barry Flanagan (June 1963)

**A stack of several hundred blank sheets of paper—one for each day on which a concept was rejected.**

    — work by Christine Kozlov

**You can only make absolute statements negatively.**

    —Ad Reinhardt[1]

Operative: this word only has meaning in regard to the possibilities. Which suggests that you can't get out of the context of art even if you're misguided enough to want to try.[2]

**There's no such thing as anti-art; there's only art.**
　　—Victor Burgin

**Art's only claim is for art. Art is the definition of art.**
　　—Joseph Kosuth[3]

**There is just one art, one art-as-art.**
　　—Ad Reinhardt[4]

Art is the only sure means of judging art. Art criticizes art (i.e. it elucidates it, reshuffles it, re-arranges it, re-enlivens it). Art stays within the area of art; the area of art expands by accretion, it does not alter through redirection. Pseudo-art continually aspires to non-art conditions: hence "anti-art," "technologic art," "pop art," etc., etc. The art is either there or it's not; the labels—"anti," "technologic," "pop" and so on—direct attention away from the issue into less critical areas. (E.g. Lichtenstein is more involved with art than with pop: pop in Lichtenstein's work is a metaphor for presentation, which is not-art. His real endeavor is corrective and critical. His public Pop image is misleading and irrelevant and nothing much to do with him anyway.) Pseudo-art is involved with avenues of escape from art. An art position can harden into a pseudo-art position. Similarly, involved criticism can harden into pseudo-criticism. Greenberg's concept of Novelty Art movements similarly acts as if to obfuscate ideas which operate within the context of art but outside Greenberg's concept of "Modernism." (The longer this term retains currency the more ironic its modes of employment become.)

For Greenberg to imply that one cube sculpture can usefully be differentiated in value from another only in terms of its visual quality—i.e. through the comparative "rightness" of its size, surface, etc.—is patently ridiculous.[5] (For a start, how can there be a specific and meaningful size for a cube, relative to other cubes?) Two separate but identical cubes could be two very different works of art at different dates or even in two different places at the same date (maybe that distinction has no meaning anyway). It seems pointless to pretend that one can come to a work of art with no prior information about anything except a narrow range of earlier art objects, or to pretend that certain kinds of information—specifically about probable intentions—can be screened off at the moment of "aesthetic contemplation." Any information which the artist provides will inevitably become a part of the spectator's area of consideration—and this includes titles, however flippantly added.

Certain artists, in taking a "my-life-is-my-art" attitude, are doing no more (nor less) than making explicit the extreme and inevitable consequences of this truism. There is of course no inherent virtue in this: it's only fatalism after all. To counter this, art has always thrown up new strategies by means of which certain endeavors can be made to read as relatively specific. This is often a question of medium—e.g. the distinct and various means of presentation for Joseph Kosuth's *Art as Idea as Idea.* Ironically, the more in-series the condition of the work presented, the more a considered presentation is needed to render the work accessible as something specific. To put it another way, the more explicit the strategy, or the more evident the distinction between strategy and purpose, the heavier the demand for a strategy which will stand up to scrutiny. Art of this kind does not evade criticism; it challenges it out in the open.

The critic's policy is characteristically to divide and rule: divide the presentation from the idea and rule the presentation (or the presentation of the presentation), confident that few will notice that the idea has been sacrificed. It is a sad irony that the critic, knowing that literacy will tend to be mistaken for intelligence by those who are less literate, can always rely on literary presentation to characterize his status as one involved with art.

Alas, information supplied by the artist is not all, however indiscriminate, that comes up for consideration: in the end, the spectator's experience of the work of art will come to include information imposed upon the art work by writers and others. Mud does stick. Fried's criticism is now a part of Noland's art. No wonder the better artists tend to protect their work from indifferent exposure; i.e. to protect the idea from indiscriminate presentation of its presentation. The notion of "cubes" obscures the endeavor of Braque and Picasso and no critic's initiative will prize it loose.

Artists tend to become indifferent to the continued currency of such labels perhaps only because for them words lose their meaning faster and become abstract. This situation may not last much longer. Duchamp's ironic instructions, anti-informative legends and complex nonsensical puns pointed the way—through the looking-glass as it were—towards an investigation of language on art's terms; i.e. within the context of art—not literary—ideas. Just now language seems potentially operative as never before within the primary art context.

The artist's indifference to literacy is the one hope for the salvation of language as a means to illuminate art. By the same token, the artist's comparative indifference to traditions of critical or art-historical thought invests him with a sole authority for illuminating past endeavors in art. The rest is archaeology at one extreme and public relations at the other. At best the perceptive critic informed about art history can do no more than give a literate exposition of the effect of a current art endeavor upon our understanding of the significance of earlier work.

Art alone is engaged with other art on equal terms.

Most of what is seen as Art is just Picturesque. Picturesque situations are established by the evidence of solutions—"formal resolution," "style," "character," "brushwork" etc.—rather than by dilemmas.[6] Everything I easily think of as a way of making art involves the picturesque. Much writing on art is nostalgia evoked by picturesque situations. (English culture particularly has a heavy bias in favor of the literary/scenic . . . even today. How to defeat an Eng. Lit. education? How to be anyone but Wordsworth?)

The major problem is never how to do something; it's always what to do. Those who are concerned principally with how to do it have got presentation confused with art. (At the second-hand level of course this also applies to critics.) There's no excuse for this nowadays;[7] which is to say that anyone involved principally in how to do it can be taken as having opted for convention rather than creation: i.e. in the end you know you'll forget them. Criticism concerned primarily with resolution does more harm than good in the end: because the problem becomes more important than what it's about,[8] and bad artists are promoted because they have the "right" concerns (even long after these concerns have any relevance to art). This is yet another way of avoiding confrontation with art. Ideas pursued beyond their currency in art become ideas concerning the picturesque. (E.g. most formalist criticism is now defense of the picturesque.)

Criticism never holds good for long.

The only alternative to criticism is art.

**(When somebody says, "Well, where do you go from here or where do *you* go from here?" I say, "Well, where do you want to go?" There's no place to go. . . .**
—Ad Reinhardt.[9])

## NOTES

1. From an interview with Ad Reinhardt by Phyllisann Kallick, published in *Studio International* (December 1967).

2. An anti-art gesture only has iconoclastic significance within the context of art. It's only

remarkable to pick up the ball and run with it if everyone thinks you're playing soccer. Even then you're still playing games.

3. In "Art after Philosophy," *Studio International* (October 1969), conclusion.

4. From "There is just one Painting: Art-as-art dogma, part XIII," *Artforum* (March 1966).

5. "The quality of art depends on inspired, felt relations or proportions as on nothing else. There is no getting round this. A simple, unadorned box can succeed as art by virtue of these things, and when it fails as art it is not because it is merely a plain box, but because its proportions, or even its size, are uninspired, unfelt . . . . The superior work of art, whether it dances, radiates, explodes, or barely manages to be visible (or audible or decipherable), exhibits, in other words, rightness of 'form.'" (The degree of progress made in formalist criticism can be judged by comparing Greenberg's use of the concept of "rightness of form" in 1968 with Clive Bell's of "significant form" some 55 years earlier. Both usages imply that, in the face of "inspiration," linguistic precision must ultimately bow to mystification.) The passage quoted is from Greenberg's "Avant-garde Attitudes—New Art in the Sixties," the John Power Lecture in Contemporary Art, delivered at the University of Sydney on 17 May 1968 and published by the Power Institute of Fine Arts, 1969. The above passage is immediately followed by a surely wrong-headed account of Duchamp's intentions. It seems to be a characteristic enterprise of the formalist critics to put down "minimal" art on the basis of the misinterpreted intentions of one "forbear" or unrepresentative representative. For example see Fried's use of Tony Smith's (!) prose to put down the whole of minimal art (as if "minimal art" were viable as an entity anyway), in "Art and Objecthood," *Artforum* (Summer 1967).

6. "There are all kinds of things going on in art, but they have nothing to do with the pretensions of a serious painter"—Ad Reinhardt (see note 1).

7. Because there have been a lot of artists by now who have labored to make the point. It's a long list and starts with Duchamp if not earlier. In scorning the "visual thrill" in Courbet's work I don't think Duchamp necessarily meant that he thought Courbet a bad painter. Duchamp's critical propositions were aimed at "Art" and not at artists. *L.H.O.O.Q. rasé* is an underestimated key work (and pre-empts, incidentally, most of the questions later posed by Rauschenberg's *Erased de Kooning*), but it doesn't in any way devalue the *Mona Lisa;* quite the reverse: it "restores" it as if by cleaning off layers of browned varnish—it renders it operative once more.

8. I owe this way of expressing this point to Seth Siegelaub; see "On Exhibitions and the World at Large," *Studio International* (December 1969).

9. From a talk, "Art as Art Dogma," given at the ICA in May 1964. Transcript published in *Studio International* (December 1967).

This text was published in *Studio International,* 179:919 (February 1970), pp. 42–43.

GENERAL IDEA,
87 YONGE ST.,
TORONTO, CANADA.

Please record your orgasms on the enclosed chart for one month and return to GENERAL IDEA. Master charts will be made, indicating distribution and frequency patterns and applying these to non-related maps, charts, graphs. New fields of unforeseen information are thus set up. If you wish further document- ation of this project, please enclose your name and address with the chart.

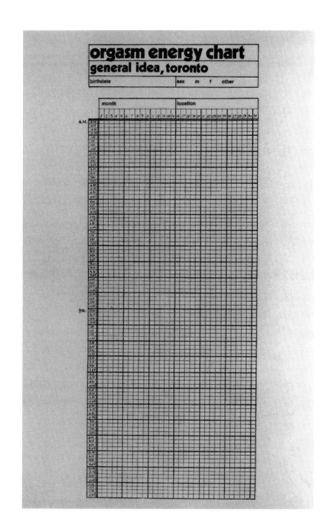

General Idea, *Orgasm Energy Chart*, 1970.

# introduction to *art in the mind*
## athena tacha spear

The exhibition *Art in the Mind* was prompted by certain consequences of recent developments in the visual arts. First of all, a significant amount of ecologic or other large outdoor art remains at the stage of projects for lack of funds, or simply because it is yet unrealizable. An even larger percentage of ecologic art enters history only through description and photographic documentation, due to its temporary nature and the inaccessibility of its location. Furthermore, a great amount of other recent art consists of acts and statements, or exists on the fringe between material reality and language. A description often evokes the work to an adequate degree. At times, the concept is as satisfactory as its execution, or even more so, because each execution is only a particular aspect of the idea. In other cases, a description is the only possible materialization of a work which otherwise would exist unperceived by our senses. Most often, the piece is constituted by a set of directions to be performed by any individual; the artistic experience may necessitate execution of the given directions, but in some instances the work can be perceived by simply imagining the results. The performed activity or part of it can be documented by photographs and other means, which are a by-product and, again, the only remainder of the real existence of the work.

It is within these premises that most idea art (including "street works") functions. However, there is still another, more specific category—pure or radical conceptual art—which uses as its exclusive medium the written language. Since one of its main objectives is to investigate and redefine the concept "art," a great deal of this writing verges upon art theory and philosophy. Most (if not all) conceptual artists started working in a visual medium, but have eliminated every trace of visual element from their present art. Yet, their work still belongs to the world of form, because it consists of *structuring* artistic thought and creating thought structures. As Sol LeWitt, one of the progenitors of conceptual art, puts it: "Since no form is intrinsically superior to another, the artist may use any form, from an expression of words (written or spoken) to physical reality, equally."[1] And in the words of Ian Burn, a younger member of the movement: "Artists are exploring language to create access to ways of seeing."[2]

In the last years, there have been a number of exhibitions which include primarily written material and photographs. Although this situation still feeds the gallery-collector system and satisfies the need of the artists to *exhibit* their works, it seems to be a highly artificial situation. The interested spectator is not given the best chance to absorb new complex thoughts by standing in front of a wall covered with endless typed or hand-scribbled pages; and the space of art museums and galleries is wasted when filled with documents. Such material belongs to publications and libraries—although it should be presented and initiated by museums and dealers. The attitude of the pioneering art dealer Seth Siegelaub[3] seems to be the most appropriate one: exhibitions of idea art can consist only of their catalogues. *Art in the Mind* follows this example. Its primary intention is to include works which are not suitable for a traditional museum (although some of them are exhibitable), and to offer a panorama of such art in its various aspects. (. . .)

## NOTES

1. Sol LeWitt, "Sentences on Conceptual Art," *Art-Language,* no. 1 (May 1969), p. 12.

2. Ian Burn, "Dialogue," in the July 1969 mimeographed publication of Art Press (New York), p. 5.

3. I am grateful to both Seth Siegelaub and Lucy Lippard for their willingness to give me information on younger artists for this exhibition.

This text was written as the introduction to the exhibition "Art in the Mind," staged at Oberlin College, Oberlin, Ohio (17 April–12 May 1970).

# introduction to *information*
## kynaston mcshine

Each artist was invited to create his own contribution to this book, a situation which meant that the material presented would be either directly related to the actual work in the show, or independent of it. Therefore, this book is essentially an anthology and considered a necessary adjunct to the exhibition. Contrary to the McLuhan thesis, books are still a major communication system, and perhaps becoming even more important, given "the global village" that the world has become. After all, *Time* magazine is available almost everywhere on Wednesday mornings.

The material presented by the artists is considerably varied, and also spirited, if not rebellious—which is not very surprising, considering the general social, political, and economic crises that are almost universal phenomena of 1970. If you are an artist in Brazil, you know of at least one friend who is being tortured; if you are one in Argentina, you probably have had a neighbor who has been in jail for having long hair, or for not being "dressed" properly; and if you are living in the United States, you may fear that you will be shot at, either in the universities, in your bed, or more formally in Indochina. It may seem too inappropriate, if not absurd, to get up in the morning, walk into a room, and apply dabs of paint from a little tube to a square of canvas. What can you as a young artist do that seems relevant and meaningful?

One necessity is, therefore, at least to move with the cultural stresses and preoccupations (as if you had a choice), particularly with the obvious changes in lifestyle. The art cannot afford to be provincial, or to exist only within its own history, or to continue to be, perhaps, only a commentary on art. An alternative has been to extend the idea of art, to renew the definition, and to think beyond the traditional categories—painting, sculpture, drawing, printmaking, photography, film, theater, music, dance, and poetry. Such distinctions have become increasingly blurred. Many of the highly intellectual and serious young artists represented here have addressed themselves to the question of how to create an art that reaches out to an audience larger than that which has been interested in contemporary art in the last few decades. Their attempt to be poetic and imaginative, without being either aloof or condescending has led them into the communications areas that *information* reflects.

Superficially considered, some might seem to be directly involved with dandyism and the "gesture," and while some are, others use these as approaches to more subtle, sophisticated, and profound ends. The activity of these artists is to think of concepts that are broader and more cerebral than the expected "product" of the studio. With the sense of mobility and change that pervades their time, they are interested in ways of rapidly exchanging ideas, rather than embalming the idea in an "object." However, the idea may reside on paper or film. The public is constantly bombarded with strong visual imagery, be it in the newspapers or periodicals, on television or in the cinema. An artist certainly cannot compete with a man on the moon in the living room. This has therefore created an ambiguous and ironic position for the artist, a dilemma as to what he can do with contemporary media that reach many more people than the art gallery.

In the reevaluation of their situation, some artists have attempted to extend themselves into their environment and to work with its problems and events. Some have become aware of their own bodies, in a way that has nothing to do with the accepted idea of the self-portrait, but more with the questioning and observing of sensations. Others have embraced natural phenomena in ways that are at times romantic and at times bordering on scientific.

An intellectual climate that embraces Marcel Duchamp, Ad Reinhardt, Buckminster Fuller, Marshall McLuhan, the *I Ching,* the Beatles, Claude Lévi-Strauss, John Cage, Yves Klein, Herbert Marcuse, Ludwig Wittgenstein and theories of information and leisure inevitably adds to the already complex situation. It is even more enriched by the implications, for example, of Dada, and more recently happenings and Pop and "minimal" art.

With an art world that knows more readily about current work, through reproductions and the wide dissemination of information via periodicals, and that has been altered by television, films, and satellites, as well as the "jet," it is now possible for artists to be truly international; exchange with their peers is now comparatively simple. The art historian's problem of who did what first is almost getting to the point of having to date by the hour. Increasingly artists use the mail, telegrams, telex machines, etc., for transmission of works themselves—photographs, films, documents—or of information about their activity. For both artists and their public it is a stimulating and open situation, and certainly less parochial than even five years ago. It is no longer imperative for an artist to be in Paris or New York. Those far from the "art centers" contribute more easily, without the often artificial protocol that at one time seemed essential for recognition.

Inevitably for art, film and videotape are growing in importance. It is quite obvious that at this point they are major mass media. Their influence has meant that the general audience is beginning to be unwilling to give the delicate responses needed for looking at a painting. Artists are beginning to use this to their advantage. They hope to introduce a large public to more refined aesthetic experiences.

The films and videotapes in this exhibition and listed in this book have often been described as "minimally structured," which means that the content is non-narrative and that the style, while being almost an extension of *cinéma vérité,* is like so much of the other work in the show, simply a method of distributing the visual information that interests the artist.

The general attitude of the artists in this exhibition is certainly not hostile. It is straightforward, friendly, coolly involved, and allows experiences which are refreshing. It enables us to participate, quite often as in a game; at other times it seems almost therapeutic, making us question ourselves and our responses to unfamiliar stimuli. The constant demand is a more aware relation to our natural and artificial environments. There is always the sense of communication. These artists are questioning our prejudices, asking us to renounce our inhibitions, and if they are reevaluating the nature of art, they are also asking that we reassess what we have always taken for granted as our accepted and culturally conditioned aesthetic response to art.

It is only too obvious that there are unpredictable implications for the established systems. For example, the whole nature of collecting is perhaps becoming obsolete, and what is the traditional museum going to do about work at the bottom of the Sargasso Sea, or in the Kalahari desert, or in the Antarctic, or at the bottom of a volcano? How is the museum going to deal with the introduction of the new technology as an everyday part of its curatorial concerns?

I have purposely made this text short and very general. *Information* will allow for a more careful and thorough analysis of all the aesthetic and social implications of the work. My essay is really in the galleries and in the whole of this volume.

This text was written as the introduction to the catalogue for the exhibition *Information*, organized by McShine and staged at the Museum of Modern Art, New York (2 July–20 September 1970).

Question:

Would the fact that Governor Rockefeller
has not denounced President Nixon's
Indochina policy be a reason for you not
to vote for him in November ?

Answer:

If 'yes'
please cast your ballot into the left box
if 'no'
into the right box.

17

Hans Haacke, *MOMA-Poll,* 1970.

# alice's head: reflections on conceptual art
## jack burnham

(. . .)

Conceptual art resembles literature only superficially. What it really characterizes is a decided shift in sensory ratios. As a result Conceptualism poses a paradox: Can art free itself from the effects of the page in type only by adopting the printed form?

The problem with vulgar McLuhanism is that it makes more sense than any refined theory of media. Our civilization, according to McLuhan, was "founded upon isolation and domination of society by the visual sense."[1] Thus printing is tied to the limits of perspectival space. He hypothesizes that in the last century vestigial illusionism has slowly been supplanted by the synesthesia of "tactile space," culminating most recently in a desire for total environmental involvement or, specifically, a "reality high." For McLuhan, reality is more than the immediate environment; it is extended by "field space" or all the electronic devices that provide global awareness. Moreover since field space is pervasive, invisible, and non-causal, it makes no logical separation betwen the mind of the perceiver and the environment. "Live in your head" means that the printed page is to Conceptualism what the picture plane is to illusionistic Realism: an unavoidable belaboring of the point, inelegant communication. Printed proposals are make-do art; Conceptual art's ideal medium is telepathy. Analogously, at the present time conversational computer programs function through typewriter terminals; eventually computer communication will be verbal or direct neural relay. Notably, no one considers a terminal printout to be literature.

Reasons for the emergence of Conceptualism vary in complexity and deal mainly with the historical development of art. They range from Joseph Kosuth's functional reductivism to the practical consideration that gallery and museum exhibitions are increasingly planned, not through the selection of existent work, but on the basis of submitted proposals, implying that the artist's prime or gestural relationship to his materials is secondary and the intellectual cognizance is in many cases adequate. Quite often execution is redundant or at best for public elaboration.

A yet more basic motive may underlie Conceptualism. The biologist Ludwig von Bertalanffy writes of a growing schism between biological drives and symbolic values. One of the reasons for rapid technological change is increased proficiency in symbol manipulation, in philosophy, art, religion, literature, mathematics, and various forms of scientific logic. Belief in symbols and ideologies compels man to commit acts ordinarily against his biological well-being. We seem to be the captives of our symbol-making capabilities and their inconsistencies, as evident in such areas as the religious stand on birth control, the dynamics of thermonuclear war, economic perpetuation of harmful industrial effects, and cases for and against computer date banks. As Bertalanffy states, "The symbolic world of culture is basically un-nature, far transcending and often negating biological nature, drives, usefulness, and adaptation."[2] Beyond a fundamental reevaluation of the meaning of art, Conceptualism inadvertently asks, "What is the nature of ideas? How are they disseminated and transformed? And how do we free ourselves of the confusion between ideas and their correlations with physical reality?"

"In a preliterate society," says McLuhan, "art serves as a means of merging the individual and the environment, not as a means of training perception of the environment."[3] Conceptual art presents us with a superspatial grasp of the environment, one that deals with time, processes, and interrelated systems as we experience them in everyday life, forcing involvement with non-art habits of perception and thus fulfilling both McLuhan's models. (. . .)

Through the history of art there have been certain tacit relationships between dealer, audience, collector and artist, establishing degrees of control over the production and dissemination of a work of art. These however break down with Conceptualism, and part of an artwork becomes the assignment of new control variables over the life duration of a piece. Certainly this has been the tendency in the last ten years. All previous notions of an object's intrinsic qualities have been challenged to the point where it would be the simplest matter to reproduce some recent objects with or without the artist's consent. As Huebler states, "Anyone could reproduce an Andre or a Flavin for instance. What would he have? I believe that the sensibility behind a work of art should be broadly accessible. At the same time I believe that the collector is someone who enters into a conspiracy with the artist that is beyond the issue of accessibility, an agreement that the sensibility is an important one. This agreement may be really what the owner has that is 'original.'"[4]

It might be added that the artist is still looking toward the collector as a source of legitimacy, if not as a means of sustaining solvency. The artist is asking the collector to pay for ownership; but in the case of most Conceptual art, the commodity is pure information. Here a dilemma appears. The point of owning information is to control knowledge and use of it. Efficacious ownership of art objects depends upon sophisticated dissemination of information about those objects. What does it mean to own a piece of information that must be in the public domain to exist as art? (. . .)

Previous art usually demanded exacting control—artistry—over the parameters of production. But gradually art has become a matter of releasing control over these parameters, permitting exposure of an art situation to different intervening forces. What happens as the structure of an artist's conception is modified by unpredictable social process is, in effect, a part of the art statement. (. . .)

The Conceptualists have objectified the dissemination of art information—that is to say, the best have rethought the artist's role relative to media, museums, and collectors. This is the result of not centering interest on content but, as in information theory, on the nature of information itself. Questions of information's *predictability, improbability, complexity, message structure, dissemination, delay,* and *distortion* are factors not only for consideration, but for a work's viability as art competing with other forms of art. Optical art, Kinetic art, Luminous art, and various types of environmentalism have sought to convey standard art information by new technical means. These were usually attempts to break out of an exhausted format, but with little thought given to the relationship between methods of transmission and the art context. One of the transcending realizations of Conceptualism is that *any form of energy can or may be used to convey art information, that the sender or carrier is in fact a secondary problem to that of formulating a significant reason for its use.* (. . .)

Perhaps the future of Conceptual art is tied more to its power for influencing artistic behavior than to any success as commodity art, although Seth Siegelaub certainly does not think that way: "My influence in relation to the artists seems magnified because no one else was interested in this kind of art . . . but this is no longer true. My interest as a businessman isn't in circumventing the commercial system. I've just made pages of a book comparable to space (art situational space). Artists having their work go out as printed matter can be just as viable as selling Nolands." Yet in a more profound sense Siegelaub sees the effect that media and business have upon Conceptual art *as idea*. "Anything, any person, any idea has a focus . . . which is located in the world . . . just radiating outwards, losing strength at the edges. Watering down comes with the intermediaries between the artist and the public. That's what culture's about . . . culture is probably about watering down."

## NOTES

1. Marshall McLuhan and Harley Parker, *Through the Vanishing Point: Space in Poetry and Painting* (New York: Harper & Row, 1968), p. xxiv.

2. Ludwig von Bertalanffy, *Men and Minds* (New York: George Braziller, 1967), p. 27.

3. McLuhan and Parker, p. 243.

4. Douglas Huebler, "PROSPECT '69," exhibition catalog statement (October 1969), p. 26.

This text was published in *Artforum,* 8:6 (February 1970), pp. 37–43.

# de-aestheticization
## harold rosenberg

The sculptor Robert Morris once executed before a notary public the following document:

*Statement of Aesthetic Withdrawal*
*The undersigned,* ROBERT MORRIS, *being the maker of the metal construction entitled* LITANIES, *described in the annexed Exhibit A, hereby withdraws from said construction all aesthetic quality and content and declares that from the date hereof said construction has no such quality and content.*

*Dated: November 15, 1963*
*[signed] Robert Morris*

Not having seen *Litanies* or read the description of it in Exhibit A, I cannot say how it was affected by Morris' withdrawal or what its aesthetic condition was after the artist signed his statement. Perhaps the construction turned into what one permissive critic has called a "super-object of literalist art" or an "anti-object of conceptual art." Or perhaps it became an "anxious object," the kind of modern creation that is destined to endure uncertainty as to whether it is a work of art or not. In any case, the obvious intent of Morris' deposition was to convert *Litanies* into an object of the same order as the reductionist-inspired boxes, modules, and shaped canvases that flooded the art world in the sixties. Morris' de-aestheticized construction anticipated, for example, the demand of Minimalist Donald Judd for an art with "the specificity and power of actual materials, actual colors, actual space."

Both Morris' aesthetic withdrawal and Judd's call for materials that are more real, or actual, than others—for example, brown dirt rather than brown paint—imply a decision to purge art of the seeds of artifice. Toward that end, Morris' verbal exorcism would probably be less effective than Judd's preselected substances. For works to be empty of aesthetic content, it seems logical that they be produced out of raw rocks and lumber, out of stuff intended for purposes other than art, such as strips of rubber or electric bulbs, or even out of living people or animals. Better still, non-aesthetic art can be worked into nature itself, in which case it becomes, as one writer recently put it, "a fragment of the real within the real." Digging holes or trenches in the ground, cutting tracks through a cornfield, laying a square sheet of lead in the snow (the so-called earthworks art) do not in their de-aestheticizing essence differ in any way from exhibiting a pile of mail sacks, tacking a row of newspapers on a wall, or keeping the shutter of a camera open while speeding through the night (the so-called anti-form art). Aesthetic withdrawal also paves the way for "process" art—in which chemical, biological, physical, or seasonal forces affect the original materials and either change their form or destroy them, as in works incorporating growing grass and bacteria or inviting rust—and random art, whose form and content are decided by chance. Ultimately, the repudiation of the aesthetic suggests the total elimination of the art object and its replacement by an idea for a work or by the rumor that one has been consummated—as in conceptual art. Despite the stress on the actuality of the materials used, the principle common to all classes of de-aestheticized art is that the finished product, if any, is of less significance than the procedures that brought the work into being and of which it is the trace.

The movement toward de-aestheticization is both a reaction against and a continuation of the trend toward formalistic over-refinement in the art of the sixties, and particularly in the rhetoric that accompanied it. Asserting the nostalgia of artists for invention, craftsmanship, and expressive behavior, earthworks protest against the constricting museum-gallery system organized around a handful of aesthetic platitudes. Works that are constructed in the desert or on a distant seashore, that are not for sale and cannot be collected, that are formless piles of rubbish, or that are not even works but information about plans for works or events that have taken place are, one earthworks artist is quoted as saying, a "practical alternative to the absolute city system of art." Here the sociology of art overtly enters into the theory and practice of creation. The current defiance of the aesthetic is the latest incident in the perennial reversion to primitivism in the art of the past hundred years and the exaltation of ruggedness, simplicity, and doing what one chooses without regard to the public and its representatives. (. . .)

This text was published in *The New Yorker,* 24 January 1970, pp. 62–67.

Event.
Duration...one hour ten minutes.
Equipment. shovel,microphone,two eight millemetre film projectors,
tape recorder, video tape, amplifier, loudspeaker,coke.
Four hundred weight of coke is heaped on floor.
First film projector starts running off film of coke being shovelled.
(after 5 minutes)
Tape recorder,tape of coke being shovelled.
(after five minutes)
Microphone in shovel is switched on and shovelling started.
(after five minutes)
Video tape is started
(after 5 minutes)
Second film projector is switched on
Tape recording amplification switched from recorder to loudspeaker.
(same for duration of film,20 minutes)
Film ends
(5 minutes)
Video ends
(5 minutes)
Tape ends
(5 minutes)
Microphone in shovel switched off
Shovelling ends  one hour ten minutes after start of event.
end event.

Mary Kelly, untitled event at the New Arts Laboratory, London, 1970.

# contemporary colonial art

## luis camnitzer

I was about eighteen years old when I read the three volumes of "The Culture of the Cities" by Lewis Mumford. Of the whole work only one idea remained stuck in my mind, an idea or description with which I had identified immediately: "The bathroom is the only place of privacy we have left." It took me about five years to realize that this statement was somebody else's truth. It is true in what Mumford himself calls a "megalopolis," an overgrown monster city, but it definitely was not true in my city, Montevideo, with less than a million people—and widely spaced, at least in that time and in my background. A symptom of metropolitan culture had managed to evoke in me, an inhabitant of the colonies—through apparently intellectual means—an experience I never had had.

One day I left my country. At the time of my leaving, people used to whistle when they wanted to show public disapproval. Five years later I returned and discovered that whistling was being used for approval, the same as in the United States of America.

A gentleman in a developed country invents the "potato chip." In his own living context, he managed to enrich qualitatively the cocktail hour and quantitatively, himself. However, in the colonial context, he introduced a new habit, a notion of status, a point of identification through which the colony can relate to the metropolis and believe to feel and act the same. We can say that what happened was a cultural rape through a potato.

The examples only show fragments of a process of transculturation, a part of a vicious circle that holds: economic dependence, mono-production, the creation of artificial needs and the substitution of cultural values. It is a process that managed the ideal situation of nearly everybody actually wanting to participate in it. It creates the need of listening to the latest record, of reading the latest book, of chewing the latest chewing gum, of fitting all the metropolitan molds.

There is no need for this process to be accomplished in all social segments. From the Empire's point of view the need decreases in proportion to the amount of power held by each social segment, provided the total mechanism is well oiled.

Most of the social classes fit between the Cadillac and the Coke, some even remaining under the latter. United Press provides total, instantaneous and universal information. But in the same act, it also leaves total, instantaneous and universal ignorance.

The artist is an integral part of these informed and isolated social segments. In the colonial areas, in a role which is not very defined—somewhere between a buffoon and a spokesman—he is one of the leaks through which the informative pressure of the Empire keeps filtering through. It is strange that the phrase "Colonial Art" is filled with only positive connotations and that it only refers to the past. In reality it happens in the present, and with benevolence it is called "international style." With less courtesy, it tends to be epigonous, derivative, and sometimes even opportunistic.

There is a rhetoric and a mental process of the Empire which are very particular and which are not new. As president of the U.S.A., Quincy Adams, said in 1842: "The moral obligation to proceed to commercial exchanges between nations is solely based on the Christian premise that obliges us to love our neighbor." At the time, the conclusion of this concept was that since China was not Christian, it was bellicose and anti-social, since "The fundamental principle of the Chinese Empire is anti-commercial." This way, the moral justification was set down for what was called the "opium war," a war mainly between Britain and China, but with strong profits for the western and Christian civilization.

Commodore Perry went with four battleships to isolationist Japan to offer a commercial treaty. Seven months later, in February of 1854, he returned with an increased squadron to look for the answer.

As with Commerce, Art is above stingy political games: "it helps the communication and understanding of the people," "it is a common denominator for understanding." "The world is smaller every day," and under the rug of this phrase one sweeps the moment-by-moment growing difference between the cultural needs of economically developed countries and those underdeveloped or developing.

The achievements of the Metropolis have international validity automatically. To speak in the U.S.A. of a Jasper Johns or of a Rauschenberg as a good local artist, with all the implications of provincialism, sounds offensive and insulting. Both are universal luminaries and "art does not have frontiers." The size of the transculturation problem may be indicated by the fact that "art does not have frontiers" is no longer a figure of speech, a saying, but rather, a commonplace.

The distortion is even deeper. The United States of America, with 6% of the world population, consumes 50% of the world consumer goods. In addition to the necessary military consequences to maintain that situation, this rather monstrous proportion allows the United States of America to also fix the conditions of the market for those goods. The art-consumer goods do not escape the rule.

An empire has a culture to disseminate, even when this culture is only a collection of habits. In the metropolis, art consumer goods are created which originate from an "existing culture." The creation of these goods, which we can call "cultural products," and their consumption, determine a series of rules both rigid and functional. Their results remain accumulated in what we call "history of art." This "history" is metropolitan in nature, and when local histories appear in other places, they are compiled with the same measuring sticks. Who determines what is universal, also is who determines how it is done.

The question for the colonial artist is this—by participating in the metropolitan art game, is he really only postponing the liberation of the colony to which he belongs? There is an absurdity in creating cultural products when there is no culture to justify them. Latin America has five centuries of being a colony, without a breathing space to assume itself. The task is still there—to build its own culture, to find a cultural identity. The artist, instead of working on this problem, holds the same attitude which Chinese restaurants have in western countries: a Chinese restaurant submits willingly to the image the metropolitan culture has of it. It announces its name with Chinesely-styled letters, advertises "exotic food," and has, just in case, a page of metropolitan food listed in the menu.

Without too much scientific care, I will borrow some terms of Information Theory: originality, redundancy, and banality.

Traditionally, in art there is a careful balance of the three elements. The originality is the contribution of the artwork. The redundancy, technically a waste of repetitive information, insures the intelligent reception of the message by the public. The banality is the frame of reference, or the collection of known elements which the originality needs as a vehicle in order not to die in hermetism and incommunicability.

One of the decisions that places the artist, politically as well as among other things, is the banality system or the system he will use as a reference. The colonial artist believes that he makes this choice in total freedom. Generally speaking, however, he only chooses out of three possibilities, and the three of them are based on manufacturing cultural products. That is how the paradox comes about that politically aware artists keep working for the metropolitan culture. The three options are: the "international style," the regional and picturesque "folklorism," and the subordination to political-literary content.

The contribution or originality of a cultural product only functions as a refinement of the culture from which it comes (for the culture itself and also for its expansion or proselytizing). It achieves a sophistication of the consuming process. The creation of cultural products in the colonial area then becomes a tool for the enrichment and sophistication of the metropolitan culture. With the growing strength of the "international style," the result becomes obvious in the productive outlook of Latin America. The aesthetic trends used are permanently lagging behind those promulgated in the imperial centers, without the corresponding evolutions which take place in those centers. It happens that in this way we have individual developments of artists with artificial breaks, which can only be explained by the date the "art magazine" arrived, or the date the "exhibition" was held with the updating information. The increase of the information stream only increases the speed of the changes. Alan Solomon, who was in charge of the American exhibit in the Biennial of Venice (where Rauschenberg won the Big Prize–exhibit flown over with military aircraft), commended a group of artists of Rosario, Argentina, because "they worked according to New York standards only with some weeks of delay." The New York painter, Frank Stella, said: "If we are the best, it is only fair that they imitate us." At the same time, colonial artists complained about the expenses of chroming and plastics in general—a fact which, according to them, put them out of the international Market. And E.A.T. (Experiments in Art and Technology) is opening branches in different underdeveloped countries, usually after the artists' own request.

The result is obviously to be a perfecting of the metropolitan imagery.

One of the reactions to the "international style," as well as willful ignoring in regard to this style, leads to folklorism. This option, instead of basing itself on the activities of the imperial cultural centers, is based on local traditions, and especially on the formal symptoms of the local traditions. There are two problems with this option. The first is that these traditions are usually not sensitive to the immediate and present reality, opening a way to escapism. Second, with few exceptions these traditions are dead. There have been too many colonizations to allow a continuity between the traditions and the artist. Usually the artist comes from the middle class, thus consuming those traditions rather than living them. The folklorist option, then, becomes as derivative as the option that follows the "international style."

The third option is the subordination to the political-literary content. This option comes from a political commitment prior to a creative decision. This in itself would be a normal process. The limitations appear when the creative process only is dedicated to the production of illustrations, didactically worried, and simultaneously follows the rules of the game indicated by the history of art. The didactic function requires a high percentage of redundance, leaving little room for originality.

The options described were in their purest form. In the international market, the winners coming from the colonies appear always to refer to more than one option at the time. In this way they probably achieve at the same time a higher degree of contribution and of communicability. But all the artists who follow these rules of the game, whatever the reference system they use, are bound by a broader system regardless of their aesthetics or their politics. It is the system of the object. A painting is a painting recognizable as such, whatever its form or its content. The same happens with any art object, even if it doesn't follow the traditional formal lines. There is a publicity machinery strong enough to transmit the norms of recognition which in every moment is called "avant-garde." The label "avant-garde" is one of these norms.

The relation between the object and the consuming of that object (which generalized gives the relation between art and society) serves as a thermometer for the functionality of art. In the capitalist, economically developed society, the art object is subject to the laws of supply and demand. The artist is placed in the production of objects with his creation, with the production of creators with his teaching. He is paid for both with very little or no philanthropy, since the power structure accepts him as important, or at least, as usable.

The situation is also reflected in the economic investment of the artist, or his patron, in the actual work production. In 1968, in the Whitney Sculpture Annual, the average investment in materials alone, per sculpture, must have reached about $200. This amount is more than the annual income of the majority of the inhabitants in underdeveloped countries.

Meanwhile, the concessions the artist has to make in the colonies are more obvious and more painful. In normal circumstances, the artist cannot live by his skills. He has one or more jobs unrelated to his art. He sells to a small national elite or to tourists. He depends on the government's philanthropy through its politically corrupt exhibitions. He always has that permanent option between his principles and the corruption and alms.

I believe the possibilities for change are two:

The first one, moderate, is to continue to use the system of reference pertaining to certain forms capable of being related to art, but not to produce cultural products, but rather to inform about data toward a culture. This means to inform about situations not necessarily aesthetic, able to affect the mechanisms that eventually will produce or define a culture. To isolate, stress, and bring to awareness of transculturating elements, and to give a notion of essences which will allow the creation of new platforms is what I feel is needed. It is what we can call a perceptual alphabetization. It implies to assume economical underdevelopment as cultural stimulus, without relative value judgments. What may be negative in economical terms is only factual in cultural terms. In this moment, a huge percentage of inhabitants of the underdeveloped areas are starving to death. But artists continue to produce full-belly art.

The second possibility is to affect cultural structures through social and political ones, applying the same creativity usually used for art. If we analyze the activities of certain guerrilla groups, especially the Tupamaros and some other urban groups, we can see that something like this is already happening. The system of reference is decidedly alien to the traditional art reference systems. However, they are functioning for expressions which, at the same time they contribute to a total structure change, also have a high density of aesthetic content. For the first time the aesthetic message is understandable as such, without the help of the "art context" given by the museum, the gallery, etc.

The urban guerrilla functions in conditions very similar to those with which the traditional artist is confronted when he is about to produce a work. There is a common goal: to communicate a message and at the same time to change with the process the conditions in which the public finds itself. There is a similar search to find the exact amount of originality which, using the known as a background, allows him to stress the message until notoriety for its effectiveness, sometimes signaling towards the unknown. But by going from the object to the situation, from the elitist legality to subversion, there appear new elements. The public, a passive consumer, suddenly in passing from object to situation has to participate actively to be part of the situation. Passing from legality to subversion, the need of finding a minimum stimulus with a maximum effect appears—an effect that through its impact justifies the risk taken and pays for it. During certain historical periods, at the level of the object, this meant dealing with and creating mysteries. At the level of situations, and in this case, it means the change of the social structure.

These coincidences are not enough to make an artist out of the urban guerilla fighter, the same way as the activity of painting is not enough to make an artist out of a painter. But there are definite cases where the urban guerilla achieves aesthetic levels, widely transcending the movement's pure political function. It is when the movement reaches this stage that it really is on the way toward creating a new culture instead of simply providing old perceptions with a new political form.

The options of traditional art fulfill socially the same function of other institutions used by the power structure to insure stability. That is why they lead to an aesthetic of balance. In a Machiavellian way, within these coordinates, a revolutionary message can be reduced to a stabilizing function. Art then becomes a safety valve for the expression of individual and collective neuroses originating in the inability of coping with the environment. Its products serve as a retarded correction of a perception braked by the system of conventions and stereotypes that stabilize society. They create a slightly updated system which, eventually assimilated by history, will require a new system, and so on without end. Art objects serve as points of identification alienated from the consumer, requiring more sympathy than empathy. The consumer, for instance, is able to identify with the moral message of a film. He applauds it, feeling that in this way he pays his quota of personal commitment without having to change the course of his life in a significant way. It is the same cathartic action offered by religion.

Instead, the aesthetics of imbalance, the one that affects structures, that demands full participation or full rejection, does not allow for the comfort of alienation.

It leads to the confrontation which will bring about change.

It leads to the integration of aesthetic creativity with all the systems of reference used in everyday life.

It leads the individual to be a permanent creator, to be in a state of constant perception. It leads him to determine his environment according to his needs and to fight in order to achieve the changes.

This text is the transcript for a paper presented to the Latin American Studies Association conference, Washington, D.C., 1969. The paper was subsequently translated into Spanish, and published in the Montevideo-based journal *Marcha* in mid-1970.

# insertions in ideological circuits
## cildo meireles

(. . .)

When, in a philosophical definition of his work, Marcel Duchamp stated that, among other things, his aim was to free "art from the dominion of the hand," he certainly did not imagine the point we would come to in 1970. Something that at first sight could easily be located and effectively combated tends nowadays to be located in an area that is hard to access and to apprehend: the brain.

It is clear that Duchamp's phrase is an example, now, of a lesson that has not been learnt correctly. Duchamp fought not so much against the domination of hands as against manual craftsmanship and, in short, against the gradual emotional, rational and psychological lethargy that this mechanicalness, this habituation would inevitably produce in the individual. The fact that one's hands are not soiled with art means nothing except that one's hands are clean.

Rather than against manifestations of a phenomenon, the fight is against the logic of that phenomenon. What one can see nowadays is a certain relief and a certain delight at not using one's hands. As if things were finally OK. As if at this specific moment, people did not need to start fighting against a much bigger opponent: the habits and handiwork of the brain.

Style, whether of the hands or of the brain (reason), is an anomaly. And with anomalies, it is more intelligent to abort them than to help them to live.

## ART-CULTURE

If Duchamp's interference was in terms of Art (the logic of the phenomenon), it is fair to say that it applied to aesthetics, and if thereby it heralded the freeing of habit from the dominion of the hands, it is right to say that any interference in this sphere nowadays (Duchamp's collocation has the great merit of forcing one's perception of Art to shift from being a perception of artistic objects to becoming more a phenomenon of thought), given that what is being done now tends to be closer to culture than to Art, would necessarily be a political interference. Because IF AESTHETICS IS THE BASIS OF ART, IT IS POLITICS THAT IS THE BASIS OF CULTURE.

This text was initially presented in the debate "Perspectivas para uma Arte Brasileira," 1970, and later published as "Inserçoes em circuitos ideológicos," *Malasartes,* no. 1 (September-November 1975), p. 15. The present translation is taken from *Cildo Meireles: IVAM Centre del Carme, 2 Febrero/23 abril 1995* (Barcelona: Generalitat Valenciana, Conselleria de Cultura, 1995), pp. 173–174.

michel claura, jeanne siegel, victor burgin, terry smith, catherine millet, max kozloff, robert smithson, seth siegelaub, lucy r. lippard, adrian piper, hans haacke

**V** 1971–1974

# interview with lawrence weiner
## michel claura

Michel Claura: For a person who does not "practice" art, the only reason to take an interest in art is that, within a specific domain, accountability can be revealed. Art is an ordinary activity, exceptional only by virtue of being privileged (in the socio-economic system in which it participates). It is important to reveal it to/in its true function, i.e., fundamentally, to assure the permanence of that system. The vanity of all the other positions facing art are founded on faith. Is this faith only in the artist?

Lawrence Weiner: It seems this hypothesis suggests a major problem. Because art is, as it always is, explicit more than specific, the role of criticism or of art writing is not to reveal, because the existence and the presentation also of art are relevant. Its role would be more that of explanation (education). Education being the job of the state (of society), criticism exists to the extent that it necessarily catalyzes that which is simply the remainder of a human activity and, in this way, transforms art so that it does not require faith (history exists concurrently with existence) in its reflection of a specific situation. The artist finds himself in the position of a naïve producer or else in that of the maker of finery for high society (history = power). Neither of these two positions suggest vanity.

M.C.: Academicism and repetition appear when the artist applies himself to the question of knowing how to achieve power. We say, in fact, that the fall into academicism and repetition is already inscribed in the first act of creation of the artist. In other words, the work of the artist does not fall into academicism and repetition. His first act is already a repetition (from art history). To arrive at power is, finally, the compensation for being a good artist (i.e., a good minion).

L.W.: If one accepts this analysis, when the least degree of power is apparent, one finds oneself in the position of a "culture-fucker". Unhappily, one does not always remember that it is one's own nest that one is soiling.

M.C.: Do you believe that about art? Why?

L.W.: It has nothing to do with what one believes or not. Art would exist whether one used it or chose to ignore it.

M.C.: Why do you make art?

L.W.: Art continues to be a viable medium of presentation for certain conclusions (issues).

M.C.: The confusion, which in our times seems so profound, originated with the practice of art as a way of life (existence) and its multiple consequences following the nonperception of this practice as the source of artistic activity. The confusion originates, in other words, out of the disturbed comfort of the bad conscience; the motor of a progressively reactionary art.

L.W.: I do not see any confusion. Those who persist with expressionism do not struggle at all with the confusion and fall into an innocuousness similar to characterizing Munich in the 30s simply as "Oktoberfest". The confusion is a type that the artist and his audience adopt because it permits them to indulge in the self-satisfying flattery of the "qualities" of their principles without feeling responsible for the horrors of humanity, for which they are pardoned.

M.C.: In what ways do you concern yourself with color?

L.W.: In terms of color.

M.C.: Do you know how many hours per day you work?

L.W.: As many hours as it takes.

M.C.: Have you ever thought of the reasons why someone would buy one of your works? Do you think that these reasons, such as they are, are important? Do they give you a sense of yourself, of your work, of art? (Do they notify you to indicate retroactively a meaning for your work, for your activity, for art?)

L.W.: The fact of buying one of my works is comparable to a signature at the bottom of a petition and is, in this sense, to accept responsibility that the conclusions, raised up to there, are correct. This would be a trap that determines the meaning in some sense since then, or likewise we can imagine a lesser reason; but, retroactively, one can show in history where the mandate of support (moral and financial) situates itself in certain matters.

M.C.: Is the context in which you show your work of any importance whatsoever? Do you take the context into consideration when you make your work?

L.W.: Art can only exist in a context where, for whatever reason, it is agreed to, or else it is invited to exist or it is permitted to exist.

M.C.: There is only a very small number of "specialists" who are interested in the artistic avant-garde. Do you think that is damaging?

L.W.: Perhaps, if, in place of saying artistic avant-garde, one says "contemporary art"; this situation (living in the past; incomprehension of the present) is dangerous for the culture in its entirety.

This interview first appeared in *VH-101*, 5 (Spring 1971), pp. 64–65. Translated by Blake Stimson, this is its first publication in English.

Allan Sekula, *Meat Theft/Disposal Piece,* 1971. Over a period of several
weeks, meat was stolen from a supermarket and stored in a freezer. The
thawed steaks were thrown beneath the wheels of freeway traffic.

19

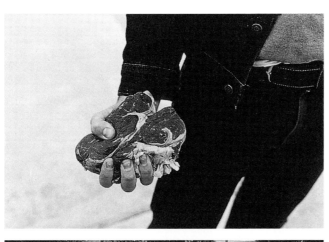

# an interview with hans haacke
## jeanne siegel

(. . .)

Jeanne Siegel: You have been called a naturalist because of your extensive interest in physical elements as well as grass, birds, ants, and animals.

Hans Haacke: I don't consider myself a naturalist, nor for that matter a conceptualist or a kineticist, an earth artist, elementalist, minimalist, a marriage broker for art and technology, or the proud carrier of any other button that has been offered over the years. I closed my little statement of 1965 with "articulate something Natural." That has an intended double meaning. It refers to "nature," and it means something self-understood, ordinary, uncontrived, normal, something of an everyday quality. When people see the wind stuff or the things I have done with animals, they call me a "naturalist." Then they get confused or feel cheated when they discover, for example, my interest in using a computer to conduct a demographic survey. This is inconsistent only for those with a naive understanding of nature—nature being the blue sky, the Rockies, Smokey the Bear. The difference between "nature" and "technology" is only that the latter is man-made. The functioning of either one can be described by the same conceptual models, and they both obviously follow the same rules of operation. It also seems that the way social organizations behave is not much different. The world does not break up into neat university departments. It is one supersystem with a myriad of subsystems, each one more or less affected by all the others.

If you take a grand view, you can divide the world into three or four categories—the physical, biological, the social and behavioral—each of them having interrelations with the others at one point or another. There is no hierarchy. All of them are important for the upkeep of the total system. It could be that there are times when one of these categories interests you more than another. So, for example, I now spend more thought on things in the social field, but simultaneously I am preparing a large water-cycle for the Guggenheim show that uses the peculiarities of the building.

J.S.: When did you first become aware of systems theory?

H.H.: Sometime in '65 or '66 I was introduced to the concept of systems. I heard about systems analysis, and the related fields of operational research, cybernetics, etc. The concepts used in these fields seemed to apply to what I had been doing and there was a useful terminology that seemed to describe it much more succinctly than the terminology that I and other people had been using until then, so I adopted it. But using a new terminology doesn't mean that the work described has changed. A new term is nothing holy, so it can't serve as a union label. On the other hand, a clear terminology can help to stimulate thinking.

J.S.: Jack Burnham has had a lot to say about systems and sculpture, yours in particular. When did you first meet him?

H.H.: I met Jack in 1962 when we were both isolated from people interested in what we were doing. Since then we have been in contact and have had a very fruitful exchange of ideas. It was Jack who introduced me to systems analysis.

J.S.: What is your definition of a system that is also a work of art?

H.H.: A system is most generally defined as a grouping of elements subject to a common plan and purpose. These elements or components interact so as to arrive at a joint goal. To separate the elements would be to destroy the system. The term was originally used in the natural sciences for understanding the behavior of physically interdependent processes. It explained phenomena of directional change, recycling, and equilibrium. I believe the term system should be reserved for sculptures in which a transfer of energy, material, or information occurs, and which do not depend on perceptual interpretation. I use the word "systems" exclusively for things that are not systems in terms of perception, but are physical, biological, or social entities which, I believe, are more real than perceptual titillation. (. . .)

A very important difference between the work of Minimal sculptors and my work is that they were interested in inertness, whereas I was concerned with change. From the beginning the concept of change has been the ideological basis of my work. All the way down there's absolutely nothing static—nothing that does not change, or instigate real change. Most Minimal work disregards change. Things claim to be inert, static, immovably beyond time. But the status quo is an illusion, a dangerous illusion politically. (. . .)

J.S.: Is there any difference in communication between social systems and physical or biological ones?

H.H.: For physical or biological processes to take their course, there is no need for the presence of a viewer—unless, as with some participatory works, his physical energy is required (he then becomes an indispensable part of the system's physical environment). However, there is no need for *anybody* to get mentally involved. These systems function on their own, since their operation does not take place in the viewer's mind (naturally this does not prevent a mental or emotional response).

The rigging of a social situation, however, usually follows a different pattern. There the process takes place exclusively in the minds of people. Without participants there is no social set. Take the "MOMA Poll" in last year's "Information" show: the work was based on a particular political situation circumscribed by the Indochina War, Nixon's and Rockefeller's involvement in it. MOMA's close ties to both, my own little quarrels with the museum as part of the Art Workers Coalition's activities, and then all the minds of the people who had a stake in this game—the Vietcong as much as the Scarsdale lady on her culture tour to the city. The result of the poll—approximately 2 to 1 against Rockefeller/Nixon and the war—is only the top of the iceberg. The figures are not quite reliable because MOMA, as usual, did not follow instructions, and the polls have to be taken with a grain of salt.

Emily Genauer gave us a little glimpse of the large base of the work in her review of the show. She wrote: "One may wonder at the humor (propriety, obviously, is too archaic a concept even to consider) of such poll-taking in a museum founded by the governor's mother, headed now by his brother, and served by himself and other members of his family in important financial and administrative capacities since its founding 40 years ago." With this little paragraph she provided some of the background for the work that was not intelligible for the politically less-informed visitors of the museum. She also articulated feelings that are shared by the top people at numerous museums. It goes like this: We are the guardians of culture. We honor artists by inviting them to show in *our* museum, we want them to behave like guests; proper, polite, and grateful. After all, we have put up the dough for this place.

The energy of information interests me a lot. Information presented at the right time and in the right place can be potentially very powerful. It can affect the general social fabric.

Such things go beyond established high culture as it has been perpetrated by a taste-directed art industry. Of course I don't believe that artists really wield any significant power. At best, one can focus attention. But every little bit helps. In concert with other people's activities outside the art scene, maybe the social climate of society can be changed. Anyway, when you work with the "real stuff" you have to think about potential consequences. A lot of things would never enter the decision-making process if one worked with symbolic representations that have to be weighed carefully. If you work with real-time systems, well, you probably go beyond Duchamp's position. Real-time systems are double agents. They might run under the heading "art," but this culturization does not prevent them from operating as normal. The MOMA Poll had even more energy in the museum than it would have had in the street—real sociopolitical energy, not awe-inspiring symbolism.

J.S.: Can you describe a social work that is not political?

H.H.: Probably all things dealing with social situations are to a greater or lesser degree political. Take *The Gallery-Goer's Residence Profile.* I asked the people that came to my exhibition to mark with a blue pin on large maps where they were living. After the show I traveled to all those spots on the Manhattan map that were marked by a blue pin and took a photograph of the building or approximately that location. I came up with about 730 photographs for Manhattan (naturally not every visitor participated in the game). The photographs were enlarged to 5″ by 7″. They will be displayed on the wall of the Guggenheim according to a geographical score. All those spots that were east of Fifth Avenue go upward on the wall from a horizontal center line, those west go downward. The respective distance from Fifth Avenue determines the sequence of pictures East and West. The Fifth Avenue spine takes up approximately 36 yards of wall space. Sometimes the photographs reach up to the ceiling, on other occasions (e.g., there is only one on the west side and none on the east side) it becomes a very jagged distribution. The "composition" is a composition determined by the information provided by the gallery-goers. No visual considerations play a role.

All this sounds very innocent and apolitical. The information I collected, however, is sociologically quite revealing. The public of commercial art galleries, and probably that of museums, lives in easily identifiable and restricted areas. The main concentrations are on the upper West Side (Central Park and adjoining blocks, and West End Avenue with adjoining blocks), the Upper East Side, somewhat heavier in the Madison–Park Avenue areas, then below 23rd Street on the East and West sides with clusters on the Lower East Side and the loft district. The photographs give an idea of the economic and social fabric of the immediate neighborhood of the gallery-goers. Naturally the Lower East Side pins were not put there by Puerto

245

Ricans. Puerto Ricans and blacks (Harlem is practically not represented) do not take part in an art scene that is obviously dominated by the middle- and upper-income strata of society or their drop-out children. I leave it up to you as far as how you evaluate this situation. You continue the work by drawing your own conclusions from the information presented.

This interview, conducted in early 1971, first appeared in *Arts Magazine,* 45:7 (May 1971), pp. 18–21.

# rules of thumb
## victor burgin

. . . all the devices at the artist's disposal are so many signs . . . the function of a work of art is to signify an object, to establish a significant relationship with an object.
—Claude Lévi-Strauss[1]

Our prevailing orthodoxy is that art signifies nothing. In presenting my own interpretation of this dogma I shall refer to a distinction which I hope is more tenable than the current "object/non–object" dichotomy.

Art's primary situation is not unique to art. It is that in which a person, or group of persons, by certain displays, seeks to alter the state of apprehension of a second person or group of persons. From this undramatic assertion it follows that the empirically observable differences between types of art are primarily differences of type, scope, and use of displays. "Sign" may not yet be substituted for "display." "Sign" implies a corollary thing signified, but in "abstract" painting and sculpture a work has no apparent significance but is rather *itself* an object of signification. As artists and critics connected with Modernism will insist that the unique art object *itself* must be brought into the proximity of our senses it should be clear that *it* is the object which is signified and that signification here takes the form of ostensive definition.[2]

Modernist works are obvious candidates for inclusion in the class of works which are denoted rather than denoting. None of the appearances of these works may be said, even metaphorically, to belong within a language. "Formal language" is that technical branch of natural language which is used to *describe* the works. The organizations of marks which constitute the works themselves are not analogous to a language; at their most coherent they represent variations upon loosely expressed compositional conventions—a quasi-syntax without semantics. However, the class of works which are denoted is by no means confined to abstract art, it also includes that ubiquitous format—the "readymade."

A bottle-rack does not function as a sign in any language, it denotes nothing but is itself "denoted as" art. The information it originally communicated has since decayed; it functions now as the historical precedent endorsing a presentational strategy which might be expressed: "By definition, an art object is an object presented by an artist within the context of art. Therefore any object which meets these conditions may serve as an art object."

Against the above background assertion, foreground activity takes the form of an attempt to find objects which are *a priori* least expected but yet which *a posteriori* will appear historically inevitable. However, within the given framework, a bottle-rack, a bridge, or the planet Jupiter all have equivalent status with any other perceptible body. Once this governing principle has been grasped, the ability to predict the imminent choice of object domain is greatly increased and so the information transmitted is proportionately decreased. The recent widespread uses of photography and natural language very often *function* as ostensive definitions in regard to a found object. A photograph of a bridge, or the word "bridge," are *operationally* ostensive here;[3] similarly, where *objet trouvé* is replaced by *évenement trouvé,* the phrase "building a bridge" also, in the final analysis, functions ostensively *if no other information is supplied.*

There is, then, a sense in which both abstract art and "operationally ostensive" postminimal art place the percipient in almost identical situations—he is simply presented with an object upon which he may impose entirely his own interpretation.[4] What is left to subjective interpretation in "ostensive" art is what is being *explicitly* referred to in the percipient's apprehension of the denoted object—the message is ambiguous. The situation may change when the work is not the *only* thing denoted but in turn selectively denotes aspects of an object domain—when it serves as a type of *definite description.*

A definite description ". . . does not indicate all properties of the object, and thus replace concrete perception; on the contrary, it actually appeals to perception. Also, definite descriptions do not even list all essential characteristics, but only as many characterizing properties as are required to recognize unequivocally the object which is meant within the object domain under discussion."[5] Obviously, a definite description must be framed in a commonly understood system of signs. A look at the types of definite description which can be transmitted by the sign systems used in art may help determine another issue, that of the type and degree of abstraction valid in art.

Carnap established a hierarchy of types of description in the ascending order, *property description, relation description, structure description:*

*A* property description *indicates the properties which the individual objects of a given domain have, while a* relation description *indicates the relations which hold between these objects, but does not make any assertions about the objects as individuals; . . . [structure descriptions are a type of relation description but] unlike relation descriptions, these not only leave the properties of the individual elements of the range unmentioned, they do not even specify the relations themselves which hold between these elements. In a structure description, only the* structure *of the relation is indicated. . . . They form the* highest level of formalization and dematerialization.[6]

At one level, the difference between Impressionism and Analytic Cubism may be seen as a difference between a concern with property descriptions in the former case and relation descriptions in the latter. Implicit in the claims which have been made for abstract art is the assumption that its concern is somehow with structure descriptions. However, art abdicated its candidacy for this sort of function when it ceased to use any commonly understood signs; that is to say, when the marks it employed consistently lay outside any language, natural or artificial. But if this type and degree of abstraction is *really* to be considered the highest aspiration of art then our greatest artists are the same individuals as our greatest mathematicians and logicians, whose concerns may most accurately be described as being with the examination and construction of formal systems *independently* of empirical references.

The orthodox line of abstract art is to hold all use of conventional signs to be "literary." It need hardly be pointed out that the function of common signs in academic painting is very different from the use of those (schematized) signs in Analytic Cubism, which was no more "about" bottles than Impressionism was "about" haystacks.

The concerns of Cubism were essentially the phenomenological concerns more recently exhibited in some Minimal sculpture of the mid-sixties. Sculpture of that period might appear more "abstract"[7] than Cubism but it performed a similar didactic and demonstrative purpose—particular geometric solids, after all, are exemplifications of commonly held structural concepts, familiar to us in diagrammatic form and signified in language by equally familiar nouns. Both Minimal and Modernist sculpture are rooted in Cubism—but whereas Modernism was content to elaborate the given sign system, with only the most residual regard for its (once) referential function, Minimal sculpture represents a continuity of focus on the referent with a consequent revision of the sign system in the interests of a more *explicit* denotation of what is attended to in the given object domain.

The accusation, "literary," has again been leveled against that recent art in which the signs employed are those of natural language. It might help, here, to consider that the way in which natural language is *used* in art is more similar to the way it is used in science than to the way it is used in literature. In the "scientific method," hypotheses are formed, observations made, and conclusions reached from which further hypotheses may be extrapolated. Any part of this rationalist-empiricist spiral may be linguistically communicated. Language here is seen as, ideally, an inert tool. In the case of natural language, what passive qualities it has are reinforced by the introduction of unambiguous technical terms (metaphor may intrude, as in "wave" in physics, but semantic drift is controlled by specific commonly agreed technical applications, so it is not in doubt that there is a difference between what is meant by "wave" in "sound-wave" and in "light-wave"). Language to science, then, is purely instrumental. This is much closer to current usage in art than are traditional literary concerns with expressive ambiguities of language.

Some confusion has also arisen in regard to what has been seen as a blurring of the distinction between "art" and "criticism." On one hand this, rather simple-mindedly, recognizes the fact that both work and comment use the same system of signs, and on the other hand acknowledges the symbiotic nature of the two activities.

*We ascertain the religion of a given society through representations, emotions, thoughts, volitions of a religious sort which occur with the members of this society; also, documents in the form of writings, pictures, and buildings are considered. Thus, the recognition depends upon the manifestation and the documentation of the object in question.*[8]

Meaning is not something which resides *within* an object but is a function of the way in which that object fits into a particular context. Any given context may "activate" differently in regard to any number of different objects; conversely, it is literally as "meaningful" to change the context as it is to change the object. In art, however, changes in the object have been more immediately effective than shifts in commentary.

If we imagine, by way of analogy, an electronic circuit into which a component (X) is plugged—we can change the state of that system by a lengthy process of rewiring or we can simply replace the component by (Y) which has a different value. This analogy crudely illustrates two points: the advantage of component replacement is in the *speed* of the operation; also, this operation introduces information from *outside* the system. (Superior speed is a characteristic advantage enjoyed by intuitive, "insight" modes of apprehension, over discursive modes—which would infer that art is exclamatory rather than declamatory. The second point is made re "significant" art.)

If we expand the analogy and consider our circuit as functioning within a complex of discrete but mutually affective circuits, then we have a picture of the cultural object "art" amongst other cultural objects within the overall structure of culture-as-a-whole at any given time and place.

Lévi-Strauss has distinguished between *individual* and *collective* creation. The former being the attempt in Western societies to form "private languages"[9] for the description of objects in order that *describing* may become *appropriating,* and with the result that art becomes at best hermetic and at worst academic. Collective creation, on the other hand, observed in certain "primitive" societies, involves the formation of rule-governed semantic systems, commonly employed and understood, for the signification of objects accessible to the community as a whole.

If we may take the word "object" here to stand for anything about which a statement may be made, so that "objects" are not only substantial things but may be states-of-mind, mythical entities, properties and classes of things, then we might in principle debate the extent to which generally accessible objects have been, and are being, signified by Western art in a more or less accessible manner. Predominantly, though, studies in art tend to be conducted along the historical axis rather than within the plane of simultaneous cultural events contemporary with the study end "pierced" by that axis. As a result, explanations of art are almost invariably *historical* and we therefore speak of art's *evolution,* and of "revolutions" in art, when we might equally well describe art's *mutations,* brought about by extra-disciplinary influences at the work's inception.

If ". . . every cultural object is reducible to its manifestations, that is, to psychological objects,"[10] then art may be seen as a fundamentally *apperceptive* operation directed towards the mental set of those psychological objects which constitute our continually contemporary sense of individuality within culture-as-a-whole—which might explain art's intellectual promiscuity; art may be a cultural *relationship* rather than a cultural *entity.* If art does operate at the intuitive rather than the discursive level, than all this would be conducted mainly through *emotional* channels: ". . . our ordinary experience of ourself and the world is infused with many shades of adversive and aversive emotions . . . if the purely factual aspect of experience needs to be organized to recurrent invariances, so does this part."[11]

". . . emotions function cognitively not as separate items but in combination with one another and with other means of knowing . . . quantity or intensity of emotion is no measure of its cognitive efficacy. A faint emotion may be as informative as an overwhelming one . . . this is something all attempts to distinguish the aesthetic in terms of amount or degree of emotion overlook."[12]

To mention the emotions is to elicit an emotional response; it is not suggested here that the function of an art work is to provide an emotional experience—life is already full of them—but rather that the "apprehension matrix" which art supplies is most predominantly emotional/intuitive. Art does not provide any new experiences, facts, or *concepts*—it "re-arranges" these things; it provides a "frame of mind" to enclose commonly accessible facts and concepts we already have.

Works which use commonly understood signs *cannot help* but signify some object beyond themselves. This referential aspect of a work might be termed the "semantic component" of the information transmitted by that work: ". . . a military order, an electrical circuitry diagram, a coded message, instructions in case of fire, a technical manual, a musical score, etc., all convey *essentially* semantic information. They prepare acts, forms of action, and in general, semantic information has a clearly utilitarian, but above all *logical* character. It sticks to acts and to meaning."[13]

The "extra-semantic" component of an art work functions as an exclamation, asserting nothing, produced in regard to an object domain identified by the semantic component of the work. The semantic component in turn asserts nothing but functions as a "label" or "pointer," thus annexing the particular content of the recipient's experience of the signified object domain. "Pointing" here, however, is more explicit, closer to "tracing," than is ostensive definition. While being explicit with regard to the recipient's own experience it must nevertheless *not* be open to refutation on empirical grounds. It is here that an uncompromised work exists as an *abstraction* from the signified object domain of that which is common to any recipient's experience of that domain.

If we reject the notion that art is a sub-class of objects, in favor of the view that art is a sub-class of *information,* then art appears in the context of a continuously contemporary informational array, formed, in large part, from our immediate perception of the external world. "Semantic labels" help orientate art information within the larger informational field. The identificational function of the semantic component should be stressed—we may conceive of a "semantic threshold" which may not be exceeded by a work if it is not to take the form of an assertion and so be subject to the criteria "true or false," thus becoming compromised in its art identity. That the tendency of a work to *diverge* in its significance is seen as a problem is evidenced by the wide use of the "self-referential" format, where signification is as far as possible recursive and *con*vergent. Such preoccupations may tempt one to make analogies with mathematics.

It has been suggested that art works represent propositions and that these have the logical form of a tautology. The analogy is partially applicable, insofar as we must acknowledge the essentially axiomatic nature of art, in that the art work is subject to no external testing but need only be consistent with the artist's own assumptions, but is less appealing if we contrast art expressions with, say, mathematical expressions. A mathematical expression is unequivocal in what it asserts and we may recognize, for example, that $(x + 1)^2 = x^2 + 2x + 1$ is tautological and that $x = x + 1$ is absurd. Art, however, is equivocal in what it asserts to such a point that we may reasonably doubt whether it actually *asserts* anything at all, and thus doubt whether $(p \vee {\sim}p)$ may be any more appropriately said to be the form of an art "proposition" than $(p \mathbin{.} {\sim}p)$; from this it follows that art is not "necessarily true" but rather that considerations of either its truth or its falsity are simply *irrelevant*.

Certainly, truth and falsity are not applicable criteria in art. The elements of a work assume, in their mutual relations, an autonomous status subject only to criteria of internal coherence. We do not ask "is it true," but only "is it valid" within the terms of its own axioms. Appreciating this we may be led to use a metaphor which seems to fit these facts and so speak of tautologies in the "language of art"—but the metaphor is misleading; art *has* no language.

Logic and mathematics may express a "frame of mind" in abstract variables and relations—logical structures absolutely independent of any experiential content which might be attributed to them—but at the levels of abstraction where art is viable, ". . . structure . . . is the content itself apprehended in a logical organization conceived as a property of the real."[14] The paradoxical nettle always to be grasped is that of reconciling the art work's status as an empty structure with its existence as an assembly of *meaningful* signs.

## NOTES

1. G. Charbonnier, *Conversations with Claude Lévi-Strauss* (London: Jonathan Cape).

2. ". . . [in] ostensive definition, the object which is meant is brought within range of perception and is then indicated by an appropriate gesture." Rudolf Carnap, *The Logical Structure of the World* (University of California Press, 1969).

3. A photograph of a bridge is a picture of a particular bridge whereas the word "bridge" does not necessarily indicate *any* existing bridge. I nevertheless hold that, encountered within an art context, the word has "nowhere to go" but to concrete particulars.

4. ". . . whatever does not belong to the structure but to the material (i.e., anything that can be pointed out in concrete ostensive definition) is, in the final analysis, subjective." Rudolf Carnap, *op. cit.*

5. Rudolf Carnap, *ibid.*

6. Rudolf Carnap, *ibid.*

7. "It is crucially important to learn to see abstraction not as the visual characteristic of a range of objects (the idea is semantically ludicrous), but as a faculty of thought." Charles Harrison, "A Very Abstract Context," *Studio International* (November 1970).

8. Rudolf Carnap, *op. cit.*

9. While we may feel we know what is meant here by "private language," it is worth emphasizing that if a "private language" is understood *only* by the person who speaks it, the use of the word "language" is inappropriate. Even interpreted liberally, assuming the term is being used metaphorically to describe some sort of personal system of encoding, we may still want to know how far it is possible to *decode,* to translate this language into terms we can all understand.

10. Rudolf Carnap, *op. cit.*

11. Ervin Laszlo, *System, Structure, and Experience* (New York: Gordon and Breach, 1969).

12. Nelson Goodman, *Languages of Art* (Oxford University Press, 1969).

13. Abraham Moles, *Information Theory and Esthetic Perception* (University of Illinois Press, 1966).

14. Claude Lévi-Strauss, quoted by Michael Lane in his introduction to *Structuralism: A Reader* (London: Jonathan Cape, 1970).

This text appeared in *Studio International,* 181:933 (May 1971), pp. 237–239.

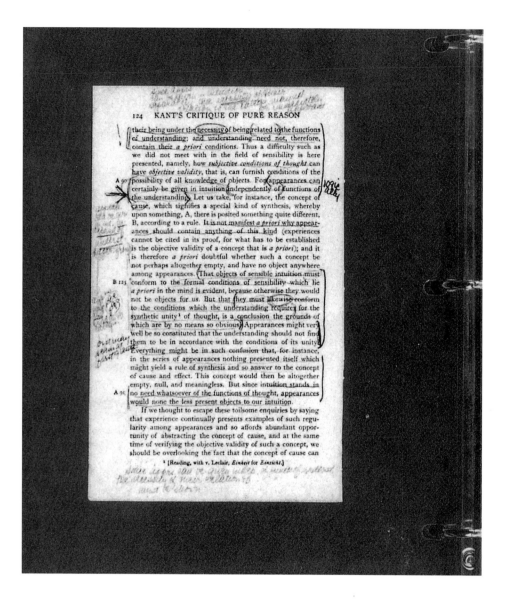

Adrian Piper, page from *Food for the Spirit,* 1971.

# propositions

## terry smith

1. Painting is not becoming obsolete, only less practiced by artists. The best artists who continue to paint feel in a liberated situation—they no longer have to carry the whole weight of artistic change and are more free to explore the infinite options still open within painting. However, they can no longer claim for painting a special status, nor any special concessions. A painting now has to be good/interesting *as art* before it is of any interest as a painting.

2. In sculpture, the closed, integrated, whole object has a function only as a freakish oddity, or as part of an environmental situation. The most fertile kind of recent sculpture (perhaps of recent art) is open-form sculpture—not objects with a core, nor even physical elements arranged coherently, but rather dispersed, thrown, placed, laid elements, disposed in real space. This kind of sculpture invokes in its perceptor a participatory sense of himself as a physical body functioning in a space continuous with that of the sculpture.

3. The basic twentieth century art program of ever-accelerating abstraction is still basic. But the idea of abstraction as reduction has been revealed as self-terminating, especially when it is pegged to the notion of each of the arts separately acting to expel their "expendable conven-

tions." Each of the arts is, in fact, going further than this—they are dispensing with their *essential* conventions (the visual arts with the visual, music with structured sound, poetry with linear print conventions, etc.).

4. In all the arts, the notion of the self-referring art object (and its associated notions of "physicality," the "real," "objecthood") has become dogma. The object (in color-painting, or colored metal sculpture, for example) is seen as the culmination of mainstream aesthetics, as an art-for-art's-sake pursuit, as a thing which embodies no more than the ritual of making it. It is claimed that this sort of art offers only closed information, is devoid of idea-content, and is merely sensual. This is clearly a false generalization about the physical object as such in art, but it does reflect the way the notion of physicality has recently dominated the way we see the potentialities of the object in art.

5. Art-for-art's-sake precious object art has become a commodity within the neo-capitalist system of exchange, of which the art market is a ludicrously exaggerated and irrational microcosm. This has been true for some years, but artists have become sensitive to it recently because it is functioning to restrict artistic innovation. An increased social consciousness amongst artists has arisen as a response to the disintegration of European, but especially American, society. Artists have become alienated from the results of their labor, and no longer want to be functionaries within such a system. This is part of the explanation for the artists' desire to produce art of a kind that cannot be handled by the art gallery/dealer system.

6. Post-object art is tremendously various. It is not a mere reaction to object-emphasizing art, but the positive assertion of myriad new forms of making art. It has not been a clean break with object art but rather a series of take-offs, via the mid-1960s work of Carl Andre, Sol LeWitt, Robert Morris, and the even earlier work of Joseph Beuys. It ranges through scatter pieces, buried sculpture, earth art, ecological art, systems art, process art, body sculpture, mail art, auto-destructive art, the art of nominating part of the world as art, conceptual art, performance art, language art, and many more.

7. The only major idea shared by all post-object artists (it is not the defining idea, nor does it characterize the most important aspect of more than a few of the pieces) is that art is an activity continuous with life, not a special sort of activity separate from life. Art should draw its form and content from our life systems, our social communication systems, our ideas of what we

are in the world. And, in doing so, it has the real option of changing the ways we see ourselves, rather than giving mere symbolic equivalents in a special code of this or that perception.

8. If the preceding proposition is true, then the ephemeral nature of much recent art should be of no concern. Artists are now free to do *more* art, and their many works and projects should be taken together so that a picture is formed of an artist's total enterprise, his quality of imagination, his consistent concerns. His activity as an artist (a thinking, making human be-ing) is what is primarily up for judgement. However, to a lesser degree, criticism is justifiably applied to the aptness or not of the sort of act through which the post-object artist chooses to convey the nature of his thinking.

9. The different sorts of new art emerging in Australia have yet to break down the limitations that have always been present in Australian art. There are still no great artists in this country, although there are some good ones. No new and profound ideas of what art can be about have been introduced here. The basic pattern is still that of stylistic change through the stimulation of change in art at the metropolitan centers. We still do not have a genuine avant-garde art in Australia (only an avant-garde relative to previous Australian art). That the new forms of art are not specifically Australian, that they are of a kind that is open, discursive, exploratory, at least establishes two of the many preconditions for a genuine avant-garde to emerge in this country.

10. In Sydney painting since late 1968 the color-form style has disintegrated as a coherent movement, but certain painters emerged from it to produce an independent post-formalist painting of quality—notably Aspden, Christmann, Johnson, Watkins, McGillick (and from Adelaide, Syd Ball).

In Melbourne, the best of the younger generation of painters have changed over the last two years in a more varied way—for example Vickers and Booth continue to strengthen for-malist painting, Guy Stuart extended his paintings to floor-slabs and mixed-materials hanging pieces, Bob Hunter his all-white painting to paper pieces, and Dale Hickey and Paul Partos gave up painting altogether for conceptual art.

The variety of the Melbourne response, and the moving across essential boundaries (like those between painting and conceptual art), reflects a different sort of art scene from that of Sydney, where initial commitments to new art are more emphatic and group activity more natural. Roughly, where Pinacotheca can bridge stylistic changes, Central Street Gallery had to close and Inhibodress to start.

However, it is now becoming increasingly evident that variety and openness of approach is becoming characteristic of all Australian art, especially sculpture.

This text appeared in the catalogue to the exhibition "The Situation Now: Object or Post-Object Art?" (Sydney: Contemporary Art Society, 1971), pp. 3–4. The exhibition was organized by Smith and Tony McGillick, and was staged from 16 July to 6 August 1971.

# interview with *art-language*

## catherine millet

Catherine Millet: The expression "conceptual art" embraces numerous activities today, diverse and almost contradictory activities, from ephemeral gestures, the anecdotal speculations on the "nonvisual," to the analytical works and the theoretical initiatives that are of interest to us. You yourselves subtitled the first issue of your periodical *The Journal of Conceptual Art* and then dropped this subtitle. What do you think of the interpretation that has been given, in general, to conceptual art? Do you continue to accept this term to designate your own activity? If so, what exact meaning do you give to the term "concept"?

Art-Language: The general usage of the term "conceptual art" has extended to the point where any distinctive meaning that it might have had has disappeared. If you are asking if we accept this term to designate our activity, the answer is frankly "no". Taken in the broadest of meanings, the term "conceptual art" can distinguish Art-Language from Pablo Picasso or from Willem de Kooning, but an answer like this does not signify more than the most hackneyed tautology.

The subtitle *The Journal of Conceptual Art* was dropped because it was associated with too varied a spectrum of artistic activity. The term "concept" could be used in another way to emphasize the importance of its problematic character. One of the possibilities could be in considering more than just one precise meaning. The writings of Frege have provided us with interesting material with respect to the notion of the concept. Frege is one of the principle theoreticians from the beginning of the century who refuted psychologism, that is unjustified psychologism. It was he who showed that it was possible to consider "sense" as an objective concept, separate from its psychological aspect.

C.M.: Ad Reinhardt, who you sometimes mention, aspired to realize "the ultimate paintings possible" with his "black paintings." For the last couple of years you yourselves have had an essentially textual production. Should we then deduce that you opted for a completely distinct terrain from the one Ad Reinhardt was developing? Of what nature is this relinquishment of all pictorial practice, of all manipulation of objects? Before being reintroduced in your work, in the first half of the sixties the work of Reinhardt above all influenced "minimal art." What do you think of that movement?

A.-L.: The particular tradition in post-war America, from Pollock and moving on to Johns, Newman, Stella, and Judd, probably reached a culmination more in the work of Reinhardt, than in any other. Reinhardt had a big influence on the theory (at the same time in his "brute" form and in his more elaborate form) that created the conditions for (what is called) "minimal art" and, consequently, to the theory which gave rise to "minimal art." Reinhardt insisted on interrogation as a constituent element of artistic practice (that is to say the opposite of what would be a pure "plastic celebration"). From this point of view the Art-Language artists situate themselves in the middle of the current of Post-War American art.

It seems clear that the work of the American artists mentioned possesses an evident component of "plastic celebration." Reinhardt in the 1950s, and particularly Judd and LeWitt in the 1960s, opened up the "interrogation" component in the logical substitutions of questions around art (for example, the relation between the object and the "idea"). The separation of the "interrogation" component and the "plastic celebration" component is very important. Initially, it was the "interrogation" component which put the "plastic celebration" component under question, but later, and perhaps in a more determinant manner the "interrogation" component put the "interrogation" component itself under question. In relation to this situation one could examine the Husserlian idea of "Epoche". (. . .)

C.M.: You have defined the linguistic field in which you work as belonging to what you call the "supporting languages" of the work of art. Do you consider language as a medium specific to art?

A.-L.: Language—supposing that we agree on what we mean by it—was, at first sight, a less ambiguous medium than the plastic method. Ambiguity has been seen at times as a necessary aspect of art. On the contrary, recent works have intended to put things in order with as much clarity as possible, and paradoxically we have become aware of the ambiguity that can inhabit language. For us, language is a medium for conserving our work in a context of investigation and interrogation. Probably, it is a specific medium of art, but above all, it would have to define a little better what is and what is not art.

C.M.: If language, the "support" of the work of art, makes this ultimately viable, it is principally thanks to its metaphorical character. Do you think that an analytic work of art, through the medium of language, can be a work of language in itself? If not, don't you run the risk that the undertaking will be considered idealist?

A.-L.: More and more, art, turning to itself in order to question its proper nature, paradoxically looks in other disciplines for the methodologies necessary to articulate those questions.

The "Epoche" as a medium (already mentioned) can be applied to the artistic paradigm of "materialization." In Art-Language there appears the necessity to develop an identical type of medium, to "put to test" the methodological and analytic models that have been borrowed from other disciplines. The most evident point of agreement, although perhaps not the most important, of Art-Language with Marxist economic analysis is that which refers to itself as the fetishism of the object. Art-Language has intended to clarify whether fetishism was or was not a necessary condition of the artistic state. The notion of the object of art as merchandise has to submit, in the first instance, to a strict classic Marxist analysis.

At this moment one of the essential preoccupations of Art-Language is that of putting to test and cleansing its language of idealist tendencies. For example, Art-Language is indebted to Anglo-Saxon analytic philosophical tradition, and in a certain way all analytic efforts which Art-Language has been able to make at any moment on the artistic condition proceeded in part from the analytic philosophical apparatus. One can examine two essential and distinct fields of this apparatus: 1) the apparatus of analytic philosophy; 2) that same apparatus as is analyzed and structured by Art-Language. Today, the problem lies more in how to formulate the questions than in the answer. Thus:

a) At whatever point it is assumed that Fine Art is in essence bourgeois, whatever our social and political convictions might be, if our artistic efforts transform themselves into objects of art we will necessarily be participating in the most extreme manifestation of the capitalist system, that is to say in classic Marxist terms, in the production of commodities.

b) Marx's categories of use value and exchange value can transform the production of art by pitting private use (private language) (use value) against public use (exchange value). The first use is subject to a critique touching on the problem of the elite; the second tries to assess whether we do or do not want a majority elite (which historically is a contradiction), that is, for more people to participate in what has traditionally been the elite sensibility (of course democracy claims for all the possibility of sharing in that elite sensibility but simple protocol of "choice" demands an alternative—in actuality art does not offer any).

c) It is possible that a majority of the writings of Art-Language are not sufficiently open to the suggestions we have described here. The actual program of Art-Language foresees the examination of those aspects.

We say that art founded in the "materialization" paradigm (and things being what they are, that is the only art there is) is a bourgeois idealist manifestation. The fact that Art-Language has attempted to formulate a means to question that paradigm does not constitute a guarantee that the "linguistic" formulation that it has developed is not equally bourgeois.

The other valuable area of investigation regarding the "materialization" paradigm, the entity that situates art, in an uninterrupted manner, in a bourgeois context, is offered by the artistic models developed in Russia between (approximately) 1917 and 1935. It is here (to the extent we can assure ourselves) that they were fully invested in the "materialization" paradigm. Thus, for Malevich, for Tatlin (it is safe to say that the two terms "materialization paradigm" and "artist" are always deployed, in some manner, as synonyms). Lenin himself was of the opinion that a new proletarian culture would be founded on the best traditions from the feudal and capitalist past. The conditioned reflex of classical art is to say that if it is art, then it is an object of art. In the case of Lenin, one can interpret it as follows: "If it is art, then they are objects of art in the manner of the past." And it should not be overlooked that Lenin and someone like Malevich had the same initial reflex. In a Stalinist state, conscious and consistent, Art-Language would arrive in the labor camps less than one or two months ahead of Jasper Johns, Noland and the others! It seems that the ontological engagement of Lenin has been as ferocious as that of Greenberg.

This interview appeared in *Art Vivant,* 25 (1971). Translated by Maya Rabasa, this is its first publication in English.

Art & Language, *Index 01,* 1972, installation details from Documenta 5, Kassel, Germany.

# the trouble with art-as-idea

## max kozloff

(. . .)

Not craftsmanly work, but the thought behind work, not sensibility, but the general and impersonal premise above sensibility: these are the priorities of much current art. They are, of course, part of a strategy, with a long tradition behind it, designed to impose greater demands on the faithful. Faith has been stringently defined as the acceptance of assumptions without the need to require evidence for them. But the mistake of this often repeated and always circular strategy in art—now, at least—is to suppose that it has no upward limits.

For the moment, though, I am more concerned with the unexpectedness of this development. And I propose to explain what there is of the unforeseen in it by resorting to a distinction between usual and unusual claims for art. Since Marcel Duchamp's ready-mades, and since his revival in the '60s, increasing store has been set on the degree and the extent to which modern art resists legitimacy. Its claims in this field may be said to deal entirely with unusual or improbable modes of production. Here, a "mode" has to do with the decisiveness with which an artist switches his operational category. A sculpture made of ground glass is certainly novel, but horseback riding, considered as sculpture, is unusual.

**I'm not a poet and I'm considering oral communication as a sculpture.**
—Ian Wilson

One of the wonders of modern artists, and sources of their prestige, has been their capacity to purge themselves of the credible, yet to behave, in a delicate balance, as if their eccentric gambits were thoroughly plausible.

Established plausibility, such as painting's, is, however, not admissible because it is a fixed mode whose practice arouses no doubts as to its legitimacy. I regret to say that the reasoning behind this is grounded on nothing more than the evident fact that painting is physically a flat surface covered variously with paint. This is to observe nothing of the subjects, styles, expressive goals or achievements in painting, matters that have no place in the new aesthetic. Robert Barry notes that he abandoned painting because he wanted to get away from framing edges and to be released from the wall. But this ordinary claustrophobia ties in with recent art's contempt for the stable and vulgarly identifies a stabilized mode with a restriction on freedom. There is an elementary confusion here, too, because the physically finite space of painting is a frame for what can be symbolically infinite.

**There are so many different situations in which to look at something that standing right before the painting or walking around a sculpture could well be the most simple kind.**
—Jan Dibbets

**Question: Does one's physical position before a work of art cancel out feeling towards or thinking about it—and how "simple" are these?**

Oddly enough, the practitioners of art-as-idea are exceedingly literal on this issue. With them, an unusual claim differentiates creators on the score of their medium of the moment, whether this be gas, philosophy, laser, post cards, Xerox, Instamatic photography, or set theory. These have their apparent limitations, too, but they have their advantages and make their point when introduced for unlikely consideration as art modes. The result is an unremitting exhaustion of possibilities of embodiment and gestures of renunciation, viewed as positive ends in themselves. (I would have guessed that this evinces a very American penchant for packaging were it not, through-and-through, an international development.) Haunted by the obsolescence and ephemeralness of his actions, the artist of unusual claims rededicates himself to inconsistency.

For though he may be very constant, even repetitive in his ideas, he is generally on record as prohibiting himself a coherent evolution furnished through style.

*Ursula Meyer:* "Would you agree that art is the more extreme the further it gets away from style?"
*Robert Barry:* "Yes, I agree. I cannot really give you my definition."

We have had styles in art for many excellent reasons, chief among which is the artist's desire to engender for us his view or views of the world. Not only does the advanced artist programmatically fail in this view, he categorically opposes any syntheses or cross–referencing of ideas. He prefers instead, deliberately undigested accretions of data, documentations without comment, the purveying of information for its own sake, and the measuring of meaningless

The documents prove nothing. They make the piece exist and I am interested in having that existence occur in as simple a way as possible. Where a thing is located involves everything else and I like that idea much more than how I "feel" about it or what it looks like.
—Douglas Huebler

quantities or changes in location of some object or phenomenon. It is all research of high selectivity and fulsome detail that goes nowhere and that neither distinguishes events nor draws them together. There has been much abstruse jargon justifying these maneuvers, but little power of abstract reasoning displayed in them. Nothing less is demanded than that we sanctify this real atomization in the name of art's prerogative. And that is what is unusual about the last four years.

Let us imagine that the affirmative goal of what has been called "Conceptual art" is to achieve for each its actings-out a social aura of uncertainty and ill-definition, the point of which is to foster new conditions of awareness and to disturb conventional notions of art's role. Something that is, or might be, operational or functioning, useful or consequential, has been taken, imitated or reconstructed from "out there," and has been appropriated within art boundaries. So that the typical response encouraged is: "Why am I asked to look upon or judge, in a special light, an incident, an activity, a process, or a thought—verbal or oral—that has no singular quality in itself?" That is the classic question posed by modern art since Courbet. And when that art was aesthetically successful, the appropriate answer was found in the imaginative transformation of initially unpromising material. In the early part of our century, this kind of question and answer process was phrased in terms of a test—a test of art's then known limits. Sixty years later, the idea that art had aesthetic limits (I do not say moral or political limits) has worn out. The social brake against anything being called aesthetic, as long as it remained aesthetic for the art world, has faded away. You can step the brake down to the floor and nothing happens. Under the circumstances, the problem of avant-garde continuity was thought to be solved by the *refusal* to transform the art subject.

There were, of course, degrees of such refusal, but of late they have become wholesale and homogeneous, regardless of the endless variables involved in an ostentatiously random focus on a motif. The untampered or unmanipulated gobbet of "real life," viewed as art, has canceled many obligations rewarding to artists who earlier made highly complex objects. But some might feel it has enhanced the illusion that artists were capable of participating directly in everyday experience and possibly of effecting the course of public events. Participatory occasions, inter-media mixes, ecological awareness, computer mimicry, environmental analyses, perceptual intensifications: these are some of the themes used by contemporary artists to solicit approval for their para-activism, their meta-engagement in the world.

I am obliged to conclude, though, that these urgent-sounding concerns decrease in credibility the more they are contoured by aestheticism. Further, the field of presence cannot be made to match ever more closely the arena of involvement without becoming uneasy by the comparison. (The converse, I might add, is not true: a murderer's deeds are not reduced in effect because he may happen to think of them in aesthetic terms.) Good art can change our consciousness through its symbolic order, but an artist cannot, in good conscience, wish away that symbolism on one level and use it for insulation and immunity on another. His flirtation with literal potency only achieves its ends involuntarily when in conflict with hard-core literalists who either do not see that art was intended, or who couldn't care less for its crazy privileges at the moment *their* symbolic structures are threatened. When Hans Haacke's photo documentation of New York landlords was censored by the Guggenheim Museum, it was an accident of this sort, induced by sensitive material. When, in an act of deliberate provocation, the Judson Flag Show artists were busted, they were testing a law, not the limits of art—so their gesture entered the political rather than the aesthetic annals of our culture.

But these exceptions do highlight the burdensome ironies faced by the immediate art audience itself. Art-as-idea's ritualization of the unusual imposes upon that audience increased depths of specious response. The unexpected is so expected that a self-defeating element is introduced into our dialogue with art. (. . .) Our over-conditioning, I think, has become debilitating.

For our commerce with art may go on nominally as it had before, but so weakened, precious, and attenuated as to make it almost a matter of indifference. (. . .) When Douglas Huebler photographs people at the moment they are told something about their appearance, the result may be a study of suddenly new, ruffled consciousness. It is a voyeuristic exercise which we may turn upon ourselves: what is the expression on our faces when we "experience" a Huebler?

Certainly it is hard to imagine it as one of shock. For the pleasures of surprise have been replaced by the comforts of the indeterminate. The taste-making class is here still on the side of the mischievous, but its enthusiasm has been very much eroded. (. . .) The once euphoric tensions and flighty instincts of the last decade have given way to politeness and pedantry. And I suspect this to be the result of a demoralization that cannot acknowledge itself.

Very few hints are taken from many works that are themselves overt scenarios of impasse and paralysis. "On Kawara selects a pre-stretched canvas for his daily work, a carefully

**Particulars related to the information not contained herein constitute the form of this action.**
—Christine Kozlov, in a telegram to the Museum of Modern Art

painted monochrome on which is noted the day's date. If the painting is not finished by midnight, it is destroyed. By October 31, 1970 eight hundred and twenty-three of these works were completed" (*Avalanche,* Spring, 1972). During a prescribed period, Vito Acconci steps up and down from a stool at the rate of thirty steps a minute, for as long as he can without stopping. John Baldessari writes, "I will not make any more boring art" over and over again. Not merely are these performances standardized in terms of their units, but they are typical of their kind. A school of legislated nihilism has grown up around them.

Mostly the acts of this school—they would pretend to enter copy books or hospital reports—seem to occur preliminary or posterior to an artist doing his thing; the middle phase, execution itself, is dropped out, or is superimposed as a name upon the aftermath or the residue. "Residual art," in fact, is a good name for what has happened. Its authors come on as compulsives, or deep in some kind of physical therapy. (. . .)

The scene is surfeited, then, with much information that goes a short way. We are barraged with data overloads, inertial lists, that are not communicative, and that are not even intelligible except by reference to a sullied faith in art. It is a turn of events that averages out a great deal of competitive energy. (The same thing, of course, happens in American culture, under the rubric of "administration.") The loss of confidence in the concrete has been screened by a downpour of minutiae. Cause and effect have been disassociated, and human action trivialized, if we accept the message of art-as-idea. But what I notice above all, is the inability of the various mediums—process, Conceptual, etc.—to come to terms with what can be said of experience. It is as if a whole language has been reduced to punctuation marks, contained on forms on which the art world inscribes its initials.

There can be no doubt that recent events in art history have led to this hermetic situation. Minimal sculpture, earthworks, happenings, "distribution" pieces, these are merely the bases of the more extreme outcomes we see today. The artist as critic, serial or systemic modes of composition, the photographic documentation offering no inherent qualities of its own, the whole evanescent, biodegradable art leavings syndrome—all these prophesied what was to come. Even more obvious, though, is the literal ransacking by the current generation of every doctrine in modern art that has opposed itself to the ideals of sensory pleasure and the values of personal imagination. Cage, Duchamp, Reinhardt, and Malevich represent extreme degrees of unrestricted or over-restricted art goals that are seen by Conceptualists to amount to very much the same thing: the principle that philosophical attitude takes precedence over unique form. But the new figures are content to describe what had earlier been necessary to show or demonstrate. They have picked clean what was once fresh in such positions through literal illustration and perpetual replay. And they treat us now to a tired litany against the possessible and the material. Not for nothing has the word "re-cycle" become an almost mystical term of art parlance. And in the film loop is found the apparatus most instrumental in effecting a mood of such unconscious desperation that it does not know any more of beginning, middle, or end.

In an extremely apparent sense, then, art-as-idea is highly conservative. It exemplifies an almost rote dependence on an art context and does nothing more than reveal passive attitudes towards advancing that context. To live off the subversiveness of the parent, to freeload from it, and to score unearned points for significance in its name: these tactics characterize recent activity. When this situation occurs in painting, instead of recondite propositions and theorems, its visibility draws immediate fire. Often ethereal in presence, the *art of ideas* is just as plainly compromised in its derivations.

As it turns out, however, a major proposition of this retread Dadaism is the longing to be free of art history. The tradition of art, after all, is culture-bound, and where is there a more effective way for the artist to declare himself independent and liberated from culture than to announce that he has disassociated himself from art history? The history of modern art is replete with artists who announced themselves impervious to historical categories. (. . .)

It is odd that their unrest manifests itself by recourse to language, and the technical language of philosophy or pseudo-science at that. To be sure, there is a short-term logic to be found in the proposal that since the history of art was a history of forms, to demolish physical form is to blink away the continuity of the historical event in art.

**To abandon the search for a new form at any price means trying to abandon the history of art as we know it. . . .**
　　—Daniel Buren

**. . . and since I am not interested in problems of forms, color and material, it goes without saying that my evolution could not be aesthetic.**
　　—Bernar Venet

I suppose this is the ultimate rebuke to formalist aesthetics whose definitions of radicalism always seemed to be incarnated by sleek, decorative artifacts. But the dialogue between art's intentions and meanings is not so much transcended as shortchanged by abandonment of a sensory guise. Aesthetic encounters have merely been transposed from the allusions that can be stimulated by art objects to a focus on the illusions of art ideology, neither of which is exempt—nor could it be—from the historical process.

One of the more extreme art-as-idea artists, Lawrence Weiner, denies neither the materiality of art, because everything an artist uses is material, nor the inevitable legitimization of his efforts by "culture." But "as what I do becomes art history the minute the culture accepts it, so it stops being art" (*Avalanche,* Spring, 1972). Like the Groucho Marx who wouldn't join a country club that would have him as a member, Weiner, less wittily, plays at being disreputable. Yet such an artist does not claim himself a pariah in any mood of ironic self-disparagement. Rather, it is assumed that art can only have art impact before it is recognized culturally as art. And it is implied that the work of the artist must be acceptable to a committed minority group by virtue of its, at least temporary, unacceptability to the "cultural" mass.

Culture, then, is often defined self-servingly by artists who would flatter their immediate sympathizers as a very exclusive club, an "inner culture." From a once fairly accurate description of how modern art became assimilated, this seduction of the sophisticates has become a formula purveyed for its own sake. Those not initially involved in the consumption of the inaugural art statement are denigrated as a kind of entombment society. Carl Andre phrases the argument quite belligerently: "Art is what we do; culture is what is done to us,"—an ungenerous half-truth. The absorption of art into a framework of meaning beyond the mystique of its practitioners, necessary to the morale of all artists, is considered suspect, inimical, even a betrayal. Doubtless there are many risky factors operating in the trade-off between the avant-garde and its wider potential audience. What we see here, however, is the attempt to institutionalize a social antagonism without observing whether a base for such antagonism any longer exists. And even more, without substantiating a subversive slogan by a subversive content.

What, after all, has Lawrence Weiner done? To take a known example, he conceived this specification for a work of art: "an abridgment of an abutment to on, near, or about the arctic circle." Lucy Lippard describes the execution of the work at Inuvik, arctic Canada: "Using whatever is at hand, in this case a cigarette package, he leans it against a broken pile of dirt." It is a tale of little consequence that loses in the telling. But from such a nonevent it is an ideological pebble's throw to Weiner's grandiose indications: "1.) The artist may construct the piece. 2.) The piece may be fabricated. 3.) The piece need not be built. Each *[sic]* being equal and consistent with the intent of the artist, the decision as to condition rests with the receiver upon the occasion of receivership."

In other words, it seems a matter of indifference whether any experience takes place at all, as long as the notion that it may take place is suggested. This insinuation, after all, is the art part. It consists of begging such questions as to why something should be done, how it should be done, and for whom. How significant that Weiner uses the economic term "receivership," a protesting too much that significance has only to be declared to exist. In an unsettling way, it deprives us of ever *finding* significance for ourselves.

For the optionality of Conceptual art is non-leading only on face value. Theoretically it represents a "further" stage in modern art where the withdrawal of constructive (in all senses of the word) decision and the rejecting of responsibility for the thing presented close the possibilities of interpretation. We are strenuously directed to see that thought itself is up for grabs. Yet it is also shrewdly anticipated that putting the exchange between the giver and the receiver in the conditional tense (may—may not) equates any conceivable outcome with any other.

Once more, therefore, the argument hinges on a bind. All "morphological" art, that is, painting and sculpture, has been superseded and demoted to the status of a historical curiosity (Kosuth) because it does not question the nature of art. But Conceptual art induces only a mood of nonexpectancy because *its* questioning has no form, only a principle, and may be said to be an affair exclusively of absolute function. This position is fanatically tautological because it collapses all distinctions among the attitude of the artist, his product, and aesthetic response. The "receiver's" experience *is* his realization of the artist's intent, just as the artist's aim is to cultivate such realization. And this explains that whatever is actually done by the artist is of no weight or consequence because then it might have content, and someone might want to bear witness to that content, empirically, in a culture where distinctions are made.

Logically, this stand is rather mysterious. Art ideas rely as surely on an *a priori* art context as art objects and it is hard to see how that context is challenged because a new language is involved. Furthermore, "absolute function," is a contradiction in terms: what serves most appropriately in one situation will not do in another. But art does not have to be logical and I am more interested in asking, in any event, why some artists today adopt this posture as a cultural attack. (. . .)

**Instead of making art I filled out this form.**
—Frederick Barthelme

Perhaps they have a common social understanding that objects alone are not what civilization deals with. But the eliminating of objects is suspect in a crew of artists who have a fear of being explicit and a horror of being held accountable. A credibility gap exists in our art life just as it does in our political world, for the reason that, in both, people are systematically abstracted from their humanity and considered as receivers of stimuli—a mass that exists only to be conditioned. Conceivably the art scene here is a frivolous microcosm of big power rhetoric and manipulations. I am impressed, in any case, by the bureaucratic tendencies of art-as-idea—the fact that ever more extraneous, repetitious, and purposeless work fills the air with crypto–efficiency.

The root of the problem, it seems to me, is the accentuation of a hidebound playfulness. The more various barriers against the acceptance of art modes are removed, the more artists are compelled to formulate their activity as a game. If Lawrence Weiner is truly the Marxist he claims to be, it is wondrous to imagine how, if at all, he related the placing of his cigarette package to the exploitation of the Eskimos he is reported to have seen all around him. One of the very few artists to comment on the toxic effects of the art game is Allan Kaprow, but his proposed escape from its pretenses is the most delusional I have heard ("The Education of the Un-Artist, Part II," *Art News,* May, 1972). His recipe, in brief, is that society would not need an art life if all urgent, purposeful, and effectual activity could be liberated by play! Our hang-ups about money, practicality, competition, and survival are the obstacles that bar entry into an exquisite world of irresponsibility. Let the artist abandon his own identity among his peers, let him missionize for indulgence in the outer world, let him become a zealot of relaxation. "Art work, a sort of moral paradigm for an exhausted work ethic, is converting into play. As a four-letter word in a society given to games, 'play' does what all dirty words do: it strips bare the myth of culture by its artists, even."

My guess, however, is that it is not the work, but the play ethic that is exhausted, at least as represented in Conceptual art. Freedom from logic, moral sanctions, and formal seriousness: none of these are issues for me as long as they do not become a reason of his being for the artist. They are among conditions under which some work has to be accomplished, but they are not a principle of art-making, nor can they be equated with content. Yet the aggressive "take-it-or-leave-it" psychology of much recent art betrays, I think, uneasiness on this score. That we are defied "to leave" the art, that we are often offered nothing, effectively, but this defiance, is the piece's justification. Why else do we have so much theory misconceived as practice, thought considered as itself an object, and hypotheses replacing experience? At this point, play becomes desperate. Unrefreshing in itself, the contrast between the frivolity of the premises and the puritanism of statement in art-as-idea is also unilluminating. It is a weird deadlock.

This essay appeared in *Artforum,* 11:1 (September 1972), pp. 261–265.

22  Fred Lonidier, *29 Arrests,* 1972, detail. Headquarters of the 11th Naval District, May 4, 1972, San Diego.

# cultural confinement
## robert smithson

Cultural confinement takes place when a curator imposes his own limits on an art exhibition, rather than asking an artist to set his limits. Artists are expected to fit into fraudulent categories. Some artists imagine they've got a hold on this apparatus, which in fact has got a hold of them. As a result, they end up supporting a cultural prison that is out of their control. Artists themselves are not confined, but their output is. Museums, like asylums and jails, have wards and cells—in other words, neutral rooms called "galleries." A work of art when placed in a gallery loses its charge, and becomes a portable object or surface disengaged from the outside world. A vacant white room with lights is still a submission to the neutral. Works of art seen in such spaces seem to be going through a kind of aesthetic convalescence. They are looked upon as so many inanimate invalids, waiting for critics to pronounce them curable or incurable. The function of the warden-curator is to separate art from the rest of society. Next comes integration. Once the work of art is totally neutralized, ineffective, abstracted, safe, and politically lobotomized it is ready to be consumed by society. All is reduced to visual fodder and transportable merchandise. Innovations are allowed only if they support this kind of confinement.

Occult notions of "concept" are in retreat from the physical world. Heaps of private information reduce art to hermeticism and fatuous metaphysics. Language should find itself in the physical world, and not end up locked in an idea in somebody's head. Language should be an ever developing procedure and not an isolated occurrence. Art shows that have beginnings and ends are confined by unnecessary modes of *representation* both "abstract" and "realistic." A face or a grid on a canvas is still a representation. Reducing representations to writing does not bring one closer to the physical world. Writing should generate ideas into matter, and not the other way around. Art's development should be dialectical and not metaphysical.

I am speaking of a dialectics that seeks a world outside of cultural confinement. Also, I am not interested in art works that suggest "process" within the metaphysical limits of the neutral room. There is no freedom in that kind of behavioral game playing. The artist acting like a B. F. Skinner rat doing his "tough" little tricks is something to be avoided. Confined process is no process at all. It would be better to disclose the confinement rather than make illusions of freedom.

I am for an art that takes into account the direct effect of the elements as they exist from day to day apart from representation. The parks that surround some museums isolate art into objects of formal delectation. Objects in a park suggest static repose rather than any ongoing dialectic. Parks are finished landscapes for finished art. A park carries the values of the final, the absolute, and the sacred. Dialectics have nothing to do with such things. I am talking about a dialectic of nature that interacts with the physical contradictions inherent in natural forces as they are—nature as both sunny and stormy. Parks are idealizations of nature, but nature in fact is not a condition of the ideal. Nature does not proceed in a straight line, it is rather a sprawling development. Nature is never finished. When a finished work of 20th-century sculpture is placed in an 18th-century garden, it is absorbed by the ideal representation of the past, thus reinforcing political and social values that are no longer with us. Many parks and gardens are re-creations of the lost paradise or Eden, and not the dialectical sites of the present. Parks and gardens are pictorial in their origin—landscapes created with natural materials rather than paint. The scenic ideals that surround even our national parks are carriers of a nostalgia for heavenly bliss and eternal calmness. Apart from the ideal gardens of the past, and their modern counterparts—national and large urban parks—there are the more infernal regions—slag heaps, strip mines, and polluted rivers. Because of the great tendency toward idealism, both pure and abstract, society is confused as to what to do with such places. Nobody wants to go on a vacation to a garbage dump. Our land ethic, especially in that never-never land called the "art world" has become clouded with abstractions and concepts.

Could it be that certain art exhibitions have become metaphysical junkyards? Categorical miasmas? Intellectual rubbish? Specific intervals of visual desolation? The warden-curators still depend on the wreckage of metaphysical principles and structures because they don't know any better. The wasted remains of ontology, cosmology, and epistemology still offer a ground for art. Although metaphysics is outmoded and blighted, it is presented as tough principles and solid reasons for installations of art. The museums and parks are graveyards above the ground—congealed memories of the past that act as a pretext for reality. This causes acute anxiety among artists, in so far as they challenge, compete, and fight for the spoiled ideals of lost situations.

This statement was originally published in the *Documenta 5* exhibition catalogue (Kassel, 1972). It subsequently appeared in *Artforum,* 11:2 (October 1972), p. 32.

# production for production's sake
## robert smithson

Gallery development starting in the late 50s and early 60s has given rise to a cultural economics that feeds on objects and ideas through a random market. The "market place of ideas" removes ideas from any physical reality. Because galleries and museums have been victims of "cutbacks," they need a cheaper product—objects are thus reduced to "ideas," and as a result we get "Conceptual Art." Compared to isolated objects, isolated ideas in the metaphysical context of a gallery offer the random art audience an aesthetic bargain. Painting and sculpture as isolated things in themselves are still carriers of class mystifications such as "quality." Overproduction takes a different form when it comes to modernist values. A group show of the followers of Anthony Caro only serves to reinforce the "quality" of Caro's sculpture. Critical mystification then reinforces that "influence" by representing or misrepresenting the idea of quality. The "object of art" becomes more a condition of a confused leisure class, and as a result the artist is separated from his own *work*. The patron of an Anthony Caro is thus conditioned by critical representations of reinforced "quality." Qualities are used to mask the value of the object, so that it is not merely an "object" among objects.

Production for production's sake, art for art's sake, sex for sex's sake are interwoven into an economic fabric that gives rise to that curious consumer called an "art lover." If you can produce art objects, idea objects, you can also produce sex objects. Andy Warhol simply produces all three at once, leaving the problems of quality for quality's sake to the more class-conscious aesthetes. By turning himself into a "Producer," Warhol transforms Capitalism itself into a Myth. Anything that you can "think" of can be turned into an object. In a fit of production hysteria, Paul Morrissey (*Village Voice,* March 2, 1972) has taken his cues from Hollywood and seized on violence for violence's sake. "We want to appeal to a mass audience, so we're using lots of violence." The many-are-called-few-are-chosen school of Michael Fried opposes such mass values. Yet, on another level the Fried school performs the same function with privileged values. Fried becomes Caro's Morrissey, whereas Morrissey becomes Warhol's Fried. Both Fried and Morrissey condition their audiences in the same way; their words may be different, "quality" and "violence," but they are both representing production for production's sake. It's not hard to imagine a film production called *Quality Violence*—opening scene: Holly Wood-lawn impales Anthony Caro, played by Brigid Polk, on one of his sculptures after a violent argument over quality. The double-headed hydra of mass and privileged values would come full circle.

This statement, written in 1972, remained unpublished until 1996 when it was included in the anthology *Robert Smithson: The Collected Writings,* ed. Jack Flam (Berkeley: University of California Press, 1996), p. 378.

# l'art conceptuel
## michel claura and seth siegelaub

Seth Siegelaub: The label conceptual art is simplistic and misleading.

Like all categories developed in order to define and assure control over aesthetic change, conceptual art does not mean anything at all. If it is possible to bring together 10, 50, 500 different artists under a single aesthetic definition—and I do not think that such is possible—a global description would be that these artists are engaged in an art whose principal characteristic is the predominant use of language; it is also the use of banal, everyday information as commentary and it is sometimes the systematic analysis of the visual aspect of our physical and intellectual environment. It differs from earlier forms of art in the sense that it does not interpret, nor change, nor add a new object to the environment, but only isolates and draws attention to existing phenomena.

In a certain sense, conceptual art could be defined as:

$$\frac{\text{Painting}}{\text{Conceptual art}} = \frac{\text{the novel}}{\text{journalism}}$$

Michel Claura: When conceptual art was defined (and this was serving as its justification) as the disappearance of the object in art, it was a fraud. 1) It is not so much in not making an object that one should be able to make the question of the object of art go away as it is in its relations with the oeuvre, its relations with art. And, more concretely, 2) what is a sheet of paper with some words on it, a book, verbal or written information; in brief, what is conceptual art if it is not a presentation of objects, as if it was a question of (and for a very good reason . . . ) objects of art?

When conceptual art was defined as an interrogation of art, it was certainly made to take the wrong course; very nearly, it would be made to believe that art's corrupt being is questioned by writing some words on its subject or to be more exact about its object (of art).

But one is never short of definitions that are as distorted as they are appealing.

## IS CONCEPTUAL ART AMERICAN?

S.S.: The debut of conceptual art is unique because it appeared simultaneously around the world. Prior to this, artistic movements were very localized with all the leaders living in the same city (and usually the same neighborhood). It could also be said, in other words, that it was impossible to be an important artist unless you lived in the "right" city. Conceptual art, which is an inappropriate name, was probably the first artistic movement which did not have a geographic center. One could think that it evolved from New York, but this is certainly due to the fact that New York was the center for artistic promotion, reviews, books, galleries, etc.

M.C.: It is certain that conceptual art existed outside the United States before it was revealed to the public. The ideology that supports this form of art is not specifically American. It could even be European rather, with its recourse to written language. And, anyway, the ideology that underlies western art seems today to subtend the art world in a much more consistent and simultaneously anterior manner.

(. . .)

## THE SUCCESS OF CONCEPTUAL ART

S.S.: There are two possible reasons why anything succeeds. One is that the thing has quality, has a certain value, is of a type evidently valuable and important. The other is the type that has been carefully and brilliantly launched by the people who profit from its success. It's up to you to make this distinction.

Beyond the question of "quality," there were a certain number of characteristics particular to conceptual art that were contributing to its success:

*1 — The work can be reproduced and printed without it deforming the intention of the work itself.*

*2 — It is (generally) very inexpensive to produce.*

*3 — It is very inexpensive to transport, causing it to not be significant for a museum or dealer putting together an international exhibition with just 200 dollars, which, obviously, made conceptual art exhibitions very attractive.*

*4 — Then, just as the problem of the transportation of the work was determined, presentation and installation was becoming an important part of the work, each artist having his own manner of "exhibiting," finding, thus, reason to travel. The problem of the "installation" contributed to increased contact between artists, museum workers and collectors.*

*5 — The work was often presented in the form of books, permitting people to possess an original work easily and without great expense.*

The initial success for conceptual art came from Europe. Even today there is very little official support for conceptual art in the United States. In fact, referring to something I know to be the case, not a single gallery in the United States was interested in conceptual art until 1971, whereas, at the same time, in Europe there was an entire team of dealers promoting conceptual art: Sperone in Italy, Fischer in Germany, Art & Project in the Netherlands, Lambert in Paris. The same is true with collectors and museums.

Conceptual art was known in the United States at first through the small books and catalogs which were often made or generated by the artists themselves and distributed by mail to the art community. In this manner, many people came to know the work of artists outside the usual circuit of galleries and museums, and the finance that implies.

In Europe, the galleries were functioning as intermediaries between the artists and the public from the beginning. They were also growing at the same time as their artists. And, in fact, they were functioning exactly as if it didn't matter which gallery, only that they were showing conceptual art.

This group of European galleries had significant success selling conceptual art, whereas only very recently in the United States, the famous galleries (Castelli, Weber, Bykert) began to show conceptual art, and these galleries were already well established prior to this.

One of the reasons why these dealers, collectors and museums hesitated before getting into conceptual art is that they did not understand how one could sell an idea. They did not understand how they might be able to reconcile their aesthetic interests and their taste for speculation. They were content to wait and observe with interest the activity as it developed.

Their European "colleagues" understood much more quickly the importance of conceptual art, and understood immediately the profit angle that they would be able to target.

The economic aspect of conceptual art is perhaps the most interesting. From the moment when ownership of the work did not give its owner the great advantage of control of the work acquired, this art was implicated in turning back on the question of the value of its private appropriation. How can a collector possess an idea? But, in fact, this question was generally "superseded," the artist gave his signature, or a certificate of ownership, even in publicity on behalf of the reputation of the purchaser.

Unhappily, the economic pattern associated with conceptual art is remarkably similar to that of other artistic movements: to purchase a unique work cheap and resell it at a high price. In short, speculation.

M.C.: The success of conceptual art in all cases in Europe since its debut has been the result, in large part, of a misunderstanding. It is presented as the art of the moment. It had the seductive appeal of intellectual pretense. It was, in fact, a mixture of trivial gags and big ideas: in place of having a painting, no more than a title is provided, but, at the same time, "it poses a problem." This provided for the instantaneous assimilation by the magic of the word: if it is "conceptual" it is interesting. Spiritual and intellectual elevation by conceptual art—there is no doubt that it was with this hope that caused a large part of the clientele to follow it. As for the critics, they made an unfettered overvaluation. They did not have, it seemed to them, any more to say except by becoming "conceptualists" as well. But it became clear that it is not easy to become a philosopher or linguist in a few months. That gave rise to some very grandiloquent language for an anthology of pedantry.

The pretension of the name is already an ideological ground for the success it received.

Also, regarding the sudden European success of this art, the other ideological basis must not be forgotten. That is, contrary to the reality of the facts, conceptual art was viewed by Europeans as an art that came from America. And for the first time, because of the ease of transportation and dissemination of the works, and also because the European dealers have been savvy, this "American" art succeeded in Europe at the same moment it emerged in the United States (and elsewhere), in place of being imported some years later as had happened previously. To first possess the new art being made at the same time in America—this was also a serious incitement for the amateur European avant-garde and a consolation for its provincial complex.

## THE POLITICS OF CONCEPTUAL ART

S.S.: Conceptual art, more than all previous types of art, questions the fundamental nature of art. Unhappily, the question is strictly limited to the exclusive domain of the fine arts. There is still the potential of it authorizing an examination of all that surrounds art, but in reality, conceptual artists are dedicated only to exploring avant-garde aesthetic problems.

M.C.: The great cleverness of conceptual art consisted in its self-presentation as a radical movement based on its renunciation of the "art object." But this radical appearance was (and is) also the limit of this form of art.

The dematerialized object is believed to be a "resolution" achieved by not doing "painting" or "sculpture" any more, when, instead, to not create, once again, is to resolve one of the many conditions of art's viability, one of the many means of sanctioning art (which permit "creativity"). As such it is evident that the absence of the object becomes an object again; by suppressing the so-called object, it cannot be ignored. Besides, what is a conceptual art work if it is not an object?

The principle that governs the artistic avant-garde is to distinguish itself from the previous avant-garde, it is to attempt to exhaust a margin that the preceding generation did not emphasize and discover.

The principle of the avant-garde is to continue art by modifying its appearance. It is, in other words, to play the game of apparent liberty; to disavow its father in order to better preserve tradition, civilization and art yet again.

This is one of the aspects of the political function of conceptual art that places it among the other avant-gardes.

This interview appeared in *XXe siècle,* no. 41 (December 1973), pp. 156–159. Translated by Blake Stimson, this is its first publication in English.

23

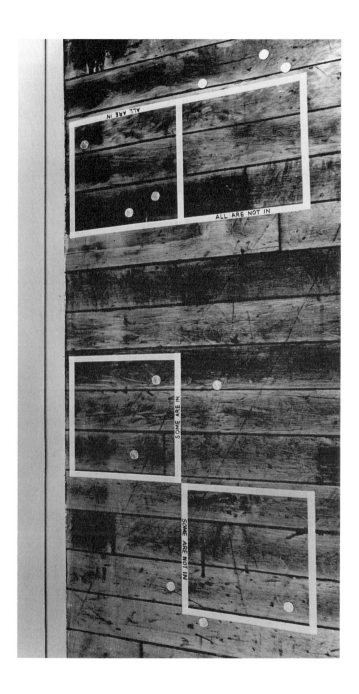

Mel Bochner, *Axiom of Indifference,* 1972–73.

## postface, in *six years: the dematerialization of the art object, 1966 to 1972*

## lucy r. lippard

Hopes that "conceptual art" would be able to avoid the general commercialization, the destructively "progressive" approach of modernism were for the most part unfounded. It seemed in 1969 that no one, not even a public greedy for novelty, would actually pay money, or much of it, for a xerox sheet referring to an event past or never directly perceived, a group of photographs documenting an ephemeral situation or condition, a project for work never to be completed, words spoken but not recorded; it seemed that these artists would therefore be forcibly freed from the tyranny of a commodity status and market-orientation. Three years later, the major conceptualists are selling work for substantial sums here and in Europe; they are represented by (and still more unexpected—showing in) the world's most prestigious galleries. Clearly, whatever minor revolutions in communication have been achieved by the process of dematerializing the object (easily mailed work, catalogues and magazine pieces, primarily art that can be shown inexpensively and unobtrusively in infinite locations at one time), art and artist in a capitalist society remain luxuries.

On the other hand, the aesthetic contributions of an "idea art" have been considerable. An informational, documentary idiom has provided a vehicle for art ideas that were encumbered and obscured by formal considerations. It has become obvious that there is a place for an art which parallels (rather than replaces or is succeeded by) the decorative object, or, perhaps still more important, sets up new critical criteria by which to view and vitalize itself (the function of the Art & Language group and its growing number of adherents). Such a strategy, if it continues to develop, can only have a salutary effect on the way all art is examined and developed in the future.

Conceptual art has not, however, as yet broken down the real barriers between the art context and those external disciplines—social, scientific, and academic—from which it draws sustenance. While it has become feasible for artists to deal with technical concepts in their own imaginations, rather than having to struggle with constructive techniques beyond their capacities and their financial means, interactions between mathematics and art, philosophy and art, literature and art, politics and art, are still at a very primitive level. There are some exceptions, among them certain works by Haacke, Buren, Piper, the Rosario group, Huebler. But, for the most part, the artists have been confined to art quarters, usually by choice. As yet the "behavioral artists" have not held particularly rewarding dialogues with their psychologist counterparts, and we have had no feedback on the Art & Language group from the linguistic philosophers they emulate. "Art use" of elementary knowledge, already accepted and exhausted, oversimplification, and unsophistication in regard to work accomplished in other fields are obvious barriers to such interdisciplinary communication.

The general ignorance of the visual arts, especially their theoretical bases, deplorable even in the so-called intellectual world; the artist's well-founded despair of ever reaching the mythical "masses" with "advanced art"; the resulting ghetto mentality predominant in the narrow and incestuous art world itself, with its resentful reliance on a very small group of dealers, curators, critics, editors, and collectors who are all too frequently and often unknowingly bound by invisible apron strings to the "real world's" power structure—all of these factors may make it unlikely that conceptual art will be any better equipped to affect the world any differently than, or even as much as, its less ephemeral counterparts. Certainly, few of the artists are directly concerned with this aspect of their art, nor can they be, since art that begins with other than an internal, aesthetic goal rarely produces anything more than illustration or polemic. The fact remains that the mere survival of something still called Art in a world so intolerant of the useless and uningratiating indicates that there is some hope for the kind of awareness of that world which is uniquely imposed by aesthetic criteria, no matter how bizarre the "visual" manifestations may initially appear to those unacquainted with the art context.

In dialogue with comments made by Lippard in 1969 published in the preface, this text served as the postface to Lippard's *Six Years: The Dematerialization of the Art Object From 1966 to 1972* (New York: Praeger, 1973), pp. 263–264.

Mierle Laderman Ukeles, *Washing, Tracks, Maintenance,* 1973. Performance at the Wadsworth Atheneum, Hartford, Conn. as part of the "Maintenance Art Performance Series."

# in support of meta-art

## adrian piper

I would like to make a case for a new occupation for artists. This occupation might exist as part of, alongside, or instead of the art itself. If it existed as part of or alongside the art, it might have the effect of giving the art a perspicuous and viable interpretation, support, or framework, although I don't see this as its intention. If, on the other hand, it were to replace the art, well and good. We could then add it as a nascent appendage to the field, and spend hours of discussion and many kilocalories deciding upon its status and implications. I will call the occupation I have in mind "meta-art." To establish something of its character, I will first give a loose account of what I mean by the term. Then I will try to sharpen the definition somewhat by contrasting it with other activities for which it might be mistaken, viz. art and art criticism. Finally I will attempt to justify the contention that we need such a thing.

1. By "meta-art" I mean the activity of making explicit the thought processes, procedures, and presuppositions of making whatever kind of art we make. Thought processes might include how we hypothesize a work into existence: whether we reason from problems encountered in the last work to possible solutions in the next; or get "inspired" by seeing someone else's work, or a previously unnoticed aspect of our own; or read something, experience some-

thing, or talk; or find ourselves blindly working away for no good reason; or any, all, or other processes of this kind.

Procedures might include how we come by the materials we use; what we do in order to get them; whom we must deal with, and in what capacity; what kinds of decisions we make concerning them (aesthetic, pecuniary, environmental, etc.); to what extent the work demands interactions (social, political, collaborative) with other people, etc. In general, by procedures I mean what we *do* to realize the work as contrasted with how and what we *think*.

Whereas getting at thought processes and procedures is largely a matter of perspicuous description of what is immediately available, getting at presuppositions is not. Here there are many possible methods, all having to do with analysis of some kind. One might be what Kant called the method of "regressive proof" which he used in the *Critique of Pure Reason*. Such an analysis would consist in beginning with the fact of the work itself, and from its properties inferring backward to the conditions necessary to bring it into existence. Luckily there is no need to insist that such conditions be transcendental. They might just as easily be social, psychological, political, metaphysical, aesthetic, or any combination thereof. Still another kind might be based on a loosely construed Hegelian method, in which the work is treated as thesis, an antithesis is posited, and a synthesis arrived at which in turn becomes thesis. The resulting dialectic attempts to specify the work with respect to the system of which it is a part. A third might be some variety of formal or informal psychological analysis: Freudian, Jungian, Reichian, etc. in terms of which we would try to make clear our subjective assumptions about the world.[1] Clearly there are others. We might do induction on the dreams we've been having, conduct ultimately *ad hominem* arguments with friends about the nature of art, etc.

The distinctions between the above are not intended to be sharply drawn. Generally what is required in meta-art is that we stand off and view our role of artist reflectively, that we see the fact of our art-making as itself a discrete state or process with interesting implications worthy of pursuing; that we articulate and present these implications to an audience (either the same as or broader than the art audience) for comment, evaluation, and feedback.

2. (. . .) Meta-art is generically related to art, art activity, and being an artist. The impulse to meta-art is unfathomable in the way the impulse to art is; meta-art is unique in just the way art-making activity is, and for the same reasons; its subject matter is, like both of these, immediately accessible to artists. But unlike art and art– making, meta-art is not completely opaque because its tools are the discursive, conceptualizing, cognitive abilities of the artist. Doing meta-art presupposes immediate and privileged access to the impulse, the activity, and the

emergence of the art. It is all of a piece with these, but in addition requires an epistemic self-consciousness about them, viz. viewing ourselves as the aesthetic objects we are, then elucidating as fully as possible the thoughts, procedures, and presuppositions that so define us.

3. Obscuring the distinction between meta-art and art criticism has resulted in the conceptions of the artist as superstar, as financial con man, as political satrap, as public relations expert. But it makes a difference whether *we* describe our own machinations and the motives and presuppositions behind them, or whether these machinations are revealed or imputed to us by a critic. The interviews in *Avalanche* attempt to circumvent or simply ignore this problem by allowing artists to speak for themselves. But this mode of self-representation is not immune to the problem of misrepresentation encountered in third-person discourse. The point I want to press is that it is one thing to handle the referents of art*works* in the third-person case, or try to educe them from the work: art itself can't, after all, protest that it is being misunderstood. But to handle artists this way is more often than not to make of them unpleasantly stylized biographical objects. This then creates near-inviolable prejudices which blind us to any genuine attempts to penetrate past the formal properties of the work for a framework in which to understand it. Artists almost always complain about the way they come off in such articles or interviews, the best intentions of the critic notwithstanding. Since they are clearly not averse to having the material revealed in the first place, the implication is that artists should take the means of revelation into their own hands. (. . .)

Because the focal point of meta-art is on the artist *qua* artist, it simultaneously accommodates all those broader referents which support the art (including its cultural, financial, social, etc. status), while circumventing the requirements of cultural anthropology to account for an entire social context. Although the values will be social, ethical, philosophical, political, as well as aesthetic, the meta-artist need merely explicate his or her particular condition in order to suggest the condition of the society.

The contrasts I have tried to bring out support a description of meta-art as artistic in its concerns, epistemological in its method, humanistic in its system of values. (. . .)

I said earlier that the values of meta-art were humanistic in character. I meant to contrast this with the narrowly aesthetic values of art, and then argue that aesthetic values alone were in fact never sufficient to explain or justify making art, when viewed in its broader social context. Our basic aesthetic proclivities may indeed be real enough; but curiously, they barely develop, if at all, in the face of poverty, overcrowding, fifth-rate education, or job discrimination. Having aesthetic proclivities presupposes gratification of survival needs; and the more we are hit by the social and political realities of the suffering of other people, the more the satisfaction of aesthetic proclivities seems a fatuous defense of our position.

In elucidating the process of making art on a personal level, meta-art criticizes and indicts the machinations necessary to maintain this society as it is. It holds up for scrutiny how capitalism works on us and through us; how we therefore live, think, what we do as artists; what kinds of social interactions we have (personal, political, financial); what injustices we are the victim of, and which ones we must inflict on others in order to validate our work or our roles as artist; how we have learned to circumvent these, if at all, i.e. how highly developed we have had to become as political animals; what forms of manipulation we must utilize to get things done; what compromises we must make in our work or our integrity in order to reach the point where such compromises are no longer necessary; whether, given the structure of this society, there can be such a point.

This is not to say that the justification for meta-art is social indictment alone. It can also be an epistemic tool for discussing the work on a broader basis which includes the aesthetic. But ultimately the justification for meta-art is social, because it is concerned with artists, and artists are social: we are not exempt from the forces or the fate of this society.

**NOTES**

1. For some recent examples, in this and other fields, from an observer's standpoint, see: Anthony Storr, *The Dynamics of Creation* (New York, 1972); Ernst Kris, *Psychoanalytic Explorations in Art* (1962); Bruce Mazlich, ed., *Psychoanalysis and History* (New York, 1971); C. Hanley and M. Lazerowitz, eds., *Psychoanalysis and Philosophy* (1971); Rosemary Mayer, "Performance and Experience," *Art* (December-January, 1973), pp. 33–36. Evaluations of some of these efforts— predominantly negative, and justifiably so, include Robert Coles, "Shrinking History, Part I," *New York Review of Books* (February 22, 1973), pp. 15–21; and Emmet Wilson in *The Journal of Philosophy* (March 8, 1973), pp. 128–134.

This essay first appeared in *Artforum,* 12:2 (October 1973), pp. 79–81.

# all the "art" that's fit to show

## hans haacke

Products which are considered "works of art" have been singled out as culturally significant objects by those who at any given time and social stratum wield the power to confer the predicate "work of art" unto them; they cannot elevate themselves from the host of man-made objects simply on the basis of some inherent qualities.

Today museums and comparable art institutions, like e.g. the I.C.A. in London, belong to that group of agents in a society who have a sizable, although not an exclusive, share in this cultural power on the level of so-called "high-art."

Irrespective of the "avant-garde" or "conservative," "rightist" or "leftist" stance a museum might take, it is, among other things, a carrier of socio-political connotations. By the very structure of its existence, it is a political institution. This is as true for museums in Moscow or Peking as for a museum in Cologne or the Guggenheim Museum. The question of private or public funding of the institution does not affect this axiom. The policies of publicly financed institutions are obviously subject to the approval of the supervising governmental agency. In turn, privately funded institutions naturally reflect the predilections and interests of their supporters. Any public museum receiving private donations may find itself in a conflict of interests. On the other hand the indirect subsidy of many private institutions through exemption from taxes and partial funding of their programs could equally create problems. Often, however, there exists in fact if not by design a tolerance or even a congruence of the respective ideological persuasions.

In principle the decisions of museum officials, ideologically highly determined or receptive to deviations from the norm, follow the boundaries set by their employers. These boundaries need not be expressly stated in order to be operative. Frequently museum officials have internalized the thinking of their superiors to a degree that it becomes natural for them to make the "right" decisions and a congenial atmosphere reigns between employee and employer. Nevertheless it would be simplistic to assume that in each case museum officials are faithfully translating the interests of their superiors into museum policy, particularly since new cultural manifestations are not always recognizable as to their suitability or opposition to the parties concerned. The potential for confusion is increased by the fact that the convictions of an "artist" are not necessarily reflected in the objective position his/her work takes on the sociopolitical scale and that this position could change over the years to the point of reversal.

Still, in order to gain some insight into the forces that elevate certain products to the level of "works of art" it is helpful—among other investigations—to look into the economic and political underpinnings of the institutions, individuals and groups who share in the control of cultural power.

Strategies might be developed for performing this task in ways that its manifestations are liable to be considered "works of art" in their own right. Not surprisingly some museums do not think they have sufficient independence to exhibit such a portrait of their own structure and try to dissuade or even censor works of this nature, as has been demonstrated. Fortunately art institutions and other cultural power agents do not form a monolithic block, so that the public's access to such works might be limited but not totally prevented.

Bertolt Brecht's 1934 appraisal of the "Five Difficulties in Writing the Truth" is still valid today. They are the need for "the courage to write the truth, although it is being suppressed; the intelligence to recognize it, although it is being covered up; the art to use it as a weapon; the judgement to choose those in whose hands it becomes effective; the cunning to spread it among them."

There are no "artists," however, who are immune to being affected and influenced by the social-political value-system of the society in which they live and of which all cultural agencies are a part, no matter if they are ignorant of these constraints or not ("artist" like "work of art" are put in quotation marks because they are predicates with evaluative connotations deriving their currency from the relative ideological frame of a given cultural power group).

So-called "avant-garde art" is at best working close to the limitations set by its cultural/political environment, but it always operates within that allowance.

"Artists" as much as their supporters and their enemies, no matter of what ideological coloration, are unwitting partners in the art-syndrome and relate to each other dialectically. They participate jointly in the maintenance and/or development of the ideological make-up of their society. They work within that frame, set the frame and are being framed.

This text was initially published as an untitled catalogue statement in *Art into Society, Society into Art* (London: Institute of Contemporary Arts, 1974). It has been reprinted in *Museums by Artists,* ed. A. A. Bronson and Peggy Gale (Toronto: Art Metropole, 1983), pp. 151–152.

sarah charlesworth, ian burn, joseph kosuth, art & language, UK, marcel broodthaers, allan sekula, martha rosler, mary kelly, benjamin h. d. buchloh

**VI** 1975–1977

# a declaration of dependence
## sarah charlesworth

We are living in a period of unprecedented destruction of languages and cultures, of nations, under the assault of highly bureaucratic states. These exert, both internally and externally, a steady pressure, reducing culture to a series of technical functions. Put another way, culture, the creation of shared meanings, symbolic interaction, is dissolving into a mere mechanism guided by signals.
—Stanley Diamond[1]

## I.

When we discuss a work of art or an art tradition, we are discussing a phenomenon which exists in an integral relationship with the entire complex of human social and historical forces defining the development of that work or tradition. This same complex of social and historical forces in turn inevitably defines the context in which that work or tradition claims significance, and ultimately functions as a force or agent in the ongoing evolution of that culture. Thus we are at once the products and the producers of the culture in which we participate. *This seems so obvious,* yet we often fail to recognize that while options may be limited, the value and function of our work may be defined by the social and economic context in which we operate; we are ourselves, individually and collectively, the constitutive agents of the social complex that defines the value and significance of our work. In the same way that we as artists are *responsible* for the notion of art, by the formulation of art works or concepts, we are in turn responsible to the culture itself in the formulation of the notion and function of art.

In speaking of a social and historical context in which any art work or tradition evolves and is transmitted, it is difficult to differentiate between the political and economic order which prevails at any particular time and place, and the ideological or intellectual traditions which have developed concomitantly; these latter more often than not serve to reinforce and sustain the political and economic order. Institutions tend to claim authority over the individuals and their activity in society *regardless of whatever subjective meaning* they may attach to their situation and endeavor. The ideological structure of society integrates and legitimizes the institutional order by explaining and legitimizing its objectivated meanings.

If we speak specifically about art in modern European and American culture, we see that its meaning, function, and value within society are clearly institutionally mediated; and that not only artistic values, but the intellectual and ideological forces which explain, interpret and legitimize art practice have their origins in the very same traditions that presuppose that institutional order. Thus the structural system of the art-world, which provides a context for the social signification of art, is itself contextually situated in a social system, the structure of which it in turn reflects. At this point, attempts to question or transform the nature of art beyond formalistic considerations must inevitably begin to involve a consideration not only of the presuppositions inherent in the internal structure of art models, but also a critical awareness of the social system which preconditions and drastically confines the possibility of transformation.

If we recognize the institutional structure of a complex society to be (culturally) all-embrasive, then we may begin to see that in attempting to redefine, alter or redirect the social definition or function of art—the manner and channels through which we can effectively work—we are encountering a firmly entrenched and highly developed institutional order: not just when confronting the obvious bureaucratic structure of the New York art world, but encountering the force of that order on every level, from such specific factors as the persistence of socially convenient (marketable) formal models of art (i.e. painting and sculpture) to more abstract socially convenient (non-controversial) theoretical models (formalism, art for art's sake), to the most blatant sociological fact that cultural power is clearly allied with economic power, and that to a large extent the internalizations of the dictates of the productive system regarding patterns of legitimation and consumption are the very means by which individuals surrender their critical faculties to that system.

A certain ideological inversion or mystification which Marx calls false consciousness is apparent in the very fact that in discussing art, we commonly describe the sphere of influence in the following manner: as one moving *outward* from the individual artist, who, acting out of personal feelings or convictions, expresses himself/herself by way of a statement, traditionally in the form of a discrete work or art product, the social recognition and validation of which is dependent on some internal properties, termed "quality," which bear upon its visual or histori-cal characteristics, *outward* through a system of institutions responsive to its self-evident merit; which in turn circulate and promote the work accordingly, to the benefit of all those culturally refined and sensitive enough to partake of its virtues. Hence the artist, as well as his product and the abstract sphere of his influence, are assumed "transcendent," that is, somehow respon-sive to and effective of abstract psychic and social conditions somewhat removed from the mundane conditions of "everyday life." The historical, social, and psychological factors which bear upon the artist are viewed from the perspective of predominantly after-the-fact analysis, the domain of various somewhat less "transcendent" (presumably more "objective") specialists who interpret and speculate on the myriad social and historical influences and implications manifest in the personal history, life style and oeuvre of the particular subject under study— those factors which bear upon and are implicit in the process of validation or interpretation seldom being taken into account. The art work as a symbolic token of the struggle of the individual artist and the spiritual and social dilemmas which that individual struggle in turn reflects, becomes in a sense a sanctified cultural relic, presumably embodying in itself some elusive, imaginative spirit.

One wonders, of course, why it is the *tokens* of struggle toward meaning and not *the struggle itself* to which we respond (or how much spirit we can touch upon when these tokens become the stock in trade of a sophisticated cultural elite). That this conception is naive and idyllic and totally out of keeping with the rather more complex situation in which cultural phenomena emerge, develop, and function ought to be readily apparent; however, attempts to construct a more accurate basis for understanding are not without problems. One obvious alternative model to this ideological Disneyland is of course a (very broadly speaking) material-ist schema, in which material processes, specifically the mode of production and distribution of goods, services and capital within and amongst societies is the primary and overriding factor of which all mental and spiritual attitudes and formulations are (consciously or unconsciously) in large part the product. "All parts of the ideological superstructure, art being one of these, are crucially determined both in content and style by the behavior of a more basic structure which is economic in nature."[2] But it would be deterministic, in this case, to suppose that the mere economic dependence of the artist, a certain *external* tie which links producer to consumer (and vice-versa), is the full extent of that relationship, that the economic and social conditions of production are explicit and can be dealt with as such; but rather they are *implicit and internalized* to such a degree that they inform *every aspect of our self and social consciousness* upon which all praxis is founded. The artist may then be unwittingly supportive of ideals or conditions in relation to which he sees himself neutral or even opposed.

While a materialist critique and the dialectical method it implies is eminently useful as a tool by which to reorient our inquiries, to attempt to situate our self-presumptions, to gauge the implications and ramifications of our critical or practical stance, we should at the same time recognize the historical (and ideological) nature of this tradition/model, as well as the one from and to which we bring it to bear. A dialectical or immanent critique, however, takes seriously the principle that it is not ideology itself which is untrue but rather its pretension to correspond to reality. There can be no method of escape, no science, no dialectic, no objective criteria which are not in turn subjectively assumed. The issue then becomes not so much a question of how we can achieve a "value-free" or "objective" model or theory of art practice as it is a question of what values and conditions of learning we in fact promote and provide through our practice of art.

*I can no more reduce the "spirit of art" to which I am still responsive, to an entirely materialistic function than I can conversely assume it to be neutral or independent of material conditions. I am wary of the individualism and subjectivism which pervades our self and social consciousness, which I believe (when assumed uncritically) is actually a factor which perpetuates the oppression of individuals in our society. Concurrently I would argue that it is only when individuals begin to accept a responsibility for the social implications of their actions that a collective spirit or consciousness conducive to social change can occur. While being critical of the idealistic and presumptive notion of freedom and transcendence which informs the modernist paradigm, I myself work within the context of that art, that tradition; in part because I am responsive to certain ideals which that endeavor represents and recognize therein a certain emancipatory and self-reflexive capacity lacking to varying degrees in other disciplines. My own work is tempered with realism only to the extent to which I feel continually compelled to re-examine or redirect my course in relation to such ideals.*

*Throughout this essay I use the pronoun "we," and thereby incorporate myself and others into some abstract community, and assume a certain sympathy amongst the members so included. This is in part a function of the fact that I see myself as a participant in a real community which in my case might be centered around my involvement with* The Fox *and my working relationship with other participants; but I also address and appeal to a larger community which is made up of other individuals with whom I share a common tradition, a similar historical and cultural locus, who see themselves and/or have come to be recognized variously as artists, critics, dealers, curators, professors, students and so on. All are at least potentially in a position to make critical choices which will affect not only the internal character but also the social dynamic of contemporary and future art activity. To a large extent, we learn what our purposes are through the systems which we use, just as we learn what is required for survival through the interaction of those systems and our experience in trying to do things. For each of us there is a certain element of contradiction involved in the majority of personal and professional choices that we make, a certain tension between self survival/self interest and social interest/species survival. Some of us feel this conflict more intensely than others and we have varying interests and values at stake. It is important, however, that we begin to recognize and elucidate the criteria and implications of choice rather than continue to apologize, rationalize, and obfuscate. None of us, neither artist, critic, dealer, curator, nor "patron of the arts," can be said to be free of conflict of interest when it comes to the making of the cultural phenomena "art."*

If art is viewed as one aspect of culture or one form of "symbolic action," then the logic embodied in this particular system and the meanings which we attribute to our actions must be considered in relation to, or more precisely as evolving within and contributing to, a larger context of social meaning. But characteristic of our liberal tradition, both on an intellectual or ideological level (political liberalism, empiricism, logical positivism) as well as on an intuitive or common sense level, is a tendency toward an emphasis on the individual fact or item at the expense of an awareness of the relational or contextual aspects in which such a seemingly discrete fact or item occurs. This tendency has been manifest in contemporary art both in our conceptualization of art as an autonomous and self regulatory discipline, an assembly of static objects of contemplation, as well as in our inclination to interpret the symbolic or gestural content of our actions in a dissociated and superficial manner.

Viewed from one perspective, the history of Modern art has been a long revolution against the complacency, sentimentality and tedium of bourgeois culture, a rebellion against the self-assuming and rhetorical aspects of traditional forms, against the threat of subsumption or diversion of political or social non-art concerns—a veritable march of progress in the name of freedom, of individuality, of *art*. On a symbolic level, this is apparently so; on a theoretical level as well. *But* is not the very logic through which we hail the theoretical and symbolic tokens of "revolutionary spirit" while embracing those very tokens in an attitude of blind acceptance and self-complacency, a tribute to the *failure* of that art—and the logic it embodies—

to adequately comprehend and respond to the exigencies of a very real social and ideological predicament that, none the less, transcends and subsumes that art? Freedom and independence is not something you can posit and proceed to assume, but a condition fought for and seldom won.

## II.

Implicit in our understanding of modernist art is the assumption that art values and objectives might somehow be viewed as dissociated or neutral in relation to the social sphere in which they operate. Andre Malraux pointed out that "the middle ages had no more idea of what we mean by fine art than Greece or Egypt. In order that this idea could be born it was necessary for works to be separated from their function . . . the most profound metamorphosis began when art had no other end than itself."[3] In keeping with this tradition, when we speak of function or meaning when discussing art work we refer to the function or meaning of that work not so much in relation to a larger sphere of social praxis, but rather within the isolated and abstracted province "art." *The struggle of modernism in the West has been, above all else, a struggle to establish an independent and autonomous context of meaning at once in opposition to and in disregard of the existent social order.* Thus when Ad Reinhardt was to proclaim the one permanent revolution in art is always a negation of the use of art for some purpose other than its own, and that all progress and change in art is toward the one end of art as art-as-art, he was, as he claims, echoing an ideal which has characterized the writings of a majority of artists and theorists of the modern era. In 1834, Theophile Gautier in his preface to *Mademoiselle De Maupin* (frequently considered the first real manifesto of the art for art's sake movement), likewise argued for the elimination of all utilitarian and moral purpose for art, in favor of anarchistic individualism, which he regarded as the reflection of unique romantic genius; he was in turn responding to an idealistic conception of disinterested and pure beauty, formulated earlier still by Kant.

It is a curious and romantic notion that somehow by ignoring that which is repugnant within the existing order, we might quite logically be immune to its effect. But more curious still is the fact that this profoundly romantic and idealistic attitude, in which the problems of the apprehension of beauty, pure and independent of moral or utilitarian concerns, a primarily aesthetic and metaphysical preoccupation descended from the Enlightenment, should survive in an age when the creation of beauty and aesthetic enjoyment are no longer the self-proclaimed ends of art. Although the notion of *l'art pour l'art* now appears an outdated and naive preoccupation, a romantic struggle against bourgeois ideals of social utility, we must begin to question the degree to which this idealistic 19th-century construct has been internalized—in not only early modern, but even the most current art-model. As Arnold Hauser points out, "What was once a revolt against classical rules has become a revolt against all external ties. . . . from the standpoint of the direct aesthetic experience, autonomy and self-sufficiency appear to be the essence of the work of art, for only by putting itself completely in the place of reality, only by forming a total self-contained cosmos, is it able to produce a perfect illusion. But this illusion is in no way the whole content of art and often has no share in the effect it produces. The greatest works of art forego the deceptive illusion of a self-contained aesthetic world and point beyond themselves."[4]

Leaving aside the question of "great works," is it not true that in forwarding an ideal self-image of autonomy (both in our concept of discrete self-contained art works and art values in general—in the face of all manner of evidence to the contrary), we are in effect now perpetuating those same bourgeois values such self confinement was originally deemed to escape? Even the question of bourgeois values is growing increasingly moot. *There is a great deal more to be frightened of at this point than the taint of an impure art.* When the power of validation and legitimization of human enterprise occurs more and more within an institutionalized system, where corporate power and investment potential are becoming increasingly the social consensus by which we signify meaning, it is clear that no private vision, no personal iconoclastic gesture can withstand.

Much "theoretical" or "analytical" work in the past few years has served to focus our attention on the conventional or conceptual underpinnings of our contemporary art practice. So-called conceptual art represents, amongst other things, an attempt to redefine art value or significance in terms of its ideational rather than physical ("experiential") attributes, but, as has been apparent for some time, to the extent that conceptual art is dependent upon the very same mechanisms for presentation, dissemination, and interpretation of art works, it *functions in society* in a manner not unlike previously more morphologically oriented work. Thus the *extent* to which its significance as art (or as idea) is dependent upon or inferred by its existence within the traditional context, its value or function within the culture is conditioned primarily by patterns of response *traditionally associated* with that context. This is a world in which honor is ritually bestowed, values assumed and rarely created. "Art as idea" was once a good idea, but art as idea as art product, alas, moves in the world of commodity-products and hardly the realm of "idea." The significance that early conceptual work bore in relation to previously held assumptions regarding formal requisites of traditional art practice is not to be denied, but formalistic innovation in and of itself is of questionable value. Since it is assumed that the intentional aspects of an artist's endeavor extend only to the making of a work or a proposition, and its placement or "documentation" within the prescribed context, the use or function of that work (aside from its existence as art history) is no longer an aspect of art. The artist is thus severed, except on a symbolic level, from his culture. *He responds to and assumes responsibility for an art in isolation.*

If art "lives" primarily by affecting other art (as is often claimed), then there is no mechanism by which such an art can reorient or redefine itself except out of a logic internal to the closure "art." Thus we are confined to a large extent to the progressive reduction and expansion of inherent formal relations; such "conceptual innovations" as may occur are subsumed within the system to which they refer. A tradition keyed to the demands of the competitive market, responding to the stylistic or formal elements of innovation, sees no use or value in the implications of change beyond the historical progressivity which it denotes. This is the ultimate consumership: *Ideas become the property of the inventor, and as such are no further use to the community once claimed.*

We move away from the tyranny of the picture frame only to discover that of the gallery, the market, and so on, and as it begins to become apparent that the privileging of the art object cannot be dissociated from the privileging of the context and tradition in which the object appears; we begin to wonder whether the very sense of that history or sociality, which is the shape and dynamic of our discipline, is not so much the momentum of a free and critical consciousness as the order of a definitive social and economic reality, the pervasiveness of which we have scarcely begun to grasp.

Inversely, we might begin to inquire whether the retreat from the objectification, commodification and institutionalization of traditional art models, which has characterized the tactics of certain more (theoretically) radical segments of the art community, is not so much a function of the realization of inherently noxious qualities which those models possess, as the instinctive recoil against *that which they represent:* the commodification and institutionalization of human history and endeavor. While such activities now appear naive and unsuccessful on the one hand, in mistaking for ethic or style that which is in fact part of a more profound social and economic reality, they *do* signify a positive and potentially liberating capacity; that is, the will to change, to re-examine, and, more importantly, to "call to arms" the tools that make radical and contextual critique conceivable. Suppose we imagine this capacity as a medium, a methodology, and not an end in itself. We can *learn* as much, in a sense, through the "failure" of concept art as we do through its partial success; while being critical of the (self) presumptive and reductionist aspects of formalist tradition, we exist as its inevitable heir.

## III.

Our dilemma at this point is profound and problematic in its circularity. If we assume any theoretical stance or critical viewpoint (by which we mean to assess a previous or other presumably "more naive" position), we must do so by use of a logic which justifies or lends authority to our current more "sophisticated" outlook. This new position claims precedence over antecedent or rival theories, and yet does so at the expense of obscuring its own presumptions. Thus we are always in a position of revealing the "false" foundations of one logic while claiming another similarly founded. This is, of course, where traditional Marxist social "science" as well as many sociological or anthropological models, particularly the structuralist models, break down. You cannot, on the one hand, claim that all knowledge is culturally determined, socially derived and then in turn claim the objective validity of your own theory. In this sense the dialectic becomes immanently useful as an ideal working model but in practice something of an impossibility. So we proceed amidst contradiction.

Dialectical critique implies that one cannot view any object or subject at rest, for in the very act of viewing or depicting our object, we grasp self and subject as situated in the same historical moment from whence we depart. "Faced with the operative procedures of the nonreflective thinking mind (whether grappling with the philosophical or artistic, political or scientific problems and objects), dialectical thought tries not so much to complete and perfect the application of such procedures as to widen its own attention to include them in its awareness as well; it aims, in other words, not so much at solving the particular dilemmas in question, as converting those problems into their own solutions on a higher level, and making the fact and the existence of the problem itself the starting point of new research."[5]

That this model does represent at any given moment a logical closure which is immensely problematic in application is readily apparent; but its emancipatory as well as normative potential in the ideal is compelling. What is called for is not the replacement of one authoritative model with another but rather the gradual creation of a community, a discourse, an art, which is not so much the reflection of our competitive and antagonistic pursuits as it is a common vehicle through which we might continually examine not only our own values and assumptions, but those of the culture of and to which we ideally speak. We might see therefore not so much to regulate our cultural praxis in relation to the existent norms, as to understand, elucidate, and evaluate the normative import of those activities in which we are historically, presently, well as potentially engaged. Thus the philosophy, the theory, the strategy and the ethics of practice become one with praxis itself. And yet this union of theory and practice in the ideal is always subject to and modified by conditions in relation to which we must continually re-evaluate our position. It is a dynamic and self-regulatory critical theory by which we attempt to understand and evaluate our own (art) practice in relation to social practice in general, and to evaluate social and historical conditions as they are effective of and become apparent in our practice of art.

If it is true that "the creation of a thing for the sake of a thing is itself an objective human relationship to itself and to man,"[6] then it is on the level of this relationship which we must question our function, for it no longer has much meaning to speak of the thing (art) in itself.

At the dawn of the 19th century, Hegel predicted that art would no longer, as in the past, be connected with the central concerns of man. Hegel saw the role of art becoming increasingly marginal as science moved into a stronger and more central position within society. Art, according to Hegel, would cease to be serious, as it became increasingly pure and disengaged. By moving into a marginal position, art would not lose its quality as art, but it would nonetheless cease to have direct relevance to the existence of man.

We have lost touch—not only with ourselves and with each other but with the culture of which we are a part. It is only by confronting the problem of our alienation, making *this* the subject of our work, that our ideals take on new meaning. We move to become one again with culture in our sense of shared concerns.

## NOTES

1. Stanley Diamond, "Anthropology in Question," *Reinventing Anthropology,* ed. Dell Hymes (New York: Random House, 1969).

2. Berel Lang and Forest Williams, *Marxism and Art* (New York: David McKay Co., 1972).

3. Andre Malraux, *Les Voix du Silence.*

4. Arnold Hauser, *The Social History of Art* (New York: Alfred A. Knopf, 1951).

5. Fredric Jameson, *Marxism and Form* (Princeton: Princeton University Press, 1971).

6. Karl Marx, *Economic and Philosophical Manuscripts of 1844,* ed., Dirk J. Struik, trans., Martin Mulligan (International Publishers Co.).

This text appeared in *The Fox,* 1:1 (1975), pp. 1–7.

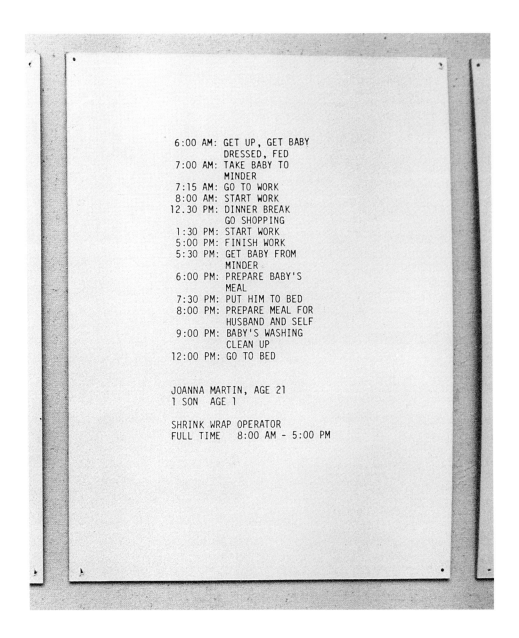

```
 6:00 AM: GET UP, GET BABY
          DRESSED, FED
 7:00 AM: TAKE BABY TO
          MINDER
 7:15 AM: GO TO WORK
 8:00 AM: START WORK
12.30 PM: DINNER BREAK
          GO SHOPPING
 1:30 PM: START WORK
 5:00 PM: FINISH WORK
 5:30 PM: GET BABY FROM
          MINDER
 6:00 PM: PREPARE BABY'S
          MEAL
 7:30 PM: PUT HIM TO BED
 8:00 PM: PREPARE MEAL FOR
          HUSBAND AND SELF
 9:00 PM: BABY'S WASHING
          CLEAN UP
12:00 PM: GO TO BED


JOANNA MARTIN, AGE 21
1 SON   AGE 1

SHRINK WRAP OPERATOR
FULL TIME   8:00 AM - 5:00 PM
```

Mary Kelly, *Daily Schedules* (1 of 14) from *Women and Work,* 1975, detail.

# the art market: affluence and degradation
## ian burn

Impending economic crisis has forced many deeply lurking problems into the open.[1] Art sales are declining and there is an air of pessimism. The sense of opulence of the 1960s has gone to dust. As artists, we have tended to understand the art market only in its reward capacity, preferring to ignore the "dismal science" of economics. But no longer, it seems. While it may once have seemed an exaggeration of economic determinism to regard works of art as "merely" commodities in an economic exchange, it is now pretty plain that our entire lives have become so extensively constituted in these terms that we cannot any longer pretend otherwise. Not only do works of art end up as commodities, but there is also an overwhelming sense in which works of art *start off* as commodities.

Faced with this impasse, we need alternate historical perspectives in order to throw light on some of the most basic of social relations, to perceive the lacuna between what we think we do and what we actually do in the world. The historical relations of up-to-date modern art are the market relations of a capitalist society. That much I believe is obvious to everyone. What we have seen more recently is the power of market values to distort all other values, so even the concept of what is and is not acceptable as "work" is defined *first and fundamentally* by the market and only secondly by "creative urges" (etc.). This has been the price of internalizing an intensely capitalistic mode of production.

Given this, shouldn't we be scrutinizing certain historically unique aspects of our market relations? How have these wrought fundamental changes in the "art" produced? I know many of us are grateful beneficiaries of this market. Nonetheless, we have all ended up victims of its capriciousness, the "principles" of modern art having trapped us in a panoptical prison of our own making. Simply, this is the realization that if the arts were really democratized, we as producers of an elite art would no longer have any means of functioning—wanting to abolish elitism in modern art is tantamount to wanting to abolish modern art itself.

## WHILE WE'VE BEEN ADMIRING OUR NAVELS

Within the moneyed structure of modern art, the collector or speculator or investor does not openly purchase my (as an artist) labor power; both my labor and means of production remain my own property and I sell only the product of my labor.[2] What this suggests to me is that, in New York today, I am operating on the principles of a lower or earlier stage of economic development, an atomistic stage of competitive market capitalism. However, when faced with the larger marketing structure in which we all live and which is far more highly developed, we become easy game for exploitation by that market. As we well know, a monopolistic inter-national market was already operating under full steam by the time conditions arose which made it possible to incorporate the art-marketing system—hence the transformations involved were unavoidably more rapid, the changes unavoidably more aggressive and antagonistic to each of us.

This is just one of the many paradoxical social contradictions I find myself in—that I am a producer still working under the illusions of one marketing system, while being a con-sumer in another, more overwhelming system. To me the most disturbing question is: to what extent have the modern market relations permeated my atomistic production? That is, what are the changes this has brought about and what are the consequences in my life? An answer to this may be pointed to in the actual functioning of a work of art in the market.

From the locus of the market, the work of art represents commodity capital; it acquires a market price which, being a function of manipulated demand and supply, virtually always deviates from the price of production—the concept of any sort of an "equilibrium market" where the market price is equal to the price of production is (almost) unheard of in the art community (that is, price would equal the sum of the cost of materials and wages for person-hours worked on the merchandise). But why should an equilibrium market be inconceivable to me? Or—the flip side of that—how is it that the work of art is so readily manipulated in the market? There are a number of feasible answers, some reflecting attitudes like the romantic rejection of a per-hour value being put on artists' time (which reflects the fact that artists' time has never been commodified).

Nonetheless, this is quite beside the point when the art market is acknowledged as an area of direct speculative investment: investing in oil wells gives you few opportunities for increasing the odds of striking oil (though you may manipulate the "worth" of your stocks); but investing in particular artists or styles admits ample opportunities to manipulate the odds in your favor. The degree to which this can be done is a peculiarity of the art market. You see, it is only my initial contract with the market that involves production, after that the work is strictly in an exchange market (not involving production), and it is this exchange market which determines the production "value" (what I get for my work). It is hard to think of any other form of production so exclusively determined by performance in an exchange market, and at the same time so free of legal restrictions—and hence manipulable. Consequently, to me it appears that the work of (fine) art has become the ideal exchange commodity in our society.

Clearly, in talking like this, I am thinking particularly of the market for "promising" artists. A distinction must be allowed between this sort of "risk" investment market, where profits can and do rise spectacularly, and the "secure" investment market involving established artists (dead or alive) where turnover profit is smaller but guaranteed. The latter relies on there being a relatively limited supply, while the former relies on a continuing supply and where future price increase is capitalized on through resale of current production. With this in mind, it is not so surprising that, inspired by our market-dependent culture, there has been such an upsurge in investing in the "risk" area. It is also not surprising that so many "promising" artists are arrested by the market success at just that stage of early development, unable to freely develop any further. I am also familiar with how difficult it is to know that this is what is happening to you, and even more difficult to be able to admit it.

Being readily manipulable, what are the further consequences for the work of art when the market is, in addition, monopolistic? Capitalism as it developed in the United States is at its most powerful and aggressive stage—where we as individuals are constantly made to act as puppets who merely maximize consumption. It has long been accepted that, for this system of marketing to work efficiently, it can't help but be exploitative of its producers. In the United States, particularly over the past fifteen years, it seems to have been able to create demands for certain types of art, then monopolize the prices and the production in these styles. In some ways this was inevitable, given the problem of survival for the art market with its center in New York. In the circumstances of atomized production, the market was forced to provide the monopolizing framework.

But this sort of manipulative marketing has forced alienating consequences into my social life as an artist. A monopoly creates conditions which could never come about otherwise: I am "created" by the market as merely part of a labor force, an unorganized one, but still a labor force. The size of this force has, significantly, augmented itself out of all proportion to the present market demand (compare the number of artists working in New York now to, say, the number twenty-five years ago). And remember all the while that, for market efficiency, the supply must meet the demand and demand is now governed by market manipulation, not the market by demand.[3] Moreover, once the market conceives of me as merely a unit in a labor force, I am also aware I can be replaced at any time by an equivalent (as defined by the market) unit. So organizational efficiency begins to dominate me to the extent that my subjective worth and "work" become defused.

This increased labor force represents an expanded market, something which is also apparent when we recall once again that twenty-five years ago the market for American art was largely a national one which has since developed into an international market with gigantic foreign sales. Such expansion, initially dependent on competition, has the effect of systematically and diabolically destroying the competitive nature of the market. In the old market, it would seem to me, artists competed more openly to sell their products and, despite an ever-growing incentive to calculate as to the market and its buyers, the market was still dominated by private patrons. But in the new monopoly, we "compete" differently. Perhaps I can suggest how by pointing briefly to the emergence of corporate monopolies in the United States in the early part of this century. For the first time, each individual was conceived as being "trained so as to be effective individually as an economic unit, and fit to be organized with his fellows so they can work efficiently together."[4] The old individualism was transformed into a new "economic individualism," which placed monetary self-interest above all else . . . this was to be the "true individualism." Thus my individualism was to be the result of my specialization in the service of the corporately organized society, and my specialization was the result of newly organized compulsory educational systems. Such was the rhetoric of the shift from the "irresponsible waste" of a competitive market to the monopolistic market of corporate industry through which the power of concentrated wealth was foreseen as the way to the great American dream.

Now that strikes me as roughly the way in which, more recently, the art market has developed: the "new" artist no longer conceives of a *personal* relation to the market. It becomes merely an economic, hence more impersonal, relation. This means my role of "artist" has become one befitting a trained and efficient economic unit, my "work" has become a mere reflex of my specialized role, and I am encouraged to regard the market as really none of my business.

As a result, the market has evolved its own autonomy, rapidly and independently of the persons supplying it. This is the difference I mentioned above: whereas once (and not so long ago) the market was a somewhat more personal matter for the artist, it has become impersonal and independent of the artist and, in an emphatically economic world, this impersonal market has grown to such an extent that it now can dominate and dictate to the artist.

Putting this into a familiar New York perspective: we have all been enticed by the prospect of endless market expansion which it seems, oddly enough, we have internalized in the idea of an endlessly innovative avant-gardist growth. This supports the power of the market by providing subtly pervasive means of cultural and intellectual control, through implicit direction and the supplying of a categorical check on the "evolution" of art. In addition, the unprecedented concentration of capital invested by the market in this avant-gardist elite has successfully had the effect of reducing "unnecessary" competition, if not eliminating it altogether. Today it is surely beyond any doubt that this popular idea of a "permanent revolution" in art is actively designed never to fulfil any personal and social relationship. From this point of view, it is a set of empty gestures which threaten none of the market requirements and end up being a sheer celebration of the new individuality, arrogantly and, finally, stupidly set against the idea of sociality.

It is also blatant how this concentration of production and capital has opened the way for monopolistic values and dubbed styles, and the ability of a few to manipulate absolute power in respect to these styles. This reflects, on other levels, the transformation into monopoly of free competition (or its aesthetic corollary, "free expression," a catchphrase we have all been psychologically duped with). In big business, "competition" has simply come to mean tempting customers away from rivals by product "differentiation" or by fancy service or better advertising or corporate images—and the art business today fairly accurately mirrors the same practices.

But what about all those much-lauded "innovations" the media has been ramming down our throats for so long? In most economic models, innovation appears as a new method of commodity production which has effect either in labor-saving or capital-saving—the innovator is considered as *necessary,* a logical mechanism in the system, creating more division of labor by creating other means of production and thus achieving a temporary monopoly. Which again entails more production, larger markets and maximal profits—the constant dynamic behind market expansion. Consequently, in art, innovation becomes an even more tyrannical "logic," since it has been made to adhere to a false model of technological progress. The market capitalizes on "innovation" for its own sake, strictly as a profit maximizing factor, transforming it into a rather blatant, however prestigious, commodity on the market. I am certainly self-consciously familiar with how "high art" has been rhetorically infected with the need to innovate and personally aware of being made to feel the pressure to innovate, on pain of extinction.

So where does that leave me? Like a lot of others, I am revolted by the torpidity of the status quo on the one hand—and on the other, by any desperate reactions to escape that status being celebrated as part of the "innovative logic" of the system! Meanwhile we are vulgarly lionized by institutions created in the belief that capitalism is divine and should not be tampered with and which are part of a market now so powerful that even the most iconoclastic work can be comfortably celebrated. With these conditions, wouldn't it be sheer lunacy for me to maintain that my market relations are just incidental?[5]

## WE HAVE BEEN CAPITALIZED AND MARKETED

There are a number of things I can no longer ignore. The emergence of the international art market along its present lines has been incontestably an arm of a necessary expansion of the United States capitalist system and consolidation of marketing areas after the Second World War. As pointed out above, the impersonal nature of the market forces it to expand without reference to the consumers or producers. Furthermore, considering some of the sources of the capital backing it, it is perhaps hardly surprising that American art achieved its "internationalism"[6] at a time when it also functioned as a weapon to fight the "menace of communism" (that is, the main threat to American domination of major marketing areas of the world).[7] This was a period when various ideals were perverted into an aesthetic ideology to sustain the emerging social and economic order. All was recent enough for most of us to be able to reconstruct how this internationalism created a "common interest" of selling to foreign investors, and how mutual advantage burgeoned into corporate interest. This common interest demanded more efficient production and organization—the outcome being, in the United States, that the consolidation of the business of art intuitively followed the lines of the model of bureaucratic corporate industry. This doesn't mean we have a concretized bureaucracy; it means the people running the various parts of the business of art, indeed ourselves, have internalized the bureaucratic method so that it now seems "natural" to separate functions, roles, relationships from the people who perform (etc.) them. So we intuitively achieve the corporate spirit of bureaucratic organization without any of its overt structures; by such means, our "high culture" has reified itself in a remote and dehumanizing tradition.

Looking at my situation today, I am obviously faced with functionally different circumstances from those of the early 1950s. In that period, in order to create a privileged art, it was necessary to produce something markedly different from what Europe was producing—this was reminiscent of the old competitive spirit: to succeed, it had to be different. But the bureaucratization and new corporate marketing techniques (involving art criticism, the trade journals, galleries and museums, art schools and all) changed that, so today we see the idea of "international high culture" demanding a uniformity dominated by New York art. To create a successful (that is, privileged) art, I must now affirm and perpetuate at least one of the dominant styles. It is hard for me to be blind to the fact that what has happened to recent art closely parallels the entrenchment of the giant multinational corporations. But, I want to restate, this has been achieved primarily on tacit agreements and not on the typically overt bureaucratic techniques—proving once more how little surveillance a system like this requires once the principles have been internalized and everyone has "like-minded" interests. This allows imperialism to operate in its most despicable state—where the specific character and subjectivity of any one place is disregarded and the "universality" of New York corporate uniformity is proclaimed.

In my mind, one depressing result of "incorporating" modern art has been the proportionately greater increase in the numbers of drab "non-production workers" (middle-people) compared with the increase in (sometimes equally drab) "production workers." This is just part of the marketing structure's expansion. But the consequences are pervasive: by bureaucratizing, the market has developed a bureaucratic or corporate "taste," essentially rendering personal or individual taste impossible. I can best illustrate this by pointing to the network of modern art museums which have sprung up like automobile sales-rooms throughout the Western world, all spouting the same rhetoric of "freely developing, democratic, cultural, educational enterprises." This has lost all relation to me as an artist. The museums, run by the new culturecrats, have become overlording institutions utilizing all the packaging techniques of the greatest consumer society in order to sell "culture" (at a price); they openly serve as showcases propagandizing the global ambitions of our selling "successes." The old "gunboat diplomacy" has been replaced by the new "modern art diplomacy" (for example, the Museum of Modern Art's International Program).

In case it appears I am overstating the role of United States capitalism in all this, let me emphasize the obvious, that the history of modern art from its beginnings was nurtured within a number of industrialized societies, not just America. Looking closer at that history, with its unrelenting emphasis on an "art-for-art's-sake" ideology, we become conscious of the ever-increasing role played by a neutered formalism—at the expense of our possibility of content. The stress on exclusively formal innovation had the aftermath of content in its last gasp being reduced to such vacua as "color," "edge," "process," "ideas," "image," etc. plus a lot of fatuous jargon about qualities symbolized through these (c.f. especially Greenberg's account of modernism, but also most issues of *Artforum* and other magazines). This is formalism taken to its ultimate empty conclusions: it is what we have lauded as pure art . . . the impossibility of content, of saying anything whatsoever. The tradition of formalism has left me largely incapable of expressing through "my art" those very things about which I have the greatest misgivings—and so incapable of changing anything through "my art." These ideological fetters have conclusively eradicated every possibility of a social practice in relation to art, even the thought of it—the expression of modern art has become the rejection of society and of our social beings. Now, obviously the United States isn't to blame for all of this, but it certainly deserves a lot of the credit for bringing it to a remarkable and unprecedented pitch. No longer just producing an art for a privileged middle-class, it has burgeoned into a spectacularly elitist art, remote even from its own producers' actual lives and problems.

What can you expect to challenge in the real world with "color," "edge," "process," systems, modules, etc. as your arguments? Can you be any more than a manipulated puppet if these are your "professional" arguments? Moreover, when you add to this picture thousands upon thousands of artists in all corners of the modern art empire tackling American formalism in the belief that it is the one "true art"—that's when it is possible to see how preposterous and finally downright degrading it has become![8]

Needless to say, it is easy for me to identify with some points of the classic nineteenth-century theses about alienation. There it was argued that alienation is the process whereby human values are projected outside of us and achieve an existence independent of us, and over us, and this is an essential condition for the functioning of capitalism. We are all familiar with the romanticized notions about the work of art "embodying the soul of the artist." Well, perhaps historically this has taken on mythic proportions, but there is a very real sense in which everything produced ought to bear some personal relation to who makes it. However, once my work of art enters the art market, it takes on a power independent of me and this strikes me as a form of estrangement from what I have produced, an alienation from my own experiences; and the more I produce the more I deprive myself of my "means of life." Yet I find I can only maintain myself by continuing in the same fashion. So, while I may retain economic ownership over my labor and means of production (thus giving me a sense of "freedom"), I am still psychologically and socially alienated from what I produce. Once entering the market, it becomes an object foreign to me—but without the market I don't recognize it, because it is defined via the market which I have internalized. Don't we all experience this to greater or lesser degrees? As a result, myself-as-an-artist has become a stranger to me, a figure over whom I have little power or control. This is today's blunt reality of alienation. No longer merely having lost the product of our labor, our ability to create is profoundly impaired . . . and this is also expressed in my relation to you, and burgeons in the relation you can have to what I produce.

Often-heard remarks implying that it is not enough to be "just an artist" are merely public admissions that, as a role in society, "artist" is a sterile one. More pointedly, this sheds light on the prevailing concept of "artist": it has become an integral part of the meaning of the concept "artist" that it is politically conservative (or, at its more adventuristic, reactionary), and that remains its sole possible political role—hence its continuing great value as propaganda for an imperious culture. This is clearly reflected in the desperation of more and more artists to escape their political impotence, in their attempts to reconcile the paradoxicality of their lives wrought by being hopefully "radical" in politics but necessarily "conservative" in art.[9]

The inside story of this is that there is no "radical theory" in the arts today, and there can be none while the present state of affairs prevails. That also explains something about the extreme poverty of "critical theory," since a critical theory which sets itself the task of revealing the various forms of conflict and exploitation needs to be informed by some (prospect of) radical theory, something which denies the current ideology and economic class values embodied in modern art. Current and recent art criticism has become at best a means of policing and regulating, at worst a sheer celebration of the impotence of the status quo.

In this light, most of the chatter about "plurality" in the contemporary scene comes over as so much liberal claptrap. What use is a sort of "freedom" which can have no other effect than reinforcing the status quo? B. F. Skinner's suggestion that freedom is just a feeling resulting from doing what you have been conditioned to do has many echoes too close to home. Furthermore, by ignoring its own realities, contemporary art criticism has collusively abetted these alienating processes. On the other hand, as artists we have to add our own careerist irresponsibility in allowing ourselves to become first inured and then dominated by our commitment to hacks in the trade art journals, who blithely use the commodity language of formal criticism to "compete" in discovering new marketable qualities.

The galleries also, of course, have an alienating function, having achieved social ascendancy in this system and become more numerous and better organized. Belonging to a gallery which "competes" for us in the market means accruing some economic benefits while further reifying ourselves in an alienating role. Again, as artists we find ourselves forced into acting out a role, one that anyone else might fill just as readily. Reliance on skills becomes less important and the need for maintaining and fulfilling the requirements of the role function becomes more and more "real" and time-consuming. This is the bureaucrat's existential nightmare and, make no mistake, we do have the artist-as-bureaucrat today.

Finally, we must not forget to emphasize that the journals, the galleries and dealers have no more or less a stake in these hierarchical and careerist economics than we ourselves do— and so we have no privileged right to shake our fists at any of them.

## BUT THROUGH REALIZING OUR SOCIALIZATION

I want now to take this further and talk about other conditions I am aware of, but which are even more difficult at present to characterize. Hence the following remarks may be more symptomatic than diagnostic. In the progressive history of capitalism, the concentration of labor always creates conditions for the socialization of labor. Now, most of us are familiar with the novel phenomenon in New York recently of "quasi-factory" conditions of art production accompanied by the "factory-related" community, SoHo. It is plain that the currently "necessary" concentration of production goes hand in hand with a concentration of population, and also prompts a relocation of the market outlets. I doubt there has ever been such a concentrated community of artists in contrast to a community of people of mixed occupations and interests. One reaction to this is to assume that our present generation of artists identify their reality only with their roles of "artist"—which, given the remarks above, is disturbing. If this is so, it implies that the "other self" or "bureaucratized artist" in all of us has triumphed and we have become inescapably reified in that role. However, the point to stress is this: the development of a "factory-like" community, which sustains and encourages an exploitative market, also creates uniquely different social conditions for that community and in turn may lead to social and political awareness of the power of the community.[10]

One noticeable outcome of this concentration and (some sort of) socialization of "art labor" is the recent tendency to "unionize," to form associations and organize the community to have some efficacy of its own—and I think it is the first time conditions on such a scale have existed where the idea of an artists' union could be regarded as in any way realistic. There are a number of examples: the old Art Workers' Coalition, the SoHo Artists' Association, growing numbers of co-op galleries ("worker-controlled factories") set up in opposition to traditionally impersonal galleries ("managerial organizations") and so on. Two instances I am slightly familiar with raise a barrage of questions. The first is biased toward "production workers," the second is specifically a "non-production workers" case. The following comments are made in the context of my earlier remarks and in the light of how I see my own "community" affairs.

In the case of the National Art Workers' Community, while I am very sympathetic to most of their proposed aims (as published in the *Art Workers News,* vol. 4, no. 6, September

1974), I am simultaneously appalled that the model taken for the proposed association or "union" is that of American trade unions, organizations which historically have allowed their political roles to be eroded away to that of "mere" economic bargain-hunters. Trade unions traditionally have been firstly social and political movements and secondly economic forces— thus economic betterment was generally conceived in terms of political action and social change. In the United States, however, unions have tended to conceive of their "force for social change" through *sharing* corporate power rather than seeking change. So, ultimately, at the point of official acceptance of collective bargaining, unions have emerged as monopolies themselves and strong allies of corporate industry, often forcing even more monopolistic exploitation and practices into the market.

This insidious but by no means rare separation of "socioeconomic" (or "culture") from "politics" is openly represented in the NAWC proposals: "The goal . . . is to improve the socio-economic status of visual artists through:

*1 — improving the standard of living of the artist through expanding the demand for art;*
*2 — promoting the recognition of the artist as a working professional . . ."*

Isn't this labor organizing for the same reasons that capital does and for no other? Living in a consumer society under a state of siege, incessantly being urged to consume more . . . do we want to persuade others into an even more conspicuous consumption of artworks? What of the tacit equation of an "economic standard of living" with "quality of life"? At what point might we be prepared to forego the lifestyle of the haute bourgeois artiste, or is that what we really mean by "professionalism"? Are there no questions to be asked about a private property system operating in the fine arts? And so on.

The second example of disavowing social-political roles was displayed in the PASTA (the Professional and Administrative Staff Association) strike at the Museum of Modern Art here in New York. In an interview published in *Artforum* (December 1973), representatives of the strike committee revealed an inability to cope with the political reality of their context, a refusal to entertain such radical questions as the key role played by the museum in the promotion of a bureaucratized, alienating "high culture." Under what conditions can we support job preservation and betterment policies in an already over-bureaucratized and over-privileged art? In what ways would we be better off as a result of the bureaucratic power being spread more evenly among the upper echelon staff? To whose advantage is it finally to see the museums function more efficiently? I find it hard to believe it is for my advantage. And what about all those questions concerning the culpability of the roles that the staff identify with?

What debilitates these efforts at unionizing and socialization is the tendency to pin hopes on liberal reformist programs (and not very forceful ones at that). These imply everyone confining themselves to agitation for changes which do not challenge any foundations of the organizing structure, changes which are compatible with the preservation of these foundations.

My point is that, no matter how much we empathize with these endeavors, the most critically important factor keeps getting lost. It cannot be stressed enough that a community, no matter how small, is unavoidably and importantly a political instrument, and a potentially aggressive one at that—finally perhaps the only one left to us. If we don't take advantage of this, we may be able to do absolutely nothing.[11]

## MIGHT WE BE ABLE TO TRANSFORM OUR REALITY?

So I come, finally, to a note of guarded optimism. Although there is scant evidence for it at present, I would hope for and not rule out the potential for a distinctive consciousness and solidarity developing out of a "community of artists." There are uniquely changed social conditions here in New York, so it is just possible that such a consciousness may be at odds with the status quo. In some subjective sense we may come to terms with the reality of our own experiences and "reintegrate" our fragmented existences. But that is high optimism because, against that, increasingly formidable odds are working. It is almost gratuitous to point out the stupefying indoctrination of the media and educational processes.

While a collapse of our privileged economy is hardly desirable, it seems a prospect to be faced—and one "logical" outcome is likely to be that much of the manipulated market demand for modern art may simply evaporate. That doesn't mean the market will magically cease to be monopolistic. No, only that it will have shrunk considerably, leaving a demand for a much diminished workforce. Thus we may initially experience a phenomenon similar to the cutbacks in scientific programs—an ever-larger surplus of trained "modern artists" for whom there are no "jobs" in relation to the market.[12] At the same time, one cannot help but express a masochistic curiosity about how much art will continue to be made if there is literally no market demand for it. Because, while we have been able to sell modern art to Europe and other Westernized countries, it is still moot whether it will be collected by the OPEC countries, the new capitalists challenging the United States as the major exporters of inflation. Presumably, in a world economy no longer wholly determined by the West, there are many prospects for a major economic shift in art . . . but for an art whose principal dynamic is the "stability" of the present economy, and a community of artists who all have some sort of an investment in that "stability," the effects may be (and again I masochistically hope) truly amazing.

Whatever we are able to accomplish now, my point is that transforming our reality is no longer a question of just making more art—it is a matter of realizing the enormous social vectoring of the problem and opportunistically taking advantage of what social tools we have. Of one thing I am certain: anything we might call radical theory in the arts will have to be solidly constructed in all its social dimensions. But even then it may not be a question of how much we might accomplish, since it might take something as catastrophic as a collapse in the economic structure of this society to have any substantial effect on the careening superstructure of modern American art.

**NOTES**

1. This article owes much to conversations within the Art & Language community in New York (and particularly with Mel Ramsden).

2. An exception to this would seem to be artists who are under contract to, are receiving retainers from or whose work materials are being supplied by galleries or dealers. However, this is not so much purchasing the artist's labor as an expedient to gaining exclusive marketing rights to their production—more a commitment to produce than control over production.

3. Something else which needs looking at is pricing of works of art, since prices are always in relation to a particular market structure. There is obviously no "natural" price independent of a market, and the arbitrariness of a particular price is simply the arbitrariness of a particular market. Setting a price on a work of art is establishing the mode of allocation of the rights to that work, including property rights or ownership; so, along with the discussions of property rights versus "moral rights" in relation to works of art (e.g. Carl Baldwin, *Art in America,* September-October 1974), it would seem especially pertinent to scrutinize the relations between private property, particular types of market structures and the setting of monetary price. After all, deciding how a price should be determined is essentially deciding about what sort of society we want to live in. For discussion of this, see my article "Pricing works of art," *The Fox* (April 1975).

4. President Theodore Roosevelt, 1907.

5. I am all too aware of my poor acumen in economics. This, not incidentally, reflects the fragmentation and specialization "necessary" in my education for "becoming an artist."

6. Note that "internationalism" in art is a market definition, not a cultural definition.

7. For discussion of this era, see Max Kozloff, "American Painting During the Cold War," *Artforum* (May 1973), and Eva Cockcroft, "Abstract Expressionism: Weapon of the Cold War," *Artforum* 12 (June 1974). On a broader cultural scale, see also Harold Rosenberg, *Discovering the Present* (Chicago: University of Chicago Press, 1974).

8. See, for example, Terry Smith, "American Painting and British Painting: Some Issues," *Studio International* (December 1974).

9. This point can also be made concerning the contradictions apparent in looking at art produced by feminist artists, black artists and various underprivileged groups: while their social thinking is radical, fertile and engaging, what we see of the art produced is too often as embarrassingly dull, uniform and bureaucratic as everyone else's.

10. To start with, you can't help wondering about the effect of this urbanizing on the "rugged individualism" hailed in SoHo mythology. After all, the reality of SoHo is that it is a community based on common occupations, interests and social need, but which is kept atomized by an individualism which no longer really holds . . . a specialists' corporate community made up of people who claim to dislike organization and specialization.

11. If I appear to be arguing for some sort of "social realism," that is not the case at all. Anyway, we already have the social realism of capitalism: it is in the "lesser arts" (c.f. William Morris), which have become the dominion of Madison Avenue's advertising artists. They create the propaganda educating and inspiring everyone to greater heights of commodity-mindedness and consumerism. These "lesser arts," financed directly by corporations, would not exist without such patronage. Ironically, the lesser arts dominate the possibilities of any explicit social practice (such as it is). They also provide the wedge which isolates us from the prospect of such a practice and herds us into the cloistered anti-social state of "high culture." We are neatly trapped by our own elitism.

12. There is already massive overproduction on both the selling market and the job market, with far more art produced than can be sold, while the excess of job applicants at recent College Art Association meetings speaks for itself—and this before any further job market shrinkage.

This text first appeared in *Artforum,* 13:8 (April 1975), pp. 34–37.

# 1975
## joseph kosuth

**1.**

Art changes only through strong convictions, convictions strong enough to change society at the same time.

　　　—Théophile Thoré, 1855[1]

Bolshevism, and later Nazism, offered avant-garde art the alternative of supporting a revolutionary regime through aesthetic conformity—(that is, through ceasing to exist) or attempting to revolutionize itself without any prospect of changing life, in view of the superior force of the "professional revolutionists."

　　　Either of these choices could only lead to the end of avant-gardism. Without its political shadow, the defiance of accepted social or moral norms becomes a game in which the old threats are turned into an insider's joke. Today, revolts restricted to the aesthetic are welcomed by the middle class as a solace; they revive the aroma of the exciting times when hostility and misunderstanding between artists and the public were considered dangerous.

**With the door to politics closed by totalitarianism art has to an increasing degree affirmed its dissociation from political and social purpose. In the ideologies of recent art movements art-historical reasoning has been offered as a substitute for consciousness of history. In this parody of vanguardism, which revives the academic idea of art as a separate "realm," art can make revolutionary strides without causing a ripple in the streets or in the mind of a collector.**

—Harold Rosenberg[2]

The last *Fox* poster advertised ". . . the failure of Conceptual Art" as part of the content of Number 1. The nature of that "failure" was only alluded to in various articles, and was left at that. But, in fact, I have reservations as to whether "failure" accurately describes the rather complex history of its diverse currents of artistic intent. Certainly the activities of the mass of practitioners within what is now an (art) institution is a betrayal of the impetus of its original aims. Stylistic conceptual art (hereafter SCA) is to my view superstructure begetting superstructure: a formalistic hypostatization of cultural sleepwalking; as dependent on and as expressive of the institutions of the prevailing dominating socio-political-economic ideology as is the current practice of the more traditional modes of art-making (painting and sculpture). In this article I hope to underscore an alternative reading of the past, present, (and possibly future) history of an art-practice one might call, with certain discomfort, theoretical conceptual art (hereafter TCA).

This article is not intended to constitute some sort of "last word." Given its author such a discussion can be inescapably self-serving. (I will leave it up to the reader to decide on the relative usefulness of an article of this sort as opposed to the objectively cloaked creative work done by our colleagues, those "neutered" artists, the professional critics and art historians.) No, quite the contrary: as this journal is the expression of a moment in the intersubjective space of those of us involved with it, so this article is a conversational cross-section of my learning and thinking. It is also a response to the experience of finding myself in the world in which I do—and realizing the vulnerability of my past context dependent work to "mean" what to so many it appears to. My thoughts about the future are unsure; certainly more unsure than this article implies. And this is compounded by the fact that in many ways I feel responsible—at least in part—for some of the current malaise in art-practice. My role, and the role of others, in disassembling the art-making opiate—as it is in its traditional mode—will only be appreciated if it is counter-balanced with a larger explanation of the historical necessity of our doing so.

Typical of most recent art "movements," conceptual art has had a relatively brief life. Had we known that its death would have come from acceptance, perhaps many of us would have appreciated (for as long as it continued) that the hostility and extreme defensiveness that marked its art public greeting was paradoxically its life-support system: the reaction from the vanguard establishment was itself a tacit understanding of its potential threat. The subsequent deterioration of the movement into a popular SCA pointed, at least on the surface, to an ultimate victory by the establishment. The form the victory takes is that of annexation. On a personal level for the practitioners what occurs is that the sense of authentic existence obtainable through a kind of struggle is replaced by an impersonal participatory role in cultural power brokerage and subsequent defense of that generalized cultural status quo of which, henceforth, your movement is part. The political implications of such a generalization is the identification of what you "mean" or intend with those institutions of society upon which your work is dependent.

The scientist structure upon which I based my older work was intended to provide an arena in which work *on* art could *be* art yet leave behind the aura of profound personal moments reified and vying for recognition as "masterpieces." The *activity* was art, not the residue. But what can this society do with *activity*? Activity must mean labor. And labor must give you a service or a product. Only as a *product* could what I spent my time doing be meaningful in this society. But what it meant to *me,* and to anyone really interested in art had nothing at all to do with its existence as a product. The more recent work needed galleries and museums to provide the necessary context—and this is where the problems, artistic and political, begin. On one hand, one can rightly ask: where else is the audience for this activity? Certainly the museums, galleries, and art magazines provide the stage for the interested public to make contact with the "activity." Then, on the other hand, one realizes that the museums, galleries, and art magazines transform, edit, alter and obscure the very basis of one's art.[3] Just like the other institutions in America, these institutions in *our* world are bent on maintaining the cultural *status quo.*

In the late sixties and early seventies in New York there was somewhat of a "junta" atmosphere in the art world. The Greenberg gang was attempting with great success to initiate an Official History gestalt, and there wasn't much generosity toward us "novelty" artists that didn't happen to fit into the prescribed historical continuum. Fortunately, there were very few younger artists that *did* fit into his historical continuum, which is what collapsed the movement—in spite of the tremendous appeal of Greenberg's brand of formalism to academics and other upper middle class professionals. Exponents of the "party line" had saturated all aspects of the art establishment. There was Lawrence Rubin selling it in his gallery, and William Rubin curating it at the MOMA; Greenbergers were on the grant-giving panels, and were published relentlessly in the magazines—from *The Hudson Review* to *Artforum*. At *Artforum*, under Phil Leider, they decided that if they would just ignore us maybe we would go away—their hegemony being what it was at the time. We didn't. If one did get reviewed you could be sure it would be a hatchet job. The token coverage of "novelty" art was usually reserved for the weakest possible examples within any tendency deemed threatening enough to Official History to deserve coverage. Anything positive generally consisted of trying to reveal the "classic" lurking within the misfit—most of the "antiform" artists were seduced, and their work affected, by such annexation. This annexing finally was forced on the formalists insofar as they were now forced to be formalists *theoretically*, but had to liberalize their practice since there were too few non-"novelty" painters or sculptors of any merit around to keep them all working. Perhaps it was that or perish. So the art critical establishment began to consider the work of younger artists (Serra, Heizer, Sonnier, Nauman, Hesse, etc.) which could be embraced in some fashion by formalist criticism—regardless of the artists' intentions. With the exception of two articles by Jack Burnham, conceptual art was by and large ignored during this period. The recent appearance of articles such as "Artists as Writers" by Lawrence Alloway (*Artforum*, March 1974) in which TCA was totally omitted, increasingly made it clear the omissions were still (small p) political. My work has seemed to be particularly useful as a negative example, so much so that it began to get humorous in its predictability.[4] (Finally, I suppose to avoid admitting past errors, when "Conceptual Art" could no longer be ignored *Artforum* came up with their *own* "Conceptual Artists." Sort of how the Russians came up with Husak to "lead" Czechoslovakia. They've pretty much still continued to ignore the work which has been around for years and constituted most of the early and even not-so-early conceptual art exhibitions here and abroad.)[5] So much for provincial bitching.

With little exception the work which gets attention (SCA) has been made "cute" and palatable. The use of language is seen as "a new kind of paint." Most of the objections have been laid out years ago in *Art-Language*.[6] What has been important about TCA has been that it has a theoretical force that recent movements have not had. It has allowed for the possibility of new work on a *collective* basis (with that "collectivity" being the product of ideological self-awareness), and not simply on the traditional stylistic tract of individual histories. What has emerged from an understanding of TCA's infrastructure (and obviously by extension art's) has been the necessity for an *alternative supporting social structure*. What began in the mid-sixties as an analysis of the context of specific objects (or propositions) and correspondingly the questions of *function*, has forced us now, ten years later, to focus our attentions on the society and/or culture in which that specific object operated. Our "radicalization" has, rather cold-bloodedly, evolved from our work. Such a recognition increasingly forces us to confront the high problem-aticity of participation with the establishment avant-garde in our work. As the Rosenberg quote above points out, the relationship between the present avant-garde and the historical role of the revolutionary artist is similar to the relationship between the forthcoming Bicentennial Celebration and what it meant to be an American and fighting in Concord in 1775.

To turn to the case of my own work, any description must appreciate its formalization through a stratification of "overviews," with these overviews operating as models of art. The initial study of anthropology was for me a way of viewing art itself as a context: though I found the lack of self-reflexivity in academic cultural anthropology seriously undermining its capacity to provide a model which wasn't *itself* an artifact. The "objective" reality of the scientistic, architectonic model is, by construction, incapable of the sort of reflexivity mandatory of a real model of art. It is in this way that one can possibly see an evolution toward a more Marxian and critical overview of American art and culture.

To the extent that one speaks of art in this century one understands modernism to have been authentic to it. I don't think that is controversial. The self-consciousness of modernist art-practice was a "motor" for the complex unconscious mediation of social reality with human action as "meaning" *internally;* beyond which—as a symbolic language—the *external* societal structure could support the contradictions; thus taking us to the present crisis. I think it is no accident that the art which I am describing in this article (TCA), as the first to address itself to a conscious self-reflexive dialectic with society/culture, is the one and the same that was so radically concerned with the internal or infrastructural mechanism of art. Whether *any* such concern would follow that direction is at best unclear, but what is clearly of paramount impor-tance to such a trajectory is the particularities (methodological and otherwise) of a significantly altered conception of art-practice priorities.

## 2.

*. . .* **A language is at the same time the product and the instrument of speech: their relationship is therefore a genuinely dialectical one.**
— Roland Barthes

"Formalism" was at issue in Conceptual Art (CA) in more ways than the apparent ones. With Greenbergian formalism what is at issue is a belief that artistic activity consists of *superstructural* analysis (prominent traditional modes of art are taken as "givers" and the issue is to attempt to understand the nature of art qua technical praxis of those traditional modes). CA, which might be described as a formalism of another sort, has as its basis *infrastructural* analysis, and it is in this context that one understands the endeavor to "question the nature of art." It is necessary to such an infrastructural analysis to locate one's activity in artistic endeavor since Abstract Expressionism, after which work began to appeal to *the logic of modernism* for art status rather than appealing to the tradition of western painting for art status.

In my past few articles I have tried to explain my activities, and the activities of Art & Language, in terms of my notion of an "anthropologized art."[7] An "anthropologized art," in keeping with my previous discussion of it, must concern itself with exposing institutional contradictions and thereby obliterating art ideologies which presuppose the autonomy of art. The understanding is that such art is dependent on an even more embracing ideology which presupposes institutions of equally autonomous value. An "anthropologized art" is an art which is not "naive" towards its own ethno*logic,* and which has as its practice the construction of a model which, though tautological in the particularities of its own structure, nevertheless functions dialectically *in situ*—that is, culture *qua* art. That it meets the demands of the ethno*logic* and alters existing norms of art is a demonstration of its dialectical functioning. *Its* alteration by the institutional supports of those "norms of art" (galleries, museums, and magazines) is as well a demonstration. An "anthropologized art" must therefore accelerate the dynamic to such a degree that this larger (operational) dialectical model exposes and isolates those institutional supports on one hand, and thereby simultaneously articulates with clarity that dimension of western civilization's ethnologic we call art, on the other.

Painting has become a "naive" art form because it can no longer include "self-consciousness" (theoretically *as well as* that of historical location) in its program. Such a self-consciousness necessitates that the prevailing "language of art," like any language, must be transparent to be believed. Sixties art was the dissolution of the language of art as painting and sculpture into opacity. With CA emerged (out of what was only implicit in "minimalism") a *competitive* paradigm or model of artistic activity. The work closest in time to "minimalism" *appealed* to the innate structure or "logic" of western civilization, more recent work (TCA) has increasingly consisted of *revealing,* through praxis (action on the superstructural level), that "logic." The older scientistic, analytic model was *passive* (*relied* on institutions for meaning); whereas the dynamic of the new work must, in part, consist of *revealing* the contradictions, and as such has as its task the dismantling of the mythic structure of art as posited in the present day cultural institutions.

The motor of art is that it is engaged. That is, the notion of art coming out of art speaks exactly of this. Art's existence is on a level of praxis, and as such it is a continuous working model of culture. But our art, even if it is to be a model of culture, is not static, but an operating, continually changing, model. One of our tasks is to re-establish an equilibrium between its internality and its externality. It must be *in the world*. By not being *in the world* it is culturally naive.

In some respects CA was a tacit recognition that visual iconography was "used up" for surface structural purposes. What then became the surface structure in TCA was *methodological choice* in the description of whether what was being described *was* art—which is in keeping with the understanding that this was not appealing to the traditions of artmaking procedure (painting and sculpture) but to the deepest structure of the "logic" of western civilization: that is, to *culture* itself. What was felt, I think, was the need for a radical surgery—a tracheotomy to bypass the blockage of meaninglessness that this society by way of its institutions (of which painting is one) had come to represent.[8]

(New) art begins with a reference to tradition (or culture, or "*langue*"). That is, it appeals to tradition for "believability"; it then proceeds to exist in terms of being a *representative itself* of tradition—taking its meaning *from* while it simultaneously gives meaning *to* "tradition." Yet the dependency of perception on theory forces the work of art into a state of continuous change in meaning. In this way it functions as a cultural road map, appearing to exist isomorphically to human consciousness as a memory of it (with the experience of art more like the experience of memory than of an actual event); speaking of itself as "tradition" it speaks of the institutions of society—the social reality—with such a specific static embodiment of "reality" as to imply the possibility of transcendent "conversations" on a cosmic level (contemplation) if only for a moment—while the *promise* of such conversations floats on as an ideology.

## 3.

Mythic variants and their contents may be progressively engendered by the logic of myth itself. In all cases, however, they remain comparative and relational, either within the specific confines of their respective ethnographic settings or in those relatively autonomous instances when myths "reflect upon themselves and their interrelation."
—Bob Scholte

No doubt everything in the folk tale originates with the individual, just as all sound changes must; but this necessary fact of invention in the first place is somehow the least essential characteristic of folk literature. For the tale does not really become a folk tale, given the oral diffusion of this literature, with its obvious dependence on word of mouth circulation, until the moment when it has been accepted by the listeners who retain it and pass it on. Thus the crucial moment for the folk tale is not that of the parole, that of its invention or creation (as in middle class art), but that of the *langue;* and we may say that no matter how individualistic may be its origin, it is always anonymous or collective in essence; in Jakobsonian terminology, the individuality of the folktale is a redundant feature, its anonymity a distinctive one.

—Fredric Jameson

It might be useful to consider certain aspects of my past work within this discussion of an "anthropologized art." Central to much of my work has been a somewhat special use of the notion of tautology. This notion of a tautology as a formal (art) model can only be understood *operationally* as an hermeneutic. The formal "map description" of it forces us to call it a tautology, but an understanding of it as a dynamic (dialectic) sees it as an hermeneutic. By hermeneutic here I am thinking of Scholte's notion of an hermeneutic approach as one which "considers a tie between historical consciousness and ethnological understanding—between experience and reality—to be fundamental to any textual interpretation. . . ." Its own paradigmatic foundations are reconstituted throughout the model in such a way as to offer (systemically include) an autocritique implicit in its own self-reflexivity.

The convenience of structuring models of art along the lines of a tautology have to do with the specific needs of a "non-naive" art-practice. If the "artist-anthropologist" has as his/her task the construction of models which "expose" our ethnologic while simultaneously being "accepted" by it and thereby mediating each other into a totality, an understanding of Modernism (in which the ethnologic of this civilization *qua* art has been most exposed) returns us in fact (though one might want to describe it differently) to my argument of artistic functioning—naive as it is—in "Art after Philosophy."[9]

Both the usefulness and the inappropriateness of tautology as a description can be made more clear in the attempt to map out the functioning of my past *Investigations.* Consider the following: we first have the need to formally construct the model so that, even if only perceptually (operationally), it can be grasped as a whole. Previous art did this literally in a visual way. Comprehension can be understood as "holistic." In my models "operationality" was pervasive. The smallest operational unit in each proposition was designed to function (operate "meaningfully") in unison with other units. These units or stratifications of meaning were all totally dependent on each other. Shifts of meaning from unit to proposition to investigation to all ten *Investigations* to contemporary art to Modernism to western civilization, etc. were structured to force *meaning* to be dependent on context *at every level,* and from the outside. And on the inside, the units (as well as the other ways they functioned) consisted of textual material, usually "theory" but not always. These were self-referential in order to be self-reflexive of the model (and art) itself. Its space consisted of "psychological space" at a unitary level (comprehension of the text) yet the construction from adding all the parts (units) to make a "whole" had no iconic meaning; the model's physicality was not rarified and made magical. Outside of the personal meaning of entering its "psychological space" no specific proposition could be "seen" any more or less than any Investigation could be "seen." Indeed, its interdependency from unit to proposition to Investigation meant that the act of "seeing" my work meant "seeing" art.[10] In this way there was a direct operational relationship between the particular (a unit) and the general (art and culture).

While I always considered my writing on art a part of my role as an artist—interdependent with the models—I nevertheless have maintained that to quasi-gesturally profess one's functioning *as a writer* (this being the praxiological in-the-world agent) as continually the "model" (from the point of view of praxis) of art *qua* artist sets up too clear and in fact an inappropriate distinction between the meaning of the *activity* and the import of the content of what was being written. Further, in Art & Language, there has been the problem of mystification which follows writing so special as to be too inaccessible to be "influential" on generally applied conceptions of art-practice; thus furthering the notion that the artistic significance of the group is the generalizable "script-making activity" rather than what is actually being said.

Language when used within the context of a "model" of art cannot be considered operationally similar to its use in explicated "art theory." "Modelistic" use of language is not the voluntary and full conscious literal content-communication which it is often mistaken to be. Certainly there is a level of specific meaning to what is stated. But its significance as a model of art is *relational,* not literal; though those relations cannot be understood independent of specific meaning, it is understood only when it is understood *in its totality.*

Throughout my work there has been a realization that "model" must *clearly* exist as such, as internalizations and capable of a contrast to *external* art criticism or aesthetics. (What separates the critic and art historian from the artist is his/her demand to have an *external* relationship to art-practice; the myth of scientific "objectivity" has demanded this—in some ways one can define the artist as one who tries to affect change from the *inside,* and the historian/critic as one who tries to affect it from the *outside.* There can be little doubt as to why the historian/critic is increasingly viewed as a "cultural policeman.") *Theory as praxis* to be more fully understood must withstand transformation in being reversed: praxis as theory—meaning what contextually (semantically) functioned *as art* was *a theory* of art.

The historically evolving unconscious rules of language were understood to have a homologous relationship to what I have called the "logic" of culture. Thus, the attempt to formalistically disassociate our work from our society's iconographic surface structure (and attempt to arrive at some kind of "non-style") partially explains the reasoning behind (in Saussure's terms) the attempted use of the *signifier* as the *signified*—what else could more clearly focus our attention on the *system of art itself*?

A TCA praxis which doesn't include a distinction between implicit theory ("models") and explicit theory (articles) is incapable of clearly establishing the interdependence between the two. Insofar as art-practice itself can only be historically understood as *model construction* then explicit theory itself becomes the model (with its meaning understood to be implicit— that is, as not being what is *actually* said in the texts themselves). The point perhaps being that unless one sets up the models as part of a conscious and controlled (relative to the endeavor) program inclusive of a self-reflexive and self-critical dynamic, formalistically functioning *explicitly*, then alternatively what emerges uncritically is a model arrived at via (social) practice. Thus one can begin to see that what has been Art & Language's weakness according to one mapping is its potential strength according to another.

Art & Language's role as an (art) model builder in the past is then subject to interpretation. What does make Art & Language extremely important is the implicit social critique in its methodology. I don't refer here to "collaboration"—this was in no way unique to Art & Language, and the unevenness of participation in practice makes "collaboration" a misnomer in signifying what's special about the group. As Mel Ramsden recently put it:[11]

*I still insist on the social roots of the problem. "The group" forced to compete in an individualistic antagonistic self-interested (Adam Smith you Scottish Bastard) world. For example: "having a show" is a one or two man endeavor. You need impact and gestalt. The whole thing is epistemologically individualistic. That's that. One reason for the collapse of A&L was that it moved from the journal (which was a "group effort") to gallery shows which suddenly meant 15 or 14 out of the 16 people were standing around pretending they knew what was going on. There's nothing wrong with leaders, it's just when others see them leading and you following that we get screwed up. Again, these problems are social, not "merely psychological."*[12]

The importance of Art & Language remains as an ideological (art) collective. I say "collective" and not community, but one could say the collective consists of two communities—one in England and the other in New York. The recent collapse of the spirit of Art & Language as *one* community has come about through work by the New York group which concerns itself with issues anchored in the specificity of their New York lives and the larger artists' community here. *The Fox* is obviously one expression of this work. It has forced us into the real world, or to put it better, it has shown us that Art & Language spans *two* real worlds: and that the gulf between the two communities is, indeed, as wide as the Atlantic.

How can we make the transition from a praxiological life-world in which our work *along with us* is commodified (i.e. money and fame) to one in which "payment" takes the form of an acknowledgment by the community in which one lives implicitly by the act of adaptation. That means seeing how one's work affects the world in which one lives, and learning *along with others* from its effect, and appreciating that effect not as simply an extension of oneself (power) but as a part of a larger historical complexity which connects the location of your life with that of others. Perhaps it is here where one begins to understand the import of the (artistic) ideological collective of which Art & Language is a prototype and emerging model.

## 4.

**... with the events of recent years Marxism has definitely entered a new phase of its history, in which it can inspire and orient analyses and retain a real heuristic value, but is certainly no longer true in the sense it was believed to be true.**
—Maurice Merleau-Ponty

The shift from the individual craftsman to the "ideological community" has as its pivotal base an understanding of a changed sense of *responsibility*. It is one result of the *generalizing* aspect of theoretical work, paramount as it has been to Conceptual Art. Initially, as Harold Rosenberg suggests, CA was self-consciously historical. Particularly among the early Conceptual artists, we were united not by a shared involvement in the technical issues of painting, for instance, but rather by a collective sense of a historical location: a view of art *overlooking* the flatlands of painting and sculpture. In thinking of artist's groups as a human community, one thinks of how painters are forced to underscore their *differences* from other painters; the struggles being how to maintain one's own identity within the generalization of painting. In CA what was felt, in the beginning at least, was not a sense of solidarity among technicians—that was wide open with everyone trying to stay out of everyone else's way—but rather a sense of solidarity in our sameness, what we shared: being members of the first generation to be young enough to be capable of breaking our ties with modernism. The myth of modernism, which includes painting and sculpture, collapsing at our heels, left only its shock waves: the sense of a more direct relationship with the cultural bias of western civilization, left for us to try to express in some historical way. It is impossible to understand this without understanding the sixties, and appreciate CA for what it was: the art of the Vietnam war era. Perhaps there is some interwoven nature to the myth of America and the myth of modernism, and when both have been sufficiently unwoven the autonomy of art may be seen for what it is: one colored strand and part of a larger fabric.

The particularities of art have, before modernism, made such a comprehensible depiction (if only a partial one) of the infrastructure of art apart from the traditional modes of superstructural art-making unthinkable. Those "particularities" of the mythic structure of art have in this century constituted a continuous and profound, even if indirect, critique of Marxism. The lack of an accommodation of one to the other might in fact be characteristic, on a level of post-revolutionary societal fracturing, of Marxism's *own* programs (as separated from its critique of Capitalism) as ultimately unworkable in profoundly human terms.

As far as any real politics are concerned I have no hope for the Soviet Union and her "satellites."[13] Like America, they have forgotten what their revolutions meant. A country that must look to its past for honor is not a happy place in which to live. I must simply refuse to accept, as well, the scenario which only allows for "bourgeois" thought or Marxist thought. I think the *use* of Marxism is instructive, and Marxism in general must be taken into account. The conspicuous inability of Anglo-American intellectual enterprise to do so is singularly significant and perhaps its major weakness. Yet any anthropology, "marxian" or otherwise, cannot avoid the realization that Marxism and Capitalism both are representative of the 19th century life-world, and both present day Russia and America exist as monuments to the unreality and unworkability of both as systems at this point at the three-quarter mark of the 20th century. Our task is now clear: our generation must assemble its knowledge from any and all available sources and *find a viable alternative* to Capitalism and Communism. *The failure of our generation continues to be its inability to do so.*

Our youth was spent in an environment clouded over by the prospect of a nuclear holocaust: our children face an equally grisly, and more likely, prospect: life under the merged bureaucracies of multi-national corporations and Communist state capitalism—the "peaceful" world of which Kissinger's "detente" speaks. Such an arrangement is simply an accommodation among rulers to facilitate themselves *remaining* rulers. What is the *alternative* to this encroaching space-age feudalism: I wish I knew.

Eventually, of course, I must return this conversation to art. It is my "location" and in many ways how I organize my understanding of the world. (Perhaps that's what "work" of any kind is all about). My attacks over the years on tradition must be understood as attacks on particular (and popular) *conceptions* of tradition. Art is a description of reality by way of an interpretation of tradition. It is in the interpretation that one judges the value of the activity—as a real depiction of the social reality. In this sense "real" work is an historical fusion of an individual's (or individuals') lived reality with the constituted "optimism" inherent in a civilization's ethnologic. One can begin to see the struggle of the earlier stage—the relationship of the active agent *in* history *to* history. The fight, too, is for the status of existence (meaning) that young art and the young artist in his/her role as mediators between a "past" and a "future" understand as the confrontation with civilization. Here, at this stage, the artist-philosopher meets momentarily the artist-shaman and contacts the inherently revolutionary nature of art-praxis—until again, that parent Society seduces with a further re-description of reality.

I have said that the artist "depicts" reality by a description of tradition in terms unique for his/her historical location. My reading of art history tells me that I now find myself capable of seeing for art (out of art) a tradition independent of and unmolested by a social coloration (meaningfully mediated) which describes *and re-enforces* the presently unacceptable social status-quo. In this sense the Marxists are correct when they claim that art cannot be apolitical. When I realize this I must ask myself: if art is necessarily political (though not necessarily *about* politics) is it not necessary to make one's politics explicit? If art is *context* dependent (as I've always maintained) then it cannot escape a sociopolitical context of meaning (ignoring this issue only means that one's art drifts into one). For this it is necessary to make one's politics explicit (in some way) and work toward constructing a socio-political context of one's own in which (cultural) actions are anchored for meaning. It is in this sense that *The Fox* is a "political" journal. The desire is to consider art, and the lives of artists, in relation to (a) social philosophy. One begins to understand, increasingly, how the notion of a "category" of politics is at best a temporary device and at worst a naive relationship vis-à-vis the world. And further, an understanding of art is forced by a realization that a "political" reading of art (as I outline here) is an integral aspect of the internalizing feature (of artistic activity) towards a rich and comprehensive (though "located") understanding of the nature of art. Such an understanding is necessary if we find that there is something in art of importance to mankind/womankind which must be preserved. A defense of art in terms of its current formalization is necessarily prescriptive, and politically repugnant.

**NOTES**

1. Théophile Thoré, quoted in Linda Nochlin, "The Invention of the Avant-Garde: France, 1830–80," in *Avant-Garde Art,* ed. T. B. Hess and J. Ashbery (New York: Collier Books, 1968), p. 3.

2. Here quoted from Harold Rosenberg, "Collective, Ideological, Combative," in Hess and Ashbery, pp. 90–91.

3. I count curators, dealers, and historian/critics among my friends, but I think non-artist art "professionals" are in an extremely problematic situation vis-à-vis the system. Particular individual efforts are noteworthy, occasionally even heroic, but a re-thinking of one's role in society is in order for *everyone.*

4. One of *Artforum*'s more dismal chapters has been the James Collins episode. Collins' overnight conversion from an Art & Language sycophant to an *Artforum* sycophant (and useful anti-CA hatchet man) attests to both *Artforum*'s power and sense of expediency. Collins ended a response to Rosetta Brooks saying that discourse ". . . between the covers of magazines like *Artforum* seems like a proper location to me. There, unlike self-edited Conceptual Art magazines, the Editor can always say 'No.'" Of course at *Art-Language* we said "No" too—to *him,* several times. Hence the fanaticism of a sour grapes convert. His naive belief in the absolute and legitimate authority of non-artist art magazine editors, by the way, is pathetic coming from someone whose opportunism has propelled him on to yet another career as an artist. This time around, though, "theory" has been replaced by sex appeal.

5. It's very instructive for artists to see which work the critics find most usable for *their* craft. Take a look at old *ArtNews* and *Artforum*s. Since such magazines are usually in the hands of the prevailing art establishment, the critics tend to act as lawyers for the maintenance of the status quo. The practice seems to be to use the *weakest* examples of any threatening new development to argue against, thereby facilitating a put-down of the whole movement. You can't expect these more malleable artists to object to the sudden windfall that's come their way, given the set-up of the art world, but by now artists at least should realize the myth of "objective" criticism/history to be understood for what it is: creative work *competitive* with the artist's, yet repressive and tenaciously self-serving in its role as "administrator" for the artist's community.

6. [Kosuth seems to be referring to his own "Introductory Note" and Terry Atkinson's "From an Art & Language Point of View," *Art-Language,* 1:2 (February 1970), pp. 25–60.]

7. "The Artist as Anthropologist," "(Notes) on an 'Anthropologized' Art," and Statement for the Congress of Conceptual Art, *Art After Philosophy and After: Collected Writings, 1966–1990,* ed. Gabriele Guercio (Cambridge, Mass.: The MIT Press, 1991), pp. 107–127, 95–101, 93–94.

8. The current re-interest in painting—perhaps best exemplified by Brice Marden and Robert Ryman—is a result, ironically, of the "success" (taken as historically "right") of CA in Europe. Several intelligent dealers, supporters of CA, but dealers nonetheless, accepted the demise of painting sufficiently to pose the question: "So, then who are the last young painters?" Art market momentum, being as it is oblivious to "content," and fueled by a basic bourgeois preference of an art of decoration to that of an art of complexity, is rolling on of its own accord. Painting, which

asks no questions—even about the nature of art—has its cultural neutrality at the service of the dominant ideology.

9. There are of course many, many problems with "Art after Philosophy." One of the ones that comes to my mind at this moment is that while objecting to the romantic paradigm of the artist—being as it is a device for rendering artists powerless in any meaningful social sense—I seemed to swallow whole the scientistic ideology which by necessity must relegate the artist to such a position in the first place. It is the same ideology that we see, when described economically or politically, as culturally eclipsing our lives of their meaning. Of course one *can* write alternate historical schemes to Greenberg's (or anyone else's) aesthetic historical continuums. We *shouldn't* because we end up, unavoidably, as formalist bed-partners. While obviously I still do not hold to the scientistic, positivistic epistemology that is exhibited in "Art after Philosophy," there is an aspect to my discussion of artistic functioning which, at least in spirit, I feel is useful—though limited as it is to our understanding at the time. The overall, somewhat propagandistic, purpose of that article was to provide an understanding of the theoretical basis for a great deal of art-making activity eliminated from the art historical schema of Greenbergian formalism. Those that have criticized my theory as a "continuation of the 'art for art's sake' doctrine, resuscitated by Ad Reinhardt in the 60's" unhappily miss the complexity of the argument, and rely too heavily on my acknowledged (and for that matter continuing) respect for Reinhardt. It's also pretty ignorant, come to think of it, of the significance of Reinhardt's work. Rosetta Brooks, as quoted above, has her own axe to grind. She and John Stezaker—the artist whose mission she identifies as her own—go to great lengths to dismiss "Art after Philosophy" for rather transparent reasons which might best be described as "Oedipal" (read Stezaker).

10. Or seeing nothing at *all* in the form of tables, chairs, and my "summer reading."

11. In a letter I received this summer.

12. The journal Mel Ramsden refers to, *Art-Language,* allowed for individual effort as part of a collective ideological front which it constituted as the "party organ." The *Art-Language* which has re-appeared more recently has been victimized to some extent by the "social problems" similarly manifested in as well as acerbated by the group's participation in the gallery and museum system. My own relationship with Art & Language has been both a part of the problem, and (as I contend) a part of the solution.

13. Not that work isn't continuously being done to improve the Marxist model, nor for that matter that there aren't perhaps better working models than the Soviet Union (Yugoslavia, China, or Cuba). One can only look longingly, and momentarily, at anarchism or utopian socialism.

This essay was first published in *The Fox,* vol. 1, no. 2 (1975), pp. 87–96.

Checking the card catalog at UCSD Central Library I found only five titles on occupational health in Sept. 1975.

One way to look at the occupational health and safety issue is to see it as a game in which players try to maximize their gains and minimize their losses. There are two advantages to using the game model as a way of understanding what is going on. First, it is in fact the model used by many of those in the real world who act upon and affect health and safety on the job. We might gain some valuable insights into their way of thinking if we adopt their perspective here. Second, the game model allows us to see all the participants' actions in terms of a very specific and measurable goal; that accounts for its usefulness to them as well as to us as observers. "Game theory" as it is used in the economic sphere is a complicated affair, but for our purposes all we need to do is isolate and look at a set of specific actions, or "moves," that can be made. Dealing with specifics prevents ambiguity, making things more clear-cut-either resources are allocated to protecting health and safety and the rates of occupational illness and injury go down or resources are not allocated and the rates stay the same or go up.

Fred Lonidier, *The Health and Safety Game: Note and Scrapbook,* 1979, detail; and *The Health and Safety Game,* 1975, detail.

# having-your-heart-in-the-right-place-is-not-making-history
## art & language, UK

Let us not cite history. Our logic and time is new. I see no collective ideals, nothing outside personal truth to identify with . . .

By choice I identify myself with working men. I belong by craft yet my subject of aesthetics introduces a breach. I suppose that is because I believe in a workingman's society in the future and in that society I hope to find a place. In this society I find little place to identify myself economically . . .

Ihave strong social feelings but propaganda is not necessarily my fate . . .

The most important thing to know is who you are and what you stand for and to acknowledge this identity in your time. Concepts in art are your history; there you start.

—David Smith, an artist with his heart in the right place

So the artist has no history outside concepts in art, and sees no "collective ideals," yet he identifies—by choice—with working men and "believes in" a "workingman's society in the future" in which he'll have a place! Is identification a matter of choice? A historical identification (i.e. identifying oneself idealistically with a history which one does not believe he can join in making) is more determinism parading as ideology; "If-I-could-I-would-ism." Smith was just being sentimental about (American) history. The technology of modern art is bourgeois technology. In talking about "belonging by craft" Smith was referring to the expropriation of manufacturing modes for bourgeois ends. Judd, Morris, Andre and others (not to mention all those new-materials sculptors in England and elsewhere) have continued the process of expropriation (media-topicalization comes to mean the same thing). One might see Minimal Art, Process Art, Back-to-Nature Art, Jacking-off Art, Doing-things-for-People-Art, Conceptual Art, etc., as sophisticated means of bringing economically intractable commodities (albeit in symbolic forms) into the market place to be "valued." Naiveté is the "concerned" artist's best defense in face of the commercialization of his activity.

Something stronger is needed than the kind of idealism which Smith proclaims, and which his successors have upheld. Belief in the objective conditions for the achieving of socialism is more than a mere matter of faith. When Rosa Luxemburg attacked the opportunist policies of the reformist Eduard Bernstein, she implied that he was guilty of a kind of defection, a stepping aside from the more demanding currents of history. If too many people give up it won't happen. Liberal-reformist projections of history are self-fulfilling prophecies, perhaps because they are essentially normative. We're talking about two kinds—two "strengths" (c.f. Hintikka) of belief. Belief in a socialist future is not like saying the creed, more like sticking to your guns. David Smith was just affirming an empty faith (belief). Putting your historical productivity where your mouth is is something different. History is not made by accident, while one's not watching what he's doing. The concept of making history requires purport and purpose. The required purpose is purpose indexed to a defensible projected view of historical reality.

Artists merely "realizing their socialization" are just people pursuing the pathology of a scandal. Ideological speculation becomes ideological action *only* when it generates class conflict and invests class struggle. ". . . The bourgeoisie maintains itself not only by virtue of force but also by virtue of the lack of class consciousness, the clinging to old habits, the timidity and lack of organization of the masses" (Lenin—"Letters on Tactics") Artists are members of an essentially bourgeois social section and thus cannot participate in progressive class struggle so long as they retain and promote the "integrity" of mere intra-social interests. For the artist, ideological interaction must follow upon class analysis and upon ideological penetration of class barriers.

There is a paradox here. One cannot defensibly be "doing it for them"; one must be doing it for oneself. The artist/intellectual's interests must be (must have been) transformed into those of the progressive class, and this transformation must be (will be, if it is real transformation) free of complacent "backwardness"; i.e. it must entail ineradicable change in productive function and class orientation.

Q. *"But who are you doing it for?"*

A. *"I'm not doing it for anyone. I'm just trying to make history. Socialization must involve historical projectivity, and 'history is classes.' 'Wanting to have it so' can invest (and thus can be) 'making history'; but we have to be talking about more than just good intentions!"*

During this century artists have mostly been non-combatants so far as effective class struggle is concerned. This is not to be accounted for by positing some mythical status as classless, or non-aligned, un-ideological beings. "End-of-ideology" (or "-of-philosophy" or whatever) fixations are themselves tediously ideological and deviously self-serving. It's just that art has been bogged down in social-sectional (merely "cultural") interests for so long now that artists have become accustomed to coprophagic forms of life and are generally unable or unwilling to see out over the edge of the cess-pit towards a *feasible* socialist future. For too long now artists have been by definition members of a non-working class. (So long as there has been a proletariat, artists have not been part of it. As the historical identity of the proletariat has developed, so the class-orientation of the artist has been attenuated.) Yet to be defensible now, artists' projects must be projects in and for action along class lines. Under present circumstances, the progressive artists will be those who seek, as however distant a prospect, the dictatorship of culture by the working classes. As a member of a bourgeois social section, the artist can thus only act progressively in the symptomatic and historical paradoxicalness of his own social practice.

One has to have a view of what should happen, in history, and sort one's tasks accordingly. It's no good just carrying-on with good intentions. The progressive intellectual's task is to generate ideological *conflict.* One's field of feasibly progressive action may be limited to superstructural (ideological) intervention (i.e. one has more potentially useful tasks to perform as a member of the intelligentsia than as a foot-soldier who can't shoot straight), but if one's ideological action doesn't include acceptance of the possible practical outcome of ideological conflict, then it is mere monkeying-about.

For instance, the dictatorship of culture by the working class will inevitably involve the progressive artist in persuading some of his social-sectional colleagues to desist, in compelling those who won't be persuaded, and in "disenfranchising" those who won't be compelled. The "radical" who does not accept this is just a liberal in Woolf's clothing. 1900-style Transcendental Socialism—the arty idealization of "human nature" as involving the potential of universal creativity—just won't do inside a concept of creativity as involving the making of history, and a concept of history as involving class struggle. (How about Joseph Beuys' solution to Ulster's troubles: set up free schools where the proletariat can be distracted by the realization of their own true creativity? What does he think they're going to do? Sculpting in fat and felt and talking to dead animals don't map easily onto the culture of the Six Counties.)

It's hard to see how social transformation can be achieved without some putting to death. This is not bloodlust but realism. It seems clear that there are those who will never be persuaded that they have no right to be greedy. They are themselves realists of a sort. There can indeed be *no* equity of provision of "opportunities" where the appropriation of material *and ideological* commodities is concerned, at least certainly not without a transformation so radical as wholly to revise the terms of reference for the concept of opportunity, and it's unlikely that this could be countenanced by those who proclaim the importance of opportunity as presently construed.

While we might not wish to sanction labor camps, we could be sympathetic to a view of them as places where you send those who *won't* be put to work. (And we all have colleagues . . .) Nor would we fight for freedom of speech if that just meant fighting for the right to express *merely* superstructural (idealistic, asocial) concepts of "human rights." We might even see mental hospitals as not inappropriate places of residence for those dissident intellectuals who see dissidence as a mere function of individuality of intuition; i.e. it's more defensible to use them as prisons for those who are already the prisoners of their own minds than as centers of "treatment" for the victims of medically irrelevant demarcations imposed by "liberal" medicine in defense of property and social harmony.

This is the point at which the social democrat gets frightened and sells out in the name of (bourgeois) "humanism." "But I wanted *peaceful* transformation. If it can't be nonviolent it won't be what I wanted. And what about my Art? I thought I was fighting for the right to go on doing my thing . . . ."

This essay was first published in *The Fox,* 1:3 (1976), pp. 75–77.

# the timeless lumpenness of a radical cultural life
## art & language, UK

. . . The timeless lumpenness of a radical cultural life; the gangrenous excrescence, stylishly exposed in the quiet salons. The market for the dry delicacies of pretentious gentility, the overfed opinion, the corpulent choice, the leisured appropriation, "society" and society in harmony are an objective condition of the class struggle. The privileged low-life of high culture is the massification of the people, is the enemy of inquiry, is an insult to, and sometimes an egregious product of, the achievement and goals of working-class movements, a denial of the real objectives of the working-class movement. It is not, however, the life of the unwitting fool. It has its own agencies.

The conditions of the production of high culture are not somehow apart from these machinations in brutality . . . and the artists are not exempt from the charge of connivance at the proliferation of force, violence: the barbarism of imperialism. Their "status" as an economic *hors concours* serves the aim of the ruling classes in their continuing domination. It avails no one of a glimpse of "freedom." It is a status which allows a parvenu sincerity, the treachery of the successful product, to be deified in a fideism of "culture," a fideism in the interests of the ruling class.

Don't think that artists are somehow the victims of an underdetermined predestination: their attempts to fix forever their relations with "the rest of the world," irrespective of social change, are the last defensive gasps of an entirely static instrument of capitalism: empty-headed, it parasitizes the ectoderm of social change in the effort to be the better fed by its masters.

And radical artists produce articles and exhibitions about photos, capitalism, corruption, war, pestilence, trench-foot and issues, possessed by that venal shade of empiricism which guards their proprietorial interests. Most people laugh easily at old fools' hack aestheticism; the by now undifferentiated mass of presence and piety. It is similarly easy to avoid debate with the serious, anorexic autohagiographers who've shoved (?) and wheedled their way into the (what?) praxis of a ludicrous and equivalent "specialism." The air (and the ether) is toxic with the confident exhalations of their apprehension. Club-foot-Ph.D.-standards-as-style is nothing new in the global sales-pitch. American football helmets and meaningless photos are serious objects of contemplation (and . . . ) if you happen to be obsessed by your career as the nexus of historiography. Heaven knows, anything must go; and it even goes against the sanction imposed by the appropriate Lebensphilosophie: the manieres of "semiotique" and the manieres of "social purpose" even sell that short. The artist, the bourgeois ideologist without "virtue," is just like anyone else without "virtue:" his "terror" is gratuitous and ultimately suicidal.

This essay was published in *Art-Language*, 3:3 (June 1976), cover page 1.

# It's worth
# thinking about . . .

To finance the system of conspicuous expenditure, an extraordinary credit network has been set up, which, when considered, reveals much of our real class situation. The earners of wages and salaries are alike in this, that most of them become quickly involved in a system of usury which spreads until it is virtually inescapable.

How many supposedly middle-class people really own their houses, or their furniture, or their cars? Most of them are as radically unpropertied as the traditional working class, who are now increasingly involved in the same process of usury.

In part it is the old exaction, by the propertied, from the needs of the unpropertied, and the ordinary middle-class-talk of the property and independence which make them substantial citizens is an increasingly pathetic illusion.

One factor in maintaining the illusion is that much of the capital needed to finance the ordinary buyer comes from his own pocket, through insurance and the like, and this can be made to look like the sensible process of accumulating social capital.

What is not usually noticed is that established along the line of this process are a group of people using its complications to make substantial profit out of their neighbours' social needs.

As we move into this characteristic contemporary world, we can see the supposed new phenomenon of classlessness as simply a failure of consciousness.

# Class consciousness
## think about it

Victor Burgin, *Think About It,* 1976. Published in *Studio International,* March/April 1976.

# to be *bien pensant* . . . or not to be. to be blind

## marcel broodthaers

What is Art? Ever since the nineteenth century the question has been posed incessantly to the artist, to the museum director, to the art lover alike. I doubt, in fact, that it is possible to give a serious definition of Art, unless we examine the question in terms of a constant, I mean the transformation of art into merchandise. This process is accelerated nowadays to the point where artistic and commercial values have become superimposed. If we are concerned with the phenomenon of reification, then Art is a particular representation of the phenomenon—a form of tautology. We could then justify it as affirmation, and at the same time carve out for it a dubious existence. We would then have to consider what such a definition might be worth. One fact is certain: commentaries on Art are the result of shifts in the economy. It seems doubtful to us that such commentaries can be described as political.

Art is a prisoner of its phantasms and its function as magic; it hangs on our bourgeois walls as a sign of power, it flickers along the peripeties of our history like a shadow-play—but is it artistic? To read the Byzantine writing on the subject reminds us of the sex of angels, of Rabelais, or of debates at the Sorbonne. At the moment, inopportune linguistic investigations all end in a single gloss, which its authors like to call criticism. Art and literature . . . which of the moon's faces is hidden? And how many clouds and fleeting visions there are.

I have discovered nothing here, not even America. I choose to consider Art as a useless labor, apolitical and of little moral significance. Urged on by some base inspiration, I confess I would experience a kind of pleasure at being proved wrong. A guilty pleasure, since it would be at the expense of the victims, those who thought I was right.

Monsieur de la Palice is one of my customers.[1] He loves novelties, and he, who makes other people laugh, finds my alphabet a pretext for his own laughter. My alphabet is painted.

All of this is quite obscure. The reader is invited to enter into this darkness to decipher a theory or to experience feelings of fraternity, those feelings that unite all men, and particularly the blind.

**NOTES**

1. Monsieur de la Palice is the character of a French folk song who pronounces truisms. A typical *lapalissade* would be "Two hours before his death, he was still alive."

Initially published in *Le privilège de l'art* (Oxford: Museum of Modern Art, 26 April–1 June 1975); this translation by Paul Schmidt appeared in *October,* no. 42 (Fall 1987), p. 35.

# documentary and corporate violence
## allan sekula

A small group of contemporary artists are working on an art that deals with the social ordering of people's lives. Most of their work involves still photography and video; most relies heavily on written or spoken language. I'm talking about a representational art, an art that refers to something beyond itself. Form and mannerism are not ends in themselves. These works might be about any number of things, ranging from the material and ideological space of the "self" to the dominant social realities of corporate spectacle and corporate power. The initial questions are these: "How do we invent our lives out of a limited range of possibilities and how are our lives invented for us by those in power?" If these questions are asked only within the institutional boundaries of elite culture, only within the "art world," then the answers will be merely academic. Given a certain poverty of means, this art aims toward a wider audience and toward considerations of concrete social transformation.

    We might be tempted to think of this work as a variety of documentary. That's all right as long as we expose the myth that accompanies the label, the folklore of photographic truth. The rhetorical strength of documentary is imagined to reside in the unequivocal character of the camera's evidence, in an essential realism. I shouldn't have to point out that photographic meaning is indeterminate; the same picture can convey a variety of messages under differing presentational circumstances. Consider the evidence offered by bank holdup cameras. Taken automatically, these pictures could be said to be unpolluted by sensibility, an extreme form of documentary. If the surveillance engineers who developed these cameras have an aesthetic, it's one of raw, technological instrumentality, "Just the facts, ma'am." But a courtroom is a battleground of fictions. What is it that a photograph points to? A young white woman holds a submachine gun. The gun is handled confidently, aggressively. The gun is almost dropped out of fear. A fugitive heiress. A kidnap victim. An urban guerilla. A willing participant. A case of brainwashing. A case of rebellion. A case of schizophrenia. The outcome, based on the "true" reading of the evidence, is a function less of "objectivity" than of politics maneuvering. Reproduced in the mass media, this picture might attest to the omniscience of the state within a glamorized and mystifying spectacle of revolution and counterrevolution. But any police photography that is publicly displayed is both a specific attempt at identification and a re-minder of police power over "criminal elements." The only "objective" truth that photographs offer is the assertion that somebody or something—in this case, an automated camera—was somewhere and took a picture. Everything else is up for grabs.

Someone once wrote of the French photographer Eugene Atget that he depicted the streets of Paris as though they were scenes of crime. That remark serves to poeticize a rather deadpan, non-expressionist style, to celebrate the photographer in his role as detective, search-ing for clues. Documentary photography has amassed mountains of evidence. In this pictorial presentation of "fact," the genre has contributed much to spectacle, to retinal excitation, to voyeurism, and only a little to the critical understanding of the social world. A truly critical social documentary will frame the crime, the trial and the system of justice and its official myths. Artists working toward this end may or may not produce images that are theatrical and overtly contrived, they may or may not present tests that read like fiction. Social truth is some-thing other than a matter of convincing style.

A political critique of the documentary genre is sorely needed. Socially conscious artists have much to learn from both the successes and the mistakes, compromises, and collaborations of their Progressive Era and New Deal predecessors. How do we assess the close historical partnership of documentary artists and social democrats? The co-optation of the documentary style by corporate capitalism (notably the oil companies and the television networks) in the late 1940's? How do we disentangle ourselves from the authoritarian and bureaucratic aspects of the genre, from its implicit positivism? (All of this is evidenced by any one second of an Edward R. Murrow or Walter Cronkite telecast.) How do we produce an art that elicits dia-logue rather than uncritical, pseudo-political affirmation?

Looking backward, at the art-world hubbub about "photography as a fine art," we find a near-pathological avoidance of any such questioning. A curious thing happens when documentary is officially recognized as art. Suddenly the audience's attention is directed toward mannerism, toward sensibility, toward the physical and emotional risks taken by the artist. Documentary is thought to be art when it transcends its reference to the world, when the work can be regarded, first and foremost, as an act of self-expression on the part of the artist. A cult of authorship, an auteurism, takes hold of the image, separating it from the social conditions of its making and elevating it above the multitude of lowly and mundane uses to which photography is commonly put. The culture journalists' myth of Diane Arbus is interesting in this regard. Most readings of her work career along an axis between opposing poles of realism and expressionism. On the one hand, her portraits are seen as transparent vehicles for the social or psychological truth of her subjects; Arbus elicits meaning from their persons. At the other extreme is projection. The work is thought to express her tragic vision (a vision confirmed by her suicide); each image is nothing so much as a contribution to the artist's self-portrait. These readings coexist, they enhance one another despite their mutual contradiction. I think that a good deal of the generalized aesthetic appeal of Arbus' work, along with that of most art photography, has to do with this indeterminacy of reading, this sense of being cast adrift between profound social insight and refined solipsism. At the heart of this fetishistic cultivation and promotion of the artist's humanity is a certain disdain for the "ordinary" humanity of those who have been photographed. They become the "other," exotic creatures, objects of contemplation. Perhaps this wouldn't be so suspect if it weren't for the tendency of professional documentary photographers to aim their cameras downward, toward those with little power or prestige. (The obverse is the cult of celebrity, the organized production of envy in a mass audience.) The most intimate, human-scale relationship to suffer mystification in all this is the specific social engagement that results in the image; the negotiation between photographer and subject in the making of a portrait, the seduction, coercion, collaboration, or rip off. But if we widen the angle of our view, we find that the broader institutional politics of elite and "popular" culture are also being obscured in the romance of the photographer as artist.

Fred Lonidier is one of a small number of photographers who set out deliberately to work against the strategies that have succeeded in making photography a high art. Their work begins with the recognition that photography is operative at every level of our culture. That is, they insist on treating photographs not as privileged objects but as common cultural artifacts. The solitary, sparely captioned photograph on the gallery wall is a sign, above all, of an aspiration toward the aesthetic and market conditions of modernist painting and sculpture. In this white void, meaning is thought to emerge entirely from within the artwork. The importance of the framing discourse is masked, context is hidden. Lonidier, on the other hand, openly brackets his photographs with language, using texts to anchor, contradict, reinforce, subvert, complement, particularize, or go beyond the meanings offered by the images themselves. These pictures are located within a narrative structure. I'm not talking about "photo essays," a cliché-ridden form that is the noncommercial counterpart to the photographic advertisement. Photo essays are an outcome of a mass-circulation picture-magazine aesthetic, the aesthetic of the merchandisable column-inch and rapid, excited, reading.

Fred Lonidier's *Health and Safety Game* is about the "handling" of industrial injury and disease by corporate capitalism, pointing to the *systemic* character of everyday violence in the workplace. Some statistics: one in four American workers is exposed on a daily basis to death, injury and disease-causing work conditions. According to a Nader report, "job casualties are statistically at least three times more serious than street crime." (So much for TV cop shows.)

An observation: anyone who has ever lived or worked in an industrial working-class community can probably attest to the commonness of disfigurement among people on the job and in the street. Disease is less visible and has only recently become a public issue. I can recall going to the Chicago Museum of Science and Industry and visiting the coal mine there. Hoarse-voiced men, retired miners, led the tourists through a programmed demonstration of mining technology. When the time came to deal with safety, one of the guides set off a controlled little methane explosion. No one mentioned black-lung disease in this corporate artwork, although the evidence rasped from the throats of the guides.

Lonidier's "evidence" consist of twenty or so case studies of individual workers, each displayed on large panels laid out in a rather photojournalistic fashion. The reference to photojournalism is deliberate, I think, because the work refuses to deliver any of the empathic goodies that we are accustomed to in photo essays. Conventional "human interest" is absent. Lonidier is aware of the ease with which liberal documentary artists have converted violence and suffering into aesthetic objects. For all his good intentions, for example, Eugene Smith in *Minamata* provided more a representation of his compassion for mercury-poisoned Japanese fisher-folk than one of their struggle for retribution against the corporate polluter. I'll say it again: the subjective aspect of liberal aesthetics is compassion rather than collective struggle. Pity, mediated by an appreciation of great art, supplants political understanding. It has been remarked that Eugene Smith's portrait of a Minamata mother bathing her retarded and deformed daughter is a deliberate reference to the Pieta.

Unlike Smith, Lonidier takes the same photographs that a doctor might. When the evidence is hidden within the body, Lonidier borrows and copies x-ray films. These pictures have a brutal, clinical effect. Each worker's story is reduced to a rather schematic account of injury, disease, hospitalization, and endless bureaucratic run-around by companies trying to shirk responsibility and liability. All too frequently we find that at the end of the story the worker is left unemployed and under-compensated. At the same time, though, these people are fighting. A machinist with lung cancer tells of stealing samples of dust from the job, placing them on the kitchen griddle in a homemade experiment to detect asbestos, a material that his bosses had denied using. The anonymity of Lonidier's subjects is a precaution against retaliation against them; many are still fighting court cases.

Lonidier's presentation is an analog of sorts for the way in which corporate bureaucrats handle the problems of industrial safety, yet he subverts the model by telling the story from below, from the place occupied by the worker in the hierarchy. The case-study form is a model of authoritarian handling of human lives. The layout of the panels reflects the distribution of power. Quotes from the workers are set in type so small that they are nearly unreadable. The titles are set in large type: "Machinist's Lung," "Egg-Packer's Arm." The body and the life are presented as they have been fragmented by management. Injury is a loss of labor power, a negative commodity, overhead. Injury is not a diminishing of a human life but a statistical impingement on the corporate profit margin.

The danger exists, here as in other works of socially conscious art, of being overcome by the very oppressive forms and conditions one is critiquing, of being devoured by the enormous machinery of material and symbolic objectification. Political irony walks a thin line between resistance and surrender.

Nevertheless, Lonidier's work documents monopoly capitalism's inability to deliver the conditions of a fully human life. One realizes that the health and safety issue goes beyond the struggle for compensation, enforcement of safety standards and improved working conditions. Against violence of this scale, violence directed at the human body, at the environment and at working people's ability to control their own lives, we need to counterpose an active resistance to monopoly capitalism's increasing power and arrogance.

This text appeared in *Dialogue/Discourse?Research,* exh. cat (Santa Barbara Museum of Art, 1979), n.p. An expanded version of this essay was published as "Dismantling Modernism, Reinventing Documentary (Notes on the Politics of Representation)," in *Massachusetts Review* (Summer 1978).

*The Curator has arrived. This is business. Carole and Karl must 'sense' him out. They present a professional face, not to betray their underlying hesitancy and doubt. This is Art after all.*

DRAGGING UP OLD ARGUMENTS AND MARKETING THEM AS NEW MYSTERIES

I still like my previous work. It was good for what it was. I can't feel bad about it. But we've changed. I also think it's important to understand that our previous work led up to our present position. What I mean is, we reached a point with that work at which it became totally impossible to generate ideas except for the monotonous reiteration of a single "essence"—the formalist *ad absurdum.* When this dawned on us we started to question why. . .

There is a sense of "crisis" in the air. A lot of artists are confused and uncertain. It accounts for the reactionary painting that has come about recently, the return of old dogmas, the veneration of Malevich. . .

That's a good point. Either you become a reactionary, dragging up old arguments and marketing them as new mysteries, or you subvert the conditions that produce that "crisis." Art either becomes aesthetic—the maintenance of the status quo—or political.

Karl Beveridge and Carole Condé, *It's Still Privileged Art,* 1976, detail.

# to argue for a video of representation. to argue for a video against the mythology of everyday life

## martha rosler

I

Where do ideas come from? All the myths of everyday life stitched together form a seamless envelope of ideology, the false account of everything thinkable. Ideology is a readymade always ready to stand in for a closer understanding of the world and its workings. The myths of ideology cushion us, it is true, from the paranoia that is engendered by mistrust of cultural givens. But they are not nurturant. The interests served by ideology are not human interests properly defined; rather, ideology serves society in shoring up its particular form of social organization. In class society, ideology serves the interests of the class that dominates. Through the channels of mass communication, which it controls, our dominant class holds its own ideology up to our whole society as the real and proper set of attitudes and beliefs. The impetus is then strong for everyone to identify her/himself as a member of the "middle class," a mystified category standing in for the image of the dominant class. We have all come to aspire to the condition of the petty bourgeoisie: to be, paradigmatically, "one's own boss." Thus the legitimate desire for control over one's own life is flattened out, transmuted into a desire to own one's own business—or, failing that, to construct a "private" life in opposition to the world out there.

The eradication of craft skills and of *economically productive* family activity has lessened people's chances to gain a sense of accomplishment and worth and has increased our vulnerability to the blandishments of advertising, the most potent educational institution in our culture. As the opportunities for personal power on a human level diminish for all but a relatively small part of the population, self-confidence, trust, and pleasure conceived in straightforward terms are poisoned, and we are increasingly beguiled by an accordionlike succession of mediations between ourselves and the natural and social world, mediations in the form of commodities. We are each promised personal power and fulfillment through consumption; we are as nothing unless clothed in a culture that is conceived of as a congeries of packages, each of which presents us with a bill. In pursuit of meaning and satisfaction we are led to grant the aura of life to things and to drain it from people: *we personify objects and objectify persons.* We experience alienation from ourselves as well as from others. We best comprehend ourselves as social entities in looking at photos of ourselves, assuming the voyeur's role with respect to our own images; we best know ourselves from within in looking through the viewfinder at other people and things.

The culture of corporate capitalism has metamorphosed architecture: each of us is the row to be hoed, the field to be sowed. The upward-aspiring bourgeoisie and upper ranks of the working class are led to develop superfluous skills, such as gourmet cooking or small-boat navigation, whose real significance is extravagant, well-rationalized consumerism and the cultivation of the self but which, in seeking legitimation, mimic skills once necessary to life; skills which, moreover, were tied to a form of social organization that we think of as less alienated and more familiar than our own. In pursuit of meaning, also, we are led to see meaning where there is only emptiness and sham, strength where there is only violence or money, knowledge where there is only illusion, honesty where there is only a convincing manner, status where there is only a price tag, satisfaction where there is only a cattle prod, limitless freedom where there is only a feed lot. Our entire outlook is conditioned by the love and the terror of consumption.

Commodity fetishism, the giving over of self to the thing, is not a universal trope of the human psyche; it is not even a quirk of character. It is both the inescapable companion and the serviceable pipe dream of capitalist social organization; it is Our Way of Life. It is built into the structure of society, originating in the production process and the social relations it engenders, in which one's very ability to make or to do something is transformed into a commodity of sorts in itself, salable to the boss in exchange for "wages."

How does one address these banally profound issues of everyday life? It seems to me appropriate to use the medium of television, which in its most familiar form is one of the primary conduits of ideology—through both its ostensive subject matter and its overtly commercial messages. I am trying to enlist "video," a different form of television, in the attempt to make explicit the connections between *ideas* and *institutions,* connections whose existence is never alluded to by corporate TV. Nevertheless, video is not a strategy, it is merely a mode of access.

## II

Video itself is not "innocent." It too is a form of cultural commodity that often stands for a celebration of the self and its powers of invention. Yet video is useful in that it provides me with the opportunity to construct "decoys," entities that engage in a natural dialectic with TV itself. A woman in a bare-bones kitchen, in black and white, demonstrating some hand tools and replacing their domesticated "meaning" with a lexicon of rage and frustration is an antipodean Julia Child. A woman in a red and blue Chinese coat, demonstrating a wok in a dining room and trying to speak with the absurd voice of the corporation, is a failed Mrs. Pat Boone. An anachronistically young couple, sitting cramped and earnest in their well-appointed living room, attempting to present a coherent narrative and explanation of their daughter's self-starvation, are any respectably middle-class couple visited by misfortune and subjected to a "human interest" news-show interview. A woman and child in a studio-constructed no-space, being handed can after package after can of food as Christmas charity, are a faded echo of *Queen for a Day.* An operatic presentation of a woman put through an ordeal of measurement tenuously alludes to a monumentally stretched-out version of *Truth or Consequences.*

One of the basic forms of mass culture, including television, is the narrative, especially the first-person narrative. (Melodramas, situation comedies, soap operas and so on seem to me to embody a form of first-person narrative in their protagonists.) Narrative is a homey, manageable form of address, but its very virtue, the air of subjectivity and lived experience, is also its fault. The rootedness in the *I,* which is (predictably) the most seductive encoding of *convincingness,* suggests an absolute inability to transcend the consciousness of a single individual. And consciousness is the realm of ideology, so that the logic of the first-person narrative, in particular, suggests that there is no appeal from ideology, no *metacritique.* Given the pervasive relativism of our society (according to which only the personal is knowable and all opinions are equally valid) the first-person narrative implies the unretrievability of objective truth. (The validity which we grant to "public" figures of all kinds, which tends to include the scientific and medical establishment, is the opposite term of this pair of oppositions.) At most, one version or another of the dominant ideology is implicitly reinforced, on the basis of what happens to the protagonists or the other figures with whom they interact.

Yet this inability to speak truth is the failure not so much of narrative per se as of the *naturalism* that is taken to be narrative's central feature. Break the bonds of that naturalism and the problem vanishes. One can provide a critical dimension and invoke matters of truth precisely through reference to the ideological confusions that naturalism falsifies by omission. A character speaking in contradictions or failing to manage the socially right sequence of behaviors can eloquently index the unresolvable social contradictions—starvation in the midst of plenty, the subtly aggressive impersonality of institutional charity, the racism, sexism, and national chauvinism of some of the basic tenets of "scientific" intelligence testing—that are the source of ideological confusions.

In choosing representational strategies I aim for the distancing (*ostranenie,* the *Verfremdungseffekt*), the distantiation occasioned by a refusal of realism, by foiled expectations, by palpably flouted conventions. Tactically I tend to use a wretched pacing and a bent space; the immovable shot or, conversely, the unexpected edit, pointing to the mediating agencies of photography and speech; long shots rather than close ups, to deny psychological intent; contradictory utterances; and, in acting, flattened affect, histrionics, or staginess. Although video is simply one medium among several that are effective in confronting real issues of culture, video based on TV has this special virtue; it has little difficulty in lending itself to the kind of "crude thinking," as Brecht used this phrase, that seems necessary to penetrate the waking daydreams that hold us in thrall. The clarification of vision is a first step toward reasonably and humanely changing the world.

This text was written for an exhibition, "New American Film Makers: Martha Rosler," at the Whitney Museum of American Art in 1977. It was distributed to the audience of this show in the form of a pamphlet.

# notes on reading the *post-partum document*
## mary kelly

### THE DISCOURSE OF THE WOMEN'S MOVEMENT

The *Post-Partum Document* is located within the theoretical and political practice of the women's movement, a practice which foregrounds the issues of subjectivity and ideological oppression. More specifically, the *Document* is identified with the tendency that bases the notion of ideological oppression on a psychoanalytic theory of subjectivity, that is, the unconscious.[1] Freud's discovery of the unconscious had crucial implications for theorizing the process by which human subjects become constituted in ideology. If there is no ideology except in practice and by a subject, then ideological oppression is not merely false consciousness. The ideological refers not only to systems of representation but also to a nonunitary complex of social practices which have political consequences. Moreover, these consequences are not given as the direct effect of the means of signification employed in a practice. They depend on a political analysis of what is signified.[2]

For the purposes of such an analysis, the *Post-Partum Document* is the product of a practice of signification, and as such, it does not reflect but reworks the feminist ideology in which it was founded. This is primarily the ideology of consciousness-raising groups that still form a major part of the women's movement. The *Document* reiterates, at one level, the unique contribution that consciousness-raising made to political practice in general by emphasizing the subjective moment of women's oppression.[3] But, at another level, it argues against the supposed self-sufficiency of lived experience and for a theoretical elaboration of the social relations in which femininity is formed. In this sense, the *Post-Partum Document* functions as part of an ongoing debate over the relevance of psychoanalysis to the theory and practice of both Marxism and feminism. Furthermore, the debate includes a critique of the patriarchal bias underlying some of the theoretical assumptions on which the *Document* is based.[4]

## THE DISCOURSE OF THE MOTHER-CHILD RELATIONSHIP

The *Post-Partum Document* describes the subjective moment of the mother-child relationship. An analysis of this relationship is crucial to an understanding of the way in which ideology functions in/by the material practices of childbirth and child care. Feeding or dressing a child depends as much on the interchange of a system of signs as teaching him/her to speak or write. In a sense, even the unconscious discourse of these moments is "structured like a language."[5] This underlines the fact that intersubjective relationships are fundamentally social. More precisely, every social practice offers a specific expression of a general social law and this law is the symbolic dimension which is given in language.[6]

In patriarchy, the phallus becomes the privileged signifier of this symbolic dimension.[7] Although the subject is constituted in a relation of "lack" at the moment of his/her entry into language, it is possible to speak specifically of the woman's "negative place" in the general process of significations or social practices that reproduce patriarchal relations within a given social formation. In childbirth, the mother's negative place is misrecognized insofar as the child is the phallus for her.[8] This imaginary relation is lived through, at the level of ideology and in the social practice of child care, as proof of the natural capacity for maternity and the inevitability of the sexual division of labor.[9]

The documentations of specific moments such as weaning from the breast, learning to speak, and entering a nursery demonstrate the reciprocity of the process of socialization, that is, the intersubjective discourse through which not only the child but also the mother is constituted as subject.

## THE DISCOURSE OF WOMEN'S PRACTICE IN ART

The *Post-Partum Document* forms part of the "problematic" of women's practice in art. The problematic includes a symptomatic reading of the visual inscriptions of women artists. Such a reading, based as much on absences as presences, suggest the way in which the realm of "the feminine" is bounded by negative signification in the order of language and culture. Because of this coincidence of language and patriarchy, the feminine is, metaphorically, set on the side of the heterogeneous, the unnamable, the unsaid. But the radical potential of women's art practice lies precisely in this coincidence, since, insofar as the feminine is said, it is profoundly subversive.[10]

However, the *Post-Partum Document* is not an excavation of female culture, or a valorization of the female body or of feminine experience as such; it is an attempt to articulate the feminine as discourse, and therefore places the emphasis on the intersubjective relationships which constitute the female subject.[11] Currently in women's art practice, there is a proliferation of forms of signification where the artist's own person, in particular her body, is given as a signifier, that is, as object. In the *Document,* as a means of distantiation, the figure of the mother is not visibly present. Although it is a self-documentation of the mother-child relationship, here between myself and my son, the *Post-Partum Document* does not describe the unified, transcendental subject of autobiography, but rather, the decentered, socially constituted subject of a mutual discourse. Moreover, this subject is fundamentally divided. There is a conscious/unconscious split which has operations characteristic of both sides: the signifying processes or drives on the one hand, and the social constraints such as family structures or modes of production on the other.[12] The means of signification used in the *Document* are scriptovisual in order to articulate the gap left by this split, that is, to show how the unconscious processes irrupt into a signifying practice and cut across the systematic order of language and, also, to show the difficulty of the symbolic order for women.

In the *Post-Partum Document,* the art objects are used as fetish objects, explicitly to displace the potential fetishization of the child and implicitly to expose the typically fetishistic function of representation.[13] The stained liners, folded vests, child's markings, and word imprints have a minimum sign value in relation to the commodity status of representational art, but they have a maximum affective value in relation to the libidinal economy of the unconscious. They are "representations," in the psychoanalytic sense, of the cathected memory traces.[14] These traces, in combination with the diaries, speech events, and feeding charts, construct the discourse of the mother's lived experience. At the same time, they are set up in an antagonistic relationship with the diagrams, algorithms, and footnotes which construct the discourse of feminist analysis. In the context of an installation, this analysis is not meant to definitively theorize the *Post-Partum* moment, but rather to describe a process of secondary revision. In a sense, this text is also included in that process not as a topology of intention, but as a rewriting of the discourse of the *Document* which is at once a repression and a reactivation of its consequences.

## NOTES

1. The *Post-Partum Document* is most closely associated with the debate that surfaced after the publication in 1974 of Juliet Mitchell's book, *Psychoanalysis and Feminism,* and in particular with a Lacanian reading of Freud, which was in strong evidence as a theoretical tendency at the Patriarchy Conference in London in May 1976. A seminar entitled Psychoanalysis and Feminism was organized during the showing of the *Post-Partum Document* at the ICA New Gallery in October 1976. The relevance of psychoanalysis to ideology, feminine psychology, and art practice was discussed by a panel on which I was a participant along with Parveen Adams, lecturer in psychology, Brunel University; Susan Lipshitz, psychologist, The Tavistock; filmmaker Laura Mulvey; and writer Rosalind Delmar.

2. Paul Q. Hirst, "Althusser's Theory of Ideology," *Economy and Society* 5 (November 1976), p. 396; see also section on "Representation," pp. 407–411.

3. Rosalind Coward, "Sexuality and Psychoanalysis," unpublished paper, 1977.

4. For a useful outline of the debate see the Editorial Collective's article on "Psychology, Ideology, and the Human Subject" in *Ideology and Consciousness* 1 (May 1977), pp. 5–56. The critique concerns Lacan's acceptance of the "universality of language," c. f. Luce Irigary, *Speculum de l'Autre Femme* (Paris: Editions de Minuit, 1974). See also "Women's Exile: An Interview with Luce Irigary," trans. Couze Penn, *Ideology and Consciousness* 1 (May 1977), pp. 62–76.

5. See Jacques Lacan, "The Insistence of the Letter in the Unconscious," in *Structuralism* (New York: Anchor Books, 1970), pp. 287–323.

6. Julia Kristeva, "The System and the Speaking Subject," *Times Literary Supplement* (October 12, 1973).

7. For an elaboration of the consequences in terms of sexual difference, see Jacques Lacan, "La Signification du phallus," *Ecrits* (Paris: Editions du Seuil, 1966), pp. 685–695.

8. Misrecognition here refers specifically to Lacan's sense of the term as in "the function of misrecognition which characterizes the ego in all its structures," and not to ideological "misrec-

ognitions." See Jacques Lacan, "The Mirror Phase as Formative of the Function of the I," *New Left Review* 5, vol. 47–52 (1968), pp. 71–77.

9. The sexual division of labor is not a symmetrically structured system of women inside the home, men outside it, but rather an intricate, most often asymmetrical, delegation of tasks which aims to provide a structural imperative to heterosexuality. Mary Kelly, *Post-Partum Document,* "Footnotes and Bibliography," (ICA New Gallery, 1976), p. 1.

10. See Julia Kristeva, "Signifying Practice and Mode of Production" in *La Traversée de Signes* (Paris: Editions du Seuil, 1975), trans. and intro. Geoffery Nowel-Smith, *Edinburgh Magazine* 1 (1976).

11. In "Art and Sexual Politics" I defined the forms/means of signification employed in women's art practice in terms of the underlying structures of "feminine narcissism," based metaphorically on Freud's description of narcissistic object choice in "On Narcissism: An Introduction" (1914), *Collected Papers* 4, p. 47. See also "Women's Practice in Art," Susan Hiller and Mary Kelly in conversation, *Audio Arts* 3, no. 3 (1977), and "Women and Art," *Studio International* 3 (1977).

12. Julia Kristeva, "The System and the Speaking Subject," *Times Literary Supplement* (October 12, 1973), c. f. the splitting of the subject, Marcelin Pleynet, "de Pictura," trans. Stephen Bann, *20th Century Studies* (December 1977).

13. See Stephen Heath on fetishism and "representation" in classic cinema and popular photography, "Lessons from Brecht," *Screen* 15 (Summer 1974); see also Laura Mulvey, "Visual Pleasure and Narrative Cinema," *Screen* 16 (Autumn 1975).

14. J. Laplanche and J. B. Pontalis, *The Language of the Self* (London: Hogarth Press, 1973), p. 200. For Freud, the idea/presentation/representation is to be understood as what comes from the object and is registered in mnemic systems, and not as the act of presenting an object to consciousness; ibid., p. 247, memory trace/mnemic trace is used by Freud to denote the way in which events are inscribed upon the memory, they are deposited in different systems and reactivated only once they have been cathected; ibid., p. 62, cathexis is an economic concept pertaining to the fact that a certain amount of psychical energy is attached to an idea or group of ideas, a part of the body, or an object.

This text was written for a seminar entitled "Psychoanalysis and Feminism," held at the Institute of Contemporary Arts, London, during the exhibition of *Post-Partum Document (PPD) I-III* (1976). It was first published in *Control Magazine,* no. 10 (1977), pp. 10–12.

Michael Corris, cover image for *Red Herring* no. 1, 1977.

# moments of history in the work of dan graham
## benjamin h. d. buchloh

Asked about the essential features of his work, Graham answered by calling it "photojournalism,"[1] an ironical quotation of a term Marcel Duchamp had once used to describe his own activities. Thus Graham voluntarily followed a misunderstanding and misnomer that his work had stirred since his earlier publication in 1965. Still in 1970, the critic Lucy Lippard could ask during a discussion with Carl Andre, Jan Dibbits and Douglas Huebler: "Dan, you've been called a poet and a critic and a photographer. Are you an artist now?"[2]

But even his own contemporaries, artist-friends of the Minimal phase whose work had found in Dan Graham's analytical criticism since 1965 a rarely qualified protagonist, refused—by misinterpreting his own visual art production—the recognition of changing basic concepts within the visual arts since 1965. Dan Flavin, for example, even though having been among the first to have been seriously interested in Graham's work and the first who published one of his photographs, wrote on Graham's *Homes for America* (1966): "Your fine photographic approach seems to recall the consistently clear and plain deviceless reportage of Henri Cartier-Bresson, which you apply not to people, as he did, but to their 'feats' of banal vernacular architecture and landscape."[3] This false classification is of particularly revealing historical irony as it shows that from a minimalist's perspective photographical information/documentation obviously could not even be conceived as possibly being "art" (unless "photographical" art).

Moreover the misapprehension reveals an unconscious attempt to eliminate radically innovative implications of post-minimalist art activity by relating Graham's photographs to a particularly restorative ideology of photography, namely Cartier-Bresson's idea of the "Decisive Moment." Whereas these photographers tend to celebrate their passive-receptive activity as a medium of the one historical moment, which they try to conserve in its photographical transubstantiation, it is Graham's intention, quite to the contrary, to construct functional models of recognition of actual history by his (photographical) media.

*Homes for America* (1966), which we consider along with Graham's *Schema* (1966) to be the most complex and relevant of his early works, shall serve as an example. This piece of "photojournalism," which he referred to as "the transition from earlier 'conceptual' pages in magazines and the 1967–1979 articles," takes off from the by then growing recognition that information about the artworks is disseminated primarily by reproduction in (art) media, as for example Carl Andre had described it in 1968: "The photograph is a lie. I'm afraid we get a great deal of our exposure to art through magazines and through slides, and I think this is dreadful, this is anti-art because art is a direct experience with something in the world and photography is just a rumor, a kind of pornography of art.[4] It is precisely at this anti-art point of "pornography" that Graham starts his inquiry, and it is significant for his post-minimalist attitude that he almost literally inverts Andre's disgust with the media and turns it into a basis for his own artistic strategies and works.

Graham has commented on this key work in a description which in itself repeats the intertwinement of the various formal and (art) historical relations and dialectical inversions of the work:

*First it is important that the photos are not alone, but part of a magazine layout. They are illustrations of the text or [inversely], the text functions in relation to/modifying the meaning of the photos and the text are separate parts of a schematic [two-dimensional grid] perspective system. The photos correlate [to] the lists and columns of serial information and both "represent" the serial logic of the housing developments whose subject matter the article is about. Despite the fact that the idea of using the "real" outdoor environment as a "site" on which to construct "conceptual" or "earth works" [remember the article was written some years before Smithson's and Oppenheim's works], I think the fact that* Homes for America *was, in the end, only a magazine article, and made no claims for itself as "Art," is its most important aspect.[5]*

Thus the informational frame of an art magazine's coverage becomes the "found" formal structure. This is however juxtaposed with the subject matter of a found "reality" structure—

the miserableness of everyday industrial housing. At the same time its formal stylistic qualities—the serial order of the cubic house forms, their permutational principles of single but repetitive elements (whose sum constitutes the "wholeness" of a given formation)—reflect in an obviously ironic and ambiguous manner the formal and stylistic principles of minimal sculpture. The dialectical combination of reality structure and formal structure, this capacity of reading "buildings and grammars"—i.e. reality systems and formal systems—which is most typical and significant for all of Graham's early writings and conceptual works, ranges them into a category of structure as simulacrum of the object of history, as Barthes has defined it, ". . . a pointed, international simulacrum, because the imitated object reveals something which remained invisible or even more incomprehensible with the mere object. . . . This simulacrum is intellect added to the object; and this addition has anthropological value as it is the human being itself, its history, its situation, its freedom and the resistance which nature opposes to his mind."[6]

The general understanding and delayed recognition of Graham's work may have had one reason in the work's specifically "non-aesthetical" form of appearance, which are not only a result of Graham's functionalizing of formal concerns, but which are probably also the result of an entirely different approach to those historical sources of constructivism that had become a point of reference in American art since Stella and which had finally received a "formalist" reading by the generation of the minimal artists, if only reluctantly acknowledged, like in a sentence by Donald Judd in 1974: "With and since Malevich the several aspects of the best art have been single, like unblended Scotch. Free."[7]

## DAN GRAHAM AND THE MINIMAL HERITAGE

"The split between art and real problems emerged in the Sixties in an essentially apolitical and asocial art—to the extent that, for most artists, political engagement meant moving to an extra art activity. . . . The neutrality which this art assumes excludes the possibility of critical relation to a capitalist form of life."[8]

Formalism in aesthetic practice and the correlating equivalent, and entrepreneurs' morality have not been the original position of the Minimal generation. They had not only oriented their formal and material strategies according to constructivist axioms, but also attempted to reactivate their socio-political implications. This meant demanding an objective functionalism of materials which had to originate from technological products and processes, an unlimited capacity of technical reproduction as well as its dialectical counterpart, namely the idea of the unique and specific work which could only find its actual function and realization in a particular segment of the time/space continuum, and finally the abolition of the artwork's commodity status and the attempt to replace its exchange and exhibition value with a new concept of functional use value.

Even though Flavin may not have understood or appreciated Graham's work, this is not true for the opposite: Graham has frequently pointed out how important his knowledge and understanding of Flavin's work has been to his own development as an artist. And it remains an open question whether the work of the elder artist offered in fact the complexity of aspects that Graham discerned in it, or whether he read those aspects into the work that should become the key issue in his own artistic production, thus anticipating his own future development by projecting it onto the historical screen of the predecessor's work. Especially the transformation of "formalist" terms into a more "functionalist" context could be called to be one of the essential qualities Graham's work has introduced into the visual arts around 1965. For example Flavin's (and equally Andre's and LeWitt's) notion of "place"—the fact that the work referred to the gallery space as the spatial container—and the notion of "presence" which had meant in Flavin's work that an installation was contingent on its present time situation, furthermore being specifically conceived for one particular architecture situation, became key issues in Graham's early conceptual work as well as in his critical analytical writings which preceded his development of performance, film and video works.

This transformation from plastic-material modes of analyzing perceptual (aesthetical) processes to literal-verbal analyses and conceptualization takes place obviously in Graham's descriptions of the work of Andre, Flavin, Judd, Nauman, Serra and LeWitt, which Graham wrote and published starting in 1965. Therefore it seems adequate to read these texts more as artistic arguments indicating the development of new forms of aesthetic work rather than as art criticism. On a first level of reading, these critical texts open up a historical perspective through their minute descriptive precision, in as much as they show basic principles of Minimalism to be derivatives of constructivist fundamentals. All of these for example appear as though catalogued in Graham's analysis of Carl Andre's sculpture *Crib, Compound, Coin* (1965) as well as in a description of Flavin's work, both published in 1967: "Fluorescent light objects in place are re-placeable in various contingently determined interdependent relations with specific environmental relations and are also replaceable from their fixture and in having a limited existence. The components of a particular exhibition upon its termination are re-placed in another situation—perhaps put to a non-art use as a part of a different whole in a different future."[9]

Or even more systematically and explicitly on Andre:

*The component units possessed no intrinsic significance beyond their immediate contextual place-ment being "replaceable." Works are impossessible by the viewer in the monetary sense, the sense of an artist being possessed of a vision or of satisfying personal inner needs of the viewer. Un-weighted with symbolic transcendental or redeeming monetary values, Andre's sculpture does not form some platonically substantial body, but is recoverable; for which no one may be poetically transported from view when the exhibition is terminated (the parts having been recovered and perhaps put to an entirely non-related use as part of a whole in a different future).*[10]

A second reading would be the historicity of the writings themselves, from a present point of view, their acuity in the way they denote almost systematically all the elementary principles of visual thinking as they had been developed by minimal art practice. At the same time these texts connote by the very precision of their verbal apprehension of the visual factic-ity, the change of the artistic procedure into concepts of verbalized materiality and materialized language. This has been quite accurately observed by Robert Smithson, who as early as 1967 seems to have seen, more clearly than Flavin, the historical and aesthetic implications of Gra-ham's writings and photographical works as being those of a new definition of art axioms (updating modes of aesthetic production to the general standards of means of recognition) and thus further approaching them to their use value potential: "Like some of the other artists Graham can 'read' the language of buildings (*Homes for America,* 1966), . . . The reading of both buildings and grammars enables the artist to avoid out-of-date appeals to "function" or "utilitarianism."[11]

In most of his writings Dan Graham has reflected on the double nature of those pro-cesses, in as much as they could be formalized and integrated into the context of his work by referring to them with the term "in-formation," thus indicating that to him formal procedures as well as their material content are invisible units. The materiality of the formal processes in Graham's works could therefore be called "specific" in the sense originally coined by Donald Judd for painterly-sculptural works of the minimal phase: "Materials vary greatly and are sim-ply materials—formica, aluminum, cold-rolled steel, plexiglas, red and common brass and so forth. They are specific. Also they are usually aggressive."[12]

Graham's critical analysis of the formal and material heritage of minimal aesthetics not only seems to have led him to the discovery that these artists' ideas about materiality were in fact rather traditional and positivist (oriented at a constructivist craft ethos), but moreover he seems to have acknowledged that their original radicality in questioning the role of the artwork in its social context had been given up and that minimal work had been restored easily into the commodity status, acquiring exchange value in as much as they gave up their context-bound idea of use value. Therefore, the materials of reality are with Graham no longer simply "found objects" or the "ready-made elements" of technological everyday reality as they are in Flavin's fluorescent lights or even Andre's metallurgical elements (these being much more technologically "cultivated" than their elementary "natural" look might at first reveal), but rather the found structures beyond visible reality and its seeming concreteness, thus determining reality, however, with a more subtle and effective impact: equally the psycho-physiological motivations of subjective behavior of the socio-economical conditions of objective political practice, or even more precisely, the omnipresent mechanisms of interdependence of those systems in the acutely observed situations of their joined effects.

Graham's authentically "conceptual" early magazine publications, which were written before the critical articles on fellow artists, had the conventional standard magazine page as a formal ground and common denominator; they were in a sense about "themselves." These works like *Figurative* (1965), *Schema* (1966) or *Detumescence* (1966), which were among the first artworks—if not the very first at all—to be published in magazine-advertisement form, sum up the reflection of Minimal presuppositions by translating them into an entirely different formal language. The historical distance and degrees of differentiation that have been actually achieved by Graham's theoretical thought as well as by his aesthetical production can be easily understood by comparing Judd's position regarding materials of art objects and Graham's attitude towards the materiality of art in his *Other Observations* (1969), a text written as a later comment on his *Schema* (1966), which reads in parts almost as a word for word comparative study and critique of minimalist formal thought and its transformation:

*A page of* Schema *exists as a matter of fact materiality and simultaneously semiotic signifier of this material (present): as a sign it unites, therefore, signifier and signified. (. . .) In the internal logic, there is the paradox that the concept of "materiality" referred to by the language is to the language itself as some "immaterial" material (a kind of mediumistic ether) and simultaneously is to it as the extensive space. There is a "shell" placed between the external "empty" material of place and the interior "empty" material of "language," (systems of) information (in-formation) exist halfway between material and concept, without being either one.*"[13]

The consequent radicality of Graham's formal procedure to reduce *Schema* to a mere formula of self-referential reflectivity, finds its dialectical material equivalent in his decision to publish this work in the context of a (art) magazine advertisement, as Graham has pointed out in later notes on *Schema:* "But, unlike a Stella painting, for example, the variants of *Schema* are not simply self-referential. This is because of the use of the magazine system support. Magazines determine a place or a frame of reference both outside and inside what is defined as 'Art.' Magazines are boundaries (mediating) between the two areas . . . between gallery 'Art' and communications about 'Art.'"[14]

Thus Graham is clearly attempting to include the analytical reflection of those determining elements which had been ignored before, the different aspects of the socio-economical framework as well as the individual's psychological framework which conditions the production as well as the reception of the artwork, and by inverting his perspective from formalist concerns to functionalist strategies makes them the very subject matter of his art. Again Graham's own retrospect comment is most illuminating in regard to the transformational changes that his work initiated in comparison to the given (art) historical conditions:

*It was interesting then, that aesthetically (but not functionally, that is, in material, economic terms) some of the Minimal Art seemed to refer to the gallery interior space as the ultimate frame or structural support/context and that some Pop Art referred to the surrounding media-world of cultural information as framework. But the frame (specific media-form or gallery/museum as economic entity concerned with value) was never made structurally apparent. Schema's strategy was to reduce these two frameworks, to coalesce them into one frame so that they were made more apparent and the "art product" would be radically de-valued. I wanted to make a "Pop" Art which was more literally disposable (an idea which was alluded to in Warhol's idea of replacing "quality" for "quantity"—the logic of a consumer society), I wanted to make an art-form which could not be reproduced or exhibited in a gallery/museum. And I wanted to make a further reduction of the Minimal object to a not necessarily aesthetic two-dimensional form (which was not painting or drawing): printed matter which is mass reproduced and mass disposable information. Putting it in magazine pages meant that it also could be "read" in juxtaposition to the usual second-hand art criticism, reviews, reproductions in the rest of the magazine and would form a critique of the functioning of the magazine (in relation to the gallery structure).*[15]

Therefore Graham's *Schema* (1966) and the later comments like *Other Observations* (1969) or his *Magazine/Advertisements* (1969), starting with the sentence "Art is a social sign," have to be read along with Daniel Buren's *Limites critiques* (1969) (published in English as *Critical Limits* in 1973)[16] as one of the first and most relevant attempts of that period to make art's most extraneous, repressed and camouflaged conditions obvious and invert them to become art's subject matter. Ahead of Hans Haacke's somewhat comparable reflections twenty years ago (published under the title of *Framing and being framed: 7 Works 1970–75,* Halifax/ New York, 1975) Graham's framework analysis differs considerably from both Buren's and Haacke's work. Different from Buren who reflects on the historical and museological determinations of the artwork, and other than Haacke who takes as well the social conditioning of art reception into consideration as well as art's historical transformation by becoming an object of capital investment, Graham analyzes in particular the general social conditions of production and reproduction of (art) information, and their formal and material consequences (see also later his *Income/Outflow,* 1969).

Graham's processes—in comparison to Judd's *Specific Objects*—are specific in a threefold manner: first in regard to their proper epistemological and historical context (i.e. the visual arts) as they dialectically reflect and transcend the given conditions of minimal aesthetics; second in their relation to objective methodology, which consciously and clearly inserts them into a context of more general principles of (recognition) production, like for example their explicit dependence on semiology. And finally Graham's works could be called specific because of their very concrete reference to a particular segment of reality. It is not at last for this reason that Graham's works, his "specific processes," seem to lack any surface of visual-aesthetic attractivity, which would more easily allow them to be read in a cultural context of art history. On the other hand their lack of surface aesthetics, rooted in their potential function, their insistence on the idea to reinvest the artwork with a potential use value, makes them more similar to certain works of productivist art than superficial comparison might recognize. It is precisely this lack of aesthetic attraction which denounces all forms of reconciliation that more craft-oriented artworks bring into the world as cultural commodities. Their service to the dominating principles are among others the attempt to restore art into its traditional role, namely that of functioning as the mere decorum of the ruling order.

## GRAHAM'S "SUBJECT MATTER" AND POST-MINIMALISM

Dan Graham's complication of critical paraphrases, which was first published in 1969 in his privately edited *End Moments* under the title "Subject Matter," indicated in its subtitle the paradigmatical change which was going on in the visual arts around 1965: "1. the subject (rather than the object), 2. matter (as process not as object)." This collection of "art-critical" writings which includes one of Graham's earliest pieces on Donald Judd (1964) as well as his at the time latest analysis of his viewing experience of a performance work by Bruce Nauman

(1969), goes further than the pieces discussed in its attempt to overcome the Minimalist presuppositions. *Subject Matter* in part has even to be considered as a reviewing and critical reflection of Graham's own work of the *Schema* period that he felt still somehow to be part of the "non-anthropomorphic ideology of late 60's New York Minimal Art." Parallel to these writings Graham initiates his own first activities within which he transformed the notions of visual and spatial concretions into the less "aesthetical" but yet more concise and immediate perceptual modes of experience, "acted out" by actual performers. Graham's concern for the immediacy of the perceptual experience shows that he consequently pursued the reductivist approach to art that had been induced by Stella and had been at issue all through Minimalism and that he quite necessarily arrived at a concern for the "behavior" of people themselves, their actual practice of perception (the subject) instead of a concern for their behavior in relation to a perceived sculptural object. As Graham has been most lucidly describing and analyzing the gradual shift from the Minimal object into the post-minimal processual attitudes, he seems to have undergone in his own work a similar change, however, quite as specific and consistent in his attitude, as his works of the *Schema* period had been. Again the starting point of reflection goes back to Graham's perception of Flavin's work as he had been describing it in retrospect: "I liked that as a side effect of Flavin's fluorescents the gallery walls became a 'canvas.' The lights dramatized the people (like 'spotlights') in a gallery—throwing the content of the exhibition onto the people in the process of perceiving: the gallery interior cube itself became the real framework. . . ."[17]

In Graham's essay on Sol LeWitt this reading of a sculptural work and its apprehension in a manner which is announcing the future development that Graham's own art was going to take, is even more explicit: "As the viewer moves from point to point about the art object the physical continuity of the walk is translated into illusive self-representing depth: the visual complication of representations 'develops' a discrete, non-progressive space and time. There is no distinction between subject and object. Object is the viewer—the art and subject is the viewer, the art. Object and subject are not dialectical oppositions but one self-contained identity: reversible interior and exterior termini. All frames of reference read simultaneously: object/subject."[18]

This reveals at the same time the absolutely consequent logic of the extension of "formalist" concerns into the more "functional" reality of Graham's later performance activities as it elucidates the strictly non-literary and non-theatrical quality of Graham's understanding of performance activities. "Acting" in the context of visual arts is relevant only in as much as it performs the elementary procedure of perceiving the network of relationships between performer and perceiver, both being simultaneously subject and object, as Graham had observed in detail when confronted with the works of Bruce Nauman and his performance practices whose description in *Subject Matter* clearly shows the process of assimilation and transformation of Nauman's impact on Graham's future work. In a comment on *Subject Matter*, in particular its parts concerning the musical and performance influences on Graham's thought, he has clearly described the importance of these phenomena for his own development:

*I had the idea of the reciprocal inter-dependence of perceiver (spectator) and the perceived art-object/or the artist as performer (who might in the case of Nauman present himself as or in place of this "object"). In his new subject-object relation the spectator's perceptual processes were correlated to the compositional process (which was also inherent in the material . . . thus a different idea of "material" and the relation of this materiality to nature(-al) processes was also developed). This change in compositional process came from the developments in music and dance . . . where the performer or performance was the center of the work, executed and perceived in a durational time continuum. This was the opposite of Minimal Art's durationless "presence" . . . a series of discontinuous instances, related by a generating self-contained compositional idea (which was a priorio to the performance or execution of the piece). From music also came the idea of the physiological presence . . . a work about the perceptual process itself, taking place simultaneously as an external phenomenon and inside the brain as part of the brain's interior process. . . . Subject Matter was written at the same time as my first films and performances. I wanted to explain these new types of works I was relating to.*[19]

The outlines of Graham's interests and strategies of his formal enterprises appear in the writings and in the works as what one could call a microscopical analysis of segments of the processes of history itself, their given structures as well as the modes of perceiving them, as well as the perceptives of analyzing and transforming them. And it is to the degree that the analysis succeeds in mediating the patterns of a given reality structure (individual behavior, modes of interaction like for example the subtle processual revealing of stereotyped male-female role behavior in his video-performance *Two Consciousness Projections* (1972), the gradual increase of awareness of group behavior versus individual behavior in performances like *Intention/Intensionality Sequence* (1972) and the open structure inducing and elucidating the mechanisms of group identification in his *Public Space/Two Audiences* (1974)—their processual mechanics as well as their reified dynamics) that the works open up an instrumental perspective of further historical proceedings (thus endowing the viewer with what he experiences as their artwork quality, their aesthetical value).

## EPILOGUE OF THE IDEA OF USE VALUE

A spindle maintains itself as use value only by being used for spinning. Otherwise, by the specific form which has been given to the wood or metal, both the work which produced the form and the material which was shaped by the form, would be spoiled for use. Only by being applied as a medium of active work, as an objective moment in its very being, are the use value of wood and metal as well as the form, maintained.

—Karl Marx, *Notizen zur Grundrisse der Kritik der Politischen Ökonomie* (Moscow, 1938

Use value in art-aesthetic's most heteronomous counterpart—defining the artistic activity as organ of history, as instrument of materialist recognition and transformation, determines itself primarily and finally by its historical context: as it can only result from the most advanced state of aesthetic reflection it must function at the same time within the specific conditions of a given particular historical situation. For example the artist as engineer in revolutionary Russia was in fact a functional and aesthetic necessity, whereas the constructivist engineering aesthetics forty years later in the era of monopoly necessarily functions merely as art. Those restorations however on the formal surfaces of social reality effect the contrary of their original intentions as can be clearly seen in the development of architecture since Constructivism and the Bauhaus. On the other hand, if artistic production gives up altogether the idea of use value, it abolishes its own inherent potential to cause dialectics within the reality of cultural history, thus producing mere artistic facticity incapable of initiating further processes of development. This seems to be true of much current post-conceptual work, either the so-called "new" painting and sculpture and even more so the photographic stories and the new theatricality of performances,—all of which show the features of a decadence in art which is deprived of its inherent and innate demand to cause effects in reality, to exist otherwise than just aesthetically, to have a function potential of historical recognition (thus much present-day art is either infantile or demonic pretension, either decorative or dramatic, as it has nothing "to do" but being "art" and somewhat new). These works' false vivacity, which seems to denounce the rigorous abstraction of the best conceptual art and reacts against the tautological cul de sac of conceptual academicism at its worst, does not seem aware of the fact that art, once having been transformed onto the level of language, had achieved a state of most advanced (potential) communicatability and thus endowed the artwork with its highest form of abstract use value potential. One could hypothetically argue then, that if present-day aesthetic language does not maintain either notion in its acute and necessary tendency and claim for a new body of material reality, as well as the general level of abstraction achieved by language and its counterpart the concretion of a specific use value potential (as it does most efficiently in the recent works of Dan Graham or equally in those of Michael Asher, Daniel Buren and Lawrence Weiner) then art ignorantly gives in to the general conditions of production and therefore, on the level of superstructure, reflects and shares their dilemma: "Boredom, resulting from the experience of destroyed use value, until now a problem of the privileged, has now also become a problem of the masses. The avoidance of proletarian revolution enables the capitalist development to take a final step in completing its basic apory: namely to produce wealth by destroying use value. What will be left over in the end is the unresisted and unquestioned production of simple trash."[20]

## NOTES

1. See Gregory Battcock, ed., "Photographs by Dan Graham," *Minimal Art* (New York, 1968), p. 175.

2. Lucy Lippard, *Six Years, the Dematerialization of the Art Object* (New York, 1973), p. 155.

3. Dan Flavin, "Some Other Remarks," *Artforum* (December 1967), p. 27. Sol LeWitt at the same time seems to have had quite a different understanding of Graham's photographical work which is proved by the fact that he included one of Graham's photographs as illustration for his "Paragraphs on Conceptual Art," *Artforum* (Summer 1967).

4. Willoughby Sharp, "Interview with Carl Andre," *Avalanche,* 1970.

5. Dan Graham in a letter to the author.

6. Roland Barthes, "L'activité structuraliste," *Essais Critiques* (Paris, 1964), p. 216.

7. Donald Judd, "Malevich," *Complete Writings* (Halifax/New York, 1975), p. 212.

8. Karl Beveridge and Ian Burn, "Donald Judd," *The Fox,* no. 2 (1975), p. 129 ff.

9. Dan Graham, *Dan Flavin,* cat. Museum of Contemporary Art, Chicago, 1967, reprinted partly in: Dan Graham, *End Moments* (New York, 1969), p. 15.

10. Dan Graham, "Carl Andre," *Arts Magazine,* no. 3 (New York, 1967), p. 34.

11. Robert Smithson, "A Museum of Language in the Vicinity of Art," *Art International,* no. 3 (1968), p. 22.

12. Donald Judd, "Specific Objects," Contemporary Sculpture (1965), *Arts Yearbook* VII, pp. 74–83. Reprinted in Judd, *Complete Writings,* p. 181.

13. Dan Graham, "Other Observations," *For Publication* (Los Angeles: Otis Art Institute of Los Angeles County, 1975), n.p.

14. Dan Graham in a letter to the author.

15. Ibid.

16. On his relationship to the work of Daniel Buren, Graham commented as follows: "I found out about Buren's theory and works many years later. I think of them as a clear advancement of Flavin's, Judd's, LeWitt's positions. It now seems to me that some of the ideas in *Schema* fore-shadow aspects of Buren's theory/practice (I don't think he knew about the piece until 1970 . . . although it is possible that he did, as it was published in *Art & Language* in 1968)." (In a letter to the author.)

17. Ibid.

18. Dan Graham, "Sol LeWitt—Two Structures," *End Moments,* p. 65.

19. In a letter to the author.

20. Wolfgang Pohrt, *Theorie des Gebrauchswertes* (Frankfurt, 1976).

This essay was first published in "Moments of History in the Work of Dan Graham," in *Dan Graham: Articles* (Eindhoven: Van Abbemuseum, 1978), pp. 211–216.

ian burn, cildo meireles, ian wilson, dan graham, adrian piper, robert barry, victor burgin, deke dusinberre, seth siegelaub, daniel buren, michel claura, art & language, mary kelly, terry smith, joseph kosuth, michael corris, martha rosler, blake stimson

**VII**   memoirs of conceptual art

# the 'sixties: crisis and aftermath (or the memoirs of an ex-conceptual artist)

## ian burn

How has official history dealt with the 1970s? There were no new "isms" generated, no rapid turnover of styles to which we were made accustomed during the 1950s and 1960s. Is the art of the 1970s to suffer a fate similar to that of the 1930s, which has so often been presented as innovatively dull and empty, not worthy of much consideration? The real character of the art in many countries during the Depression years is made up of the production of vital and socially creative imagery—but the political sympathies explicit in much of the work made it too "impure" for the art historians of the book publishing industry during the Cold War and afterwards.

It has not been difficult to observe the falsification of the history of the 1970s, even while that history was taking place. The ever-prolific art magazines were filled with revivals of 1950s and 1960s styles, incorporating minor modifications to satisfy a market need for "change." That same work filled the galleries, was displayed and acquired by the museums, supported by the state funding bodies and bought by the modern Medicis. In Australia, it has been little different—the magazines, the various survey exhibitions and institutional purchasing policies, together with recurring events like the Sydney Biennale, have constantly set out to convince us that nothing else was going on.

It is well accepted that capitalism has created the most effective form of censorship ever: if something does not reach the marketplace (or any of its agencies), then it does not exist! Plainly, anyone who accepts that as a criterion for writing history (or making history "visible," as curators and others do) is a fool, though more likely than not a very successful one. Nonetheless, it is still history with a ghetto mentality.

Any historian aspiring to a more comprehensive history of the 1970s must not merely account for the art market push, but also for the diverse, experimental and culturally rich work which has mushroomed outside of marketing constraints and avant-garde ideals: the community-oriented art and cultural activities, the work of numerous women's groups, the street murals and theater, the activities of artists working within trade union contexts and with social and political activist groups, and more. An important element in such an historical account, however, will be an analysis of the developments critical to the later 1960s. In this essay I will outline one basis for such an analysis, focusing on the ideological character of the crisis in art which unfolded between roughly 1965 and 1969 and its implications relevant to any account of the 1970s.[1]

The massive economic and political expansion of the United States already begun by the Second World War came to a close towards the later part of the 1960s. Under the leadership of the United States, the capitalist world shifted into the period of crisis and reconstruction still being experienced. During the 1950s and 1960s, political/cultural life was being shaped by the struggle between conservative forces and Cold War liberalism.[2] The shift of influence towards more liberal ideals confronted, but was unable to provide answers to, the social crises which throughout the 1960s took on increasingly public forms: black nationalism, the civil rights movement, student radicalism, the hippies and "counter-culture"; providing a common meeting ground was the burgeoning anti-war movement. Each evening, while eating their dinners, Americans watched their military defeating the communist hordes in Vietnam—yet the ultimate victory never came and the official lies continued. More and more people felt moral outrage at the continuing American atrocities, as well as a spreading anger at the many other oppressive and repressive aspects of the American way of life.

Since the Second World War, the corporate forces of American capitalism had been making a concerted effort to create an explicit identification of the needs of individuals with the interests of corporations. Hence anything which rejected the basis of that identification was seen as *political*—for example, lifestyles, individual feelings, quality of life, spontaneity, anti-institutionalism, "free-form" expression, drug-associated cultures. In conflict with the passively aggressive impersonalism of corporate styles and values, a new feeling of personal-social responsibility was surfacing. In the broadest sense, these diverse cultural expressions converged on a common attitude of anti-institutionalism.

Within this radicalizing climate, the social consciousness which developed tended to value highly the ideals of spontaneity and individualism, which at times appeared as virtually an ideology of personal psychology. Jerry Rubin argued, for example, that politics is how you lead your life, not for whom you vote. The revolution was to happen by each of us transforming our own consciousnesses—sometimes referred to as "communism of the mind." These attitudes found cultural expression on a wide front, from the seeking of alternate lifestyles and the counter-cultural forms to the still-elegant adjustments within elite intellectual production, including the officially sanctioned high art styles.

By the mid-1960s the sanctioned styles of avant-gardism were Pop Art, Color Field or Hard Edge painting (or Post-Painterly Abstraction) and Minimal Art. For the ambitiously avant-garde younger artist these formed the horizon of options to be "worked through and beyond," but they were also the styles which would function to legitimize the next avant-garde developments.

Looking back over the rapidly and successfully institutionalized avant-garde art of the later 1960s, a strong sense of crisis remains in the work, appearing on a wide front and seeming to connect political and social consciousness to aesthetic attitudes. The art did not merely passively reflect the larger social milieu, but was in fact undergoing its own crisis as a necessary climax to its own recent history. This artistic crisis, while very much part of the pervasive condition throughout American society, needs to be examined in terms of its specific character in order to unravel its participation in the larger crises but also to identify how the issues were experienced and confronted in terms of artistic production. In other words, both the "autonomy" of high cultural forms and their "integration" into a corporate capitalist culture have to be accommodated.

The symptoms of the crisis within avant-garde art surfaced within particular characteristics. In the following, I have set out to describe them in the terms in which they seemed to be experienced at the time.

## THE DESKILLING OF THE PRACTICE OF ART

Each of the early 1960s styles was marked by a tendency to shift significant decision-making away from the process of production to the conception, planning, design and form of presentation. The physical execution often was not carried out by the artist, who instead could adopt a supervisory role. While the execution frequently entailed quite rigorous control and technical proficiency, the scope of required skills was severely limited . . . or else it demanded skills of workers in other-than-art fields, where there was little advantage to be gained by the artist acquiring and competing with those skills.

This mode of production encouraged artists to devalue not just traditional skills but the acquisition of any skills demanding a disciplined period of training. Younger artists were faced with the conclusion that it was unnecessary to acquire any more than the few skills demanded to reproduce the particular style to which they were committing themselves. While persuasive arguments can be made in favor of discarding "anachronistic" practices in the face of "space-age" technologies, what is so often overlooked is that skills are not merely manual dexterity but forms of knowledge. The acquisition of particular skills implies an access to a body of accumulated knowledge. Thus deskilling means a rupture within an historical body of knowledge— in other words, a dehistoricization of the practice of art.

This problem is an enduring one. For example, in Australia, the growth period for Australian art schools (as elsewhere) was during the 1960s and early 1970s, a time when American influence was at its peak. Preference for tenured positions in these schools was more often than not given to artists whose work directly acknowledged American influences. During the 1970s, the tendency was for art students to be taught traditional skills (e.g. figure drawing, composition, perspective, color theory, knowledge of materials and techniques) on an ever-decreasing scale. This, I would argue, is a heightened problem in Australia, since the concept of an avant-garde has scarcely gained a tradition here. It has not been uncommon during the past decade for students to experience an avant-garde context during their art school years, but to find difficulty in sustaining such attitudes outside of the school and to then discover that they have not been taught skills to allow them to work in any other way.[3]

## THE DECREASED IMPORTANCE OF THE PHYSICAL OBJECT

The devaluing of traditional skills threw into question the status of the work of art as a privileged object, as a special thing-in-itself. With few or no artistically valued manual skills involved in the production of the work, it was hard to sustain the idea that the object itself was the exclusive embodiment of a special creative process.

Moreover, the official styles of the early 1960s deflected importance away from the physical work of art itself, giving more weight to the conception of the work, the process by which it was produced, its context of display or its sheer existence ("presence"). The power of the work became the power it could reflect through its immediate institutionalized context (galleries, museums, glossy magazines), or through contexts it invoked associations with, for example, the "international style" which had become identified with the new corporate architecture, design and public-relations image; the advertising and symbolism of multinational corporatism; the mass-reproduced imagery of the media, etc. Within the styles themselves, the tendency towards simplification and paring-away of "non-artistic" elements gave the illusion of an essence being revealed; however, in retrospect, it has become clearer that the "essence" lay not within a rigorous tradition of art but more within the realm of a repressive corporate way of life.

For one to accept the power of these early 1960s styles implied (whether one was conscious of it or not) acceptance of the dominance of the corporate world over the individual. To challenge this entailed attempting to create a "personal" power of similar nature and strength. To place significance back on to the object again was a "regressive" step in terms of avant-garde logic. Yet how was one to conceive of the continuing practice of art as the production of objects lacking any importance in themselves?[4]

## THE DEVALUATION OF SUBJECT MATTER AND RECOGNIZABLE IMAGERY

Under these circumstances, subject matter could not be retained in any traditionally significant role. More often than not, this entailed subject matter itself being excluded or substituted for by a set of formal qualities. If a recognizable image was used (as by the Pop artists), then its "meaning" could not be read literally. For example, the image of Coca-Cola bottles was used, not because of what it depicted, but for what it represented or symbolized. The image-associated power sought by the artists could not be satisfied by (say) the image of a local Tarax soft drink bottle, but only by the "international" (multinational) symbol of corporate identity and domination.

## THE NEGATION OF THE ARTIST AS SUBJECT

The corporate-like institutions of the New York art world and its international art marketing system were increasingly acting to determine the public "meaning" of works of art. The artist's prerogative to determine a "meaning" of his or her work had been eroded—indeed, it seemed to have been surrendered almost willingly. Moreover, the body of knowledge of art traditionally acquired in association with its practice was being increasingly taken over by the new growth industries of art history departments, the publication of criticism, the contemporary museums and galleries. The perpetuation of many careers in these areas demanded that the territorial claims be defended by all conceivable means.

Thus success as an artist implied more than ever that one did not merely produce "good art" but that one had to produce "history." Indeed (and this has been commented on by other writers) there is much evidence of an expanding "art historical" consciousness in the attitudes of American artists from the 1940s onwards—a tendency which became strident during the 1960s. This was not a broad and culturally diverse sense of history but a particular history conceived as a narrow lineage of styles, in respect of which the artist's task was to invent the next (formally) "logical" step. By conceiving of one's work as "instant art history," one necessarily conceives of oneself as merely an object of that history—not as a thinking, acting subject.

The tenets of the styles encouraged artists to eliminate all personal reference and marks; the finished product hid rather than revealed the artist. Similarly, the viewer was faced with little to engage—increasingly a detailed familiarity with the recent avant-garde tradition was presupposed in order for the viewer to appreciate a work. One contemplated not the work but oneself experiencing an inability to engage the work. In other words, the nature of the work encouraged viewers to experience themselves self-consciously but not as thinking, acting subjects.

## THE COMMERCIALIZATION OF ART

From the mid-1950s, art became big business on an unprecedented scale. The international art market centered in New York grew into a multi-million-dollar industry and money literally poured through the market. The sheer impact of this on the process of art production itself has yet to be accounted for adequately.[5] Yet, by the mid-1960s, it was an unavoidable experience for any artist involved with avant-garde art and conflicted openly with the moralizing idealism of the artist in bourgeois society. Such intense commercialization was widely regarded as spelling corruption and the prostitution of the artist . . . and every artist had a story to prove the point.

The agent of corruption was identified—albeit rather shortsightedly—as the commercial gallery system, while its role and interdependence in the larger marketing totality of museums, curators, historians, magazines, critics, collectors, private and state patronage was generally ignored. The perpetuation of galleries depended on the trading of unique objects, which might be acquired as property and/or investment. Thus artists were faced with this dilemma: to continue to produce physically large objects, or indeed any objects at all, implied a commitment to producing the commodities on which galleries thrived; it implied conforming to the priorities of the property/investment art market.

## SEXUAL AND RACIAL DISCRIMINATION IN ART

Since about the 1870s, women students have outnumbered men in art schools, yet the institutions and the history of art have continued to be dominated by men. Rising feminist consciousness during the 1960s led to a long overdue questioning and challenging of the male-dominated status quo. Discrimination against women artists was shown to be in evidence in the museums and galleries, the magazines and the writing of art history. Paralleling this, cases were made concerning discrimination against black artists in the United States, though with different class and cultural complexities existing in their circumstances.

While white male chauvinism was a fact of the marketplace, it was also the case that the discriminatory values of the market had been "internalized" as a normal functioning and dynamic of the official avant-garde movements of the 1950s and early 1960s. These styles were blatant in their enshrinement of stereotyped "masculinity"—the qualities sought and experiences embodied, the associations of particular materials, the ambience of power, the relation to and manipulation of public spaces and so on. It can be seen as no accident that male artists almost exclusively dominate Pop Art, Hard Edge painting and Minimalism. With the devaluation of the role of the artist as a thinking, acting subject, the artist's ability to act to overcome the male-biased values became impossible without challenging an entire framework and tradition.

Thus one frequently found those discriminatory values being reproduced by both male and female artists, despite their other intentions. Much has been written on discrimination against women artists, but more analysis is needed concerning the ideological biases of the dominant ideas and values in specific circumstances of art.

## THE SOCIAL DISENGAGEMENT OF THE ARTIST

The styles discussed are overt in their separation of art from any notion of politics. The mounting politicization of a growing sector of the American people, including artists, led to a realization by some artists that the officially sanctioned styles could not be used in any fashion to express a critical view of American society. In other words, the artists' major means of expression was "voiceless," incapable of conveying their outrage at the United States' involvement in Vietnam. Admittedly, for many, this was a quite acceptable situation—not because they endorsed those militarist actions, but because of the widely held belief that art naturally and rightly "transcended" such issues.

Such styles should be seen as part of what has been called "the affirmative culture," acquiescing to and by default endorsing all aspects of American society. For artists with commitments or investments in such styles, social and political protest became an activity engaged outside of art production. This, perhaps more than any other factor, gave a focus to the sense of crisis. The social and political upheavals affected many of the artists and, increasingly, there appeared an awareness of the conflict between their personal political views and the aesthetic ideology expressed through their work.

## THE AMERICANIZATION OF ART

With greater financial support ensuing from a privileged access to the market—as well as favored treatment by aspiring contemporary museums around the capitalist world—American artists had begun to travel widely. Increasingly they found themselves subjected to accusations of "cultural imperialism." Many of the artists began to be sensitive to this accusation, even if not very sensitive to the actual problem. There was, however, a gradual realization on the part of some artists that the work they were presenting, disseminating and publicizing did not "transcend" the society in which it was produced, but was indeed intensely nationally chauvinistic.

This chauvinism followed similar lines of monopolistic self-interest which obsessed the corporate empires. One of the more offensive examples was the assumption that the particular styles produced in the United States were really "international," while anything else was not.[6] What needs more considered elaboration is the extent to which the official styles had come to reproduce the American corporate way of life, the sort of person it made you as you produced that kind of art, as you viewed and appreciated it.[7] Perhaps this was less obvious to people in the United States, given the dominant role played by corporate values within everyday life. But the quite explicit use of this art by corporately-persuaded institutions like the Museum of Modern Art in New York made its Americanistic values all too apparent in other countries.[8]

The specific character of the American styles of the 1960s separated them from most prior styles. The adoption of any one of those styles implied a concentrated but narrow range of possible options. Diverse cultural and individual backgrounds tended to be negated or suppressed. There was, for example, little room left within the styles for "Australianizing" Pop Art,

Colorfield or Minimalism. The outcome was, in places like Australia, that a generation of young artists tended to become alienated from their own cultural specificity.[9]

The above characterizes some of the main aspects of the crisis of the late 1960s in a generalized (and incomplete) fashion. What it does begin to suggest is the *complexity* of the issues as they were being experienced at the time. It also conveys a sense of the *interrelatedness* of the issues, and the manner in which aesthetic questions collided with social and political ones.

Given this situation, the process of sorting out which of the issues were the priorities depended largely on the conscious experiences of particular artists. For example, faced with a realization of the deskilling process, it is perhaps not surprising to discover a renewed interest in various forms of realist painting, including Photo-Realism. The latter evolved a particular mode of painting which permitted an obvious display of skill in depiction or imitation, yet without any real engagement with or emotional commitment to the subject matter, thus maintaining a continuity with the recent abstract tradition. Interest in a particular subject matter was generally because it offered the conditions for a display of a particular skill.

The rejection of the traditional status of the physical work of art was conceived in a variety of ways. Conceptual Art provided some of these (which will be elaborated on later), but also Body Art, Environments and Performances can all be interpreted in part as responding to this priority.

The devaluation of subject matter and recognizable imagery in turn led to a reconsideration of images. This is especially apparent in relation to the expanded interest in photography—not just art photography, but photographic images in every sense including the historical. This has occurred in a context in which more critical means of reading or analyzing imagery are becoming widely accepted. These means integrated, among other things, the formal(ist) tools of analysis associated with the early 1960s styles together with ideological readings of the subject matter, thus creating a more critical mode of reading images which has influenced artists and photographers, as well as writers and some areas of art history.

The crisis in terms of the artist's self-perceived role led some to reject the objectification of the role in favor of acting as more responsible (initially moralistically so) subjects. This attempted to reclaim responsibility for the public "meaning" of what one produced, and in general attempted to conceive of the practice of art in relation to broader-ranging ideas, to a less restrictive intellectual context.

The reaction to the commercialization of art was wide and took many forms. It is enough here to point to the more obvious, ranging from the rapid development of artist-run galleries and co-ops to the phenomenon of Earthworks, artworks whose material form is created *in situ* outside of the expected precincts of art. However, the more successful responses gradually built up financial supports outside of traditional patronage structures and directed their production towards specific, non-art audiences.

The challenge to sexual discrimination has been better documented than any other aspect of the crisis, mainly within feminist art publications such as *Lip* (Australia), *Heresies* and *Feminist Art Journal* (both New York). But of at least as much importance has been the nature of the work developed from the social and working relations within various women's collectives, which more than anything else has given weight to the critique of male chauvinist values.

The social and political disengagement implied by the dominant styles of the 1950s and early 1960s led artists to utilize diverse means to reconstruct their practices in more socially responsible ways. These included reconstructions within the avant-garde tradition, like so-called Political Art, to greater interest in political posters, street murals and community-oriented art, to social activist and unequivocally political involvement.[10]

Finally, in revulsion against the Americanization of contemporary art practices, there emerged in many countries a reconsideration of the national, regional and local cultural forms and traditions. From that ground, conscious struggle against the imposition (and blithe or unwitting acceptance) of the values and forms of American culture has gathered strength. In addition, it has been realized that if work is produced in a context where it is liable to be reproduced and even exhibited "around the world," then its "meaning" cannot be simply that which is interpreted through its original context. For example, the impact that a Minimal sculpture has in a place like Australia is as much a part of its "meaning" as the effect it has in New York. In other words, work which is conceived to function on an "international" level should be defined by the accumulation of international "meanings." If particular kinds of work reproduce imperialistic relationships in other contexts, then that is part of the work's "meaning."

In the above, the connections made are the obvious and often more simplistic ones. Yet the majority of the connections are neither simple nor obvious. Nor for that matter were these developments all simultaneous. Nonetheless, the above provides a number of indications of ways in which artists were acting and reacting within that crisis ambience.

A specific case is now considered in the light of the above discussion. The reasons for choosing Conceptual Art are many, not merely personal involvement at the time. Conceptual Art participated and responded within the crisis atmosphere perhaps more self-consciously than other contemporary work.

From one point of view, Conceptual Art can be seen as an amalgam of attempts to critically analyze and dissect the situation in which artists were working, to assume responsibility for articulating these ideas and develop ways of incorporating that critical perspective into the work of art itself. By these means, it was hoped to transform the practice of art itself. Such intellectual Luddism was unashamedly idealistic, and in retrospect the inadequacies of those initial critiques are patent—and more symptomatic of the situation than remedial. Thus the piecemeal rationality built up into a composite irrationality. Nonetheless, Conceptual Art did contribute significantly in laying out a groundwork from which more penetrating analyses of current art practices began to be realized.

This is not the place to lay out a "history" of the development of Conceptual Art or to elaborate a list of "major" works. There are books and articles providing adequate enough surveys of work and which establish the individual "heroes" for the market and history.[11] (The discussion which follows, however, presupposes some familiarity with that material.)

More than a decade has passed since Conceptual Art became a public and institutionalized style. Most styles of the 1960s have since come under microscopic scrutiny through voluminous writings in magazines and books—often the kind of writing which would embarrass artists were it not at the same time directly connected to their "success." But Conceptual Art has been conspicuous by its comparative lack of discussion and the poverty of such discussion as has appeared. Reasons for this must include the role and historical position that Conceptual Art adopted during the critical period. More than any other style during the 1960s, Conceptual Art constituted itself upon *social* criteria. While the work was often disguised within apparently formalist objectives, its character still contained a social dimension of a kind incompatible with the ethos of other styles associated with the avant-garde tradition of the period.

There was no materialist analysis of the conditions of art production—indeed, the understanding was far from that and can be seen as quite overtly Utopian. Thus perhaps the most significant thing that can be said to the credit of Conceptual Art is that it *failed*. In terms of its development, it failed to fulfil certain initial expectations and ideals, and its goals were in many ways unattainable. How this unfolded can be shown through discussing some of the more general tendencies within Conceptual Art.

Firstly, Conceptual Art was a specific reaction against the entrenched art marketing system. As pointed out earlier, the art object had become the symbol of commercialization and commodification of art—and the gallery was seen as the context in which that process occurred. There was in Conceptual Art a genuine attempt to produce a kind of art which eschewed such absorption by the market; in fact, it saw itself in the process of divesting itself of the materialist aspects of the market. Lucy Lippard's notion of the "dematerialization" of the art object is perhaps the most widely known description of this process and was influential on a number of artists. However, the concept of "dematerialization"—as she defined it, "a deemphasis on material aspects (uniqueness, permanence, decorative attractiveness)"—remains highly problematic.[12] What was witnessed with Conceptual Art was an absolute separation of mental or intellectual work from manual work, with a revaluing of the intellectual and a devaluing of the manual. It is hard to avoid the analogy with the role of management in industry but would we say that the mental work of management was a "dematerialization" of the manual work? Of course not: the mental work represents the withdrawal of mental decision-making out of manual production, in order that management might more readily control production and workers. If the analogy is applied back to Conceptual Art, one is left with endless questions about why art should mimic that structure, why at this particular time, and so on.

While "dematerialization" perhaps may be appropriate for describing some works, it is clearly inappropriate for others. Certain works saw the object as a problem, not because it was an object but because of its *special* or *privileged* status, a status which removes art objects from their everyday settings and renders them immune to commonsense assumptions. This attack on the object at least did acknowledge that the object existed within particular relationships, though there was little grasp of any means of transforming those relations. But the outcome did lead to realizations about the contradictory, the arbitrary and capricious nature of the category of art.

But there is a further consideration concerning the indictment of the role of the object. From the present vantage-point, it is obvious that there was a marked failure to distinguish between objects and commodities—and in particular a failure to appreciate that one does not need to have an object in order to have a commodity. Ideas can and do exist as commodities in societies like ours. What really counts is not whether something has a physical form, but rather the nature of the economic and social relations in which a particular form of production is embedded. Thus this attack on the object was more a moralistic and emotive stance than a course of action based on social necessity.[13] Its moralism remained individualistic and its necessity conformed too readily to the avant-garde ambience.[14]

Secondly, Conceptual Art represented a tendency to use forms which were potentially more "democratic" (i.e. the forms of mass communication and media). Works of art were (re)produced which existed solely or primarily in art magazines, catalogues or books, thus potentially reaching a wider audience, faster, than an object exhibited in a gallery. Moreover, the art accrued some of the cultural aura associated with the media. This decision reflected a desire to move away from unique objects, to produce art which could not be owned in the traditional sense—often all one needed to do was to rip a page out of a magazine and pin it on the wall in order to "own" it. Elitism was equated with the unique object and the utilization of media forms which did not encourage uniqueness seemed a way to escape the elitist tag.

The 1960s were a time when Marshall McLuhan was widely read, although the political naiveté of his "global village" ideas was not as yet widely apparent. He asserted that the medium was the message. If the medium is the message, that effectively negates the potential of the content.[15] But to avant-gardists committed to the search for formal innovation, this justified a "contentless" trek through the many possible media forms . . . from hiring men to walk Paris streets carrying sandwich boards covered with stripes to a tape-recording of a mathematics lecture playing continually in an art gallery to telegrams to friends assuring them of the artist's continued existence to billboards in the middle of a New Mexico desert quoting to passing motorists a section of the Synopsis of Categories of *Roget's Thesaurus.* It also led many artists into publishing their own books and journals, and to adopt that form as the primary outlet for their ideas and art.[16]

Thirdly, tendencies within Conceptual Art gave expression to more direct and personal relationships. This was a sort of self-externalization, or avant-garde "humanism," set against the overwhelming impersonalism of Pop, Color Field and Minimalism. However, what was allowed to count as personal and individual was constrained by a narrow and particular concept of the individual, one which conformed to the definition of the individual in a mass consumer society. Not surprisingly, this aspect of Conceptual Art often led to excesses, ranging from the recounting of whimsical personal anecdotes to narcissistic obsessions. Nonetheless this still represented a reclaiming, in part, of a personal/social relationship and expression within the practice of art.

Fourthly, given the withdrawal from the production of unique objects, more collectively organized work became possible and numerous artists began working in groups. Not only was that possible, but work could emerge which reflected the collective socialization process—that is, which grew "out of" the working interaction between the artists in the group.

The fifth point concerns the process of self–re-education by artists and the development of a more critically informed understanding of their own situation. This was another aspect of reclaiming a more actively subjective and self-liberating role for the artist. Despite the naiveté of much of it, it opened doors which had been shut for some time. It encouraged efforts to demystify the art process and to acquire intellectual tools which might assist in this task.

Other points can be made, but the above comments indicate the social and the "progressive" implications of particular attitudes in Conceptual Art. They suggest how, within that particular movement during the late 1960s, artists participated in the broader crisis in American society through a self-conscious struggle to resolve particular social issues in relation to their own means of production.

But each of the above attitudes contained implications which could only undermine the position held. For example, how long can you use mass media forms before becoming aware of the political and economic functioning of mass media in a capitalist society?[17] How long do you need to work collectively before realizing that genuinely collective work is antagonistic to the social relations of a capitalist society? How long can you give expression to your most personal feelings within an alienating market structure before realizing you are also alienating your own personal feelings? After you realize that the market can operate by selling ideas just as readily as it sells objects as commodities, how long can you continue to believe you are being subversive towards the market?

In other words, Conceptual Art evolved in a context of trying to find a resolution to the issues experienced within that crisis atmosphere. But within its development new contradictions emerged which made impossible a resolution as part of the avant-garde tradition of modern art. In this manner, Conceptual Art failed . . . though its failure is significant. Nor can one blame the victims for complicity. That some artists have invented successful careers as Conceptual artists and others have continued to cling to unsuccessful careers cannot impinge on the profound inability to resolve those contradictions.

Conceptual Art had a dual character: on the one hand, the social nature of the work was progressive; on the other, its structural adherence to the avant-garde geography was conservative. Insofar as art history has chosen to notice only the latter, its reactionary aspect has dominated interpretations.[18]

But the other history no longer exists as art history. For those who took the inevitable steps beyond Conceptual Art—and stepped outside of the market-dominated avant-garde heritage—part of the understanding of the necessity of this was arrived at *as a function of* Conceptual Art and not despite it. The real value of Conceptual Art lay in its *transitional* (and thus genuinely historical) character, not in the style itself.

## NOTES

1. The term "crisis" is being used in its social sense here. At the time, the experience of any crisis for artists was largely intuitive and for many perhaps indistinguishable from the kind of "crisis" associated with any formal or avant-garde shift. However, with hindsight, the crisis had significant dimensions to it which move it beyond that aesthetic category.

2. See, for example, Irving Horowitz's discussion of the period in *Ideology and Utopia in the United States 1956–1976* (New York: Oxford University Press, 1977). Daniel Bell's widely read thesis on "The End of Ideology in the West" in *The End of Ideology* (New York: Collier Books

1960), can be located as a key text heralding the triumph of (the ideology of) liberalism. The way he argues this should be read at first hand. (Against this can be placed the many shifts away from liberal ideals in the West during the 1970s and early 1980s.)

One of the ways the shift towards liberalism affected artists was that it legitimized the "split" between art and political commitments. The need was no longer felt to vocally deny the role of a social content in art, as the Abstract Expressionists had. For the younger artist, the liberal ideals informing their art "transcended" such issues.

3. A rather obvious consequence can be seen in many of the street murals being done by artists. Often they show a marked lack of proficiency with traditional skills, which is not a function of expediency. Hence they fall into an uncomfortable area displaying neither fully developed skills nor the naiveté of untrained community-produced murals.

4. Similar ideas can be found in other areas of cultural production, from the "transcendence" of the materialist values of Western society deriving from Eastern religious beliefs, to some of the ideas advocated within sections of the New Left, particularly by Herbert Marcuse. Marcuse, for example, supported the notion of an avant-gardism of ideas, while rebelling against the dictates of "repressive reason" in which brute facts and mere objects became an outrage to the imagination, an attitude which extended into a moralistic "horror of objects."

5. I have made several attempts to deal with this issue, none of which are very successful; e.g. "The Art Market: Affluence and Degradation," *Artforum* (April 1975); "Pricing Works of Art," *The Fox* no. 1 (1975); and "Don Judd," *The Fox* no. 2 (1975) (co-written with Karl Beveridge). Donald Kuspit has also obliquely addressed the problem in "Pop Art: a Reactionary Realism," *Art Journal* (Fall 1976), and "Authoritarian Abstraction," *Journal of Aesthetics and Art Criticism* (Fall 1976).

6. For example, Donald Judd: "I think that American art is far better than that anywhere else but I don't think that situation is desirable. Actually, it's international art in America and the best thing that could happen would be equal international art elsewhere." *Studio International* (February 1970).

7. The beginnings of such an elaboration can be found in M. Kozloff, "American Painting during the Cold War," *Artforum* (May 1973), and J. Tagg, "American Power and American Painting," *Praxis* no. 2 (1976). For a handy discussion of the context in which artists produced in the 1960s, see W. Van Ness, "The Minimal Era" *Arts in Society* (Fall/Winter 1974).

8. See, for example, E. Cockroft, "Abstract Expressionism: Weapon of the Cold War," *Artforum* (June 1974). For further elaboration, see W. Hauptman, "The Suppression of Art during the McCarthy Decade," *Artforum* (October 1973).

9. To give one instance, consider the character of subsequent developments of many of the artists who exhibited in the "The Field" exhibition at the National Gallery of Victoria, Melbourne, 1968, and contrast this with the character of the development of Australian artists of the 1940s and 1950s.

10. For a useful account of this, see T. Schwartz, "The Politicalization of the Avant-Garde," *Art in America* (November-December 1971).

11. The most widely available books are U. Meyer's *Conceptual Art* (New York: Dutton, 1972), and L. Lippard's *Six Years: the Dematerialization of the Art Object* (New York: Praeger, 1973).

12. The concept was first discussed publicly in an article by L. Lippard and J. Chandler in *Art International* (February 1968). For a contemporaneous critique of this concept, see Lippard, *Six Years,* pp. 43–44.

13. For example, in an interview in 1969, Lawrence Weiner said: "I do not mind objects, but I do not care to make them. . . . Industrial and socioeconomic machinery pollutes the environment and the day the artist feels obliged to muck it up further, art should cease being made. If you can't make art without making a permanent imprint on the physical aspects of the world, then art is not worth making. In this sense, any permanent damage to ecological factors in nature not necessary for the furtherance of human existence, but only necessary for the illustration of an art concept, is a crime against humanity" (Meyer, *Conceptual Art,* p. 217)

14. We should not underestimate the role of avant-gardism in shaping the attack on the art object. Avant-gardism projects its own "necessity," locating the artist within an alienated sense of necessity, "a necessity of one's own un-necessity." The residual strength of the concept in Conceptual Art is apparent in the historicist statements of some of the artists. Robert Barry (speaking of his own radio-wave transmission artworks): "I guess it was the first invisible art" (Meyer, *Conceptual Art,* p. 36); Joseph Kosuth: "I am perhaps the first artist to be out of the grip of the 19th century" (catalogue statement, l969); Douglas Huebler: "I was one of the first people to use language with photography," (*Journal,* Southern California Art Magazine, no. 15, p. 38). Such comments are the function of "an-historical" consciousness: to establish precedents with no matter how trivial a formal innovation could be assumed to be enough to guarantee a place in art history. Given this, to do away with the object was also probably the most avant-garde option open to artists at the time.

15. There may be an interesting parallel between McLuhan and Clement Greenberg which could be developed through a comparison of McLuhan's notion that the medium is the message and that each medium is unique, with Greenberg's argument that the task of the modernist artist is to isolate the unique features of painting.

16. As a dealer in the late 1960s, Seth Siegelaub held "exhibitions" of his artists in which the exhibition consisted solely of a catalogue of the works being published. Siegelaub's own history is not without interest: he moved from being a fairly straight dealer to a shrewd promoter of a group of New York Conceptual artists (Barry, Weiner, Huebler and Kosuth), to an involvement in artists' rights and art politics, to a subsequent role within a group in Paris publishing a range of left cultural critiques. In this fashion, Siegelaub parallels the history of many artists who moved through Conceptual Art to more direct engagements with "real-world" issues. By comparison, the Conceptual artists he was promoting have proven to have far more conservative ideals and histories.

17. For example, many people involved in the various protest movements advocated using the media all the time. But one of the most divisive techniques of the mass media is over-exposure. The Situationists criticized the deliberate use of the mass media: "The revolt is contained by over-exposure. We are given it to contemplate so that we shall forget to participate."

18. For example, Lippard, in the "Postface" to her book, *Six Years,* complains that her earlier hopes were shattered by the rapid commercial success enjoyed by Conceptual artists. At that time, she chose to acknowledge only that work which had broached the market.

This essay was first published in *Art & Text,* 1:1 (Fall 1981), pp. 49–65.

# statements
## cildo meireles

I remember that in 1968, 1969 and 1970 we knew we were beginning to touch on what was interesting—we were no longer working with metaphors (representations) of situations; we were working with the real situation itself. On the other hand, the kind of work that was being done tended to volatilize, and that was another characteristic. It was work that, really, no longer had that cult of the object, in isolation; things existed in terms of what they could spark off in the body of society. It was exactly what one had in one's head: working with the idea of the public. At that time we were putting everything into our work, and it was being directed towards a large, indefinite number of people: that thing that is called the public. Nowadays, in fact, there is the danger of doing work knowing exactly who will be interested in it. The idea of the *public,* which is a broad, generous notion, was replaced (through deformation) by the idea of the *consumer,* which is the part of the public that has acquisitive power. Really, the *Inserçoes em circuitos ideológicos* (Insertions into ideological circuits) arose out of the need to create a system for the circulation and exchange of information that did not depend on any kind of centralized control. A language. A system essentially opposed to that of press, radio and television, typical examples of media that actually reach an enormous audience, but in their circulation system there is always a certain control and a certain channelling of the insertion. In other words, there the "insertion" is performed by an élite that has access to the levels on which the system is developed: technological sophistication involving huge amounts of money and/or power.

The *Inserçoes em circuitos ideológicos* had taken shape as two projects: the *Coca-Cola* project and the *Cédula* (Banknote) project. The work started with a text I wrote in April 1970 and it sets out precisely from this position: 1) in society there are certain mechanisms for circulation (circuits); 2) these circuits clearly embody the ideology of the producer, but at the same time they are passive when they receive insertions into the circuit; 3) and this occurs whenever people initiate them. The *Inserçoes em circuitos ideológicos* also arose from the recognition of two fairly common practices: chain letters (letters you receive, copy and send on to other people) and the bottles flung into the sea by victims of shipwrecks. Implicit in these practices is the notion of a circulating medium, a notion crystallized most clearly in the case of paper money and, metaphorically, in returnable containers (soft drink bottles, for example).

As I see it, the important thing in the project was the introduction of the concept of "circuit," isolating it and fixing it. It is this concept that determines the dialectical content of the work, while interfering with each and every effort contained within the very essence of the process (medium). In other words, the container always carries with it an ideology. So, the initial idea was the recognition of a (natural) "circuit" that exists and on which it is possible to do real work. Actually, an "insertion" into this circuit is always a kind of counter-information.

It capitalizes on the sophistication of the medium in order to achieve an increase in equality of access to mass communication and also, one must add, to bring about a neutralization of the original propaganda (whether produced by industry or by the state), which always has an anaesthetic effect. It is a contrast between awareness (insertion) and anaesthesia (circuit), considering awareness as a function of art and anaesthesia as a function of industry. Because any industrial circuit normally is far-reaching, but it is alienating/ed.

Of course, art has a social function and has more ways of being densely *aware.* A greater density of awareness in relation to the society from which it emerges. And the role of industry is exactly the opposite of this. As it exists today, the power of industry is based on the greatest possible coefficient of alienation. So the notes on the *Inserçoes em circuitos ideológicos* project specifically contrast art and industry. (. . .)

The way I had thought of it, the *Inserçoes* would only exist to the extent that they ceased to be the work of just one person. In other words, the work only exists to the extent that other people practice it. Another thing that arises then is the idea of the need for anonymity. By extension the question of anonymity involves the question of ownership. You would no longer work with an object, because the object would become a practice, something over which you could have no kind of control or ownership. And it would try to raise other matters: firstly, it would reach more people to the extent that you no longer needed to go to the information because the information would come to you; and consequently there would be the right conditions for "exploding" the notion of a *sacred space*. (. . .)

Insofar as museums, galleries or pictures form a sacred space for representation, they become a Bermuda Triangle: anything you put there, any idea, is automatically going to be neutralized. I think people tried primarily to make a commitment with the public. Not with the purchaser of art (the market). But with the audience sitting out there in the stalls. The hazy face, the most important element in the whole structure. Working with the wonderful possibility that the plastic arts provide of creating a new language to express each new idea. Always working with the possibility of transgression in terms of reality. In other words, making works that do not simply exist in an approved, consecrated, sacred space; that do not happen simply in terms of a canvas, a surface, a representation. No longer working with the metaphor of gunpowder itself. You would no longer work with the object, because the object would be a practice, something over which you could have no kind of control or ownership.

This text is taken from statements made by Meireles in a recorded interview with Antônio Manuel. This extract was originally published in Ronaldo Brito and Eudoro Augusto Macieira de Sousa, *Cildo Meireles, arte brasileira contemporânea* (Rio de Janeiro: FUNARTE, 1981), and more recently in *Cildo Meireles: IVAM Centre del Carme, 2 febrero/23 abril 1995* (Barcelona: Generalitat Valenciana, Conselleria de Cultura, 1995), p. 174, from which these extracts are taken.

# conceptual art

## ian wilson

The difference between conceptual art and poetry, literature, and philosophy is that conceptual art takes the principles of visual abstraction, founded in the visual arts, and applies them to language. When it does that a nonvisual abstraction occurs.

Nonvisual abstraction is more difficult to grasp than visual abstraction. Although it occurs in all forms of language, it is never focused on.

Nonvisual abstraction is difficult to grasp because we continue to look for something. This tendency of looking for visual meaning, or trying to use the visual faculty, causes meaninglessness to occur.

Nonvisual abstraction is difficult to appreciate because it deals with the most difficult objective to comprehend. It endeavors to inspire a consciousness of being which is formless.

Nonvisual abstraction is at the heart of conceptual art.

Nonvisual abstraction is formless.

There still is content in visual abstraction, but nonvisual abstraction has no content.

A concept without content is formless.

True conceptual art does not compromise itself by re-entering the traditional context of the visual arts. No matter how nonvisual or abstract a work may be, when it is put on a gallery wall language becomes an object to be looked at and not read. Print becomes a visual object to the extent it is physically removed from the reader.

Conceptual art presented in a typeface larger than 12 points causes a reference to a place other than the consciousness of the reader.

When consciousness is related to place and time it is limited to place and time.

Consciousness withdrawn from external references is beyond space and time.

Conceptual art is beyond space and time.

Space and time have nothing to do with the nature of consciousness. They are superimposed upon it.

True conceptual art shows a reality without dimension, without form.

At the outset it was misunderstood that conceptual art meant any art that was involved in ideas, or that had an idea involved in its construction, be it a photograph, painting, or sculpture. This is not so.

Conceptual art is not about ideas. It is about the degree of abstraction of ideas.

The idea "car" is not as appropriate as the idea "infinity." It is not as abstract.

Abstraction is concerned with the present.

The true present is without references of space and time.

The conceptual artist is someone who has been trained rigorously in visual abstraction and brings this into the area of language.

The conceptual artist raises the consciousness of abstraction in language.

The conceptual artist points to abstraction as an expression of the evolving consciousness. By removing all social and political references this evolving consciousness searches for a means to see through an opaque language.

The nature of abstraction is so obscure that it had to be discovered by a primary research such as the visual arts. Poetry, literature, and philosophy have used abstraction but it was never focused on for itself. Once the principles of abstraction were understood, the only way they could be further developed was for the artist to move into language.

The artist is forced to go beyond visual abstraction and enter language the better to express an evolving ability to grasp a nonvisual world.

Sol LeWitt's statements about conceptual art are important. They are, however, general enough to include physical execution of ideas.

Joseph Kosuth's writings on conceptual art go further. Although still concerned with the visual presentation of ideas, he shows the essential nature of an idea to be removed from its physical execution. However, we must move further into a more precise definition of the nonvisual and formless nature of conceptual art.

True conceptual art moves beyond visual and physical execution of ideas no matter how abstract, beyond figurative and inanimate ideas: true conceptual art is found within the formless abstractions of language.

The development of art is the development of abstraction, and the development of abstraction is the movement into a formless language.

Language is the most formless means of expression. Its capacity to describe concepts without physical or visual references carries us into an advanced state of abstraction.

Conceptual art is concerned with the internal, intellectual nature of a concept. The more removed from external references, the stronger the concept.

The nature of concepts is antithetical to sensual reality. Conceptual art, when it is taken seriously, separates consciousness from the exterior world.

Concepts are, however, involved in our every day. A person in the street is a concept. We are always associating concepts with physical reality. Good conceptual art isolates the concept. Everyday thought is composed of both concepts and the relationship of concepts to the external world. There is a clear distinction between the two. Conceptual art makes this distinction.

Art that has visual aspects is concerned with references exterior to the concept as well as the concept. Good conceptual art is concerned with just the concept.

When a concept is made strong, that is, removed from external references, consciousness is cut off from the physical world. The awareness of consciousness removed from external objects is an awareness of energy, an awareness of being: the conscious mind aware of itself.

Consciousness of a person or an inanimate object is not the heart of consciousness. The heart of consciousness is a state of being which is formless.

That which is neither known nor unknown is without form. What is grasped is an awareness of being.

Being is the awareness of consciousness.

Reality is the formless heart of consciousness.

Consciousness focused into the present becomes conscious of itself.

At the moment consciousness becomes aware of itself it withdraws. Withdrawn from the concept, consciousness itself is the object.

Visual art presents an exterior point for the viewer to focus on. Good conceptual art leaves nothing. The reader is suspended, and it is from this vacuum that true consciousness emerges.

Normally consciousness is related to forms. Abstraction reduces that relationship. Non-visual abstraction reduces it further.

Language is made transparent by abstraction.

The heart of consciousness is shown by a transparent language.

A nonvisual abstraction such as "that which is neither known nor unknown" reduces logical thought totally and in this way allows intuitive insight to occur.

Thought without an object of thought is a formless concept.

The nature of the inspired state is shown in a formless concept.

When consciousness becomes aware of itself it becomes inspired.

The inherent potential of a universal concept is a means of expression whose physical existence does not compete or eclipse the subtle consciousness involved in comprehending a formless concept.

The concept of infinity is a very beautiful concept. Although unseen it provokes us to try to comprehend it, forcing us to enter the inspired state. The inspired state being that state in which reality is understood.

Formless and without content, the structure of a universal concept approaches the structure of the inspired state.

Nonvisual abstraction allows an appreciation of the inspired state that figurative art doesn't. It articulates the formless nature of the inspired state.

Nonvisual abstraction shows the inspired state to exist independently of the physical world. Physical objects may raise consciousness to the inspired state, but it exists independently of these objects.

Good conceptual art realizes the force of its own reality.

True conceptual art is aware of the force of the moment in which it exists. For example: *Ruptured* (Lawrence Weiner, 1969). It is persistent, unique, allusive, harmonious . . . (Robert Barry, 1970); meaning . . . = that which exists in the mind . . . (Joseph Kosuth, 1968); 1 = 1 and 1 + 1 = 2 is 1 2 . . . (Hanne Darboven, 1971).

In the best conceptual art only very pure concepts are used.

Passing toward the center of conceptual art, idea-oriented figurative writing, photography, and painting are on the remote periphery. Passing the visual realm of color and natural form we pass closer to the center. We have already passed idea-oriented performance and social and political writing. We have passed abstract color painting. We pass black and white abstract painting. Approaching the limit of visual abstraction we pass from three into two dimensions and into language descriptions of abstract physical objects and events. Passing beyond metaphor, beyond criticism, beyond art, beyond space and time, we come upon the formless abstractions of language. Infinite and formless what is presented is neither known nor unknown.

This is the center. This is the heart of conceptual art.

This text was published in *Artforum,* 22:6 (February 1994), pp. 60–61.

# my works for magazine pages: "a history of conceptual art"

dan graham

I became involved with the art system accidentally when friends of mine suggested that we open a gallery. In 1964, Richard Bellamy's Green Gallery was the most important avant-garde gallery and was just beginning to show people such as Judd, Morris and Flavin. Our gallery, John Daniels, gave Sol LeWitt a one-man show, as well as doing several group-shows which included all the "proto-Minimalist" artists whether they already showed at Green Gallery or not. We had also plans to have a one-man exhibition of Robert Smithson—then a young "Pop" artist. However, the gallery was forced to close due to bankruptcy at the end of the first season.

If we could have continued for another two years, with the aid of more capital, perhaps we might have succeeded. Nevertheless, the experience of managing a gallery was particularly valuable for me in the fact that it afforded the many conversations I had with Dan Flavin, Donald Judd, Jo Baer, Will Insley, Robert Smithson and others who, if they were not able to give works for thematic exhibitions, supported the gallery by recommending other artists and by dropping by to chat. In addition to a knowledge of current and historical art theory, some of these artists had an even greater interest, which I shared, in intellectual currents of that moment such as serial music, the French "New Novel" (Robbe-Grillet, Butor Pinget, etc.), and new scientific theories. It was possible to connect the philosophical implications of these ideas with the art that these "proto-Minimal" artists and more established artists such as Warhol, Johns, Stella, Lichtenstein and Oldenburg or dancers such as Yvonne Rainer or Simone Forti, were producing.

The fall after the gallery failed I began experimenting myself with art works which could be read as a reaction against the gallery experience, but also as a response to contradictions I discerned in gallery artists. While American "Pop" art of the early 1960s referred to the surrounding media world of cultural information as framework, "Minimal" art work of the middle through late 1960s would seem to be referring to the gallery's interior cube as the ultimate contextual frame of reference or support for the work. This reference was only compositional; in place of a compositional reading interior to the work, the gallery would compose the art's formal structure in relation to the gallery's interior architectural structure. That the work was equated to the architectural container tended to literalize it; both the architectural container and the work contained within were meant to be seen as non-illusionistic, neutral and objectively factual—that is, as simply material. The gallery functioned literally as part of the art. One artist's work of this period (although not always his later work) examined how specific, functional architectural elements of the gallery interior prescribed meaning and determined specific readings for the art defined within its architectural frame: Dan Flavin's fluorescent light installations.

Lighting—light fixtures—within the architectural setting of the gallery/museum are normally disregarded, or considered merely functional or minor interior decoration. As gallery space is meant to appear neutral, the lighting, which creates this neutrality as much as the white walls, and at the same time is used to highlight and center attention on the art work on the wall or floor, is kept inconspicuous. While the background in general makes the art works visible, the lighting literally makes the work visible.

The lighting system, within which the specific light fixtures of a gallery arrangement function, is both part of the gallery apparatus and part of the larger, existing (non-art) system of electric lighting in general use:

**I believe that the changing standard lighting system should support my idea within it.**
—Dan Flavin, "Some Remarks," *Artforum*, 1967.

Flavin's installations make use of this double functioning (inside and outside the gallery/art context) as well as the double connotation of lighting as minor decoration (interior decoration) and anonymously functional creator of the gallery's neutrality.

I believe that art is shedding its vaunted mystery for a common sense of keenly realized decoration. Symbolizing is dwindling—becoming slight. We are pressing downward toward no art—a mutual sense of psychologically indifferent decoration—a neutral pleasure of seeing known to everyone.

—Dan Flavin, "Some Remarks," *Artforum,* 1967.

His arrangements of light fixtures in a gallery space depend for significance, contextually, upon the function of the gallery, and the socially determined architectural use of electric lighting. Use of electric light is related to a specific time in history. Flavin has observed that when the existing system of electric lighting has ceased to exist, his art would no longer function. Being a series of standardized, replaceable units, which, in Flavin's words, "can be bought in any hardware store," his arrangements of fluorescent tubes within the interior or adjacent exterior architectural frame of the gallery exhibition-space function only in situation installation and upon completion of the exhibition cease to function artistically.

Perhaps I misread the implications of these works by suggesting a conscious intention to examine the relation of the value of art to the question of the gallery in which it was exhibited. I also felt that the "solution" which Marcel Duchamp had found to this problem of art's "value" was unsatisfactory.

In his "readymades," Duchamp brought objects which were not considered as art when placed outside the gallery, into the gallery to prove dialectically that it is in fact the gallery which gives the object its value and meaning. Instead of reducing gallery objects to the common level of the everyday object, this ironic gesture simply extended the reach of the gallery's exhibition territory. In bringing the "non-art" object into the gallery, Duchamp wished to place both the conventional function of the gallery to designate certain objects as "art" and to exclude others in apparent contradiction.

Essentially Duchamp attempted to question the aristocratic function of art and the art gallery as an institution. Because this question was only presented on a logical abstract level, his critique was itself immediately integrated back into the institutional system of gallery or museum art, becoming a kind of "idea" art. A further problem with Duchamp's analysis is the resolution of the contradiction between gallery art and art in relation to its social value based on an historical concept; the condition of art is seen as neither social or as subject to external social change. By contrast, Flavin's fluorescent light pieces are not merely *a priori* philosophical idealizations, but have concrete relations to specific details of the architectural arrangement of the gallery, details which produce meaning.

In addition, Duchamp saw the problem of value and meaning in art as a simple binary opposition, inside the gallery or outside in the world. He failed to link this opposition of art and so-called "non-art" to more ambiguous phenomena such as the reproduction of the art object by the media, which was mediated upon by the critic Walter Benjamin in the 1930s and was even earlier an important aspect of Constructivist art.

Through the actual experience of running a gallery, I learned that if a work of art wasn't written about and reproduced in a magazine it would have difficulty attaining the status of "art." It seemed that in order to be defined as having value, that is as "art," a work had only to be exhibited in a gallery and then to be written about and reproduced as a photograph in an art magazine. Then this record of the no longer extant installation, along with more accretions of information after the fact, became the basis for its fame, and to a large extent, its economic value.

From one perspective, the art object can be analyzed as inseparably connected to the institution of the gallery, or museum; but from another perspective it can be seen as having a certain independence, as it belongs also to the general cultural framework which the magazine is a part of. Magazines specialize in a way which replicates other social and economic divisions. Any magazine, no matter how generalized, caters to a certain market or a specific audience in a particular field. All art magazines are directed to people who are involved in the art world professionally in one way or another. Furthermore, the art magazine itself is supported by advertisements which, with one or two exceptions, come from art galleries that are presenting exhibitions. It follows that in some way the advertisers have to be taken care of in that their shows have to be reviewed and made a matter of record in the magazine. Thus these shows and works are guaranteed some kind of value and can be sold on the market as "art." The fact that sales do take place yields enough money for the gallery to purchase more advertisements in art magazines and to sustain the art system in general.

Art magazines ultimately depend upon art galleries for their economic support, just as the work shown in galleries depends on photographic reproduction for its value in the media. Magazines determine a place or are a frame of reference both outside and inside. Magazines specialize in a "field" in a way which replicates other social and economic divisions—for instance, the specialized "world" of art and artists termed the "art" world. Each magazine, no matter how generalized, always caters to a certain market or a certain audience in a certain field; *Sports Illustrated* caters to those who are interested in sports, the *American Legion* magazine caters to members of the American Legions. All art magazines cater to people who professionally or institutionally are involved in the art world—either as artists, dealers, collectors, connoisseurs, writers, they all have a professional interest. And the art magazine itself is supported by advertisements.

If "Minimal" art took its meaning from the notion that the gallery is an objective support, by comparison "Pop" art took its meaning from the surrounding media-world of images. "Pop" art also made an ironic comment about popular culture to itself. What "Pop" pointed out was that the information media, such as magazines, could be used dialectically with the art system. That is, a work could function in terms of both the art language and the popular language of the media at the same time, commenting upon and placing in perspective the assumptions of each. I designed works for magazine pages which would both be self-defined and would relate, through their context, to the surrounding information on the other printed pages. (. . .)

I wanted to make a "Pop" art which was more literally disposable (an idea which was alluded to in Warhol's idea of replacing "quality" for "quantity," the logic of a consumer society). I wanted to make an art-form which could not be reproduced or exhibited in a gallery/ museum, and I wanted to make a further reduction of the "Minimal" object to a not necessarily aesthetic two-dimensional form (which was not painting or drawing): printed matter which is mass-reproduced and mass-disposable information. Putting it in magazine pages meant that it also could be "read" in juxtaposition to the usual reproduction art, art criticism, reviews, reproductions in the rest of the magazine and form a critique of the magazine (in relation to the gallery structure).

Magazines have issues which appear at regular time intervals; a magazine's contents continuously change to reflect present-time currency: magazines deal with curent events. While gallery art is defined by its enclosure as "timeless," magazines presuppose a notion of present-time (timeliness) which only has value as it is current, each successive issue defining "new" or "up-to-date" in terms of the representative moment. However, the notion of news is not merely dependent upon the internal institution, but equally upon the institutions which generate its news content and finance its existence through the purchasing of advertisements. For the art magazine, it is the art gallery whose definition of "Art" and whose advertisements uphold the existence of the art magazine.

This text first appeared in Gary Dufour, *Dan Graham,* exh. cat. (Perth: The Art Gallery of Western Australia, 1985), pp. 8–13.

# on conceptual art
## adrian piper

I turned to language (typescript, maps, audio tapes, etc.) in the 1960s because I wanted to explore objects that can refer both to concepts and ideas beyond themselves and their standard functions, as well as to themselves; objects that both refer to abstract ideas that situate those very objects in new conceptual and spatiotemporal matrices, and also draw attention to the spatiotemporal matrices in which they're embedded. Also, with language I could construct works in thought that would have been impossibly expensive and time consuming to construct in physical materials (see "Flying" for more of this). My earliest conceptual pieces were very derivative of Sol LeWitt's work. Sol's sensibility in general has influenced me enormously. I see less connection with other conceptual artists working at that time. For me my earliest conceptual work succeeded insofar as it illuminated the contrast between abstract atemporality and the indexical, self-referential present. All the *Concrete Space-Time-Infinity Pieces* played with the idea of the indexical present, and it's continued to be a very central preoccupation of my work. The work failed when the ideas were too concretely involved and complex. At the level of abstraction, freewheeling conceptual idiosyncrasy works only when it's simple and pure. Becoming a working philosopher has helped me purify and simplify the conceptual presentation of my artwork. The main issues and preoccupations of my work have become increasingly focused on political content, specifically racism, racial stereotyping, and xenophobia. This is one direct consequence of having chosen to work with materials, that is, language and conceptual symbols, that can refer to content beyond themselves: It forces a choice of content, and therefore a recognition of what content is most pressingly important. And the indexical present has provided the major strategy of my work, which is direct, immediate, and confrontational. Racism is not an abstract, distanced issue out there that only affects all those unfortunate other people. Racism begins with you and me, here and now, and consists in our tendency to try to eradicate each other's singularity through stereotyped conceptualization.

This text was first published in *Flash Art,* 143 (November-December 1988), p. 115.

# statement
## robert barry

If there was anything important about conceptual art? If there was one thing? It was the way the work questioned the entire system. It really dug deep and revealed the relation between art and the viewer. What being an artist was about, and what conceptual art was about, was testing the limits of one's perception, pushing it as far as possible, to the point of invisibility. I think conceptual art was the end of modern art. I think modern art was going out on a limb and then cutting off the limb to see what would happen.

This statement was published in *Flash Art,* 143 (November-December 1988), p. 115.

# yes, difference again: what history plays the first time around as tragedy, it repeats as farce
victor burgin

In the late 1960s, "Conceptual Art"—a heterogeneous phenomenon—emerged both as a new chapter in the old story of bad relations between modernism and the "historical avant-garde" (Dada, surrealism, 1920s Soviet art, and so on) and, contradictorily, the termina stage of that same modernist progress towards complete self-reference. On the one hand (in common with the historical avant-garde) most conceptualist works represented a rejection of the commodity form of art, of the confinement of art within the museum (its separation from everyday life), and of an identity defined by a style. On the other hand the most celebrated conceptualist (and stylist) of the period, Joseph Kosuth, concluded his manifesto "Art After Philosophy" (*Studio International,* October 1969) with: "Art's only claim is for art. Art is the definition of art." Kosuth subsequently joined the editorial board of *Art-Language*—in appearance a British journal of analytic philosophy, devoted to the dissection of statements about art. *Art-Language* differed from other philosophical journals, however, in that the articles it contained were written not by professional philosophers but by artists—who in using the journal to conduct internal doctrinal disputes in public, and to launch denunciations and excommunications, behaved, again, much in the manner of the avant-gardes of the 1920s and '30s.

In the early 1970s, in response to an *Art-Language* attack, I put my own disagreement with what I saw as their hermetic avant-gardism in a short essay ("In Reply," *Art-Language,* Summer 1972). I argued: "No art activity is to be understood apart from the codes and practices of the society which contains it; art in *use* is bracketed ineluctably within ideology." The terms "code," "practice," "ideology," signal the presence of a different emerging framework for visual art in the early 1970s. In Europe, conceptualism coincided with that more fundamental critique of commodity society for which the 1968 "Events of May" now serve as an emblematic moment. One subsequent path of European conceptualism was into an involvement with the transformations of "left" cultural theory in the wake of 1968. In common with several other British artists and film-makers (for example, Mary Kelly, Laura Mulvey and Peter Wollen) my work became a "working through" of political and theoretical positions informed at first by Althusserian Marxism and Barthesian semiotics, but which were quickly brought into conjunction with feminism and psychoanalysis. It was under the impact of feminism in particular that, in the mid-1970s, there was a move away from the "knowing" discourse of a Marxist class-political analysis towards forms of work which were, as Peter Wollen put it, "interjected into the place *of* which questions are asked, rather than that *from* which questions are asked." This work focused particularly on the ideological construction of the individual *subject* of social processes. In 1984 some of this work was exhibited in New York as part of the New Museum exhibition "Difference: On Representation and Sexuality."

In the early 1980s, one source of the great hostility which met the work in the "Difference" show—from almost all cultural political positions represented in New York—was its "conceptualist" appearance. . ."Not photographs and text *again,*" groaned one (leftist) critic. I asked him if he ever complained, "Not moving images and sound again," when viewing films. For many "political conceptualists" the machine-printed photograph and the typewritten text had offered, for a period, a "zero degree" of style in which authorial expression could be subsumed to issues of content. In time, inevitably, this strategy itself became a recognizable style. To then continue to work in a style which had become *dépassé* was to emphasize that style was no longer a concern. What was at issue in the work was not a transient *aesthetic* form but a long-established *semiotic* form—text/image—encountered in most aspects of the everyday environment. The *work* of such "works of art" was upon systems of representations which were not confined within the institutions and practices of "art." On that opening night at the New Museum it was my biggest surprise of the evening that the futility of applying *traditional* formalist and expressive criteria to such works—taken for granted in London—was not understood in New York, even by the "left." (The "difficulty" of the work was also disliked. What seemed to be valued most on the New York art left was a clear political "statement"—specific *indictments* were best—accomplished with as much visual flourish as could be mustered.) Apart from attracting hostility from the left, the low-key, *démodé,* appearance of most of the "Difference" work was also anathema to enthusiasts of the then fashionable neo-expressionism. The renaissance of conservative values towards the close of the 1970s had produced a New Right and a "New Spirit in Painting," "new object" sculpture, and "neo-geo" followed. Today, "neo-conceptualism" is in fashion. What is "new" about this latest work, however—when compared with the conceptualism of the 1960s and '70s—is precisely what makes it the *same* as the stylistic revivals which immediately preceded it. Nothing has changed between neo-expressionism and neo-conceptualism, except *appearances*—their position with respect to the various economic and ideological apparatuses of art is the same. This is to observe that *history* has been evacuated from these purloined forms. "Art history" is not *just* a set of coffee-table volumes from Rizzoli, but this is precisely what these stylistic revivals would have us believe. Conceptual art, having spent its critical momentum, had (in Shklovsky's image) completed its "journey from poetry to prose"; today's neo-conceptualism has picked up the inert mass and carried it further—to a point where historical differences are flattened, a point of historical *indifference,* the terminal point of *platitude.* The original conceptual art is a failed avant-garde. Historians will not be surprised to find, amongst the ruins of its utopian program, the desire to resist commodification and assimilation to a history of styles. The "new" conceptualism is the mirror-image of the old—*nothing but* commodity, *nothing but* style. We once again have occasion to observe, "What history plays the first time around as tragedy, it reappears as farce." (. . .)

This statement was published in *Flash Art,* 143 (November-December 1988), p. 115.

# working with shadows, working with words

## deke dusinberre, seth siegelaub, daniel buren, and michel claura

Deke Dusinberre: Would you want to start by talking about personal origin, personal moments of inspiration for art practice?

Seth Siegelaub: No. I would want to talk about the larger political context within which I grew up. The context for me during my early working life in the United States was the Vietnam War, it was an important factor in my growing up. Whether it was an important factor in the art world as such remains to be seen.

D.D.: So you suggest we start from those social and political points?

S.S.: Well, that to me, in the United States, was a very important background for what was going on in the art world. It was probably so in varying degrees for Larry Poons and everybody else too, but I think it was particularly critical for the kind of art that we're talking about.

Daniel Buren: I think it's true of all people of my generation. From the time that I was seventeen or eighteen with the Korean War and then after that the Algerian War, there has been a succession of violent and controversial events which have formed the central point for daily actions and thoughts in France. This happened from my youth right through to its peak which, although different, was still political; that is, the events which led up to May '68. So for people of my generation, even if it has not been totally conscious, I think a lot of our way of thinking, our attitudes, reactions, etc., have been framed by those successive colonial wars.

D.D.: Would you go so far as to make a direct relationship between that cultural/political environment and an art practice such as Conceptual Art?

D.B.: I am sure it is important although I would not draw a direct line. Personally, I was both very engaged and skeptical about the drawing of that kind of engagement into the production of art. I was strongly critical of those contemporaries of mine in France who brought into art a formal concern with these sorts of problems. For the most part their work consisted of large figurative paintings which described an attitude to the events we have been mentioning. My dissatisfaction with the idea of taking an artwork as a flag for a certain kind of political engagement was that in political terms such a gesture was meaningless. However, there is a strong relation with what I was able to do at the time, if we take into account the kind of consciousness we are talking about. I guess that the bridge was, and this is something which I shared with other people in other places, the question that if one was concerned with the political situation, what would it mean to take the art world itself as a political problem? Is that micro-system a total revelation or reverberation of the general system? If it is not, where does the weight of the political system make itself felt within the art world? I think producers from different cultures and different countries, and I'm thinking particularly of America, shared this total rejection of a practice which put political concern into "art shapes." Up until then that had been the only way to deal with issues of this kind. Focusing on something which seemed to have little or nothing to do with this concern allowed us to question where politics was actually feeding into the production of art, its reception, its structure and its context. I guess that, vaguely, under the stupid name of Conceptual Art, a certain Sixties sensibility did criss-cross between Europe and America. Obviously there were different cultural emphases, but the connections were there.

S.S.: You have to use the term politics in two ways. Daniel is alluding to this although I don't think we've made it quite clear yet. There is "political" in the superficial sense in which one speaks of the traditional left/right oppositions of social forces, and "political" in the deeper sense which refers to a conscious questioning of what is going on around you, not just in the sense of left/right or imperialist/anti-imperialist, but in terms of the kind of relationships that exist between people, between people and things, between people and institutions. This latter sense calls up in art, as in any other context, a whole range of issues. That moment in the late Sixties, particularly in the United States in any case, was very full of these kinds of questions.

They were *l'air du temps* you might say. A lot of people, even those doing traditional things like Pop Art, were talking about such relationships. The Vietnam War brought into question a whole range of things—the traditional role of the United States, or maybe of France for Daniel and Michel, the role of imperialist power, the wider under standing of world relationships. This also nourished the traditional "art attitude" which, at least as it has been presented in the twentieth century, is one of contestation, too. But that would be the false route: that the artist would naturally be against a power structure is the most superficial kind of trap, and is one that particularly concerns Daniel. As I say, the deeper aspects of this questioning of relationships were of concern to many artists, not just Conceptualists, although Conceptualism was perhaps able to attack these problems more frontally than painting could ever do, since it took too much for granted in its very nature.

Michel Claura: How and when would you make the connection between the political surroundings and the fact that at that time people created, so to speak, a new, dematerialized form of art? You described the context, you described the fact that artists were concerned with that context and politically involved against what was going on, but to what extent is that reflected by this move towards a non-object based form of art work?

S.S.: It is not a one-to-one relationship, but there are certain underlying links. For example, the sort of question that could conceivably have been posed at that time was: What could be the connection between a subject like democracy and a kind of art? With reference to this, there is certainly something which is very dear to me about materiality. The process of making a work of art which, although not necessarily less *material,* certainly, in a crude sense, costs less, opens up the possibility of who can make it. It also has to do with how it can be seen, how it can be shown, and a lot of other things which go with that.

D.B.: It was difficult not to be affected by the political situation however hard you tried to avoid it. I think one of the things which links a lot of the people who came to prominence in the mid to late Sixties, quite apart from any formal distinction that could be made, is an economic restriction which is seen in the use of poor materials, of no materials at all, in exhibition outside the gallery, and so on. Remember also that in economic terms those were boom years. It wasn't that artists were simply against the idea of money, they were working in an atmosphere in which one found the widely held belief that the West was set for a future of permanent economic growth. 1968 was the first point at which people realized that this was not true and that we were running towards catastrophe. Unfortunately that has been true of most of the time between then and today. The interesting thing in terms of the art world is that there was a group of people at that time, all of whom were working in a way which had almost nothing to do with aesthetics and which concerned itself with the question of how one can make something from nothing. There were people working with shadows—no cost; people working with words—no cost; people working with bits of wood found lying in the street or hedgerows—no cost; etc., etc. Of course, and perhaps this is something we should discuss elsewhere, a lot of this stuff became chic and expensive, stylish and academic. But if you take it as the emergence of a connection between the sensibilities of people who, in most cases, did not at that time know each other, it is very interesting to see it in terms of the economy of means.

S.S.: You wouldn't want to rush too quickly to say that that was democracy, but that seemed to me at the time to be an important factor. You can say that of all art movements when they're young—putting bits of wood together in Paris in 1910 was new, too—but I think we're talking about something quite, quite different in the late Sixties.

D.B.: I would see that in a way as being in the very standard tradition of the avant-garde. This kind of total contradiction between a society which believed that all was possible, that progress would continue for ever, and a group of artists, not necessarily homogeneous or with shared interests, working on things which were of no cost, usually with no technique, no technology, very fugitive, more or less also against possession, even if that did turn into bullshit for most of them. But if you see the impulse and the opposition it's interesting, it is in the tradition of the avant-garde, it's a reaction against society as a whole . . .

S.S.: . . . as opposed to just a form of art. You could say that a lot of avant-gardisms have been directed at their immediate predecessors and have developed in relation to, antithesis or contravention of them. Here was something which didn't have that quality, it dealt with something else. I suppose in terms of generations, the people who came immediately before would be Carl Andre and, as a borderline case, Sol LeWitt: minimal sculptors anyway. Conceptualism wasn't developed in opposition to that, and, in fact, there are a lot of people who fall just on the line between the two. Conceptualism was a much more fundamental calling into question of things. That's what is so interesting about it and is probably why we're having this conversation.

D.B.: We also know that, historically, attacking the object, attempting to escape from it, is a twentieth-century phenomenon. It comes in cycles and was not new in the Sixties. However, as things get older they can get more radical, and even though it may have been working on familiar principles it was, for a moment, a more radical questioning of the object than anything which had gone before. From a personal point of view, it led to a lot of suspicion. I wrote at the time that although the impulse seemed a good and interesting one, we should be careful not to withdraw the object simply because the object itself was under question. In other words, I was suspicious of the term Conceptual Art because it was easy to place under its umbrella a lot of objects which were much less interesting than a painting. Also because I thought then, and still think, that if the problem of the object is one of the most interesting to challenge, you don't solve that problem by doing non-object work. The idea that something was more interesting simply because there was nothing to see was a ridiculous one, but was dangerous because even if it wasn't what most of the artists thought, it was the notion adopted by many observers at the time. Many of the people who championed that view eventually turned back to things which had nothing to do with it. Force of economic obligation and the frustration of the public and the art world have had something to do with this. They are not the only reasons, but they did partly open the door for the production of the most reactionary art that we have seen over the past ten years. I am sure that in a few years' time the art of this period will appear as some of the least interesting and most reactionary of the entire century.

D.D.: Can you be more specific about the kind of art you mean?

D.B.: During the past decade we have seen, more or less under the term postmodernism, the production and acceptance of something which is diametrically opposed, even in ideological terms, to the spirit of the mid-Sixties. This is not to say that the mid-Sixties were beautiful, this is bad; I'm more interested personally in what happened in the mid-Sixties, but that's beside the point. What is objective, and not personal, is to say that these two movements are radically separate. What one, with all its mistakes and tentativeness, was trying to say, the other is opposing very loudly, very brilliantly. Expressionistic painting, reactionary sculpture, and so on. Even though the term Conceptual Art is itself ridiculous, it refers to something important. What these people were reacting against was a caricature of Conceptual Art, and what they accomplished in doing so was the erasure of 70 years of art. We have seen the return of the nineteenth-century *pompiers* in the production of a certain type of painting today—Schnabel, Clemente, Lupertz, I could go on, not forgetting Kiefer. They show an evident step back, not only compared to Conceptualism, but 70 years of art.

S.S.: It's also interesting to note not just the painters but the immediate art world environment within which they operate. It has changed so dramatically, particularly for me as someone who has not lived the last twenty years in the art world. It has changed in part due to frustrations which may have been potential rather than real, but which existed in the kind of art we started to talk about at the beginning. But also, the nature of the art world in reference to the real world has changed. The art that is produced within it connects to money, to business, to fashion, to the hype which characterizes a lot of the advanced capitalist culture today.

The relationship is very, very close. There is a very high turnover in every sense of the word, emotionally, artistically, and economically. So the art world has changed dramatically and with that change it has brought with it a certain kind of art, or it has searched for a kind of art which responds to that kind of hype shit. I'm sure that Conceptual Art corresponds to a certain moment within the art world too, a certain kind of art showing, or lack of it, particularly.

D.B.: We started by saying that everyone was concerned in their own place with these problems. This was true in a personal sense, but it was also true that this was forced upon everyone. Personally, today I have the same kinds of commitments. They are not perhaps so brilliant but they are no worse than they were. What I see, though, is that this commitment is no longer part of the context, and when you dare to say the sort of thing which comes naturally to me about connections which exist between what is happening in the world and what is happening in the art world, you almost look like a zombie. Few people will ever bother to enter into discussion, preferring to think, even if it is not true, that this is an old story all washed up. I'm not talking about myself and a situation in which someone can say to me, "Look, you said that twenty years ago, forget it." People of all ages who speak of these things from an interesting and new perspective have a very hard time getting themselves understood or even followed. It will change again no doubt, but the present situation I find astonishing.

S.S.: All art movements since the late nineteenth century have started with a group of people. It is impossible to promote one great artist. Once they have been established by Kahn-weiler or Castelli or Betty Parsons it is possible for the public to perceive the personality of each individual artist. This process of individualization of each artist's *troc* becomes more and more the focus of art at the expense of exactly these kinds of social determinants which are not one to one. The mechanisms of art promotion do everything to try and avoid the context we are trying to understand here, at the expense of great artists. The business of art history is the valorizing of individual artists and the selling of them. Even looking at the problem is difficult because it is so obfuscated and blurred. No-one wants to hear that there were fifty people thinking about this kind of thing in the Sixties, they just want to know who the fucking genius was and who they're going to make money with. The kind of questions we are considering are asked by some people of nineteenth-century painting, but to do the same for the period in which we live is very difficult. Everything works against the kind of analysis which attempts to find a commonality.

D.B.: We can go further. This kind of thing, whether it is a fantasy, degenerate, or what-ever, did provoke and create a new style. Seth was able to do a show which was a catalogue; it was possible to put on a show simultaneously in Paris, London, New York and New Mexico;

it was possible to do a show in a small village. Today, the door has been opened to a new academicism within curatorship. I do not think all that is unconnected to the fact that one can now think that a possible use for the Gare d'Orsay is as museum. In the Sixties there was an explosion: we could show anywhere, and anyone could show. This could be ridiculous, but it was also part of the spirit: everyone was an artist, or could be. Today there is little enthusiasm for the stimulation of production, but a huge enthusiasm for the creation of museums. This increase in the number of art centers is one of the legacies of that period, and it implies a change in the audience, since such centers would not exist without people to attend. People operating in the wider context understood better what to do with those ideas than the artists did. This is a paradox which affects what I do today since as an artist you come *after* the proposal of a context. I think this is extremely funny, interesting, tricky and dangerous. The effort which this requires from architects, keepers, curators, directors, collectors takes place in a system which has no common measure with the art world of twenty years ago.

M.C.: Is the question not, in fact, whether Conceptual Art ever existed? Thinking of the fact, for instance, that, perhaps with one or maybe two exceptions, I cannot remember any artist ever accepting himself to be a conceptual artist? Am I right?

S.S.: I think Joseph (Kosuth) did.

M.C.: He's the only one to my knowledge. Nonetheless, people have been talking about Conceptual Art for quite a while, including a period of a few years in which they spoke of it as a sort of threat. To some extent because of the combination that existed at the time, which opened up more freedom for exhibitions, I just wonder whether it was because of this that art suddenly became so fashionable. When you say that it opened up this variety of types of exhibition—do it anywhere, by yourself, whenever—does this not have a lot to do with the fact that art has become a real thing in economic terms? It would be paradoxical if, because of something which never existed, one saw the emergence of art as reactionary as you describe, but there is another way of demonstrating that conceptual art never existed: it has never achieved power, even within the art world.

D.B.: The power has been taken from the ends of the artist and transferred to the ends of the curator, museum director, magazine editor, or whoever. There is one example of this which I like because it is so extraordinary. After 1967 even people with totally antagonistic works were able, with somebody's help or on their own, to show anywhere. It was interesting and was difficult and it was totally for a little élite—a bakery is a vitrine for an exhibition, the apartment of a friend is a beautiful place to show, etc. All of this was put by and almost forgotten as stupidity, or naiveté. During the Seventies things gradually moved back to the museums, and galleries became more and more important. All of a sudden in 1986 you have a museum by itself which finds a way to get money and prestige to put on the exhibition "Chambres d'Amis." And what is that exhibition? It isn't one artist in the museum, or two. *Seventy* artists show their work in the private houses of seventy people in the city of Ghent. In '67–68, several artists with no commitment say, "We cannot find a gallery, let's show outside." Twenty years later, the director of a museum makes the ludicrous decision that to show in a private house is more public than to show in a museum (I don't know exactly what that means, but it was stated in the catalogue), he persuades seventy artists, even those of my generation who more or less invented the idea to show in these houses, and seven months later is given the biggest award to a director for the concept of his exhibition!

D.D.: Twenty years ago, when people showed in those contexts, what was the relation between the art they showed and the space they used, and was it the same as that which obtained in Ghent?

D.B.: Each of the people in Ghent was, by force, obliged to do something in relation to that situation, and in that, of course, I included the possibility that the relationship could be antagonistic. But no one was doing any oil painting and using the bakery as a vitrine. Everything they did was done for a coherent reason; it wasn't interesting or chic.

S.S.: Another difference is that in this case it is the museum director who is, in effect, the major figure, the artist if you like. Twenty years ago it wasn't like that.

D.B.: Everything you did as an organizer was done more or less through a process of osmosis, but don't forget that you are a perfect example of what is now the cliché. Everyone really has copied you in the worst way, which is to be the chief and the artist of the show.

S.S.: It was my lack of economic means and *l'air du temps* which created the relationship that existed between the kind of shows I did and the artists with whom I was involved. It was an attempt to get away from the gallery because my feeling at the time, as it is now in the case of publishing, is that a space becomes sacralized. The economics of the situation is such that you need to fill a space with eight or ten shows a year, and it is inconceivable that you can do that and remain interested in all of the work you show. You didn't run a gallery, the gallery ran you; it was just another form of alienated work experience. The gallery came to determine the art to the extent that painters would paint paintings to fit the walls of their dealer. I simply took the responsibility of working with the artists whose work was around and bubbling up. Osmosis is probably the best way of describing what went on.

D.D.: Do you three think, then, that there was such a thing as the Conceptual Art movement or was it a fiction?

S.S.: I think all art movements are fictions in that sense. They are promotional and, ultimately, economic devices. It's perfectly normal for a group of people to get together in order to work, discuss and help each other, whether to raise crops in 2000 B.C. or to make art in 1988, but the art world refers to these things as movements for purely economic reasons. It's something that I think Newman referred to as the hardening of the categories; the world just has to have these little boxes, and I hate them. I hate them. It is just an easy way of describing something so that you don't have to deal with it.

D.B.: And I think that because most of the people at that time were concerned with these issues it was difficult for them to accept this kind of labeling. All recent movements, from Pop Art onwards, have an image. By contrast, the success of a word like conceptualism lies in the total depreciation of the products which lie behind it.

S.S.: The other thing about categories is that they prevent you from seeing the reality. They give you the impression that each generation has one thing going on and that that's all that's happening, they prevent you from looking. It's a formalist and ultimately reactionary way to view the world.

D.B.: Even though the exhibitions at the time drew on a group of forty, fifty or sixty artists, I am sure that history will see conceptualism in terms of the work of four or five artists who work in a particular way.

S.S.: One of the reasons there is an interest in this kind of art is that economically it has not been successful in the way that other art has and in the way that its reputation might suggest. There is, therefore, a romantic side to its image: that of the poor artist.

D.D.: When did this fictional movement cease even to be a fiction? When did it lose steam?

D.B.: In a personal sense it decayed very quickly. The first period was '65–70, and then in the Seventies there were a lot of things which followed on. We couldn't call that a second generation, but there were people who were just too young who were influenced by our generation. As a fashion it carried on until the late Seventies, and even after that it was still being used as a recommendation, and this big wave of painting and sculpture rose up from those who stupidly thought we had tried to erase these things from the planet. The move against Conceptualism started earlier though. Conceptualism featured strongly in the 1969 Prospekt alongside Arte Povera and some Minimalism, and this was followed by "When Attitudes Become Form," and a number of other shows. By 1972 or '73, however, Prospekt was full of painting, a gesture which collapsed totally because the general mood was still for questioning art, questioning objects. In 1980, with a very different kind of product, painting came back into consideration.

S.S.: A very important facet of this work was that if you wanted to show it you had to deal with these people. It was never a question of just sending something somewhere. The way the economics worked out, it was cheaper to send the artist than to send the work.

M.C.: That is also where Conceptual Art became human. People had to be on the spot, but quite often they were there just to be around.

D.B.: Speaking of the romantic aspect of things, people saw no direct relationship between having a show and selling something. It was absolutely not wrong, not something to feel guilty about, if you had a show and sold nothing at all. It was not wrong to sell either. Traveling meant that it was about human relations. Don't forget the museums deal with objects and in those terms they are pretty good. They know how to classify a thing, how much it weighs, how much it costs, but when you invite some*body*, all these things are erased, they have no idea how to proceed.

This discussion appeared in *Art Monthly,* no. 12 (December 1988–January 1989), pp. 3–6.

# we aimed to be amateurs
## art & language

The fact that this event has been divided into old folks and young suggests that Conceptual Art has been identified and processed if only in a working sense. We wish to resist this suggestion by pointing out some of the difficulties entailed. Actually, what we want to resist is the thought that Conceptual Art is or was a readily recognized and ordered artistic style which remains inviolate in the hands of some purists and which has been variously abandoned or aetiolated by others like ourselves. And I want to suggest that one of the implications of this is that the renovated form of Conceptual Art is no more than a nostalgic husk; a look; text and various neo-neo-Dada bits and pieces.

What is quite interesting about some old Conceptual Art is its paradoxical relationship with the well-policed and the professional. I'd argue that there exists some set of inverse relations between what might be called the prevailing (historical) self-images of Conceptual Art and conceptual artists, and what might be called its vividness, or aesthetic effectiveness. Some conceptual artists, for example, radically appropriated some of the strange appurtenances of another professionalism like lawyers', managers' and therapists': suits. These were often inexpert borrowings, indeed so callow as to reduce the resulting appearance to no more than an adolescent posture—an ironical spectacle, perhaps. Some continued (and continue) this in their more conspicuous adult life. It is and was a quick way to the collector's and curator's heart: *his* world becomes coextensive with the internal dialogue of the artist. Of course there was a lot of art which was called "conceptual" which was simply compulsive and obsessive and which more or less automatically eschewed such an executive-impersonating professionalism. (But the "cold" professional and the compulsive obsessive are not always unadjacent in the culture of Conceptual Art.) What I'm trying to say is that notwithstanding its "professionalized" later self-image (and perhaps because of its early efforts which were often rather sad and aspiring), old Conceptual Art is vivid in virtue of its cognitive and cultural character as displaced and exiled, unable-to-be-professional-really.

This is not unconnected to the fact that, in general, it was practiced—and certainly animated—by relatively young people. This is not a claim for conceptual art as youth culture at all. It is an observation that "early" Conceptual Art, in its culturally radical, relatively untransformed form, is more or less *essentially* the work of people who saw themselves as in process. That is to say, people with a high degree of mobility, low security (and a relatively low perceived need for security), high discursivity, amenability to dialogical situatedness, possessed of a relatively meager economic base; fairly active in their efforts to extricate themselves from unwanted structurally-ordered determinations, and so on. These are, perhaps, additional conditions which might separate Professor Rorty's "strong poets" from Professor McIntyre's "managers and therapists" . . . or perhaps a way of pointing the way to such a separation. It would be pleasant, for example, if we could extract the strong poet from the patronage of the university: strong (adolescent) poets . . . as inept and aspiring adolescent managers and therapists perhaps.

In highly volatile cultural circumstances, the cost of failure and similar risk is often perceived to be bearable, while there is relatively little pressure to produce objects of a negotiably middle-sized dry sort. And for many conceptual artists there was certainly little real pressure to act with any mechanical consistency concerning the formal appearance of any of their "products" which eventually found themselves in the public domain. This is not the apotheosis of youth culture. It is merely that being young tends to coincide with these conditions being present. What is clear is that Conceptual Art was *vivid* insofar as it approached the condition of what might be thought of as an exotic variant of *amateur* art activity. This does not mean "amateur" in the sense of subservient to the grand style *passé,* nor does it mean "primitive" in the sense of untutored or somehow "naive." This later sense is, however, important in some way or at some point—as may be clear later.

And continuing on the *via negativa,* I do not use "amateur" in the sense of a gentleman amateur's lofty and privately-funded disinterest. And while I have no sense of Jamesian clarity as to how this amateur might finally be specified, I do mean to suggest someone who signs up for the game without any guarantees as to where it will end—what the result will be—and, for that matter, without being sure where and when it began. This is not so much a world of collaborative and self-abnegating security (or hiding), so much as one of openness and inquisitiveness and contingency concerning one's self-description—an openness which runs the risk of being composed out-of-cultural-character. It is such that the materials upon which ingenuity is turned are acquired without shame or a sense of posterity, image or face. (. . .)

Conceptual Art might for the moment be regarded as more or less non-pictorial, more or less physically or formally reduced post-Minimal art, which was exhibited (called "New Art" or something) between about 1968 and 1974, and which enjoyed avant-garde pre-eminence at that time.

But many kinds of work are captured by this gloss. There are, for example, various incarnations of what might be called Minimal-ish, or ultra-minimal-ish *mad* art. This obsessive-compulsive iterative stuff (iterative on the page or panel, or iterative in a matrix of time and place) is in its discursive poverty, its fraudulently aesthetic (and essentially Modernist) silence, always "mature." It is work without internal or discursive complexity, work whose "development" is transacted in predicates which exclude or sidestep a sense of "ordinary" connected human political development. To describe this work as "callow" would be more or less a waste of time as it is simply callow (non-complex and relatively undifferentiated, relatively autonomous) culture. There was also another species of "mad" art. It's possessed of a little more internal complexity than the former sort. This is a variety exemplified by Broodthaers—in his role as the presumed heir to that other great proto-conceptualist, René Magritte. What Broodthaers did was to orchestrate a quasi-literal world—a world of socio-personal props. Very Belgian, a bit jokey, and reliant on the power of the literal object to fire meaning and desire. Deleuzean machines, perhaps. There is no "no" among the possible predicates which these flimsy machines might provoke or bear. This is one of the variants in the curatorial (indeed the highly managerial) spectacle of mad art: the corollary of the fraudulently ascetic compulsive-obsessive. It is art which is, again, always "mature." The suggestion that this or that example of work is somehow immature or inchoate is more or less uninformative. (. . .)

I guess—or hope—that I'm staggering towards something a bit more positive or constructive than the remark that Conceptual Art was a mess, not something "identifiable" like Cubism . . . I am not suggesting that the late 1960s and early 1970s are immune to retrodiction, but rather that what is interesting about (some) Conceptual Art (and what makes Conceptual Art interesting) is that it is radically incomplete.

This means that all or most claims that Conceptual Art can be isolated as some sort of discrete historical well-formed epoch are false unless severely limited *and* apparently almost paradoxical, that any attempt to invest the use of certain textual-type materials associated with certain artists who became (a bit) prominent in the late 1960s and early 1970s with some sort of present cultural pre-eminence—resisted only by reactionaries—is doomed to bathos and failure.

So what is to be extracted from this? Perhaps something like the following. Conceptual Art does not correspond *tout court* to some sort of linguistic turn in artistic practice. It does represent an appropriation of certain dialogic and discursive mechanisms by artists who sought thereby critically to empower themselves and others, and to that limited extent it represents a linguistic turn. But Conceptual Art did not reduce (or attempt to reduce) the pictorial to the linguistic (or textual). The point is, rather, that the gaps and connections, the lemmas and absurdities between the pictorial and the textual, are spaces in which much cultural aggravation was and is possible. The eruption of the text into the cultural and historical space of the picture or the painting is an exemplary moment. A dialogic—and consequently more or less linguistic—sense of work and action provides a considerable critical purchase upon the prevailing stereotypes of artistic personality and practice, and even upon what is to count as artistic practice in a social context. And these considerations bear quite powerfully upon what it is to claim historicity for any Conceptual Art. Again, what is interesting about some Conceptual Art is its resistance to (its own) history.

And what is odd about what I am saying is that it both seeks to identify Conceptual Art as some activity engaged in by young people from a position of internal exile at a particular time (and at a particular time in their lives), *and* attempts to refuse the proposition that the morale of this moment died with the passing of 1974 or whatever. Perhaps this is not as odd as it seems.

. . . And now, I suppose I am talking largely about Art & Language's work, and in particular that now somewhat vexatious group of works known as *Indexes*.[1] I will not dwell on the anecdotal nostalgia with which certain small-business inspired ex-colleagues have sought both to infiltrate and to derogate these projects, except to say that it is far from edifying to witness these former friends, who departed Art & Language out of a perfectly understandable combination of economic necessity and what might be called incipient ideological difference, now reduced to the production of an apologetics in the interests of a pathological monomaniac whose only project is at best the settling of imaginary scores.

To be sure, these *Indexes* did not contain very much pictorial or iconic material. They consisted mainly of text or of text-like material. This was text, or rather conceptual material, which was always in internal exile, paradoxically situated both within (just within) and beyond the borders of disciplines as traditionally defined and institutionally policed (as were the artists themselves, with one notable exception). And it was from this internal exile that far from stable artistic meta-languages were generated; unstable because there was and is no prioritization of concepts that live in the borders which define them internally. There are writers and critics who have seen this dialogical implosion as representing a strange bureaucratization of Art & Language's and *inter alia* of Conceptual Art's practice. To these, I would say that far from representing grounds for the denunciation of a demonic authoritarianism, these indexing projects are and were Conceptual Art's best chance (a) of an internal complexity which might be capable of resisting the management culture these writers allege to fear, and (b) of an anti-hegemonic and non-purist critical path for a morale which was falling apart in a dying culture: the best chance of maintaining internal exile, and of insuring Conceptual Art (or some relatively young artists) against co-option and worse. The margins of the index-projects were such as to model *inter alia* some rather fugitive (though compelling) forms of solidarity: talkative and aggressive non-proprietorial tolerance. Others have tried to suggest that a lively (or something) anarchy was evident as the productive ethos of Conceptual Art, insofar as it is represented by the work of Art & Language, and that this was brought to an end by the organization mentality of the *Index*. This is a tawdry distortion. The *Index* ruined the atmosphere for the small-business tendency. It should be added that small-business can acquire any political odor according to expedient. Indeed, a recent criticism of the *Index* is a monument to a career almost medieval in its capacity to grub for a niche, a place at some table or any. The *Index* had the tendency to proliferate tables and places in surprisingly uncentered locations; in an exile unlikely to satisfy the mechanical aspirations of small-business—and intolerable to small-business gone historical.

The *Index* provided unforeseen resonances, conversations and cultural misfortune or embarrassment: exile and hybridity; distance from the putative cultural center. Therein lies the class character of these projects. On the one hand, the *garagiste* tendency faced loss by appropriation (or expropriation) followed by implosion, on the other hand, very little work at the time aspired to (or stood much chance of achieving) the necessary qualifications for co-option. The projective mechanism was relentlessly to pull things away from the accultured center. (And remember, almost everyone involved had started life very far from that center.) This pulling away occurred even when (though this was quite rare) the autonomous character of a given item was more or less commensurable with the mechanisms of co-option, actual or potential. The artists were tied, as it were, to a machine which exiled and bastardized them in virtue of its power to operate as a function-spitting container. The workers had no need to learn to overcome their real (one might say structurally induced) discomfort with the fine things which allegedly preceded them, nor did they need to devise the latter's structurally successful replacement.

And it is exile, this generative context of hybridity and malingering, which is conceivably the only vivid and continuing legacy of Conceptual Art: its post-imperialist confusion. It is perhaps understandable that those who would seek to persist with an historical account, more often an historicistic account, cast about with various attempts and purifications and convergences, are the acculturated representatives of the cultural interests of the remaining globally imperialistic paranoid power, witting or not. The manipulative strivings of Conceptual Art's last purist seem to owe almost as much to the nitty gritty of American foreign policy in the 1950s as to some unavoidable mental disorder. The "theme," if you like, of internal exile which is played out, no doubt upon the surface of cultural margins, is no more than worthless provocation unless it is the prospect of the annihilation of the artist herself. "*We Aim to be Amateurs*" is a surface enfolded in the unabated compilation of the Index. This is exile which entails the derogation and loss of hard won competence, not the promise of Napoleonic return and final triumph. A history of pie in the sky is a history of expectation and loss, of allusions and displacements. The history of Conceptual Art had better be a story of some artists and how they tried to account for themselves. This will be a story of neither pies nor skies.

## NOTE

1. The name Art & Language designates the collaborative artistic and literary work of Michael Baldwin and Mel Ramsden. It also identifies collaboratively written work of these two and Charles Harrison. It has done this for almost 17 years.

The name is derived from that of the journal *Art-Language* (first published in Coventry in May 1969) which had its origin in the work and conversation of Terry Atkinson and Michael Baldwin (from 1966) in association with Harold Hurrell and David Bainbridge. These were its original editors. Art & Language was used subsequently to identify the joint and several artistic works of these four in an effort to reflect the conversational basis of their activity which, by late 1969, already included contributions from New York by Joseph Kosuth, Ian Burn and Mel Ramsden.

The facts of who did what, how much they contributed and so on, are more or less well known. They are by no means a secret. The (small) degree of *anonymity* which the name originally conferred continues to be, however, of historical significance.

As the distribution of the journal and the teaching practice of the editors and others developed, the conversation expanded and multiplied to include by 1971 (in England) Charles Harrison, Philip Pilkington, David Rushton, Lynn Lemaster, Sandra Harrison, Graham Howard, Paul Wood, and (in New York) Michael Corris and later Paula Ramsden, Mayo Thompson, Christine Koslov, Preston Heller, Andrew Menard and Kathryn Bigelow.

The name Art & Language sat precariously all over this. Its significance (or instrumentality) varied from person to person, alliance to alliance, (sub)discourse to (sub)discourse—from those in New York who produced *The Fox* (1974–76) to those engaged in music projects or to those who continued the original journal. There was a confusion: Terry Atkinson departed for his own reasons in 1974 and by 1976 a dialectically fruitful confusion had become a chaos of competing individualities and concerns.

In a practice which tried to eschew the pomp and power of control, decisive action had become necessary if any vestige of Art & Language's original ethos was to remain. There were those who saw themselves excluded from this who departed for individual occupations in teaching or as artists. There were others immune to the troubles who simply found different work. There were yet others whose departure was expedited by those whose practice had continued to be identified with the journal *Art-Language* and its artistic commitments. While musical activities continued with Mayo Thompson, and the literary conversational project continued (and continues) with Charles Harrison, by late 1976 the genealogical thread of this artistic work had been taken into the hands of Michael Baldwin and Mel Ramsden, with whom it remains.

This paper was initially delivered by Art & Language (Michael Baldwin, Charles Harrison, Mel Ramsden) to the conference "Who's Afraid of Conceptual Art," at the Institute of Contemporary Arts, 19 March 1995. It was subsequently published in *Art-Language,* new series no. 2 (June 1997), pp. 40–49. The only footnote in this text was initially published as "Summary" in *Art & Language* (Paris: Galerie Nationale du Jeu de Paume, 1993), pp. 147–148.

# a conversation about conceptual art, subjectivity and the *post-partum document*

## mary kelly and terry smith

Terry Smith: There are very few artists still practicing now whose work, however transformed, remains shaped—in its basic parameters, perhaps—by that moment in the early 1970s when it seemed possible to achieve what we then called "praxis": to fuse theory and practice, to evolve a theoretical practice as art, to do art-theoretical work. I recall that David Antin once picked out the most enterprising work of the 1960s as *performative*—I think he had in mind happenings, performance work, maybe even his and Ian Wilson's speech pieces—or *processual*—which meant actions or environments displaying natural systems, such as Hans Haacke's early work—or *procedural*—all those nominations of a series of actions, or sequence of thoughts, logical strings, ranging from scripts for performances to Richard Long's walks, or Huebler's social measurement mappings. Another term, *propositional* practices, needs to be added to pick up the essential character of language-based conceptualism. This was emphasized by Joseph Kosuth in the second issue of *Art-Language,* when he tried to distinguish the work which he and the English originators of Art & Language were doing from artists in what they called the Seth Siegelaub stable (Andre, Weiner, Barry, Huebler, et al.).

These four terms are useful pointers to the forms of practice then, but I believe that content was—as always—crucial. Right from the mid-1960s, the driving template, if you like, was to work on the concept of art, to test the possibilities for art practices which would be metadiscursive, and to use languages of various kinds to that end. So Art & Language-type work, for example, was initially an *analytic* practice, developing propositions about the possibilities for art practice, first through interrogating imagined or actualized theoretical objects, then through examining imagined theories and theories of imagining, or, better, of theorizing. In the early 1970s, however, things shifted. Analytical work continued, but it became also *synthetic* in the sense that the practice was expanded to become an inquiry into subjects and experiences which were much broader than art and its languages, and, of course, into theories for thinking, for speaking, these subjects and experiences. This is an obvious impact of the social movements of the 1960s.

Examples of this shift would be Hans Haacke, obviously. Less obvious, but important, is the trajectory of Art & Language work itself, especially in New York and then Australia from 1975–6. But it happens all over the world, in Central Europe, in Latin America, for example, sometimes earlier, sometimes later. The conceptual-political connection occurs as a split, or a displacement, or as a nexus, depending on the local context. I see your *Post-Partum Document* very much in this context.

Mary Kelly: When I started work on *Post-Partum Document* in 1973 I was curious about the parallels with Art & Language work in England. They were very influential, as was the work of Kosuth in New York. I did want to shift the emphasis from the notion of the analytical proposition to a more synthetic process. This is a much more complex argument than simply saying that I was going to reintroduce life into art. Your own terms for understanding Conceptual Art—where you set up the idea of a practice concerned with interrogating the conditions of existence for its own interrogation—make a lot of sense to me. In my case, obviously, the founding condition is an investigation of the subject. This was coincident with the kinds of questions being asked outside of art, by Marxism and feminism. The very first piece that I did, called *Introduction to the Post-Partum Document,* used found objects. Previous conceptual work had remained rather distant from that kind of materiality.

That was one of the first big departures from the established conceptual aesthetic. Another was the decision to not use photography. I wanted to emphasize what was effectively, emotionally loaded about this relation that I was documenting. But, then, when I superimposed the Lacanian schema over the baby vests, I don't think that, at the very first moment, I knew exactly how controversial—or even consequential—this juxtaposition would be. It began as a very insistent and almost intuitive attempt to bring the desire—you could say—for theory (itself very, very embryonic as far as its use in the women's movement was concerned at that time) together with the cathexis of the everyday experience of mothering. *Post-Partum Document* was the first work that I know of to introduce Lacanian references so explicitly, but there isn't a significant division here between the emotional effect of theory and the emotional effect of objects, between the ability of material objects to be fabricated or organized theoretically and for a theory to have its materiality. There's a certain breaking down of these discrete domains by bringing them together.

T.S.: Putting it that way makes me want to set out a little more fully how I see the unfoldings of Conceptual Art. Not exactly in phases, or cut and dried periods, but the first significant moves of conceptualism occurred, I believe, between 1965 and 1969 and were—it is often forgotten—object-directed. Paradoxically, of course—or better, through a doubling. You remember that a lot of people, then, were working at the edges of minimalism or performance or anti-form sculpture or environmental art or earthworks, in ways supplementary to the work which we saw as achieving style under those headings, inspired by it but wanting to maintain a distance from the specifics of the incorporating processes operating in each case. Well, one move was to create impossible objects, things that might, for example, embody the morphological characteristics of any artwork but only those, or consist of the general characteristics of every artwork but none of the specifics. Some of these, like Nauman's, were emotional objects, with somatic psychic residue. But most were theoretical objects, instantiating speculation about art itself. Like algebraic solids, or DNA models. This is where language became so crucial. Early Art & Language work—the impossible objects made, or conceived, by those who first formed Art & Language in Coventry and elsewhere in England, and those in Melbourne, New York and elsewhere who joined the group or did related work—was about examining the conditions for producing just those kinds of objects. The next move—although some had already made it before 1969—was to interrogate the conditions for the interrogation of what it was to produce those kinds of objects. This doubled meta-discursivity is, to me, the key to language-based, or analytic, conceptualism.

M.K.: But how did this relate to the social, psychoanalytic and experiential emphases I was suggesting?

T.S.: It was as if a commitment to pure experimentality, to radical interrogation of everything in its most specific forms, was enough . . . we assumed that the articulation between these would take care of itself, would just, somehow, happen. It took many of us until the early 1970s to realize how wrong we were. This was partly an impact of feminism, partly because the crisis of capitalism then was even deeper than we had thought.

M.K.: For me, the impossible objects you talk about were still unitary rather than relational. For instance, in the *Document,* the intersubjective object was the speech of the child. The pre-condition for that investigation—that is, of language—is already put in place, but not as a question of how we come to be speaking subjects, and how that becoming positions us as men or women.

T.S.: You're right, subjectivity in this sense was largely lacking from the first two moments of Conceptual Art . . .

M.K.: The significance of the relation between the psychic and the social was made obvious to me by its absence in Art & Language work in England, in Kosuth's work. . . . I saw that space as being open.

T.S.: It became increasingly obvious to some of us in Art & Language as well, although there was a huge reluctance to embrace psychoanalysis. There was an assumption, shared by most of us engaged in public sphere politics, including the varieties of Marxism, even anarchism, that whatever happened in that sphere would override the private, or should. There was perhaps also a masculinist suspicion of what seemed an invitation to confusion in "the personal is the political." A fear of loss of power, not unfounded. On the other hand, Freudian psychoanalysis, institutionalized or not, did not seem self-evidently the royal road to a political solution. Instead, we became deeply concerned with indexical processes, with understanding what was at stake in regarding ourselves as a language-embedded, language-producing community. We set the measurement routines of formal language-logics, and the analyses of ordinary language, against the actual chaos of our own conversations.

M.K.: The linguistic theories that seem to predominate initially in the art world were positivistic. But there was already, in France, the development of semiotics. I was part of that trajectory because of my associations with people in film as well as other women in the movement who were interested in the relations between semiotic linguistics and psychoanalysis. I remember when I published the first writing about the *Document* in *Control Magazine* in 1977. Steve Willett's magazine was a perfect example of this information theory attitude towards language, yet it was flexible enough to include my writing. Semiotics is, perhaps, the tendency that predominates now or, at least it did, through the 1980s. But in the period that we're talking about it was just being introduced in a way that was rather confrontational. Even within the women's movement psychoanalytic theory was not at all accepted. In the early 1970s it started to come out, when Ros Coward and Juliet Mitchell and others insisted on its uses for feminism—it was very hotly debated. So, the key contexts of the *Document* were the relations it had to linguistic theories in the art world and to the questions of socialization raised in the women's movement. In both cases, there was an insistence on certain shifts, most specifically focussed on that impossible object which Freud called the unconscious, and the body of theory appropriate to it, that is, psychoanalysis.

I wanted to go back to the discussion of Art & Language and ask how far you think they went with what you call the synthetic proposition?

T.S.: Well, I suppose it began in the early 1970s with the move into indexing in England, and the Annotations and Blurting projects in New York. The shift is that the work became conversations not only about the concept of art, and about the conditions for interrogating it, but about the art world, about political change and its impact on our practice. To some degree they were about language and subjectivity, about the formation of speakers, about what we called the *idiolect*—pursuing the implications of the idea that each person had their own particular way of speaking—but you could also say this as *ideolect* and thus pick up subjectivization, or interpellation, through ideology: the subject spoken by the state, of and by official language-use. Not by the "beginnings" of speech, as Lacan has it. By 1974 Ian Burn, Mel Ramsden and I were writing an issue of *Art-Language* which began from social speech but became a conversation about international politics, provincialism, individualism, the modernist art machine, etc. Certainly in New York these were the great points of debate—as is obvious in such formations as the Artists Meeting for Cultural Change. But these happened late in New York, artists' unions had sprung up, as you know from your experience in London, all over the place.

As to the form of such work, it became less propositional, and, indeed, less procedural. The time for issuing instructions for "actions" other people might take was well past. Frankly, it became very difficult to produce public work—that is, find forms of display—that seemed adequate to the social work of the conversations. Yet the desire to do so was crucial: the turn, or re-turn, of conceptual artists to political practice in the mid-1970s is a major move, one which has driven much of the significant art done since. For me, your earlier project *Women and Work* and the *Post-Partum Document* come out of a similar moment in England.

M.K.: *Women and Work* was an installation which documented the divisions of labor in the metal box industry during the implementation of Equal Pay legislation. For me, it was clearly related to Haacke's *Shapolsky Real Estate* project. But neither it nor *Post-Partum Document* is usually seen as a conceptual work, is it? Rather, as the product of a certain moment in feminist art—usually the one after the moment in which it was produced. It was made in the 1970s, yet is normally seen as representing the shift in feminist art into more theoretical concerns around 1980. Sometimes it seems that the particular moment of a work's reception—in the United States—is more definitive than the moment of its creation. In this case, it eclipses even the scandal of *Post-Partum's* first reception: the "Bricks and nappies" controversy when it was shown at the Institute of Contemporary Art in London in 1976.

T.S.: Cultural imperialism rides again! I see *Post-Partum Document* as primarily conceptual work, definitely in its form: it's organized to track various activities, that is, procedurally. Its organizational logic is presumed to be larger than the subject or the person doing the tracing. It's processual in that its subject—motherhood—is itself normally figured as a natural process. Yet the procedures you follow, or set out, seem to cut against any sense of natural flow, seem placed against the instinctual. There is a kind of manic restraint, a withholding, an initial distancing which nevertheless hopes to surprise some otherwise inaccessible information or attitudes along the way. This mood is typical of procedural work from the late 60s onwards.

Some people probably did read the *Document* as about natural forces, and were shocked by its cognitive armature. To me, it's a work of theory, in the sense that it shows theory at work in your daily life, actively constructing the sort of relations involved in having children, being a mother. Mothering is a theoretically informed practice in a absolutely saturated way. Dr. Spock, or Penelope Leach, anyone?

Another Conceptual Art aspect of the *Document* is that it enables—in fact, obliges—the spectator to experience theory, to relate to what's happening via theory as the only way of grasping what's going on.

M.K.: Right, the *Document* follows, in your terms, typical procedural forms, tracing events such as feeding every hour, every day, or taping the linguistic exchanges between mother and child. This might look developmental, but what I always call the pseudo-scientific discourse is countered by the reference to the Lacanian diagram. In the Footnotes "Experimentum Mentis" sections I introduced a different theorization of that moment which was much more connected to the debate around psychoanalysis and feminism. The Art & Language indexes, although they might have touched on questions that moved outside of aesthetics, still seemed to me to remain within the discourse of the fine art institutions. The installation of the *Document* was intended to be polemical with the Art & Language *Index.* My idea was that you would go to the Footnotes for information, but rather than a system of internal referencing, it would raise issues which related to the social movements of the time.

T.S.: That's important, but a response might be that if you look closely at the *Index,* or many other conceptual works right from the mid-1960s, you will find that systemization always has one or two random terms in it, or that its structural regularity is aimed at provoking, even generating, some kind of dyssytemic irrationality. The craziness of things in the world. The randomness of structures. The irreality of the real. These were what drew us—more and more, especially in the early-mid 1970s. So it's not an obsession with order, but a thirst towards a catacrexic disordering of pictures . . .

M.K.: For some people, the *Document* was a catacrexic disordering of motherhood.

T.S.: Yes, mothering appears in an environment of manic intensity!

M.K.: And once you take the discourse to that extreme it almost turns itself inside out, it's hardly recognizable as coming out of that procedural method.

T.S.: I was also thinking about Adrian Piper's work in the early 1970s. It, too, focussed on identity-formation, confronting people on the street, glancing off a connection with them. Somewhat like what she is doing now, but in forms that were more singular, and less to do with racism, from memory.

M.K.: Aside from her, there were very few artists doing performance work in rigorously theoretical ways. I'm thinking of Gina Pane's *Sentimental Actions,* or Vito Acconci's *Following Piece,* where the question of subjectivity did come into it.

T.S.: Subjectivity was one route that early language-based Conceptual Art didn't take. Nauman was exceptional. By '69 at least he was casting bits and pieces of body space, setting up those harrowing performance rooms, or observational spaces, where sometimes recorded statements operated as a kind of surveillance-voice. They weren't widely known then, but they were part of the first, analytic move of conceptualism in that they were very much about the spectator in space in relation to an object. The degree of psychic, unconscious, actually traumatic emphasis was unusual for conceptualism. As it was in Acconci.

M.K.: This junction, where performance-oriented work had taken on in some way the question of subjectivity, and conceptual work had developed a kind of theoretical, procedural rigor, is exactly what I wanted to come together in the *Document.* It had the procedural look of Conceptual Art, but fundamentally it engaged with the kinds of issues that predominated in performance work.

T.S.: I want to return to the question of power distributed according to gender in those days. There was an appalling lack of space for women artists in the early "thrust" (I have to say) of conceptualism. This led to some blinkered perceptions, which still echo. Hanne Darboven's work, for example, was seen as a screen of pseudo-language, as something decorative that would never become meaningful. It ended up as a general sign for obsessiveness. Yet in the late 1980s she exhibited a series which interspersed photographs of library spaces with her usual sequences of written pages . . .

M.K.: But her work amounts to much more than just, say, foregrounding obsession. It's the concentrated intensity of the activity which has power. She lets that quality become quite clear as having a level on which, while entirely subjective, is also completely determined by something outside of scientific discourse, although she never states that very explicitly.

T.S.: As if her books were being written by forces outside of her? They do seem runic.

M.K.: The perception of her work has been very male dominated, perhaps.

T.S.: This is a serious issue because in a certain sense she has been figured as someone whose work had the look of Conceptual Art, but none of the content. Another instance of historical gendering?

I wonder how this might come up in relation to the *Post-Partum Document*? One point of view, perhaps masculinist, would presume that its subject—motherhood—is a domain of social experiencing, bodily feeling, emotional diversification, etc. which is both specific to each individual, and also widespread. Not universal, but quite fundamental, basic if anything is, miasmic. So you were faced with the possibility of this project roaming in every direction. Against this chaotic yet bounded prospect you set your methods of regulation, which posit flows, and escaping from regulation. Nothing like a flow escapes from the look of the *Document,* or from its mode of presentation. But flows do erupt in the way many people responded to it, especially to its message about motherhood—which does seem at the heart of what most people take to be natural—being constructed. Many, including me, reacted by reading the work itself as closed: how could motherhood be subject to this cool, withdrawn, unemotional analysis? Maybe our response was one of shocked displacement from the realization that motherhood—even motherhood!—was not a natural but social, psychic, linguistic construction.

M.K.: It is what I was saying earlier about the affective force of the idea, that it should be taken on—as you would say—as part of the interrogation of the conditions of interrogation as such. It's not divided up into some neat masculinity/femininity, theory/practice binary, but is a rather chaotic, anarchic, impositional structure of drives and desires that I continue to be interested in. All of my work has, I think, a certain tension between ordering and losing control.

T.S.: True, but even as far back as Sol LeWitt's first sentences, or Dan Graham's late 1960s poem projects, an anti-analytic relativism was present.

M.K.: If that's the case then the move to subjectivity in the *Document* should have seemed a logical step. For many, it seemed to go too far . . .

T.S.: You must had have people criticizing you for dealing with, and very clearly valuing, motherhood, when lots of women thought of it as a total trap, an anti-feminist way to go. And for doing so in a way that was intensely and obviously theoretical in its mode of address.

M.K.: Well, in one sense that dilemma just put me squarely in the old tradition of the avant-garde transgression. Yet part of the point of conceptualism, you remember, was to change the distribution of interpretative power in the art world, to restore some of it to artists. Certainly to try to influence the ways it would be institutionally received. What amazes me now, looking back, is how little control you do have, finally.

T.S.: The other side of the dilemma for some viewers was the very fact of the subject—motherhood—being made so central in such a sustained way in the *Document* when among the women whom I was closest to at the time, the idea of motherhood—while not necessarily ruled out in practice—was certainly not seen as a likely, or even possible, subject for art. By introducing such material, such a central subjectivity, the *Document* signals a major break with the main concerns of early conceptualism.

## REFERENCES

Ian Burn, Mel Ramsden, and Terry Smith, "Draft for an Anti-Textbook," *Art-Language* 3:1 (September 1974).

Rosalind Coward and John Ellis, *Language and Materialism, developments in semiology and the theory of the subject* (London: Routledge & Kegan Paul, 1977).

Charles Harrison, *Essays on Art & Language* (Oxford: Blackwell, 1991).

Mary Kelly, *Footnotes and Bibliography, Post-Partum Document* (London: Institute of Contemporary Art, 1976).

Mary Kelly, "Notes on Reading the *Post-Partum Document*," *Control Magazine* 10 (1977).

Mary Kelly, *Post-Partum Document* (London: Routledge & Kegan Paul, 1983).

Joseph Kosuth, "Introductory Note by the American Editor," *Art-Language* 1:2 (February 1970).

Juliet Mitchell, *Psychoanalysis and Feminism* (New York: Pantheon, 1974).

Terry Smith, "Art and Art & Language," *Artforum* 12:6 (February 1974).

This discussion took place in Chicago on 10 March 1995. It is previously unpublished.

# intention(s)
## joseph kosuth

### INTENTION (ARTISTS)

**Intention is the forward-leaning look of things. It is not a reconstituted historical state of mind, then, but a relation between the object and its circumstances.**
   —Michael Baxandall[1]

When art historians, even the best of them, write about intention there seems to be a presumption that you have *two* things: the work of art and the artist's intentions. As an artist I find this, perhaps more than any other single thing, the major division now between how artists understand their work and how art historians see them. While the primacy of the object has long been questioned by artists, it remains the basis for much of the art-historical enterprise. This difference in the two disciplines, I feel, has been brought into focus by the issues raised by the context of art with which my own work has been long associated: Conceptual art. Paradoxically, it is some recent writing on this movement which has now brought art-historical writing into a crisis of meaning of its own.

Conceptual art, simply put, had as its basic tenet an understanding that artists work with meaning, not with shapes, colors, or materials. Anything can be employed by the artist to set the work into play—including shapes, colors, or materials—but the form of presentation itself has no value independent of its role as a vehicle for the idea of the work.[2] Thus, when you approach the work you are approaching the idea (and therefore the intention) of the artist directly. The "idea," of course, can be a force that is as contingent as it is complex, and when I have said that *anything* can be used by (or as) a work of art, I mean just that: a play within the traditional constraints of morphology, media, or objecthood.

Art can manifest itself in all of the ways in which human intention can manifest itself. The task for artists is to put into play works of art unfettered by the limited kinds of meanings which objects permit, and succeed in having them become not the autonomous texts of structuralism, but the production of artists as authors within a discourse, one concretized through subjective commitment and comprised of the making process. It is the historically defined agency of the artist working within a practice that sees itself as such a process, in which an artist's work becomes believable *as art* within society. To do that, work must satisfy deeper structures of our culture than that surface which reads in the market as tradition and continuity. The more enriched our understanding of that "text" of art becomes, so does our understanding of culture. A focus on meaning, by necessity, has focused our concerns on a variety of issues around language and context. These issues pertain to the reception and production of works of art themselves. The aspect of the questioning process that some now call "institutional critique" began here, too, and it originated with Conceptual art's earliest works.[3]

The relevance of this to the question of intention is in what it implies: the disappearance, perhaps with finality, of the threshold between what had been the art *object* (that which is now simply art) and the intentions of its maker. Indeed, there can no longer really be a separation between the work and the intention of the artist: the work of art, in this case, is *manifested* intention. Ultimately, we might want to ask, of course, if intention is the text itself, or the production of the screen upon which the greater social text appears—even if the fragments and overlaps are of many projections: race, creed, gender.

Recently I have corresponded with an art historian who wrote her master's thesis on my *Passagen-Werk,* a large installation I did for Documenta IX, in Kassel.[4] In one letter, discussing artistic intention, she writes, "the relativizing position of the art historian says 'even if we can know what the artist intended, it isn't that important. What is important is the work of art and how it generates meaning.'" I don't doubt her assessment, but reading her letter I felt again the distance between the art historian's approach and mine. What this suggests is that the art-historical process is a kind of conspiracy, even if unwittingly so, to politically disenfranchise my activity as an artist. If my intention is denied at its inception, then my responsibility for the meaning I generate in the world as an artist is also nullified. The artist becomes just another producer of goods for the market, where the work finds its meaning.

This, it seems to me, was exactly where we came into the picture in the sixties, when Noland, Olitski, et al. would never need to leave their studios; just paint 'em and ship 'em out, and let Clement Greenberg and his minions provide the meaning. For them, art and politics were separate, and their practice reflected that. What is seldom discussed is how one looked at those paintings and *saw* the theory. I think this greatly explains why, for so many now, such work is held in the low esteem it is. Perhaps I should make clear that I am not suggesting that artists are the only ones capable of discussing works of art. On the contrary, art historians and critics play an important role in the struggle of the work's "coming to meaning" in the world. But that is the point: they represent the world. That is why a defining part of the creative process depends on the artists to assert their intentions in that struggle.

One of the greatest lessons defending the primacy of the intention of the artist, and the increasing importance of writing by artists on their work, is provided by this period of the sixties.[5] Our more recent experience of the return to painting in the eighties reminds us again of the bankruptcy of a form of art that relies on its meaning to be provided by other than its makers. If Conceptual art means more than a style, its defining difference is established here in the rethinking of artistic responsibility in the production of meaning.[6] Without this, the politics which inform work remain homeless, only a topic among others that distinguishes style.

Artists working within such a practice have a particular responsibility not to permit their work at its inception to be defined "by the world." What the work *is* (that is, what distinguishes it from what preceded it) must be established by the artist before "the world" includes it within all that is given. "The world" begins as a process of institutionalization, and the art-historical and critical establishment is its first moment: without it there would be no "professional" artists. Here is where one finds the true "aesthetics of administration," and it is a structural, and apparently inescapable, feature of the process of a work coming into the world.

Only a state of deep denial could keep an artist from avoiding the fact that seeing isn't as simple as looking: the text the viewer brings to a work organizes what is seen. The production of that "text" has become a primary part of the artistic meaning-making process. The productive result of this understanding, beginning with Conceptual art, has been precisely the emergence of an "art of intention" as I discussed above. If the actual people standing behind works of art—who provide the belief, in a sense, as they take subjective responsibility for the meaning of what is produced—think that an object "speaks for itself," they are sorely mistaken. The (making) process of putting a proposition (that signifying action which may or may not employ the object, performance, video, text, et al.) "into play" is only *one* of the responsibilities of the artist. The act of putting it into the world is empty unless an artist also fights for its meaning. This informational framing of the proposition itself increasingly becomes part of the artistic process. Thus, a key to the changed role of intention and the artist's self-perception of his or her practice, is the role of writing by artists. (. . .)

There is another consideration of artistic intention, also important. It is *part* of the intention of this particular artist for the works to engage the viewer/reader's participation in the meaning-making process. By bringing with them what they do in their approach to the work, they thereby complete it. They are every work's "local" site. This role would be rendered passive, and would provide only a moment of consumption, without work which is anchored to a larger process of signification. Thus the speaker is designated, embedded in the human meaning which artistic intention constitutes. No speaker, no listener.

## INTENTION (ART HISTORIANS)

In considering this exchange of the objective voice for the subjective one, I, of course, contemplated the genre of confessional writing. But that seemed too obvious, too easy. Instead I decided on ventriloquism. I would write as though through the first-person account of many other characters, actual historical characters, whose narratives I would, by the mere fact of bringing them into the orbit of my own subjectively developed voice, suspend somewhere between history and fiction.
　　—Rosalind Krauss[7]

It's a dangerous moment for artists. The models of art historians writing on contemporary art give every indication of being in transition. The inherited model of art history's self-conception, part of its professional "unconscious," as it were, is one in which an old apparatus has not yet been completely dismantled. It implied that art historians speak with an authority which is "objective and scientific." The art-historical enterprise's links to academia do not contradict such authority, which originated with the internalized values of a regnant science upon which intellectual life in the university was founded. The social sciences must mimic the hard sciences, the assertion went, as this is the economy of academic standards and discipline. Thus, the question remains, does the art-historical enterprise speak with the voice of objectivity, even when its mission is contradictory to it?

That contradiction becomes increasingly pronounced as the works of artists are approached in a distinctively new way: as inspiration for the production of essentially subjective, creative texts by *auteur* writers on art. A rather ironic development, considering that the "death of the author" discussed by Barthes and Foucault decades ago hasn't prevented the stylish use of French theory otherwise. Such theory, although making claims as art-historical text, betrays a hope that their production will gain status itself as a cultural object, post-*S/Z*. (Keep the power, have the fun?) It's one thing to commingle discourses, but, within this transformed discipline, what, finally, is the intention of the art historian that emerges? That seems a fair question, since the result of such writing on individual works (or, for that matter, an activity spanning a lifetime) selected for this treatment can be both deeply unfair and inaccurate.[8]

Perhaps what has initiated this transmigration of models, or, should I just say it, the source of this *license,* has been critical theory. It is one thing, however, to anchor one's writing within a discourse such as critical theory, with its position theoretically compelled to something like consistency vis-à-vis, for example, the originary and the historical narrative. At least their texts have a perceivable principled basis and there is no confusion about the writing of history in its more "objective" conventional form. One can then perceive the (ethical) space within which the writer is operating: reader/buyer beware. Here, all "texts" are equal, the work and the text it generated all being a part of the same surface, and any claims of objectivity are suspended as they are made irrelevant.

The hybrid of which I speak combined such a license with a conventional form of authority. This practice occupies a very different and self-servingly ambiguous ethical space. Having a mixed parentage has given us an interesting patrimony: rather like little Frankensteins of *Art-Language* (a license at least partially sired by Charles Harrison's fictive histories of the Art & Language group), we have another, and mutant, form of art theory as art, except this time it is not the production of artists but of art historians. Maybe I'm partly to blame, writing as I did in *Art-Language* in 1970 that "This art both annexes the function of the critic, and makes a middleman unnecessary."[9] I didn't realize at the time, however, that the art historians might join our ranks *under cover.* This emerging professional class of writers seems to want celebrated careers *like* those of artists while they keep their protective perch, and its detached view, with the perquisites and power of recorders of history. It appears that there is a palpable, if admittedly vague, dimension of something like a "conflict of interest" if those given the responsibility to inscribe history are under a powerful and conflicting need to, instead, *make* it.

This leaves us with a brand of art-historical "intentions" which begin to produce an ambiguous ethical relationship with the artist, in curating as well as writing. The history of recent art history leads one to conclude that there is a conservatism which pervades the art-historical and critical establishment, in which convention necessitates a view of artists as bewildered children playing with lumps of wet clay, in dire need of the paternal art-historical and critical presence to swoop down and make sense of it all. If you are one of the artists who risk standing up to this conception, prepare to be vilified.[10] As I've asked myself and others before: is our production, as artists, really only *nature,* from which critics, as historians, make their own "culture"? And doesn't it violate society's sense of fair play that they are permitted to do so behind a mask of implied "objectivity" without having to take the kind of *subjective* responsibility for the production of consciousness which artists have historically had to, and which has previously distinguished the two activities?

Who now seriously believes that the decisions made by such art historians in the performance of their craft are really any less subjective than those made by an artist, given the career needs and the social relationships of art historians such writing reflects? Previously there seemed to be some kind of moral imperative for art historians to be above such considerations out of a sense of professionalism. Having it both ways seems, at this receiving end, like an extremely unjust, and even corrupt, development. I always thought that critics, as journalists, could discuss the meaning of an artist's present production with the public in ways that indicated that the critics either got it or didn't (and artists could either deal with that or not). The assumption was that, in the long run and after the smoke cleared, at least the historians could be counted on to be basically fair and accurate in saying who did what and when, why, whom it influenced, and the like. I assumed that the trail of evidence one leaves as a practicing artist with a public life would, in some sense, secure an honest record.[11] That record is, however, nothing more than a history of the intentions of particular individuals living in a given moment. The record of those intentions is the anchor, perhaps, which puts weight on the ethical responsibility of the art-historical enterprise. Without the meanings which such a record suggests, our cultural production as artists is reduced to being a playpen, a free-for-all of interpretation, institutionalizing history as a creative act—but only for its writers.

Finally, the reason we don't really consider the paintings by monkeys and children to be art is because of intention; without artistic intention there *is* no art. The subjective presence which stands behind a work of art and which takes responsibility for its meaning something, which I have discussed here, is what makes it authentic as a work. This is the human power which informs, in a sense gives life, to what would otherwise be empty forms and objects. Just as the grunts and groans of language would be gibberish as only physical properties of sound in themselves, within a system of relations they become meaningful. There is a tenacious formalism lurking in the art historian's argument which wants art as a language dead—archaic and unreadable, its meaning the province of whoever *owns* it—for they are free to make a decorative trophy of it and that would be its final meaning. In this view it is the role of the art-historical process to locate the value of art in the cadavers of passing artistic forms and materials, an institutionalizing process which severs the language from its speaker, so that it can give up its meaning to the market.

**NOTES**

1. Michael Baxandall, *Patterns of Intention: On the Historical Explanation of Pictures* (New Haven, London, 1985), p. 42.

2. I would cite my work from 1965–66, the Protoinvestigations, of which *One and Three Chairs* would be a representative example. This work, using deadpan "scientific-style" photographs which were always taken by others, also employed common objects and enlarged texts from dictionary definitions. The elements were never signed, with the concept of the work being that this "form of presentation" would be made and remade. The reason for this was an important part of my intention: eliminate the aura of traditional art and force another basis for this activity to be approached as art, conceptually. Ownership of the work is established by the production instructions which double as a certificate. This *is* signed, but as a deed of ownership, not as a work of art. Thus, I've made it clear that these certificates are never to be exhibited, and they rarely are. The art itself, which is neither the props with which the idea is communicated, nor the signed certificate, is only the *idea* in and of the work. As it was for other artists at that time, the issues of modernism were rapidly becoming opaque. One effect of this work was to "sum up" modernism for me, and once that was visible I was able to use that view to get past it, as the work which followed shows. Thus, for me, this work was both a "summation" of modernism and the way out of it.

3. The use of tautology in the Protoinvestigations has generated a variety of confused responses. One aspect of this work was the attempt to actualize a Wittgensteinian insight: by drawing out the relation of art to language, could one begin the production of a cultural language whose very function it was to *show*, rather than *say*? Such artworks might function in a way which circumvents significantly much of what limits language. Art, some have argued, *describes* reality. But, unlike language, artworks, it can also be argued, simultaneously describe *how* they describe it. Granted, art can be seen here as self-referential, but significantly, not *meaninglessly* self-

referential. What art shows in such a manifestation is, indeed, *how* it functions. This is revealed in works which feign to *say*, but do so as an art proposition and reveal the difference (while showing their similarity) with language. This was, of course, the role of language in my work beginning in 1965. It seemed to me that if language *itself* could be used to function as an artwork, then that difference would bare the device of art's language game. An artwork then, as such a *double* mask, provided the possibility of not just a reflection on itself, but an indirect *double* reflection on the nature of language, through art, to culture itself. "Do not forget," writes Wittgenstein, "that a poem, even though it is composed in the language of information is not used in the language-game of giving information." Whatever insights this early work of mine had to share, it did, and it initiated within the practice an essential questioning process which is now basic to it. It should be obvious that the "baring of the device" of the institutions of art would begin at the most elemental level: the point of production itself, the artwork. Seeing the artwork, in such a context, forced a scrutiny of its conventions and historical baggage, such as the painting/sculpture dichotomy. First inside the frame and then outside. One goal of a work such as *The Second Investigation,* 1968 was to question the institutional forms of art. If the work that preceded this confronted the institutionalized form of authority of traditional art, this work pressed the point *out* of the gallery and museum into the world, using public media.

4. See Deborah Zafman, "Joseph Kosuth's *Passagen-Werk (Documenta-Flânerie):* An Installation of Ideas," M. A. thesis (Berkeley: University of California, 1994).

5. Ad Reinhardt painted black paintings. But anyone who knew him, who knew how he thought about art, would tell you that he was more than just a producer of paintings; he was a producer of meaning. It is this *total* activity as an artist which ultimately provided those paintings with a cultural life *as* it preserved Reinhardt's reasons for making them, which you see when you look at them. By his ceaseless participation in panel discussions, his lectures, his texts such as "Rules for a New Academy," his teaching, and his cartoons, he made it very difficult for others to co-opt his work for their own purposes. Indeed, his work had to resist a critical atmosphere in which work that was outside of a certain orthodoxy was either made to fit, or was dismissed. The limits of Clement Greenberg's vision are probably witnessed with no greater clarity than in his statement on Reinhardt, that he "has a genuine if small gift for color but none at all for design or placing" (quoted in the regrettable text of Yve-Alain Bois, "The Limit of Almost," in *Ad Reinhardt,* exhibition catalogue [New York: Museum of Modern Art, 1991], p. 18).

6. In the context of such a practice, I see an insurmountable contradiction for those colleagues of mine who have permitted art historians and critics to provide the theoretical basis for their work. What is thus brought into question is the very grounds of its authenticity.

7. Rosalind Krauss, "We Lost It at the Movies," *Art Bulletin,* 76, no. 4 (1994), p. 579.

8. My own activities as an artist have recently been subjected to what I can only call an organized form of abuse by writers associated with *October* who seem to want to keep the voice of authority presumed by the former while having the "creative" flexibility of the latter. See, e.g., *October,* no. 55 (Winter 1990); no. 57 (Summer 1991); no. 69 (Summer 1994); and no. 70 (Fall 1994). This has continued as well, in various public lectures, panel discussions, and exhibition catalogues by the same writers.

9. Joseph Kosuth, "Introductory Note by the American Editor," *Art-Language* 1, no. 2 (1970), 1–4, especially 2–3, repr. in idem, *Art after Philosophy and After: Collected Writings, 1966– 1990,* ed. Gabriele Guercio (Cambridge, Mass., 1991), pp. 37–70.

10. See "Conceptual Art and the Reception of Duchamp," Round Table, in *October,* no. 70 (Fall 1994), as an example. We know that there is a place for polemics. What I feel I can reasonably object to is when my work and historical position are intentionally misrepresented as a consequence of the *polemical mission* of writers who enjoy an authority as institutionally affiliated historians. Is it not an ethical issue when academic validation, which at least has the implication of scholarly disinterest, is used for such purposes?

11. After nearly thirty years as an artist, I have recently been surprised to learn that this may not be true, a least in the short run, if certain individuals, for ad hominem motives or careerist expediency, decide otherwise. We need to keep in mind that such writing lowers the level for *all* of us. The concern is that it becomes part of a record, one which is restated (and restated again, eventually taking on the quality of a "fact") as a natural process of the art-historical enterprise itself. The vendettas of such fashions of history (and their petty and personal banalities) may fade from memory, but their historical view may not. Perhaps whatever altruism remains might force our reconsideration of the dubious value of what may have been written as a result of such intentions. Indeed, we need to ask: are these *art-historical* intentions, or are they something else?

This text was published in *Art Bulletin,* 78: 3 (September 1996), pp. 407–412.

# inside a new york art gang: selected documents of art & language, new york

## michael corris

## INTRODUCTION

Twenty years ago the New York section of Art & Language collapsed. Since then, a number of inflammatory polemics, post-mortems and serious attempts to tackle the complexities and contradictions of that community have been published. Like the workings of the Soviet Polit-buro and the details of the Communist Party's international relations with its counterpart in the capitalist West, the internal history of Art & Language, New York—or "ALNY" as it was known to us—has remained a mystery. For years, the composition of narrative accounts of Art & Language has mainly been the preserve of British participants writing from the stand-point of the British wing of the group ("ALUK," as it was known to us). The story of how things got done in ALNY and its relationship to its English cousins has always been colored by this fact. Inspired by the rich historical rewards being reaped by historians thanks to recent access to the archives of the Soviet Communist Party, I have decided to enact my own modest version of *Glasnost* for the benefit of art critics and historians everywhere.

Much of the following may strike the reader as claustrophobic gossip; "chatter" that is incomprehensible and possibly irrelevant to contemporary interpretive projects. I would resist such an assessment. According to Ann Stephen, Ian Burn imagined an art history based on artists' anecdotes. It is a notion that is anything but arbitrary; in fact, Burn was simply reiterating what we in "ALNY" had always taken to be a *constitutive* feature of our practice. We had always put those unfairly debased and mongrelized discourses of anecdote and gossip to good use. In the context of our practice they remained powerful agents for debunking the myth of Modernism as we saw it. Gossip was the way we blocked our resources from turning into exalted "topics"; anecdote was how we defeated art-historical rationalization.

On the other hand, those aspects of our past practice which are truly challenging and controversial have remained obscured. These include the story of why some of us nominated radical politics to be a cure for art. Many of the documents excerpted below have never before been published, yet they provide the necessary context to explain why, during the mid-1970s, many of us turned our backs on art. Admittedly, some of us went down in flames; individuals such as Jill Breakstone, Preston Heller and Andrew Menard dropped out of art entirely. Ian Burn, on the other hand, was one amongst us who deliberately interrupted an art world career for the possibility to develop a practice of social and political consequence within a broader cultural field. For readers already familiar with his career in Australia since 1977, I hope that the relevance of these documents to that work is obvious.[1]

## DOCUMENT I, APRIL 1975

The first text is typical of many which addressed ALNY's complex, difficult and often bitter relationship to their English cousins. The projects realized by ALNY between 1972 and the publication of *The Fox* in 1975 were more often than not viewed condescendingly by our transatlantic counterparts. During the early 1970s, for instance, ALNY's "Handbook" was severely criticized by Michael Baldwin and others for its allegedly unreconstructed model of intersubjectivity. A similar jibe was made public by ALUK in a little-known review reporting on an ALNY exhibition in London and published in *Studio International.* That review prompted an angry missive from Mel Ramsden to Baldwin. On another occasion, Burn was attacked by Baldwin for publishing an article in *Artforum* titled "The art market: affluence and degradation" (April 1975). The excerpt which follows—"Strategy is political: Dear Michael . . ." is part of Burn's reply to Baldwin's presumptive reading of ALNY's context and work.[2] According to Burn, the latter failed to acknowledge "the pragmatic/contextual parameters of the article, that it was written in socio-political conditions differing in some fundamental ways from your own." ALUK's repeated misreading of our practice had become a problem by 1974; for most of us, this proved to be a major factor contributing to our decision to launch and sustain *The Fox* as an alternative to *Art-Language* journal.

*. . . To talk about tactics and strategy is to recognize the significance of location and occasion. Then our differences tend to be culturally mediated, not ideologically. Don't make the silly mistake in thinking everything that is against the Bolsheviki is counter-revolutionary. . . . You do rely overly on "class conflict" . . . in America? It was no accident that Marx took England for his model of social classes—just as it's also not incidental his concepts of conflict and revolution derived mainly from the experiences of France. But the English class system, the blend of crude plutocratic reality with sentimental aroma of aristocratic legend? . . .*

*. . . This isn't denying class struggle at all, but making the point that in the US you just don't have highly stratified classes—hence it's not a very reliable basis for analysis. Marx's class theory clings to a binary class model, though often he's forced to speak of "intermediate" classes (your "social sections"). That may be fine in a monolithic social structure, such as perhaps still exists in England, but here it's more complex and highly confused. . . .*

*It's not a case of trying to resolve surface contradictions (. . . perhaps proliferate them?). The cultural restrictions on generation from deep structure, of need be, produce contradictions. This is especially so if one adopts (for whatever reasons) the critically-complicit attitude of Alice-in-Wonderland empiricism. The NY environment, with its unilateral media network, sustains culturally-doctrinaire points of reference which anyone who lives here does "experience"—and these form the basis of "common" or "shared" experience. Deontic (etc.) imperatives notwithstanding. Idealism is futile in New York, it's why you finally leave New York! . . .*

*You know as well . . . the only hope of any sort of authentic [sic] practice lies in being able to keep our dialogue going . . . more conversations . . . the moment we let it go, fade away, we don't have any hope and can just as well be thrown onto the garbage heap of Modern Art.*

*Keeping it going also means getting it to penetrate other people's conversations, activities, contexts, lives . . . as long as it co-opts other speakers . . . "you were dead; theirs was the future. But you could share in that future if you kept alive the mind . . ." (Orwell, another petty bourgeois). And you said that the dialogical-historical vectors of . . . (etc.) can be mediated* theoretically. *I suppose you (we) are seeing that as they exist from the paradoxicalness of any "practico-" realm . . . you end up trading expensive Marxism for expensive theory . . . still the old problem, still the only option. So we try to bargain . . . less-expensive theory (*The Fox, *at $2), and perhaps bits of vulgar determinism do stick to it. But, given the occasion, that's important. It's never gratuitous . . . far from indulging in utopian panaceas; we are, as it were, trying to practice* *(create) the conditions . . . we haven't arrived at our own content—subverting form-as-content is political, that's all.* But we won't end up as more objects of history . . . yet. . . .

## DOCUMENT II, 1975

The following item by Annette Kuhn appeared in the *Village Voice*—a well-known New York liberal weekly now owned by Rupert Murdoch—in early 1975.

*"Us old warlords of conceptual art have gotten together," says Joseph Kosuth. The 30 and under group—Sarah Charlesworth, Michael Corris, Preston Heller, Kosuth, Andrew Menard and Mel Ramsden, all loosely second generation conceptualists—is about to give birth to* The Fox, *a quarterly magazine of reviews and articles on the politics of art. The first issue, coming out April 15, has a run of 4000 and costs $2. Kosuth, who shows at the Castelli Gallery, is banging the war drums when he says the magazine is "going to be the formalization of the schism between theoretical conceptualists and the stylists."*

## DOCUMENT III, 1975

*"I've been here in Maryland for over a week," writes Mel Ramsden in the summer of 1975. "It's given me time to think. The following are some thoughts—more or less straight off the top of my head, concerning the 'political' thrust of the recent work. I'm talking about NYAL. One of the things I finally sorted-out down here, after a fair amount of soul-searching, was that—speaking for myself—I have to break contact with ALUK—but that's incidental."*

*Some of my worries appear to me—insofar as we step-up the moral if not moralizing side of the work—to be typical of the worries of the post-war American left. We haven't looked hard enough at the paradoxes of the US left though we've picked up a lot of the lingo. For instance, the impossibility of striking a* real *balance between the articulation of ideals and the recognition of social realities led Sweezy, Baran, Mills, Marcuse, the SDS [Students for a Democratic Society] to moods of despair. Right now I share that despair, because I am part of that left. I share the ideals of the left. Even-though-my-field-is-art I wish to politicise-that-category-and-relate-it-to-the-whole.*

*Notice I said* paradoxes *above. A paradox is not a dilemma, nor is it a contradiction. With these latter two we can still* choose. *You choose one and lose or suffer the alternative. The result may not be exactly happy but the choice is still logically possible. A paradox is different, it totally bankrupts* choice. *Nothing is possible and a self-perpetuating oscillation is set in motion. Faced with our current situation, recognizing social realities, considering the way I want to act, paradoxes follow paradoxes. This is nothing new but it is increasingly leading to a kind of pandemoniacal despair. A moral anguish which so far I refuse to romanticize, but I will if it keeps me out of the looney bin. . . .*

*The question remains: who do we direct our activism at and who is it for? Do we simply assail "the art-establishment"? Our very own privileges? In which case, who listens? Joseph's [Kosuth] and Sarah's [Charlesworth] radical academics? Terry Smith's radical academics? Michael's [Corris] Marxist chums? Maybe, maybe? The greatest subversion of the privileged* Kunstwelt *would be to refuse to make art for that* Kunstwelt *whilst making an art as ambitious as that* usually seen in the Kunstwelt. *I have no idea of course how to do this.*

## DOCUMENT IV, DECEMBER 1975

In the fall, 1975, Art & Language New York received a postcard from the artist Lawrence Weiner bearing the cryptic message: "a meeting is desired." Weiner was the go-between acting on behalf of a larger group of artists and critics, including Lucy Lippard, Carl Andre, Sol LeWitt, Miriam Schapiro and a collective of African-American artists calling themselves the "Black Emergency Cultural Coalition." These individuals and groups, and many others, formed the nucleus of a coalition named "Artists Meeting for Cultural Change" (AMCC). AMCC was a very loose "coalition" of mostly artists and art workers who met regularly at Artists Space (155 Wooster Street, New York City) on Sunday evenings. The meetings were open, and anyone was able to participate in the ensuing discussions. "Such a process demands commitment," writes Sarah Charlesworth in 1976, "and very irregular attendance of participants poses obstacles to developing group consciousness and effectiveness." The following is the first official communiqué of the coalition, addressed "To the American Art Community from Artists Meeting for Cultural Change," from which the present text is taken.

Next September, as one of its four Bicentennial exhibitions, the Whitney Museum of American Art in New York City will present a show entitled *Three centuries of American art—* a package deal, originating in April at the De Young Museum in San Francisco.

But this show isn't simply another example of bureaucratic mediocrity as it is entirely culled from the private collection of John D. Rockefeller III and includes no Black artists and only one woman artist.

Try and imagine Rockefeller and his staff of experts quaintly constructing a history of American art from the complacent viewpoint of the power elite. What this show is not is *Three centuries of American art;* it is, however, a blatant example of a large cultural institution writing the history of American art as though the last decade of cultural and social reassessment had never taken place.

We, the undersigned, strongly object to the collusion of the De Young and Whitney Museums and John D. Rockefeller III in using a private collection of art, with its discriminatory omissions, to promote upper class values and a socially reactionary view of American art history.

*Several of us met on 5 December with Tom Armstrong, director of the Whitney, to discuss our objections to this show. We stressed that such a celebration of exploitation and acquisition was hardly an appropriate homage to our long-buried revolution. Mr. Armstrong instinctively resorted to bureaucratic diversionary tactics, stated "I'm not willing to go into a dialogue with you or your groups," and left us completely unsatisfied. On 8 December, a larger art community meeting was called to discuss possible actions against the Whitney and other museums and cultural institutions around the nation which are using the Bicentennial to reinforce the values, taste, prestige and power of the ruling class . . .*

We will be picketing the Whitney on 3 January 1976 at 2.00 p.m. *Additional strategies to be employed in the next year include: picketing to coincide with key American history holidays, alternative street exhibitions and an alternative catalogue, a slide show for education purposes and letters to Congresspersons. This letter is the first step in setting up a national network to protest such misuse of art and artists for the Bicentennial—and afterwards.*

Ad Hoc Women Artists Committee, Art & Language, *Art Worker's News,* Artists & Writers Protest, Black Emergency Cultural Coalition, Creative Women's Collective, *The Fox,* Guerrilla Art Action Group, WEB, Women in the Arts, Women's Art Registry.

Carl Andre, Benny Andrews, Rudolf Baranik, Arnold Belkin, Karl Beveridge, Camille Billops, Willie Birch, Vivian Browne, Ian Burn, Sarah Charlesworth, Michael Chisholm, Carole Conde, Michael Corris, Peter Frank, Leon Golub, Hans Haacke, Suzanne Harris, Alex Hay, Preston Heller, Elizabeth Hess, Jene Highstein, Leandro Katz, Joseph Kosuth, Nigel Lendon, Sol LeWitt, Lucy Lippard, Andrew Menard, Irving Petlin, Mel Ramsden, Ginny Reath, Miriam Schapiro, Joan Semmel, Jackie Skiles, Pat Steir, May Stevens, Mayo Thompson.

## DOCUMENT V, 1975–76

A questionnaire authored by Mel Ramsden and Mayo Thompson was circulated within the group sometime during late 1975 and early 1976. Thompson—who had recently become involved with Art & Language in New York—had previously spent some time in Great Britain working with Michael Baldwin, Lynn Lemaster, Philip Pilkington and others on a number of songs which would be released during the summer of that year as *Music-language*. The title *Red faces* refers to a projected "opera" about the tragi-comic consequences of the group's—and by extension, all artists'—contradictory class location. The original document, from which the present text is taken, lists twenty-four questions. *Red faces* was never completed.

*Your reply's [sic] to the following list of questions will provide us with the base for your participation in* Red faces. *Take as much space as you want—just reply in the way you think appropriate—only for Christ's sake don't get creative or contrive to "write songs." Answer whatever questions you want . . . extrapolate. The questions are sort of arbitrary—extracted from a modest text on organization. They don't ooze relevance and there are no booby-traps:*

*1. Do you think there is a ruling class conspiracy in the United States? If so, what is it that in your view constitutes that conspiracy? (Rather than "conspiracy," consider "ruling class complex.")*

*2. Liberal institutions make use of radicals and dissenters to give a diversified veneer to their own, in fact repressive institutions. Do you think a)* The Fox *pack is being or will be used in this way, and b) if so, what would it take for* The Fox *pack to move on to a higher logical-institutional space—assuming we're not already in that space. Another way of putting this might be: how do we escape a merely inverse relation to the art-world or, how do we move from dependent critical theory to autonomous radical theory? . . .*

*8. How do you feel about the fact that M. Ramsden and M. Thompson are scripting* Red faces *and formulating these questions? . . .*

*12. Do you think "being an artist" is a description of an ontologically special mind with a fundamental mental endowment called "creativity" or do you think being an artist is a* social contribution? *Is this the same as saying: being an electrician doesn't describe what that person is, it descries their social contribution? In saying creativity is either a state of mind or a social contribution should this in fact be framed in either/or terms? Could you imagine any situation in which these either/or terms could be heuristic-propagandistic. What purpose could be served by insisting on an either/or formulation? . . .*

## DOCUMENT VI, 1975

The Anti-Imperialist Cultural Union (AICU) began to recruit members from AMCC [Artists Meeting for Cultural Change] during the winter of 1975. Composed almost exclusively of African-Americans who had been active in the Black Nationalist organizations which emerged after the Newark Riots following the assassination of Dr. Martin Luther King, the AICU sought to enlarge their social base to include SoHo artists to form a new, "mass organization." A leading figure in the AICU was Amiri Baraka (aka LeRoi Jones, the well-known beat poet), of the Congress of Afrikan People (CAP) and, later, the Revolutionary Communist League (RCL). The following is taken from an early draft of the organization's Principles of Unity submitted by CAP.

*We propose the name Anti-Imperialist Cultural Union for this organization. As Georgi Dimitrov pointed out to the Union of Bulgarian Writers: "Its task is to develop devotion and love for the people, intensifying the general aversion to fascism and all people's enemies, to scourge everything that is rotten and noxious for the healthy people's organism (parasitism, vulgar careerism and petty egoistic political intrigues)." (We also propose that the character of the organization be that of a mass organization made up of people in various organizations, individuals and class strata, all joined together around a common issue.)*

*"Anti-Imperialist" because our class stand opposes Imperialism wherever it exists, "Cultural" in order to include all the arts and artists who through their creative labor take the raw materials found in the life of the people and shape them into the ideological form of literature and art serving the masses of the people, and "Union" to reflect the proposed mass character of the organization. We unite to take revolutionary action to end our oppression and exploitation caused by the system of Imperialism. . . .*

Presented by the Congress of Afrikan People

## DOCUMENT VII, MARCH 1976

In March 1976, a series of meetings on the issue of ALNY's organizational form took place. At that time, a number of provisions were put forward in draft form with the intention to force the issue of collaboration under the name "Art & Language." Since his association with Art & Language in the late 1960s, Kosuth's "independent" practice had always been a contentious issue for many members of the group; but it was probably Kosuth's alleged opportunism with respect to *The Fox* that provided the straw that broke the camel's back. With the numbers involved in *ALNY/The Fox* now into double digits, the potential danger of this sort of "sectarianism" to the cohesion of the group was exacerbated. The "provisions" for a new form of organization were translated into French and publicly displayed for the first time on the occasion of an exhibition of "(Provisional) Art & Language" at Eric Fabre Gallery, Paris in April 1976 of a project initiated and produced by the "subgroup" constituted by Michael Corris, Preston Heller and Andrew Menard. Excerpts of minutes of the meeting of Monday, 2 March 1976 as transcribed by Nigel Lendon are presented here.

Draft for Form of Organization

*1 — All work which is "made public" will be represented under the collective name. This applies to exhibitions, publishing articles, teaching and any other working [sic] which has a "public" form.*

*2 — All work which is "made public" has to be discussed and accepted by the general body. This will set up a framework for criticism/self-criticism of work (something which has been lacking in the past). In this matter the will of the general body has to prevail.*

*3 — Working "publicly" in an individualistic manner will be considered as self-disqualification from this process . . .*

Questions still to be clarified:

*1 — The key question . . . economic issues*
*2 — "Decentralized" working*
*3 — Collective work, meaning? . . .*
*4 — The question of teaching, and other forms of speaking in public; that is, when the content and direction of what we say is not known in advance; do we represent, in "informed" good faith, what we believe to be the group's position? (in this transitional period, before positions are clarified?)*
*5 — "The will of the general body;" does this mean unanimous (prior?) decision?—or the consensus of those members who can reasonably meet to discuss, subject to later review, reversal or criticism by the general body?*

6 — *What is, who constitutes the "general body"?—it was suggested that only those "working"*
*qualify for inclusion, which would seem to rest on a formal question of a definition of "work."*

## DOCUMENT VIII, AUGUST 1976

In 1975, (Provisional) Art & Language received an invitation from Carlo Ripa di Meana, the director of La Biennale di Venezia, to exhibit as part of the "Aperto" section. During spring 1976, we discussed the production of a large red cloth banner to bear the following inscription in white: "Ars Longa, Vita Brevis Est. Welcome to Venice: the dictatorship of the bourgeoisie 'eternalizes' local color." The plan was to display the banner on the exterior of one of the venues of "Aperto."

Olle Granath, a curator associated with the Biennale, expressed his horror at the possibility of such an installation actually taking place. In a telegram dated 20 May and addressed to the group in New York, he stated: "I only want to communicate to you that there is no possibility to put your 'banner' outside the pavilion of the exhibition, it has to be put inside." Flora Lewis reported on the Biennale in *The New York Times* of 25 August 1976, from which the present text is taken.

Venice Biennale's Revival Offers Vitality
   *. . . Two competing, antagonistic American groups were also permitted to enter contributions.*
   *One, whose leader calls himself Joseph Kossuth [sic], brought a batch of huge posters headlined "Where Do You Stand?" Pointing out the importance of knowing one's "social location," it offers a series of multiple-choice pre-packaged reactions to the whole Biennale.*
   *They run the gamut from rejection of it all, because by the very fact of being organized it represents authority and is therefore anti-revolutionary, through varying degrees of artistic arrogance and philistine confusion ("nothing makes any sense to me" is one choice) to rejection of it all because art is a private matter and must not be tainted by social commentary or politics.*
   *The other American group, called The Fox, protested bitterly against such a leaven of humor. But Mr. di Meana managed to assuage them by allowing them to put up a huge red banner outside the old shipyard at Giudecca, where the "international contemporary" exhibition has been organized, and where graphics are to be shown next month. The banner proclaims, "Welcome to Venice: the dictatorship of the bourgeoisie 'eternalizes' local color."*

*Mr. di Meana said The Fox group arranged some open meetings with Italian workers, students and others to explain the depth of their commitment, as artists, to social concerns.*

*"They were completely sincere," he said, "but to such highly politicized people as Italians you can't be candid in that way. The Italians just didn't trust them, they were so naive."*

## DOCUMENT IX, 1976

ALNY has been in a virtually continuous state of crisis since March 1976, when the group adopted a number of formal principles which effectively disqualified Charlesworth and Kosuth from continued membership. By June, some of us argued for an organizational structure closer to a federation: less disciplined than a party, but more cohesive than an amalgamation of sub-groups. At all times, these discussions were taking place in the context of a deep involvement with the so-called Marxist-Leninist-Maoist left. Throughout the June meetings, one can chart the relation to "class struggle;" the need to analyze and act upon our contradictory class "location," and to sort-out "social-sectional tasks" with respect to the "proletariat," to socialism, and to . . . "revolution." We were generally contemptuous of the "revisionist" stance of "cultural" workers pressing for a "cultural" revolution in advance of a political revolution. In short, many of us promoted a startlingly romantic workerism, and by so doing rehearsed and prolonged the most pernicious illusions of the 1960s left for the benefit of the art world.

During June 1976, (Provisional) Art & Language (PA&L) met in the basement of Carol Conde's and Karl Beveridge's residence at 49 East First Street, Manhattan. Present over the weeklong course of meetings were Karl Beveridge, Jill Breakstone, Carol Conde, Michael Corris, Preston Heller, Andrew Menard, Nigel Lendon, Mel Ramsden, Paula Ramsden and Mayo Thompson. As the meetings progressed, the atmosphere of the discussions grew progressively more tense, polarized, and argumentative. It became clear to most of us by the end of the week that the true purpose of these meetings was to force the issue of the "semi-autonomy" of the sub-groups. This issue was refracted through a discussion of "class" and the nature of our class location as artists.

The two positions which emerged at these meeting are attributable to the positions held by each of two dominating blocs or "sub-groups." Referred to at one point by Mayo Thompson as the "minority" and "majority," this allusion to the historically prior ideological struggle of the Mensheviks and Bolsheviks was clear. The position consistently voiced by Ramsden and Thompson positioned PA&L as undeniably petit-bourgeois; nor, however, incapable of doing progressive work within and around our social-sectional "base." The second position, articulated mainly by Corris, Heller and Menard, mapped the artists'—and by implication, the groups'—class location within a more transitional space. To support this claim, the notion of the "proletarianization" of the petit-bourgeois professional was muted. It was a favored concept of Menard's, and one that would make its influence felt in the pages of *Red-Herring*, especially in that publication's latter numbers.

The group was virtually evenly split between those who wished to continue to work in and around the art world and its institutions and those who were willing to jettison such a commitment once and for all. Those who supported the latter offered up a program of voluntary merger with suitable "working class"—oriented mass organizations and/or "pre-party" formations. The principal candidates for amalgamation at the time were the AICU [the Anti-Imperialist Cultural Union] and the RCL [the Revolutionary Cultural League]. As a self-styled "mass organization," the AICU was already well known to us. Dismissed by Baldwin months earlier as "Maoist pipsqueaks," the AICU was nevertheless held in some esteem by PA&L. The RCL, in contrast, was not a mass organization, but a "pre-party" formation; it was not open to White volunteers, only "auxiliary" members.

The following text, taken from an unpublished position paper authored by Andrew Menard, is a reflection on the internal history of the group since March 1976. It was circulated between the end of June and mid September, 1976; precisely on the cusp of the final fragmentation of (Provisional) Art & Language.

*At first glance it almost seemed that the March meetings, culminating in the provisions and ushering in our second phase, were not simply a means of purging Joseph [Kosuth] and Sarah [Charlesworth], but a resolution of the contradictions defining our first phase, a "negation of a negation." While it was necessary to expose the opportunist-cum-anarchist finery of Joseph and Sarah as the ideological equivalent of the "layered look"—liberalism—it was also necessary to take a bead on opportunism within the group in general. So we developed the idea of "collectivization": making work public under one name only and generating work from the center of the table. More importantly, the provisions were* the first explicit standard of membership *the group had ever developed, and thus appeared to be a strategy of sorts, a more or less inarticulate groping towards "party unity." Though the provisions were seen as "procedural constraints," applying only until we reached "further clarity in relation to organizational form," they were constantly evoked in discussions during the second phase. Both the method of generating work and the work itself were constantly judged according to this standard. As such, it was assumed that adhering to the provisions would "resolve," or begin to "resolve" the accelerating contradiction of the group's laissez-faire form and its increasingly "Socialist" content. If anything went wrong it meant we weren't adhering to the provisions, not that the provisions themselves might be inadequate.*

*Unfortunately the provisions were inadequate, from the very start. Instead of resolving the contradictions of the first phase, they both embodied and intensified those contradictions. This is because they never resolved the principal contradiction of the first phase—the contradiction between our material base in the glittering bourgeois world of Culture and Highbrow Conversation and our historical projectivity towards (the advanced sectors of) the working class. In fact, caught on the horn of this principal contradiction, the provisions both embodied and intensified, not resolved, every contradiction of the first phase. At best it was two steps forward, one step back; hardly a "negation of a negation" . . .*

*Yes, the provisions were stillborn, I think we can all agree on that. Their main function was to intensify the contradiction between our social base and our historical projectivity, and the contradiction between sub-group sectarianism and group unity. (Without the acrimony, and with less confusion about form and content, the June showdown might have gone the other way, might have united us: the contradiction between a completely exploded group and a completely unified one was white-hot at the time.) By doing this the provisions made both contradictions more obvious. At the same time, they exposed their own limitation as a resolution of these contradictions. It's time to get rid of them. They were like John Ford trying to remake "October." (Whatta you mean a wagon-train isn't a revolutionary cadre . . .). A strategy shouldn't be primarily economistic and spontaneous to the core, it should be political and principled. It's time to develop that strategy.*

## DOCUMENT X, 1976

In early September, Breakstone, Corris, Heller, and Menard jointly drafted a statement to AMCC in the name of (Provisional) Art & Language (PA&L). A confrontation at Ramsden's loft over the above-mentioned communiqué resulted in the aforementioned sub-group's disenfranchisement, as Ramsden asserted what he took to be his "historical" prerogative to the "name" Art & Language. Burn responded incredulously to what he considered to be an absurdly transparent pretext to void the group of its supposedly "destabilizing" elements. The encounter was brief, brutal, and to the point and from the point of view of Ramsden and Thompson effectively "resolved" the organization's contradiction that had dogged PA&L since the end of March. In retrospect, these "problems" were present, to a greater or lesser extent, since ALNY's inception. When the dust finally settled, Beveridge, Breakstone, Burn, Conde,

Corris, Heller and Menard re-grouped as a new editorial collective. The collective immediately began work to publish a tabloid-format magazine, titled *Red-Herring*. A not-for-profit foundation—the "Cultural Information Foundation" (CIF)—was established for the purpose of securing and administering funds from the New York State Council on the Arts (NYSCA) and the National Endowment for the Arts (NEA). In January 1977 the premiere issue of *Red-Herring* was launched; it was distributed through the same channels as its predecessor, *The Fox*. The following is excerpted from "Organization: a working paper," a text collectively developed during the fall, 1976 although largely the work of Burn.

*Many artists are, for many reasons, organizing themselves into "groups," "unions," communalities, or perhaps just talking possibilities. But, for the most part, "organization" has no particular significance per se. No aspiring "rank and file"-high-culture-social-section-alliance can be realistic if its principles of organization fail to take into account the class historical nature of the process it is initiating. Those enlisted in the high-cultural ranks know the contradictions mounted by a predatory capitalist culture: the intentions of our working are carefully, and violently misrepresented. We become forces opposed to ourselves. We are exploited at the same time that we are forced into exploitative relations to others. We are unable to translate human needs into social outcomes. Our social alienation forces us into adopting forms of psychological expression . . .*

*What happens when artists try to reacquire a bit of control? Say you picket a museum, say the Whitney Museum in protest against the showing of John D. Rockefeller III's collection as "a history of American art." Take a good look at the basis of such an action. It is first of all a protest against the cultural forms which are used to "represent" us. As an action in concert, it's a social action against one small aspect (incident) of the prevailing culture-spectacle. At the same time, it does amount to the action of a broad spectrum in a social section . . .*

*We are not cultural "workers"; we are only marginally "workers." Admittedly, "culture" and "society" are not easy to separate in any hard and fast way. There are however particular reifications which must be excluded from social possibility. What passes for "social content" in our social section is pretty much embroiled in the political character of all other superstructural forms, compromising any notion of "social content." A fixed, and so false distinction between "social consent" and "political form" is—given the necessity of class analysis, given our social section—a mystification of our historical dislocation from the means of production . . .*

*It would be easy to organize everyone's chip-on-the-shoulder, then sit on it and exploit it to maintain a continuous organization. What for? A "union" or any other form of organization can't be built on membership passivity; form must be sorted out on principles of participation and on what we organize against. Such principles cannot presuppose exclusive or hierarchical forms. If this is really about ideology, that point can't be stressed enough. No productive forms are "inherently more valuable" then others, the measure is history, social-historical "impact."*

## POSTSCRIPT

By early 1977, the original founders of ALNY had scattered to the four winds: Ian, Avril, and Daniel Burn set off for Australia; Mel, Paula and Anne Ramsden made their way back to the South Midlands of Great Britain. Those involved with ALNY during the early to mid 1970s followed suit, or re-grouped in New York. Mayo Thompson and Christine Kozlov emigrated to Great Britain; for a time working with Michael Baldwin, Mel Ramsden and Charles Harrison. Carole Conde, Karl Beveridge, the late Jill Breakstone, Preston Heller, Andrew Menard and myself remained in New York for a few years to continue to publish *Red-Herring* and work in the milieu of left and ultra-left "mass" organizations and Maoist "pre-party" formations. What remained of the "left wing" of the AMCC splintered and gravitated towards more extensive organizations, including the AICU, the League for Proletarian Revolution, and the dissident wing of the Transit Workers Union of New York City. In late 1978, the *Red-Herring* editorial collective was riven with internal conflicts as well; the contentious issue being, ironically, the continued autonomy of the magazine in the face of overwhelming pressures to throw our lot in with those for whom culture was nothing more than a political weapon. By 1979 former *Red-Herring* editors such as Andrew Menard had effectively united with the AICU and helped to publish a thoroughly Zhdanovite cultural magazine titled *Main Trend*. There were other players, of course; and other trajectories. Kathy Bigelow, who had established relations with ALNY during 1975, eventually moved west to establish herself as a director in Hollywood; Alex Hay, associated with ALNY for a brief period around 1975–76, took off for the southwest. Terry Smith and Nigel Lendon—both of whom had spent one year in NY and had worked closely with Ian Burn and others in ALNY—returned to Australia.

A farewell party for the Ramsdens and the Burns in early 1977 held at Karl Beveridge and Carol Conde's Lower East Side loft was the last, bittersweet moment of congregation. Sometime later, during the early to mid 1980s, I struck up a correspondence with Ian Burn. It was not until 1985 that I was once again face-to-face with Mel and Paula Ramsden, Michael Baldwin and Lynn Lemaster. Finally, I renewed my acquaintance with Christine Kozlov in London during the summer of 1989; just this year I encountered Mayo Thompson for the first time in nearly two decades.

**NOTES**

1. See my "The artist out of work?" *Word and Image* 9, no. 2 (April/June 1993), for a contextualization of the practices and ideological debates of Art & Language in terms of a wider history of Conceptual Art.

2. The full version of Burn's reply was published in *Art-Language* 3, no. 2 (May 1975), pp. 81–87.

This text appeared in *Artists Think: The Late Works of Ian Burn* (Sydney and Melbourne: Power Publications, in association with Monash University Gallery, 1996), pp. 60–71.

# statement
## martha rosler

From an early age I felt oppressed by a conspiracy of silences, silences about things in the wider world most of which were perpetually present, unspoken but forming the unmarked boundaries of the possible. I felt the passivity and fatalism that went along with this silence. I was also moved by my private responses to images, responses apparently shared by no one, to look deeply into images and to mine what was unspoken and unacknowledged there.

In my teens I was deeply influenced by contemporary poetry, which addressed in direct and angry words the betrayal of people by "society" and by public figures. The poet's universe was marginal, but it was part of the New York bohemian world, which included musicians, performers and artists, makers of Happenings and events outside the ordinary art-world venues of slick dealerships and highbrow museums. It wasn't even the world of John Ashbery, Denise Levertov, already of an older generation—though it did draw in Robert Creeley, Robert Duncan, Charles Olson, some Black Mountain figures—but of Jackson MacLowe and Leroi Jones, Diane Wakoski and Diane DiPrima, Paul Blackburn, Meg Randall, and the people to whom I was closest, David Antin and Jerome Rothenberg. (Sometimes referred to as Deep Image poets. This is not negligible.) They led me to Jess and Ray Johnson, and also to Pop, Warhol, Allan D'Arcangelo, George Maciunas, Yoko Ono and Fluxus, to Carolee Schneeman, and of course to Duchamp. It brought me an infusion of rationalism and calculation. Before this, seeing de Chirico, Delvaux, Cornell, and Magritte, I thought I might relinquish Abstract Expressionism for surrealism. I made boxes and little peep shows. I learned to ground this surrealism in a materialist analysis and therefore a rationalized space.

By the mid-60s I was drawing sustenance from the political movements. I felt impelled to reject the pseudo-scientific "experimental" approach to making art, roughly derived from physics but focused on aesthetic problem solving and individual perception. I soon realized that the work that had the most meaning for me, that drew deep, was engaged with the imagery of the "other" world of power, control, and ideological articulation. I found myself drifting away from the tight-knit community of poets, their parallel world of dis engagement and rejection only occasionally ruptured by organized expressions of anger and protest over the violence directed against the black movement and against the Vietnam War. I was unconcernedly alienated from the high art world, like so many other people making art at the time.

I moved to California and was in the right place at the right time to become part of the powerfully intertwined women's and antiwar movements. Still, the left remained overly suspicious of artists for their unreliability and individualism, maddening traits that I continue to value, though I might name them somewhat differently, since artists' experience with commissars hasn't been particularly productive in the long run. I was making work both at the margins of a community and from within it. I was making photo montages that I didn't call "art," though I didn't doubt they were, and I had no intention of placing them in the art world— that was the point. Instead, I wanted them to be agitational arguments meant to persuade.

These works themselves engaged with the notion of looking deep "inside the visible," for in looking at the imagery of the polite world of mainstream magazines, of newspapers and television, I saw worlds of power and wealth on some pages and on other pages, or in other slots, a world of victimized or dispossessed people. I saw men in suits and women in lingerie. I thought of this as the mythologies of everyday life, which kept mental images segregated from one another, serving to shore up ideological absurdities that kept life on an even keel in one neighborhood while around the corner the world was erupting. I kept thinking that if we could imagine Mrs. Jones as the woman machine-gunned with her kids in Vietnamese thatch, we would understand why it was a moral and political outrage. (Especially after Yugoslavia I realize that I misunderstood the nature and conditions of empathy.)

I put my photomontages in underground newspapers and on flyers. When they were appropriated by other publications I was pleased by the anonymity of it. Those I didn't use publicly I showed to my friends. At present, the ones that were made in convenient sizes continue to exist, though some are damaged, while those made on, say, 8-foot sheets of mason-ite I abandoned.

The triumph of postwar modernism had been so complete that its notions of art had been naturalized and essentialized, unnamed. Even through the early seventies, the words modernism and postmodernism went unmentioned in art schools. There was no framework there for helping me articulate my responses to public events; when I applied to graduate school in Southern California in the early 1970s, a friend suggested I apply on the grounds of wanting to make political photomontage respectable; her partner, a senior faculty member, emphatically suggested I apply with paintings and writing. I entered as a painter. However, I felt isolated in the studio in a way I did not when I worked with photography, video, performance, and installation. I continued making antiwar photomontages that I still refused to put in the art world on the grounds of the obscenity of such a move, though I had showed other works in museums and "alternative spaces."

Because of our rejection of art world institutions and our determination to change the art system, a few of us felt we should write. In effect we became designated writers for the group. Writing seemed a natural and ordinary move for artists, since few critics were friendly, and even favorable reviews were primarily rewritten press releases. Writing about art was part of our art practice—and there were often words in my work—but I didn't intend to hypo-statize my writing as "theory." (The ad hoc nature of all of this is the ineradicable stamp of origins.) This was before high theory was industrialized and institutionalized within the university, before the conviction that art ought to be theory-driven, a conviction that now prevails in much of the discontinuous academy constituting professional art training. If we were proselytizing, we were doing so by making and showing work, by giving talks, and by teaching, teaching, teaching. The search for fame, fortune, and security was the last things on our covertly, quietly apocalyptic minds.

My interest in alternative methods of engagement led me to make videotapes for distribution outside the art world and to produce postcards—following Ray Johnson and Ellie Antin. Although I didn't know of anyone else using a narrative postcard form without images, lots of people were interested in doing video in the way that I was. The 60s alternative art movement was born of the artist's desire for autonomy, energized by social activism and drawing inspiration from the counter-cultural Zeitgeist. But the way that this has been written into art history is skewed toward precisely those institutions on which huge numbers of artists turned their backs. For example, the artists who showed their videotapes in one or two New York galleries instead of making them for distribution, the artists whose work was destined from its inception for New York art galleries, the photogra phers who made coffee-table books and showed their images of poverty, carnage, or emptiness in the Museum of Modern Art, appear as central figures in a history of art production that in no sense depended upon them or even saw them as central to the discourse or the praxis. This is a problem for art historians. But it is why I became persuaded to put these "non Art works" into a museum, a gallery, a dealership, and at least for now into art history. As Allan Kaprow observed pungently long ago, there is no art more Art than Non Art.

## II

My son the comix artist has recently interviewed me for a 'zine, called *Maxine,* "a literate companion for churlish girls and rakish women." Here's part of their call for submissions for an issue focusing on AMBITION: "Do you have it? . . . What, did it fly out the window the last time you weren't called on in math class? Or do you think the whole concept was concocted by the forces of consumer capitalism and keeps us chained to deadening cycles of production, consumption and display? Are you actually propelled through the spiral of life by something much cooler?" He added, "What has the word 'ambition' meant in your life? Have you found it important to be ambitious regarding your art and career?" My answer, unstated as such, was that everything that had organized my work precisely precluded answering a question posed in those terms, to us repressed and repressive. Now I recognize the words but don't know the answer.

## III

This is an odd moment for the system of art. Through most of the 80s the demands of capital shaped and reshaped this system, but the recession in the industrial powers after the '87 crash brought the eventual withdrawal of big capital. But the art system has not effectively reshaped itself. Artists entered the 80s with an inflated sense of control over their production, supported by a bustling field of artist-founded or artist-run centers, a fair number of grant-giving organizations respecting artists' ideas of what art was, and a sufficient critical establishment writing in trade journals. Dealers were held in some disdain, since few enough showed interest in what artists thought was hot. But the boom of the 80s tipped that world over. By the end of the decade there were plenty of dealers but almost no more critics, and most major art journals had become homes for academic adjuncts while cultural-studies journals, staffed by echt academics, proliferated. By the mid-90s many galleries had closed. If in the 70s the art world still spoke the language of bohemian avant gardism, in the 80s it was driven by a kind of bravura cynicism and by the end of the 80s, a necessary though quasi-balkanized politics of identity had taken hold. (*The New York Times* this week suggested that as the education of potential art audiences is curtailed, politics becomes the subject of art because it is easier to understand. I suppose this is a version of the socialist realism apologia—pose familiar arguments in recognizable terms.) For artists, what is the new paradigm?

In 1981, Russell Jacoby, in a symposium on intellectuals in the 80s, wrote that "in the long march through the institutions, the institutions won." He was writing about the decline of a transformative intellectual discourse and practice that he traced to left intellectuals' having found refuge in the academy—and the academy exacted its own price, namely, careerism and therefore caution. He comments, "Bankers guard the escape routes. Universities not only monopolize intellectual life, they bankrupt independent producers. In an economy of $3 trillion, the means of support for nonacademic intellectuals relentlessly shrinks. . . . Today even painters, dancers and novelists are usually affiliated with academic institutions." Following his caution that "a blind anti-academicism feeds and is fed by anti-intellectualism; there is no excuse for promoting either," he went on to observe that "as the world speeds towards renewed class antagonisms, decay and perhaps catastrophe, academics may be busily browsing through the department stores of knowledge, eyeing the goods and each other."

This text was presented at the College Art Association annual meeting in Boston, February 1996. It is previously unpublished.

# "dada—situationism/tupamaros—conceptualism": an interview with luis camnitzer

## blake stimson

Blake Stimson: Please tell me a little bit about the conceptual art book project you are working on.

Luis Camnitzer: The working title is "Dematerialization and Resistance: The Use and Misuse of Conceptualism in Latin American Art." It puts together many of the assorted premises that have informed my work since the sixties, among them: that art is an instrument to implement ethical beliefs and therefore part of an individual's political strategy, that certain forms of urban guerrillas expressed themselves with an aesthetic surplus that transcended military needs, that in Latin America visual arts cannot be fully understood without their relation to politics and poetry, and that the periphery has autonomous cultural parameters that cannot always be understood within the constraints given by canonical thought.

When I started reviewing my materials for the piece on conceptualism I found a scrap paper with a note from 1970 outlining a lineage which read "Dada—Situationism/Tupamaros—Conceptualism," reflecting some of my concerns. So, the idea of breaking away from the enclosed conceptual art stylistic definition was always there. Since then my paradigmatic figures have become Simón Rodríguez, the tutor of Simón Bolívar, and the Tupamaro movement, with pedagogy as the primary model for communication.

While it is true that the art pressures from the center are always present on the periphery (it is part of the relation of dependence first established by colonialism), this does not mean that central aesthetics have to serve, or do serve, the same purposes here, or that expressions on the periphery can be comprehended through the tools and values of the center. Thus, canonical "conceptual art" filters and distorts the perception of some manifestations that may overlap with it by means of superficial stylistic symptoms. Also, art history is usually written with a central clock running as a reference. I believe in the importance of local time-keeping when one tries to understand local events, which sometimes throws a monkey wrench into the neat original-derivative classification.

B.S.: Can you tell me more specifically what it was about the "enclosed conceptual art stylistic definition" that you were responding to in your work at the end of the 1960s? Were there particular art works or particular artists that represented that position for you? If so, how did that response manifest itself in your work and thinking?

L.C.: When I started to do "conceptual" work in 1966 I was not yet aware of works by other people. In my case the work developed as a reaction to the industrial finish of minimal art and the expense involved in the production of those pieces. I figured that carrying that thinking process to an extreme, I could conceive of taking the Empire State Building and have it redone in the shape of a "u." In that thought experiment I decided a) that it was economically immoral, b) that it betrayed my roots coming from a developing country, c) that the piece would be totalitarian in its relation to the public and d) that the enunciation of the idea sufficed and generated an appropriate and less intimidating image in the reader's mind. I was not interested in a "style" and in fact, when the term "conceptual" became fashionable, a group that I was a member of (The New York Graphic Workshop, with my ex-wife Liliana Porter—from Argentina—and José Guillermo Castillo—from Venezuela) discussed how, for us, "contextual art" would be a much more fitting term.

By then it was clearer what other artists were doing and that conceptual art was being treated as another discrete art historical movement rather than as an attitudinal break. I was not working "against" any artists symbolizing this, but basically ignoring them (which does not mean that I wasn't contaminated by them). So the art was not coming from a reaction to my peers. My interest in pursuing my work was to find an all-encompassing system rather than an exclusionary one, in which a minimum input would achieve a maximum reaction. Thus there was room for pedagogy, for politics, and for humor, perception, philosophy or whatever I felt like. The important issues were a) to help create a politically active and enlightened public, b) to demystify art and help the viewer become a creator, c) to liberate the viewer of the ownership imperative and d) to hopefully get society to a point in which artists would not be needed as mediators with reality so that I could pursue other things like veterinary or carpentry. I was suspicious of analytical art movements, that would try to construct a view of the world on a fragmentary aspect of things. I had seen pop art (at the time) as a synthesis approach (anything could fit into pop without disturbing it, any pop addition to another aesthetic would make it pop) and hoped to find a more ambitious "unifying field" or theory.

B.S.: What exactly did you and your associates do to help create a more politicized public? What role did your work play in this? When you say "help" does that suggest you were in active collaboration with other social movements, political organizations, etc.? If so, which?

L.C.: I hope I didn't sound too presumptuous in the previous (or any other) answer; your question makes me very self-conscious now because works and actions always end up being modest and with little or no consequence. I guess the biggest group effort was what started, in 1970, as the Museo Latinoamericano and then had a splinter group (to which I belonged) called MICLA (Movimiento por la Independencia Cultural Latino Americana). It was to be sort of a virtual museum that grouped Latin American artists in New York and included about thirty people, initially fighting against the Center for Interamerican Relations (now Americas Society) and what we perceived as misuse of Latin American intellectuals. The main action was the organization of an international boycott of the São Paulo Biennial to protest torture in Brazil and the publication of "Contrabienal," an exhibition in a book with work of those protesting. You will find more information in the paper. Another one, also in 1970, was to organize (with artist Julio Leparc and others) a demand of the organizers of the First Print Biennial of Puerto Rico to display a text dedicating the show to the liberation of the Latin American people. The text was signed by more than half of the participants and by three of the four artists that received prizes. Philip Morris was sponsoring the exhibit and decided to buy all the works of the Biennial so not to have to deal with the demand.

On a personal level it was more the standard denunciation bit many others were doing as well and which I am still doing today. In 1968 I made a series of etchings, each one bearing the name of some leader killed during Latin American resistance (Che, Marighela, Albizu Campos, Camilo Torres, etc.). In 1969 I did the "Masacre de Puerto Montt," an installation about the killing of squatters in the south of Chile by Frei's army, using xeroxed words on the wall and floor naming soldiers, weapons and bullet trajectories. The exhibit was in the Museum of Fine Arts, and in a gallery of the Ministry of Culture in Chile I exhibited the etchings and other works. The exhibitions took place during student upheavals and beatings. Liliana Porter was exhibiting with me and we forced the gallery to publish an accusatory document on the occasion of the show. The same year we were both invited to participate in an exhibit in the Instituto Di Tella in Buenos Aires. One piece of mine was to print on the big street window, taking the place of a title for the whole exhibit, the phrase "Arte Colonial Contemporáneo" (Contemporary Colonial Art), thus appropriating and criticizing the show itself. In the show room I had an area defined as "common grave" with tape and stenciled letters, and "fragment of a friend" stenciled on the angle of wall and floor, taking the position of a fallen body. This addressed directly the Argentine dictatorship. The Institute also sent out four mail-exhibits with cards bearing instructions on what to do with them, all the usages being (poetically) anti-dictatorship. Liliana Porter approached things in a less overt political fashion. She had painted shadows of people looking at the wall where they were painted, so that real shadows mixed with painted ones and everything cancelled out. Her mailings were shadows printed on cards to be completed with the objects (a glass, an olive, etc.).

When we were invited, as The New York Graphic Workshop, to exhibit in the "Information" show, we faced the conundrum of being co-opted into the mainstream. At the same time we were aware that it was career-suicide to turn the invitation down. Our solution was to announce a mail exhibit in the museum, have people put their address on envelopes provided there, and have the museum mail them the mail piece. The announcement sheet said: "The New York Graphic Workshop announces its mail-exhibition #14." The mailed piece was the exact sheet with only one letter changed: instead of "announces" it said "announced." We felt that with that we were in it without being in it and that we may upset the Museum's budget (we never found out how many mailings they had to make on our behalf). So, when I said "help create a politically active and enlightened public" I meant it in relatively quiet and intimate way, not thinking of mass rallies.

B.S.: Can you tell me more about the Instituto Di Tella and its role during the later 1960s in the development of what has come to be called "Latin American Conceptualism"?

L.C.: The Institute was an offspring of the Di Tella conglomerate, a company which produced a wide range of products including a variation of Fiat cars. The institute was created in 1958 and had several divisions, including music under Ginastera, an industrial design sector that looked up to the Design School of Ulm (the director of Ulm, succeeding Max Bill in 1956, was Tomás Maldonado, a prestigious Argentine painter) and visual arts, directed by Jorge Romero Brest, which started in 1960. Romero Brest was the most charismatic and, in certain ways, influential art theoretician in Latin America. He was extremely eloquent, challenging, eccentric, vaguely Marxist in his thought structure, successfully flirtatious with upper society ladies and a cynic. He formed many of the more important art critics of the generation following (Marta Traba for example) and wrote many books, although I cannot say that he left a systemic thought as a legacy (I would have to reread his stuff from that angle). His role through the Institute was to make Buenos Aires a center for cutting edge modernism and avant-garde art, and he succeeded. I am writing from what I remember, so this is not real history, but the first Lygia Clark, Tapies and Nevelson among other things, I saw because of Romero Brest's work in Di Tella. However, his cultural role was not a clear one from a political point of view and got mixed reactions from radical young artists. In part he was seen as providing needed primary sources of information. In part he was seen as serving as a conduit for cultural colonization. He always sponsored new and young artists, he promoted the "Otra Figuración" group (Noé, Deira, De la Vega and Macció) in 1961 (the forerunners of neo-expressionism), and he was sympathetic to anything new and liable of gathering attention. One cannot say that he or the Institute emphasized conceptualist expressions for any programmatic reason. People like Greco, Ferrari, Carreira, Bony, Jacoby, Plate, Lamelas and many others, all were working in that direction and it was only natural that the Di Tella would exhibit them.

The Di Tella had a yearly experimental exhibit. In 1968 Romero Brest's ideas about the exhibit conflicted with the projects presented by some of the artists and he asked them to revise their presentations. Some did, some refused, some protested publicly with letters (Pablo Suárez proclaimed his letter a piece of art). One of the revisions was by Roberto Plate, whose piece was the building of two simulated bathrooms where people started writing graffiti, mostly political, which led the regime to seal the rooms. This led all the other artists to remove their works as well. "Tucumán Arde" took place several months after that and included many of the artists that had been in the show. At this point, the Di Tella (and Romero Brest) became the symbol for the opposite of what "Tucumán Arde" stood for. When I visited in 1969, I was not fully aware of the state of affairs. I had known Romero Brest for nearly ten years (he had seen my beginnings as an artist, expressionist wood cuts and had told me that they were OK, but that I still needed to suffer to achieve any quality) and, during what was a social visit, he invited us to participate in the "Experiencias 1969" exhibition. I accepted and then, finding out more about what was going on and unable to withdraw, decided to make a point by "titling" the exhibition "Contemporary Colonial Art."

B.S.: I know that the Di Tella Institute funded exchange between Argentinean and New York art circles. How did that impact the ways in which conceptualism emerged? For example, Lucy Lippard has referred repeatedly to being politicized by her visit to Rosario and her meeting with the Tucumán Arde group. Since you were working both in New York and South

America at this time can you tell me your understanding of how it was that conceptualism emerged as a vital aesthetic sensibility in both contexts at the same time? In what ways can we tie the two developments together? In what ways should we keep them distinct?

L.C.: The Di Tella was interested in a New York–Buenos Aires exchange, and an exhibit "New Art of Argentina" was organized in 1964 in conjunction with the Walker Art Center and "Beyond geometry" in the Center for American Relations in 1968. For a while it had a yearly competition with a national and an international prize, the latter given to artists like Nevelson, Noland and Rosenquist, and I know that Sol Lewitt went at some point. However, this does not seem the conduit for conceptualism and I think that I would rather keep a division and deal with distinct phenomena. After all Alberto Greco was doing his "vivo dito" in 1962 and he claimed that he had signed bathrooms in Paris as early as 1954. Ferrari did his written painting in 1964; Costa, Jacoby and Escari did their fictional happening (one that only happened through the appearance of concerted reviews in different magazines about a news item that didn't really take place) in 1966.

Many of the participants in "Tucumán Arde" resented being absorbed into a movement that followed them without crediting them for having preceded it. Much of Latin American conceptualism was a consequence of an anti-colonialist and anti-imperialist stance and to co-opt it into the New York movement seems not only historically tricky because of the dates involved, but may also be interpreted as offensive by many artists. Argentina was always nationalistic to the extreme of chauvinism and even in the left there was an odd mixture of enlightened socialist views combined with retrograde patriotism. Most of the conceptualists were focused on Argentina. Many had gone through some kind of geometry and minimalism and sometimes had U.S. art influence during that phase, but the entry into conceptualist stances was one of cleansing, not of following.

B.S.: I want to shift the discussion slightly by raising the question of form. Mari Carmen Ramírez argues in her MoMA catalog essay that conceptualism held particular appeal for Latin American artists not only because of its institution-critical ambitions (which served the politicized contexts in, for example, Argentina and Brazil), but also, specifically, for its attenuated materiality "suited to the . . . economic precariousness of Latin America" (p. 158). If we grant this point, it seems to me, questions of who came first and of center and periphery are less important, at least from historical and critical perspectives. That is, we might see two distinct developments within the history of modernism, responding to, among other things, that history (the figure of Duchamp, for example, and the historic avant-gardes of the 1920s and 30s). The political circumstances were different in the two contexts, as you have pointed out, but so were the economic circumstances and the sense of confidence in the art economy. In 1968, for example, the U.S. was still riding a boom and the art world was experiencing an unprecedented infusion of cash from a new wave of very ambitious collectors, the rise of corporate sponsorship and from a renewed emphasis on government funding represented most notably by the NEA. Could you comment on the different economic circumstances at work in the two contexts and how they differently and similarly influenced (what we might agree, for the purposes of discussion, to refer to as) "the dematerialization of art"?

L.C.: Well, that is precisely the point I tried to tell Alex Alberro when we had our conversation a couple of years ago. It is the same point that made Jane Farver, Rachel Weiss and me want to organize the Queens Museum exhibit and, earlier, what many years ago prompted me to start writing about this. There are local clocks and many histories on this, not even just two. China elaborated its own version in the 1980s, so did Korea, and Japan started somewhere in the 1950s. And if you accept Lettrist and Situationist contributions as part of this history(ies), the configuration becomes even richer within the mainstream itself. And in Latin America it also becomes complicated to put everything into one mold: Brazil, benefiting from concrete and neo-concrete poetry had approached this very early. So did Argentine artists, for somewhat different reasons. Chile and Venezuela found their way a decade later. Colombia had one artist in the late 1960s (Salcedo) and another one in the early and mid 1970s (Caro).

Some countries never felt the need to engage in conceptualist activities. But in each of the cases what happened was not necessarily conditioned by what *Artforum* had to say, but mostly by what questions were to be answered locally (I am talking here not about artists following fads, but the culturally more important ones). Among those questions economy was a crucial one. Economy, on one hand, was used as a determinant for politics and, on the other, a determinant for production. Many artists did react to the affectation of reproducing an "affluent finish" typical of the hegemonic mainstream. Somewhere I mentioned that "arte povera" was more influential for some artists because of the evocations of the title than for the actual work. But it was not just a "make do" approach based on modest available media. That would have immediately led to the craftsy-identity stuff and the recycling approach in installations (particularly Cuba, Chile and some in Mexico) that came about in the 1980s in Latin America. It was more of a political assumption of a poverty coinciding with an absence of a serious art market (serious in the sense of an ability to support artists). Good artists were educated in their countries and then funded to travel to the cultural centers, rather than funded to contribute locally. That was taken for granted and, for me at least, it took some political enlightenment to discover that there was something wrong about this setup. But we shouldn't be too schematic. There were anti-institutionalist artists (in the broadest sense) in the U.S. and there were artists that tried to find their niche of originality in Latin America. So when I am laying all this out, it is more about a differences in general patterns and cultural aims and impacts, perforated by many individual exceptions.

B.S.: Yes, I think we can grant the different clocks theory but it is important too to characterize the networks of influence and common or related experience between different regions—New York–Buenos Aires, for example—and to understand why these various practices which we are assuming can all be grouped together under the rubric "conceptualism" emerged when they did and as they did. This does not mean we need to fall back on a strict innovator/follower model or even a center/periphery model but I also think we don't want to assume, even as a general pattern, that artists in Latin America were responding to local and global political issues while artists in New York were responding to *Artforum*. The question then becomes, what historical determinants do they share and how are they inflected by local circumstances? If we don't grant a shared history (above and beyond a shared art history) to the developments in question then the "conceptualism" that they share is rendered a matter of coincidence or merely stylistic. We might, for example, venture the following very general claim—that the conceptualism which emerged in New York and Argentina (as well as other places) represents an aesthetic radicalism that somehow corresponds to the (very different but nonetheless simultaneous) radicalization of the larger political cultures in the two contexts. A compelling historical question, it seems to me, is why artists in Argentina made the jump to throw their lot in with workers and activists (most notably in the 1968 Tucumán Arde event) and redefined their aesthetic in response to the heated political climate developing around them when artists in New York, by and large, did not develop an aesthetic position that sided directly with the Civil Rights Movement and the protests against the war that were transforming their milieu.

L.C.: I did not say or imply that North American artists were following *Artforum*. Some were and some were not, but *Artforum* (and I use it really as a metaphor for the direction of the flow of artistic information) was avidly read by many on the periphery and probably more in Argentina than in other Latin American countries, since particularly Buenos Aires had high cosmopolitan pretensions. So, if we were to discuss abstract-expressionism we would have a different conversation (I remember the impact in Uruguay, especially combined with informalism and the Spanish "arte-otro") and I don't think that this kind of art-making would have happened without influence. However, Pop art was well pushed as well and basically fell flat under the same conditions. I would say that to some extent at that particular time, conceptualism was a matter of coincidence more than of mutual knowledge (if we use 1964 as a reference), particularly in the political stream. Some, no doubt, were by some magazine information or returning tourist but in general, Latin America has a tradition which would lead to this art regardless of what was happening in that particular stream in other countries.

The dynamics toward radicalism were given from preceding international and national movements: there were Argentine destructionists in 1961, Greco was a link with "nouveau realisme," and then there were the political conditions. In Brazil, concrete poetry took place in the 1950s and fed from Antropofagia in the 1920s. I think that all of that (and that is why I take Simón Rodríguez as a paradigm), the fusion of poetry, politics and art in a long tradition, makes a local clock for conceptualism particularly relevant. I agree we should not leave out "shared historical determinants" and the percentages vary from individual to individual as much as artist groups to artist groups, etc. But there is always the danger of unilateralness in the definition of sharing. It took the U.S. half a century to "share" the ideas of university reform and one can say that in fact they never really shared but finally "discovered." The history of this belated "insight" illustrates the dangers of presumption in a definition of sharing and also explains your question about lack of coordination of art with the civil rights movement. The lack of politicized academic tradition explains the blandness of artistic positions during civil rights and Vietnam protests (I am separating art from artists-as-citizens here) in the U.S. vs. the presence and integration of political issues in Latin America.

This interview was conducted by e-mail, January-February 1998. It is previously unpublished.

jeff wall, benjamin h. d. buchloh, charles harrison, adrian piper, mari carmen ramírez, thomas crow

**VIII** critical histories of conceptual art

# dan graham's kammerspiel
## jeff wall

Dan Graham's unrealized (and possibly unrealizable) project *Alteration to a Suburban House* (1978) generates a hallucinatory, almost Expressionist image by means of a historical critique of conceptual art. In this work, conceptualism is the discourse which fuses together three of the most resonant architectural tropes of this century (the glass skyscraper, the glass house and the suburban tract house) into a monumental expression of apocalypse and historical tragedy.

In 1978, when the denunciation of conceptual art began to be openly articulated by advocates of new subjective, narcissistic and frankly commercial attitudes, Graham constructed a profoundly expressive work on the basis of conceptualism. At a moment when conceptualism's suppression of the expressive element in art, once seen as the movement's radical achievement, is decried as the source of its failure and collapse, Graham transformed conceptual methods into their opposites, drawing unexpected conclusions from them. These conclusions, embodied in the *Alteration* project, suggest a new historical moment in regard to conceptual art, the emergence of a new period in its interpretation and its historical significance.

Graham begins from the failure of conceptualism's critique of art. But his intention is not to celebrate that failure and throw away the lessons of the radical art of the 1960s in a theatricalized revival of the myth of authenticity. Rather, he intends with the *Alteration* project to build a critical memorial to that failure. In the very spirit of the movement memorialized, he builds it as a counter-monument.

In developing the *Alteration* project, Graham begins from a distressed recognition of conceptualism's failure of its own aim, which was to rebuild art from its core outward. He reflects upon the forces unleashed in art by that failure, and his artistic language as a whole emerges from his struggle within the crisis of radical modernism, exemplified for his generation by conceptual art. What is the content of this notion of crisis?

Conceptualism intensified and clarified attitudes developed by the pair of artistic movements which emerged from the decline of Abstract Expressionism in a Culture Industry setting. The Minimalist *and* the Pop artists based themselves on a repudiation of the extravagant inwardness of the Forties generation. Both groups stressed the impingement of the division of labor upon the image of the unified and organic artistic process taken over by Abstract Expressionism from its European sources. Both were "Constructivist" in this regard, and therefore implicitly re-opened an artistic argument which characterized the early decades of this century. That argument developed around the *form* art would take as society was liberated from the rule of capitalism, then seen to be in its "death-agony." But the common aspect of Pop and Minimal art which most affected the younger artists who became "conceptual" was precisely the two's inability to free themselves from the social aloofness and emotional indifference characteristic of post-1945 American art, as expressed above all in Greenbergian formalism (the institutional orthodoxy of the corporatized art business). Minimalism's suburbanite asceticism and the smirking ironies of Pop representationalism each took on the aura of serenity imposed from above, of cultural "normalization," characteristic of Cold War and corporate culture as seen by the young artists inspired by the anti-Vietnam upheaval and May '68. Conceptual art emerged from the disappointment and dissatisfaction with these art movements over the fact that the social forces and ideas which had been stirred and revived by the aggressively mechanistic and anti-expressive aspects of the new art, did not extend into the kind of radically explosive and disruptive expression desired within the cultural New Left. In the eyes of the conceptualists, the cultural shock effects of Minimal and Pop art had, by the late 60s, given rise only to a new, more complex and distressed version of the art-commodity. This guilt-ridden commodity could do no more than dramatize its own problematic and marginal character as source of surplus value and as transcendent form.

In this process of self-dramatization, there is a reversion to an earlier, unresolved dilemma of European modernism. The problem of the artistic critique of social unfreedom disappointed or frustrated by political disasters and transformed thereby into monumental emblems of social and spiritual crisis (rather than breaking through into symbolizing liberation) was the problem faced by all the great modern movements of the "heroic" period of revolutionary upheaval (1905–25). As the somber history of Abstract Expressionism shows, this tragic emblematicism was enshrined as the highest and most sublime value in the "triumph of American painting." The liberating shock of the assault of Pop and Minimal art on the enclosures of earlier work was aggravated and turned in a more critical direction by the subsequent spectacle of the great Rauschenbergs, Judds and Flavins taking their places in museums alongside the Picabias, Lissitzkys and Rothkos. This re-awakening of critical historical thought in the art of the 1960s corrodes the legitimacy of the very works which initiated the process most directly. Conceptual art's central intent is of course to interrogate the basis of that legitimacy. The question thus posed was: "What is the process in which the cultural crisis is not resolved socially, but transmuted into sublime fixation upon immobilized symbols and fetishes?"

Once again—and here the conceptualists resumed aspects of the Surrealist-Constructivist terms of critique—the styles of modern art are attacked because of the institutions for which they are seen to form a kind of essential facade. Conceptual art interrogates modern art as a complex of institutions which produce styles, types of object, and discourse, rather than questioning art in the academies' terms, of works of art first and foremost.

This interrogation is inconceivable outside the critical context in which conceptualism developed. The political upheavals of the 1960s provided a fissure through which ideas, traditions and methods of critical thought could make a dramatic return to the cultural field, as they had been suppressed and discredited by anathema and terror during the period which witnessed the collapse of liberationist ideals that animated European modernism and saw the rise of totalitarian regimes in the 1930s.

In general, conceptual art draws its themes, strategies and content from the politicized cultural critique identified broadly with the New Left. The assault on the institutions of art takes up, on the one hand, the revival of Frankfurt School ideas of the encirclement and falsification of avant-garde culture and its traditional critical con sciousness by the Culture Industry, and on the other hand, upon Situationist strategies of guerilla activism, which found their most complete expression in the student revolts of 1968. Thus, in a sense, the historical character and limitations of conceptualism stem from its intellectual and political location mid-way between the *Dialectic of Enlightenment* and the *Society of the Spectacle*. That is, it is between the acerbic defeatism of the Adorno-Horkheimer position, which sees art as a transcendent concretion and emblem of existing unfreedom, and the desperate anarchism of Debord's indignant cultural terrorism. The actual works of art which organize themselves most deliberately around this dynamic, display its dual tendencies. They struggle toward political immediacy in the sense of New Left activism and the "productivist" desire for resolution of social conflict, for a break or leap. At the same time, they tend toward concretization of the cultural dilemma of the falsification and ruination of art by mimicking that ruination; reflecting it in their own structure.

The functionalistic and activistic aspect of radical conceptualism attempts to break the vicious circle of falsification in a dialectical inversion, one which has its direct precedents in the reductivism of so much 60s art. This reductivism emphasized the work of art's resemblance to non-art and is the direct precondition for the "dematerialization" of the work of art into critical language. The transformation from emblematics to a directly critical and discursive form of expression is conceptualism's central achievement.

The critical language developed within conceptualism is con structed from the discourses of publicity, journalism, academicism, and architecture. Artists like Graham, Buren, Weiner or Kosuth understand architecture as the discourse of siting the effects of power generated by publicity, information and bureaucracy in the city. While conforming to the idea of emphasizing critical or analytical language as the antipode to the isolated, auratic art object, these artists treat this language not as a theoretical object (thus formulating a treatise as a work of art, as did Art-Language), but rather in terms of its physicality, modes of production and enforcement in the urban arena. In this way, conceptualism participated in the development of the New Left's critique of academicism's and publicity's interdependence. The insight conceptualism made explicit in many works was that both the university system and the media monopolies (having been purged of socially-critical ideas during the Cold War period) had become primary support-systems for new art in the same process in which they themselves were inscribed in a complex of bureaucratic structures of authority and knowledge whose essential cognitive structure—one could almost say their epistemology—is publicity. The best-appreciated of this art, Kosuth's for example, presents a condensed image of the instrumentalized "value-free" academic disciplines characteristic of American-type universities (empiricist sociol ogy, information theory, positivist language philosophy) in the form of 1960s high corporate or bureaucratic design.

Conceptualism's exhibition strategy self-consciously presents the museum-gallery system—the institutional complex whose architectural look was foregrounded by Minimalism—as the crucial arena of this new synthesis. This is inseparable from the strategy of appropriating existing media forms such as magazines, TV and billboards. In all this, the kinship with Pop is evident. However, unlike Pop, conceptualism attempts to incriminate the art business as the mechanism through which a corporatization of aesthetic production and thought is being carried out. This is understood as a social and political crisis in art in which crucial elements of the critical traditions of modernism are being liquidated.

The strategies of Graham, Buren or Kosuth are, each in their own way, informed (through the issues raised by the institutionalization of Minimalism and Pop) by the combination of concepts drawn from the Frankfurt School tradition with related, historicist, critiques of urbanism. This combination took the form of linked studies in the development of state and scientific institutions (as mechanisms of social power and control) and research into the methods of siting these institutions within the modern city (or, more accurately, of the rebuilding of the modern city in terms of the strategic siting of these institutions). In Graham's case, these areas of thought are most directly identified with the writings of Barthes in the 1960s and of Foucault and Tafuri through the 1970s. The influence of the Frankfurt School, but most particularly of Walter Benjamin, is evident in the connections these authors make between their specific objects of study and the psychosocial effects of these objects, wherein mechanisms of power and domination are internalized by the atomized urban masses and involuntarily reproduced as profound estrangement.

These issues are expressed artistically in the rapid turning of conceptual artists toward techniques and procedures identified with the communications monopolies and state "information" agencies—the "new media" of 60s art. Through the appropriation of these media antagonistic to those of traditional art, conceptualism attempts to break out of the institutional enclave of "Art" and intervene actively in the complex of social forces constituted by urban communication and representation systems. This intervention is constantly stimulated through critique of other art.

Minimal art is recognized as more than simply a new formalism (because of the echo of Constructivism it retains), but it is criticized for being no real negation of formalism. Minimalism is seen as a transitional form dominated by a Romantic and mystified concept of negativity, though one which is preferred to the chronic affirmativeness of Pop. There is frustration and disappointment over the fact that the Minimalist "heroes" never make a decisive break from the positivism dominant within American formalism. Minimalism therefore appears to be no more than a "negativistic" version of formalism. Even by the end of the 1960s it had become clear that the Constructivist elements in Minimalism were only a feeble residue of socially-aggressive aspects of the original movement, filtered through Bauhaus streamlining and American "systems" ideas. Minimalism, far from striving (in the Constructivist spirit) to break open its constricting architectural shell and assert itself as antithetical to constriction, endeavored above all to come to terms with its austere and elegant architectural containers, to glamorize them by means of a self-dramatizing acquiescence. The Minimal object, in this light, expresses the silencing of the Constructivist ideal, and the celebrated experiential shock provoked by a Morris, for example, is (historically speaking) the shock of unfulfilled promises of freedom. The space held open by this absence of freedom is then occupied by the mute Minimal object, whose effect is precisely to demarcate the historical void which has brought it into existence. The problematic "objecthood" of Minimal art is an outcome of this and derives from another contradiction. Judd, for example, implied a social commentary by handing over the fabrication of his work to professionals. But at the same time, by means of his critical writings, he insulated the resulting object from the very same social discourse of meaning he invoked by directing attention to the effects of the division of labor. Thus, he posited the work as an irreducible, somewhat ineffable, very concrete "presence" (Morris' term). Minimalism's critics promptly recognized the resulting exhibitionism of the works as a symptom of their actual social reduction to the mystified state of a commodity soliciting fetishization. This "reductivism" was then criticized for its armored inwardness and indifference toward the social considerations it incited and which actually sustained it as important art.

Nevertheless, reductivist tendencies formed a primary fascination in the 60s because they resulted in the production of austere and mechanistic objects whose aggressive passivity and stylish indifference toward the spectator evoked feelings of alienation and dehumanization reminiscent of those experienced in everyday life. So, the response of the conceptualist critique was twofold and contradictory. On the one hand, it grasped the fact that the exhibitionistic "objecthood" of reductivist art accomplished only the reproduction of alienation and anxiety. It saw that anxiety was not really constituted as a subject of the work (which because of its bonds with formalism, could not admit of course to having a "subject" at all), but was concocted as a theatrical effect. The spectator was subjected to it as he was to publicity and commands in relation to objects in "normal" social life. On the other hand, the conceptualist critique recognized this theatrical effect as having created at least an up-to-date physical art-form which implied (however involuntarily and indifferently) concepts about the relationship between the experience of art and the experience of social domination. These concepts were rapidly turned against the art which had helped to stimulate them. In this process, narcissism and fetishistic regression were identified with the theatricalized status of art objects in general. Conceptual art as "anti-object" is the result. However, the recognition of the capitalist market as the foundation of all forms of domination in culture is the insight which could be sustained in the conditions of enormous inflation characterizing the period beginning in the early 70s.

Speculative, inflation-driven capital enclosed and reorganized the art world, spectacularly driving up the prices on a broad front. Thus the anti-objects of conceptualism were "absorbed" and "negated" (to use the Marcusian terms of the period) as critical intervention by the aura of value imposed upon them by speculation. Conceptual art's feeble response to the clash of its political fantasies with the real economic conditions of the art world marks out its historical limit as critique. Its political fantasy curbs itself at the boundary of market economy.

The struggle to transcend the commodity-form within capitalism is an ideal and, at best, carries some value as a utopian vision. But there is a negative aspect of this avant-garde utopianism which must be accounted for. Namely, the role of this fantasy of transcendence was of an ideal *not* to be realized. In the atmosphere of rising social conflict which characterized that moment of the invention of conceptualism, the unrealizability of this fantasy could act as a utopian prod and challenge: a stimulus to further audacity. However, after circa 1974, as the political tide began its shift away from challenge toward retrenchment and the rise of contrary cultural trends, the utopian ideal was transformed into its opposite—disillusionment. This transformation produced a collapse of great implosive force. The implosion of the ideal was thus the exact precondition for the new regime in the art world, the ironically self-conscious but nonetheless compulsive submission to marketing that is the central characteristic of the period from the mid-70s to the present.

Paradoxically it is therefore the feeble or imploded utopianism of conceptualism which brings it close to Pop. In conceptual art the accepted forms of institutionally purified social knowledge are packaged according to design. Display codes are systematically appropriated as material in a strategy of mimicry. In this sense conceptualism is the *doppelgänger* of Warhol-type "Popism" in its helplessly ironic mimicry of the mechanisms for control and falsification of information and social knowledge whose despotic and seductive forms of display are copied to make art objects.

Neither Pop nor conceptualism can posit their social subject matter in good faith. No ironic social content is considered to be a residual property of 1930s art. "Modernist" art in the American sense begins from the idea that that era is not only "over" (dissolved by the advent of post-war "neo-capitalism") yet moreover, that it was nothing but an abysmal historical aberration produced by the clash of inherently totalitarian European political ideas, "Communism" and "Fascism." In this perspective American-type "modernism" is the most crystalline cultural reflection of the idea of neo-capitalism with its proclamation of the transcendence of the era of capitalist crises through technocratic totalization and state-supported private monopolies, and its blissful anticipation of the "end of ideology." The social indifference of so much post-1945 American art is symptomatized at least in part by the aesthetic ideal of remoteness which recurs in it, from Newman to, say, Jack Goldstein. This is a reflex of the trauma of the collapse, circa 1939, of the ideal of an integrated modernist art which could speak critically about the world.

Thus, if Pop is the amnesiac and cynical "social realism" of the new bureaucratic and monopolistic so-called neo-capitalist order, conceptual art is its melancholy Symbolism. In presenting its forgotten card-files and print-outs, its "caskets" of information, conceptual art recapitulates a kind of Mallarméanism: social subjects are presented as enigmatic hieroglyphs and given the authority of the crypt. This identification of publicity, bureaucracy and academicism with cryptic utterances expresses an awareness of the participation of bureaucracies and universities in a corporate death-machine, an awareness which animated the student anti-war movement. The deadness of language characterizing the work of Lawrence Weiner or On Kawara, for example, is exemplary and necessary. The failure to express *is* its expression, and in this dialectic, conceptual art becomes emblematic. However, these emblematics rescue themselves from complete capitulation to resignation by their anti-monumentalism.

What is unique about conceptual art is its reinvention of defeatism; of the indifference always implicit in puristic or formalistic art. The gray volumes of conceptualism are filled with somber ciphers which express primarily the inexpressibility of socially-critical thought in the form of art. They embody a terrible contradiction. These artists attempted to break out of the prison-house of the art business, its bureaucracy and architecture, and to turn toward social life. But in that process they reassumed the very emptiness they wished to put behind them. This is because they had been led (by the protest movements) to once again identify their own vanguardism with the moral necessity of political opposition, in imitation of earlier modernism. At the same time they had not broken with the dominant neo-capitalist perspective, which implied that this struggle was a histori cal anachronism, a moral exorcism meaningless outside a ritualistic sense of artistic heroism. The radical conceptualists were thus socially mortified by the reawakened moral implications of their own vanguardism. The emblematicism to which they capitulate is precisely that of mortification. Much of the art they made (with its "mausoleum look") is involuntarily expressive of its own self-conscious immobilization before the forms of power it is compelled to confront.

In bringing the tomb-like aspect of Minimalist exhibitionism out from the "dead" gallery space into "life"—on billboards, in newspapers and so on—conceptual art carries out into the city only the mortified remains of social art silenced by three decades of political "normalization." Conceptualism's display of these remains can only be exhibitionistic; the expression of its bad conscience. Exhibitionism and public distress are therefore the final indicators that this work is art at all, in the serious sense of the past. Nothing in either its actual social content or its mimetic appearance can really establish this any longer. Rather, in its rueful immobilization before the *mechanisms* of falsification of language (under the perspective of neo-capitalism) it represents the terminus-point of serious modern art.

However, in its very immobilization, conceptual art reflects the emergence of certain significant preconditions for the development of revolutionary ideas in society. The re-emergence of critical social thought into currency in America in the later 1960s, after a long period of eclipse and suppression, indicates that a new stage in the social struggle as a whole was germinating at that time. The period of the stabilization of imperialism behind the U.S. dollar, which began in 1944–45—the so-called "post-war era"—had reached its end with the dollar crises of the late 60s and early 70s. The current period of uncontrollable world financial destabilization and political conflict had begun. With the end of that era of stabilization based upon inflationary "credit" economic policies, there also ends the basis upon which all the ruling class' cultural strategies of control in the realm of ideas and representations could function. Essentially, the termination of the period of paper-money prosperity and co-optation through various funding schemes dates from around 1970, although the *effects* of this basic transformation were (generally) sufficiently mediated that they could be ignored within the art world until recently. "Reaganomics" and the wholesale assault on all the social and cultural institutions which owe their existence to the post-war combination of New Deal corporatism and inflationary public spending on culture are making it clear that the cultural presuppositions of two or three generations of artists have entered a period of fundamental crisis.

Conceptual art's attempts at a new social art in the early 1970s must be seen in the context of these developments, which placed enormous obstacles in the way of the directions those artists wished to pursue. Thus, the inadequacy of their artistic formulation of these issues is a profound and decisive one. The failures of conceptual art, measured against the possibilities the movement had only glimpsed, are, even as failures, the most incisive reflection of the gap which had opened in the historical and political memory of modernism after 1939.

This failed and unresolved aspect of conceptualism remains crucial. The movement appears today above all as incomplete. Its first response to the political upheaval which began in the 1960s, was an appropriation of mechanical and commercial techniques in an assault upon "Art," and constitutes the basis of both its radicalism and its faculty of historical memory. But insofar as it was unable to reinvent social content through its socialization of technique, it necessarily fell prey to the very formalism and exhibitionism it had begun by exposing (though it managed in the process to drive that formalism to a new level of internal decomposition). Involuntarily conceptualism had been encapsulated as a "radical purism." By the mid-1970s, this led to a fundamental split in the movement, one which announced the collapse of the whole thing. Some artists like Barry or Huebler easily shed the final trappings of historicism and interventionism and moved into orthodox commodity production, albeit of a refined and mildly ironic type. Others, such as *The Fox* group, attempted to extend the political argument. Most of this work foundered in the sterile academicism constituting the dregs of the New Left. This late "leftist" conceptualism was only able to produce negatively polemical, or "self-referential" indictments reiterating the idea of their own unthinkability as works of art. Bureaucratic immobilization was absolutized in the dreariness of the movement's final phase.

This lackluster spectacle, however, brought conceptualism face to face with its essential nemesis, "Popism." By the mid-1970s, the economic and social ascendancy of Pop had legitimated Warhol's interpretation of ironic mimicry above all others, and led to the eruption of an aesthetic of compulsive and unreflective mimicry of all forms of culture, especially the "successful" and "effective" ones, across the whole art market. As the conceptualist struggle for historical memory succumbed, the antithetical cultural forces it wished to defeat burst forth with unprecedented vigor in the "poet-conceptual pluralism" of the late 1970s and the business-fetishism of the past four or five years. Everything is forgotten, everything is possible, everything is "great." But the issues at stake in conceptual art's collapse make that movement perceptible as the crucial axis of transition between the distraught quietism of the "New York School" and an explosive revival of *both* revolutionary and counter-revolutionary ideas in art. This makes conceptualism representative of the end of New York–type art.

Conceptualism's transcendence of the New York mythos is the source of its almost organic internationalism. By the very premises of its perspective of a bureaucratic world culture industry, it breaches definitively the authority of the old idea of national styles in art, to which all other movements of the period ultimately reverted. The bureaucratic look of conceptual art permitted it to free itself from dependence upon American corporate design insignia and production systems, which still identify Pop and Minimal art so closely with the New York School look. Conceptualism makes explicit the Europe-America dialectic out of which all the critical theory of the period emerged. (. . .)

This essay was first published in Gary Dufour, *Dan Graham,* exh. cat. (Perth: The Art Gallery of Western Australia, 1985), and reprinted in Jeff Wall, *Dan Graham's Kammerspiel* (Toronto: Art Metropole, 1991), pp. 7–83.

# conceptual art 1962–1969: from the aesthetic of administration to the critique of institutions
## benjamin h. d. buchloh

This monster called beauty is not eternal. We know that our breath had no beginning and will never stop, but we can, above all, conceive of the world's creation and its end.
—Apollinaire, *Les peintres cubistes*

Allergic to any relapse into magic, art is part and parcel of the disenchantment of the world, to use Max Weber's term. It is inextricably intertwined with rationalization. What means and productive methods art has at its disposal are all derived from this nexus.
—Theodor Adorno

A twenty-year distance separates us from the historical moment of Conceptual Art. It is a distance that both allows and obliges us to contemplate the movement's history in a broader perspective than that of the convictions held during the decade of its emergence and operation (roughly from 1965 to its temporary disappearance in 1975). For to historicize Conceptual Art requires, first of all, a clarification of the wide range of often conflicting positions and the mutually exclusive types of investigation that were generated during this period. But beyond that there are broader problems of method and of "interest." For at this juncture, any historicization has to consider what type of questions an art-historical approach—traditionally based on the study of visual objects—can legitimately pose or hope to answer in the context of artistic practices that explicitly insisted on being addressed outside of the parameters of the production of formally ordered, perceptual objects, and certainly outside of those of art history and criticism. And, further, such an historicization must also address the currency of the historical object, i.e., the motivation to rediscover Conceptual Art from the vantage point of the late 1980s: the dialectic that links Conceptual Art, as the most rigorous elimination of visuality and traditional definitions of representation, to this decade of a rather violent restoration of traditional artistic forms and procedures of production.

It is with Cubism, of course, that elements of language surface programmatically within the visual field for the first time in the history of modernist painting, in what can be seen as a legacy of Mallarmé. It is there too that a parallel is established between the emerging structuralist analysis of language and the formalist examination of representation. But Conceptual practices went beyond such mapping of the linguistic model onto the perceptual model, outdistancing as they did the spatialization of language and the temporalization of visual structure. Because the proposal inherent in Conceptual Art was to replace the object of spatial and perceptual experience by linguistic definition alone (the work as analytic proposition), it thus constituted the most consequential assault on the status of that object: its visuality, its commodity status, and its form of distribution. Confronting the full range of the implications of Duchamp's legacy for the first time, Conceptual practices, furthermore, reflected upon the construction and the role (or the death) of the author just as much as they redefined the conditions of receivership and the role of the spectator. Thus they performed the postwar period's most rigorous investigation of the conventions of pictorial and sculptural representation and a critique of the traditional paradigms of visuality.

From its very beginning, the historic phase in which Conceptual Art was developed comprises such a complex range of mutually opposed approaches that any attempt at a retrospective survey must beware of the forceful voices (mostly those of the artists themselves) demanding respect for the purity and orthodoxy of the movement. Precisely because of this range of implications of Conceptual Art, it would seem imperative to resist a construction of its history in terms of a stylistic homogenization, which would limit that history to a group of individuals and a set of strictly defined practices and historical interventions (such as, for example, the activities initiated by Seth Siegelaub in New York in 1968 or the authoritarian quests for orthodoxy by the English Art & Language group).

To historicize Concept Art (to use the term as it was coined by Henry Flynt in 1961)[1] at this moment, then, requires more than a mere reconstruction of the movement's self-declared primary actors or a scholarly obedience to their proclaimed purity of intentions and operations.[2] Their convictions were voiced with the (by now often hilarious) self-righteousness that is continuous within the tradition of hypertrophic claims made in avant-garde declarations of the twentieth century. For example, one of the campaign statements by Joseph Kosuth from the late 1960s asserts: "Art before the modern period is as much art as Neanderthal man is man. It is for this reason that around the same time I replaced the term 'work' for *art proposition*. Because a conceptual *work* of art in the traditional sense, is a contradiction in terms."[3] (. . .)

## SOL LEWITT'S STRUCTURES

It would seem that LeWitt's proto-Conceptual work of the early 1960s originated in an understanding of the essential dilemma that has haunted artistic production since 1913, when its basic paradigms of opposition were first formulated—a dilemma that could be described as the conflict between structural specificity and random organization. For the need, on the one hand, for both a systematic reduction and an empirical verification of the perceptual data of a visual structure stands opposed to the desire, on the other hand, to assign a new "idea" or meaning to an object randomly (in the manner of Mallarmé's "transposition") as though the object were an empty (linguistic) signifier. (. . .)

. . . It should be noted, however, that the strange admixture of the nominalist position of Duchamp (and its consequences) and the positivist position of Reinhardt (and its implications) was not only accomplished in 1965 with the beginnings of Conceptual Art but was well-prepared in the work of Frank Stella, who in his *Black Paintings* from 1959 claimed both Rauschenberg's monochrome paintings and Reinhardt's paintings as points of departure. Finally, it was the work of Sol LeWitt—in particular work such as his *Structures*—that demarcates that precise transition, integrating as they do both language and visual sign in a structural model.

The surfaces of these *Structures* from 1961 to 1962 (some of which used single frames from Muybridge's serial photographs) carried inscriptions in bland lettering identifying the hue and shape of those surfaces (e.g., "RED SQUARE") and the inscription itself (e.g., "WHITE LETTERS"). Since these inscriptions named either the support or the inscription (or, in the middle section of the painting, both support and inscription in a paradoxical inversion), they created a continuous conflict in the viewer/reader. This conflict was not just over which of the two roles should be performed in relation to the painting. To a larger extent it concerned the reliability of the given information and the sequence of that information: was the inscription to be given primacy over the visual qualities identified by the linguistic entity, or was the perceptual experience of the visual, formal, and chromatic element anterior to its mere denomination by language?

Clearly this "mapping of the linguistic onto the perceptual" was not arguing in favor of "the idea"—or linguistic primacy—or the definition of the work of art as an analytic proposition. Quite to the contrary, the permutational character of the work suggested that the viewer/reader systematically perform all the visual and textual options the painting's parameters allowed for. This included an acknowledgment of the painting's central, square element: a spatial void that revealed the underlying wall surface as the painting's *architectural* support in actual space, thereby suspending the reading of the painting between architectural structure and linguistic definition.

Rather than privileging one over the other, LeWitt's work (in its dialogue with Jasper Johns's legacy of paradox) insisted on forcing the inherent contradictions of the two spheres (that of the perceptual experience and that of the linguistic experience) into the highest possible relief. Unlike Frank Stella's response to Johns, which forced modernist self-referentiality one step further into the ultimate *cul de sac* of its positivist convictions (his notorious statement "what you see is what you see" would attest to that just as much as the development of his later work),[4] Sol LeWitt's dialogue (with both Johns and Stella, and ultimately, of course, with Greenberg) developed a dialectical position with regard to the positivist legacy.

In contrast to Stella, his work now revealed that the modernist compulsion for empiricist self-reflexiveness not only originated in the scientific positivism which is the founding logic of capitalism (undergirding its industrial forms of production just as much as its science and theory), but that, for an artistic practice that internalized this positivism by insisting on a purely empiricist approach to vision, there would be a final destiny. This destiny would be to aspire to the condition of tautology.

It is not surprising, then, that when LeWitt formulated his second text on Conceptual Art—in his "Sentences on Conceptual Art" from the spring of 1969—the first sentence should programmatically state the radical difference between the logic of scientific production and that of aesthetic experience:

*1 — Conceptual artists are mystics rather than rationalists. They leap to conclusions that logic cannot reach.*

*2 — Rational judgments repeat rational judgments.*

*3 — Irrational judgments lead to new experience.*[5]

## ROBERT MORRIS'S PARADOXES

**The problem has been for some time one of ideas—those most admired are the ones with the biggest, most incisive ideas (e.g., Cage & Duchamp) . . . think that today art is a form of art history.**
—Robert Morris, letter to Henry Flynt, 8/13/1962

Quite evidently, Morris's approach to Duchamp, in the early 1960s, had already been based on reading the readymade in analogy with a Saussurean model of language: a model where meaning is generated by structural relationships. As Morris recalls, his own "fascination with and respect for Duchamp was related to his linguistic fixation, to the idea that all of his operations were ultimately built on a sophisticated understanding of language itself."[6] Accordingly, Morris's early work (from 1961 to 1963) already pointed toward an understanding of Duchamp that transcended the limited definition of the readymade as the mere displacement of traditional modes of artistic production by a new aesthetic of the speech act ("this is a work of art if I say so"). And in marked distinction from the Conceptualists' subsequent exclusive focus on the unassisted readymades, Morris had, from the late 1950s when he discovered Duchamp, been particularly engaged with work such as *Three Standard Stoppages* and the *Notes for the Large Glass (The Green Box)*.

Morris's production from the early 1960s, in particular works like *Card File* (1962), *Metered Bulb* (1963), *I-Box* (1963), *Litanies,* and the *Statement of Aesthetic Withdrawal,* also entitled *Document* (1963), indicated a reading of Duchamp that clearly went beyond Johns's, leading towards a structural and semiotic definition of the functions of the readymade. As Morris described it retrospectively in his 1970 essay "Some Notes on the Phenomenology of Making":

*There is a binary swing between the arbitrary and the nonarbitrary or "motivated" which is . . . an historical, evolutionary, or diachronic feature of language's development and change. Language is not plastic art but both are forms of human behavior and the structures of one can be compared to the structures of the other.*[7]

While it is worth noticing that by 1970 Morris already reaffirmed apodictically the ontological character of the category "plastic" art versus that of "language," it was in the early 1960s that his assaults on the traditional concepts of visuality and plasticity had already begun to lay some of the crucial foundations for the development of an art practice emphasizing its parallels, if not identity, with the systems of linguistic signs, i.e., Conceptual Art.

Most importantly, as early as 1961 in his *Box with the Sound of Its Own Making*, Morris had ruptured both. On the one hand, it dispenses with the Modernist quest for medium-specific purity as much as with its sequel in the positivist conviction of a purely perceptual experience operating in Stella's visual tautologies and the early phases of Minimalism. And on the other, by counteracting the supremacy of the visual with that of an auditory experience of equal if not higher importance, he renewed the Duchampian quest for a nonretinal art. In *Box with the Sound of Its Own Making*, as much as in the subsequent works, the critique of the hegemony of traditional categories of the visual is enacted not only in the (acoustic or tactile) disturbance of the purity of perceptual experience, but it is performed as well through a literalist act of denying the viewer practically all (at least traditionally defined) visual information.

This strategy of a "perceptual withdrawal" leads in each of the works from the early 1960s to a different analysis of the constituent features of the structured object and the modes of reading it generates. In *I-Box*, for example, the viewer is confronted with a semiotic pun (on the words *I* and *eye*) just as much as with a structural sleight of hand from the tactile (the viewer has to manipulate the box physically to *see* the *I* of the artist) through the linguistic sign (the letter I defines the shape of the framing/display device: the "door" of the box) to the visual representation (the nude photographic portrait of the artist) and back. It is of course this very tripartite division of the aesthetic signifier—its separation into object, linguistic sign, and photographic reproduction—that we will encounter in infinite variations, didactically simplified (to operate as stunning tautologies) and stylistically designed (to take the place of paintings) in Kosuth's *Proto-Investigations* after 1966.

In *Document (Statement of Aesthetic Withdrawal)*, Morris takes the literal negation of the visual even further, in clarifying that after Duchamp the readymade is not just a neutral analytic proposition (in the manner of an underlying statement such as "this is a work of art"). Beginning with the readymade, the work of art had become the ultimate subject of a legal definition and the result of institutional validation. In the absence of any specifically visual qualities and due to the manifest lack of any (artistic) manual competence as a criterion of distinction, all the traditional criteria of aesthetic judgment—of taste and of connoisseurship—have been programmatically voided. The result of this is that the definition of the aesthetic becomes on the one hand a matter of linguistic convention and on the other the function of both a legal contract and an institutional discourse (a discourse of power rather than taste).

This erosion works, then, not just against the hegemony of the visual, but against the possibility of any other aspect of the aesthetic experience as being autonomous and self-sufficient. That the introduction of legalistic language and an administrative style of the material presentation of the artistic object could effect such an erosion had of course been prefigured in Duchamp's practice as well. In 1944 he had hired a notary to inscribe a statement of authenticity on his 1919 *L.H.O.O.Q.*, affirming that "... this is to certify that this is the original 'ready-made' *L.H.O.O.Q.* Paris 1919." What was possibly still a pragmatic maneuver with Duchamp (although certainly one in line with the pleasure he took in contemplating the vanishing basis for the legitimate definition of the work of art in visual competence and manual skill alone) would soon become one of the constituent features of subsequent developments in Conceptual Art. Most obviously operating in the certificates issued by Piero Manzoni defining persons or partial persons as temporary or lifetime works of art (1960–61), this is to be found at the same time in Yves Klein's certificates assigning zones of immaterial pictorial sensibility to the various collectors who acquired them.

But this aesthetic of linguistic conventions and legalistic arrangements not only denies the validity of the traditional studio aesthetic, it also cancels the aesthetic of production and consumption which had still governed Pop Art and Minimalism.

Just as the modernist critique (and ultimate prohibition) of figurative representation had become the increasingly dogmatic law for pictorial production in the first decade of the twentieth century, so Conceptual Art now instated the prohibition of any and all visuality as the inescapable aesthetic rule for the end of the twentieth century. Just as the readymade had negated not only figurative representation, authenticity, and authorship while introducing repetition and the series (i.e., the law of industrial production) to replace the studio aesthetic of the handcrafted original, Conceptual Art came to displace even that image of the mass-produced object and its aestheticized forms in Pop Art, replacing an aesthetic of industrial production and consumption with an aesthetic of administrative and legal organization and institutional validation.

## EDWARD RUSCHA'S BOOKS

One major example of these tendencies—acknowledged both by Dan Graham as a major inspiration for his own "Homes for America" and by Kosuth, whose "Art after Philosophy" names him as a proto-Conceptual artist—would be the early book work of Edward Ruscha. Among the key strategies of future Conceptual Art that were initiated by Ruscha in 1963 were the following: to chose the vernacular (e.g., architecture) as referent; to deploy photography systematically as the representational medium; and to develop a new form of distribution (e.g., the commercially produced book as opposed to the traditionally crafted *livre d'artiste*. (. . .)

Accordingly, even in 1965–66, with the earliest stages of Conceptual practices, we witness the emergence of diametrically opposed approaches: Joseph Kosuth's *Proto-Investigations* on the one hand (according to their author conceived and produced in 1965);[8] and a work such as Dan Graham's *Homes for America* on the other. Published in *Arts Magazine* in December 1966, the latter is a work which—unknown to most and long unrecognized—programmatically emphasized structural contingency and contextuality, addressing crucial questions of presentation and distribution, of audience and authorship. At the same time the work linked Minimalism's esoteric and self-reflexive aesthetics of permutation to a perspective on the architecture of mass culture (thereby redefining the legacy of Pop Art). The Minimalists' detachment from any representation of contemporary social experience upon which Pop Art had insisted, however furtively, resulted from their attempt to construct models of visual meaning and experience that juxtaposed formal reduction with a structural and phenomenological model of perception.

By contrast, Graham's work argued for an analysis of (visual) meaning that defined signs as both structurally constituted within the relations of language's system *and* grounded in the referent of social and political experience. Further, Graham's dialectical conception of visual representation polemically collapsed the difference between the spaces of production and those of reproduction (what Seth Siegelaub would, in 1969, call primary and secondary information).[9] Anticipating the work's actual modes of distribution and reception within its very structure of production, *Homes for America* eliminated the difference between the artistic construct and its (photographic) reproduction, the difference between an exhibition of art objects and the photograph of its installation, the difference between the architectural space of the gallery and the space of the catalogue and the art magazine.

## JOSEPH KOSUTH'S TAUTOLOGIES

In opposition to this, Kosuth was arguing, in 1969, precisely for the continuation and expansion of modernism's positivist legacy, and doing so with what must have seemed to him at the time the most radical and advanced tools of that tradition: Wittgenstein's logical positivism and language philosophy (he emphatically affirmed this continuity when, in the first part of "Art after Philosophy," he states, "Certainly linguistic philosophy can be considered the heir to empiricism . . ."). Thus, even while claiming to displace the formalism of Greenberg and Fried, he in fact updated modernism's project of self-reflexiveness. For Kosuth stabilized the notion of a disinterested and self-sufficient art by subjecting both—the Wittgensteinian model of the language game as well as the Duchampian model of the readymade—to the strictures of a model of meaning that operates in the modernist tradition of that paradox Michel Foucault has called modernity's "empirico-transcendental" thought. This is to say that in 1968 artistic production is still the result, for Kosuth, of artistic intention as it constitutes itself above all in self-reflexiveness (even if it is now discursive rather than perceptual, epistemological rather than essentialist).[10]

At the very moment when the complementary formations of Pop and Minimal Art had, for the first time, succeeded in criticizing the legacy of American-type formalism and its prohibition of referentiality, this project is all the more astounding. The privileging of the literal over the referential axis of (visual) language—as Greenberg's formalist aesthetic had entailed—had been countered in Pop Art by a provocative devotion to mass-cultural iconography. Then, both Pop and Minimal Art had continuously emphasized the universal presence of industrial means of reproduction as inescapable framing conditions for artistic means of production, or, to put it differently, they had emphasized that the aesthetic of the studio had been irreversibly replaced by an aesthetic of production and consumption. And finally, Pop and Minimal Art had exhumed the repressed history of Duchamp (and Dadaism at large), phenomena equally unacceptable to the reigning aesthetic thought of the late 1950s and early '60s. Kosuth's narrow reading of the readymade is astonishing for yet another reason. In 1969, he explicitly claimed that he had encountered the work of Duchamp primarily through the mediation of Johns and Morris rather than through an actual study of Duchamp's writings and works.[11]

As we have seen above, the first two phases of Duchamp's reception by American artists from the early 1950s (Johns and Rauschenberg) to Warhol and Morris in the early 1960s had gradually opened up the range of implications of Duchamp's readymades.[12] It is therefore all the more puzzling to see that after 1968—what one could call the beginning of the third phase of Duchamp reception—the understanding of this model by Conceptual Artists still foregrounds intentional declaration over contextualization. This holds true not only for Kosuth's "Art after Philosophy," but equally for the British Art & Language Group, as, in the introduction to the first issue of the journal in May 1969, they write:

*To place an object in a context where the attention of any spectator will be conditioned toward the expectancy of recognizing art objects. For example placing what up to then had been an object of alien visual characteristics to those expected within the framework of an art ambience, or by*

*virtue of the artist declaring the object to be an art object whether or not it was in an art ambi-*
*ence. Using these techniques what appeared to be entirely new morphologies were held out to*
*qualify for the status of the members of the class "art objects."*

> *For example Duchamp's "Readymades" and Rauschenberg's "Portrait of Iris Clert."*[13]

A few months later Kosuth based his argument for the development of Conceptual Art on just such a restricted reading of Duchamp. For in its limiting view of the history and the typology of Duchamp's oeuvre, Kosuth's argument—like that of Art & Language—focuses exclusively on the "unassisted readymades." Thereby early Conceptual theory not only leaves out Duchamp's painterly work but avoids such an eminently crucial work as the *Three Standard Stoppages* (1913), not to mention *The Large Glass* (1915–23) or the *Etants donnés* (1946–66) or the 1943 *Boîte en valise*. But what is worse is that even the reading of the unassisted readymades is itself extremely narrow, reducing the readymade model in fact merely to that of an analytical proposition. Typically, both Art & Language and Kosuth's "Art after Philosophy" refer to Robert Rauschenberg's notorious example of speech-act aesthetics ("This is a portrait of Iris Clert if I say so") based on the rather limited understanding of the readymade as an act of willful artistic declaration. This understanding, typical of the early 1950s, continues in Judd's famous lapidary norm (and patently nonsensical statement), quoted a little later in Kosuth's text: "if someone says it's art, then it is art. . . ." In 1969, Art & Language and Kosuth shared in foregrounding the "analytic proposition" inherent in each readymade, namely the statement "this is a work of art," over and above all other aspects implied by the readymade model (its structural logic, its features as an industrially produced object of use and consumption, its seriality, and the dependence of its meaning on context). And most importantly, according to Kosuth, this means that artistic propositions constitute themselves in the negation of all referentiality, be it that of the historical context of the (artistic) sign or that of its social function and use:

*Works of art are analytic propositions. That is, if viewed within their context-as-art, they provide*
*no information what-so-ever about any matter of fact. A work of art is a tautology in that it is a*
*presentation of the artist's intention, that is, he is saying that that particular work of art is art,*
*which means, is a definition of art. Thus, that it is art is true a priori (which is what Judd means*
*when he states that "if someone calls it art, it's art").*[14]

(. . .)

## A TALE OF MANY SQUARES

The visual forms that correspond most accurately to the linguistic form of the tautology are the square and its stereometric rotation, the cube. Not surprisingly, these two forms proliferated in the painterly and sculptural production of the early- to mid-1960s. This was the moment when a rigorous self-reflexiveness was bent on examining the traditional boundaries of modernist sculptural objects to the same extent that a phenomenological reflection of viewing space was insistent on reincorporating architectural parameters into the conception of painting and sculpture. (. . .)

As the central form of visual self-reflexiveness, the square abolishes the traditional spatial parameters of verticality and horizontality, thereby canceling the metaphysics of space and its conventions of reading. It is in this way that the square (beginning with Malevich's 1915 *Black Square*) incessantly points to itself: as spatial perimeter, as plane, as surface, and, functioning simultaneously, as support. But, with the very success of this self-referential gesture, marking the form out as purely pictorial, the square painting paradoxically but inevitably assumes the character of a relief/object situated in actual space. It thereby invites a viewing/reading of spatial contingency and architectural imbeddedness, insisting on the imminent and irreversible transition from painting to sculpture.

This transition was performed in the proto-Conceptual art of the early- to mid-1960s in a fairly delimited number of specific pictorial operations. It occurred, first of all, through the emphasis on painting's *opacity*. The object-status of the painterly structure could be underscored by unifying and homogenizing its surface through monochromy, serialized texture, and gridded compositional structure; or it could be emphasized by literally sealing a painting's spatial transparency, by simply altering its material support: shifting it from canvas to unstretched fabric or metal. This type of investigation was developed systematically, for example, in the proto-Conceptual paintings of Robert Ryman, who employed all of these options separately or in varying combinations in the early- to mid-1960s; or, after 1965, in the paintings of Robert Barry, Daniel Buren, and Niele Toroni.

Secondly—and in a direct inversion and countermovement to the first—object-status could be achieved by emphasizing, in a literalist manner, painting's *transparency*. This entailed establishing a dialectic between pictorial surface, frame, and architectural support by either a literal opening up of the painterly support, as in Sol LeWitt's early *Structures,* or by the insertion of translucent or transparent surfaces into the conventional frame of viewing, as in Ryman's fiberglass paintings, Buren's early nylon paintings, or Michael Asher's and Gerhard Richter's glass panes in metal frames, both emerging between 1965 and 1967. Or, as in the early work of Robert Barry (such as his *Painting in Four Parts,* 1967, in the FER-Collection), where the square, monochrome, canvas objects now seemed to assume the role of mere architectural demarcation. Functioning as decentered painterly objects, they delimit the *external* architectural space in a manner analogous to the serial or central composition of earlier Minimal work that still defined internal pictorial or sculptural space. Or, as in Barry's square canvas (1967), which is to be placed at the exact center of the architectural support wall, a work is conceived as programmatically shifting the reading of it from a centered, unified, pictorial object to an experience of architectural contingence, and as thereby incorporating the supplementary and overdetermining strategies of curatorial placement and conventions of installation (traditionally disavowed in painting and sculpture) into the *conception* of the work itself.

And thirdly—and most often—this transition is performed in the "simple" rotation of the square, as originally evident in Naum Gabo's famous diagram from 1937 where a volumetric and a stereometric cube are juxtaposed in order to clarify the inherent continuity between planar, stereometric, and volumetric forms. This rotation generated cubic structures as diverse as Hans Haacke's *Condensation Cube* (1963–65), Robert Morris's *Four Mirrored Cubes* (1965) or Larry Bell's simultaneously produced *Mineral Coated Glass Cubes,* and Sol LeWitt's *Wall-Floor Piece (Three Squares),* 1966. All of these (beyond sharing the obvious morphology of the cube) engage in the dialectic of opacity and transparency (or in the synthesis of that dialectic in mirror-reflection as in Morris's *Mirrored Cubes* or Larry Bell's aestheticized variations of the theme). At the same time that they engage in the dialectic of frame and surface, and that of object and architectural container, they have displaced traditional figure-ground relationships.

The deployment of any or all of these strategies (or, as in most cases, their varying combination) in the context of Minimal and post-Minimal art, i.e., proto-conceptual painting and sculpture, resulted in a range of hybrid objects. They no longer qualified for either of the traditional studio categories nor could they be identified as relief or architectural decoration—the compromise terms traditionally used to bridge the gap between these categories. In this sense, these objects demarcated another spectrum of departures towards Conceptual Art. Not only did they destabilize the boundaries of the traditional artistic categories of studio production, by eroding them with modes of industrial production in the manner of Minimalism, but they went further in their critical revision of the discourse of the studio versus the discourse of production/consumption. By ultimately dismantling both along with the conventions of visuality inherent in them, they firmly established an aesthetic of administration.

The diversity of these proto-conceptual objects would at first suggest that their actual aesthetic operations differ so profoundly that a comparative reading, operating merely on the grounds of their apparent analogous formal and morphological organization—the visual topos of the square—would be illegitimate. Art history has accordingly excluded Haacke's *Condensation Cube,* for example, from any affiliation with Minimal Art. Yet all of these artists define artistic production and reception by the mid-1960s as reaching beyond the traditional thresholds of visuality (both in terms of the materials and production procedures of the studio and those of industrial production), and it is on the basis of this parallel that their work can be understood to be linked beyond a mere structural or morphological analogy. The proto-conceptual works of the mid-1960s redefine aesthetic experience, indeed, as a multiplicity of *nonspecialized* modes of object- and language-experience. According to the reading these objects generate, aesthetic experience—as an individual and social investment of objects with meaning—is constituted by *linguistic* as well as by *specular* conventions, by the institutional determination of the object's status as much as by the reading competence of the spectator.

Within this shared conception, what goes on to distinguish these objects from each other is the emphasis each one places on different aspects of that deconstruction of the traditional concepts of visuality. Morris's *Mirrored Cubes,* for example (once again in an almost literal execution of a proposal found in Duchamp's *Green Box*), situate the spectator in the *suture* of the mirror reflection: that interface between sculptural object and architectural container where neither element can acquire a position of priority or dominance in the triad between spectator, sculptural object, and architectural space. And insofar as the work acts simultaneously to inscribe a phenomenological model of experience into a traditional model of purely visual specularity and to displace it, its primary focus remains the sculptural object and its visual apperception.

By contrast, Haacke's *Condensation Cube*—while clearly suffering from a now even more rigorously enforced scientist reductivism and the legacy of modernism's empirical positivism—moves away from a specular relationship to the object altogether, establishing instead a bio-physical system as a link between viewer, sculptural object, and architectural container. If Morris shifts the viewer from a mode of contemplative specularity into a phenomenological loop of bodily movement and perceptual reflection, Haacke replaces the once revolutionary concept of an activating "tactility" in the viewing experience by a move to bracket the phenomenological within the determinacy of "system." For his work now suspends Morris's tactile "viewing" within a science-based syntagm (in this particular case that of the process of condensation and evaporation inside the cube brought about by temperature changes due to the frequency of spectators in the gallery).

And finally, we should consider what is possibly the last credible transformation of the square, at the height of Conceptual Art in 1968, in two works by Lawrence Weiner, respectively entitled *A Square Removal from a Rug in Use* and *A 36" × 36" Removal to the Lathing or Support*

*Wall of Plaster or Wallboard from a Wall* (both published or "reproduced" in *Statements,* 1968), in which the specific paradigmatic changes Conceptual Art initiates with regard to the legacy of reductivist formalism are clearly evident. Both interventions—while maintaining their structural and morphological links with formal traditions by respecting classical geometry as their definition at the level of shape—inscribe themselves in the support surfaces of the institution and/or the home which that tradition had always disavowed. The carpet (presumably for sculpture) and the wall (for painting), which idealist aesthetics always declares as mere "supplements," are foregrounded here not only as parts of their material basis but as the inevitable future location of the work. Thus the structure, location, and materials of the intervention, at the very moment of their conception, are completely determined by their future destination. While neither surface is explicitly specified in terms of its institutional context, this ambiguity of dislocation generates two oppositional, yet mutually complementary readings. On the one hand, it dissipates the traditional expectation of encountering the work of art only in a "specialized" or "qualified" location (both "wall" and "carpet" could be either those of the home or the museum, or, for that matter, could just as well be found in any other location such as an office, for example). On the other, neither one of these surfaces could ever be considered to be independent from its institutional location, since the physical inscription into each particular surface inevitably generates contextual readings dependent upon the institutional conventions and the particular use of those surfaces in place.

Transcending the literalist or perceptual precision with which Barry and Ryman had previously connected their painterly objects to the traditional walls of display, in order to make their physical and perceptual interdependence manifest, Weiner's two squares are now physically integrated with *both* these support surfaces and their institutional definition. Further, since the work's inscription paradoxically implies the physical displacement of the support surface, it engenders an experience of perceptual withdrawal as well. And just as the work negates the specularity of the traditional artistic object by literally withdrawing rather than adding visual data in the construct, so this act of *perceptual* withdrawal operates at the same time as a physical (and symbolic) intervention in the institutional power and property relations underlying the supposed neutrality of "mere" devices of presentation. The installation and/or acquisition of either of these works requires that the future owner accept an instance of physical removal/withdrawal/interruption on both the level of institutional order and on that of private ownership.

It was only logical that, on the occasion of Seth Siegelaub's first major exhibition of Conceptual Art, the show entitled "January 5–31, 1969," Lawrence Weiner would have presented a formula that then functioned as the matrix underlying all his subsequent propositions. Specifically addressing the relations within which the work of art is constituted as an open, structural, syntagmatic formula, this matrix statement defines the parameters of a work of art as those of the conditions of authorship and production, and their interdependence with those of ownership and use (and not least of all, at its own propositional level, as a *linguistic definition* contingent upon and determined by *all* of these parameters in their continuously varying and changing constellations:

*With relation to the various manners of use:*
*1. The artist may construct the piece*
*2. The piece may be fabricated*
*3. The piece need not to be built*
*Each being equal and consistent with the intent of the artist the decision as to condition rests with the receiver upon the occasion of receivership*

What begins to be put in play here, then, is a critique that operates at the level of the aesthetic "institution." It is a recognition that materials and procedures, surfaces and textures, locations and placement are not only sculptural or painterly matter to be dealt with in terms of a phenomenology of visual and cognitive experience or in terms of a structural analysis of the sign (as most of the Minimalist and post-Minimalist artists had still believed), but that they are always already inscribed within the conventions of language and thereby within institutional power and ideological and economic investment. However, if, in Weiner's and Barry's work of the late 1960s, this recognition still seems merely latent, it was to become manifest very rapidly in the work of European artists of the same generation, in particular that of Marcel Broodthaers, Daniel Buren, and Hans Haacke after 1966. In fact an institutional critique became the central focus of all three artists' assaults on the false neutrality of vision that provides the underlying rationale for those institutions.

In 1965, Buren—like his American peers—took off from a critical investigation of Minimalism. His early understanding of the work of Flavin, Ryman, and Stella rapidly enabled him to develop positions from within a strictly painterly analysis that soon led to a reversal of painterly/sculptural concepts of visuality altogether. Buren was engaged on the one hand with a critical review of the legacy of advanced modernist (and postwar American) painting and on the other in an analysis of Duchamp's legacy, which he viewed critically as the utterly unacceptable negation of painting. This particular version of reading Duchamp and the readymade as acts of petit-bourgeois anarchist radicality—while not necessarily complete and accurate—allowed Buren to construct a successful critique of both: modernist painting and Duchamp's readymade as its radical historical Other. In his writings and his interventions from 1967 onwards, through his critique of the specular order of painting and of the institutional framework determining it, Buren singularly succeeded in displacing both the paradigms of painting and that of the readymade (even twenty years later this critique makes the naive continuation of object production in the Duchampian vein of the readymade model appear utterly irrelevant).

From the perspective of the present, it seems easier to see that Buren's assault on Duchamp, especially in his crucial 1969 essay *Limites Critiques,* was primarily directed at the conventions of Duchamp *reception* operative and predominant throughout the late 1950s and early '60s, rather than at the actual implications of Duchamp's model itself. Buren's central thesis was that the fallacy of Duchamp's readymade was to obscure the very institutional and discursive framing conditions that allowed the readymade to generate its shifts in the assignment of meaning and the experience of the object in the first place. Yet, one could just as well argue, as Marcel Broodthaers would in fact suggest in his catalogue of the exhibition "The Eagle from the Oligocene to Today" in Düsseldorf in 1972, that the contextual definition and syntagmatic construction of the work of art had obviously been initiated by Duchamp's readymade model first of all.

In his systematic analysis of the constituting elements of the discourse of painting, Buren came to investigate all the parameters of artistic production and reception (an analysis that, incidentally, was similar to the one performed by Lawrence Weiner in arriving at his own "matrix" formula). Departing from Minimalism's (especially Ryman's and Flavin's) literalist dismemberment of painting, Buren at first transformed the pictorial into yet another model of opacity and objecthood. (This was accomplished by physically weaving figure and ground together in the "found" awning material, by making the "grid" of vertical parallel stripes his eternally repeated "tool," and by mechanically—almost superstitiously or ritualistically, one could say with hindsight—applying a coat of white paint to the outer bands of the grid in order to distinguish the pictorial object from a readymade.) At the same time that the canvas had been removed from its traditional stretcher support to become a physical cloth-object (reminiscent of Greenberg's notorious "tacked up canvas [which] already exists as a picture"), this strategy in Buren's arsenal found its logical counterpart in the placement of the *stretched* canvas leaning as an object against support wall and floor.

This shifting of support surfaces and procedures of production led to a wide range of forms of distribution within Buren's work: from unstretched canvas to anonymously mailed sheets of printed striped paper; from pages in books to billboards. In the same way, his displacement of the traditional sites of artistic intervention and of reading resulted in a multiplicity of locations and forms of display that continuously played on the dialectic of interior and exterior, thereby oscillating within the contradictions of sculpture and painting and foregrounding all those hidden and manifest framing devices that structure both traditions within the discourse of the museum and the studio.

Furthermore, enacting the principles of the Situationist critique of the bourgeois division of creativity according to the rules of the division of labor, Buren, Olivier Mosset, Michel Parmentier, and Niele Toroni publicly performed (on various occasions between 1966 and 1968) a demolition of the traditional separation between artists and audience, with each given their respective roles. Not only did they claim that each of their artistic idioms be considered as absolutely equivalent and interchangeable, but also that anonymous audience production of these pictorial signs would be equivalent to those produced by the artists themselves.

With its stark reproductions of mug shots of the four artists taken in photomats, the poster for their fourth manifestation at the 1967 Biennale de Paris inadvertently points to another major source of contemporary challenges to the notion of artistic authorship linked with a provocation to the "audience" to participate: the aesthetic of anonymity as practiced in Andy Warhol's "Factory" and its mechanical (photographic) procedures of production.[15]

The critical interventions of the four into an established but outmoded cultural apparatus (represented by such venerable and important institutions as the Salon de la Jeune Peinture or the Biennale de Paris) immediately brought out in the open at least one major paradox of all conceptual practices (a paradox, incidentally, which had made up the single most original contribution of Yves Klein's work ten years before). This was that the critical annihilation of cultural conventions itself immediately acquires the conditions of the spectacle, that the insistence on artistic anonymity and the demolition of authorship produces instant brand names and identifiable products, and that the campaign to critique conventions of visuality with textual interventions, billboard signs, anonymous handouts, and pamphlets inevitably ends by following the pre-established mechanisms of advertising and marketing campaigns.

All of the works mentioned coincide, however, in their rigorous redefinition of relationships between audience, object, and author. And all are concerted in the attempt to replace a traditional, hierarchical model of privileged experience based on authorial skills and acquired competence of reception by a structural relationship of absolute equivalents that would dismantle both sides of the equation: the hieratic position of the unified artistic object just as much as the privileged position of the author. In an early essay (published, incidentally, in the same 1967 issue of *Aspen Magazine*—dedicated by its editor Brian O'Doherty to Stéphane

Mallarmé—in which the first English translation of Roland Barthes' "The Death of the Author" appeared), Sol LeWitt laid out these concerns for a programmatic redistribution of author/artist functions with astonishing clarity, presenting them by means of the rather surprising metaphor of a performance of daily bureaucratic tasks:

*The aim of the artist would be to give viewers information. . . . He would follow his predetermined premise to its conclusion avoiding subjectivity. Chance, taste or unconsciously remembered forms would play no part in the outcome. The serial artist does not attempt to produce a beautiful or mysterious object but functions* merely as a clerk cataloguing the results of his premise *(emphasis added)*.[16]

Inevitably the question arises how such restrictive definitions of the artist as a cataloguing clerk can be reconciled with the subversive and radical implications of Conceptual Art. And this question must simultaneously be posed within the specific historical context in which the legacy of an historical avant-garde—Constructivism and Productivism—had only recently been reclaimed. How, we might ask, can these practices be aligned with that historical production that artists like Henry Flynt, Sol LeWitt, and George Maciunas had rediscovered, in the early '60s, primarily through the publication of Camilla Gray's *The Great Experiment: Russian Art 1863–1922*.[17] This question is of particular importance since many of the formal strategies of early Conceptual Art appear at first glance to be as close to the *practices* and *procedures* of the Constructivist/Productivist avant-garde as Minimal sculpture had appeared to be dependent upon its *materials* and *morphologies*.

The profoundly utopian (and now unimaginably naive) nature of the claims associated with Conceptual Art at the end of the 1960s were articulated by Lucy Lippard (along with Seth Siegelaub, certainly the crucial exhibition organizer and critic of that movement) in late 1969:

*Art intended as pure experience doesn't exist until someone experiences it, defying ownership, reproduction, sameness. Intangible art could break down the artificial imposition of "culture" and provide a broader audience for a tangible, object art. When automatism frees millions of hours for leisure, art should gain rather than diminish in importance, for while art is not just play, it is the counterpoint to work. The time may come when art is everyone's daily occupation, though there is no reason to think this activity will be called art*.[18]

While it seems obvious that artists cannot be held responsible for the culturally and politically naive visions projected on their work even by their most competent, loyal, and enthusiastic critics, it now seems equally obvious that it was precisely the utopianism of earlier avant-garde movements (the type that Lippard desperately attempts to resuscitate for the occasion) that was manifestly absent from Conceptual Art throughout its history (despite Robert Barry's onetime invocation of Herbert Marcuse, declaring the commercial gallery as "Some places to which we can come, and for a while 'be free to think about what we are going to do'"). It seems obvious, at least from the vantage of the early 1990s, that from its inception Conceptual Art was distinguished by its acute sense of discursive and institutional limitations, its self-imposed restrictions, its lack of totalizing vision, its critical devotion to the factual conditions of artistic production and reception without aspiring to overcome the mere facticity of these conditions. This became evident as works such as Hans Haacke's series of *Visitors' Profiles* (1969–70), in its bureaucratic rigor and deadpan devotion to the statistical collection of factual information, came to refuse any transcendental dimension whatsoever.

Furthermore, it now seems that it was precisely a profound disenchantment with those political master-narratives that empowered most of '20s avant-garde art that, acting in a peculiar fusion with the most advanced and radical forms of critical artistic reflection, accounts for the peculiar contradictions operating within (proto) Conceptual Art of the mid- to late 1960s. It would explain why this generation of the early '60s—in its growing emphasis on empiricism and its skepticism with regard to all utopian vision—would be attracted, for example, to the logical positivism of Wittgenstein and would confound the affirmative petit-bourgeois positivism of Alain Robbe-Grillet with the radical atopism of Samuel Beckett, claiming all of them as their sources. And it would make clear how this generation could be equally attracted by the conservative concept of Daniel Bell's "end of ideology" and Herbert Marcuse's Freudo-Marxist philosophy of liberation.

What Conceptual Art achieved at least temporarily, however, was to subject the last residues of artistic aspiration toward transcendence (by means of traditional studio skills and privileged modes of experience) to the rigorous and relentless order of the vernacular of administration. Furthermore, it managed to purge artistic production of the aspiration towards an affirmative collaboration with the forces of industrial production and consumption (the last of the totalizing experiences into which artistic production had mimetically inscribed itself with credibility in the context of Pop Art and Minimalism for one last time).

Paradoxically, then, it would appear that Conceptual Art truly became the most significant paradigmatic change of postwar artistic production at the very moment that it mimed the operating logic of late capitalism and its positivist instrumentality in an effort to place its autocritical investigations at the service of liquidating even the last remnants of traditional aesthetic experience. In that process it succeeded in purging itself entirely of imaginary and bodily experience, of physical substance and the space of memory, to the same extent that it effaced all residues of representation and style, of individuality and skill. That was the moment when Buren's and Haacke's work from the late 1960s onward turned the violence of that mimetic relationship back onto the ideological apparatus itself, using it to analyze and expose the social institutions from which the laws of positivist instrumentality and the logic of administration emanate in the first place. These institutions, which determine the conditions of cultural consumption, are the very ones in which artistic production is transformed into a tool of ideological control and cultural legitimation.

It was left to Marcel Broodthaers to construct objects in which the radical achievements of Conceptual Art would be turned into immediate travesty and in which the seriousness with which Conceptual Artists had adopted the rigorous mimetic subjection of aesthetic experience to the principles of what Adorno had called the "totally administered world" were transformed into absolute farce. And it was one of the effects of Broodthaers' dialectics that the achievement of Conceptual Art was revealed as being intricately tied to a profound and irreversible loss: a loss not caused by artistic practice, of course, but one to which that practice responded in the full optimism of its aspirations, failing to recognize that the purging of image and skill, of memory and vision, within visual aesthetic representation was not just another heroic step in the inevitable progress of Enlightenment to liberate the world from mythical forms of perception and hierarchical modes of specialized experience, but that it was also yet another, perhaps the last of the erosions (and perhaps the most effective and devastating one) to which the traditionally separate sphere of artistic production had been subjected in its perpetual efforts to emulate the regnant episteme within the paradigmatic frame proper to art itself.

Or worse yet, that the Enlightenment triumph of Conceptual Art—its transformation of audiences and distribution, its abolition of object status and commodity form—would most of all only be short-lived, almost immediately giving way to the return of the ghostlike reapparitions of (prematurely?) displaced painterly and sculptural paradigms of the past. So that the specular regime, which Conceptual Art claimed to have upset, would soon be reinstated with renewed vigor. Which is of course what happened.

## NOTES

1. As is usual with stylistic formations in the history of art, the origin and the name of the movement are heavily contested by its major participants. Barry, Kosuth, and Weiner, for example, vehemently denied in recent conversations with the author any historical connection to or even

knowledge of the Fluxus movement of the early 1960s. Nevertheless, at least with regard to the invention of the *term,* it seems correct when Henry Flynt claims that he is "the originator of concept art, the most influential contemporary art trend. In 1961 I authored (and copyrighted) the phrase 'concept art,' the rationale for it and the first compositions labeled 'concept art.' My document was first printed in *An Anthology,* ed. La Monte Young, New York, 1962." (La Monte Young's *An Anthology* was in fact published in 1963.)

A second contestant for the term was Edward Kienholz, with his series of *Concept Tableaux* in 1963 (in fact, occasionally he is still credited with the discovery of the term. See for example Roberta Smith's essay "Conceptual Art," in *Concepts of Modern Art,* ed. Nikos Stangos [New York: Harper and Row, 1981], pp. 256–270.)

Joseph Kosuth claims in his "Sixth Investigation 1969 Proposition 14" (published by Gerd de Vries, Cologne, 1971, n.p.) that he used the term "conceptual" for the first time "in a series of notes dated 1966 and published a year later in a catalogue for an exhibition titled 'Non-Anthropomorphic Art' at the now defunct Lannis Gallery in New York."

And then there are of course (most officially accepted by all participants) Sol LeWitt's two famous texts from 1967 and 1969, the "Paragraphs on Conceptual Art," first published in *Artforum,* vol. 5, no. 10, pp. 56–57 and "Sentences on Conceptual Art," first published in *Art & Language,* vol. 1, no. 1 (May 1969), pp. 11–13.

2. For a typical example of an attempt to write the history of Conceptual Art by blindly adopting and repeating the claims and convictions of one of that history's figures, see Gudrun Inboden, "Joseph Kosuth—Artist and Critic of Modernism," in *Joseph Kosuth: The Making of Meaning* (Stuttgart: Staatsgalerie Stuttgart, 1981), pp. 11–27.

3. Joseph Kosuth, *The Sixth Investigation 1969 Proposition 14* (Cologne: Gerd De Vries/Paul Maenz, 1971), n.p.

4. Stella's famous statement was of course made in the conversation between Bruce Glaser, Donald Judd, and himself, in February 1964, and published in *Art News* (September 1966), pp. 55–61. To what extent the problem of this dilemma haunted the generation of Minimal artists becomes evident when almost ten years later, in an interview with Jack Burnham, Robert Morris would still seem to be responding (if perhaps unconsciously) to Stella's notorious statement:

*Painting ceased to interest me. There were certain things about it that seemed very problematic to me. . . . There was a big conflict between the fact of doing this thing, and what it looked like later. It just didn't seem to make much sense to me. Primarily because there was an activity I did in time, and there was a certain method to it. And that didn't seem to have any relationship to the thing at all. There is a certain resolution in the theater where there is real time, and* what you do is what you do. *(emphasis added)*

Robert Morris, unpublished interview with Jack Burnham, November 21, 1975, Robert Morris Archive. Quoted in Maurice Berger, *Labyrinths: Robert Morris, Minimalism, and the 1960s* (New York: Harper & Row, 1989), p. 25.

5. Sol LeWitt, "Sentences on Conceptual Art," first published in 0–9, New York (1969), and *Art-Language,* Coventry (May 1969), p. 11.

6. Robert Morris as quoted in Berger, *Labyrinths,* p. 22.

7. Robert Morris, "Some Notes on the Phenomenology of Making: The Search for the Motivated," *Artforum,* vol. 9 (April 1970), p. 63.

8. In the preparation of this essay, I have not been able to find a single source or document that would confirm with definite credibility Kosuth's claim that these works of the *Proto-Investigations* were actually produced and existed physically in 1965 or 1966, when he (at that time twenty years old) was still a student at the School of Visual Arts in New York. Nor was Kosuth able to provide any documents to make the claims verifiable. By contrast these claims were explicitly contested by all the artists *I* interviewed who knew Kosuth at that time, none of them remembering seeing any of the *Proto-Investigations* before February 1967, in the exhibition *Non-Anthropomorphic Art by Four Young Artists,* organized by Joseph Kosuth at the Lannis Gallery. The artists with whom I conducted interviews were Robert Barry, Mel Bochner, Dan Graham, and Lawrence Weiner. I am not necessarily suggesting that the *Proto-Investigations* could not have been done by Kosuth at the age of twenty (after all, Frank Stella had painted his *Black Paintings* at age twenty-three), or that the logical steps fusing Duchamp and Reinhardt with Minimalism and Pop Art leading up to the *Proto-Investigations* could not have been taken by an artist of Kosuth's historical awareness and strategic intelligence. But I am saying that none of the work dated by Kosuth to 1965 or 1966 can—until further evidence is produced—actually be documented as 1965 or 1966 or dated with any credibility. By contrast, the word paintings of On Kawara (whose studio Kosuth visited frequently at that time), such as *Something,* are reproduced and documented.

9. "For many years it has been well known that more people are aware of an artist's work through (1) the printed media or (2) conversation than by direct confrontation with the art itself. For painting and sculpture, where the visual presence—color, scale, size, location—is important to the work, the photograph or verbalization of that work is a bastardization of the art. But when art concerns itself with things not germane to physical presence, its intrinsic (communicative)

value is not altered by its presentation in printed media. The use of catalogues and books to communicate (and disseminate) art is the most neutral means to present the new art. The catalogue can now act as the primary information for the exhibition, as opposed to secondary information *about* art in magazines, catalogues, etc. and in some cases the 'exhibition' can be the 'catalogue.'" (Seth Siegelaub, "On Exhibitions and the World at Large" [interview with Charles Harrison], *Studio International,* [December 1969].)

10. This differentiation is developed in Hal Foster's excellent discussion of these paradigmatic differences as they emerge first in Minimalism in his essay "The Crux of Minimalism," in *Individuals* (Los Angeles: The Museum of Contemporary Art, 1986), pp. 162–183.

11. Joseph Kosuth, "Art After Philosophy" (Part II), in *The Making of Meaning,* p. 175.

12. As Rosalind Krauss has suggested, at least Johns's understanding at that point already transcended the earlier reading of the readymade as merely an aesthetic of declaration and intention:

*If we consider that Stella's painting was involved early on, in the work of Johns, then Johns's interpretation of Duchamp and the readymade—an interpretation diametrically opposed to that of the Conceptualist group outlined above—has some relevance in this connection. For Johns clearly saw the readymade as pointing to the fact that there need be no connection between the final art object and the psychological matrix from which it issued, since in the case of the readymade this possibility is precluded from the start. The* Fountain *was not made (fabricated) by Duchamp, only selected by him. Therefore there is no way in which the urinal can "express" the artist. It is like a sentence which is put into the world unsanctioned by the voice of a speaker standing behind it. Because maker and artist are evidently separate, there is no way for the urinal to serve as an externalization of the state or states of mind of the artist as he made it. And by not functioning within the grammar of the aesthetic personality, the* Fountain *can be seen as putting distance between itself and the notion of personality per se. The relationship between Johns's* American Flag *and his reading of the* Fountain *is just this: the arthood of the* Fountain *is not legitimized by its having issued stroke-by-stroke from the private psyche of the artist; indeed it could not. So it is like a man absentmindedly humming and being dumbfounded if asked if he had meant that tune or rather another. That is a case in which it is not clear how the grammar of intention might apply.*

Rosalind Krauss, "Sense and Sensibility," *Artforum,* vol. 12 (November 1973), pp. 43–52, n. 4.

13. Introduction, *Art-Language,* vol. 1, no. 1 (May 1969), p. 5.

14. Joseph Kosuth, "Art after Philosophy," *Studio International,* nos. 915–917 (October-December 1969). Quoted here from Joseph Kosuth, *The Making of Meaning,* p. 155.

15. Michel Claura, at the time the critic actively promoting awareness of the affiliated artists Buren, Mosset, Parmentier, and Toroni, has confirmed in a recent conversation that the reference to Warhol, in particular to his series *The Thirteen Most Wanted Men,* which had been exhibited at the Ileana Sonnabend Gallery in 1967, was quite a conscious decision.

16. Sol LeWitt, "Serial Project #1, 1966," *Aspen Magazine,* nos. 5–6, ed. Brian O'Doherty, 1967, n.p.

17. The importance of this publication in 1962 was mentioned to me by several of the artists interviewed during the preparation of this essay.

18. Lucy Lippard, "Introduction," in *955,000* (Vancouver: The Vancouver Art Gallery, January 13–February 8, 1970), n.p.

This essay was first published in Claude Gintz, *L'art conceptuel: Une perspective,* exh. cat. (Paris: Musée d'Art Moderne de la Ville de Paris, 1989), and reprinted in *October,* 55 (Winter 1990), pp. 105–143.

# conceptual art and critical judgement
## charles harrison

In the short historical sight of postmodern culture, certain works of Conceptual Art are now seen as having "stood the test of time"—a measure applied by the likes of Sir Ernst Gombrich to distinguish the very different objects of their attention. The evidence for this assertion comes with the staging of retrospective surveys, with the publication of tentative art-historical accounts and, most tellingly, with the growth of a competitive market in "established" works of the crucial period—a moment located between 1965 and 1975, or, for the less gullible, between 1967 and 1972. Coincidentally, a consensus appears to be forming around the thesis that Conceptual Art was a movement of critical significance in the development of modern art. For Benjamin Buchloh, for instance, writing in 1989, "Conceptual Art truly became the most significant paradigmatic change of post–World War II artistic production. . . . "

It should occasion no surprise that the curatorial and commercial ratification of individual works and careers coincides with art-historical establishment of the movement as a whole. It does not follow, however, that retrospective views are now readily organized into a consensus. Some awkward questions remain to be addressed—questions concerning the relationship between historical representation and qualitative assessment.

The avant-garde of the late 1960s and early '70s has rightly been associated with a certain subversiveness as regards the conventions of artistic quality. To the extent that the question of qualitative discrimination has genuinely been shown to be otiose or irrelevant to the enterprise of Conceptual Art, no good purpose is served by reintroducing it. But it needs to be acknowledged that the market discriminates and is discriminating whether or not critics, historians and others consider it proper or relevant to discriminate. If the critical character of Conceptual Art is inseparable from those wider forms of critique of conventions which where brought to a head in '68, it may also be observed, firstly that Conceptual Art failed during the 1970s and '80s to achieve any plausible public presence outside the art-world, and secondly that the economic substrate of the art world was among those repositories of power and influence which survived the sixties untransformed. In face of this unfaltering power on the part of the market (the very power which it was once thought by some that Conceptual Art would challenge or subvert), it would seem a matter of mere piety to accord works of Conceptual Art any privileged critical status, for example on the grounds of their supposed radicalism as forms of distribution. By the same token, it can be said that the positions of militant relativism or self-conscious pluralism adopted by critics in recent years are not alternative to any actual grounds or mechanisms of assessment, but rather that they coincide with forms of abdication or self-induced blindness in face of the obligations and difficulties which qualitative assessment continues to entail.

I do not mean to bemoan the passing of any certainties. Unless we can countenance the aesthetic as an essential and underlying value, we must accept that criteria for judgement of art will change. They will change in response to changes in art or, more realistically, in response to those changes which change art itself. Appropriate evaluative criteria are not discovered as abstractions nor do they emerge as well-formed sets. They are elaborated in practice, in the process of critical reading, and they are recognized in forms of difference from those principles of judgement which, for one reason or another, have become dogmatic or bureaucratic or simply ineffective. In addressing the issue of critical judgement, therefore, the aspiration of this essay is not to furnish a set of protocols for recognition of the "best" Conceptual Art. It is simply to explore those conditions by which relevant criticism may itself be determined, and towards which it may need to be responsive.

To claim significance for Conceptual Art as a movement is implicitly to assert some relationship of strong critical distinctness between the representative works of that movement and whatever is taken as establishing the normal ground of the practice of art at the time in question. And this is to say that a relationship of mutual implication will hold between on the one hand one's view on the art-historical priorities and interests of the modern period in general and the early 1960s in particular, and on the other the grounds on which one singles out certain works as representative of the critical character of Conceptual Art. It is the point of view of this text that no account of Conceptual Art can be adequate if it is not adequate in its understanding of Modernism. (By Modernism I mean not those vagrant forms of commentary which announce what it is that artists can get away with this year, but Modernism as substantial history and theory, which has been close to practice and informative to practice.) This is not to say that Conceptual Art was in any sense the necessary outcome of Modernism. Rather, it is to assert that the representative critical character of Conceptual Art was established by reference to the epistemological character of Modernist theory, to the ontological character of Modernist production and to the moral and ideological character of Modernist culture, and that the historical significance to be accorded to Conceptual Art is therefore relative to an estimation of the status and character of Modernism in the 1960s.

It is the further contention of this essay that by the mid-1960s Modernism as theorized in dominant forms of criticism and as represented in dominant institutions was a) morally and cognitively exhausted, and b) materially entrenched; and, in consequence, that there could be no critically adequate form of continuation of the practice of art which did not avail or imply a) an account of the practical exhaustion of Modernist protocols for the production of authentic culture, and b) an account of the mechanisms by which the effective power of those protocols was nevertheless sustained. According to this view of the determining conditions of the time, the task in hand was twofold—albeit the respective requirements were not necessarily distinct in practice. The first requirement was to establish a critique of the aesthetics of Modernism. This entailed the development of appropriate art-theoretical and art-historical tools. The second requirement was to establish a critique of the politics of Modernism. This entailed the application of socio-economic forms of analysis.

In thus framing the critical determinations upon the development of Conceptual Art, I have in mind the various collaborative practices and individual enterprises which composed the early work of Art & Language. The sustained project of Art & Language developed, awkwardly, unsystematically and unevenly, and occasionally elegantly and systematically, as a kind of critical resistance to the dogmatization of the aesthetic and to those political and theoretical prescriptions by which the agents and clients of Modernism sought to protect its failing conceptual apparatus. In particular this form of Conceptual Art involved skeptical and elliptical re-examination of two assumptions central to the theoretical and ideological character of

Modernism. The first assumption is that the authentic experience of art—the experience by which the very function of art is defined—is a disinterested response to the work of art in its phenomenological and morphological aspects, which is to say that the experience is cast in the self-image of the sensitive, empiricistic and responsible (bourgeois) beholder. The second assumption is that modern art develops along a fixed trajectory marked by the gradual reduction of its means. According to this second theoretical assumption, the tendency to reduction may be retrospectively perceived in the self-critical developments of "major" art. Unsurprisingly, apparent exceptions to this rule have normally been disqualified in Modernist theory on the grounds that the sensitive and responsible beholder is unable to accord them the status of major art. From the point of view of Art & Language, the character of Modernism as an ideology of art was thus seen as established by the relationship of mutual dependence between a historicistic model of the development of art and an account of aesthetic experience as involuntary and disinterested. The historicistic matrix, that's to say, was the "empirical" validation not of some objective canon but rather of an arbitrary manipulative power—the power perceived by Art & Language as exercised in the image and agency of the beholder.

This manipulative agency could not be resisted in artistic acts which were mere orthogonal projections of the historical matrix, and which thus aligned themselves, however covertly, with the mechanisms of validation. In the view of Art & Language in the later 1960s, Modernism had become a system which made the objects of its own attention. It followed that the requirement for a critically interesting artistic practice was not simply that it should evade the more evident protocols of Modernist aesthetic judgement, but that it should be opaque—other—vis-à-vis that account of the history of art which represented the progressive reduction of means as a logic of development. The tendency of some American artists was to advance ideas and statements as "art" either by virtue of some neo-Duchampian procedure of selection or nomination, or on the principle that they constituted radically reduced—"Post-Minimal"—forms of object. The tendency of Art & Language was to treat such procedures of nomination and reduction not as the manifestations of a transformed aesthetic, but as symptomatic of the very system they were designed to supplant—that's to say as cases of a Modernist historicism reduced to absurdity. The "texts-as-paintings" and "dematerialized objects" were seen as resting upon an assumption of the theoretical continuity of art (and of the practical continuity of a public already enchanted with avant-garde art). Such forms of Conceptual Art—typically represented in Seth Siegelaub's now mythologized January 1969 exhibition— were regarded for the most part as ingenious forms of business-as-normal, and thus as offering no fertile or open ground for a differential critical elaboration. By 1969 it was already clear that nomination was a dead duck. It required that the relations between language and the world be treated as secure and unquestionable. From the point of view of Art & Language the relevant logical grammar was in urgent need of wholesale re-examination and renewal.

It was the position of Art & Language in the later 1960s that given a) the beholder's status as the personification of the Modernist moral and aesthetic disposition, and given b) the exhaustion of Modernism as a discursive system, the possibility of critical transformation in the practice of art implied not the exploitation but the ruination of those mechanisms of validation which were identified with the beholder. To imagine a transformed art was thus to imagine the experience of art as a possibly different form of experience and to imagine the public as a constituency of which different dispositions and competences could be expected or predicated. It followed both that different competences would have to be exercised in the production of art and that these would have to be exercised upon some different range of discursive and aesthetic materials. It was a distinguishing feature of the most critically challenging works of Conceptual Art that they were opaque to the intuitive responses of the Modernist connoisseur, *even in his Post-Minimalist guise.* Viewed under their phenomenal and morphological aspects they remained insignificant, inconstant or absurd. Into the resulting aesthetic void they instilled the demand for a reading—that is to say, a demand which the modernized beholder could not satisfy without abandoning the grounds of his own authority.

The search for new material was one which variously preoccupied the larger avant-garde of the later 1960s. Among those that were found were some from earlier avant-garde episodes which had been marginalized in the process of establishment of the Modernist historical canon—forms of enterprise which had been derogated as "impure" on the grounds of their adjacency to the theatrical, the narrative or the political. Thus the period of development of Conceptual Art coincided with a recuperation of the critical and informal aspects of such earlier avant-garde movements as Dadaism, Constructivism and Surrealism. Consequent shifts in the conceptual relations of mainstream and margins have been observable in recent art-historical perspectives on the twentieth century. In some Eurocentric accounts, the moment of Conceptual Art is seen as marking the end of that long American diversion which Modernism is taken to have been, as effecting the re-identification of the history of modern art with an authentic avant-garde tradition, and even as reestablishing the status of such disregarded antecedents as the Fluxus group and the Nouveaux Réalistes. Recently there have been attempts to represent Conceptual Art as a form of Situationist "terror." In the more sophisticated of these revisionist accounts, attention is drawn to the prominence accorded to European philosophy and literary theory among the favored intellectual materials of the Conceptual Art movement.

Such rewritings are understandable as corrective responses to the absurd and purblind chauvinism of the American art—and art-critical world—a chauvinism which of recent years has fed and grown gross upon the form of Modernist apostasy initiated by Minimalism—but they are not adequate to the larger view. However decisive American writers and curators may have been in establishing critical and art-historical protocols, Modernism does not refer to a uniquely American moment or agency, nor does it mean American art rather than French art. Modernism is a system of representation, complexly connected to a system of distribution, within which European and American art alike are (mis)represented. Modernism is ideological, and as ideology American Modernism has been powerful and hegemonic. It does not follow, however, that all claims on behalf of the work of, say, Jackson Pollock or Donald Judd are hegemonic mystifications, nor does it follow that the work of, say, Lucio Fontana or César has been underestimated. Such accounts as would equate the critique of Modernism solely with resistance to American cultural hegemony tend to be notably uninstructive as regards those conditions which Modernist theory itself has explicitly sought to address—conditions of continuity and qualitative depth in modern art over the course of more than a century. The authority of Modernist history is not overthrown by a narrative of alternative practices; the Modernist concern for continuity and depth is not effectively countered by advancing trivial forms of persistence to the status of major art; nor is the claim to disinterestedness which lies at the heart of Modernist aesthetic preferences significantly undermined by claiming a supervening non-aesthetic virtue for those forms of art which can be seen as overtly tendentious.

To say that critique of the notion of disinterested value was a preoccupation of the Conceptual Art movement is not to allow that all or some Conceptual Art can be automatically conscripted to anyone's interests, however critically virtuous they may believe those interests to be. Nor is it to make a virtue of tendentiousness in Conceptual Art. Tendentiousness does not necessarily equate with discursiveness, nor are political themes simply *available* to counter the dogmatization of the aesthetic. Crudely tendentious Conceptual Art may be faulted on grounds not entirely dissimilar to those which might apply to a crudely tendentious Cubist painting. Tendentiousness normally entails a sacrifice of depth and complexity for the sake of transparency and immediacy. The point is not that the pursuit of significant formal or intentional identity necessarily involves submission to some universal aesthetic value, nor that art has to be seen to absolutize or to dehistoricize the contingent (or the "political"). The point is rather that unless the given contingent material is such as to be transformable by the artistic system, it is probably better treated in some other practical sphere; while if the supposed artistic system is such as to impose no limits upon the admission of the contingent or the political, it is probably not worth considering as art. And Conceptual Art is nothing if there is no power to its claim to be occupying the space of art. What I mean by this is that Conceptual Art is not art at all unless its objects are intentional objects under some description; and it is not art of any critical interest unless it enforces recognition of a transformation amongst that range of descriptions under which something may be seen as intentional.

There are of course those who would claim that the radicalism of Conceptual Art lay not in its occupation but rather in its displacement of the space of art—a displacement effected precisely by breaking down the barriers between the aesthetic and the political and between the over-specialized high arts and the more notionally "popular" (through in fact simply more readily distributable) arts of publicity. From this point of view the concern for quality is seen as a form of abnegation of the requirement of effectiveness. This argument is all very well, but the works at issue tend either to establish themselves in a thoroughly conventional world of art or to be absorbed without aesthetic remainder into the larger world they purport to invade. (Artists cited in support of such arguments include Burgin, Haacke, Holzer and Kruger.) In the first case the works thus represented are subject to whatever institutional or fashionable criteria may happen to prevail. In the second case they do indeed put themselves beyond the concerns of qualitative judgement, but only by failing to be of interest as intentional objects under some critically significant description. In neither case do they offer any novel address or alternative to the requirement of depth in art. This is to say that they do nothing to resist the form of manipulative agency associated with the image of the beholder.

If a case is to be made for the art-historical significance of Conceptual Art, it seems clear that it will not be enough either to reproduce the protocols of late-Modernist aesthetics under a new Post-Minimalist disguise, or to replace judgement with claims for non-cognitive effectiveness. The case will have to be one which, while it resists the *conventions* of quality associated with the ideology of Modernism, nevertheless admits the possibility—and difficulty—of evaluating works of Conceptual Art as intentional objects under a range of relevant descriptions. And this will entail some assessment of the *readings*—and not simply of the category-mistakes—which works of Conceptual Art avail. The demand for intelligent readings rather than involuntary responses is still instinct in those works of Conceptual Art which have remained interesting (and in that sense "stood the test of time"). That demand should not now be replaced or forgotten in the name of some automatic art-historical authenticity.

This is not a plea for the restoration of connoisseurship on some already-discredited basis (such as the self-serving fiction that art speaks for itself to the innately sensitive). Rather it is to affirm that need for interpretative reading (*Verstehen*) which was implicitly asserted in

political subject matter—was demoted by Greenbergian formalism to in
the "purity" or impeding the "transcendence" of a work. If a "pure" work
content, then the artist could not express formally the self-consciously di
toward content—issues, events, concepts, conditions—that had characte
nic art. So the only stance an artist could legitimately take was an unself-
participatory one: In this scheme of things, the artist's role was to "engag
lessly with the formal and material properties of his (almost always a "l
critic's role was to articulate the aesthetic rationale of the work thereby c
content and abdicating the self-conscious stance to the critic, artists aban
ities of conscious control over their creative efforts and their meaning.
from the Freudian unconscious, was all that was left to them.

How could the thematic fulcrum of European modernism be
American modernism? If the centrality of social content is a constar
Giacometti, and de Kooning, as I have suggested, then postmodernis
tendency to reductivism *of content* characterized the development of m
Such a radical shift in priorities cannot be explained as part of the inter
itself. Instead it is necessary to look at the external social and politic
American formalists were responding.

The ideological use of American art for cold war propaganda
has been charted frequently.[1] But the reaction to recent U.S. governr
"politically sensitive" subject matter in contemporary American art na
son specifically with Senator Joseph McCarthy's successful campaign
wing artists and intellectuals as communist sym pathizers in the 19
the rationalization that political content was incompatible with the
functioned as a form of self-censorship among art professionals just
does now. As it does for us, it gave art professionals in the 1950s a r
become politically engaged, not to fight back, not to notice the infiltr
by complex social and political realities, and not to try to come to
creative work—that is, not to work creatively with them as artists alv
it gave them a reason to relegate whatever political convictions and
have had to a corner of their lives in which they would not threa
opportunities. In short, the ideology of Greenbergian formalism to
McCarthyism to render politically and socially impotent a powe
change—visual culture—whose potential government censors ha
clearly than artists do; and rationalized that impotence to the castra

the early work of Art & Language and which has been stressed in the continuing work associated with that name. What is meant here by reading is not the willful digression of the self-enchanted, but rather the critical elaboration of the object of thought, where the object of thought is recognized as the other, both as regards the self-image of the observer and as regards any given historical narrative or tableau.

The need for strong interpretative reading is now all the more urgent in face of two prevailing recent tendencies: the first—characteristic of the new ruling class of the eighties and early nineties—is to identify rational judgement and preference with the "findings" of the market; the second—characteristic of a new left clerisy—is to fetishize causal inquiry (*Verklären*) as the means to uncover authentically subversive meanings. However mutually distinct they may believe their ends to be, the respective adherents of these two tendencies have the same ideal object in view: the unimpeachable work of art which confirms their picture of history and authenticates their image of themselves.

It is an important function of interpretative reading that it serves to distinguish the cognitively critical from the factitiously avant-garde. As regards the art of the past twenty-five years, this is a matter of specific moment to the business of discrimination between various candidates for attention. The suppression of the beholder was not simply a matter of making things which were radically unartistic or radically political—and in that sense unamenable to being beheld. Nor did it simply mean envisaging a different constituency. It meant establishing the grounds for a different form of transaction. As envisaged by Art & Language, the distinguishing critical feature of Conceptual Art lay in the requirement of collaboration or silence it made of its imagined public, and in the transformed image which it thus offered spectators of themselves as historical beings: the image of people placed on their mettle before the material presented to view: of people challenged to act upon that material, and to take thought upon, the conditions of thought—or to keep quiet.

This essay was published in the catalogue for the exhibition *Art conceptuel formes conceptuelles* (Paris: Galerie 1900–2000 and Galerie de Poche, 1990), pp. 538–545.

# the logic of modernism
## adrian piper

There are four interrelated properties of Euroethnic art th:
development of modernism, and in particular the develo;
United States within the last few decades: (1) its appro pria
its self-awareness, and (4) its commitment to social con
strong conceptual and strategic con tinuities between the hi
in particular—and recent developments in American art v
ter. Relative to these lines of continuity, the peculiarly Am
as Greenbergian formalism is an aberration. Characteriz
general and explicitly political subject matter in particu
currency as an opportunistic ideological evasion of the th;
ship and Red-baiting in the 1950s. To the extent that th
subject matter has prevailed in the international art con
ceeded in supplanting the long-standing European tradi
gagement with a peculiarly pharmaceutical conception (

Relative to this long tradition of combining social
pean modernism's American equivalent, Greenbergian f(
ture. From its status as the linchpin of a work, social

strategy of importing back to Europe the artistic embodiment of unself-conscious social in-
effectuality under the guise of an extracted essence of critically sophisticated formal appropriation was perfectly suited to its Marshall Plan agenda of cultural and political imperialism.

Since the McCarthy era and the heyday of Greenbergian formalism, American art has
been restoring its social content through the back door. Minimalism's geometrical simplicity
and formal reductiveness was an explicit repudiation of the abstract aesthetic theorizing projected onto art by formalist critics in the Greenbergian camp. Emphasizing the concrete,
unique particularity of the specific object, its spatiotemporal immediacy and imperviousness
to abstract critical speculation, minimalism mounted an individualist attack on aesthetic stereotyping that echoed analogous attacks on race and gender stereotyping that first surfaced in
the white American mainstream in the early 1960s. In so doing, minimalism reasserted the
primacy of the object itself as content of the work.

In the mid-1960s, Sol LeWitt further developed this notion of self-reflexive content: By
insisting on the primacy of the idea of the work over its medium of realization, LeWitt created
the context in which the cognitive content of a work could have priority over its perceptual
form. And by using the permutation of selected formal properties of an object—its sides,
dimensions, or geometrical shape—as a decision procedure for generating the final form of
the work as a permutational system, LeWitt moved that system itself, and the idea of that
system, into the foreground of the work as its self-reflexive subject matter. Here it is not only
the object as a unique particular that has primacy, but that object as the locus and origin of
the conceptual system it self-reflexively generates.

From there it was only a short step to conceptual art's insistence in the late 1960s on the
self-reflexive investigation of concepts and language themselves as the pri mary subject matter
of art. And because self-consciousness is a special case of self-reflexivity, it was then an even
shorter step to the self-conscious investigation of those very language users and art producers
themselves as embedded participants in the social context: For Joseph Kosuth and the Art &
Language group, this natural progression was from linguistic analysis of the concept of art to
discursive Marxist critique of the means of art production; for Hans Haacke, it was from self-
sustaining material systems to self-sustaining political systems; in my own work, it was from
my body as a conceptually and spatiotemporally immediate art object to my person as a gen-
dered and ethnically stereotyped art commodity. The reemergence of self-consciously distanced,
critical art with explicit social content in the early 1970s, then, was a natural outgrowth of the
reaffirmation of content latent in minimalism and the self-reflexive subject-matter explicit in
conceptual art. The cognitive and formal strategies of minimalism, and their evolution in the
work of Sol LeWitt and first-generation conceptualists, reestablished the link with European

modernism by restoring distanced self-awareness as a central value of artistic production—a self-awareness that is inevitably as social, cultural, and political as it is formal in its purview.

Meanwhile, the repressive McCarthyite ideology of Greenbergian formalism continues to gain adherents in post-cold war Europe, where many thoughtful and intelligent art professionals are alarmingly eager to discard Europe's variegated social and historical traditions as sources of continuity and cultural memory, in favor of the American substitute. This substitute is, of course, willful amnesia; that is, simply to deny that there is anything to remember or grasp that can't be resolved in a twenty-two-minute sitcom or merchandised in a thirty-second commercial. The erasure of content—particularly political content—was a Madison Avenue inspiration long before it was a gleam in Clement Greenberg's eye. The continuing European susceptibility to 1950s American cultural imperialism is particularly regrettable in a historical period in which Europe's turbulent social, political, and demographic changes offer such fertile conditions for artistic social engagement. Europe is now undergoing the same sustained assault from outside on its entrenched mythologies, conventions, and social arrangements that mainstream white America did from the civil rights movement, the counterculture, feminism, and anti–Vietnam war protesters in the 1960s. As the United States has, Europe will need a period of sustained cultural processing of these events by its artistic communities in order to learn how best to represent these changes to itself. It would be unfortunate if European art professionals chose to follow America's lead again, in ideologically blindfolding the visual arts in this undertaking. The American habit of somnambulism about its criminal past is such that it took the American art world decades to reawaken the aesthetic vocabulary of social resistance and engagement narcotized by Greenbergian formalism. In Europe, by contrast, this vocabulary is more deeply rooted in the artistic tradition of self-conscious criticality and more firmly buttressed by well-preserved artifacts of cultural memory. Let us hope it will be sufficient antidote against renewed American attempts to export yet one more "new world order" for cross-cultural consumption.

**NOTE**

1. See, for example, Max Kozloff, "American Painting during the Cold War," *Artforum* 11 (May 1973), pp. 43–54; Eva Cockcroft, "Abstract Expressionism: Weapon of the Cold War," *Artforum* 12 (June 1974), pp. 39–41; Serge Guilbaut, *How New York Stole the Idea of the Avant-Garde* (Chicago: University of Chicago Press, 1983).

This essay was written in 1992 and first published in *Flash Art,* 26:168 (January-February 1993), pp. 56–58, 118, 136.

# blueprint circuits: conceptual art and politics in latin america

## mari carmen ramírez

Circuit: . . . a course around a periphery . . . space enclosed within a circumference . . . a system for two-way communication.[1]

In 1972, taking stock of the status of Conceptual art in Western countries, the Spanish art historian Simón Marchán Fiz observed the beginnings of a tendency toward "ideological conceptualism" emerging in peripheral societies such as Argentina and Spain.[2] This version of Conceptual art came on the heels of the controversial propositions about the nature of art and artistic practice introduced in the mid-1960s by the North Americans Robert Barry, Mel Bochner, Douglas Huebler, Joseph Kosuth, Sol LeWitt, and Lawrence Weiner, as well as the British group Art & Language. These artists investigated the nature of the art object as well as the institutional mechanisms that support it, and their results tended to de-emphasize or eliminate the art object in favor of the process or ideas underlying it. North American Conceptual artists also questioned the role of museums and galleries in the promotion of art, its market status, and its relationship with the audience. This exposure of the functions of art in both social and cultural circuits has significantly redefined contemporary artistic practice over the last thirty years.

For Marchán Fiz, the distinguishing feature of the Spanish and Argentine forms of Conceptualism was extending the North American critique of the institutions and practices of art to an analysis of political and social issues. At the same time when he made these observations, the radical edge of North American Conceptual art's critique was obscured by the generalizing, reductive posture of Kosuth's "art-as-idea-as-idea."[3] In Kosuth's model the artwork as conceptual proposition is reduced to a tautological or self-reflexive statement. He insisted that art consists of nothing other than the artist's idea of it, and that art can claim no meaning outside itself. Marchán Fiz contrasted the rigidity of this self-referential, analytical model with the potential of "ideological conceptualism" to reveal political and social realities. For artists, he saw in this hybrid version of Conceptualism the possibility of an exit from the tautological impasse which, in his view, had deadlocked the practice of Conceptual art by 1972.

In Latin America Marchán Fiz was referring specifically to the Argentine Grupo do los Trece, but the version of Conceptual art he described has flourished not only in Argentina but in Uruguay, Chile, and Brazil since the mid-1960s.[4] As with any movement originating in the periphery, the work of Latin American political-conceptual artists—in its relationship with the mainstream source—engages in a pattern of mutual influence and response. It is both grounded in and distant from the legacy of North American Conceptualism in that it represents a transformation of it and also anticipated in many ways the forms of ideological conceptualism developed in the late 1970s and 1980s by feminist and other politically engaged artists in North America and Europe.[5] To investigate the reasons for this complex interaction is to delve into the ways in which the peripheral situation and socio-historical dynamic of Latin America imprinted a new logic onto the most radical achievements of center-based Conceptual art.

Marchán Fiz's insight can illuminate the development of Conceptual art in Latin America. Two generations of political-conceptual artists are discussed in his essay: the first—exemplified by the Argentine Victor Grippo, the Uruguayan Luis Camnitzer, the Brazilian Cildo Meireles, and the Chileans Eugenio Dittborn and Gonzalo Díaz—witnessed the emergence of Conceptual art and the political upheavals of the 1960s in the United States and Latin America; the second group—which includes the Chilean Alfredo Jaar and the Brazilian Jac Leirner—emerged in the 1980s and experienced the demise of and aftermath of the political dictatorships whose rise to power the previous generation had seen.[6] Taken as a whole, the work of both groups embodies a series of systematic inversions of important propositions of North American Conceptual art, "counter-propositions" that function as "exits" from the ideological impasse seen by Marchán Fiz.

## STRATEGIC CIRCUITS: UNFOLDING POLITICS

In a recent interview with the critic Sean Cubitt, Eugenio Dittborn described the function of his Pinturas Aeropostales (Airmail Paintings) as a means of *traveling* "to negotiate the possibility of making visible the invisible: *the distance*." Traveling "*to negotiate a meaning*," he added, is the political element of his work; more precisely, it is "*the unfolding of that politics*."[7] A preoccupation with bridging distances, crossing borders, and violating limits is also evident in Alfredo Jaar's description of his photo-light-box installations as a body of production that deals with "the extraordinary, widening gap between Us and Them, that striking distance that is, after all, only a mental one."[8] Each of Jaar's installations features evidence of his travels to remote sites in order to research and document a theme. Understood conceptually, "traveling," in the work of Dittborn and Jaar, as in that of Camnitzer, Díaz, Grippo, Leirner, and Meireles, established an "inverted route" that reverses the cultural polarity of "South" and "North" that has persistently subordinated Latin America to Europe and North America.

The closing of the gap between "center" and "periphery," between "first" and "third" worlds—constructs that convey the disparities between highly industrialized and still-developing nations—has been at the heart of Latin American concerns since the colonial period. Geography and colonialism dictated a history based on cycles of journeys and displacements, circulation and exchange, between the metropolitan centers of Europe and the colonies of Latin America and the Caribbean. Forced into cultural and political subordination, the practices of art were locked in endless rounds of copy/repetition, adaptation/transformation, and resisting or confronting the dominant powers. With this background, the history of modern art in Latin America since the 1920s can be seen as a constant search to open a space for change amid the web of economic and cultural circuits that continues to determine the experience of artists in this region.[9]

The political-conceptual artists considered here are distinguished by their deliberate assumption of the peripheral condition as the starting point of their work.[10] (. . .) Coming of age in the midst of the postwar development effort known as *desarrollismo*, which significantly reorganized the socioeconomic structures of major Latin American countries,[11] this group also lived through the promise of liberation from the political and economic stranglehold of the United States. Employing "dependency theory" to analyze their situation, they envisioned an emancipated role for Latin America in the "first world" order. Such optimism coincided with the shift of the art world's center from Paris to New York, reducing the distance—at least geographically—between that center and the Latin American periphery. The artistic environment of New York would play a pivotal role in the emergence of Conceptual and other experimental tendencies in Latin America by offering the large number of Latin American artists who arrived there in the 1960s freedom from the official conservatism of artistic institutions in their native countries.[12] It is important to note that unlike Brazil, where the early work of Hélio Oiticica and Lygia Clark had anticipated many experimental trends, Argentina, Chile, and Uruguay had little artistic experience to support the emergence of the radical practice of Conceptual art.[13] By contrast, the openly irreverent postures of such New York artists as Robert Rauschenberg, Jasper Johns, Jim Dine, Andy Warhol, and Robert Morris offered a context in which to engage openly in artistic experimentation. In general, the work of these North American artists offered a critique of formalism and a recovery of the iconoclastic legacy of Marcel Duchamp, both of which would strongly appeal to Latin American artists. Being in New York also placed in perspective both the social and artistic problems of Latin American countries.[14]

The generation that rode the optimism of the 1960s, however, experienced frustration of its hopes for Latin America. Between 1964 and 1976, six major countries in South America fell under military rule, including Brazil, Chile, and Uruguay, where authoritarian regimes not only abolished the rights and privileges of democracy but also institutionalized torture, repression, and censorship.[15] The critic Nelly Richard has analyzed how the fall of Chile's president, Salvador Allende, in 1973, coupled with General Augusto Pinochet's seizure of power, shattered the existing framework of social and political experiences linked to democracy. This abrupt transformation of social structures brought about a "crisis of intelligibility," as Richard calls it. Subjected to strict rules of censorship, artists concerned with the production of art relevant to the country's recent history had no recourse but "to seek alternative ways to recover the meaning of that history, which had been replaced by the Grand History of the Victors."[16] Richard's description can be extended to countries like Argentina and Uruguay, which, until the mid-1960s, had known some degree of democracy.

All of the artists discussed here experienced authoritarianism, in its psychological and material forms, either as internal or external exiles.[17] Translating this experience artistically in a significant way could proceed only from giving new sense to the artist's role as an active intervener in political and ideological structures. (. . .)

The appeal Conceptual art held for these artists rested on two factors: first, its equation of art with knowledge that transcends the aesthetic realm, which enabled them to explore problems and issues linked to concrete social and political situations; second, its critique of the traditional institutions and agents of art, which opened the way for an elaboration of a form of art suited to the political and economic precariousness of Latin America.[18] Instead of serving

as vehicles to dissect the commodification of art under capitalism, the fundamental propositions of Conceptual art became elements of a strategy for exposing the limits of art and life
under conditions of marginalization and, in some cases, repression. Hence, these artists developed a series of strategic inversions of the North American conceptual model, thereby determining the political character of their art.

## BARGAINING CIRCUITS: NEGOTIATING MEANINGS

**If M. DUCHAMP intervened at the level of Art (logic of phenomena), . . . what is done
today, on the contrary, tends to be closer to Culture than to Art, and that is necessarily a
political interference. That is to say, if aesthetics grounds Art, politics grounds Culture.**
—Cildo Meireles[19]

In the work of most of the Conceptual artists under consideration, the aims of bridging distance to negotiate meaning evolved into a deliberate tactic of *insertion* into prevailing artistic
and ideological circuits. This was done in order to expose mechanisms of repression and dis-
rupt the status of Latin American identity as a commodity exchanged along the axis between
center and periphery. The development of such a conceptual strategic language, however, eventually situated the work of these artists in a paradoxical relation to a fundamental principle of
European and North American Conceptual art: the dematerialization of the discrete object of
art and its replacement by a linguistic or analytical proposition. Latin American artists inverted
this principle through a recovery of the object, in the form of the mass-produced Duchampian
readymade, which is the vehicle of their conceptual program.[20] Meireles' Coca-Cola bottles,
bank notes, and leather boxes; Grippo's potatoes; Dittborn's found photographs and Airmail
Paintings; Camnitzer's text/object combinations; Díaz's found objects and appropriated emblems of the advertising world; Jaar's light-boxes, mirrors and frames; Leirner's accumulations
of "trash" provide us with curious twists of the Duchampian idea. Such objects are visual counterparts to the thought processes suggested by conceptual propositions. Following Duchamp,
the artists were concerned not so much with the production of artistic objects but with the
appropriation of already existing objects or forms as part of broad strategies of signification.[21]

The inversion of North American Conceptual art's analytic propositions can be attributed to these artists' explorations of the implications of Duchamp's legacy, which had already
been investigated, with different results, by both Conceptual and Pop art. As Benjamin Buchloh has argued, with regard to analytic Conceptual art, the revival of the readymade led to an

analysis of the self-reflexive or self-referential qualities of the object. This analysis originated in a narrow reading of Duchamp's original intention; the significance of the readymade was reduced to the act that created it: "It's art because I say so."[22] On the other hand, in the case of such Pop artists as Andy Warhol, appropriation of the idea of the readymade led to the exaltation of marketable commodities, represented by the Coca-Cola bottle or Campbell's soup can, as icons of a market-driven culture.[23] Both approaches to the readymade can be seen as grounded in a passive attitude toward the prevailing system, which this group of political-conceptual artists aimed to subvert. Thus, in Latin American work, the ready-made object is always charged with meanings related to its functions within a larger social circuit. That is the Latin American conceptual proposition. In most cases the infusion of broader meanings is achieved by removing the object from circulation, physically transforming it, and, in the case of Meireles, reintroducing it into an everyday circuit. Through such acts as silk-screening messages onto actual Coca-Cola bottles and bank notes (Meireles); sewing and stitching together large quantities of trash (Leirner); enlarging, cropping, and juxtaposing found photographs (Dittborn); or wrapping and staining commercial cardboard boxes with red dye that simulates blood (Camnitzer), the artist reinscribes meaning into the commodity object. In this way, the readymade, as these artists employ it, goes beyond Pop art's fetishization of the object, turning it into a conveyor of political meanings within a specific social context. Once transformed, the object is inserted into a proposition where it operates through the following linguistic mechanisms: explicit message, metaphor, and analogy. (. . .)

## EXITING CIRCUITS: "RECYCLED CONTEXTS"

**In tautology there is a double murder: one kills rationality because it resists one; one kills language because it betrays one. . . . Now any refusal of language is a death. Tautology creates a dead, a motionless world.**
—Roland Barthes[24]

The political logic of the Latin American version of Conceptual art described thus far rests on two factors. On the one hand, it posits the recovery of the object and its insertion into a conceptual proposition or a physical space. This trait can be interpreted as anachronous to the extent that it runs counter to the general trend of mainstream Conceptual art, which moved toward the abolition of the art object. The constant presence of the object in the work of the artists discussed suggests that the reasons for the difference have to do with the demands of the

Latin American context. The grounding of artistic languages in extra-artistic concerns has indeed been a constant of the avant-garde in Latin America since the 1920s. It was not only an intrinsic part of the process of tearing apart or recycling forms transmitted from cultural and political centers but a logical step in the act of constructing a tradition with the copy as its starting point. On the other hand, Benjamin Buchloh has suggested that the obsession with "facticity" of North American Conceptual art practices can derive only from the concept of an "administered society" typical of "late" capitalism.[25] The absence in Latin America of the social conditions supporting an administered society makes it an unsuitable model, perhaps even antithetical to a Latin American context. The elaboration of a Conceptual art practice aimed at exposing Latin American political and social realities thus involved a series of inversions of the mainstream model of Conceptual art. Along with the examples already discussed, the differences between the two can be summarized by the following oppositions:

| Latin American | North American |
| --- | --- |
| Contextualization | self-reflexivity |
| Referentiality | tautology |
| Activism | passivity |
| Mediation | immediacy |

One could argue that if Duchamp's propositions found a fertile ground in Latin America, it was because a refusal to abandon the specificity and communicative potential of the aesthetic object was deeply embedded in the modern art tradition initiated by the Mexican Mural Movement and later embraced by the group of political-conceptual artists. However, Duchamp's radical subversion of art as institution, implicit in the provocative creation of the readymade, is reenacted in these artists' works as an ironic tactic aimed at exposing a precarious activity: that of artistic practice in the frequently inoperative conditions of Latin America. Therefore, utilizing the readymade as a "package to communicate ideas,"[26] as Camnitzer has called it, ultimately points to an underlying concern with "devaluation," the loss of the object's symbolic value as a result of an economic or ideological process of exchange (as opposed to the North American artists' preoccupation with the process of commodification). Thus, the acts of "reinsertion" carried out by these artists are intended to reinvest objects with social meaning. The ready-made, then, becomes an instrument for the artists' critical intervention in the real, a stratagem by which patterns of understanding may be altered, or a site established for reinvesting reality with meaning. The readymade also turns into a vehicle by which aesthetic activity may be integrated with all the systems of reference used in everyday life.[27]

Such a reintegration could proceed only from rejecting the idea that the sphere of art is autonomous, thereby recovering the ethical dimension of artistic practice. The ultimate aim of this form of art can be seen as the elaboration of a system of signs, symbols, and actions through which the artist can intervene in what Jaar has called "the process of production and reproduction of meaning and consciousness."[28] Unlike previous models of Latin American political art that relied on the content of the art's "message," the politics of this art requires "unfolding": deconstructing linguistic and visual codes, subverting meanings, and activating space in order to impress on the viewer the effects of the mechanisms of power and ideology. By presenting the work itself as a space (whether physical or metaphoric), this art recovers the notion of the audience. That is to say, it regains for the artist the possibility of engaging in active communication through the artistic object or installation. In these circumstances, the viewer, as a socially constituted recipient, becomes an integral part of the conceptual proposition of the artist.

For these artists the act of replacing tautology with meaning is grounded in the larger project of exiting exhausted political and ideological circuits through the revitalizing of contexts—artistic, geographic, economic—in which they practice their art. This project, in turn, reveals a complex understanding of the realities of Latin America in relation to those of the first world. The deep goal of the work lies in the way it manages "to place in crisis the history of its own culture without forgoing a commitment to that same culture."[29] No longer confined, however, to national boundaries, or split between national and international forces, center and periphery, first and third worlds, it exposes the relations among these constructs, their interdependence. To achieve this aim requires an active negotiation of meaning between them. The Latin American "inverted" model of Conceptual art thus reveals a practice which not only is inscribed in a different framework of development but responds to the misalignment of global politics. Through its capacity to blend central and peripheral sources in the structure and function of a work, it challenges the authority of the "center" as originator of artistic forms.

The practice of a revisionist Conceptual art, seen in the work of this select group of Latin American artists, represents the recovery of an emancipatory project. At a time when the "logic" of "late" capitalism has annihilated the goals of the historic avant-garde, and when most forms of contemporary art have run up the blind alley of self-referentiality, the range and possibilities of such an enterprise should not be overlooked in the United States, where the original propositions of Conceptual art were born.

## NOTES

1. *Webster's Third New International Dictionary* (Springfield, Mass.: G. & C. Merriam Company, 1981), p. 408.

2. Simón Marchán Fiz, *Del arte objetual al arte de concepto: Las artes plásticas desde 1960* (1972; reprint ed., Madrid: Ediciones Akal, 1988), pp. 268–271. This book provides one of the first comprehensive discussions to appear in Spanish of the Conceptual art movements in Europe and North America.

3. A number of authors in recent years have criticized the apolitical reductiveness of Conceptual art, both in its original versions and in recent revivals. For instance, Hal Foster, in *Recodings: Art, Spectacle, Cultural Politics* (Seattle: Bay Press, 1985), p. 103, has noted that the practices of Conceptual artists that focus on general assumptions governing the institution of art in "late" capitalism are compromised by "present[ing] the exhibitional limits of art as socially indiscriminate and sexually indifferent." Benjamin Buchloh has offered a detailed analysis and critique of those practices in "Conceptual Art, 1962–1969: From the Aesthetics of Administration to the Critique of Institutions," *October* 55 (Winter 1990), pp. 105–143. Other recent critics who have commented on these issues include Robert C. Morgan, "The Situation of Conceptual Art," *Arts* 63 (February 1989), pp. 40–43. Of the artists being considered in the present essay, Alfredo Jaar has offered the most cogent critique of this aspect of Conceptual art practice in the following statement: "Conceptual art's greatest failure was definitely its provincialism, . . . in the sense that Tzvetan Todorov has used the term, . . . a failure to recognize that many provinces and capitals do exist. . . . All the dominant assumptions about art were challenged, but this was done practically behind closed doors, in an extraordinary [*sic*] exclusive fashion, almost in an arrogant way, and blind to a number of political events that transformed the world. For the conceptualists, obviously, life was elsewhere." Alfredo Jaar, "Alfredo Jaar," *Flash Art International* 143 (November/December 1988), p. 117.

4. Marchán Fiz, *Del arte objetual al arte de concepto,* pp. 269–270. The Grupo de los Trece was constituted in Buenos Aires in 1971 following a visit by the Polish director Jerzy Grotowski. The group was based at the Centro de Arte y Comunicación (CAYC), directed by Jorge Glusberg, and included the artists Jacques Bedel, Luis F. Benedit, Gregorio Dujovny, Carlos Ginzburg, Victor Grippo, Vicente Marotta, Jorge González Mir, Luis Pazos, Juan Carlos Romero, and Horacio Zabala. For a summary, of the history, and objectives of the group, and illustrations of works by its members, see "El Grupo de los Trece," in Gabriel Levinas, ed., *Arte argentino contemporáneo* (Madrid: Editorial Ameris, 1979), pp. 197–201.

5. A glance at the catalogues that accompanied two of the most influential surveys of Conceptual art ever mounted, *Live in Your Head: When Attitudes Become Form, Concepts—Processes—Situations—Information* (Bern: Kunsthalle Bern, 1969), and Kynaston L. McShine, ed., *Information* (New York: The Museum of Modern Art, 1970), reveals an almost complete absence of political concerns, though these would emerge later in the work of Marcel Broodthaers, Daniel Buren, and Hans Haacke, and in that of feminist artists. Even then, excepting the later work of Haacke, Barbara Kruger, Louise Lawler, and Martha Rosler, political or ideological issues were limited to critiques of the institutions of art and rarely addressed politics.

6. Other important artists who contributed to the consolidation of this form of art in Latin America include, in Brazil, Anna Bella Geiger, Rubens Gerchman, Mario Ishikawa, and Regina Vater; in Argentina, León Ferrari and the group Tucumán Arde; in Uruguay, Clemente Padin and Nelbia Romero; in Chile, Virginia Errazuriz, Carlos Leppe, Catalina Parra, and the CADA group, which included Juan Castillo, Lotty Rosenfeld, and others; and in Colombia, Antonio Caro. Also important were Felipe Ehrenberg and the numerous artistic collaboratives of the 1970s in Mexico. See Jorge Glusberg, *Arte en la Argentina: Del pop-art a la nueva imagen* (Buenos Aires: Ediciones de Arte Gaglianone, 1985); Nelly Richard, "Margins and Institutions: Art in Chile Since 1973," *Art and Text* 21 (May-July 1986), pp. 17–114; Aracy Amaral, *Arte pare quê? A preocupaçao social na arte brasileira, 1930–1970* (Sao Paulo: Nobel, 1984); Walter Zanini, *Circunambulatio* (Sao Paulo: Museu de Arte Contemporanea da Universidade de Sao Paulo, 1973); *6 jovem arte contemporânea* (Sao Paulo: Museu de Arte Contemporânea da Universidade de Sao Paulo, 1972); *8 jovem arte contemporânea* (Sao Paulo: Museu de Arte Contemporânea da Universidade de Sao Paulo, 1974); Shifra M. Goldman, "Elite Artists and Audiences: Can They Mix? The Mexican Front of Cultural Workers," *Studies in Latin American Popular Culture* 4 (1985), pp. 139–54; *De los grupos los individuos: Artistas plásticos de los grupos metropolitanos* (Mexico City: Museo de Arte Carrillo Gil, 1985).

7. Sean Cubitt and Eugenio Dittborn, "An Airmail Interview," in Guy Brett and Sean Cubitt, *Camino Way: The Airmail Paintings of Eugenio Dittborn* (Santiago: Eugenio Dittborn, 1991), p. 28.

8. Alfredo Jaar, "La géographic ça sert, d'abord, à faire la guerre (Geography = War)," *Contemporánea* 2 (June 1989), inside cover.

9. This point is argued by Charles Merewether in "The Migration of Images: Inscriptions of Land and Body in Latin America," in *America: Bride of the Sun* (Antwerp: Koninklijk Museum voor Schone Kunsten, 1992), pp. 197–222.

10. Dittborn has explained, "Como todo trabajo de arte que quiere dar cuenta de la periferia en la que se produce y circula, mi obra se ha propuesto asumir creativamente el irrecuperable atraso, asi como la multiestratificación de esta periferia (As with any work of art that wants to take into account the periphery in which it is produced and circulated, my work has proposed to creatively assume the irreparable backwardness as well as the multiple stratifications of this periphery)."—*Chile vive* (Madrid: Círculo de Bellas Artes, 1987), p. 282.

11. See Néstor Garcia Canclini, *Culturas híbridas: Estrategias pare entrar y salir de la modernidad* (Mexico City: Editorial Grijalbo, 1989), pp. 65–93.

12. Of the artists considered in this essay, Camnitzer has lived in the New York area continuously since 1964, and Meireles resided in New York in 1970 and 1971. Reflecting on why he moved there, Camnitzer has stated, "New York seemed fascinating: the center of the empire. The measuring stick for success was set by the empire and not in the colonies." Cited in Carla Stellweg, "'Magnet—New York': Conceptual, Performance, Environmental, and Installation Art by Latin American Artists in New York," in Luis Cancel et al., *The Latin American Spirit: Art and Artists in the United States, 1920–1970* (New York: Bronx Museum of the Arts and Harry N. Abrams, 1988), p. 285. For an overview of other Latin American Conceptual artists active in New York during this period, see Stellweg, "'Magnet- New York,'" pp. 284–311; and Jacqueline Barnitz, Florencia Bazzano Nelson, and Janis Bergman Carton, *Latin American Artists in New York since 1970* (Austin: Archer M. Huntington Art Gallery, University of Texas, 1987), pp. 13–19.

13. For details see Jacqueline Barnitz, "Conceptual Art and Latin America: A Natural Alliance," in *Encounters/Displacements: Luis Camnitzer, Alfredo Jaar, Cildo Meireles* (Austin: Archer M. Huntington Art Gallery, University of Texas, 1992), pp. 35–48.

14. Several Latin American artists in New York created experimental work under the auspices of the New York Graphic Workshop, which was established by Camnitzer, Liliana Porter, and José Guillermo Castillo in 1964 and was dissolved in 1970 (author's telephone interview with Luis Camnitzer, September 24, 1992). The workshop was founded on a form of political activism that rejected the commodity status of art, seeking instead to make it accessible to a mass audience through prints. The workshop launched the idea of serial graphics in which a single element could be assembled in many ways, a concept described by the acronym FANDSO (Free Assemblage, Nonfunctional, Disposable, Serial Object). See Luis Camnitzer, *Art in Editions: New Approaches* (New York: Pratt Center for Contemporary Printmaking and New York University, 1968). Shifra M. Goldman has analyzed the activities of the N.Y.G.W. in "Presencias y ausencias: Liliana Porter en Nueva York, 1964–1974," in *Liliana Porter: Obra gráfica, 1964–1990* (San Juan: Instituto de Cultura Puertorriqueña, 1991), pp. 1–22.

15. The constitutional government of Brazil was overthrown by a military coup in 1964, and the nation was subsequently ruled by military dictators until 1985; Uruguay was ruled by a de facto military dictatorship from 1973 to 1985; Argentina experienced a succession of military governments after the coup of 1966; and Chile was governed from 1973 until 1989 by the dictator General Augusto Pinochet. Peru was under military rule from 1968 to 1980, Bolivia from 1971 to 1982, and Ecuador from 1972 to 1980. See Beverly Adams, "The Subject of Torture: The Art of Camnitzer, Nuñez, Parra, and Romero." Master's thesis, University of Texas, Austin, 1992, pp. 21–38.

16. Richard, "Margins and Institutions," p. 17.

17. Camnitzer was in New York when Uruguay's democratic government fell in 1973. Even though he did not return, the event indelibly marked his life and experience in the United States. Dittborn and Díaz remained in Chile throughout the military regime of Pinochet. Jaar lived through the fall of Allende and left Chile for New York in 1982; Meireles remained in Brazil for the duration of the military dictatorship, with the exception of the two years he spent in New York; Grippo lived through the black years in Argentina; Leirner has lived through the return of democracy to Brazil and the subsequent period of deep economic and social crisis.

18. The theme of art and torture in the work of Camnitzer, Dittborn, and other artists from South America has been analyzed by Beverly Adams in "The Subject of Torture" and by Charles Merewether in "El arte de la violencia: Un asunto de representación en el arte contemporáneo," *Art Nexus* 2 (October 1991), pp. 92–96, and 3 (January 1992), p. 132–135.

19. "Se a interferência de M. DUCHAMP foi ao nivel da Arte (logica do fenômeno), . . . uma vez que o que se faz hoje tende a estar mais próximo da culture do que da Arte, é necessariamente uma inteferência politica. Porque se a estética fundamenta a Arte, é a Politica que fundamenta a Cultura." Cildo Meireles, "Arte-Cultura," *Malasartes* 1 (September/October/November 1975), p. 15.

20. Conceptual artists do, of course, utilize objects in their work: photographs, video and audio tapes, drawings, maps, and diagrams, which function as "documents" that record the conceptual proposal.

21. Camnitzer, for instance, referred to form itself as being important only insofar as it could serve the purposes of content, and Meireles spoke of his attempts to develop a language of *inserção* rather than "style." See Luis Camnitzer, "Chronology," in Camnitzer, Mosquera, and Ramírez, *Camnitzer Retrospective,* p. 52; and Meireles, in Brito and Marcieira de Sousa, *Cildo Meireles,* p. 24.

22. Buchloh, "Conceptual Art 1962–1969," pp. 124–127.

23. For analysis of the relationship of Meireles, Leirner, and other Brazilian artists to Warhol, see Paulo Herkenhoff, "Arte e money," *Revista galena* 24 (October 1989), pp. 60–67.

24. Roland Barthes, *Mythologies,* trans. Annette Lavers (New York: Hill and Wang, 1972), pp. 152–153.

25. Buchloh, "Conceptual Art, 1962–1969," pp. 128–129.

26. Luis Camnitzer, "Contemporary Colonial Art," paper presented at the Annual International Congress of the Latin American Studies Association, Washington, D.C., 1970. Meireles also used the term *package* to refer to his conceptual propositions with ready-mades.

27. See Luis Camnitzer, "Chronology," in Camnitzer, Mosquera, and Ramírez, *Camnitzer Retrospective,* p. 53.

28. Jaar, "Alfredo Jaar," p. 117.

29. Merewether, "Migration of Images," p. 202.

This essay appeared in Waldo Rasmussen, *Latin American Art of the Twentieth Century,* exh. cat. (New York: Museum of Modern Art, 1993), pp. 156–167.

# unwritten histories of conceptual art
## thomas crow

Historical objectification ought to be sped up while there is still a collective experience and memory which can assist in the clarity of an analysis while, simultaneously, opening up a space to ask fundamental questions regarding history-making.
—Michael Asher, 1989[1]

Almost every work of serious contemporary art recapitulates, on some explicit or implicit level, the historical sequence of objects to which it belongs. Consciousness of precedent has become very nearly the condition and definition of major artistic ambition. For that reason artists have become avid, if unpredictable, consumers of art history. Yet the organized discipline of the history of art remains largely blind to the products of this interest and entirely sheltered from the lessons that might accrue from them.

That art historians of a traditional cast should display little interest in new art, however historically informed, is of course a familiar story: within living memory, all art produced since 1600 was merged into the single category of "post Renaissance." But recent changes in art history have not greatly altered the situation, despite the growing prominence in the discipline of theorists pursuing a postmodern vision of culture. Their particular postmodernism has not grown from within visual art itself, but derives instead from the contentions within literary theory, most of all the drive to relax the distinctions between a canon of great authors and the universe of other texts once excluded from the teaching and learning of literature. Influential voices, impressed by that example, have lately recommended that the idea of a history of art be set aside, to be replaced by a forward-looking "history of images," which will attend to the entire range of visual culture. One benefit of such a change, the argument goes, will be that "the cultural work of history of art will more closely resemble that of other fields than has been the case in the past," and that transformation temptingly "offers the prospect of an interdisciplinary dialogue . . . more concerned with the relevance of contemporary values for academic study than with the myth of the pursuit of knowledge for its own sake."[2]

This is a fair definition of what postmodernism has come to mean in academic life. But as a blueprint for the emancipation of art history, it contains a large and unexamined paradox: it accepts without question the view that art is to be defined by its essentially visual nature, by its working exclusively through the optical faculties. As it happens, this was the most cherished assumption of high modernism in the 1950s and 1960s, which constructed its canon around the notion of opticality: as art progressively refined itself, the value of a work more and more lay in the coherence of the fiction offered to the eye alone. The term visual culture of course represents a vast vertical integration of study, extending from the esoteric products of fine-art traditions to hand bills and horror videos, but it perpetuates the horizontal narrowness entailed in modernism's fetish of visuality. Its corollary in an expanded history of images (rather than art) likewise perpetuates the modernist obsession with the abstract state of illusion, with virtual effects at the expense of literal facts.[3]

What is plainly missing in this project is some greater acknowledgment of the challenges to modernist assumptions that changed the landscape of artistic practice from the later 1950s onwards. The postmodern art historian of the 1990s cites for support "consequences of the theoretical and methodological developments that have affected other disciplines in the humanities."[4] But the revival of Duchampian tactics in the hands of artists like Jasper Johns, Robert Morris, and Donald Judd long ago erased any effective elite/vernacular distinctions in the materials of art, while at the same time opening contexts and hidden instrumental uses of art to critical scrutiny. The great theoretical advantage of this activity, as opposed to doctrines imported from other disciplines, was its being made from existing art and as such requiring no awkward and imprecise translation in order to bear upon the concerns of art history. Nor could these practical artistic ventures be contained within the category of the image, a fact which a succeeding generation of overtly conceptual artists then took as fundamental. The "withdrawal of visuality" or "suppression of the beholder," which were the operative strategies of conceptualism, decisively set aside the assumed primacy of visual illusion as central to the making and understanding of a work of art.[5]

During the early 1970s, the transitory, hazardous, and at times illegal performances staged by Chris Burden remained, apart from a select group of collaborators, unavailable to spectatorship.[6] The photographic documentation by which such events were subsequently publicized serves to mark the inadequacy of recorded image to phenomenon. Conceptual work of a materially substantial and permanent character was no more amenable to the category of visual culture. Works like the *Index* of the Art & Language group dared the spectator to overcome a positively forbidding lack of outward enticement in order to discover a discursive and philosophical content recorded in the most prosaic form possible.

Even in discrete objects in traditional formats, there is something of a tradition— stretching from Elaine Sturtevant to Sherrie Levine—whereby the visual appeal of painting or photography is acknowledged but expelled by tactics of replication.[7] Perhaps as revealing as any theoretical exegesis is a bantering remark made in a recorded conversation between two collectors, both perceptive enough to have supported Sturtevant:

*I am sure that you have often noticed that visitors to your apartment—like the visitors to our loft—shrug off the Warhol or the Stella before you tell them that it is Sturtevant. Watch how their eyes roll! Their hair stands on end! Their palms collect sweat! Over and over they fall to fighting, arguing, debating. If this isn't the shock of the new, then the term is meaningless. Art is involved with so much more than visual appearance, as television has very little to do with the eye, or radio with the ear.*[8]

His interlocutor replies, with equal accuracy and equal heat, that Sturtevant suffered abuse and ostracism during the 1960s and 1970s for having so acutely defined the limitations of any history of art wedded to the image. Those now defining themselves as historians of images rather than art have so far shown little capacity to grasp the practice of artists on this level, certainly none that adds anything to that already achieved by the practitioners themselves. Instead, they reproduce the exclusions traditional to their discipline, validating the past centrality of painting and its derivatives, which are most easily likened to the image world of the modern media and to unschooled forms of picturing.

But Conceptualism, which long anticipated recent theory on the level of practice, can be encompassed only within an unapologetic history of art. Its arrival in the later twentieth century recovered key tenets of the early academies, which, for better or worse, established fine art as a learned, self-conscious activity in Western culture. One of those tenets was a mistrust of optical experience as providing an adequate basis for art: the more a painting relied on purely visual sensation, the lower its cognitive value was assumed to be. The meaning of a work of art was mapped along a number of cognitive axes, its affinities and differences with other images being just one of these—and not necessarily the strongest. Art was a public, philosophical school; manipulative imagery serving superstitious belief and private gratification could be had from a thousand other sources.

It was only in the later nineteenth century that the avant-garde successfully challenged a decayed academicism by turning that hierarchy on its head: the sensual immediacy of color and textured surfaces, freed from subordination to an imposed intellectual program, was henceforth to elicit the greater acuity of attention and complexity of experience in the viewer. The development of conceptual art a century later was intended to mark the limited historical life of that strategy, but postmodern theory has had the effect of strengthening conventional attachments to painting and sculpture. The art market quite obviously functions more comfortably with discrete, luxury objects to sell; and the sec ondhand, quotation-ridden character of much of the neotraditionalist art of the 1980s has been well served by theorists (Jean Baudrillard being a leading example) who have advanced the idea of an undifferentiated continuum of visual culture.

The aspirations of Conceptualism have been further diminished by a certain loss of heart on the part of its best advocates, who are united in thinking (amid their many differences) that the episode is essentially concluded. Benjamin H. D. Buchloh has voiced this general conclusion when writing that Marcel Broodthaers

*anticipated that the enlightenment-triumph of Conceptual Art, its transformation of audiences and distribution, its abolition of object status and commodity form, at best would only be short-lived and would soon give way to the return of the ghost-like re-apparitions of (prematurely?) displaced painterly and sculptural paradigms of the past.*[9]

Charles Harrison, editor of the journal *Art & Language,* laid down the requirement for any Conceptual art aspiring to critical interest that it conceive a changed sense of the public alongside its transformation of practice. But on precisely these grounds, he finds the group's own achievement to be limited: "Realistically, *Art & Language* could identify no *actual* alternative public which was not composed of the participants in its own projects and deliberations."[10]

In Jeff Wall's view, that isolated imprisonment was the cause of the pervasive melancholy of early Conceptualism: both "the deadness of language characterizing the work of Lawrence Weiner or On Kawara" and the "mausoleum look" embodied in the gray texts, anonymous binders, card files, and steel cabinets of Joseph Kosuth and *Art & Language.* "Social subjects," he observes, "are presented as enigmatic hieroglyphs and given the authority of the crypt," pervasive opacity being an outward betrayal of art's rueful, powerless mortification in the face of the overwhelming political and economic machinery that separates information from truth.[11] The ultimate weakness of this entire phase of art for him lies in its consequent failure to generate any subject matter free from irony. For both Harrison and Wall, their pessimistic verdicts on the achievements of Conceptual art have led them to embrace monumental pictorialism as the most productive way forward, a move that sustains the idea of an encompassing visual culture as the ultimate ground for discussion.

These three names represent the most formidable historians of Conceptual art, and their strictures must be treated with all possible seriousness. If the history of Conceptual art is to maintain a critical value in relation to the apparent triumph of visuality, it must meet the conditions implied in their judgment on its fate: 1) it must be living and available rather than concluded; 2) it must presuppose, at least in its imaginative reach, renewed contact with lay audiences; and 3) it must document a capacity for significant reference to the world beyond the most proximate institutions of artistic display and consumption.

(. . .)

**NOTES**

1. From text by Michael Asher in Claude Gintz, ed., *L'Art conceptuel, une perspective* (Paris: Musée d'Art Moderne de la Ville de Paris, 1989), p. 112.

2. Editors' introduction in Norman Bryson, Michael Ann Holly, and Keith Moxey, eds., *Visual Culture: Images and Interpretations* (Hanover, N.H.: University Press of New England, 1994), p. xvii.

3. The classic polemic advancing this position is Michael Fried, "Art and Objecthood," in Gregory Battcock, ed., *Minimal Art* (New York: Dutton, 1968), pp. 116–147.

4. Bryson et al, *Visual Culture,* p. xvii.

5. These two formulae are the coinages of Benjamin H. D. Buchloh and Charles Harrison respectively.

6. The most notorious instance is *Shoot* (1971), to which could be added *TV Hijack* (1972),

*747, Icarus* and *Trans-Fixed* (1973); see Anne Ayres and Paul Schimmel, eds., *Chris Burden: a twenty-year survey* (Newport Beach, Calif.: Newport Harbor Art Museum, 1988), pp. 53–54, 59–60, 66.

7. See the discussion in Crow, "The Return of Hank Herron: Simulated Abstraction and the Service Economy of Art," in *Modern Art in the Common Culture* (New Haven: Yale University Press, 1996), pp. 69–84.

8. Douglas Davis in Eugene W. Schwartz and Davis, "A Double-Take on Elaine Sturtevant," *File,* December 1986, n. p. Davis also relates the remarkable story of Duchamp's reaction, in the year before his death, to Sturtevant's restaging of his performance *Relache.*

9. Benjamin H. D. Buchloh, "From the Aesthetic of Administration to Institutional Critique," in Gintz, *L'Art conceptuel,* p. 53.

10. Charles Harrison, "Art Object and Artwork," in Gintz, *L'art conceptuel,* p. 63.

11. See Jeff Wall, *Dan Graham's Kammerspiel* (Toronto: Art Metropole, 1991), p. 19. William Wood offered helpful comments on this and other points in this essay.

This essay first appeared in Catherine Gudis, *Oehlen Williams 95* (Columbus, Ohio: Wexner Center for the Arts, 1995), and was subsequently included in Thomas Crow, *Modern Art in the Common Culture* (New Haven: Yale University Press, 1996), pp. 212–242.